To Rosie, Clare, Camila, Sofia, Eliana, Julian, Carson, and Owen

BRIEF CONTENTS

Contents

CHAPTER 2

CHAPTER 5   The Moral Aspects of Leadership   141

CHAPTER 6 Enhancing Teamwork within the Group   170

CHAPTER 7 The Leader as a Motivator and Coach   202

Preface

Welcome to the seventh edition of *Principles of Leadership*. The new edition of this text is a thorough update of the sixth edition, which has been used widely in both graduate and undergraduate courses in leadership.

In recent years, leadership has become a course by itself after long having been a key topic in several disciplines. Many scholars and managers alike are convinced that effective leadership is required to meet most organizational challenges. Today, organizations recognize that leadership transcends senior executives. As a result, organizations require people with appropriate leadership skills to inspire and influence others in small teams, task forces, and units at all organizational levels.

Without effective leadership at all levels in organizations, it is difficult to sustain profitability, productivity, and good customer service. In dozens of different ways, researchers and teachers have demonstrated that leadership does make a difference. Many curricula in business schools and other fields, therefore, now emphasize the development of leadership skills. With the recent exposures of the dark side of business leadership, such as CEOs finding ways to create fortunes for themselves at the expense of employees and stockholders, more attention than ever is being paid to the values and personal characteristics of leaders. Toward that end, this text continues its emphasis on the qualities of effective leaders, including an entire chapter on leadership ethics and social responsibilities.

PURPOSE OF THE TEXT

The purpose of this text is implied by its title—*Principles of Leadership*, seventh edition. It is designed for undergraduate and graduate courses in leadership that give attention to research findings about leadership, leadership practice, and skill development. The text best fits courses in leadership that emphasize application and skill building. *Principles of Leadership* is also designed to fit courses in management development that emphasize the leadership aspect of management. In addition, it can serve as a supplement to organizational behavior or introductory management courses that emphasize leadership.

The student who masters this text will acquire an overview of the voluminous leadership literature that is based both on research and experience.

Information in this text is not restricted to research studies and syntheses of research and theories; it also includes the opinions of practitioners, consultants, and authors who base their conclusions on observations rather than empirical research.

What the text is *not* also helps define its nature and scope. This book does not attempt to duplicate the scope and purpose of a leadership handbook by integrating theory and research from several thousand studies. At the other extreme, it is not an evangelical approach to leadership espousing one leadership technique. I have attempted to find a midpoint between a massive synthesis of the literature and a trade book promoting a current leadership fad. *Principles of Leadership*, seventh edition, is designed to be a mixture of scholarly integrity, examples of effective leadership in action, and skill development.

Principles of Leadership is not intended to duplicate or substitute for an organizational behavior text. Because almost all organizational behavior texts are survey texts, they will mention many of the topics covered here. My approach, however, is to emphasize skill development and prescription rather than to duplicate basic descriptions of concepts and theories. I have tried to minimize overlap by emphasizing the leadership aspects of any concept presented here that might also be found in an organizational behavior or management text. Often when overlap of a topic exists, the presentation here focuses more on skill development than on a review of theory and research. For example, the section on motivation emphasizes how to apply basic explanations of motivation such as expectancy theory and equity theory, but I do not present an overview of motivation theories as is found in an organizational behavior text.

One area of intentional overlap with organizational behavior and management texts does exist: a review of all basic leadership theories. In such instances, however, I emphasize skill development and ideas for leadership practice stemming from these older theories.

FEATURES OF THE BOOK

To accomplish its purpose, this textbook incorporates many features into each chapter in addition to summarizing and synthesizing relevant information about leadership:

- **Chapter Outlines** giving the reader a quick overview of the topics covered
- **Learning Objectives** to help focus the reader's attention on major outcomes
- Boldfaced **key terms**, listed at the end of the chapter and defined in a **Glossary** at the back of the textbook
- Real-life and hypothetical **examples** throughout the textbook
- **Leader in Action** inserts describing the leadership practices, behaviors, and personal attributes of real-life leaders
- **Leadership Self-Assessment Quizzes** relating to both skills and personal characteristics
- **Leadership Skill-Building Exercises**, including role plays, to emphasize the activities and skills of effective leaders
- End-of-chapter **Summaries** that integrate all key topics and concepts

- End-of-chapter **Guidelines for Action and Skill Development**, giving additional suggestions for improving leadership skill and practice
- **Discussion Questions and Activities** suited for individual or group analysis
- Two **Leadership Case Problems** per chapter, which illustrate the major theme of the chapter and contain questions for individual or group analysis
- **Role plays** accompanying almost all the case problems to help reinforce the opportunity for learning interpersonal skills within the case problems
- A **Leadership Portfolio** skill-building exercise in each chapter that instructs the student to record progress in developing leadership skills and behaviors

Framework of the Text

The text is a blend of description, skill development, insight development, and prescription. Chapter 1 describes the meaning, importance, and nature of leadership, including leadership roles and the importance of followership. Chapter 2 discusses effective leadership in international and culturally diverse settings. Chapter 3 identifies personal attributes associated with effective leaders, a subject that has experienced renewed importance in recent years. Charismatic and transformational leadership, an extension of understanding the personal attributes of leadership, is the subject of Chapter 4.

Chapter 5 focuses on leadership ethics and social responsibility. Chapter 6 describes how leaders foster teamwork and empower team members. Chapter 7 discusses motivating and coaching skills. Chapter 8 surveys behaviors and practices associated with effective leadership in a variety of situations, and describes leadership styles. Chapter 9 extends the study of styles by describing the contingency and situational aspects of leadership. Chapter 10 analyzes the tactics leaders use to influence people. Chapter 11 describes how leaders use power and politics.

The next three chapters deal with specific leadership skills: communication (including nonverbal, social media, and cross-cultural communication) and conflict resolution skills (Chapter 12); creativity and innovation (Chapter 13); and vision and strategy creation and knowledge management (Chapter 14).

Chapter 15 concludes the book with an overview of approaches to leadership development and learning. In addition, there is a discussion of leadership succession and the challenges facing a new leader.

CHANGES IN THE SEVENTH EDITION

The seventh edition of *Principles of Leadership* is a thorough update of the sixth edition. Some of the changes in this edition reflect the recent leadership information I felt should be included in the new edition. Many changes, however, reflect suggestions made by adopters and reviewers. For example, several reviewers suggested that I place more emphasis throughout the textbook on leadership via Internet interactions, including social media, ethics, and cross-cultural ideas. To make way for the new material, I have selectively pruned older examples and research findings, and deleted some concepts that seem to be only slight variations of another concept in the text. The following list highlights the changes in the seventh edition, in addition to updating research and opinion:

Changes Throughout the Text

- A role-playing or other experiential activity linked to twenty-eight end-of-chapter cases
- All fifteen chapter introductions are new
- All fifteen Leader in Action boxes are new
- Nineteen new cases
- More emphasis on leaders of less well-known firms, middle managers in larger firms, and small-business owners
- New research findings presented in each chapter
- New examples throughout
- Eight Guidelines for Action and Skill Development either replaced or supplemented with additional information
- Twenty-one new Skill-Building Exercises
- Five new Leadership Self-Assessment Quizzes

Content Changes Within Chapters

Chapter 1 identifies several new job titles for leaders; information about relationship building electronically; the flexible leadership theory of Gary Yukl; and the multilevel nature of leadership. Chapter 2 now contains information about how diversity programs help local economies; the increased demand for U.S. workers with second-language skills; and modifying products and services for targeted demographic groups. Chapter 3 adds the core self-evaluations as a leadership trait; aggressiveness and financial decision making among male CEOs; as well as emotional intelligence and emergent leadership. Chapter 4 adds information about the effects of charisma; several company vision statements; and social networking for displaying charisma. Chapter 5 adds information about how motivated blindness can contribute to unethical behavior; the importance of an ethical code for a leadership career; how middle-level leaders can be philanthropists; and the financial scandals of 2008.

Chapter 6 presents information about coaching the entire team; the value of occasionally conducting face-to-face meetings for virtual teams; the cross-cultural aspects of building teamwork; and how leader status relates to LMX. Chapter 7 includes information about leadership and employee engagement and the problems created by using unethical and dysfunctional shortcuts to attain goals. The chapter also presents new information about how to make feedback less intimidating. Chapter 8 presents information about modifying one's leadership style to fit the occasion and organizing for collaboration. Chapter 9 presents information about the form of organization as a moderator of leadership style; how LMX relates to contingency theory; avoiding the unintended negative consequences of LMX; and the importance of decisiveness during a crisis. Chapter 10 now organizes the ethics of influence tactics in the categories of positive, neutral, and negative. The influence tactic of apprising is new.

Chapter 11 adds information about how gaining power can reduce stress; the value of a small number of high-quality contracts; positive psychological capital; and abusing power. Chapter 12 adds several new subjects: communication networks for leaders (both face to face and the social media); the problem of converting an excess of nouns into verbs; brainstorming and bartering for negotiation; and telepresence as a form of videoconferencing. Chapter 13 now adds discussions on how both the right and left brain are needed for creativity; on limits to thinking outside the box; on the morality of enhancing creativity; on financial rewards for innovation; and on how being perceived as creative might block receiving a leadership assignment. Chapter 14 touches on these new subjects: how much time to spend planning the future; research about leadership effectiveness and strategy implementation; and the strategy of environmental sustainability as the role of transformational versus transactional leadership for organizational learning. Chapter 15 includes several new topics: catalytic learning ability and leadership potential; effective mentoring behaviors; the importance of having more than one mentor, and succession planning at Procter & Gamble.

Supplements

Several supplements that facilitate teaching accompany this edition.

Instructor's companion website at login.cengage.com. This password-protected website provides valuable resources for designing and teaching your course. Content includes downloadable files from the instructor's manual, PowerPoint® slides for downloading, links to the text-specific video segments from the DVD, and the video guide.

Instructor's Manual. This manual features chapter outlines and lecture notes, possible answers to discussion questions and case questions, and comments on exercises in the text.

Computerized Test Bank. This computerized version of the test bank allows instructors to select, edit, and add questions, or generate randomly selected questions to produce a test master for easy duplication. Online Testing and Gradebook functions allow instructors to administer tests via their local area network or the Internet, set up classes, record grades from tests or assignments, analyze grades, and compile class and individual statistics. This program can be used on both PC and Mac.

PowerPoint® slide presentation. These slides have been specially developed for this book to enhance the teaching and learning experience. The Premium PowerPoint slides embed multimedia content including graphics, tables, links, and more.

DVD. The video package focuses on important leadership and teamwork skills and concepts found throughout the text. A Video Guide with segment overviews and discussion questions is also available.

Students will also have access to support materials that have been developed to help them obtain a strong understanding of the Leadership course.

Premium Student Website. In addition to the companion site (www.cengage-brain.com), you can also choose to package your text with the Premium Student Website. This PIN code–protected website is an optional package, and provides students with value-added content, including student-facing PowerPoint® slides, interactive quizzes and games, flash cards, leadership assessments, and more. Ask your sales representative about this optional package, or visit login .cengage.com to add Leadership to your bookshelf and access the Premium Student Website.

Acknowledgments

Any project as complex as this one requires a team of dedicated and talented people to see that it achieves its goals. First, I thank the many effective leaders whom I have observed in action for improving my understanding of leadership. Second, I thank the following professors who offered suggestions for improving this and previous editions:

Steve Barnett, *Unitec New Zealand*
Steven Barry, *University of Colorado–Boulder*
John Bigelow, *Boise State University*
Meika Bowden McFarland, *Albany Technical College*
Bruce T. Caine, *Vanderbilt University*
Felipe Chia, *Harrisburg Area Community College*
Jeewon Cho, *Montclair State University*
Conna Condon, *Upper Iowa University*
Emily J. Creighton, *University of New Hampshire*
Michael de Percy, *University of Canberra*
Rawlin Fairbough, *Sacred Heart University*
Michael Fekula, *The Citadel*
Janice Feldbauer, *Austin Community College*
Justin Frimmer, *Jacksonville University*
Barry Gold, *Pace University*
George B. Graen, *University of Cincinnati*
Stephen G. Green, *Purdue University*
Nathan Hanson, *Palm Beach Atlantic University*
James R. Harris, *North Carolina Agricultural and Technical State University*
Paul Harris, *Lee College*
Nell Hartley, *Robert Morris College*
Linda Hefferin, *Elgin Community College*
Winston Hill, *California State University, Chico*
Katherine Hyatt, *Reinhardt University*
Avis L. Johnson, *University of Akron*
Marvin Karlins, *University of South Florida*
Nelly Kazman, *University of La Verne*
David Lee, *University of Dayton*
Alan Lockyer, *Unitec New Zealand*

Brian McNatt, *University of Georgia*
Ralph Mullin, *Central Missouri State University*
Linda L. Neider, *University of Miami*
Andreas Nilsson, *Umeå School of Business, Sweden*
Rhonda S. Palladi, *Georgia State University*
Jeff Perlot, *Green River Community College*
Joseph Petrick, *Wright State University*
Mark Phillips, *University of Texas at San Antonio*
Judy Quinn, *Kutztown University*
Diana Rajendran, *Swinburne University of Technology at Lilydale*
Clint Relyea, *Arkansas State University*
Gary Renz, *Webster University*
Howard F. Rudd, *College of Charleston*
Silvia Sala, *University of Massachusetts at Loweel*
Tom J. Sanders, *University of Montevallo*
Robert Scherer, *Wright State University*
Marianne Sebok, *Community College of Southern Nevada*
Charles Seifert, *Siena College*
Kimberley L. Simons, *Madisonville Community College*
Randall G. Sleeth, *Virginia Commonwealth University*
Steven Tello, *University of Massachusetts at Lowell*
Ahmad Tootoonchi, *Frostburg State University*
David Van Fleet, *Arizona State University West*
John Warner, *University of New Mexico*
Velvet Weems-Landingham, *Kent State University—Geauga*

The editorial and production team at Cengage Learning also receives my gratitude. By name they are Erin Joyner, Scott Person, Conor Allen, Jennifer King, Ruth Belanger, Jonathan Monahan, and Kristin Meere. Sara Planck of Matrix Productions and Rebecca Roby also receive my gratitude for their contributions to this book. Writing without loved ones would be a lonely task. My thanks, therefore, also go to my family members—Drew, Douglas and Gizella, Melanie and Will, Rosie, Clare, Camila, Sofia, Eliana, Carson, Julian, and Owen.

A.J.D.

ABOUT THE AUTHOR

Andrew J. DuBrin is a professor of management emeritus in the College of Business at the Rochester Institute of Technology, where he teaches courses and conducts research in leadership, organizational behavior, and career management. He also served as department chairman and team leader in previous years. He received his PhD in industrial psychology from Michigan State University.

DuBrin has business experience in human resource management and consults with organizations and individuals. His specialties include leadership, influence tactics, and career development. DuBrin is an established author of both textbooks and trade books, and he has contributed to professional journals. He has written textbooks on organizational behavior, management, human relations, organizational politics, and impression management. His trade books cover many topics, including charisma, team play, coaching and mentoring, office politics, and self-discipline.

Principles of Leadership

The **Meaning** and **Relevance** of **Leadership**

1

LEARNING OBJECTIVES

After studying this chapter and doing the exercises, you should be able to

- Explain the meaning of leadership and how it differs from management.
- Describe how leadership influences organizational performance.
- Pinpoint several important leadership roles.
- Identify the major satisfactions and frustrations associated with the leadership role.

- Describe a framework for understanding leadership.
- Recognize how leadership skills are developed.
- Pinpoint several traits, behaviors, and attitudes of a successful follower.

CHAPTER OUTLINE

Andre Sougarett is a serious-minded, highly focused engineer who is also the manager of the government-owned El Teniente copper mine in Chile. One day news broke that thirty-three men were trapped deep within a gold mine in his country. Three days after the event, Sougarett was summoned by Chile's president, Sebastian Pinera. The president's orders were clear—the forty-six-year-old engineering leader would be in charge of the rescue operation.

Whether the miners were dead or alive, it would be the responsibility of Sougarett and his chosen team to complete the rescue operation as rapidly as possible. Sougarett faced enormous pressure because he had to decide where and how to drill through multiple layers of volcanic rock to reach the exact spot where the miners were located.

At the mine, the methodical Sougarret encountered a mass of confusion and anxiety. Loads of people, including rescue workers, police workers, and firefighters, were milling around, along with relatives desperately seeking word about the status of the trapped miners. Sougarret's first move—in order to get the rescue mission started and decrease some of the confusion—was to ask the rescue workers to leave until they might be needed later. He also requested any available maps of the mine.

Sougarett's team began by involving a risk manager, and the team grew to 300 people in the next several weeks. At the moment Sougarret was placed in charge of the rescue operation, seven companies were already assigned to the task. Sougarret kept on those he thought could make the biggest contribution.

A key part of the rescue operation was building three shafts. At the end it was Plan B, a 28-inch wide shaft, that reached the miners first, beating the estimate of how long the rescue operation would take by a couple of months. A remaining step was to encase the top of the funnel in steel pipes and test the workability of the escape capsule. At this point, Sougarett was no longer apprehensive. "The last stage for me was like butter," he said.

In reflecting on the Chilean miracle, a business reporter said, "… the saving of those men gave us something we don't see enough, a brilliant example of human excellence—of cohesion, of united and committed action, of planning, of execution, of caring. They used the human brain and spirit to save life."[1]

The description of Andre Sougarret touches on many leadership topics to be covered in this book, including the ideas that providing direction is part of a leader's job, that technical expertise is an important leadership role, and that a superior leader can help workers get through a crisis.

Our introductory chapter begins with an explanation of what leadership is and is not. We then examine how leaders make a difference, the various roles they play, and the major satisfactions and frustrations they experience. The chapter also includes an explanation of how reading this book and doing the various quizzes and exercises will enhance your own leadership skills. It concludes with a discussion of followership—giving leaders good material to work with.

THE MEANING OF LEADERSHIP

You will read about many effective organizational leaders throughout this text. The common characteristic of these leaders is their ability to inspire and stimulate others to achieve worthwhile goals. Therefore, we can define **leadership** as the ability to inspire confidence and support among the people who are needed to achieve organizational goals.[2]

A Google search of articles and books about leadership in organizations indicates 14 million entries. In all those entries, leadership has probably been defined in many ways. Here are several other representative definitions of leadership:

- A process in which an individual influences a group of individuals to achieve a common goal
- The influential increment over and above mechanical compliance with directions and orders
- An act that causes others to act or respond in a shared direction
- The art of influencing people by persuasion or example to follow a line of action
- An effort to maintain control and power over others
- The principal dynamic force that motivates and coordinates the organization in the accomplishment of its objectives[3]
- A willingness to take the blame (as defined by legendary football quarterback Joe Montana)[4]
- First figuring out what's right, and then explaining it to people, as opposed to first having people explain to you what's right, and then just saying what they want to hear (as defined by former New York mayor and presidential candidate Rudy Giuliani)[5]

Importantly, leadership is not only found among people in high-level positions. Quite the contrary: Leadership is needed at all levels in an organization and can be practiced to some extent even by a person not assigned to a formal leadership position. For example, working as a junior accountant, a person might take the initiative to suggest to management that they need to be more careful about what they classify as a true sale. A current analysis suggests that for improved business results to come about, it will be because managers below the "C suite" (such as CEO, COO, and CFO) take the initiative and risks to drive the company in a different direction. Change needs to come about from leaders at lower levels, rather than relying exclusively on leadership from the top.[6]

Part of understanding leadership is recognizing that new job titles for leaders and managers continue to emerge, reflecting new responsibilities for leaders. Here are three examples of leadership positions with relatively new titles:

- Chief Customer Officer—works with a small staff to enhance customer retention.
- Chief Revenue Officer—oversees corporate advertising accounts at a media company, such as Time Inc.
- Director of Social Media—works with a small staff to directly spearhead advertising and publicity on social media websites.

The ability to lead others effectively is a rare quality. It becomes even more rare at the highest levels in an organization because the complexity of such positions requires a vast range of leadership skills. This is one reason that firms in search of new leadership seek out a select group of brand-name executives with proven track records. It is also why companies now emphasize leadership training and development to create a new supply of leaders throughout the firm.

Leadership as a Partnership and Shared Responsibility

The current understanding of leadership is that it is a partnership between leaders and group members, including a sharing of leadership responsibility. According to Peter Block, in a **partnership**, the leader and the group members are connected in such a way that the power between them is approximately balanced. Block also describes partnership as the opposite of parenting (in which one person—the parent—takes responsibility for the welfare of the other—the child). Partnership occurs when control shifts from the leader to the group member, in a move away from authoritarianism and toward shared decision making.[7] Four things are necessary for a valid partnership to exist:

1. *Exchange of purpose.* In a partnership, every worker at every level is responsible for defining vision and values. Through dialogue with people at many levels, the leader helps articulate a widely accepted vision.
2. *A right to say no.* The belief that people who express a contrary opinion will be punished runs contrary to a partnership. Rather, a person can lose an argument but never a voice.
3. *Joint accountability.* In a partnership, each person is responsible for outcomes and for the current situation. In practice, this means that each person takes personal accountability for the success and failure of the organizational unit. (See Joe Montana's definition of leadership, stated earlier.)
4. *Absolute honesty.* In a partnership, not telling the truth to one another is an act of betrayal. When power is distributed, people are more likely to tell the truth because they feel less vulnerable.

Block's conception of leadership as a partnership is an ideal to strive toward. Empowerment and team building—two major topics in this book—support the idea of a partnership. Also, many leadership theorists and managers agree that the leadership role within a team is seldom the responsibility of one person. Rather, several individuals within the team may serve as leaders, both by formal assignment and informally. Leadership may shift, depending on whose expertise is the most relevant at the moment,[8] such as one member of a marketing team having advanced expertise in using social media for product promotion.

Looking at leadership as a partnership is also important because it is linked to an optimistic view of group members who want to perform well for the good of the organization.

Leadership as a Relationship

A modern study of leadership emphasizes that it consists of a relationship between the leader and the people being led. In the words of popular leadership theorist Ken Blanchard, "Leadership isn't something you do to people. It's something you do with them."[9] Research indicates that having good relationships with group members is a major success factor for the three top positions in large organizations. James Kouzes and Barry Posner conducted an online survey asking respondents to indicate, among other responses, which would be more essential to business success in five years: social skills or Internet skills.

Seventy-two percent indicated social skills, and 28 percent, Internet skills. The authors concluded that the web of people matters more than the web of technology.[10] (Yet a person who lacks Internet skills may not have the opportunity to be in a position to manage relationships.) Building relationships with people is such an important part of leadership that the theme will be introduced at various points in this text.

How leaders build relationships has changed somewhat in the modern era of Web 2.0 and its emphasis on interacting with people electronically. It is common practice for leaders to give recognition and praise via e-mail or a posting on the company social media site, or a public social media site such as Facebook or Twitter. As a representative example, at Cisco Systems managers are encouraged to communicate with group members through blogging, uploading videos, and using company-created social networking tools.[11]

Leadership Versus Management

To understand leadership, it is important to grasp the difference between leadership and management. We get a clue from the standard conceptualization of the functions of management: planning, organizing, directing (or leading), and controlling. Leading is a major part of a manager's job, yet a manager must also plan, organize, and control.

Broadly speaking, leadership deals with the interpersonal aspects of a manager's job, whereas planning, organizing, and controlling deal with the administrative aspects. Leadership deals with change, inspiration, motivation, and influence. Table 1-1 presents a stereotype of the differences between

TABLE 1-1 Leaders versus Managers

LEADER	MANAGER
Visionary	Rational
Passionate	Businesslike
Creative	Persistent
Inspiring	Tough-minded
Innovative	Analytical
Imaginative	Deliberative
Experimental	Authoritative
Warm and radiant	Cool and reserved
Initiator	Implementer
Acts as coach, consultant, teacher	Acts as a boss
Does the right things	Does things right
Inspires through great ideas	Commands through position
Knows results are achieved through people	Focuses on results
Focuses on uplifting ideas	Focuses on plumbing

Source: Genevieve Capowski, "Anatomy of a Leader: Where Are the Leaders of Tomorrow?" *Management Review*, March 1994, p. 12; David Fagiano, "Managers Versus Leaders: A Corporate Fable," *Management Review*, November 1997, p. 5; Keki R. Bhote, *The Ultimate Six Sigma* (New York: AMACOM, 2002); "Leaders: Salespeople in Disguise?" *Manager's Edge*, Special Issue, 2007, p. 3; Henry Mintzberg, *Managing* (San Francisco: Berrett-Koehler Publishers, 2009), pp. 8–9.

leadership and management. As is the case with most stereotypes, the differences tend to be exaggerated.

According to John P. Kotter, a prominent leadership theorist, managers must know how to lead as well as manage. Without being led as well as managed, organizations face the threat of extinction. Following are several key distinctions between management and leadership:

- Management produces order, consistency, and predictability.
- Leadership produces change and adaptability to new products, new markets, new competitors, new customers, and new work processes.
- Leadership, in contrast to management, involves having a vision of what the organization can become and mobilizing people to accomplish it.
- Leadership produces change, often to a dramatic degree, such as by spearheading the launch of a new product or opening a new market for an old product. Management is more likely to produce a degree of predictability and order.
- Top-level leaders are likely to transform their organizations, whereas top-level managers just manage (or maintain) organizations.
- A leader creates a vision (lofty goal) to direct the organization. In contrast, the key function of the manager is to implement the vision. The manager and his or her team thus choose the means to achieve the end that the leader formulates.[12]

If these views are taken to their extreme, the leader is an inspirational figure, and the manager is a stodgy bureaucrat mired in the status quo. But we must be careful not to downplay the importance of management. Effective leaders have to be good managers themselves or be supported by effective managers. A germane example is the inspirational entrepreneur who is so preoccupied with motivating employees and captivating customers that he or she neglects internal administration. As a result, costs skyrocket beyond income, and such matters as funding the employee pension plan and paying bills and taxes on time are overlooked. In short, the difference between leadership and management is one of emphasis. Effective leaders also manage, and effective managers also lead.

Management guru Henry Mintzberg, a professor at McGill University, strongly supports based on firsthand observation the position that the difference between leadership and management should not be overdrawn. Mintzberg writes:

> How would you like to be managed by someone who doesn't lead? That can be awfully dispiriting. Well, then, why would you want to be led by someone who doesn't manage? That can be terribly disengaging; how are such "leaders" to know what is going on?[13]

An example of how a company might recognize the difference between leadership and management took place at the Boston investment firm GMO LLC. The company brought on the first chief executive in its thirty-two-year history, Marc Mayer. His role was to take care of running the company (management) so that senior officials could focus more on navigating the treacherous market (strategic leadership).[14]

THE IMPACT OF LEADERSHIP ON ORGANIZATIONAL PERFORMANCE

An assumption underlying the study of leadership is that leaders affect organizational performance. Boards of directors—the highest-level executives of an organization—make the same assumption. A frequent antidote to major organizational problems is to replace the leader in the hope that the newly appointed leader will reverse performance problems. Here we will review some of the evidence and opinion, pro and con, about the ability of leaders to affect organizational performance.

Research and Opinion: Leadership Does Make a Difference

The idea that leaders actually influence organizational performance and morale seems plausible, and there has been a moderate amount of research and opinion that deals with this issue. Think back to the story of the chief engineer who spearheaded activities to rescue the miners in Chile. It is difficult to imagine that the rescue would have been accomplished without an effective leader and manager in charge. Here we look at a sample of the existing research and opinion on the topic of leaders making a difference on performance.

The Center on Leadership & Ethics at Duke University conducted a survey about executive leadership based on 205 executives from public and private companies. One of the issues explored was whether leadership actions can affect performance. It was concluded that they can indeed, but only if the leader is perceived to be responsible and inspirational. Such behaviors included engaging employees in the company's vision, and inspiring employees to elevate their goals. Another contributor to organizational performance was promoting an environment in which employees have a sense of responsibility for the entire organization.[15]

The *flexible leadership theory* developed by Gary Yukl, a professor of management at the University of Albany, also provides insight as to when leaders contribute to organizational performance. One proposition of the theory is that organizational performance is stronger when the influence of middle- and lower-level leaders on important decisions is commensurate with their unique, relevant knowledge.[16] The implication is that involving leaders throughout the organization in making decisions improves company performance—if these leaders are knowledgeable about the problem to be resolved. (This proposition contrasts with leadership advisers who think that anybody should be encouraged to participate in decision making.)

A leader who appears to adhere to the flexible leadership theory proposition just mentioned is Mary Berner, the chief executive of Reader's Digest Association. She and her team are doing their best to revitalize the once prominent *Reader's Digest*, as well as the approximately one hundred other magazines the association publishes. Middle-level managers throughout the global organization contribute relevant knowledge to editorial, production, and financial decisions.[17] The contribution of these many leaders helped the Reader's Digest Association work its way through bankruptcy in 2009–2011.

In another study, a group of researchers analyzed 200 management techniques as employed by 150 companies over 10 years. The aspect of the study evaluating the effects of leadership found that CEOs influence 15 percent of the total variance (influencing factors) in a company's profitability or total return to shareholders. The same study also found that the industry in which a company operates also accounts for 15 percent of the variance in profitability. So, the choice of a CEO leader is as important as the choice of whether to remain in the same industry or enter a different one.[18]

An analysis of the franchise industry points to the importance of leadership. The report noted that it can be difficult to pinpoint a specific formula for franchise success, yet conversations with successful franchise operators emphasized the importance of enthusiasm, leadership, and an ability to work with people. (Enthusiasm and the ability to work with people are important components of leadership.) One of the franchisers included in the report was Steven J. Greenbaum, the founder of PostNet International Franchise Corp., which offers copying, printing, packing, and shipping services. According to Greenbaum, "Leadership is critical. You are required to have a vision of what the business can be, and communicate the vision to the company officers and franchisees."[19]

An overview of research on managerial succession over a recent twenty-year period provides more support for the idea that leadership has an impact on organizational performance. A consistent relationship was found between who is in charge and how well an organization performed as measured by a variety of indicators. Using different methodologies, these studies arrived at the same conclusion that changes in leadership are followed by changes in company performance. Statistical analyses suggest that the leader might be responsible for somewhere between 15 percent and 45 percent of a firm's performance.[20]

Leadership researcher Bruce J. Avolio from the University of Washington, along with four colleagues, conducted a comprehensive synthesis of 200 studies about the impact of leadership. The studies analyzed included those conducted in laboratories and in work settings. The many outcomes of leadership studied included outcomes such as the satisfactions of subordinates and organizational performance. One of the many study findings was that the leader's activities had a 66-percent probability of achieving a positive outcome.[21]

How leaders impact organizational (or unit) performance is the essential subject of this book. For example, good results are attained by developing teamwork and formulating the right strategy.

Research and Opinion: Formal Leadership Does Not Make a Difference

In contrast to the previous argument, the anti-leadership argument holds that the impact of the leader on organizational outcomes is smaller than the impact of forces within the situation. To personalize this perspective, imagine yourself appointed as the manager of a group of highly skilled investment bankers. How well your group performs could be attributed as much to their talent and to economic conditions as to your leadership. The three major arguments against the importance of leadership are substitutes for leadership, leadership irrelevance, and complexity theory.

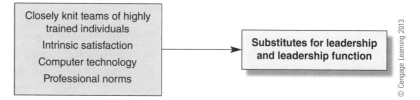

FIGURE 1-1 Substitutes for Leadership.

Substitutes for Leadership   At times, competent leadership is not necessary, and incompetent leadership can be counterbalanced by certain factors in the work situation. Under these circumstances, leadership itself is of little consequence to the performance and satisfaction of team members. According to this viewpoint, many organizations have **substitutes for leadership**. Such substitutes are factors in the work environment that provide guidance and incentives to perform, making the leader's role almost superfluous,[22] as shown in Figure 1-1.

1. *Closely knit teams of highly trained individuals.* When members of a cohesive, highly trained group are focused on a goal, they may require almost no leadership to accomplish their task.
2. *Intrinsic satisfaction.* Employees who are engaged in work they find strongly self-motivating, or intrinsically satisfying, require a minimum of leadership. Part of the reason is that the task itself grabs the worker's attention and energy. The worker may require little leadership as long as the task is proceeding smoothly.
3. *Computer technology.* Some companies today use computer-aided monitoring and computer networking to take over many of the supervisor's leadership functions. The computer provides productivity and quality data, and directions for certain tasks are entered into the information system. (We could argue here that the computer is being used to control, rather than to lead, workers.)
4. *Professional norms.* Workers who incorporate strong professional norms often require a minimum of supervision and leadership. A group of certified professional accountants may not need visionary leadership to inspire them to do an honest job of auditing the books of a client or advising against tax fraud.

Leadership Irrelevance   Jeffrey Pfeffer, a professor of organizational behavior at Stanford University, theorizes that leadership is irrelevant to most organizational outcomes. Rather, it is the situation that must be carefully analyzed. Pfeffer argues that factors outside the leader's control have a larger impact on business outcomes than do leadership actions.[23] In recent years, the sales of smart phones have surpassed the sale of personal computers, including laptops and tablet computers. The sales boom in these could be better attributed to an outside force of handheld communication technology becoming so essential for so many people than to inspirational leadership within telecommunications companies.

Another aspect of the leader irrelevance argument is that high-level leaders have unilateral control over only a few resources. Furthermore, the leader's control of these resources is limited by obligations to stakeholders like consumers and stockholders. Finally, firms tend to choose new organizational leaders whose values are compatible with those of the firm. The leaders therefore act in ways similar to previous leaders.

Jim Collins, who has extensively researched how companies endure and how they shift from average to superior performance, also doubts the relevance of leadership. According to his earlier research, corporate leaders are slaves of much larger organizational forces. Collins makes the analogy of children holding a pair of ribbons inside a coach and imagining they are driving the horse. It is not the leader's personality that makes a difference; more important is the organization's personality.[24]

Another argument for leadership irrelevance is that in the modern organization effective leadership means widespread collaboration in obtaining ideas, rather than the heroic leader doing all the innovating. According to this point of view, instead of centralizing leadership in the hands of a few, authority and power are shared, and people lead themselves.[25] (The concept of shared leadership was mentioned above in relation to leadership as a partnership, and will surface at several places in the text.)

The leader irrelevance argument would have greater practical value if it were recast as a *leader constraint theory*, which would hold that leaders are constrained in what they can do but still have plenty of room to influence others.

Complexity Theory Similar to the pessimistic outlook of leader irrelevance is the perspective of *complexity theory*, which holds that organizations are complex systems that cannot be explained by the usual rules of nature. Leaders and managers can do little to alter the course of the complex organizational system. The same view holds that forces outside the leader or manager's control determine a company's fate. Managers cannot predict which business strategies or product mixes will survive. The best they can hope for is to scramble or innovate in order to adapt to outside forces. Ultimately, all companies will die, but at different times, because it is the system, not leadership and management, that dominates.

Another aspect of complexity theory that challenges the importance of the leader is that organizational members are not passive workers in need of direction and emotional support. Instead, they are active agents who influenced coworkers and are influenced by them. The same people are capable of dealing with harsh realities, such as the need to adapt to new technology, without direction from above.[26]

A useful perspective on whether leadership makes a difference is to ask the right question as framed by J. Richard Hackman and Ruth Wageman. Instead of asking if leaders make a difference, we should be asking under what conditions leaders make a difference.[27] A crisis mode is an example of a situation in which a strong leader usually makes a difference, such as getting field units back on track after a hurricane or product recall.

LEADERSHIP ROLES

Another way to gain an understanding of leadership is to examine the various roles carried out by leaders. A *role* in this context is an expected set of activities or behaviors stemming from one's job. Leadership roles are a subset of the managerial roles studied by Henry Mintzberg and others.[28] Before reading ahead to the summary of leadership roles, you are invited to complete Leadership Self-Assessment Quiz 1-1.

LEADERSHIP SELF-ASSESSMENT QUIZ 1-1

Readiness for the Leadership Role

Instructions: Indicate the extent to which you agree with each of the following statements, using the following scale: 1, disagree strongly; 2, disagree; 3, neutral; 4, agree; 5, agree strongly.

1. I like having people count on me for ideas and suggestions.

    1   2   3   4   5

2. I have definitely inspired other people.

    1   2   3   4   5

3. It's a good practice to ask people provocative questions about their work.

    1   2   3   4   5

4. It's easy for me to compliment others.

    1   2   3   4   5

5. I have many more friends and followers on social working websites than do most people.

    1   2   3   4   5

6. I like to cheer people up even when my own spirits are down.

    1   2   3   4   5

7. What my team accomplishes is more important than my personal glory.

    1   2   3   4   5

8. Many people imitate my ideas.

    1   2   3   4   5

9. Building team spirit is important to me.

    1   2   3   4   5

10. I would enjoy coaching other members of the team.

    1   2   3   4   5

11. It is important to me to recognize others for their accomplishments.

    1   2   3   4   5

12. I would enjoy entertaining visitors to my firm even if it interfered with my completing a report.

    1   2   3   4   5

13. It would be fun for me to represent my team at gatherings outside our unit.

    1   2   3   4   5

QUIZ 1-1 (continued)

14. The problems of my teammates are my problems too.

   1   **2**   **3**   **4**   **5**

15. Resolving conflict is an activity I enjoy.

   1   **2**   **3**   **4**   **5**

16. I would cooperate with another unit in the organization even if I disagreed with the position taken by its members.

   1   **2**   **3**   **4**   **5**

17. I am an idea generator on the job.

   1   **2**   **3**   **4**   **5**

18. It is fun for me to bargain whenever I have the opportunity.

   1   **2**   **3**   **4**   **5**

19. Team members listen to me when I speak.

   1   **2**   **3**   **4**   **5**

20. People have asked me to assume the leadership of an activity several times in my life.

   1   **2**   **3**   **4**   **5**

21. I have always been a convincing person.

   1   **2**   **3**   **4**   **5**

22. I enjoy imagining a bright future for a group to which I belong.

   1   **2**   **3**   **4**   **5**

23. Several people have told me that I have good ability to see the big picture.

   1   **2**   **3**   **4**   **5**

24. I am willing to listen to people gripe and complain about their job.

   1   **2**   **3**   **4**   **5**

25. I enjoy the opportunity to work with people from cultures different than my own.

   1   **2**   **3**   **4**   **5**

Total score: _____

Scoring and Interpretation: Calculate your total score by adding the numbers circled. A tentative interpretation of the scoring is as follows:

- **90–100:** High readiness for the leadership role
- **60–89:** Moderate readiness for the leadership role
- **40–59:** Some uneasiness with the leadership role
- **39 or less:** Low readiness for the leadership role

   If you are already a successful leader and you scored low on this questionnaire, ignore your score. If you scored surprisingly low and you are not yet a leader, or are currently performing poorly as a leader, study the statements carefully. Consider changing your attitude or your behavior so that you can legitimately answer more of the statements with a 4 or a 5. Studying the rest of this text will give you additional insights that may be helpful in your development as a leader.

Leading is a complex activity, so it is not surprising that Mintzberg and other researchers identified ten roles that can be classified as part of the leadership function of management.

1. **Figurehead.** Leaders, particularly high-ranking managers, spend some part of their time engaging in ceremonial activities, or acting as a figurehead. Four specific behaviors fit the figurehead role of a leader:
   a. entertaining clients or customers as an official representative of the organization
   b. making oneself available to outsiders as a representative of the organization
   c. serving as an official representative of the organization at gatherings outside the organization
   d. escorting official visitors

2. **Spokesperson.** When a manager acts as a spokesperson, the emphasis is on answering letters or inquiries and formally reporting to individuals and groups outside the manager's direct organizational unit. As a spokesperson, the managerial leader keeps five groups of people informed about the unit's activities, plans, capabilities, and possibilities (vision):
   a. upper-level management
   b. clients or customers
   c. other important outsiders such as labor unions
   d. professional colleagues
   e. the general public

   Dealing with outside groups and the general public is usually the responsibility of top-level managers.

3. **Negotiator.** Part of almost any manager's job description is trying to make deals with others for needed resources. Four illustrative negotiating activities are as follows:
   a. bargaining with superiors for funds, facilities, equipment, or other forms of support
   b. bargaining with other units in the organization for the use of staff, facilities, equipment, or other forms of support
   c. bargaining with suppliers and vendors for services, schedules, and delivery times
   d. bargaining with job candidates about starting compensation and benefits

4. **Coach and motivator.** An effective leader takes the time to coach and motivate team members, and sometimes to inspire large groups of people inside the organization. This role includes five specific behaviors:
   a. informally recognizing team members' achievements
   b. providing team members with feedback concerning ineffective performance
   c. ensuring that team members are informed of steps that can improve their performance
   d. implementing rewards and punishments to encourage and sustain good performance
   e. inspiring people through such means as being charismatic, creating visions, telling interesting stories, and being highly ethical

5. *Team builder.* A key aspect of a leader's role is to build an effective team. Activities contributing to this role include:
   a. ensuring that team members are recognized for their accomplishments, such as through letters of appreciation
   b. initiating activities that contribute to group morale, such as giving parties and sponsoring sports teams
   c. holding periodic staff meetings to encourage team members to talk about their accomplishments, problems, and concerns

6. *Team player.* Related to the team-builder role is that of the team player. Three behaviors of team players are:
   a. displaying appropriate personal conduct
   b. cooperating with other units in the organization
   c. displaying loyalty to superiors by fully supporting their plans and decisions

7. *Technical problem solver.* It is particularly important for supervisors and middle managers to help team members solve technical problems. Two activities contributing to this role are:
   a. serving as a technical expert or adviser, such as helping the group make optimum use of social marketing to promote the company
   b. performing individual contributor tasks on a regular basis, such as making sales calls or repairing machinery

8. *Entrepreneur.* Although not self-employed, managers who work in large organizations have some responsibility for suggesting innovative ideas or furthering the business aspects of the firm. Three entrepreneurial leadership role activities are:
   a. reading trade publications and professional journals to keep up with what is happening in the industry and profession
   b. talking with customers or others in the organization to keep aware of changing needs and requirements
   c. getting involved in situations outside the unit that could suggest ways of improving the unit's performance, such as visiting other firms, attending professional meetings or trade shows, and participating in educational programs

9. *Strategic planner.* Top-level managers engage in strategic planning, usually assisted by input from others throughout the organization. Carrying out the strategic-planner role enables the manager to practice strategic leadership. The strategist role is concerned with shaping the future of the organization, or a unit within the larger organization. Specific activities involved in this role include:
   a. setting a vision and direction for the organization and providing innovative ideas to pursue
   b. helping the firm deal with the external environment
   c. helping develop organizational policies

10. *Executor.* In carrying out the executor role, the leader makes things happen, often helping translate plans into action. Parts of this role include:
   a. translating strategy into action, such as helping develop action plans
   b. making change happen
   c. holding people accountable to ensure that productive work is accomplished

A common thread in the leadership roles of a manager is that the managerial leader in some way inspires or influences others. An analysis in the *Harvard Business Review* concluded that the most basic role for corporate leaders is to release the human spirit that makes initiative, creativity, and entrepreneurship possible.[29] An important practical implication is that managers at every level can exercise leadership. For example, a team leader can make an important contribution to the firm's thrust for efficiency by explaining to team members how to minimize duplications in a mailing list. Leadership Skill-Building Exercise 1-1 provides an opportunity to apply role analysis to yourself.

LEADERSHIP SKILL-BUILDING EXERCISE 1-1

My Leadership Role Analysis

Here is an opportunity for you to think through your current level of skill or potential ability to carry out successfully the ten leadership roles already described. Each role will be listed along with a reminder of one of its key aspects. Check next to each role whether it is an activity you could carry out now, or something for which you will need more experience and preparation. For those activities you check as "capable of doing it now," jot down an example of your success in this area. For example, a person who checked "capable of

doing it now" for Role 7, technical problem solver, might have written: "I helped the restaurant where I was an assistant manager bring in more revenue during off-peak hours. I promoted an early-bird supper for senior citizens."

Few readers of this book will have had experience in carrying out most of these roles. So relate the specific roles to any leadership experience you may have had, including full-time work, part-time work, volunteer work, clubs, committees, and sports.

LEADERSHIP ROLE	CAPABLE OF DOING IT NOW	NEED PREPARATION AND EXPERIENCE
1. Figurehead (Engage in ceremonial activities; represent the group to outsiders.)	☐	☐
2. Spokesperson (Answer inquiries; report information about the group to outsiders.)	☐	☐
3. Negotiator (Make deals with others for needed resources.)	☐	☐
4. Coach and motivator (Recognize achievements; encourage; give feedback and advice; inspire people.)	☐	☐
5. Team builder (Contribute to group morale; hold meetings to encourage members to talk about accomplishments and concerns.)	☐	☐
6. Team player (Correct conduct; cooperate with others; be loyal.)	☐	☐
7. Technical problem solver (Help group members solve technical problems; perform individual contributor tasks.)	☐	☐
8. Entrepreneur (Suggest innovative ideas and further business activity of the group; search for new undertakings for the group.)	☐	☐
9. Strategic planner (Set direction for others based on external environment.)	☐	☐
10. Executor. (Makes things happen, often helping translate plans into action.)	☐	☐

Interpretation: The more of the ten roles you are ready to perform, the more ready you are to function as a manager or to perform managerial work. Your study of leadership will facilitate carrying out more of these roles effectively. For purposes of skill development, choose one of the roles in which you need preparation and experience. Read some information in this text or elsewhere about the role, and then practice that role when the opportunity arises. Or create an opportunity to practice that role. For example, assume you have a valuable skill such as gathering followers on a social media website. During the next couple of weeks, coach a beginner in creating effective social media posts.

Up to this point, we have described the meaning of leadership, how leadership affects organizational performance, and the many activities carried out by leaders. You have had an opportunity to explore your attitudes toward occupying the leadership role and to personally apply leadership role analysis. We now further personalize information about leadership.

The accompanying Leader in Action helps illustrate both leadership roles and the fact that a leader can make a difference.

LEADER IN ACTION

CEO Martin Mucci of Paychex Wants to Make a Difference

A large number of employees cheered when insider Martin Mucci was named president and chief executive officer of Paychex Inc. in 2010. Paychex is an established provider of payroll, human resource, and benefits outsourcing services for small to medium-sized business firms. Company founder and philanthropist Tom Golisano said "Marty Mucci has earned the opportunity to be the CEO in this company, based on his character, his level of accomplishment, and his ability to be an inspiring leader." John Morphy, senior vice president, chief financial officer, and treasurer commented, "Having Marty means you have someone people will respect, and he spends a lot of time with the people and cares about them. At the same time, he'll make decisions he needs to make on an expedient basis."

Tor Constantino, a former colleague at a communications company, added that Paychex is bound to succeed with Mucci at the head. "He's a force of nature from a business perspective," Constantino said. "He has a very savvy background and an excellent grasp of customers and employees and how to get the most out of individuals. For a top-quality organization to land such a stellar executive as Marty is only going to mean good things for Paychex in the future."

In accepting the CEO assignment, Mucci said, "I am excited about the opportunity to take Paychex to the next level of performance. We have more than 12,000 dedicated employees and an experienced management team, and I look forward to working together to build in the company's history of success."

Mucci said he like to be involved in just about every facet of the organization, and stay on top of almost everything. "Board members were looking for a long-term builder for the business, to grow the business and do it in a steady, continuous run," said Mucci, who has been with Paychex since 2002 as senior vice president of operations. "I believe I can do that and I accept the challenge to continually build the company over the long haul."

Mucci said that Paychex will prosper through growing its client base through better sales execution, as well as having the right products. He added that the company planned to grow its payroll client base through acquisition and sales. Paychex was also exploring whether there were markets other than payroll and human resources outsourcing it could penetrate. Mucci wondered if there were other things like offering accounting software and credit-card processing that small businesses need.

In talking about the CEO role, Mucci said that he relished having responsibility for getting results. He pointed out that having already had oversight of 8,000 of the 12,000 employees he had a good sense of the people.

"Paychex and the culture that's been built over almost 40 years will see changes but it'll remain mostly the same. You don't break something that's successful. I got into the job to make a difference, and that is just more success and the long-term growth of the business.

If it takes changes in people or processes or products, we'll do it."

Mucci holds an MBA from the Simon School of the University of Rochester, and was previously vice president of operations for Paychex. His other business experience includes being the CEO of a telephone company, and the president of telephone operations for Frontier Communications.

QUESTIONS

1. In what ways does Mucci hope to make an impact as a leader?
2. Which leadership roles does Mucci see himself as occupying?
3. How qualified does Mucci appear to be to hold the CEO position of Paychex?

Source: Story created from facts in the following sources: Matthew Daneman, "Mucci's Goal: Build Sales Quickly, Repeat," *Democrat and Chronicle Business*, October 20, 2010, pp. 5B, 6; Nate Dougherty, "Numbers Guy: Martin Mucci Will Focus on Restoring Sales Growth at Paychex," *Rochester Business Journal* (www.rbj. net), October 22, 2010, pp. 1–6; "Paychex Names Martin Mucci President and Chief Executive Officer," *Business Wire* (www.techzone360. com/news), September 30, 2010; "Paychex Names Martin Mucci CEO, President," *Fairport-East Rochester Post* (www.fairport-erpost. com), September 30, 2010, p. 1.

THE SATISFACTIONS AND FRUSTRATIONS OF BEING A LEADER

The term *leader* has a positive connotation for most people. To be called a leader is generally better than to be called a follower or a subordinate. (The term *follower* has virtually disappeared in organizations, and the term *subordinate* has fallen out of favor. The preferred term for a person who reports to a leader or manager is *team member*, *group member*, or *associate*. Researchers, however, continue to use the terms *subordinate* and *follower* for technical purposes.) Yet being a leader, such as a team leader, vice president, or COO (chief operating officer), does not always bring personal satisfaction. Some leadership jobs are more fun than others, such as being the leader of a successful group with cheerful team members.

Because most of you are contemplating becoming a leader or moving further into a leadership role, it is worthwhile to examine some of the potential satisfactions and frustrations many people find in being an organizational leader.

Satisfactions of Leaders

The types of satisfactions that you might obtain from being a formal leader depend on your particular leadership position. Factors such as the amount of money you are paid and the type of people in your group influence your satisfaction. Leaders often experience seven sources of satisfaction.

1. *A feeling of power and prestige.* Being a leader automatically grants you some power. Prestige is forthcoming because many people think highly of people who are leaders. In some organizations, top-level leaders are addressed as Mr., Mrs., or Ms., whereas lower-ranking people are referred to by their surnames. Yet most leaders encourage others to address them by their first names.

2. *A chance to help others grow and develop.* A leader works directly with people, often teaching them job skills, serving as a mentor, and listening to personal problems. Part of a leader's job is to help other people become managers and leaders. A leader often feels as much of a people helper as does a human resource manager or a counselor. Kip Tindell, founder of the Container Store, says that one of the most rewarding aspects of his job is enriching people's lives.[30]

3. *High income.* Leaders, in general, receive higher pay than team members, and executive leaders in major business corporations typically earn several million dollars per year. A handful of business executives receive compensation of over $100 million per year and several have received over $150 million as compensation for being fired. If money is an important motivator or satisfier, being a leader has a built-in satisfaction. In some situations a team leader earns virtually the same amount of money as other team members. Occupying a team leadership position, however, is a starting point on the path to high-paying leadership positions.

4. *Respect and status.* A leader frequently receives respect from group members. He or she also enjoys a higher status than people who are not occupying a leadership role. Status accompanies being appointed to a leadership position on or off the job. When an individual's personal qualifications match the position, his or her status is even higher.

5. *Good opportunities for advancement.* Once you become a leader, your advancement opportunities increase. Obtaining a leadership position is a vital first step for career advancement in many organizations. Staff or individual contributor positions help broaden a person's professional experience, but most executives rise through a managerial path.

6. *A feeling of being in on things.* A side benefit of being a leader is that you receive more inside information. For instance, as a manager you are invited to attend management meetings. In those meetings you are given information not passed along to individual contributors. One such tidbit might be plans for expansion or downsizing.

7. *An opportunity to control money and other resources.* A leader is often in the position of helping to prepare a department budget and authorize expenses. Even though you cannot spend this money personally, knowing that

your judgment on financial matters is trusted does provide some satisfaction. Many leaders in both private and public organizations control annual budgets of several million dollars.

Dissatisfactions and Frustrations of Leaders

About one out of ten people in the work force is classified as a supervisor, administrator, or manager. Not every one of these people is a true leader. Yet the problems these people experience often stem from the leadership portions of their job. Many individual contributors refuse to accept a leadership role because of the frustrations they have seen leaders endure. These frustrations include the following:

1. ***Too much uncompensated overtime.*** People in leadership jobs are usually expected to work longer hours than other employees. Such unpaid hours are called casual overtime. People in organizational leadership positions typically spend about fifty-five hours per week working. During peak periods of peak demands, this figure can surge to eighty hours per week.

2. ***Too many headaches.*** It would take several pages to list all the potential problems leaders face. Being a leader is a good way to discover the validity of Murphy's law: "If anything can go wrong, it will." A leader is subject to a batch of problems involving people and things. Many people find that a leadership position is a source of stress, and many managers experience burnout.

3. ***Facing a perform-or-perish mentality.*** Many leaders face an enormous amount of pressure to either perform or be fired. These pressures often can be found in companies owned by private equity (or buyout) firms. The head of each company owned by an equity firm is expected to make the company profitable through such means as slashing costs, boosting sales in international markets, and paying down debt. There is also considerable pressure on the CEO to improve operations by making them more efficient.[31]

4. ***Not enough authority to carry out responsibility.*** People in managerial positions complain repeatedly that they are held responsible for things over which they have little control. As a leader, you might be expected to work with an ill-performing team member, yet you lack the power to fire him or her. Or you might be expected to produce high-quality service with too small a staff and no authority to become fully staffed.

5. ***Loneliness.*** As former Secretary of State and five-star general Colin Powell says, "Command is lonely." The higher you rise as a leader, the lonelier you will be in a certain sense. Leadership limits the number of people in whom you can confide. It is awkward to confide negative feelings about your employer to a team member. It is equally awkward to complain about one group member to another. Some people in leadership positions feel lonely because they miss being one of the gang.

6. ***Too many problems involving people.*** A major frustration facing a leader is the number of human resource problems requiring action. The lower your leadership position, the more such problems you face. For example, the

office supervisor spends more time dealing with problem employees than does the chief information officer. If you do not like dealing with people problems, you are not suited for a leadership or management position.[32]

7. ***Too much organizational politics.*** People at all levels of an organization, from the office assistant to the chairperson of the board, must be aware of political factors. Yet you can avoid politics more easily as an individual contributor than you can as a leader. As a leader you have to engage in political byplay from three directions: below, sideways, and upward. Political tactics such as forming alliances and coalitions are a necessary part of a leader's role. Another troublesome aspect of organizational politics is that there are people lurking who want to take you out of the game, particularly if you are changing the status quo. These enemies within might attack you directly in an attempt to shift the issue to your character and style and avoid discussing the changes you are attempting to implement. Or your superiors might divert you from your goals by keeping you overwhelmed with the details of your change effort.[33] In addition, backstabbers may agree with you in person but bad-mouth you to others.

8. ***The pursuit of conflicting goals.*** A major challenge facing leaders is to navigate among conflicting goals. The central theme of these dilemmas is attempting to grant others the authority to act independently, yet still getting them aligned or pulling together for a common purpose.[34] Many of the topics relating to these conflicting goals are discussed at later points in the text.

9. ***Being perceived as unethical, especially if you are a corporate executive.*** The many corporate financial scandals made public in recent years have led to extreme perceptions that CEOs, in particular, are dishonest, unethical, and almost criminal in their behavior. Even if 95 percent of corporate leaders are honest and devoted to their constituents, the leader still has to deal with the possibility of being perceived as dishonest.

A FRAMEWORK FOR UNDERSTANDING LEADERSHIP

Many different theories and explanations of leadership have been developed because of the interest in leadership as a practice and as a research topic. Several attempts have been made to integrate the large number of leadership theories into one comprehensive framework.[35] The framework presented here focuses on the major sets of variables that influence leadership effectiveness. The basic assumption underlying the framework can be expressed in terms of a simple formula with a profound meaning:

$$L = f(l, gm, s)$$

The formula means that the leadership process is a function of the leader, group members (or followers), and other situational variables. Bruce J. Avolio emphasizes that leadership is a function of both the leader and the led and the complexity of the context (setting and environment).[36] In other words, leadership

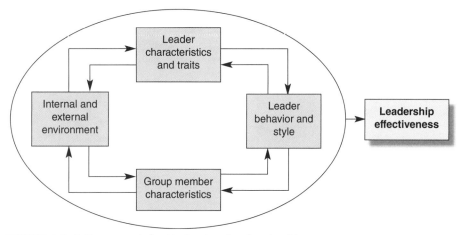

FIGURE 1-2 A Framework for Understanding Leadership.

Source: Managing Today! by Stephen P. Robbins, © 1997. Reprinted by permission of Prentice-Hall, Inc. Upper Saddle River, N.J.

does not exist in the abstract but takes into account factors related to the leader, the person or persons being led, and a variety of forces in the environment. A charismatic and visionary leader might be just what a troubled organization needs to help it achieve world-class success. Yet a group of part-time telemarketers might need a more direct and focused type of leader to help them when their telephone calls mostly meet with abrupt rejection from the people solicited.

The model presented in Figure 1-2 extends this situational perspective. According to this model, leadership can best be understood by examining its key variables: leader characteristics and traits, leader behavior and style, group-member characteristics, and the internal and external environment. At the right side of the framework, **leadership effectiveness** refers to attaining desirable outcomes such as productivity, quality, and satisfaction in a given situation. Whether or not the leader is effective depends on the four sets of variables in the box.

Beginning at the top of the circle, *leader characteristics and traits* refers to the inner qualities, such as self-confidence and problem-solving ability, that help a leader function effectively in many situations. *Leader behavior and style* refers to the activities engaged in by the leader, including characteristic approach, that relate to his or her effectiveness. A leader who frequently coaches group members and practices participative leadership, for example, might be effective in many circumstances.

Group member characteristics refers to attributes of the group members that could have a bearing on how effective the leadership attempt will be. Intelligent and well-motivated group members, for example, help the leader do an outstanding job. The *internal and external environment* also influences leadership effectiveness. A leader in a culturally diverse environment, for example, will need to have multicultural skills to be effective. All of the topics in this text fit somewhere into this model, and the fit will be more obvious at some places than at others. Table 1-2 outlines how the elements of the leadership model line up with chapters in the text.

TABLE 1-2 Relationship between Chapter Topics and the Framework for Understanding Leadership

COMPONENT OF THE MODEL	RELEVANT CHAPTER OR CHAPTERS
Leader characteristics and traits	Chapter 3, "Personal Attributes of Leaders"
	Chapter 4, "The Charismatic and Transformational Aspects of Leaders"
	Chapter 5, "The Moral Aspects of Leadership"
	Chapter 12, "Communicating with Others and Resolving Conflict"
	Chapter 13, "The Creative and Innovative Aspects of Leaders"
Leader behavior and style	Chapter 5, "The Moral Aspects of Leadership"
	Chapter 6, "Enhancing Teamwork within the Group"
	Chapter 8, "Leadership Actions, Attitudes, and Styles"
	Chapter 10, "How Leaders Exert Influence"
Group member characteristics	Chapter 7, "The Leader as a Motivator and Coach"
	Chapter 9, "How Leaders Respond to the Situation at Hand"
Internal and external environment	Chapter 2, "Global and Cross-Cultural Leadership"
	Chapter 11, "How Leaders Attain and Maintain Power"
	Chapter 14, "Thinking Strategically and Managing Knowledge"
	Chapter 15, "The Development of Leaders and Succession Planning"

The arrows connecting the four sets of variables in Figure 1-2 suggest a reciprocal influence among them. Some of these linkages are stronger than others. The most pronounced linkage is that a leader's characteristics and traits will typically influence the leader's style. If a given individual is extraverted, warm, and caring, it will be natural for that person to adopt a people-oriented leadership style. Another linkage is that the group members' characteristics might influence the leader's style. If the members are capable and self-sufficient, the leader is likely to choose a leadership style that grants freedom to the group. It will be easier for the leader to empower these people. A final linkage is that the internal and external environment can influence or mediate the leader's traits to some extent. In an environment in which creativity and risk taking are fostered, leaders are more likely to give expression to their tendencies toward creative problem solving and risk taking.

A key point of this model is that leadership is a multilevel phenomenon. The leader interacts with group members one at a time, and also with the group. At the same time, leadership takes place in the context of the organization and the external environment. As noted by leadership scholars Francis J. Yammarino and Fred Danjsereau, leadership involves a movement from one level (person level) to a higher level (leader-follower group level).[37] After that come the organizational and societal levels. A brief example of leadership as a multilevel phenomenon follows:

> Team leader Ashley decides to coach team member Li on how to express her ideas more forcibly when making a PowerPoint presentation. Ashley recognizes that Li is shy, so she moves slowly with her coaching. Ashley also recognizes that she is working with a supportive team, so she thinks that the team will be encouraging toward Li in whatever progress she makes. In addition, Ashley recognizes that the organization as a whole encourages assertiveness, so she feels justified in coaching Li toward being more assertive in her presentations. Yet at the same time Ashley understands that Li was raised in a culture (society level) that values humility and timidity so she does not push Li too fast to make improvements.

SKILL DEVELOPMENT IN LEADERSHIP

Leadership skills are in high demand. Executives who recruit candidates for high-level management jobs list leadership skills as the top attributes they want. Leadership skills are also sought in candidates for entry-level professional positions.[38] Although students of leadership will find this information encouraging, developing leadership skills is more complex than developing a structured skill such as inserting an additional memory card into a computer. Nevertheless, you can develop leadership skills by studying this textbook, which follows a general learning model:

1. *Conceptual information and behavioral guidelines.* Each chapter in this textbook presents useful information about leadership, including a section titled "Guidelines for Action and Skill Development."

2. *Conceptual information demonstrated by examples and brief descriptions of leaders in action.* Students can learn much from reading about how effective (or ineffective) leaders operate.

3. *Experiential exercises.* The textbook provides an opportunity for practice and personalization through cases, role plays, and self-assessment quizzes. Self-quizzes are emphasized here because they are an effective method of helping you personalize the information, thereby linking conceptual information to yourself. For example, you will read about the importance of assertiveness in leadership and also complete an assertiveness quiz.

4. *Feedback on skill utilization, or performance, from others.* Feedback exercises appear at several places in the text. Implementing some of the skills outside of the classroom will provide additional opportunities for feedback.

5. *Practice in natural settings.* Skill development requires active practice. A given skill has to be practiced many times in natural settings before it

LEADERSHIP SKILL-BUILDING **EXERCISE 1-2**

My Leadership Portfolio

Here, we ask you to begin developing a leadership portfolio that will be a personal document of your leadership capabilities and experiences. In each chapter, we will recommend new entries for your portfolio. At the same time, we encourage you to use your imagination in determining what constitutes a suitable addition to your leadership portfolio.

We suggest you begin your portfolio with a personal mission statement that explains the type of leadership you plan to practice. An example might be, "I intend to become a well-respected corporate professional, a key member of a happy and healthy family, and a contributor to my community. I aspire to lead many people toward constructive activities." Include your job résumé in your portfolio, and devote a special section to leadership experiences. These experiences can be from the job, community and religious activities, and sports. (See Leadership Self-Assessment Quiz 1-2.)

becomes integrated comfortably into a leader's mode of operation. A basic principle of learning is that practice is necessary to develop and improve skills. Suppose, for example, that you read about giving advice in the form of questions, as described in Chapter 7. If you practice this skill at least six times in live settings, you will probably have acquired an important new skill for coaching others.

Leadership Skill-Building Exercise 1-2 gives you the opportunity to begin developing your leadership skills systematically.

LEADERSHIP SELF-ASSESSMENT **QUIZ 1-2**

The Leadership Experience Audit

Instructions: Readers of this book vary considerably in their leadership, managerial, and supervisory experience. Yet even readers who have not yet occupied a formal leadership position may have had at least a taste of being a leader. Use the following checklist to record any possible leadership experiences you might have had in the past or have now.

- Held a formal leadership position, such as vice president, department head, manager, assistant manager, team leader, group leader, or crew chief
- Seized the opportunity on the job to take care of a problem, although not assigned such responsibility
- Headed a committee or task force
- Was captain or co-captain of an athletic team
- Held office in a club at high school, career school, or college
- Was editor of a campus newspaper or section of the newspaper such as sports
- Organized a study group for a course
- Organized an ongoing activity to sell merchandise at people's homes, such as for Avon, Mary Kay, or Tupperware

QUIZ 1-2 (continued)

- Worked in multilevel sales and recruited and guided new members
- Organized a charity drive for a school or religious organization
- Organized a vacation trip for friends or family
- Took charge during a crisis, such as by helping people out of a burning building or a flooded house
- Was head of a choir or a band
- Headed a citizens' group making demands on a company or the government
- Organized a group of friends to help out people in need, such as physically disabled senior citizens
- Other

Interpretation: The more experiences you checked, the more leadership experience you already have under your belt. Leadership experience of any type can be valuable in learning to work well with people and coordinate their efforts. Many CEOs in a variety of fields got their start as assistant fast-food restaurant managers.

FOLLOWERSHIP: BEING AN EFFECTIVE GROUP MEMBER

To be an effective leader, one needs good followers. Leaders cannot exist without followers. As we mentioned at the outset of this book, the word *followers* suffers from political incorrectness, yet it is a neutral term as used by leadership researchers. A point of view that represents a modern view of leadership, as explained by J. Richard Hackman and Ruth Wageman, is that leaders are also followers and followers also exhibit leadership. Each boss is also a subordinate, such as a team leader reporting to a middle manager.[39] And each subordinate will often carry out a leadership role, such as heading up a short-term project—or even organizing this year's holiday party. Another perspective on followers is that they are the people who get things done; that the bright ideas of leaders would go nowhere without the doers.[40]

Most of the topics in our study of leadership are aimed at inspiring, motivating, and influencing group members to want to achieve organizational goals. It is also valuable, however, to focus on three key aspects of being an effective group member: types of followers, the personal characteristics of productive followers, and the importance of collaboration between leaders and followers.

Types of Followers

A major challenge in being a leader is to recognize that followers differ substantially in talent and motivation. Similarly, a challenge in becoming an effective follower is to understand your basic approach to being a group member. Barbara Kellerman offers a typology that helps explain how followers differ from one another. She focuses on the defining factor of the level of engagement with the leader or group to arrive at five types of follower, as

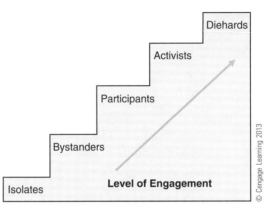

FIGURE 1-3 Followers Classified by Level of Engagement.

illustrated in Figure 1-3. At one end of the continuum is "feeling and doing nothing." At the other end is "being passionately committed and deeply involved."[41]

1. *Isolates* are completely detached, and passively support the status quo by not taking action to bring about changes. They do not care much about their leaders and just do their job without taking an interest in the overall organization. Isolates need coaching, yet sometimes firing them is the only solution.

2. *Bystanders* are free riders who are typically detached when it fits their self-interests. At a meeting, a bystander is more likely to focus on the refreshments and taking peeks at his or her personal text messages. Bystanders have low internal motivation, so the leader has to work hard to find the right motivators to spark the bystander into action.

3. *Participants* show enough engagement to invest some of their own time and money to make a difference, such as taking the initiative to learn new technology that would help the group. Participants are sometimes for, and sometimes against, the leader and the company. The leader has to review their work and attitudes carefully to determine whether or not the participant is being constructive.

4. *Activists* are considerably engaged, heavily invested in people and processes, and eager to demonstrate their support or opposition. They feel strongly, either positively or negatively, about their leader and the organization and act accordingly. An activist might be enthusiastic about reaching company goals, or so convinced that the company is doing the wrong thing that he or she blows the whistle (reports the company to an outside agency). The leader has to stay aware of whether the activist is for or against the company.

5. *Diehards* are super-engaged to the point that they are willing to go down for their own cause, or willing to oust the leader if they feel he or she is headed in the wrong direction. Diehards can be an asset or a liability to the leader. Diehards have an even stronger tendency to be whistleblowers than do activists.

A diehard, for example, might take it on her own to test the lead quantity of paint in children's furniture sold by the company. Leaders have to stay in touch with diehards to see if their energy is being pointed in the service of the organization.

The categorization of followers just presented adds a touch of realism to understanding the challenging role of a leader. Not everybody in the group is supercharged and eager to collaborate toward attaining organizational goals.

Essential Qualities of Effective Followers

As observed by Robert E. Kelley, effective followers share four essential qualities:[42]

1. *Self-management.* The key to being a good follower is to think for oneself and to work well without close supervision. Effective group members see themselves as being as capable as their leaders.
2. *Commitment.* Effective followers are committed to something beyond themselves, be it a cause, product, department, organization, idea, or value. To a committed group member, the leader facilitates progress toward achieving a goal.
3. *Competence and focus.* Effective followers build their competence and focus their efforts for maximum impact. Competence centers on mastering skills that will be useful to the organization. Less effective group members rarely take the initiative to engage in training and development.
4. *Courage.* Effective followers establish themselves as independent, critical thinkers and fight for what they believe is right. A good follower, for example, might challenge the company's policy of taking ninety days to make good on accounts payable, or of recruiting key people almost exclusively from people with demographic characteristics similar to those of top management.

This list is illustrative, since almost any positive human quality would contribute directly or indirectly to being an effective group member or follower. Another way of framing the qualities of effective followers is to say that such followers display the personal characteristics and qualities of leaders. Although leaders cannot be expected to change the personalities of group members, they can take steps to encourage these qualities. Interventions such as coaching, empowerment, supportive communication, and frequent feedback would support effective followership.

Collaboration Between Leaders and Followers

A key role for followers is to collaborate with leaders in achieving organizational goals. As described by leadership guru Warren Bennis, the post-bureaucratic organization (a type of organization that came after the bureaucratic era, such as team-based organizations) requires a new kind of alliance between leaders and the led. When high-level leaders do not make all of the decisions but solicit input from knowledgeable group members, leaders and followers work together more closely.[43]

A related point here is that the new leader and the led are close allies. Great leaders are made by great groups; every organizational member needs to contribute energy and talent to help leaders carry out their roles successfully.

SUMMARY

Leadership is the ability to inspire confidence in and support among the people who are needed to achieve organizational goals. Leading is a major part of a manager's job, but a manager also plans, organizes, and controls. Leadership is said to deal with change, inspiration, motivation, and influence. In contrast, management deals more with maintaining equilibrium and the status quo. Leadership is often regarded as a partnership or collaboration between leaders and group members.

Many people attribute organizational performance to leadership actions. Some research evidence supports this widely accepted view. For example, one study showed that leadership actions can affect performance, but only if the leader is perceived to be responsible and inspirational. Others argue that certain factors in the work environment, called substitutes for leadership, make the leader's role almost superfluous. Among these factors are close-knit teams of highly trained workers, intrinsic satisfaction with work, computer technology, and professional norms. Another anti-leadership argument is that the leader is irrelevant in most organizational outcomes because the situation is more important and the leader has unilateral control over only a few resources. Moreover, since new leaders are chosen whose values are compatible with those of the firm, those values actually are more important.

Complexity theory argues that leaders and managers can do little to alter the course of the complex organizational system. The system, rather than the leader, dictates that all companies ultimately die.

Examining the roles carried out by leaders contributes to an understanding of the leadership function. Ten such leadership roles are the figurehead, spokesperson, negotiator, coach and motivator, team builder, team player, technical problem solver,

entrepreneur, strategic planner, and executor. An important implication of these roles is that managers at every level can exert leadership.

Leadership positions often are satisfying because they offer such things as power, prestige, the opportunity to help others, high income, and the opportunity to control resources. At other times being a leader carries with it a number of frustrations, such as facing a perform-or-perish mentality, insufficient authority, having to deal with human problems, and too much organizational politics. The leader also has the difficult task of balancing workers' need to be independent with their need to commit to a common purpose.

The framework for understanding leadership presented here is based on the idea that the leadership process is a function of the leader, group members, and other situational variables. According to the model, leadership can best be understood by examining its key variables: leader characteristics and traits, leader behavior and style, group member characteristics, and the internal and external environment. Leadership effectiveness is dependent on all four sets of variables. Another point of the model is that leadership is multilevel, involving the individual, the small group, and the organization. The society and culture might also need to be taken into account.

Leadership skills can be developed by following a general learning model that involves acquiring conceptual knowledge, reading examples, doing experiential exercises, obtaining feedback, and practicing in natural settings.

A major challenge facing leaders is that followers differ substantially in characteristics, including level of engagement from feeling and doing nothing to total passion, commitment, and involvement. To be an effective leader, one needs good followers with characteristics such as self-management, commitment, competence and focus, and courage. A key role for followers is to collaborate with leaders in achieving organizational goals. The post-bureaucratic organization requires a new kind of alliance between leaders and the led.

KEY TERMS

leadership	**substitutes for leadership**
partnership	**leadership effectiveness**

 GUIDELINES FOR **ACTION** AND **SKILL** DEVELOPMENT

Vast amounts of information have been gathered about leaders and leadership, and many different leadership theories have been developed. Many leadership research findings and theories are confusing and contradictory. Nevertheless, from this thicket of information emerge many useful leadership concepts and techniques to guide you toward becoming a more effective leader.

As you work toward leadership effectiveness, first be familiar with the approaches to leadership described in this text. Then choose the formulation that seems best to fit the leadership situation you face. For example, if you are leading a team, review the information about team leadership. Typically, an effective leader needs to combine several leadership approaches to meet the demands of a given situation. For instance, a leader might need to combine creative problem solving and emotional support to members to help the team rebound from a crisis.

The eclectic (choosing from among many) approach we recommend is likely to be more effective than accepting an idea such as "there are six secrets to leadership success."

Discussion Questions and Activities

1. What forces in the environment or in society have led to the surge in interest the subject of leadership in recent years?
2. Give an example of how you have exerted leadership on or off the job in a situation in which you did not have a formal leadership position. Explain why you describe your activity as leadership.
3. What would a boss of yours have to do to demonstrate that he or she is an effective leader and an effective manager?
4. Identify a business or sports leader who you think is highly effective, and explain why you think he or she is highly effective.
5. Based on an informal survey, many people who were voted "the most likely to succeed" in their high school yearbooks became leaders later on in their career. How can you explain this finding?
6. Top-level leaders of major business corporations receive some of the highest compensation packages in the work force. Why are business leaders paid so much?
7. If so much useful information is available about leadership, why do we still find so many managers who cannot gain the respect of their subordinates?
8. Which of the ten leadership roles do you think you are the most suited for at this stage in your career? Explain your reasoning.
9. A twenty-five-year-old manager of a branch of a fast-food restaurant was told by her boss that she was not an effective leader. She replied, "For $25,000 a year, how can you expect me to be an effective leader?" What do you think of her argument?
10. In what way might being an effective follower help prepare a person for becoming an effective leader?

LEADERSHIP CASE PROBLEM A

Mike Todman Makes a Splash at Whirlpool

By the time the financial crisis hit, the brutal economy forced its executive leadership team to stay focused on a recently drafted strategic plan to turn its business around. Michael A. Todman, president of Whirlpool International, recalled the overarching goal: "Let's control the things we can. We had already changed our business model, and we had to make some really tough decisions."

Senior management concentrated on three priorities: aligning costs to meet the demands of the turbulent business climate; managing cash for greater liquidity; and maximizing market share by targeting consumers in a more effective, efficient manner. As a result, the company abandoned brand advertising, shifting to promotional and point-of-sales methods. "We spent our time talking directly to them so we used more digital media," Todman said.

To underscore the urgency, management also ramped up internal communications. It was critical to make and implement decisions at a faster pace and, at the same time, secure employee buy-in. So board members met once a month instead of six times a year while managers spent more time meeting with the rank and file. "Philosophically, our approach is to be straight, be honest, tell people exactly what is going on," said Todman.

During the challenging financial period, Todman focused on the North American market. He also completed the integration of Maytag into the Whirlpool product line. Todman focused on revamping the product line by closing costly plants and educating the entire staff on both companies before introducing the new models. Todman oversees brands in Europe, Latin America, and Asia with duties that include management of global information systems and global strategic initiatives, including efficiency and innovation.

Jeff Fettig, Whirlpool Corp. CEDO and chairman, said, "Mike has a number of strengths. First, he's got great expertise in being a global leader. He knows how to operate effectively with different cultures and different people. He also knows our operations very well—our strengths and weaknesses, what we can do and what we can't do—so he's instrumental in helping us to set the right priorities and then running disciplined operations to help us deliver our expected results."

Born and raised in St. Thomas, U.S. Virgin Islands, Todman has been described as a robust man with a gentle demeanor that's not easily ruffled. His colleagues describe him as consistent, engaging, and extremely personable. A Whirlpool executive said about Todman: "He's able to analyze really complex business problems and make the right decisions so that the company can make money."

Communication is an integral part of Todman's management style: dissecting trend information, disseminating company goals and objectives, and pushing employees to think more broadly, more creatively, but as an interconnected unit that functions across the globe. It's a twenty-four-hour job, he says of managing the various time zones through phone calls and video conferencing. Todman spends two weeks out of every month in the marketplace visiting the team as well as customers. "I understand how consumers are living and that keeps you on the pulse."

Todman has a bachelor's degree in business administration from Georgetown University. He joined Whirlpool in 1993 in London as director of finance, eventually running the customer service business in Europe. For his leadership role in helping bolster Whirlpool's financial performance through his strategic vision in accessing global markets and ability to effectively drive innovation, Todman was selected as the 2010 *Black Enterprise* Corporate Executive of the Year.

Questions

1. In what way is Michael A. Todman exercising leadership?

2. Identify at least three leadership roles Todman emphasizes as president of Whirlpool, International.

3. To what extent does it appear that Todman is showing a good balance between strategic thinking and focusing on people?

4. What advice might you offer Todman to be even more successful as the head of Whirlpool?

Source: Black enterprise by SCOTT Copyright 2010. Reproduced with permission of BLACK ENTERPRISE MAGAZINE.

ASSOCIATED ROLE PLAY

Dealing with Dissent

CEO Mike Todman is conducting a town-hall meeting with about 200 employees at a Whirlpool factory in the United States. Five minutes into the meeting, an employee holding up a U.S. flag says in a loud voice, "Excuse me Mr. Todman, but I object strongly to something you and the other executives are doing. We are manufacturing too many of our products overseas. We are killing jobs for Americans." One student plays the role of Todman, who wants to listen to employee concerns but is not about to change company strategy. Another student plays the role of the dissenter who thinks of himself as a true patriot.

Run the role play in front of the class for about five minutes. The course instructor and other students will provide feedback on how well the dissenter got across his or her point and how well CEO Todman dealt with the situation.

LEADERSHIP CASE PROBLEM B

The Subprime Department Blues

Mary Chen had been the manager of the subprime mortgage department of a large bank for several years. Although her department was small, she and top-level management thought that their mission was important. As Chen explains it, "We make it possible for people with less than prime credit ratings to become homeowners. We create mortgages for honest, hardworking people who for many reasons do not have excellent credit records. So our group is doing some good in this world, despite a few foreclosures here and there."

As interest rates climbed on adjustable rate mortgages (ARMs), the number of late payers tripled, and the number of foreclosures doubled. Every day the media pounded the subprime lenders, blaming them for a potential recession and a sharp decline in the stock market.

Supervising the people in her department became increasingly more difficult. As Chen said, "As the subprime mess progressed, I saw fewer smiles in my department. Workers were calling in sick more frequently. One-half the people in the department requested a transfer to the mortgage department that provided mortgages to customers with first-rate credit records. Even my best workers looked stressed out."

Malcolm Flynn, a mortgage specialist with four years' experience, described the working conditions in the subprime department in these words: "This is bad. We feel we are looked upon like we are drug dealers. People think we are rotten because we lent money to people who didn't have the means to pay back the loan.

"Most of us won't admit the kind of work we are in when talking to people outside the bank. We come to work every day hoping the work will be more fun, but it never is."

When Chen discussed the morale problems she was facing within her group, her manager advised Chen to be a "better leader." Her manager also said that a true leader can guide a group through rough times.

Chen thought to herself, "This advice looks good on paper, but I don't know what to do next."

Questions

1. What advice might you offer Mary Chen to pick up morale in her department?
2. Which leadership roles should Chen emphasize to lead the group out of its funk?
3. To what extent do you believe the statement of Chen's manager that "a true leader can guide a group through rough times"?

ASSOCIATED ROLE PLAY

Cheering Up the Team

One student plays the role of Mary Chen who decides to hold a morale-building session at ten o'clock on a Friday morning. She is serving bagels, doughnuts, fresh fruit, and beverages, including a couple of energy drinks. Chen's intent is to cheer up the group, and help them recognize how important their work is to society. Several other students play the roles of department members with mixed attitudes toward their work. Run the role play for about eight minutes. Observers will concentrate on how successful Chen appears to have been, and how effective group members were in expressing their feelings.

▶❚❚ LEADERSHIP VIDEO CASE DISCUSSION QUESTIONS

To view the videos for this activity, you'll need access to the CourseMate that is available for this text. To get access, visit www.CengageBrain.com.

After viewing "The Fruit Guys," answer the following questions.

1. Chris Mittelstaedt, founder and CEO of The Fruit Guys, takes on many roles in his position. Of the ten leadership roles identified by Henry Mintzberg and others which three roles do you think Chris uses the most often? Explain.

2. Do you believe that Chris Mittelstaedt receives any of the satisfactions of leaders as mentioned in Chapter 1? Why or why not?
3. As Chapter 1 mentions, "a key role for followers is to collaborate with leaders in achieving organizational goals." Do you think that followers at The Fruit Guys have the opportunity to collaborate with company leaders such as Chris Mittelstaedt?
4. Would you enjoy working at The Fruit Guys? Why or why not?

NOTES

1. Story created from facts in the following sources: Vivian Sequera, "Veteran Engineer Behind Chile Rescue," The Associated Press, October 16, 2010; Terri A. Scandura, "Leadership Lessons from the Chilean Mine," *The Miami Herald* (www.miamiherald.com), October 25, 2010; Peggy Noonan, "Viva Chile! The Left No Man Behind," *The Wall Street Journal*, October 16–17, 2010, p. A17; Tim Padgett Anthony Espositio, and Aaron Helsen, "5: The Chilean Miners," *Time*, December 27, 2010–January 3, 2011, p. 105.

2. W. Kan Kim and René A. Maubourgne, "Parables of Leadership," *Harvard Business Review*, July–August 1992, p. 123.
3. Derived from a literature review in Bernard M. Bass (with Ruth Bass), *The Bass Handbook of Leadership: Theory, Research, and Managerial Applications*, Fourth Edition (New York: The Free Press, 2008), pp. 15–23.
4. Jeffrey Zaslow, "Joe Montana: Leadership, Says the Legendary Quarterback of Four Super Bowls, Means 'Being Willing to Take the Blame,'" *USA Weekend*, January 30–February 1, 1998, p. 15.

5. Brian M. Carney, "Of Tax Cuts and Terror," *The Wall Street Journal*, June 30–July 1, 2007, p. A7.

6. James Kelly and Scott Nadler, "Leading from Below," *The Wall Street Journal*, March 3–4, 2007, p. R4.

7. Peter Block, *Stewardship: Choosing Service Over Self-Interest* (San Francisco: Berrett-Koehler Publishers, 1993), pp. 27–32.

8. Tamara L. Friedrich et al., "A Framework for Understanding Collective Leadership: The Selective Utilization of Leader and Team Expertise within Networks," *The Leadership Quarterly*, December 2009, pp. 933–958.

9. Quoted on page 2 of the February 2006 issue of *Black Enterprise*.

10. James M. Kouzes and Barry Z. Posner, *The Leadership Challenge*, 3rd ed. (San Francisco: Jossey-Bass, 2002), p. 20.

11. "Cisco: Making the Change with Web 2.0," *Executive Leadership*, February 2009, p. 1.

12. John P. Kotter, *A Force for Change: How Leadership Differs from Management* (New York: The Free Press, 1990); "Managing + Leading = True Leadership," *Executive Leadership*, September 2004, p. 8; Edwin A. Locke and Associates, *The Essence of Leadership: The Four Keys to Leading Successfully* (New York: Lexington/Macmillan, 1991), p. 4.

13. Henry Mintzberg, *Managing* (San Francisco: Berrett-Koehler Publishers, 2009), p. 8.

14. Diya Gullapalli, "GMO Taps 1st CEO in 32-Year History," *The Wall Street Journal*, Februay 13, 2009, p. C9.

15. *Duke University Executive Leadership Survey*, Center on Leadership & Ethics, March 2009, pp. 1–17.

16. Gary Yukl, "How Leaders Influence Organizational Effectiveness," *The Leadership Quarterly*, December 2008, pp. 708–722.

17. Richard C. Morais, "Impatience," *Forbes*, June 16, 2008, pp. 128–132.

18. Nitin Nohria, William Joyce, and Bruce Roberson, "What Really Works," *Harvard Business Review*, July 2003, p. 51.

19. Ellen Shubart, "Success Hinges on Vital Skills Like the Human Factor," *The Wall Street Journal* (Special Advertising Section), March 29, 2007, p. D6.

20. Robert B. Kaiser, Robert Hogan, and S. Bartholomew Craig, "Leadership and the Fate of Organizations," *American Psychologist*, February-March 2008, p. 103.

21. Bruce J. Avolio, Rebecca J. Reichard, Sean T. Hannah, Fred O. Walumbwa, and Adrian Chan, "A Meta-Analytic Review of Leadership Impact Research: Experimental and Quasi-Experimental Studies," *The Leadership Quarterly*, October 2009, pp. 764–784.

22. Jon P. Howell, David E. Bowen, Peter W. Dorfman, Steven Kerr, and Philip Podaskoff, "Substitutes for Leadership: Effective Alternatives to Ineffective Leadership," *Organizational Dynamics*, Summer 1990, p. 23.

23. Jeffrey Pfeffer, "The Ambiguity of Leadership," *Academy of Management Review*, April 1977, pp. 104–112.

24. Cited in Jerry Useem, "Conquering Vertical Limits," *Fortune*, February 19, 2001, p. 94.

25. Thomas H. Hout, "Are Managers Obsolete?" *Harvard Business Review*, March–April 1999, pp. 161–162. (Books in Review)

26. Mary Uhl-Bien and Russ Marion, editors, *Complexity Leadership: Conceptual Foundations* (Charlotte, N.C.: Information Age, 2008).

27. J. Richard Hackman and Ruth Wageman, "Asking the Right Questions about Leadership," *American Psychologist*, January 2007, p. 43.

28. Updated and expanded from Henry Mintzberg, *The Nature of Managerial Work* (New York: Harper & Row, 1973); Kenneth Graham Jr. and William M. Mihal, *The CMD Managerial Job Analysis Inventory* (Rochester, N.Y.: Rochester Institute of Technology, Center for Management Development, 1987), pp. 132–133; Mary Jo Hatch, Monika Kostera, and Andrzej K. Koźmiński, "The Three Faces of Leadership: Manager, Artist, Priest," *Organizational Dynamics*, vol. 35, no. 1, 2006, pp. 49–68; Dave Ulrich, Norm Smallwood, and Kate Sweetman, *The Leadership Code: Five Rules to Lead By* (Boston: Harvard Business Press, 2008).

29. Christopher A. Bartlett and Sumantra Ghosal, "Changing the Role of Top Management Beyond Systems to People," *Harvard Business Review*, June 2002, pp. 132–133.

30. Cited in Justin Fox, "Employees First!" *Time*, July 7, 2008, p. 45.

31. Emily Thornton, "Perform or Perish," *BusinessWeek*, November 5, 2007, p. 40.

32. Eilene Zimmerman, "Are You Cut Out for Management?" *The New York Times* (nytimes.com) January 16, 2011, p. 2.

33. Ronald A. Heifetz and Mary Linsky, "A Survival Guide for Leaders," *Harvard Business Review*, June 2002, pp. 65–74.

34. Thomas A. Stewart, "The Nine Dilemmas Leaders Face," *Fortune*, March 18, 1996, pp. 112–113.

35. Three examples are Martin M. Chemers, *An Integrative Theory of Leadership* (Mahwah, N. J.: Lawrence Erlbaum Associates, 1997), pp. 151–173; Francis Yammarino, Fred Dansereau, and Christina J. Kennedy, "A Multiple-Level Multidimensional Approach to Leadership: Viewing Leadership through an Elephant's Eye," *Organizational Dynamics*, Winter 2001, pp. 149–162; Bruce J. Avolio, "Promoting More Integrative Strategies for Leadership Theory-Building," *American Psychologist*, January 2007, pp. 5–33.

36. Avolio, "Promoting More Integrative Strategies," pp. 25, 31.

37. Francis J. Yammarino and Fred Dansereau, "Multi-Level Nature of and Multi-Level Approaches to Leadership," *The Leadership Quarterly*, April 2008, p. 136.

38. "12 Common Skills Sought by Employers," www.dartmouth.edu, accessed February 18, 2011; Randall S. and Katharine Hansen, "What Do Employers *Really* Want? Top Skills and Values Employers Seek from Job Seekers," *Quintessential Careers* (www.quintcareers), accessed February 18, 2011.

39. Hackman and Wageman, "Asking the Right Questions," p. 45.

40. Nancy Lublin, "Let's Hear it for the Little Guys" *Fast Company*, April 2010, p. 33.

41. Barbara Kellerman, "What Every Leader Needs to Know About Followers," *Harvard Business Review*, December 2007, pp. 84–91.

42. Robert E. Kelley, "In Praise of Followers," *Harvard Business Review*, November–December 1988, pp. 142–148.

43. Warren Bennis, "The End of Leadership: Exemplary Leadership Is Impossible Without Full Inclusion, Initiatives, and Cooperation of Followers," *Organizational Dynamics*, Summer 1999, pp. 76–78. (This statement has become increasingly true over time.)

Global and Cross-Cultural Leadership

LEARNING OBJECTIVES

After studying this chapter and doing the exercises, you should be able to

- Explain the potential ethical and competitive advantage from leading and managing diversity.
- Describe how cultural factors, including values, influence leadership practice.
- Explain the contribution of cultural sensitivity and cultural intelligence to leadership effectiveness.
- Explain how global leadership skills contribute to leadership effectiveness.
- Pinpoint leadership initiatives to enhance the acceptance of cultural diversity.

CHAPTER OUTLINE

Nippon Sheet Glass, a global supplier of glass to the auto and construction industries, made a second unusual hire for a Japanese company in a two-year period. Craig Naylor, a retired DuPont executive and foreigner to Japan, was hired as president and CEO. He was the second consecutive non-Japanese CEO hired by the company. The Nippon Glass chairman, Katsuji Fujimoto, said that Naylor "has the fundamental qualities we wish to find in a global leader, the person who will lead NSG in its next phase."

Naylor had joined DuPont of Great Britain in 1970 and steadily worked his way up the ranks of the multinational chemical company. His overseas assignments included positions in Switzerland, the United States, China, and a leadership stint in Japan from 1987 to 1991. His last position at DuPont was group vice president of the U.S.-based Electronic & Communications Technologies division.

At Nippon Sheet, Naylor has emphasized a global perspective and cultural diversity. He worked early to discard the Japanese style of management with its heavy emphasis on domestic concerns. Naylor encountered some resistance from NSG employees who did not like the practice of fast decision making that is characteristic of many British and American firms. Instead, the Japanese workers preferred a consensus approach to decision making.

After purchasing U.K. glassmaker Pilkington PLC several years ago, Nippon Sheet Glass made English its official language. At the same time, Naylor built a multicultural, multiregional team that has input into creating strategy, not just implementing strategy developed at headquarters. Naylor recalls that when he was on assignment in Japan for DuPont, his division would sometimes receive a plan to implement that lacked a local flavor. He believes strongly that effective strategy in a global corporation needs local input.

Naylor believes that most boards of multinational U.S. corporations would prefer to have a more multicultural composition, particularly with respect to board members from outside the U.S.

With respect to English being the official language at NSG, Naylor has been encouraging the staff to eliminate idioms and slang from business communications to overcome language barriers. He says, "You have to get that stuff out because it's unintelligible to the Japanese." Even if the Japanese have to develop their skills in English, the British have to make themselves understood.[1]

The story about the British executive heading a Japanese company illustrates that cultural factors, such as language and local input, are important for running a successful company. Working in another country—and thus dealing with cultural groups different from one's own—is becoming a requirement for many senior-level management positions. As mentioned previously, in recent years manufacturers have been seeking leaders who can deal with suppliers globally and negotiate cultural differences. An example is Caterpillar, a company that has expanded rapidly in China and India during the past several years.[2]

In addition, corporate success, profit, and growth depend increasingly on the management of a diverse work force both outside and within one's own country. According to the U.S. Census Bureau, by the year 2042, racial minorities will be the majority of the U.S. population and the workforce as well. European nations are also becoming more diverse because of liberal immigration policies, often designed to attract a large number of foreign workers.[3]

The various cultural and demographic groups in the workplace want their leaders and coworkers to treat them with respect, dignity, fairness, and sensitivity. At the same time, these groups must work together smoothly to serve a variety of customers and to generate an array of ideas.[4]

Because the focus on diversity includes many types of people in an opportunity to participate fully in the organization, the word *inclusion* is often used to replace *diversity*. Not only is the work force becoming more diverse, but business has also become increasingly global. Small and medium-size firms, as well as corporate giants, are increasingly dependent on trade with other countries. Furthermore, most manufactured goods contain components from more than one country, and global outsourcing has become a dominant trend.

Our approach to cultural diversity both within and across countries emphasizes the leadership perspective. Key topics include the ethical and competitive advantage of managing for diversity, how cultural factors influence leadership practices, and how cultural sensitivity and global leadership skills contribute to leadership effectiveness. This chapter also describes initiatives that enhance the acceptance of cultural diversity. The underlying theme is that effective leadership of diverse people requires a sensitivity to and enjoyment of cultural differences.

THE ADVANTAGES OF MANAGING FOR DIVERSITY

The ethical and socially responsible goals of leaders and their organizations include providing adequately for members of the diverse work force. Ethical leaders should therefore feel compelled to use merit instead of favoritism or bias as a basis for making human resource decisions. A firm that embraces diversity is also behaving in a socially responsible manner. A leader, for example, who chose to hire five developmentally disabled, unemployed individuals would be acting in a socially responsible manner. Hiring these people would transfer responsibility for their economic welfare from the state or private charity to the employer. (Some would argue that unless hiring these people is cost effective, the company is neglecting its responsibility to shareholders.)

According to research and opinion, managing for diversity also brings the firm a competitive advantage. Patricia Harris, the Global Chief Diversity Officer of McDonald's Corporation, expresses the matter quite directly: "We began to diversify our operations when it became clear to us it was the best way to sell more hamburgers in minority communities."[5] Such an advantage is most likely to accrue when diversity is built into the firm's strategy. According to long-term research conducted by Massachusetts Institute of Technology professor Thomas A. Kochan, diversity can enhance business performance only if the proper training is provided and the organizational culture supports diversity.[6] In addition, the chief executive of an organization should be the champion for valuing inclusion, and must establish this perspective and associated actions for others throughout the organization.[7]

Here we review evidence and opinion about the competitive advantage of demographic and cultural diversity.

1. *Reduction of turnover and absenteeism costs.* As organizations become more diverse, the cost of managing diversity poorly increases. Turnover and absenteeism decrease when minority groups perceive themselves as receiving fair treatment. More effective management of diversity may increase the job satisfaction of diverse groups, thus decreasing turnover and absenteeism and their associated costs. The major initiatives in managing diversity well at Allstate Corporation have substantially reduced turnover among Latinos and African Americans, both in corporate headquarters and in field locations.[8]

2. *Managing diversity well offers a marketing advantage.* A representational work force facilitates the sale of products and services, and the need for such a workforce appears to be increasing. A major component of the marketing advantage of diversity is that a work force that matches the diversity of a company's customer base has an edge in appealing to those customers. According to the Future Work Institute, the fastest-growing domestic markets in the United States for goods and services will be minority communities. One such emerging group is African immigrants, representing a fast-growing market in terms of buying power.[9]

Bank of America leaders say the banking mammoth fosters a diverse and inclusive workplace because it affords them the business advantage of understanding and satisfying the needs of their associates, customers, clients, and shareholders.[10]

Another marketing advantage is that many people from culturally diverse groups prefer to buy from a company with a good reputation for managing diversity. Allstate Insurance Company, Inc., is well known for its diversity initiatives, and the company has become the nation's leading insurer of African Americans and Latinos. Allstate leadership states that inclusive diversity is one of its core values.[11] The large number of agents and customer service representatives from these two groups facilitates attracting and retaining a high percentage of African Americans and Latinos as customers. State Farm is another example of a financial services company that promotes diversity as part of its business strategy.

3. *Companies with a favorable record in managing diversity are at a distinct advantage in recruiting and retaining talented people.* Those companies with a favorable reputation for welcoming diversity attract the strongest job candidates among women and racial and ethnic minorities. Also, a company that does not welcome a diverse work force shrinks its supply of potential candidates. An organization that strives for diversity in recruiting simply has a larger talent pool in which to search for candidates. A telling example is that in recent years companies have chosen more executive leaders who are women or who are foreigners. When companies hire culturally diverse workers and provide them with all the tools, resources, and opportunities they need to succeed, those companies are more likely to display the full talents of their work force.

4. *Heterogeneity in the work force may offer the company a creativity advantage, as well as improve its problem-solving and decision-making capability.* Creative solutions to problems are more likely to be reached when a diverse group attacks a problem. According to experiments conducted by Scott E. Page, groups of people with diverse perspectives and heuristics (rules of thumb for solving problems) consistently outperformed groups composed of the best individual performers.[12] There are limits to this conclusion. At times specialized expertise, such as in understanding complex tax regulations or how to perform laser surgery on the retina, is absolutely essential.

5. *Diversity and inclusion programs help local economies thereby boosting social responsibility.* Many large companies take the diversity initiative of purchasing from local, minority, as well as female suppliers. The substantial purchases aid the local economy in terms of the flow of money as well as employment. Joyce Ibardolasa, director of diversity and inclusion at PG&E, a San Francisco-based utility, says: "There's no doubt in my mind that spending money at minority-owned businesses has a positive net effect on local economies."[13]

Scientific research continues to refine knowledge about the advantages of diversity. An analysis of many studies found that cultural diversity had positive effects in the service industry settings (such as restaurants and hotels). In contrast, cultural diversity within a manufacturing context had slightly negative effects. A possible explanation is that in service settings, management is more proactive in addressing issues related to differences in gender, ethnicity, and age because of the frequent interaction employees have with customers.[14]

According to Frances J. Milliken and Luis L. Martins, diversity appears to be a double-edged sword: It increases both the opportunity for creativity and the likelihood that group members will be dissatisfied and fail to identify with the group.[15] (The diverse viewpoints often enhance creativity.) Another caution is that the leader of the diverse group must help members collaborate; otherwise, the advantages of diverse perspectives will be lost.[16]

To raise your level of awareness about how to capitalize on the potential advantages of diversity, do Leadership Skill-Building Exercise 2-1, which illustrates that diversity skills are another important subset of interpersonal skills associated with leadership.

LEADERSHIP SKILL-BUILDING **EXERCISE 2-1**

Capitalizing on Diversity

The class organizes into small groups of about six students, who assume the roles of the top management team of a medium-size manufacturing or service company. Each group has the following assignment: "Being socially aware, ethical, and modern in its thinking, your company already has a highly diverse work force. Yet somehow, your company is not any more profitable than the competition. As the company leaders (yourself a diverse group), today you will work on the problem of how to better capitalize on the cultural diversity within your company. Working for about fifteen minutes, develop a few concrete ideas to enable your company to capitalize on diversity." After the problem solving has been completed, the team leaders might present their ideas to the other groups.

CULTURAL FACTORS INFLUENCING LEADERSHIP PRACTICE

A **multicultural leader** is a leader with the skills and attitudes to relate effectively to and motivate people across race, gender, age, social attitudes, and lifestyles. To influence, motivate, and inspire culturally diverse people, the leader must be aware of overt and subtle cultural differences. Although such culturally based differences are generalizations, they function as starting points in the leader's attempt to lead a person from another culture. For example, many Asians are self-conscious about being praised in front of the group because they feel that individual attention clashes with their desire to maintain group harmony. Therefore, a manager might refrain from praising an Asian group member before the group until he or she understands that group member's preferences. The manager is likely to find that many Asians welcome praise in front of peers, especially when working outside their homeland.

Here we examine two topics that help a leader learn how to manage in a culturally diverse workplace: (1) understanding key dimensions of differences in cultural values and (2) the influence of cultural values on leadership style.

Key Dimensions of Differences in Cultural Values

One way to understand how national cultures differ is to examine their values or cultural dimensions. The cultural dimensions presented here and outlined in Figure 2-1 are based mostly on those included in GLOBE (Global Leadership

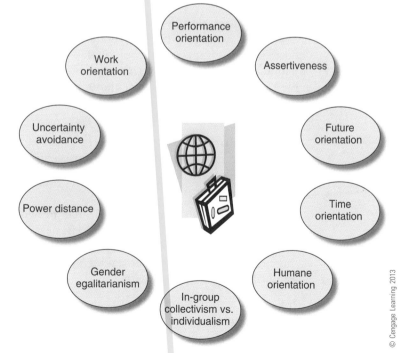

© Cengage Learning 2013

FIGURE 2-1 Dimensions of Cultural Values.

and Organizational Behavior Effectiveness), a research program in 62 societal cultures, and builds on previous analyses of cultural dimensions.[17] We also include two other dimensions useful in working with people from other cultures—attitudes toward time and work orientation. Keep in mind that these cultural dimensions are stereotypes that apply to a representative person from a particular culture, and are not meant to insult anybody. Individual differences are substantial. For example, many Americans are not assertive, and many French people are willing to work seventy hours per week.

1. Performance orientation is the degree to which a society encourages (or should encourage) and rewards group members for performance improvement and excellence. Countries high on this dimension are the United States and Singapore, whereas those low on this dimension are Russia and Greece.

2. Assertiveness is the degree to which individuals are (and should be) assertive, confrontational, and aggressive in their relationships with one another. Countries scoring high on this dimension are the United States and Austria, whereas those low on this dimension are Sweden and New Zealand. Assertive people enjoy competition in business, in contrast to less assertive cultural groups who prefer harmony, loyalty, and solidarity.

3. Future orientation is the extent to which individuals engage (and should engage) in future-oriented behaviors such as delaying gratification, planning, and making investments for the future. Singapore and Switzerland are examples of societies with longer time horizons, whereas Russia and Argentina are less future oriented.

4. Time orientation is the importance nations and individuals attach to time. People with an urgent time orientation perceive time to be a scarce resource and tend to be impatient. People with a casual time orientation view time as an unlimited and unending resource and tend to be patient. Americans are noted for their urgent time orientation. They frequently impose deadlines and are eager to get started doing business. Asians, Mexicans, and Middle Easterners, in contrast, are patient negotiators.

5. Humane orientation is the degree to which a society encourages and rewards, and should encourage and reward, individuals for being fair, altruistic, and caring to others. Egypt and Malaysia rank high on this cultural dimension, and France and Germany rank low.

6. In-group collectivism is the degree to which individuals express, and should express, pride, loyalty, and cohesiveness in their organizations and families. Asian societies emphasize collectivism, as do Egypt and Russia. One consequence of collectivism is taking pride in family members and the organizations that employ them.

7. Gender egalitarianism is the degree to which a culture minimizes, and should minimize, gender inequality. European countries emphasize gender egalitarianism, and so do the United States and Canada. South Korea is an example of a country that is low on gender egalitarianism and is male dominated.

8. Power distance is the degree to which members of a society expect, and should expect, power to be distributed unequally. Individuals who accept power and authority expect the boss to make the major decisions. These same individuals are more formal; however, being formal toward people in positions of authority has decreased substantially throughout the world in recent years. Examples of societies that score high on acceptance of power and authority are Thailand, Brazil, France, and Japan.

9. Uncertainty avoidance is the extent to which members of a society rely (and should rely) on social norms, rules, and procedures to lessen the unpredictability of future events. The stronger the desire to avoid uncertainty, the more likely people are to seek orderliness, consistency, and laws to cover situations in daily life. Examples of societies with high uncertainty avoidance are Singapore and Switzerland. Societies with low uncertainty avoidance include Russia and Greece.

10. Work orientation is the number of hours per week and weeks per year people expect to invest in work versus leisure, or other non-work activities. American corporate professionals typically work about 55 hours per week, take 45-minute lunch breaks, and go on two weeks of vacation. Americans tend to have a stronger work orientation than Europeans but a weaker one than Asians. United States employees average 1,804 hours of work per year, compared with 1,407 for Norwegian workers and 1,564 for the French. Workers in seven Asian countries including South Korea, Bangladesh, and China work 2,200 hours per year.[18]

How might a manager use information about differences in values to become a more effective leader? A starting point would be to recognize that a person's national values might influence his or her behavior. Assume that a leader wants to influence a person with a low-power-distance orientation to strive for peak performance. The low-power person will not spring into action just because the boss makes the suggestion. Instead, the leader needs to patiently explain the personal payoffs of achieving peak performance. Another example is a leader who wants to improve quality and therefore hires people who value collectivism. A backup tactic would be to counsel people who value individualism on the merits of collective action. Leadership Self-Assessment Quiz 2-1 will help you think about how values can moderate (or influence) work performance.

Cultural Values and Leadership Style

The values embedded in a culture influence the behavior of leaders and managers as well as the behavior of other workers. As Geert Hofstede explains, relationships between people in a society are affected by the values programmed in the minds of these people. Because management deals heavily with interpersonal relationships, management and leadership are affected by cultural values. Management and leadership processes may vary from culture to culture, but, being value based, these processes show strong continuity in each society.[19]

LEADERSHIP SELF-ASSESSMENT QUIZ 2-1

Charting Your Cultural Value Profile

Instructions: For each of the ten value dimensions, circle the number that most accurately fits your standing on the dimension. For example, if you perceive yourself to have a "high humane orientation," circle the 7 on the fifth dimension.

1. Low performance orientation   High performance orientation

    1   2   3   4   5   6   7

2. Low Assertiveness   High Assertiveness

    1   2   3   4   5   6   7

3. Casual time orientation   Urgent time orientation

    1   2   3   4   5   6   7

4. Low future orientation   High future orientation

    1   2   3   4   5   6   7

5. Low humane orientation   High humane orientation

    1   2   3   4   5   6   7

6. In-group individualism   In-group collectivism

    1   2   3   4   5   6   7

7. Low gender egalitarianism   High gender egalitarianism

    1   2   3   4   5   6   7

8. Low power distance   High power distance

    1   2   3   4   5   6   7

9. Low uncertainty avoidance   High uncertainty avoidance

    1   2   3   4   5   6   7

10. Low work orientation   High work orientation

    1   2   3   4   5   6   7

Scoring and Interpretation: After circling one number for each dimension, use a marker, pen, or pencil to connect the circles; this gives you a *profile of cultural values*. Do not be concerned if your line cuts through the names of the dimensions. Compare your profile to others in class. Should time allow, develop a class profile by computing the class average for each of the ten dimensions and then connecting the points. If the sample size is large enough, compare the cultural value profiles of Westerners and Easterners.

    One possible link to leadership development is to hypothesize which type of profile would be the most responsive and which would be the least responsive to your leadership.

> ## LEADER IN ACTION

McDonald's Leaders at All Levels Take Into Account Cultural Differences

Leadership at McDonald's Corp., the world's best known quick food service restaurant, is proud of the company's cultural diversity. More than 60 percent of the home office and U.S. company workforce are of a racial or ethnic minority, or are women. Approximately two-thirds of the company workforce is located outside the United States. Also, the company has the largest number of minority and women franchise owners in the quick-service industry.

McDonald's stores (restaurants) are found in 118 countries, with all of them responding to local tastes. Most of the overseas franchises are locally owned, which helps to adapt the menu to local tastes. A few examples: In Egypt, a customer can order a McFelafel; in Japan, McDonald's serves seaweed burgers; beef is not served in an Indian McDonald's; beer is served in McDonald's restaurants of Munich, Germany; and some McDonald's restaurants in France serve rabbit.

Store-level leaders and managers not only respond to the cultural tastes of customers, they also respond to the cultural values of employees. Richard Floresch, the vice president and chief human resources officer at McDonald's, explains that each manager in a particular market is going to have cultural differences in the way he or she manages. Managers in countries throughout the world are granted considerable independence in dealing with their workforces. For example, in China,

the manager might be quicker to seek approval from a superior. A manager in Brazil might respond to the expectations of the community by inviting the parents of a new teenage employee to a family night orientation. In this way, the parents can learn more about their son or daughter's job, thereby reinforcing family values.

McDonald's isn't going to tell someone how to manage people, says Floresch. "That has to be part of the cultural norm."

QUESTIONS

1. If McDonald's is still a U.S. company, why should local managers overseas worry about conforming to local cultural values?
2. If McDonald's is supposed to promote family values in such a big way, how can beer be served in any McDonald's restaurant?

Source: Story created based on facts and observations reported in the following: Aman Singh, "McDonald's Makes Diversity about the Bottom Line," *The CSR Blog* (http://blogs.forbes.com), September 8, 2010, pp. 1–3; Janet Wiscombe, "McDonald's Corp." *Workforce Management*, November 2010, pp. 38–40; Patricia Harris, "The McDonald's Diversity Story," *Guest Insights* (http://views.washingtonpost.com), November 2009, pp. 1–14; "Americanization or Cultural Diversity," *Global Envision* (www.globalenvision.org), June 22, 2007, pp. 1–5; "Diversity at McDonald's: A Culture of Inclusion and Diversity," (www.aboutmcdonalds.com). Accessed May 11, 2011.

French Managers   One example of the influence of values on management and leadership style is the behavior of French managers. France has always put a strong emphasis on class. A typical manufacturing plant in France has several classes of workers. Managers and professionals are labeled the *cadres;* first-level supervisors are called the *maîtrise;* and lower-level workers are the *non-cadres.* Within each of these classes there are further status distinctions such as higher and lower cadres. French managers who have attended the major business schools (*Grand Écoles*) have the highest status of all.

The implication for leadership style is that French managers, particularly in major corporations, are part of an elite class, and they behave in a superior, authoritarian manner. (Not every French manager follows the cultural tradition of being authoritarian, with the more modern managers being less class conscious.) The traditional style of manager would expect obedience and high respect from group members, and would tend to emphasize bureaucracy.[20]

German Managers   Another example of a distinctive leadership style related to culture is the stereotype of the German manager. German managers were studied as part of the GLOBE project. Data were collected on culture and leadership from 457 middle managers in the telecommunications, food processing, and finance industries. A strong performance orientation was found to be the most pronounced German cultural value. German middle managers thus tend to avoid uncertainty, are assertive, and are not terribly considerate of others.

German managers typically show little compassion, and their interpersonal relations are straightforward and stern.[21] (Another interpretation of these findings is that the performance orientation of German managers is so strong that they seem less interested in interpersonal relations in comparison. This does not mean that German managers and leaders are inconsiderate.) And the strong performance they expect must be packed into a short workweek!

Malaysian Managers   The characteristic leadership style of Malaysian managers is instructive because other Asian managers use a similar style. Malaysia has become important as a trading partner of both the United States and Europe, particularly because of the outsourcing movement. The following conclusions about the Malaysian leadership style were also based on the GLOBE project.[22] Malaysians emphasize collective well-being (collectivism) and display a strong humane orientation within a society that respects hierarchical differences (high power difference). The culture discourages aggressive, confrontational behavior, preferring harmonious relationships. The preferred organizational leadership style is therefore for managers to show compassion, while at the same time be more autocratic than participative. The Malaysian work group member defers to the boss and in turn is treated with respect and compassion. A Malaysian supervisor might say typically to a worker, "Here is exactly how I want this job done, but I want you to enjoy yourself and learn something valuable while doing the job."

Northern U.S. Versus Southern U.S. Managers   Differences in cultural values between regions of a large country can also have an impact. An example of a cross-regional stereotype is that managers in the southern United States are lower key and more interested in relationship building than are their brusque counterparts in the North. Leaders from the North have a reputation for efficiency and getting tasks accomplished quickly. Leaders from the South perceive such behavior as rude, pushy, and short on relationship building. "If Donald Trump was from the South, he would say, 'You're fired, but bless your heart, you've tried,'" says Joe Hollingsworth, CEO of Hollingsworth Companies in Clinton, Tennessee.[23] The point here is that Southern chivalry has worked its way into leadership style.

However, the stereotype of Southern business leaders being more laid-back and slow moving has been challenged. Business in the South may have moved more slowly in the days before air conditioning was widespread. Heat tends to slow people down. John Thompson, former CEO of Symantec Corporation and now chairman, is a Florida A&M graduate. He says there is nothing regional about attaining business results. "I was raised in the South and spent 27 years working for IBM all over the world. I don't think management style can be localized."[24]

Despite culturally based differences in leadership style, certain leadership practices are likely to work in every culture, including giving people clear directions and administering appropriate rewards for attaining goals. In support of this generalization, a conclusion reached in the GLOBE study was that "in all cultures, leader team orientation and the communication of vision, values, and confidence in followers are reported to be highly effective leadership behaviors."[25]

CULTURAL SENSITIVITY AND CULTURAL INTELLIGENCE

Some managers are more effective at leading diverse groups than others. The traits and behaviors that will be described in Chapters 3, 4, and 8 should equip a person to lead diverse groups. In addition, cultural sensitivity, cultural intelligence, and certain specific global leadership skills are essential for inspiring people from cultures other than one's own. Although they reinforce each other, here we describe cultural sensitivity and cultural intelligence separately. Global leadership skills encompass so many behaviors that they receive a section of their own.

Cultural Sensitivity

Leaders, as well as others, who are attempting to influence a person from a foreign country must be alert to possible cultural differences. Thus, the leader must be willing to acquire knowledge about local customs and learn to speak the native language at least passably. A cross-cultural leader must be patient, adaptable, flexible, and willing to listen and learn. All of these characteristics are part of **cultural sensitivity**, an awareness of and a willingness to investigate the reasons why people of another culture act as they do.

A person with cultural sensitivity will recognize certain nuances in customs that will help build better relationships with people in his or her adopted cultures. Refer to Table 12-2 in Chapter 12 for a sampling of appropriate and less appropriate behaviors in a variety of countries. (These are suggestions, not absolute rules.) Another aspect of cultural sensitivity is being tolerant of the subtle differences between cultures. Leadership Self-Assessment Quiz 2-2 gives you an opportunity to reflect on your own tolerance for cross-cultural issues.

LEADERSHIP SELF-ASSESSMENT QUIZ 2-2

My Tolerance for Cultural Differences

Instructions: Indicate how comfortable you would feel in the following circumstances: very uncomfortable (VU); uncomfortable (U); neutral (N); comfortable (C); very comfortable (VC).

	VU	U	N	C	VC
1. Working on a team with both men and women	1	2	3	4	5
2. Coaching a team or club when all the members are of a different sex than myself	1	2	3	4	5
3. Having a transsexual person for a boss	1	2	3	4	5
4. Having a person of a different race for a boss	1	2	3	4	5
5. Having an opposite-sex person for a boss	1	2	3	4	5
6. Answer 6a if you are heterosexual; 6b if you are homosexual:	1	2	3	4	5
6a. Having a gay or lesbian boss					
6b. Having a straight boss					
7. Having dinner with someone who eats what I consider to be a pet	1	2	3	4	5
8. Having dinner with someone who eats what I consider to be a repulsive animal or insect	1	2	3	4	5
9. Working alongside a teammate who I know is HIV positive	1	2	3	4	5
10. Working alongside a teammate who has served prison time for vehicular homicide	1	2	3	4	5

Total score: _____

Scoring and Interpretation:

- **40–50:** You are highly tolerant and flexible in terms of working with a broad spectrum of people. These attitudes should help you be an effective multicultural leader.

- **21–39:** Your tolerance for working with people different from yourself is within the average range. If you learn to become more tolerant of differences, you are more likely to become an effective multicultural leader.

- **10–20:** You may be experiencing difficulties in working with people quite different from yourself. As a consequence, your effectiveness as a multicultural leader might be hampered. If you seek out more diverse cross-cultural experiences, you are likely to become more tolerant of differences.

Cultural sensitivity is also important because it helps a person become a **multicultural worker**. Such an individual is convinced that all cultures are equally good and enjoys learning about other cultures. Multicultural workers and leaders are usually people who have been exposed to more than one culture in childhood. (Refer to Leadership Self-Assessment Quiz 12-2, about cross-cultural relations.) Being multicultural helps one be accepted by a person from another culture.

Sensitivity is the most important characteristic for leading people from other cultures because cultural stereotypes rarely provide entirely reliable guides for dealing with others. An American manager, for example, might expect Asian group members to accept his or her directives immediately because Asians are known to defer to authority. Nevertheless, an individual Asian might need considerable convincing before accepting authority.

Problems of cultural misunderstanding leaders should be aware of cluster in five areas.[26] *Language* differences create problems because U.S. workers (most of whom are monolingual) can become frustrated by coworkers' accents and limited English skills. Non-English speakers may feel that they do not fit well into the team. Differences in *religion* are the source of many misunderstandings. In many cultures, religion dominates life in ways that Americans find difficult to comprehend. *Work habits* vary enough across cultures to create friction and frustration. Employees in some cultures are unwilling to spend personal time on work. Problems can also stem from office rituals, such as having coffee or tea together during work breaks, or singing songs together at the start of the workday.

Women's roles may differ considerably from those in the United States. Women in many countries may not have the same independence or access to education and higher-level jobs as American women. Workers from various countries may therefore have difficulty accepting the authority of an American manager who is female. *Personal appearance and behavior* vary considerably across cultures. Grooming, office attire, eating habits, and nonverbal communication may deviate significantly from the U.S. standards. Many workers around the world may perceive American workers as overfriendly, aggressive, or rude.

A key item in personal appearance is choosing appropriate attire when working in another culture. Cultural sensitivity helps you detect what type of clothing is appropriate. Many faux pas are possible, including that many Hindus in India may be offended by a finely tooled leather belt and briefcase because steers have religious significance. In some parts of Asia, white is the color of mourning. A cross-cultural guideline for professionals is that a dark, well-made business suit and conservative accessories such as ties and simple jewelry are acceptable for business around the world.[27]

Generational differences are another manifestation of cultural differences, quite often within a leader's national culture. For example, young people typically want more frequent recognition and rewards as well as flexible scheduling. Older people might want more deference to their knowledge and experience.

The reality of greater number of *transgender* employees in the workplace requires considerable cultural sensitivity on the part of the leader or manager. (A transgender person goes beyond cross-dressing, and converts to the opposite sex through a combination of surgery and hormone treatments.) Managers may have to deal with their own tolerance toward the transgender (or transsexual) workers, as well as the tolerance and flexibility of employees and customers. A particular need for cultural sensitivity is to begin referring to an employee as "him" or "her," when the person was formerly "her" or "him."[28] A general guide is that transgender employees are rare, but are still part of a culturally diverse workforce, and they have some legal protections with respect to job discrimination.

Cultural sensitivity is enhanced by cultural training, and also by simply listening carefully and observing. A key principle is to be flexible when dealing with people from other cultures. Cultural sensitivity is also enhanced by asking questions, such as whether it is reasonable to expect people to work on Saturday and Sunday. When cross-cultural issues about performance arise, the leader/manager is advised to ask: "My job requires that I manage your performance. Your job is to meet or exceed our performance standards. How can I help you do that?"[29]

Cultural Intelligence

A refinement and expansion of cultural sensitivity is **cultural intelligence (CQ)**: an outsider's ability to interpret someone's unfamiliar and ambiguous gestures the way that person's compatriots would.[30] For example, an American might be attending a business meeting in Europe. He or she might pick up the clue that the Europeans present prefer to discuss U.S. politics and trade agreements (or current events) for an hour before discussing the business purpose of the meeting. So the cross-border visitor engages in a lively but nonpartisan discussion of politics and trade agreements. Cultural intelligence has three facets or components:

- *Cognitive CQ (head)*. The first facet of cultural intelligence is the ability to pick up some factual clues about relevant behavior such as the importance of deadlines.
- *Physical CQ (body)*. Your actions and demeanor must prove to your foreign hosts that you have entered their world by adopting people's habits and mannerisms. You might gently kiss each cheek of a French compatriot (or be kissed), and not shake hands with a Japanese work associate in Tokyo. With the latter, you might bow slightly or smile as a form of greeting.
- *Emotional/motivational CQ (heart)*. Adapting to a new culture involves overcoming obstacles and setbacks. You need the self-confidence and courage to keep trying even though your first few attempts at adapting your behavior to a group of foreign workers went poorly. You might say to yourself, "OK, when I stood very close to the Mexican workers, they didn't like it even though they stand close to each other. Maybe I looked a little stiff. I'll practice some more."

To attain the highest level of cultural intelligence, you would need competence in all three facets, and the head, body, and heart would have to work together smoothly. You would need to gather the facts, adapt your mannerism and appearance to fit the culture, and stay motivated to make refinements.

Cultural intelligence is similar to emotional intelligence, yet it goes one step further by enabling a person to distinguish among behaviors that are (a) produced by the culture in question, (b) peculiar to particular individuals, and (c) found in all human beings. Suppose you are making a PowerPoint presentation in Germany and suddenly your presentation is verbally attacked. You ask yourself, "Is this a German trait? Are these people just being hostile? Or are my slides so bad anyone would attack them?" Picking up on the cues, you decide that German corporate professionals find it normal to challenge ideas and that they are not being personal.

GLOBAL LEADERSHIP SKILLS

In general, **global leadership skills** refer to the ability to exercise effective leadership in a variety of countries. The definition stems from the idea that the essence of global leadership is the ability to influence people who are dissimilar to the leader and stem from different cultural backgrounds.[31] Such skills would therefore include the concepts already reviewed, of cultural sensitivity, being a multicultural worker, and cultural intelligence. Here we look at global leadership skills from several perspectives: a specific model, success factors in international positions, and motivating workers in different cultures.

Global leadership skills are so important that they improve a company's reputation and contribute to a sustainable competitive advantage.[32] Excellent global leaders have a leadership style that generates superior corporate performance in terms of four criteria: (1) profitability and productivity, (2) continuity and efficiency, (3) commitment and morale, and (4) adaptability and innovation. *Behavioral complexity* is the term given to this ability to attain all four criteria of organizational performance. Excellent global leaders are able to understand complex issues from the four perspectives just mentioned and to achieve the right balance. For example, when a company is facing a mature market, it might be necessary to invest more effort into being innovative than into achieving high profits.

The global leader must tap into a deep, universal layer of human motivation to build loyalty, trust, and teamwork in different cultures. Universal needs are found among people in all cultures; for example, both Dominican Republicans and Inuit want to be part of a group. Another example of a universal need is to have meaning in the work one performs. Meaningful work would therefore be another universal need, with a large percentage of people wanting to perform work they consider to be relevant. People vary considerably in what they regard as meaningful work, with some people thinking that producing pharmaceuticals is meaningful while others think the same for producing video games.

Success Factors in International Management Positions

A study was conducted of success factors in international management positions. Two traits were specifically related to success in conducting international business: sensitivity to cultural differences and being culturally adventurous.[33] Cultural sensitivity has already been described. The adventurous aspect refers to a willingness to take chances and experiment with a new culture. A Mexican American from Phoenix, Arizona, who volunteered for a six-month assignment in Johannesburg, South Africa, would be culturally adventurous. Similarly, a set of observations by DDI, Inc., specialists in executive behavior, indicated that being a *global explorer* facilitated effective leadership. The global explorer has a passion for the native culture, and will ask questions about how and why things work in the country he or she is visiting for business purposes.

Being a *contextual chameleon* is also quite important, according to DDI. As in cultural sensitivity, effective global leaders are able to adapt to unfamiliar roles and environments. *Handig* is a Dutch term for adaptability; Dutch leaders in their roles as trading mediators between nations have gained a reputation for being flexible, adaptable, and skilled. Another example of responding to the context would be to emphasize consensus-style leadership in Scandinavia because most Scandinavian workers value low power distance.[34]

A study demonstrated that deficits in emotional intelligence contributed to executive failure on assignments in Latin America, Europe, and Japan.[35] Being able to read emotions is particularly helpful when evaluating how well the person from another culture is accepting your propositions.

Tolerance for ambiguity is important for leaders in general, and especially important for developing global leadership skills. Every country he or she works in represents a new way of doing things, so the leadership has to work with only general guidelines. A leader from an American company might be visiting a Korean affiliate. He or she should probably reflect, "Koreans have high respect for authority, and at the same time have a strong work ethic. So how far should I go in asking questions? They might expect me as the leader to have all the answers. Yet at the same time, they probably want to display their knowledge." Asking Korean managers questions before the presentation might be a good idea.[36]

Another area where tolerance for ambiguity is a success factor lies within providing leadership to cross-cultural teams. One of the more pronounced cross-cultural differences is that various members of the team nay have differing attitudes toward hierarchy and authority (or power distance). Team members from some cultures may have difficulty with the flat structure of most teams. If team members defer to a higher-status team member, their behavior will be regarded as appropriate when most of the team derives from a hierarchical culture. In contrast, team members who defer to authority may damage their stature and credibility if most of the team comes from a culture of low power distance (egalitarian). One manager of Mexican heritage who belonged to a cross-cultural team lamented:

> In Mexican culture, you're always supposed to be humble. So whether you understand something or not, you're supposed to put it in the form of a question. You have to keep it open-ended, out of respect. I think that actually worked against me, because the Americans thought I really didn't know what I was talking about. So it made me feel like they thought I was wavering on my answer.[37]

A potential leadership intervention to the problem of status and hierarchy is to talk about the problem in advance, and to encourage behavior that will fit most team members. The team leader might mention several times that the structure is flat, and that all team members have an equal voice. Because cultural values control behavior so strongly, the message will have to be repeated frequently.

A confusing skill issue for many international workers is the importance of having a good command of a second language. Part of the confusion comes from the fact that English has become the standard language of business, technology, engineering, and science. For example, when Europeans from different countries assemble at a business conference, they communicate in English. However, when you are trying to influence a person from another culture, you are more influential if you can speak, read, and write well in his or her language. A command of a second language also enhances the person's charisma.

Despite all the electronic devices, including Internet translators for converting one language into another, the demand for U.S. workers who speak a foreign language continues to grow. A recent study conducted by the University of Phoenix Institute found that 42 percent of the employers surveyed expect proficiency in Chinese to be in moderate or high demand in a decade. Approximately 70 percent expect Spanish to be in demand. (Arabic and Russian were next in demand.) The study also revealed that relatively few workers thought they would develop competency in Spanish or Chinese.[38] A worker who developed such competency might therefore enhance his or her leadership credentials.

Motivating and Inspiring Workers in Other Cultures

The discussion of expectancy theory in Chapter 7 provides the best general clue to motivating people in other cultures—figure out which rewards have high valence for them. Workers who lack basic necessities in life would rather be rewarded with a scooter or bicycle than a $500 luxury fountain pen or watch. Workers will be motivated and inspired to the extent that need satisfaction will be forthcoming.

Cross-cultural trainer Nancy Settle-Murphy provides another example: Team members from the United States tend to crave popularity and approval. For Germans, the goal is to do an excellent job with great attention to detail. The implication is that German professionals prefer motivation through exciting work, whereas Americans prefer external rewards. Team members from Asian cultures are more motivated by rewards that emphasize group harmony, such as a group reward.[39] (Again we are presented with cultural stereotypes that work much of the time.)

So who is an example of a leader with global leadership skills—one person who has most of the attributes described in this section? A highly visible example is Carlos Ghosn, the chief executive of both Nissan and Renault, known as the "hottest car guy on earth." He travels around the world in a corporate jet that can fly between Paris and Tokyo nonstop. Ghosn also spends considerable time visiting the U.S. operations of Nissan. He carries two briefcases, one for Renault and another for Nissan. He crosses time zones and cultures with great facility. Born in Brazil to Lebanese parents, and college-educated in Paris, Ghosn speaks several languages and enjoys cuisine from many countries.[40]

LEADERSHIP INITIATIVES FOR ACHIEVING CULTURAL DIVERSITY

For organizations to value diversity, top management must be committed to it. The commitment is clearest when it is embedded in organizational strategy, as well as in the life and culture of the organization. Diversity initiatives should be deep rather than superficial.[41] A true diversity strategy should

TABLE 2-1 Leadership Initiatives for Achieving Cultural Diversity

1. Hold managers accountable for achieving diversity.
2. Establish minority recruitment, retention, and mentoring programs.
3. Conduct diversity training.
4. Conduct cross-cultural training.
5. Encourage the development of employee networks.
6. Avoid group characteristics when hiring for person–organization fit.
7. Modify products and services for targeted demographic groups.
8. Attain diversity among organizational leaders.

© Cengage Learning 2013

encourage all employees to contribute their unique talents, skills, and expertise to the organization's operations, independent of race, gender, ethnic background, and any other definable difference. In addition, leaders should take the initiative to ensure that many activities are implemented to support the diversity strategy. Table 2-1 lists the eight leadership initiatives for encouraging diversity that are discussed in the following text.

Hold Managers Accountable for Achieving Diversity

A high-impact diversity initiative is for top-level organizational leaders to hold managers accountable for diversity results at all levels. If managers are held accountable for behavior and business changes in the diversity arena, an organizational culture supportive of diversity will begin to develop. Accountability for diversity results when achieving diversity objectives is included in performance evaluations and when compensation is linked in part to achieving diversity results.

The Allstate Corporation exemplifies a firm that has worked hard to hold managers accountable for achieving cultural diversity within the firm. The company states that a core component of the diversity strategy at Allstate is effective education and training for all employees. The diversity education program delivers a message that focuses on inclusion and maximizing performance at the same time. All employees including managers are required to participate in a classroom and online training about diversity.[42]

Establish Minority Recruitment, Retention, and Mentoring Programs

An essential initiative for building a diverse work force is to recruit and retain members of the targeted minority group. Because recruiting talented members of minority groups and women is competitive, careful human resources planning is required.

Efforts at recruiting a culturally diverse work force must be supported by a leadership and management approach that leads to high retention. To increase retention rates, diversity consultants advise employers to strengthen cultural training programs, recognize employees' hidden skills and talents, and give diversity committees clout with top management.[43] Retaining employees is also a function of good leadership and management in general, such as offering workers challenging work, clear-cut goals, feedback, and valuable rewards for goal attainment. Mentoring is a key initiative for retaining minority-group members, as well as for facilitating their advancement.

A component of attaining culturally diverse leaders in an organization is to work with executive placement (or search) firms who have developed strong networks with successful managers from various demographic groups. The Association of Executive Search Consultants has established a resource center to help member firms to promote diverse candidates and to equal opportunity in employment.[44]

Conduct Diversity Training

Diversity training has become a widely used method for enhancing diversity within organizations. The purpose of diversity training is to bring about workplace harmony by teaching people how to get along better with diverse work associates. Quite often the program is aimed at minimizing open expressions of racism and sexism. All forms of diversity training center on increasing people's awareness of and empathy for people who are different from themselves in some important way. In recent years, diversity training has placed some emphasis on leveraging diversity to enhance business performance.[45] The enhancements to performance were described at the outset of the chapter.

Training sessions in valuing differences focus on the ways in which men and women, or people of different races, reflect different values, attitudes, and cultural backgrounds. These sessions can vary from several hours to several days or longer. Sometimes the program is confrontational, sometimes not.

An essential part of relating more effectively to diverse groups is to empathize with their point of view. To help training participants develop empathy, representatives of various groups explain their feelings related to workplace issues. Leadership Skill-Building Exercise 2-2 gives you the opportunity to engage in an effective diversity training exercise. A useful way of framing diversity training is to say that it represents a subset of interpersonal skills: Relating effectively to coworkers who are different from you in some meaningful way adds to your interpersonal effectiveness.

An extension of diversity training is helping organizational leaders develop empathy for diverse groups by having them spend time working with demographic groups different from their own. In addition to developing empathy, the executives learn to relate more comfortably with diverse groups. An extreme approach is when Rod Bond, an executive at a food service company, accompanied female colleagues to a meeting of the Women's Food Service Forum, where he was the only man among 1,500 women. Bond said, "I can begin to feel what it must have felt like to be different." Another example is that Raytheon's missile-systems division once required managers to spend a day in a wheelchair in the office. The goal of the activity was to understand the concerns of the disabled employees. Diversity specialists believe that executives should be asked to engage in activities that relate to their regular work, so they can see how diversity is relevant.[46]

LEADERSHIP SKILL-BUILDING **EXERCISE 2-2**

The Diversity Circle

Some diversity trainers use the *diversity circle* exercise to help workers appreciate diversity and overcome misperceptions. The exercise adapts well for classroom use. Form a group of about ten students. Arrange your chairs into a circle, and put one additional chair in the center of the circle. A group member who feels diverse in any way volunteers to sit in the center chair and become the first awareness subject. Because most people are diverse in some way, most people are eligible to occupy the center chair.

The person in the center tells the others how he or she has felt about being diverse or different and how people have reacted to his or her diversity. For example, an Inuit described how fellow workers were hesitant to ask him out for a beer, worrying whether he could handle alcohol. Another name for this exercise is "How I Felt Different" because each person describes how he or she felt different from others at one point in his or her life.

An equally effective alternative to this procedure is for each class member to come up in front of the class to describe a significant way in which he or she is different. After each class member has presented, a discussion might be held of observations and interpretations.

What lessons did you learn about interpersonal relations from this exercise that will help you be a more effective leader?

A frequently mentioned concern about diversity training is that it reinforces stereotypes about groups. Participants are informed about group differences, such as cultural values, and tactics might be suggested for coping with these differences—such as using more body language when relating to Latinos.

Leaders of diversity training exercises are cautioned to guard against encouraging participants to be too confrontational and expressing too much hostility. Companies have found that when employees are too blunt during these sessions, it may be difficult to patch up interpersonal relations in the work group later on. Sometimes the diversity trainer encourages group members to engage in outrageous behavior, such as by having women sexually harass men so the men know what it feels like. Key themes of negative reactions to diversity training are charges of political correctness and white-male bashing.

Even when diversity training is effective in achieving better cross-cultural understanding, and improved cross-cultural relationships, such training may not accelerate the number of minority group members and women into managerial positions. A review of 31 years of data from 830 workplaces suggested that when diversity training was mandatory and aimed at avoiding liability in discrimination lawsuits, the number of women in management, as well as minorities including Latinos and Asians, decreased.

In contrast, when diversity training is voluntary and implemented to advance a company's business strategy, the training was associated with increased diversity in management. Another key finding is that diversity training works best when it focuses on organizational skills, such as establishing mentoring relationships and giving women and minorities a chance to prove they can compete successfully in high-profile positions.[47]

Diversity training is yet another initiative that needs to be incorporated into a culture that supports inclusion for the training to have much of an Impact on the organization. In the words of diversity training pioneer, Roosevelt Thomas, "I may come out with some skills (after diversity training), but I also know that if I'm going to use these skills effectively, I must have a culture that supports their use, that affirms their use."[48]

Conduct Cross-Cultural Training

For many years, companies and government agencies have prepared their managers and other workers for overseas assignments. The method frequently chosen is **cross-cultural training**, a set of learning experiences designed to help employees understand the customs, traditions, and beliefs of another culture. Foreign language training is often included in cultural training. The multicultural leader needs to know that English is spoken differently in the United States, Great Britain, Australia, and South Africa, among other countries. Four examples follow:

- Britons say "keen" whereas Americans say "enthusiastic."
- Britons say "to table (an idea), whereas Americans say "To put (an idea) out for discussion."
- Britons say "to put (an idea) aside," whereas Americans say "To table (an idea)."
- Britons say "lift," whereas Americans say "elevator."[49]

Cross-cultural training usually includes the type of information about cross-cultural bloopers included in Chapter 12. Among the hundreds of tidbits included, depending on the target country, are how to handle chopsticks in China (never stick them straight into the rice bowl) and that it is acceptable in Finland to take a sauna with a client (that's the normal way to conduct business there).[50]

The art of facial cheek-kissing is an amusing, yet important, aspect of cross-cultural training. Americans favor handshakes for greetings, yet in most countries outside of Asia, light kisses on the cheek of the other person are more acceptable. The kisses are given to people of the same and opposite sex for greeting purposes; however, kissing a business acquaintance of the opposite sex is even more expected and appropriate. Frank Higgins, a global leader of two divisions for Nestlé USA Inc., observes, "I would be rude if I didn't kiss my female colleagues from Mexico." At the company's Zurich headquarters, Higgins triple cheek-kisses.[51]

Another development in intercultural training is to train global leaders in cultural intelligence. Following the model of cultural intelligence described earlier in this chapter, global managers receive training in the cognitive, physical, and emotional or motivational domains. The training is highly complex, with the leader being expected to learn dozens of different concepts and behaviors, as well as insights. A sampling of what training in cultural intelligence involves is as follows:[52]

A Canadian manager is attempting to interpret a "Thai smile." First, she needs to observe the various cues provided in addition to the smile gesture itself (for example, other facial or bodily gestures, significance of others who may be in proximity, the source of the original smile gesture) and to assemble them into a meaningful whole and make sense of what is really experienced by the Thai employee. Second, she must have the requisite motivation (directed effort and self-confidence) to persist in the face of confusion, challenge, or apparently mixed signals. Third, she must choose, generate, and execute the right actions to respond appropriately.

If any of these elements is deficient, she is likely to be ineffective in dealing with the Thai employee. A high CQ manager has the capability with all three facets as they act in unison.

Again, cultural intelligence is a refinement of cultural sensitivity. The international leader who remains alert to cues in the environment can go a long way toward building relationships with people from different cultures.

Encourage the Development of Employee Networks

Another leadership initiative toward recognizing cultural differences is to permit and encourage employees to form **employee network (or affinity) groups**. The network group is composed of employees throughout the company who affiliate on the basis of a group characteristic such as race, ethnicity, sex, sexual orientation, or physical ability status. Group members typically have similar interests and look to the groups as a way of sharing information about succeeding in the organization. Although some human resources specialists are concerned that network groups can lead to divisiveness, others believe they play a positive role.

Allstate has at least seven employee network groups running at any given time. Two examples are 3AN (Allstate Asian American Network), and ANGLES (Allstate Network of Gay and Lesbian Employees and Supporters). The mission statement of 3AN is "3AN develops leaders of tomorrow through professional development, networking, cultural awareness and knowledge sharing." The group's vision statement is "Leverage the diverse experiences of Asian Americans at Allstate to create value that supports Allstate."[53]

Macy's is another business firm that encourages diversity through affinity groups, also known as employee resource groups. The groups help employees network and bond across different functions and levels within Macy's. Affinity groups include those for women, African Americans, Latinos, Native Americans, Chinese-Americans, the disabled, plus gay, lesbian, and transgender employees.[54]

Employee network groups sometimes play a functional role in the organization in addition to the social role. A prime example is The Latino Employee Network (called Adelante) at Frito-Lay, the snack food division of PepsiCo. The group made a major contribution during the development of Doritos Guacamole Flavored Tortilla Chips. Adelante members provided feedback on taste and packaging to help ensure the authenticity of the product in the Latino community. The network members' insight helped make the guacamole-flavored Doritos into one of the most dramatically successful new-product launches in the history of Frito-Lay.[55] Olé!

A caution about employee network groups is that they can result in employee segregating rather than integrating themselves into the workforce, thereby defeated the purpose of diversity initiatives. The same series of studies in over 800 companies referred to above found that networking and affinity groups may simply resegregate the workplace.[56]

Avoid Group Characteristics When Hiring for Person–Organization Fit

An important consideration in employee recruitment and hiring is to find a good *person–organization fit*, the compatibility of the individual with the organization. The compatibility often centers on the extent to which a person's major work-related values and personality traits fit major elements of the organization culture. Following this idea, a person who is adventuresome and prone to risk taking would achieve highest performance and satisfaction where adventuresome behavior and risk taking are valued. Conversely, a methodical and conservative individual should join a slow-moving bureaucracy.

Many business firms today are investing time and effort into recruiting and hiring employees who show a good person–organization fit. A selection strategy of this type can lead to a cohesive and strong organizational culture. The danger, however, is that when employers focus too sharply on cultural fit in the hiring process, they might inadvertently discriminate against protected classes of workers. Specifically, the hiring manager might focus on superficial aspects of conformity to culture, such as physical appearance and which schools the candidates attended. Selecting candidates who look alike and act alike conflicts with a diversity strategy. Elaine Fox, a labor and employment attorney, cautions that "one of the biggest problems that can occur when hiring based on culture is if the culture you're comfortable with doesn't open the way for women and minorities."[57]

Leaders can take the initiative to guard against this problem. The way to circumvent it is to avoid using group characteristics (such as race, sex, ethnicity, or physical status) in assessing person–organization fit. The alternative is to focus on traits and behaviors, such as intelligence or ability to be a team player. Leaders at Microsoft emphasize hiring intelligent people only because bright people fit their culture best. Being intelligent is an individual difference rather than a group characteristic.

Modify Products and Services for Targeted Demographic Groups

Managing for diversity often means modifying products and services as to increase their appeal to targeted demographic groups. Hundreds of examples abound in everyday life including advertisements written in Spanish in newspapers and on the Internet to enhance their appeal to the Latino community. Even as ordinary an act as having a larger kosher food section in supermarkets situated in a neighborhood with many Jewish people is an example of this straightforward business tactic. State Farm Insurance exemplifies a company whose leadership emphasizes ethnic-targeted services. An advisory committee meets annually to discuss how they can better meet the needs of Hispanic customers. Rural Texas is one such focus because of its large proportion of Spanish speaking residents. Invoices for insurance are sent in both English and Spanish, and customer-service agents in the regional call center have a bilingual unit to handle calls in English and Spanish.[58]

Attain Diversity Among Organizational Leaders

To achieve a multicultural organization, firms must also practice **leadership diversity**—that is, have a culturally heterogeneous group of leaders. Many global firms have already achieved leadership diversity with respect to ethnicity. Sex is another key area for leadership diversity, with many organizations today having women in top executive positions. An organization with true leadership diversity also has a heterogeneous group of leaders in such positions as supervisors, middle managers, and team leaders. McDonald's Corp. and Xerox Corp. are two examples of well-known companies whose C-level executives include minority group members and women. One of the executive positions at McDonald's is chief diversity officer, a practice also followed by several other large business firms including PepsiCo.

SUMMARY

The modern leader must be multicultural because corporate success, profit, and growth depend increasingly on the management of a diverse work force. The ethical and social responsibility goals of leaders and their organizations include providing adequately for the members of the diverse work force.

Managing for diversity brings a competitive advantage to the firm in several ways. Turnover and absenteeism costs may be lower because minorities are more satisfied. Marketing can be improved because a representational work force facilitates selling products and services, and a good reputation for diversity management may attract customers. Companies with a favorable record in managing diversity are at an advantage in recruiting and retaining talented minority-group members. Managing diversity also helps unlock the potential for excellence among employees who might otherwise be overlooked. A heterogeneous work force may also offer an advantage in creativity and problem solving. Diversity and inclusion programs also help local economies partly because of the reliance on minority suppliers.

To influence, motivate, and inspire culturally diverse people, the leader must be aware of overt and subtle cultural differences. Differences in cultural values help explain differences among people. Ten of these values are as follows: (1) performance orientation, (2) assertiveness, (3) future orientation, (4) time orientation, (5) humane orientation, (6) in-group collectivism, (7) gender egalitarianism, (8) power distance (acceptance of formal authority), (9) uncertainty avoidance, and (10) work orientation.

Cultural values influence leadership style as well as the behavior of other workers. For example, French managers believe in a class system. Another way to understand how culture influences leadership is to compare leadership styles across cultural groups. For Malaysian managers, the preferred organizational leadership style is to show compassion while at the same time being more autocratic than participative. Cultural differences in leadership style within the same country exist also, such as the stereotype of U.S. Southern managers being more interested in building relationships than their Northern counterparts.

Cultural sensitivity is essential for inspiring people from different cultures. Part of this sensitivity is the leader's willingness to acquire knowledge about local customs and to learn to speak the native language. A person with cultural sensitivity will recognize certain nuances in customs that help him or her build better relationships with people from different cultures. Cultural misunderstandings tend to cluster in five key areas: (1) language differences, (2) religious differences, (3) work habits, (4) women's roles, and (5) personal appearance and behavior. Choosing appropriate attire for conducting business in another culture requires careful observation. Generational differences are another manifestation of cultural differences. The reality of a greater number of transgender employees requires considerable cultural sensitivity.

Cultural intelligence helps an outsider interpret someone's unfamiliar and ambiguous gestures the way that person's compatriots would. Such intelligence has three facets: (1) cognitive (head), (2) physical (body), and (3) emotional/motivational (heart).

Global leadership skills help improve a company's reputation and contribute to a sustainable competitive advantage. One model of such skills contends that behavioral complexity helps a leader attain high organizational performance. Among the success factors for international management positions are cultural sensitivity; cultural adventurousness (or being a global explorer); being a contextual chameleon (adaptation to the unfamiliar); emotional intelligence; and tolerance for ambiguity. Having a command of a second language is helpful for influencing a person from another culture.

Top management commitment to valuing diversity is clearest when valuing diversity is embedded in organizational strategy. Specific leadership initiatives for valuing diversity can be divided into eight categories: (1) hold managers accountable for diversity; (2) establish minority recruitment, retention, and mentoring programs; (3) conduct diversity training; (4) conduct cross-cultural training, (5) encourage the development of employee networks; (6) avoid group characteristics when hiring for person–organization fit, (7) modify products and services for targeted demographic groups, and (8) attain diversity among organizational leaders.

KEY TERMS

multicultural leader	gender egalitarianism	global leadership skills
performance orientation	power distance	diversity training
assertiveness	uncertainty avoidance	cross-cultural training
future orientation	work orientation	employee network (or affinity) groups
time orientation	cultural sensitivity	leadership diversity
humane orientation	multicultural worker	
in-group collectivism	cultural intelligence (CQ)	

✔ GUIDELINES FOR **ACTION** AND **SKILL** DEVELOPMENT

A major problem to manage in developing a diverse work force is for company leadership to reduce turnover among the employees they have worked so hard to recruit. A report that surveyed 490 minority professionals in finance suggests that companies that work so hard to get diverse employees in the building don't try nearly hard enough to keep them from leaving. Among the suggestions made in the report were to include communicating a clear path for employee advancement and providing suggestions for development as part of performance evaluation. The report also stated that "Professionals of color are, or perceive themselves to be, outside of the informal mechanisms of information sharing and social networks, including lunch or coffee with peers, being invited to drinks, and socializing with managers."[59]

A caution in implementing diversity management is for managers and other interviewers not to go overboard in trying to make a minority-group member feel comfortable. "When interviewers try too hard to be black, Latin, or Asian," says Martin de Campo, managing consultant with an executive search firm, "they come across as hokey." John Fujii, the president of a diversity recruiting firm, says, "The best way to make minority candidates feel comfortable is to make them feel that they have an equal opportunity to compete for a position. That's all they want."[60]

Discussion Questions and Activities

1. Some U.S. consumers object to voice-mail customer support systems that include the direction, "Press 1 for English." How should a manager respond to such a objection?
2. An Arabian friend of yours is conducting a job search to land a middle-management position. Given that so many companies are attempting to build a more culturally diverse group of managers, should your friend include a photo of himself on his job résumé? Explain your reasoning.
3. With so much business being conducted over the Internet, including e-mail, why is it important to understand cross-cultural differences in values?
4. If a business leader is regarded as charismatic by many people in one culture, to what extent do you think the leader would be perceived as charismatic in many other cultures?
5. What actions might a leader take to demonstrate that his or her interest in diversity goes beyond rhetoric?
6. Assume that a manager becomes the leader of a division in which the vast majority of the workers are under twenty-five, such as a restaurant chain. Would you recommend that the leader get some body piercing and tattoos to help establish rapport with the division work force? Explain your reasoning.
7. Many international companies have found that it is particularly helpful to hire local citizens for key management positions in a company location in another country. What advantages might a native offer to the company?
8. Assume that an outstanding sales representative works for a company that considers it unethical to bribe officials to make a sale. The sales representative is about to close a major deal in a country where bribing is standard practice. Her commission will be $60,000 for a signed contract. What should the representative do if an official demands a $4,000 *gift* before closing the deal?
9. Suppose you are a team leader and one of your team members has a strong work ethic, based on his or her cultural values. Is it fair to assign this member much more work just because he or she is willing to work longer and harder than the other team members?
10. What can you do this week to help prepare yourself to become a multicultural leader?

LEADERSHIP CASE PROBLEM A

What to Do About Louie?

Louie is the manager of a Mighty Muffler Brake service center in the Great Lakes Regions of the United States. The centers offer a wide range of services for vehicles including muffler and exhaust system replacement, brake systems, oil change, lubrication, tune-ups, and state inspection. Louie's branch is located close to a busy highway, yet stores and residential neighborhoods are also close by. His store is among the chain's highest-volume and most profitable units.

Management at Mighty Muffler is pleased with the financial management of Louie's store, yet complaints have surfaced about aspects of his relationships with employees and customers. Emma, the human resources and customer services for the company, was recently poring over the results from customer satisfaction cards mailed back to the company. She found that a few of the customer comments suggested that Louie might have made some inappropriate comments, as reflected in the following feedback:

"You did a wonderful job replacing my brakes and fixing a rattle in my exhaust system. But the manager insulted me a little by suggesting that I talk over with my husband about whether to get a new exhaust system now."

"I have no complaints about the repairs you made or the price you charged.

However, you better replace that manager of yours. He is definitely out of touch with the times. My partner and I are proud of our gayness, so we don't attempt to hide occasional public displays of affection. When your manager saw me giving my partner a light kiss on the cheek, he asked if we were from San Francisco."

"When I came back to pick up my car, I had to wait two hours even though I was told the car would be ready by 3 p.m. I also found some smudge marks on the beige leather seats. When I complained to the manager, he said, 'Granny, watch your blood pressure. It's not good for a senior citizen to get too excited.' I was never so insulted."

Concerned about these comments, Emma scheduled a trip to Louie's store to investigate any possible problems he might be having in managing cultural diversity among customers and employees. Emma explained to Louie that the home office likes to make periodic trips to the stores to see now well employee relations are going, and how well employees are working together. Louie responded, "Talk to anybody you want. I may joke a little with the boys and girls in the shop, but we all get along great."

In Emma's mind, her informal chats with workers at Louie's Mighty Muffler suggested that employee relations were generally satisfactory, but she did find a few troublesome comments. A young African American noted that when he does something particularly well, or Louie agrees with him strongly, Louie gives him a high five. In contrast, Caucasian or Latino workers will receive a congratulatory handshake or a fist bump, respectively.

A woman brake technician said that Louie is a kind-hearted boss but that he is sometimes patronizing without realizing it. She volunteered this incident: "During breaks I sometimes enter the waiting room area because we have a vending machine up front that sells small bags of nuts and raisins, which I particularly like. One day, I was about to enter the waiting room when Louie tells me to stay in the back. He said that there was a Hell's Angels–type guy waiting for his truck to be repaired, and he probably wouldn't appreciate it if he thought that a 'girl' was working on his truck. How could anybody be that sexist in today's world?"

Emma went back to the home office to discuss her findings with the CEO and the vice president of administration. Emma said that Louie is making a contribution to the firm, but that some changes needed to be made. The two other executives agreed that Louie should become a little more multicultural, but that they didn't want to upset him too much because he could easily join a competitor. Emma concluded, "So I guess we need to figure out what to do about Louie."

1. Does Louie have a problem, or are the people who made the negative comments about him being too sensitive?

2. What improvements might Louie need to make to become a truly multicultural manager?
3. What activity or program would you recommend to help make Louie more culturally sensitive?

ASSOCIATED ROLE PLAY

One student plays the role of Emma who decides to take it upon herself to coach Louie about becoming more culturally sensitive and schedules an appointment with Louie for her first coaching session. Another person plays the role of Louie, who does not quite understand the purpose of the meeting, yet agrees to the appointment. During this first coaching session, Emma will focus on getting Louie to become more aware that he should become more culturally sensitive. Louie might become a little defensive during the session. Observers will make particular note as to whether Emma is getting through to Louie.

LEADERSHIP CASE PROBLEM B

Curses, Foiled Again in France

A U.S. manufacturer of kiosk photo printers with an affiliate in Dijon, France, decided to create the position of "international liaison." This person would spend about five days per month in Dijon in the role of home-office representative. The liaison would offer some advice to European operations and function as the intermediary between the home office and Dijon.

Erin Barker, a product development manager, was a logical choice for the new position. In addition to being technically competent, Barker had good interpersonal skills and spoke French. She had studied French in high school and college and had spent one semester in France as part of her college program. In recent years, she had taken two vacations in France.

Erin still retained her position as product development manager. She planned to work at her new position about half time. Some of her responsibilities as product development manager were delegated to two specialists in the product development department. Erin was somewhat skeptical about occupying a liaison position, because it was by nature nebulous. The Dijon group would have to respect her authority because she represented company headquarters. However, the Dijon group really reported to the company CEO, not to her.

Erin prepared herself mentally for her first trip to Dijon. She gathered relevant facts and figures about the company's European business headquartered in Dijon, and listened to French language-learning CDs for two weeks. With a dry throat and determination in her heart, Erin walked into the Dijon conference room one Monday morning for her first meeting with the French group.

Barker greeted the management team at the plant in French: "Bonjour. Je suis enchanté de faire votre connaissance. Mon séjour sera pour plusieurs jours. Je voudrais apprendre votre opération. Aussi, je voudrais expliquer les opérations du siège, et répondre à vos questions." [Hello. It's a pleasure to meet you. My stay will be several days. I would like to learn about your operation. Also, I would like to explain the operations of headquarters and answer your questions.]

"Oh, how nice, you speak a little French," said plant manager Gilles Naulleau, in English. Erin was taken aback that Naulleau and the other French managers seemed intent on speaking English. She interpreted it as a sign of their not taking her interest in them seriously. Erin also thought that her first few days in Dijon were strictly ceremonial. She felt more like a visitor on a plant tour than an executive conducting business. When Erin touched on business topics such as sales and production forecasts, the Dijon representative would typically shrug and change the subject.

The following month, Erin revisited Dijon and again met with Naulleau and Pierre Chevalier, the sales manager for France. She opened the meeting with these words: "Ma dernière visite chez vous était très agréable. J'ai apprécié l'opportunité à connaître les cadres de Dijon. Maintenant je voudrais discuter les projets liés au succès de notre entreprise." [My last visit here was very pleasant. I appreciated the opportunity to get to know the Dijon managers. Now, I would like to discuss projects linked to the success of our business.] Again, Naulleau talked mostly about superficial topics, but he did respond in a few words of French. The other managers spoke among themselves in French in her presence but held back on talking about serious business issues.

Back at headquarters, Erin met with the CEO. She discussed her seemingly slow progress in getting down to serious business with the Dijon managers. The CEO then asked whether she would like the company to assign somebody else to the job. Erin responded, "I'm not willing to say goodbye to Dijon quite yet. Give me more time to prove myself."

Questions

1. How should Erin conduct herself in her future visits to the Dijon operation in order to get down to business?
2. Should the company replace Erin with another person for the position of international liaison? Explain your answer.
3. What message or messages about global business relationships do you extract from this case history?

ASSOCIATED ROLE PLAY

One student plays the role of Erin, who makes yet another visit to Dijon. She is invited to dinner with the executive group and accepts the invitation because she thinks it will be a good opportunity to demonstrate the seriousness of her purpose. Several other students play the role of the Dijon cadre of managers, who might be more interested in having a relaxed, social dinner than discussing serious business. Observers will take particular note if Erin is able to communicate the seriousness of her role.

LEADERSHIP SKILL-BUILDING EXERCISE 2-3

My Leadership Portfolio

To be an effective cross-cultural leader, you need to work effectively with people from demographic and cultural groups different from your own. Describe what experiences you have had lately in working with and/or relating effectively to a person quite different from you. If you have not had such an experience, take the initiative during the next week to relate meaningfully to a person quite different from you in terms of culture or demographic group membership. Finance major Stephanie had this to say:

> Claire, a special education teacher, lives on my block. Claire goes to work every school day in spite of being legally blind. She can read with visual assists, including reading what is on her computer screen. Yet paper forms are difficult for Claire to navigate. I telephoned Claire one night and asked her if she could use my assistance in preparing her income tax this year. Claire agreed, and it worked out well. I now feel more comfortable working side by side with a visually handicapped person. Also, I picked up some practical experience in preparing a complicated tax form.

LEADERSHIP SKILL-BUILDING EXERCISE 2-4

Positive Cross-Cultural Experiences in the Workplace

Organize into brainstorming groups to identify at least six positive cross-cultural experiences you have observed in the workplace, or would like to observe. Take an expansive view of cross-cultural to include many types of demographic factors such as wheel-chair use, visual status, and ethnic, racial, and age groups. After you have completed your brainstorming, attempt to draw conclusions from the findings. Comparing the results of your group with those of other brainstorming groups in the class will be helpful in drawing conclusions because you will have more data at your disposal.

▶ LEADERSHIP VIDEO CASE DISCUSSION QUESTIONS

To view the videos for this activity, you'll need access to the CourseMate that is available for this text. To get access, visit www.CengageBrain.com.

After watching "Texas Instruments," answer the following questions.

1. Does a diverse workforce at Texas Instruments offer the company a competitive advantage? Explain. How does the company work to attract employees from around the country and world?

2. What are the three facets or components of cultural intelligence (CQ)? Briefly define each and give an example of how each of these may be used at Texas Instruments.

3. What are universal needs? How might Texas Instruments meet these universal needs?

NOTES

1. Story created from facts and observations reported in the following sources: Mariko Sanchanta, "Cultivating Multiculturalism: At Nippon Sheet Glass, Local Flavor Is Good, Slang Is Bad," *The Wall Street Journal*, June 7, 2010, p. B6; "Nippon Sheet Glass Recognizes Need For Non-Japanese Leader," *News in Depth* (http://business.nikkeibp.co), May 6, 2010, pp. 1–2; "Nippon Sheet Glass Taps Former DuPont Exec as CEO." *Update 1* (http://news.alibaba.com), April 15, 2010, pp. 1–2.

2. James R. Hagerty, "'Lightning Bolt' Led Caterpillar to Look Outside," *The Wall Street Journal*, December 13, 2010, pp. B1, B5.

3. Dianna L. Stone, Book Review in *Personnel Psychology*, Spring 2010, pp. 260–261.

4. Jennifer Schramm, "Acting Affirmatively," *HR Magazine*, September 2003, p. 192.

5. Patricia Harris, "The McDonald's Diversity Story," *Guest Insights* (http://views.washingtonpost.com)., November 25, 2009, p. 1.

6. Fay Hansen, "Diversity's Business Case Doesn't Add Up," *Workforce*, April 2003, pp. 28–32.

7. Susan Meisinger, "Diversity: More Than Just Representation," *HR Magazine*, January 2008, p. 8.

8. Irwin Speizer, "Diversity on the Menu," *Workforce Management*, November 2004, pp. 41–45.

9. Cited in Annya M. Lott, "Future of Diversity: Cultural Inclusion Is a Business Imperative," *Black Enterprise*, August 2010, p. 75.

10. Nicole Ibarra, "Some Companies Turn to Their Diverse Workforce to Help with the Bottom Line," *Hispanic Business*, December 2007, p. 56.

11. "Allstate Diversity," www.allstate.com/diversity.aspx. © 2011 Allstate Insurance Company.

12. Scott E. Page, "Making the Difference: Applying a Logic of Diversity," *Academy of Management Perspective*, November 2007, p. 9.

13. Quoted in Frank Nelson, "U.S. Economy Gets a Life from Diversity Best Companies," *Hispanic Business*, September 2010, p. 14.

14. Aparna Joshi and Hyuntak Roh, "The Role of Context in Work Team Diversity Research: A Meta-Analytic Review, *Academy of Management Journal*, June 2009, p. 619.

15. Frances J. Milliken and Luis L. Martins, "Searching for Common Threads: Understanding the Multiple Effects of Diversity in Organizational Groups," *Academy of Management Review*, April 1996, p. 403. See also Daan van Knippenberg, Carsten K. W. De Dreu, and Astrid C. Homan, "Work Group Diversity and Group Performance: An Integrative Model and Research Agenda," *Journal of Applied Psychology*, December 2004, pp. 1008–1022.

16. Katherine J. Klein and David A. Harrison, "On the Diversity of Diversity: Tidy Logic, Messier Realities," *Academy of Management Perspectives*, November 2007, p. 31.

17. Mansour Javidan, Peter W. Dorfman, May Sully de Luque, and Robert J. House, "In the Eye of the Beholder: Cross Cultural Lessons in Leadership from Project GLOBE," *Academy of Management Perspectives*, February 2006, pp. 69–70. Similar dimensions were described in Geert Hofstede, *Culture's Consequences: International Differences in Work Related Values* (Beverly Hills, Calif.: Sage Publications, 1980); updated and clarified in Hofstede, "Who Is the Fairest of Them All?" Galit Ailon's Mirror," *Academy of Management Review*, July 2009, pp. 570–571. Dimension 10 is not included in the above research.

18. Study reported in Bradley S. Klapper, "Report: U.S. Workers Are the Most Productive," Associated Press, September 2, 2007.

19. Geert Hofstede, "The Universal and the Specific in 21st-Century Global Management," *Organizational Dynamics*, Summer 1999, pp. 35–37.

20. The observation about bureaucracy is from Javidan, Dorfman, de Luque, and House, "In the Eye of the Beholder," p. 79.

21. Felix C. Brodbeck, Michael Frese, and Mansour Javidan, "Leadership Made in Germany: Low on Compassion, High on Performance," *Academy of Management Executive*, February 2002, pp. 16–30.

22. Jeffrey C. Kennedy, "Leadership in Malaysia: Traditional Values, International Outlook," *Academy of Management Executive*, August 2002, pp. 15–26.

23. Del Jones, "North vs. South: Leaders from Both Sides of the Mason-Dixon Line Have Strong Opinions About the Styles of Their Regionally Different Peers," *USA Today*, July 9, 2004, p. 5B.

24. Ibid.

25. Robert J. House, Paul J. Hanges, Mansour Javidan, Peter W. Dorfman, and Vipin Gupta, eds., *Culture, Leadership, and Organizations: The GLOBE Study of 62 Societies* (Thousand Oaks, Calif.: Sage, 2004), p. 7.

26. Carla Johnson, "Cultural Sensitivity Adds Up to Good Business Sense," *HR Magazine*, November 1995, pp. 83–85.

27. Christina Binkley, "Where Yellow's a Faux Pas and White Is Death," *The Wall Street Journal*, December 6, 2007, p. D8.

28. Diane Cadrain, "Accommodating Sex Transformations," *HR Magazine*, October 2009, pp. 59–62.

29. "Managing Diversity: When Cultures Collide," *Managing People at Work*, sample issue, 2008, p. 7.

30. P. Christopher Earley and Elaine Mosakowski, "Cultural Intelligence," *Harvard Business Review*, October 2004, pp. 139–146.

31. Javidan, Dorfman, de Luque, and House, "In the Eye of the Beholder," p. 85.

32. Joseph A. Petrick, Robert E. Scherer, James D. Bodzinski, John F. Quinn, and M. Fall Ainina, "Global Leadership Skills and Reputational Capital: Intangible Resources for Sustainable Competitive Advantage," *The Academy of Management Executive*, February 1999, pp. 58–69.

33. Gretchen M. Spreitzer, Morgan W. McCall Jr., and Joan D. Mahoney, "Early Identification of International Executive Potential," *Journal of Applied Psychology*, February 1997, pp. 6–29.

34. David Tessmann-Keys and Richard S. Wellins, *The CEO's Guide to Preparing Future Global Leaders* (Pittsburgh, Penn.: DDI, 2008), pp. 18–19.

35. Research cited in Douglas T. Hall, Guorong Zhu, and Amin Yan, "Developing Global Leaders: To Hold On to Them, Let Them Go," *Advances in Global Leadership*, vol. 2, 2001, p. 331.

36. Javidan, Dorfman, de Luque, and House, "In the Eye of the Beholder," p. 85.

37. Jeanne Brett, Kristin Behfar, and Mary C. Kern, "Managing Multicultural Teams," *Harvard Business Review*, November 2006, p. 87.

38. Joe Light, "Help Wanted: Multilingual Employees," *The Wall Street Journal*, January 18, 2011, p. B7.

39. Cited in Simon Kent, "Go Team, Go!" *PM Network*, November 2007, p. 41.

40. Paul Ingrassia and John Stoll, "Hottest Car Guy on Earth," *The Wall Street Journal*, January 14, 2006, p. A8; Alex Taylor III, "The World According to Ghosn," *Fortune*, December 11, 2006, p. 116; Sebastian Moffett, "Renault's No. 2 Executive Quits," *The Wall Street Journal*, April 12, 2001, p. B1.

41. Todd Campbell, "Diversity in Depth," *HR Magazine*, March 2003, p. 152.

42. "Allstate Insurance Company," *Vault/INROADS Guide to Diversity Internship, Co-op and Entry-Level Programs, 2007 Edition*, pp. 65–66.

43. Marc Adams, "Building a Rainbow One Stripe at a Time," *HR Magazine*, August 1998, pp. 73–74.

44. Wendy Harris, "Executive Partners: A Company's Diversity Efforts are Only as Good as Its Search Firm," *Black Enterprise*, October 2008, p. 73.

45. Rohini Anand and Mary-Frances Winters, "A Retrospective View of Corporate Diversity Training from 1964 to the Present," *Academy of Management Learning & Education*, September 2008, pp. 356–372.

46. Phred Dvorak, "Firms Push New Methods to Promote Diversity," *The Wall Street Journal*, December 18, 2006, p. B3.

47. Research reported in Shankar Vedantam, "Most Diversity Training Ineffective, Study Finds," *Washington Post* (washingtonpost.com), January 22, 2008; Fay Hansen, "Diversity of a Different Color," *Workforce Management*, June 2010, p. 25.

48. Quoted in C. Douglas Johnson, "It's More Than the Five To Do's: Insights on Diversity Education and Training From Roosevelt Thomas, A Pioneer and Thought Leader in the Field," *Academy of Management Learning & Education*, September 2008, p. 411.

49. DeeDee Doke, "Perfect Strangers," *HR Magazine*, December 2004, p. 64.

50. Deborah Steinborn, "Cross-Cultural Training Gains," *The Wall Street Journal*, April 4, 2007, p. B5D.

51. Christina Binkley, "Americans Learn the Global Art of the Cheek Kiss," *The Wall Street Journal*, March 27, 2008, p. D1.

52. P. Christopher Earley and Randall S. Peterson, "The Elusive Cultural Chameleon: Cultural Intelligence as a New Approach to Intercultural Training for the Global Manager," *Academy of Management Learning and Education*, March 2004, p. 105.

53. "Allstate Diversity," (*www.allstate.com/diversity*). Accessed May 16, 2011.

54. Nelson, "U.S. Economy Gets a Lift," p. 16.

55. Robert Rodriguez, "Diversity Finds Its Place," *HR Magazine*, August 2006, pp. 56, 58.

56. Hansen, "Diversity of a Different Color," p. 25.

57. Lin Grensing-Pophal, "Hiring to Fit Your Corporate Culture," *HR Magazine*, August 1999, p. 52.

58. Gary D. Fackler, "The Texas Hispanic Touch," *Hispanic Business*, December 2010, pp. 35–36.

59. Michael Todd, "Report: Companies Should Help Workers Get Comfortable, Stay Awhile," *Hispanic Business*, March 2007, p. 44.

60. Julie Bennett, "'Corporate Angst' Can Generate Gaffes That Turn Off Coveted Candidates," *The Wall Street Journal*, October 21, 2003, p. D9.

Personal Attributes of Leaders

LEARNING OBJECTIVES

After studying this chapter and doing the exercises, you should be able to

- Identify general and task-related traits that contribute to leadership effectiveness.

- Describe how emotional intelligence contributes to leadership effectiveness.

- Identify key motives that contribute to leadership effectiveness.

- Describe cognitive factors associated with leadership effectiveness.

- Discuss the heredity versus environment issue in relation to leadership effectiveness.

- Summarize the strengths and weaknesses of the trait approach to leadership.

CHAPTER OUTLINE

Tamara is the chief of marketing at Venus Beverages. The company is a small niche manufacturer and distributor of soft drinks that contain a higher percentage of natural ingredients, and a lower percentage of artificial ingredients than most soft drinks on the market. Although Venus has not had much success in getting shelf space in national and regional supermarkets, the company has found a reasonable number of outlets. Among the stores selling Venus Beverages are health-food stores, conveniences stores, local grocery stores, and service stations.

At a weekly staff meeting, Brett, the chief financial officer, told the group, "I dislike playing the role of the company pessimist, but we are hurting financially. I forecast a loss of $250,000 this quarter and perhaps $900,000 for the year. We either lay off one-third the staff, or boost revenue in a hurry."

Product development manager Natalie said with a smile, "OK, maybe now the team is ready to listen to the new product I have been proposing for months. It is time to launch our new energy drink, Brazen. As you know, it will be loaded with caffeine and contain alcohol up to the legal limit. This is the fastest-growing niche in the energy-drink field. A few states are trying to block the drink, but I think the opposition will soon fade."

Tamara replied, "Natalie and Brett, I need you to listen carefully. I applaud your thinking of the company's financial welfare, but let's look at the big picture. We must all work diligently to protect the reputation of Venus Beverages. Caffeine- and alcohol-laden beverages are socially irresponsible. You have teenagers drinking them as if they were ordinary soft drinks. The caffeine masks symptoms of feeling high from the alcohol. Too many deaths have occurred from overconsumption of this type of energy drink, including fatal auto crashes.

"We need to stick to our roots of making wholesome, organic soft drinks. Let's all work together to get through our financial troubles honorably. I know we can find a solution."[1]

The vignette just presented describes a highly placed manager who has several of the leadership traits discussed in this chapter, particularly the ability to think conceptually (see the big picture), as well as being trustworthy and optimistic.

When people evaluate managers in terms of their leadership effectiveness, they often scrutinize the managers' traits and personal characteristics. Instead of focusing only on the results the managers achieve, those making the evaluation assign considerable weight to the manager's attributes, such as adherence to high standards. Many people believe intuitively that personal characteristics strongly determine leadership effectiveness.

The trait-based perspective on leadership has reemerged in recent years after having fallen out of favor for decades. Stephen J. Zacarro notes that traits tend to help understand leadership behavior and effectiveness when integrated in meaningful ways.[2] The trait-based perspective also acknowledges that the situation often influences which trait to emphasize, such as a supervisor of highly technical workers needing to emphasize problem-solving ability. In contrast, a supervisor of workers performing nontechnical, repetitive work might need to emphasize enthusiasm as a motivator.

This chapter and the following chapter concentrate on personal characteristics; Chapter 8 describes the behaviors and skills that contribute to leadership effectiveness. Recognize, however, the close association between personal characteristics and leadership skills and behaviors. For example, creative thinking ability (a characteristic) helps a leader formulate an exciting vision (leadership behavior).

Characteristics associated with leadership can be classified into three broad categories: personality traits, motives, and cognitive factors. These categories of behavior serve as helpful guides. However, they are not definitive: A convincing argument can often be made that an aspect of leadership placed in one category could be placed in another. Nevertheless, no matter how personal characteristics are classified, they point toward the conclusion that effective leaders are made of the *right stuff*. Published research about the trait perspective first appeared in the mid-nineteenth century, and it continues today. Since a full listing of every personal characteristic ever found to be associated with leadership would take several hundred pages, this chapter discusses only the major and most consistently found characteristics related to leadership effectiveness.

PERSONALITY TRAITS OF EFFECTIVE LEADERS

Observations by managers and human resource specialists, as well as dozens of research studies, indicate that leaders have certain personality traits.[3] These characteristics contribute to leadership effectiveness in many situations, as long as the leader's style fits the situation reasonably well. For example, an executive might perform admirably as a leader in several different high-technology companies with different organizational cultures. However, his intellectual style might make him a poor fit with production workers. Leaders' personality traits can be divided into two groups: general personality traits such as self-confidence and trustworthiness, and task-related traits, such as an internal locus of control.

General Personality Traits

We define a general personality trait as a trait that is observable both within and outside the context of work. That is, the same general traits are related to success and satisfaction in both work and personal life. Figure 3-1 lists the general personality traits that contribute to successful leadership.

Self-Confidence   Self-confidence improves one's performance in a variety of tasks, including leadership.[4] A leader who is self-assured without being bombastic or overbearing instills self-confidence in team members. A self-confident team leader of a group facing a seemingly impossible deadline might tell the group, "We are understaffed and overworked, but I know we can get this project done on time. I've been through tough demands like this before. If we work like a true team, we can pull it off."

Self-confidence was among the first leadership traits researchers identified, and it currently receives considerable attention as a major contributor to leadership effectiveness.[5] In addition to being self-confident, the leader must project that self-confidence to the group. He or she may do so by using unequivocal wording, maintaining good posture, and making appropriate gestures such as pointing an index finger outward.

Self-confidence is not only a personality trait. It also refers to a behavior and an interpersonal skill that a person exhibits in a number of situations. It is akin to being cool under pressure. We can conclude that a person is a self-confident leader when he or she maintains composure when dealing with a crisis, such as while managing a large product recall. The interpersonal skill comes into play in

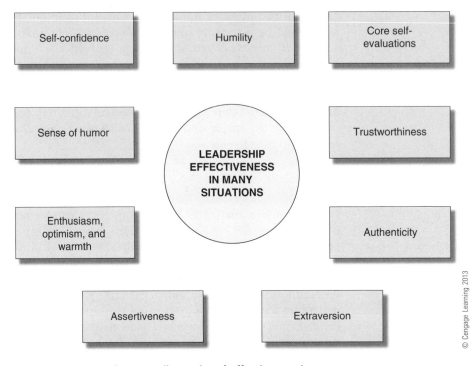

FIGURE 3-1 General Personality Traits of Effective Leaders.

being able to keep others calm during turmoil. In speaking about the suitability of job candidates who were recently military officers, Noel Tichy, director of the Global Business Partnership at the University of Michigan said, "There's a big pool of these officers who had had the kind of under-fire judgment experience that makes them really valuable."[6]

A famous example of coolness under pressure by a leader was the situation of Captain Chelsey "Sully" Sullenberger, who landed a plane intact on the Hudson River in January 2009, saving 155 lives. Several analyses of the miraculous landing suggested that it was primarily attributed to long preparation and coolness under pressure.[7]

Leadership Self-Assessment Quiz 3-1 gives you an opportunity to think about your level of self-confidence.

Humility Although self-confidence is a key leadership trait, so is humility, or being humble at the right times. Part of humility is admitting that you do not know everything and cannot do everything, as well as admitting your mistakes to team members and outsiders. A leader, upon receiving a compliment for an accomplishment, may explain that the group deserves the credit. The case for humility as a leadership trait is made strongly by Stephen G. Harrison, the president of a consulting firm, in his comment about how the definition of great leadership has changed: "Great leadership is manifested or articulated by people who know how to understate it. There is leadership value in humility,

LEADERSHIP SELF-ASSESSMENT QUIZ 3-1

How Self-Confident Are You?

Indicate the extent to which you agree with each of the following statements. Use a 1-to-5 scale: (1) disagree strongly; (2) disagree; (3) neutral; (4) agree; (5) agree strongly.

NO.	STATEMENT	DS	D	N	A	AS
1.	I frequently say to people, "I'm not sure."	5	4	3	2	1
2.	I have been hesitant to take on any leadership assignments.	5	4	3	2	1
3.	Several times, people have asked me to be the leader of the group to which I belonged.	1	2	3	4	5
4.	I perform well in most situations in life.	1	2	3	4	5
5.	At least several people have told me that I have a nice, firm handshake.	1	2	3	4	5
6.	I am much more of a loser than a winner.	5	4	3	2	1
7.	I am much more of a winner than a loser.	1	2	3	4	5
8.	I am cautious about making any substantial change in my life.	5	4	3	2	1
9.	I dread it when I have to learn how to use a new digital device, such as a smart phone or video camera.	5	4	3	2	1
10.	I freely criticize other people, even over minor matters such as their hair style or word choice.	5	4	3	2	1
11.	I become extremely tense when I know it will soon be my turn to present in front of the group or class.	5	4	3	2	1
12.	Speaking in front of the class or other group is a frightening experience for me.	5	4	3	2	1
13.	When asked for my advice, I willingly offer it.	1	2	3	4	5
14.	I feel comfortable attending a social event by myself.	1	2	3	4	5
15.	It is rare that I change my opinion just because somebody challenges me.	1	2	3	4	5

Scoring and Interpretation: Calculate your total score by adding the numbers circled. A tentative interpretation of the scoring is as follows:

- **65–75:** Very high self-confidence, with perhaps a tendency toward arrogance
- **55–64:** A high, desirable level of self-confidence
- **35–54:** Moderate, or average, self-confidence
- **15–34:** Self-confidence needs strengthening

the leadership that comes from putting people in the limelight, not yourself. Great leadership comes from entirely unexpected places. It's understatement, it's dignity, it's service, it's selflessness."[8]

Research by Jim Collins on what makes companies endure and dramatically improve their performance supports the importance of humility. He uses the term *Level 5 Leader* to describe the most accomplished leaders. Level 5 Leaders are modest yet determined to accomplish their objectives.[9]

Core Self-Evaluations Self-confidence is one way of looking at the self that contributes to leadership effectiveness. Extensive research suggests that a set of four other related self-perceptions also contribute to leadership effectiveness. **Core self-evaluations** is a broad personality trait that captures bottom-line self-assessment that is composed of self-esteem, locus of control, generalized self-efficacy, and emotional stability. All four traits are positively related to each other. Self-esteem deals with feeling positive toward the self, and generalized self-efficacy means roughly the same thing as being self-confident in many situations. Locus of control refers to whether a person feels personally responsible for events happening to him or her—as will be described later in the chapter. Emotional stability refers to having emotional control, not being neurotic, and having good mental health.

A leader with positive core evaluations is more likely to make decisions more rapidly, and pursue initiatives to implement the decisions. Such a leader will feel confident, be steady under pressure, and believe that he or she can control the external environment to some extent.[10]

Trustworthiness Evidence and opinion continue to mount that being trustworthy and/or honest contributes to leadership effectiveness.[11] An effective leader or manager is supposed to *walk the talk*, thereby showing a consistency between deeds (walking) and words (talk). In this context, **trust** is defined as a person's confidence in another individual's intentions and motives and in the sincerity of that individual's word.[12] Leaders must be trustworthy, and they must also trust group members. Given that so many people distrust top-level business leaders, as well as political leaders, gaining and maintaining trust is a substantial challenge. The following trust builders are worthy of a prospective leader's attention and implementation:[13]

- Make your behavior consistent with your intentions. Practice what you preach and set the example. Let others know of your intentions and invite feedback on how well you are achieving them.
- When your organization or organizational unit encounters a problem, move into a problem-solving mode instead of looking to blame others for what went wrong.
- Honor confidences. One incident of passing along confidential information results in a permanent loss of trust by the person whose confidence was violated.
- Maintain a high level of integrity. Build a reputation for doing what you think is morally right in spite of the political consequences.
- Tell the truth in ways people can verify. It is much easier to be consistent when you do not have to keep patching up your story to conform to an earlier lie. An example of verification would be for a group member to see if the manager really did attempt to buy new conference room furniture as promised.
- Admit mistakes. Covering up a mistake, particularly when everybody knows that you did it, destroys trust quickly.
- Make trust pay in terms of receiving rewards. Trust needs to be seen as a way of gaining advantage.

It takes a leader a long time to build trust, yet one brief incident of untrustworthy behavior can permanently destroy it. Leaders are usually allowed a fair share of honest mistakes. In contrast, dishonest mistakes quickly erode leadership effectiveness.

When a leader is perceived as trustworthy, the organization benefits. Kurt T. Dirks and Donald L. Ferrin examined the findings and implications of research during the last four decades about trust in leadership. The review involved 106 studies and 27,103 individuals. The meta-analysis (quantitative synthesis of studies) emphasized supervisory leadership based on the importance of trust in day-to-day interactions with group members. Trusting a leader was more highly associated with a variety of work attitudes of group members. The highest specific relationships with trust were as follows:[14]

- Job satisfaction ($r = .51$)
- Organizational commitment ($r = .49$)
- Turnover intentions ($r = .40$) (If you trust your leader, you are less likely to intend to leave.)
- Belief in information provided by the leader ($r = .35$)
- Commitment to decisions ($r = .24$)
- Satisfaction with the leader ($r = .73$)
- LMX ($r = .69$) (LMX refers to favorable exchanges with the leader.)

The relationship of trust to job performance was statistically significant but quite low ($r = .16$). One reason may be that many people perform well for a leader they distrust out of fear of being fired or bad-listed.

Being trustworthy and earning trust is considered so essential to effective leadership that some companies use these factors to evaluate leaders and managers. Being perceived as trustworthy is also important for entrepreneurs who are seeking investors. A study of 28 entrepreneurial ventures in the U.K. found that details matter in being trusted by potential lenders and investors. Little things that send a message of credibility include making sure that the website is polished and professional, or sending follow-up notes after a meeting with potential investors. The study also found that the most successful business founders were skilled at making symbolic gestures that signaled stability and credibility. Such gestures included holding meetings in an upscale location and having testimonials from satisfied customers on the entrepreneur's website.[15]

Leadership Self-Assessment Quiz 3-2 gives you the opportunity to examine your own tendencies toward trustworthiness.

Authenticity   Embedded in the trait of being trustworthy is **authenticity**—being genuine and honest about your personality, values, and beliefs as well as having integrity. Bill George, a Harvard Business School professor and former chairman and CEO of Medtronic, developed the concept of authentic leadership. In his words, "Authentic leaders demonstrate a passion for their purpose, practice their values consistently, and lead with their hearts as well as their heads. They establish long-term meaningful relationships and have the self-discipline to get results. They know who they are."[16] To become an authentic leader, and to demonstrate

LEADERSHIP SELF-ASSESSMENT QUIZ 3-2

Behaviors and Attitudes of a Trustworthy Leader

Instructions: Listed here are behaviors and attitudes of leaders who are generally trusted by their group members and other constituents. After you read each characteristic, check to the right whether this is a behavior or attitude that you appear to have developed already, or whether it does not fit you at present.

	FITS ME	DOES NOT FIT ME
1. Tells people he or she is going to do something, and then always follows through and gets it done.	☐	☐
2. Is described by others as being reliable.	☐	☐
3. Is good at keeping secrets and confidences.	☐	☐
4. Tells the truth consistently.	☐	☐
5. Minimizes telling people what they want to hear.	☐	☐
6. Is described by others as "walking the talk."	☐	☐
7. Delivers consistent messages to others in terms of matching words and deeds.	☐	☐
8. Does what he or she expects others to do.	☐	☐
9. Minimizes hypocrisy by not engaging in activities he or she tells others are wrong.	☐	☐
10. Readily accepts feedback on behavior from others.	☐	☐
11. Maintains eye contact with people when talking to them.	☐	☐
12. Appears relaxed and confident when explaining his or her side of a story.	☐	☐
13. Individualizes compliments to others rather than saying something like "You look great" to many people.	☐	☐
14. Does not expect lavish perks for himself or herself while expecting others to go on an austerity diet.	☐	☐
15. Does not tell others a crisis is pending (when it is not) just to gain their cooperation.	☐	☐
16. Collaborates with others to make creative decisions.	☐	☐
17. Communicates information to people at all organizational levels digitally and in person.	☐	☐
18. Readily shares financial information with others.	☐	☐
19. Listens to people and then acts on many of their suggestions.	☐	☐
20. Generally engages in predictable behavior.	☐	☐

Scoring and Interpretation: These statements are mostly for self-reflection, so no specific scoring key exists. However, the more of these statements that fit you, the more trustworthy you are—assuming you are answering truthfully. The usefulness of this self-quiz increases if somebody who knows you well also answers it about you. Your ability and willingness to carry out some of the behaviors specified in this quiz could have an enormous impact on your career because so many business leaders in recent years have not been perceived as trustworthy. Being trustworthy is therefore a career asset.

authenticity, be yourself rather than attempting to be a replica of someone else. Others respond to your leadership, partly because you are genuine rather than phony. The authentic leader can emphasize different values and characteristics to different people without being phony. For example, a corporate-level manager at Goodyear service centers might engage in more banter when he visits a service center than when meeting with financial analysts.

You are most likely to find an authentic leader among the ranks of middle managers, small-business owners, and athletic coaches in non-name athletic programs. (Observe that the models provided are not usually strongly power-oriented glory seekers.) However, George offers the example of Daniel Vasella, the former CEO and chairman of the pharmaceutical firm Novartis who switched to the position of chairman only in 2010. He helped build a global health care company that could help people through developing lifesaving new drugs. The cornerstones of the Novartis culture are compassion, competence, and competition.

George and several colleagues conducted an intensive leadership development study of 125 diverse business leaders to understand how they became and remain authentic. The authentic leaders typically learned from their experiences by reflecting on them. They also took a hard look at themselves to understand what they really believe, such as whether they really care if their workers are satisfied. The authors of the study concluded that the leader being authentic is the only way to create long-term, positive business results.[17]

Authentic leadership can also have a payoff in terms of daily interactions with group members. A study conducted with two telecom firms in China found that employees who reported to supervisors with authentic leadership behavior tended to be better organizational citizens, and were also more engaged in their work.[18] (Organizational citizenship behavior refers to a willingness to help out beyond one's job description without expecting to be rewarded.)

Extraversion   Extraversion (the scientific spelling for *extroversion*) has been recognized for its contribution to leadership effectiveness because it is helpful for leaders to be gregarious, outgoing, and upbeat in most situations. Also, extraverts are more likely to want to assume a leadership role and participate in group activities. A meta-analysis of seventy-three studies involving 11,705 subjects found that extraversion was the most consistent personality factor related to leadership effectiveness and leadership emergence.[19] (*Emergence* refers to someone being perceived as having leadership qualities.) Extraversion is also the personality trait most consistently and strongly related to the type of leadership than brings about major changes (the transformational type).[20]

Extraversion may be an almost innate personality characteristic, yet most people can move toward becoming more extraverted by consciously attempting to be friendlier toward people including smiling and asking questions. An example is, "How are things going for you today?"

Even though it is logical to think that extraversion is related to leadership, many effective leaders are laid-back and even introverted. Michael Dell, the famous founder of Dell Inc., is a reserved individual who is sometimes described as having a vanilla personality. (Dell has attempted to become more extraverted.)

Assertiveness Letting others know where you stand contributes to leadership effectiveness, and also contributes to being or appearing extraverted. **Assertiveness** refers to being forthright in expressing demands, opinions, feelings, and attitudes. Being assertive helps leaders perform many tasks and achieve goals. Among them are confronting group members about their mistakes, demanding higher performance, setting high expectations, and making legitimate demands on higher management. A director of her company's mobile phone service unit was assertive when she said to her staff, "Our cell service is the worst in the industry. We have to improve." An assertive person is reasonably tactful rather than being aggressive and obnoxious.

A potential problem with a high level of aggressiveness in male leaders is that it may lead to impulsive financial decisions. A study found that young male CEOs (in the testosterone-peaking ages under 45) tend to be impulsive, unpredictable, and ultimately destroy value for shareholders. The researchers found that young male CEOs are more likely to withdraw a bid, conduct un-friendly negotiations, and use tender offers to acquire another company. For example, young male CEOs tend to reject offers even when turning down the offer is against their best interests. The researchers concluded that this combat-ive nature stems from testosterone levels that are higher in young males.[21] (The world awaits a study among young women CEOs to serve as a control group!)

Enthusiasm, Optimism, and Warmth In almost all leadership situations, it is desirable for the leader to be enthusiastic. Group members tend to respond positively to enthusiasm, partly because enthusiasm may be perceived as a re-ward for constructive behavior. Enthusiasm is also a desirable leadership trait because it helps build good relationships with team members. A leader can ex-press enthusiasm both verbally ("Great job"; "I love it") and nonverbally (mak-ing a fist-bump or high-five gesture).

Ajay Banga, the CEO of MasterCard, exemplifies an enthusiastic executive. Shortly after joining the company as president and chief operating officer in 2009, he developed the reputation of being the company's cheerleader, shaking up its low-key culture with hugs and fist bumps in the hallway.[22]

Enthusiasm often takes the form of optimism, which helps keep the group in an upbeat mood and hopeful about attaining difficult goals. The optimistic leader is therefore likely to help bring about exceptional levels of achievement. Yet, there is a potential downside to an optimistic leader. He or she might not develop contingency plans to deal with projects that do not go as well as ex-pected.[23] An overly optimistic information technology manager, for example, might not take into account that an earthquake could hit the geographic area where company data are stored.

Being a warm person and projecting that warmth is part of enthusiasm and contributes to leadership effectiveness in several ways. First, warmth helps es-tablish rapport with group members. Second, the projection of warmth is a key component of charisma. Third, warmth is a trait that helps provide emo-tional support to group members. Giving such support is an important leader-ship behavior. Fourth, in the words of Kogan Page, "Warmth comes with the territory. Cold fish don't make good leaders because they turn people off."[24]

Sense of Humor   Whether humor is a trait or a behavior, the effective use of humor is an important part of the leader's role. Humor adds to the approachability and people orientation of a leader. Laughter and humor serve such functions in the workplace as relieving tension and boredom and defusing hostility. Because humor helps the leader dissolve tension and defuse conflict, it helps him or her exert power over the group. Self-effacing humor is the choice of comedians and organizational leaders alike. By being self-effacing, the leader makes a point without insulting or slighting anybody. Instead of criticizing a staff member for being too technical, the leader might say, "Wait, I need your help. Please explain how this new product works in terms that even I can understand."

Humor as used by leaders has been the subject of considerable serious inquiry, and here are a few recommendations based on this research:[25]

- People who occupy high-status roles joke at a higher rate than those of lesser status and tend to be more successful at eliciting laughter from others. (A possible reason that high-status people elicit more laughter is that lower-status people want to please them.)
- Self-enhancing humor (building up yourself) facilitates the leader's acquisition of power from superiors by increasing the leader's appeal.
- Self-defeating (self-effacing to the extreme) humor is negatively related to power, and may lead to the perception that the leader is too playful and not serious.
- Aggressive humor can be used to victimize, belittle, and cause others some type of disparagement—and will lead to negative outcomes such as stress and counter-hostility among group members. (No surprise to readers here.)

Leadership Skill-Building Exercise 3-1 provides an opportunity to use humor effectively.

LEADERSHIP SKILL-BUILDING EXERCISE 3-1

A Sense of Humor on the Job

This is an exercise for six persons in both scenarios.

Scenario 1: Corporate Bankruptcy. One person plays the role of the CEO of a company that makes commercial loans and advises other companies on corporate finance. He or she calls an emergency staff meeting to explain that the company must declare Chapter 11 bankruptcy because it is unable to pay its bills and loans. The CEO will attempt to lessen the gravity of the situation with some humor. The five other people, who play the roles of the staff members, should also make effective use of humor in responding to the CEO's comments.

Scenario 2: Windmill Plant Manager. One person plays the role of the head of the manufacturing plant that makes windmills to help other companies and communities reduce energy sources that send too many pollutants into the air. The manager has called a meeting to discuss some somber news: The plant has been cited by the Environmental Protection Agency for spewing too many toxic wastes into the air. Improvements must be made in a hurry. He or she should make a few humorous introductory comments that will relieve some of the tension and worry. The five other people, who play the roles of department heads in the windmill factory, should also make effective use of humor in responding to the CEO's comments.

Task-Related Personality Traits

Certain personality traits of effective leaders are closely associated with task accomplishment. The task-related traits described here are outlined in Figure 3-2.

Passion for the Work and the People A dominant characteristic of effective leaders is their passion for their work and to some extent for the people who help them accomplish the work. The passion goes beyond enthusiasm and often expresses itself as an obsession for achieving company goals. Many leaders begin their workday at 6:00 A.M. and return to their homes at 7:00 P.M. After dinner, they retreat to their home offices to conduct business for about two more hours. Information technology devices, such as personal digital assistants and cell phones, feed the passion for work, making it possible to be in touch with the office even during golf or a family picnic. The downside to extreme passion for work is that it can lead to work addiction, thereby interfering with other joys in life.

Passion for their work is especially evident in entrepreneurial leaders, no matter what size and type of business. A given business, such as refurbishing engines, might appear mundane to outsiders. The leader of such a business, however, is willing to talk for hours about tearing down old engines and about the wonderful people who help do the job.

Martha Stewart, the diva of better living, is also a highly successful executive who is known for the passion she has for her enterprise. A business executive who has observed Stewart for a long time commented, "Anyone who knows Martha knows that Martha Stewart Living Omnimedia is the very purpose of her life. Not two breaths are taken without thoughts of her business."[26]

One of the ways for an entrepreneur to inject passion into a business is to tell a *creation story*. The story should inspire people to understand how your

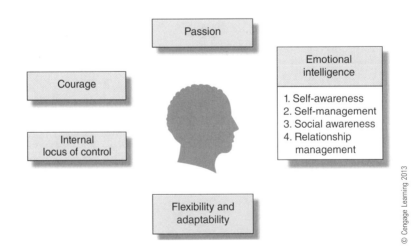

FIGURE 3-2 Task-Related Personality Traits of Leaders.

product or cause will make the world a better place. Howard Schultz, the founder and chairman of Starbucks, provides an example.[27]

> Schultz's story begins in 1961, when his father broke his ankle at work and was left without income, insurance or any way to support his family. The family's fear inspired change. Schultz grew up driven to create a company in which employees have a safety net woven of respect and dignity.

Emotional Intelligence   Many different aspects of emotions, motives, and personality that help determine interpersonal effectiveness and leadership skill have been placed under the comprehensive label of *emotional intelligence*. **Emotional intelligence** refers to the ability to do such things as understand one's feelings, have empathy for others, and regulate one's emotions to enhance one's quality of life. This type of intelligence generally has to do with the ability to connect with people and understand their emotions. Many of the topics in this chapter (such as warmth) and throughout the text (such as political skill) can be considered related to emotional intelligence.

Based on research in dozens of companies, Daniel Goleman discovered that the most effective leaders are alike in one essential way: They all have a high degree of emotional intelligence. Cognitive intelligence (or general mental ability) and technical skills are considered threshold capabilities for success in executive positions. Yet, according to Goleman, without a high degree of emotional intelligence, a person can have excellent training, superior analytical skills, and loads of innovative suggestions, but he or she still will not make a great leader. His analysis also revealed that emotional intelligence played an increasingly important role in high-level management positions, where differences in technical skills are of negligible importance. (Keep in mind, however, that most high-level managers would not have advanced to their position if they lacked good technical skills or business knowledge.) Furthermore, when star performers were compared with average ones in senior leadership positions, differences in emotional intelligence were more pronounced than differences in cognitive abilities.[28]

Four key factors in emotional intelligence are described next, along with a brief explanation of how each factor links to leadership effectiveness. The components of emotional intelligence have gone through several versions, and the version presented here is tied closely to leadership and interpersonal skills. The leader who scores high in emotional intelligence is described as *resonant*.[29]

1. *Self-awareness.* The ability to understand your own emotions is the most essential of the four emotional intelligence competencies. Having high self-awareness allows people to know their strengths and limitations and have high self-esteem. Resonant leaders use self-awareness to accurately measure their own moods, and they intuitively understand how their moods affect others. (Effective leaders seek feedback to see how well their actions are received by others. A leader with good self-awareness would recognize such factors as whether he or she was liked or was exerting the right amount of pressure on people.)

2. *Self-management.* This is the ability to control one's emotions and act with honesty and integrity in a consistent and adaptable manner. The right degree of self-management helps prevent a person from throwing temper tantrums when activities do not go as planned. Resonant leaders do not let their occasional bad moods ruin their day. If they cannot overcome the bad mood, they let work associates know of the problem and how long it might last. (A leader with high self-management would not suddenly decide to fire a group member because of one difference of opinion.)

3. *Social awareness.* This includes having empathy for others and intuition about organizational problems. Socially aware leaders go beyond sensing the emotions of others by showing they care. In addition, they accurately size up political forces in the office. (A team leader with social awareness, or empathy, would be able to assess whether a team member had enough enthusiasm for a project to assign it to him. A CEO who had empathy for a labor union's demands might be able to negotiate successfully with the head of the labor union to avoid a costly strike.)

4. *Relationship management.* This includes the interpersonal skills of being able to communicate clearly and convincingly, disarm conflicts, and build strong personal bonds. Resonant leaders use relationship management skills to spread their enthusiasm and solve disagreements, often with kindness and humor. (A leader with good relationship management skills would not burn bridges and would continue to enlarge his or her network of people to win support when support is needed. A leader or manager with good relationship management skills is more likely to be invited by headhunters to explore new career opportunities.)

It is also helpful to recognize that emotional intelligence has relevance for leaders other than those in the executive suite. Two recent studies with students taking a course in organizational behavior, and assigned small-group projects, examined how emotional intelligence was related to emergent leadership. Among the dimensions of emotional intelligence measured, it was found that the ability to understand emotions was the most consistently related to leadership emergence.[30] In other words, the study participants with the best skill in understanding emotions in others were more likely to be perceived as having leadership qualities.

If leaders do not have emotional intelligence, they may not achieve their full potential despite their high cognitive intelligence. Almost daily, a scanning of hard-copy or online newspapers will reveal an organizational leader who was disgraced or dismissed because of displaying poor emotional intelligence. Sometimes the business leader is a person of outstanding reputation and accomplishment, as is the case of Mark V. Hurd, the former chief executive of Hewlett-Packard. Hurd had become the benchmark for a top-level executive skilled in operational efficiency, squeezing costs, and maximizing profits.

His penchant for cutting costs, however, did not appear to apply to his own behavior in entertaining Jodie Fisher, a contractor to HP. Her role in 2007–2009 was to help the company with high-level executive and summit events at which Hurd was present. The specific charges that led to Hurd resigning related to expense account abuses. About $20,000 was at issue, and Hurd was willing to reimburse the company. It also appeared that Fisher was sometimes paid for no specific work. Fisher, an actress and reality-show contestant, filed sexual harassment charges against Hurd, but a company investigation cleared him of the charges. Also, Fisher resolved those claims with Hurd privately.

Hurd's severance package was about $45 million, and he was quickly hired by Oracle Corp. in a president's position. Many shareholders complained that Hurd received too generous a severance package for someone who had, in the words of the company, "violated HP's standards of business conduct."[31]

A key link to Hurd's problems and emotional intelligence is that he allowed his personal feelings toward a contractor interfere with upholding company standards that state that, before making a decision, one should consider how it would look in a news story. Despite his high cognitive intelligence, Hurd permitted his emotions to lead him into public disgrace.

Most of the leaders described in this book have good emotional intelligence. Here are two examples of making good use of emotional intelligence on the job:[32]

- Your company is approached about merging. The due diligence process suggests everything is favorable, yet your gut instinct says something is amiss. Rather than ignore your intuition, use it to motivate yourself to gather more information on the principals in the company.
- Your stomach knots as you prepare for a presentation. Your anxiety may stem from your sense that you are not well prepared. The emotionally intelligent response is to dig into the details and rehearse your presentation until the knots are replaced by a sense of welcome anticipation and confidence.

Research on emotional intelligence and leadership has also focused on the importance of the leader's mood in influencing performance. Daniel Goleman, Richard Boyatzis, and Annie McKee believe that the leader's mood and his or her associated behaviors greatly influence bottom-line performance. One reason is that moods are contagious. A cranky and ruthless leader creates a toxic organization of underachievers (who perform at less than their potential). In contrast, an upbeat and inspirational leader breeds followers who can surmount most challenges. Thus mood finally affects profit and loss. The implication for leaders is that they have to develop emotional intelligence regarding their moods. It is also helpful to develop a sense of humor, because lightheartedness is the most contagious of moods.[33]

A study with principals and teachers provided further evidence that emotional contagion is a meaningful factor in leadership. (*Emotional contagion* refers to the automatic and unconscious transfer of emotions between and among individuals.) One particularly revealing find was that principals who reported greater positive affect (emotional) at work had lower levels of turnover the following summer. The implication is that a leader who expresses positive emotion regularly is less likely to have group members quit.[34]

A concluding note about the study of emotional intelligence is that it contributes to the understanding of leadership because EI highlights the importance of leaders making effective use of emotions. Nevertheless, some proponents of emotional intelligence go too far in their claims about its importance in relation to leadership effectiveness. Specifically, we cannot overlook the contribution of general mental ability (cognitive intelligence) to being an effective leader. A recent synthesis of research studies suggests that emotional intelligence is only one of various factors (including other personality traits, cognitive ability, and functional skills) that influence what leaders accomplish.[35]

Flexibility and Adaptability   A leader is someone who facilitates change. It therefore follows that a leader must be flexible enough to cope with such changes as technological advances, downsizings, global outsourcing, a shifting customer base, and a changing work force. **Flexibility**, or the ability to adjust to different situations, has long been recognized as an important leadership characteristic. Leaders who are flexible are able to adjust to the demands of changing conditions, much as anti-lock brakes enable an automobile to adjust to changes in road conditions. Without the underlying trait of flexibility, a person might be an effective leader in only one or two situations. The manufacturing industry exemplifies a field in which situation adaptability is particularly important because top executives are required to provide leadership for both traditional production employees as well as highly skilled professionals.

Internal Locus of Control   As mentioned in relation to core self-evaluations, people with an **internal locus of control** believe that they are the prime mover behind events. Thus, an internal locus of control helps a leader in the role of a take-charge person because the leader believes fundamentally in his or her innate capacity to take charge. An internal locus of control is closely related to self-confidence. A strong internal locus facilitates self-confidence because the person perceives that he or she can control circumstances enough to perform well.

A leader with an internal locus of control is likely to be favored by group members. One reason is that an "internal" person is perceived as more powerful than an "external" person because he or she takes responsibility for events. The leader with an internal locus of control would emphasize that he or she can change unfavorable conditions, as did many courageous managers whose offices were destroyed during the World Trade Center attacks on September 11, 2001. The Great Recession of 2008–2009 (and extending into 2010) required many business leaders to assure employees that they had a plan for company survival.

Leadership Skill-Building Exercise 3-2 provides you with an opportunity to begin strengthening your internal locus of control. Considerable further work would be required to shift from an external to an internal locus of control.

Courage   Leaders need courage to face the challenges of taking prudent risks and taking initiative in general. Courage comes from the heart, as suggested by the French word for heart, *coeur*. Leaders must face up to responsibility and be willing to put their reputations on the line. It takes courage for a leader to suggest a new undertaking, because if the undertaking fails, the leader is often seen as having failed. Many people criticized the late Steve Jobs (the former Apple Inc. CEO and then Chairman) and his management team when they initiated Apple stores because they saw no useful niche served by these retail outlets. Apple stores were an immediate and long-lasting success, vindicating the judgment of Jobs and his team. The more faith people place in the power of leaders to cause events, the more strongly they blame leaders when outcomes are unfavorable.

According to Kathleen K. Reardon, courage in business is a special kind of calculated risk taking that comes about with experience. One of the requirements

LEADERSHIP SKILL-BUILDING EXERCISE 3-2

Developing an Internal Locus of Control

A person's locus of control is usually a deeply ingrained thinking pattern that develops over a period of many years. Nevertheless, you can begin developing a stronger internal locus of control by analyzing past successes and failures to determine how much influence you had on the outcome of these events. By repeatedly analyzing the relative contribution of internal versus external factors in shaping events, you may learn to feel more in charge of key events in your life. The following events are a good starting point.

1. *A contest or athletic event that you either won or made a good showing in.*

   What were the factors within your control that led to your winning or making a good showing?

   _____
   _____
   _____

   What were the factors beyond your control that led to your winning or making a good showing?

   _____
   _____
   _____

2. *A course in which you received a poor grade.*

   What were the factors within your control that led to this poor grade?

   _____
   _____
   _____

What were the factors beyond your control that led to this poor grade?

_____
_____
_____

3. *A group project to which you were assigned that worked out poorly.*

   What were the factors within your control that led to this poor result?

   _____
   _____
   _____

   What were the factors beyond your control that led to this poor result?

   _____
   _____
   _____

After you have prepared your individual analysis, you may find it helpful to discuss your observations in small groups. Focus on how people could have profited from a stronger internal locus of control in the situations analyzed.

of taking an intelligent gamble is having contingency plans.[36] For example, if Apple stores had failed, the properties could have been sold to other posh retailers, thereby reducing possible losses.

LEADERSHIP MOTIVES

Effective leaders have frequently been distinguished by their motives and needs. In general, leaders have an intense desire to occupy a position of responsibility for others and to control them. Figure 3-3 outlines four specific leadership motives or needs. All three motives can be considered task related.

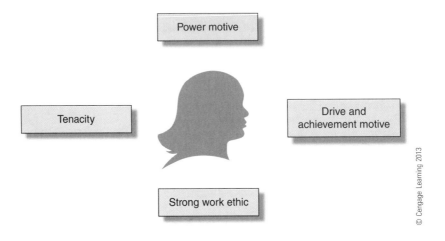

© Cengage Learning 2013

FIGURE 3-3 Leadership Motives.

The Power Motive

Effective leaders have a strong need to control resources. Leaders with high power motives have three dominant characteristics: (1) they act with vigor and determination to exert their power; (2) they invest much time in thinking about ways to alter the behavior and thinking of others; and (3) they care about their personal standing with those around them.[37] The power motive is important because it means that the leader is interested in influencing others. Without power, it is much more difficult to influence others. Power is not necessarily good or evil; it can be used for the sake of the power holder (personalized power motive) or for helping others (socialized power motive).[38]

Personalized Power Motive Leaders with a personalized power motive seek power mostly to further their own interests. They crave the trappings of power, such as status symbols, luxury, and money. In recent years, some leaders have taken up power boating, or racing powerful, high-speed boats. When asked how he liked his power-boating experience, an entrepreneurial leader replied, "It's fun, but the startup costs are about $350,000." Some leaders with strong personalized power motives typically enjoy dominating others. Their need for dominance can lead to submissive subordinates who are frequently sycophants and yes-persons.

Another characteristic of leaders with a personalized power motive is that they do not worry about everybody liking them. They recognize that as you acquire power, you also acquire enemies. In the words of successful college football coach Steve Spurrier, "If people like you too much, it's probably because they are beating you."[39]

Socialized Power Motive Leaders with a socialized power motive use power primarily to achieve organizational goals or a vision. In this context, the term *socialized* means that the leader uses power primarily to help others. As a result, he or she is likely to provide more effective leadership. Leaders with socialized power motives tend to be more emotionally mature than leaders with personalized power motives. They exercise power more for the benefit of the entire organization and are less likely to manipulate others through the use of power. Leaders with socialized power motives are also less defensive and more willing to accept expert advice. Finally, they have longer-range perspectives.[40]

It is important not to draw a rigid line between leaders with personalized power motives and those with socialized power motives. The distinction between doing good for others and doing good for oneself is often made on the basis of very subjective criteria. A case in point is John T. Chambers, the chairman and chief executive of Cisco Systems. The company he heads has long been associated with the growth of the Internet because it builds and installs equipment that makes the Internet function. If you believe that the Internet is a force for good in the world, you could argue that Chambers has a socialized power motive. At the same time, the growth of Cisco over the years has created thousands of jobs, despite a moderate downturn in recent years.

Another point of view about Chambers is that he relishes being a powerful and well-known executive. Several years ago, he created an organization structure that consists of many different councils or committees that work on different products and markets. Several observers say that Chambers' council-based approach is an effective way for him to consolidate power. The dilution of authority by spreading it across councils may prevent any one manager from gaining too much control.[41] The analysis that Chambers is grabbing power suggests a personal power motive.

The Drive and Achievement Motive

Leaders are known for working hard to achieve their goals. **Drive** refers to a propensity to put forth high energy into achieving objectives and to persistence in applying that energy. Drive also includes **achievement motivation**—finding joy in accomplishment for its own sake. Entrepreneurs and high-level corporate managers usually have strong achievement motivation. Such people have a consistent desire to:

1. Achieve through their efforts and take responsibility for success or failure
2. Take moderate risks that can be handled through their own efforts
3. Receive feedback on their level of performance
4. Introduce novel, innovative, or creative solutions
5. Plan and set goals[42]

We sometimes hear the argument that many leaders are lazy because they have delegated all the hard work to subordinates. In reality, most leaders have a lot of analytical work to do on their own, so they are working hard despite have delegated responsibility.

Tenacity and Resilience

A final observation about the motivational characteristics of organizational leaders is that they are *tenacious*. Tenacity multiplies in importance for organizational leaders because it takes a long time to implement a new program or to consummate a business deal, such as acquiring another company. Resilience is part of tenacity because the tenacious person will bounce back from a setback through continuous effort.

Prescription drug wholesaler Stewart Rahr is the former owner of Kinray, a privately held company. He attributes much of his success to his ability to overcome rejection and keep trying. In reflecting on his early days, he says, "I remember Charlie Cohen of Cohen's Pharmacy telling me, 'Nothing for you today,' and hanging up on me over and over again." Rahr's persistence eventually brought orders, if only for a few bottles of aspirin. Today his company provides drugs, bandages, and orthopedic shoes to 2,000 independent pharmacies in seven states. Despite heavy competition in the industry, Kinray has prospered. In 2010, rival Cardinal Health purchased Kinray for $1.3 billion in cash, with Rahr staying on as an advisor. Rahr is also resilient in his personal life because he is a melanoma cancer survivor.[43]

Leadership Self-Assessment Quiz 3-3 gives you the opportunity to obtain a tentative measure of your resilience.

LEADERSHIP SELF-ASSESSMENT **QUIZ 3-3**

Personal Resiliency Quiz

Instructions: Answer each of the following statements mostly agree or mostly disagree as it applies to you. In taking a questionnaire such as this, it can always be argued that the true answer to any one particular statement is "It depends on the situation." Despite the validity of this observation, do your best to indicate whether you would mostly agree or disagree with the statement.

	MOSTLY AGREE	MOSTLY DISAGREE	SCORE (SEE KEY)
1. Winning is everything.	☐	☐	_____
2. If I have had a bad day at work or school, it tends to ruin my evening.	☐	☐	_____
3. If I just keep trying, I will get my share of good breaks.	☐	☐	_____
4. It takes me much longer than most people to shake the flu or a cold.	☐	☐	_____
5. If it were not for a few bad breaks I have received, I would be much further ahead in my career.	☐	☐	_____
6. There is no disgrace in losing.	☐	☐	_____
7. I am a generally self-confident person.	☐	☐	_____
8. Finishing last beats not competing at all.	☐	☐	_____
9. I like to take a chance, even if the probability of winning is small.	☐	☐	_____
10. If I have two reversals in a row, I do not worry about it being part of a losing streak.	☐	☐	_____
11. I am a sore loser.	☐	☐	_____
12. It takes a lot to get me discouraged.	☐	☐	_____
13. Every "no" I encounter is one step closer to a "yes."	☐	☐	_____
14. I doubt I could stand the shame of being fired or being included in a company downsizing.	☐	☐	_____
15. I enjoy being the underdog once in a while.	☐	☐	_____

QUIZ 3-1 (continued)

Scoring Key: Give yourself 1 point for each statement you responded to that is in agreement with the following answer key. If your response does not agree with the key, give yourself a zero. Add your points for the 15 statements to obtain your total score.

1. Mostly disagree	6. Mostly agree	11. Mostly disagree
2. Mostly disagree	7. Mostly agree	12. Mostly agree
3. Mostly agree	8. Mostly agree	13. Mostly agree
4. Mostly disagree	9. Mostly agree	14. Mostly disagree
5. Mostly disagree	10. Mostly agree	15. Mostly agree

Scoring and Interpretation: Your score on the Personal Resiliency Quiz gives you a rough index of your overall tendencies toward being able to back bounce from adversity. The higher your score, the more resilient you are in handling disappointment, setbacks, and frustration. The following breakdown of scores will help you determine your degree of resiliency.

- **13+ *Very Resilient:*** You are remarkably effective in rebounding from setbacks, or being resilient. Your resiliency should help you lead others when setbacks arise.

- **4–12 *Moderately Resilient:*** Like most people, you probably cope well with some type of adversity but not others.

- **0–3 *Not Resilient:*** You are the type of individual who has difficulty coping with adversity. Focusing on learning how to cope with setbacks and maintain a courageous outlook could help you in your development as a leader.

COGNITIVE FACTORS AND LEADERSHIP

Mental ability as well as personality is important for leadership success. To inspire people, bring about constructive change, and solve problems creatively, leaders need to be mentally sharp. Another mental requirement is the ability to sort out essential information from less essential information and then store the most important information in memory. Problem-solving and intellectual skills are referred to collectively as **cognitive factors**. The term *cognition* refers to the mental process or faculty by which knowledge is gathered. We discuss five cognitive factors that are closely related to cognitive intelligence, as shown in Figure 3-4. The descriptor *cognitive* is somewhat necessary to differentiate traditional mental ability from emotional intelligence.

Cognitive (or Analytical) Intelligence

Being very good at solving problems is a fundamental characteristic of effective leaders in all fields. Business leaders, for example, need to understand how to analyze company finances, use advanced software, manage inventory, and deal

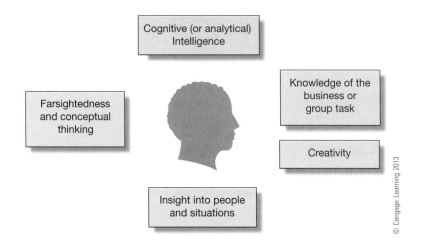

FIGURE 3-4 Cognitive Factors and Leadership.

with international trade regulations. Research spanning 100 years has demonstrated that leaders receive higher scores than most people on mental ability tests, including IQ (a term for a test score that for many people is synonymous with intelligence). A meta-analysis of 151 studies found a positive relationship between intelligence and job performance of leaders in many different settings. The relationship is likely to be higher when the leader plays an active role in decision making and is not overly stressed.

The researchers also found support for the old idea that intelligence contributes the most to leadership effectiveness when the leader is not vastly smarter than most group members.[44] Even if this fact is true, another synthesis of studies indicated that leadership status more often than not was associated with superior intelligence.[45] Again, group members prefer that their leaders be smarter than the average group member even if the difference is not huge.

Cognitive intelligence is all the more useful for leadership when it is supplemented by **practical intelligence**, the ability to solve everyday problems by using experience-based knowledge to adapt to and shape the environment. Practical intelligence is sometimes referred to as street smarts.[46] A leader with good practical intelligence would know, for example, not to deliver a vision statement on a day most of the company employees were worried about a power outage in their homes created by a massive lightning storm.

One of thousands of potential examples of a leader with good cognitive intelligence is Paula Shannon, the chief sales operator, senior vice president, and general manager at Lionbridge Technologies. The global company provides companies with translation services in more than one hundred languages. At college, Shannon majored in languages—Spanish, German, and Russian—and also studied computer science. Before Lionbridge, she worked for another language technology company.[47]

Knowledge of the Business or Group Task

Intellectual ability is closely related to having knowledge of the business or the key task the group is performing. An effective leader has to be technically competent in some discipline, particularly when leading a group of specialists. It is difficult for the leader to establish rapport with group members when he or she does not know what the group members are doing and when the group does not respect the leader's technical skills.

A representative example of the contribution of knowledge of the business to leadership effectiveness is the situation of Duncan MacNaughton, who became the chief merchandising officer for Wal-Mart Stores, Inc., in 2011. Before this position, he had held several other leadership positions in merchandising. His knowledge of the business is reflected in the plan he developed boosting sales:

We intend to make the shopping experience more fun for our customers through increasing promotional intensity by effectively utilizing action alley. In the end it's about having great products at everyday low prices. (*Action alley* refers to in-aisle displays that feature markdowns or special promotions.)[48]

The importance of knowledge of the business is strongly recognized as an attribute of executive leadership. Leaders at every level are expected to bring forth useful ideas for carrying out the mission of the organization or organizational unit. Newspaper executive Gary Pruitt explains that today is the age of architect CEOs, who have to decide whether to gut, scale down, expand, or build new divisions for their companies. "This is an era when CEOs have to be hands-on, deeply engaged and knowledgeable about operations."[49]

Knowledge of the business or the group task is particularly important when developing strategy, formulating mission statements, and sizing up the external environment. Chapter 14 deals with strategy formulation at length.

Creativity

Many effective leaders are creative in the sense that they arrive at imaginative and original solutions to complex problems. Creative ability lies on a continuum, with some leaders being more creative than others. At one end of the creative continuum are business leaders who think of innovative products and services. One example was the late Steve Jobs of Apple Inc. Jobs contributed creative product ideas to his company including endorsing the development of the iPod, followed by the iPhone and iPad. Even while on medical leave, and working from home, Jobs had been involved in product development and company strategy formulation.

At the middle of the creativity continuum are leaders who explore imaginative—but not breakthrough—solutions to business problems. At the low end of the creativity continuum are leaders who inspire group members to push forward with standard solutions to organizational problems. Creativity is such an important aspect of the leader's role in the modern organization that the development of creative problem-solving skills receives separate attention in Chapter 13.

Insight into People and Situations

Another important cognitive trait of leaders is **insight**, a depth of understanding that requires considerable intuition and common sense. Intuition is often the mental process used to provide the understanding of a problem. Insight helps speed decision making. Lawrence Weinbach, the former chairman, president, and CEO of Unisys, puts it this way: "If we want to be leaders, we're going to have to make decisions with maybe 75 percent of the facts. If you wait for 95 percent, you are going to be a follower."[50] Jeff Bezos of Amazon.com believes that the bigger the decision, such as whether or not to enter a particular business, the greater the role of insight and intuition.

Insight into people and situations involving people is an essential characteristic of managerial leaders because it helps them make the best use of both their own and others' talents. For example, it helps them make wise choices in selecting people for key assignments. Insight also enables managers to do a better job of training and developing team members because they can wisely assess the members' strengths and weaknesses. Another major advantage of being insightful is that the leader can size up a situation and adapt his or her leadership approach accordingly. For instance, in a crisis situation, group members welcome directive and decisive leadership. Being able to read people helps the manager provide this leadership. An in-demand leadership skill is to be able to read people from different cultures, and then negotiate cultural differences. In recent years, U.S. manufacturers have hired executive recruiters to find leaders with such skill because of global outsourcing.[51]

You can gauge your insight by charting the accuracy of your hunches and predictions about people and business situations. For example, size up a new coworker or manager as best you can. Record your observations and test them against how that person performs or behaves many months later. The feedback from this type of exercise will help sharpen your insights.

Farsightedness and Conceptual Thinking

To develop visions and corporate strategy, a leader needs **farsightedness**, the ability to understand the long-range implications of actions and policies. A farsighted leader recognizes that hiring talented workers today will give the firm a long-range competitive advantage. A more shortsighted view would be to hire less-talented workers to satisfy immediate employment needs. The farsighted leader/manager is not oblivious to short-range needs but will devise an intermediate solution, such as hiring temporary workers until people with the right talents are found.

Conceptual thinking refers to the ability to see the overall perspective, and it makes farsightedness possible. A conceptual thinker is also a *systems thinker* because he or she understands how the external environment influences the organization and how different parts of the organization influence each other. A good conceptual thinker recognizes how his or her organizational unit contributes to the firm or how the firm meshes with the outside world.

The CEO of PepsiCo, Indra Nooyi, believes that the single most important skill needed for any CEO today is strategic acuity (meaning conceptual thinking and farsightedness). She notes that over twenty-five years ago, when she was chosen to run the European business for PepsiCo, Roger Enrico, the company CEO at the time, said, "I'm pulling you back." When Nooyi asked why, Enrico replied, "I can get operating executives to run a profit-and-loss-center. But I cannot find people to help me re-conceptualize PepsiCo. That's the skill in shortest supply."[52]

The accompanying Leader in Action insert gives you a well-known high-tech executive to study in terms of her personal attributes.

To help personalize the information about key leadership traits presented so far, do Leadership Skill-Building Exercise 3-3.

> LEADER IN ACTION

Carol Bartz, the Well-Known Former CEO of Yahoo Inc.

Carol Ann Bartz is a high-tech executive well-known for the successes she has enjoyed, her optimism, and her frankness and colorful expressions. Shortly after being appointed as the CEO of Yahoo Inc., she pulled off one of the biggest deals of her career. She relinquished control of the Yahoo search business in exchange for a decade of revenue-sharing with Microsoft. (The Bing engine powers Yahoo searches.) The deal was criticized by stockholders and business writers, but Bartz believed that over the long run the Microsoft deal will pay off for Yahoo because so much advertising has shifted to search engines.

Bartz began her career in information technology with a B.S. in Computer Science from the University of Wisconsin. During her early career, she held sales positions at 3M and Digital Equipment Corp. Her executive experience before Yahoo included positions as vice president of Worldwide Field Operations at Sun Microsystems, and as chief executive at Autodesk.

Bartz contends that Yahoo's most important asset is its ability to reach over 600 million people in 30 countries and place ads on their computer or smart-phone screens. She is heavily sales-oriented. An executive who has known Bartz for many years said, "She is good at figuring out what people will buy, why they buy it and what you can do to make them pay more."

One of the reasons that Bartz accepted the CEO position at Yahoo is that after retiring from Autodesk in 2006, she missed the day-by-day thrills, and even the stress, of executive life. She particularly enjoys working through crises.

Bartz has had to overcome personal adversity during her business career. The second day on the job as Autodesk CEO she discovered she had breast cancer. She had a mastectomy, leaving her hospitalized for four weeks. She worked on company problems from her hospital bed. Shortly after joining Yahoo, she had a left-knee replacement.

Bartz has a reputation for unvarnished language. At Yahoo, she told employees she would "drop-kick to f——g Mars" anyone who leaked company information. In reference to giving feedback, she once comment that she believed in the puppy theory: "If a puppy pees on the rug, you don't wait six months for a performance evaluation to tell the dog what he or she did wrong."

In paying a compliment to Steve Jobs for his effort to maintain high-quality ads on Apple devices, Barz said: "The last thing you need on that beautiful iPad is to see an ad for Russian brides or teeth whitener." Her words about Jobs were less charitable with respect to Apple's restrictions on what information can be placed on its devices. She said that Apple has "obnoxious control" over what kind of ads and content are permitted to appear on some of its devices, but that the control will not endure.

ACTION (continued)

Bartz writes the occasional e-mail of encouragement to Yahoo employees. A paragraph from one of these messages is as follows:

"There sure are a lot of folks writing about us. There are some pretty incredible stories out there. I'm not letting it distract me, and you shouldn't either. Because the really incredible story to me is how far we've come to build a better Yahoo!—something you're all making a reality.

Your fearless leader,

Carol."

As Bartz worked to improve the business results of Yahoo, she told a reporter, "You don't come in and do fairy dust. You upgrade technology, you see what drives engagement." Her approach appeared to be working but too slowly for the Yahoo board who fired Bartz in September 2011.

QUESTIONS

1. What evidence is presented in this story that Bartz has good cognitive skills?

2. Which personality traits does Bartz appear to possess?

3. Assuming that she had a job available in your field, how would you enjoy reporting directly to Bartz?

Source: A variety of sources provided facts and observations to create this story, including the following: "Carol Bartz," *Forbes*, September 7, 2009, pp. 84–88; Jon Fortt, "Yahoo's Taskmaster," *Fortune*, April 27, 2009, pp. 80–84; Sarah Lacy, "And Now a Folksy Update from Carol Bartz, "Massive Outage Relegated to 'PS'," *TechCrunch* (http://techcrunch.com), October 15, 2010, pp. 1–2; Joann S. Lublin, "Some CEOs Face Big Repair Jobs in 2011," *The Wall Street Journal*, January 4, 2011, p. B6; Amir Efrati and Jessica E. Vascellaro, "No 'Fairy Dust' for Yahoo Turnaround," *The Wall Street Journal*, September 16, 2010, p. B1; Scott Morrison, "Yahoo Chief Defends Her Site, Strategy," *The Wall Street Journal*, June 25, 2010, p. B7.

 LEADERSHIP SKILL-BUILDING **EXERCISE 3-3**

Group Feedback on Leadership Traits

The class organizes into groups of about seven people. A volunteer sits in the middle of each group. Each group member looks directly at the person in the hot seat and tells him or her which leadership trait, characteristic, or motive he or she seems to possess. It will help if the feedback providers offer a few words of explanation for their observations. For example, a participant who is told that he or she has self-confidence might also be told, "I noticed how confidently you told the class about your success on the job." The group next moves on to the second person, and so forth. (We assume that you have had some opportunity to observe your classmates prior to this exercise.)

Each member thus receives positive feedback about leadership traits and characteristics from all the other members in the group. After all members have had their turn at receiving feedback, discuss as a group the value of the exercise.

THE INFLUENCE OF HEREDITY AND ENVIRONMENT ON LEADERSHIP

Which contributes more to leadership effectiveness, heredity or environment? Are leaders born or made? Do you have to have the right stuff to be a leader? Many people ponder these issues now that the study of leadership is in vogue. The most sensible answer is that the traits, motives, and characteristics required for leadership effectiveness are caused by a combination of heredity and environment. Leaders are both born and made. Personality traits and mental-ability traits are based on certain inherited predispositions and aptitudes that require the right opportunity to develop. Cognitive intelligence is a good example. We inherit a basic capacity that sets an outer limit to how much mental horsepower we will have. Yet people need the right opportunity to develop their cognitive intelligence so that they can behave brightly enough to be chosen for a leadership position.

Evelyn Williams, who directs the leadership development program at Stanford University, makes the following metaphor: "I think leadership is a combination of nature and nurture. Just as some musicians have a special talent for playing instruments, some people seem to be born with leadership abilities. But whatever their natural talent, people can certainly learn to be better musicians—and better leaders."[53]

Recent research supports the idea that genetics play a role in determining leadership potential. A study found that 47 percent of identical twins raised by different parents had the same level of leadership potential as measured by the California Personality Inventory (a popular personality test).[54]

The physical factor of energy also sheds light on the nature-versus-nurture issue. Some people are born with a biological propensity for being more energetic than others. Yet unless that energy is properly channeled, it will not help a person to become an effective leader.

Research about emotional intelligence reinforces the statements made so far about leadership being a combination of inherited and learned factors. The outermost areas of the brain, known collectively as the neocortex, govern analytical thinking and technical skill, which are associated with cognitive or traditional intelligence. The innermost areas of the brain govern emotions, such as the rage one might feel when being criticized by a customer. Emotional intelligence originates in the neurotransmitters of the limbic system of the brain, which governs feelings, impulses, and drives.

A person's genes, therefore, influence the emotional intelligence necessary for leadership. However, experience is important for emotional intelligence because it increases with age,[55] and a person usually becomes better at managing relationships with practice. As one turnaround manager said, "I've restructured five different companies, and I've learned to do it without completely destroying morale."

A final note is that some leadership traits are more difficult to awaken or develop than others, with passion for work and people being an example. Jonathan Byrnes, a consultant and senior lecturer at MIT, says that you have to have the right people to develop into leaders. "You can't teach passion for the work to someone who can't wait to go home."[56]

THE STRENGTHS AND LIMITATIONS OF THE TRAIT APPROACH

A compelling argument for the trait approach is that there is convincing evidence that leaders possess personal characteristics that differ from those of non-leaders. Based on their review of the type of research reported in this chapter, Kirkpatrick and Locke concluded: "Leaders do not have to be great men or women by being intellectual geniuses or omniscient prophets to succeed. But they do need to have the 'right stuff' and this stuff is not equally present in all people."[57] The current emphasis on emotional intelligence, charisma, and ethical conduct, which are really traits, attitudes, and behaviors, reinforces the importance of the trait approach.

Understanding the traits of effective leaders serves as an important guide to leadership selection. If we are confident that honesty and integrity, as well as creativity and imagination, are essential leadership traits, then we can concentrate on selecting leaders with those characteristics. Another important strength of the trait approach is that it can help people prepare for leadership responsibility and all of the issues that accompany it. A person might seek experiences that enable him or her to develop vital characteristics such as self-confidence, good problem-solving ability, and assertiveness.

A limitation to the trait approach is that it does not tell us which traits are absolutely needed in which leadership situations. We also do not know how much of a trait, characteristic, or motive is the right amount. For example, some leaders get into ethical and legal trouble because they allow their ambition to cross the borderline into greed and gluttony. In addition, too much focus on the trait approach can breed an elitist conception of leadership. People who are not outstanding on key leadership traits and characteristics might be discouraged from seeking leadership positions.

A subtle limitation to the trait approach is that it prompts some people to believe that to be effective, you have to have a high standing on almost every leadership characteristic. In reality, the majority of effective leaders are outstanding in many characteristics but are low on others.

A balanced perspective on the trait approach is that certain traits, motives, and characteristics increase the probability that a leader will be effective, but they do not guarantee effectiveness. The leadership situation often influences which traits will be the most important.[58] At the same time different situations call for different combinations of traits. Visualize yourself as managing a restaurant staffed by teenagers who had never worked previously. You would need to emphasize warmth, enthusiasm, flexibility, and adaptability. Less emphasis would be required on cognitive skills and the power motive.

SUMMARY

The trait-based perspective of leadership contends that certain personal characteristics and skills contribute to leadership effectiveness in many situations. General personality traits associated with effective leadership include (1) self-confidence; (2) humility; (3) core self-evaluations; (4) trustworthiness; (5) authenticity; (6) extraversion; (7) assertiveness; (8) enthusiasm, optimism, and warmth; and (9) sense of humor.

Some personality traits of effective leaders are closely associated with task accomplishment. Among them are (1) passion for the work and the people, (2) emotional intelligence, (3) flexibility and adaptability, (4) internal locus of control, and (5) courage. Emotional intelligence is composed of four traits: self-awareness, self-management, social awareness, and relationship management.

Certain motives and needs associated with leadership effectiveness are closely related to task accomplishment. Among them are (1) the power motive, (2) the drive and achievement motive, and (3) tenacity and resilience.

Cognitive factors are also important for leadership success. They include cognitive (or analytical) intelligence and knowledge of the business or group task (or technical competence.) Practical intelligence contributes to cognitive intelligence. Creativity is another important cognitive skill for leaders, but effective leaders vary widely in their creative contributions. Insight into people and situations, including the ability to make effective judgments about business opportunities, also contributes to leadership effectiveness. Farsightedness and conceptual thinking help leaders to understand the long-range implications of actions and policies and to take an overall perspective.

The issue of whether leaders are born or bred frequently surfaces. A sensible answer is that the traits, motives, and characteristics required for leadership effectiveness are a combination of heredity and environment.

The trait approach to leadership is supported by many studies showing that leaders are different from non-leaders and that effective leaders are different from less effective leaders. Nevertheless, the trait approach does not tell us which traits are most important in which situations or how much of a trait is required. Also, different situations call for different combinations of traits.

KEY TERMS

core self-evaluations	flexibility	practical intelligence
trust	internal locus of control	insight
authenticity	drive	farsightedness
assertiveness	achievement motivation	
emotional intelligence	cognitive factors	

✔ GUIDELINES FOR ACTION AND SKILL DEVELOPMENT

Because emotional intelligence is so important for leadership success, many organizations sponsor emotional intelligence training for managers. One way to get started on improving emotional intelligence would be to attend such a training program. However, like all forms of training, emotional intelligence training must be followed up with consistent and determined practice. A realistic starting point in improving your emotional intelligence is to work with one of its four components at a time, such as the empathy aspect of social awareness.

Begin by obtaining as much feedback as you can from people who know you. Ask them if they think you understand their emotional reactions and how well they think you understand them. It is also helpful to ask someone from another culture or someone who has a severe disability how well you communicate with him or her. (A higher level of empathy is required to communicate well with somebody much different from you.) If you have external or internal customers, ask them how well you appear to understand their position.

If you find any area of deficiency, work on that deficiency steadily. For example, perhaps you are not perceived as taking the time to understand a point of view quite different from your own. Attempt to understand other points of view. Suppose you believe strongly that money is the most important motivator for practically everybody. Speak to a person with a different opinion and listen carefully until you understand that person's perspective.

A few months later, obtain more feedback about your ability to empathize. If you are making progress, continue to practice. Then, repeat these steps for another facet of emotional intelligence. As a result of this practice, you will have developed another valuable interpersonal skill.

Another way of developing emotional intelligence is through *mindfulness*, which refers to being more aware of your thoughts and actions. Reflect carefully on how you react to people and what you are thinking. As with meditation, pay careful attention to the moment. For example, you might be a participant in an intense meeting, and you think of a witty comment that at first you feel cannot wait. Through mindfulness, you might decide to postpone the comment until a less intense moment.[59]

A constructive approach to applying trait theory to attain your goals in a given situation is to think through which combination of traits is the most likely to lead to positive outcomes in the situation at hand. Finding the right cluster of traits to emphasize is usually much more useful than emphasizing one trait. You might be leading a group, for example, that is worried because it needs a creative idea to become more productive. Here you might emphasize your cognitive skills, be assertive about expressing your ideas, and also express enthusiasm about the group's chances for success.

Discussion Questions and Activities

1. How much faith do voters place in the trait theory of leadership when they elect public officials?
2. Suppose a college student graduates with a major for which he or she lacks enthusiasm. What might this person do about becoming a passionate leader?
3. Explain how being highly self-confident in a given leadership situation might not be an advantage.
4. What would a manager to whom you report have to do to convince you that he or she has emotional intelligence?
5. Describe any leader or manager whom you know personally or have watched on television who is unenthusiastic. What effect did the lack of enthusiasm have on group members?
6. What would lead you to conclude that a leader was non-authentic (phony)?
7. What are your best-developed leadership traits, motives, and characteristics? How do you know?
8. Provide an example of a leader you have observed who appears to have good cognitive intelligence, yet is lacking in practical intelligence.
9. Which do you think is the most outstanding leadership trait, motive, or characteristic of the person teaching this class? Explain your answer.
10. Many people who disagree with the trait approach to leadership nevertheless still conduct interviews when hiring a person for a leadership position. Why is conducting such interviews inconsistent with their attitude toward the trait approach?

LEADERSHIP CASE PROBLEM A

Store Manager, Ensign Jimmy Badger

During his senior year in high school, Jimmy Badger decided that he would apply for a scholarship with the Naval Reserve Officers Training Program (NROTC) Scholarship Program. The prospect of having a scholarship that included the cost of tuition, textbooks, lab fees, and minor living expenses seemed outstanding. The focus of the NROTC program on developing leadership skills, including community-service activities, was another plus for Jimmy. He reasoned also that the formal education he would receive would help prepare him for a good career in whatever field he chose. Furthermore, Jimmy thought that serving his country for the six required years was an excellent idea. In his words, "If the powers that be think our country needs a Navy, I want to do my part."

Jimmy found appealing the idea that after graduation from college he would be commissioned as an Ensign in the Naval Reserve, if he committed to a minimum of five years of active duty service. After a successful four years at his chosen state university, Jimmy became submarine officer Ensign Badger. The five years in the Navy fulfilled their promise. Jimmy enjoyed working with sailors, other officers at his level, and more experienced officers. Jimmy particular enjoyed being a leader and having so much responsibility. He noted that "One mistake in a submarine can have disastrous consequences for hundreds of people."

Jimmy's superiors thought highly of his work, and they consistently give him outstanding performance evaluations (fitness reports). The one area of suggested improvement in his performance as a naval officer was that at times his performance expectations of those in his command tended to be unrealistically high. A senior officer once told him, "Ensign Badger, this is not your grandfather's Navy. You need to be a little more patient with young sailors."

When Jimmy began his job search as he approached the end of his naval service, he found that many companies were actively recruiting former military officers. The most attractive opportunities were for management positions, or management training programs that would lead quickly to a management position. After a brief job search, Jimmy accepted a management training position at one of the best-known home-improvement chains.

From the start of the training program, Jimmy knew that he had made a good career choice. He believed strongly that his command experience in the Navy, as well as his formal education and part-time jobs, were a strong combination for being successful as a store manager. Jimmy began by working as a store associate for three months in order to learn the business from an entry-level perspective. Next, he was appointed as manager of the tool department at one store for nine months.

Jimmy's giant step into a leadership position took place when was appointed as the store manager at a medium-size store in the chain, located in Denver, Colorado. In his first meeting with the department managers and other key personnel, Jimmy told them, "I am so pleased to have command of this store. I will soon be asking you for your suggestions as to how to make our store one of the highest-performing units in the company. Communication with me will be constant. My BlackBerry will be turned on 24/7 to listen to your problems, as well as to inform you of any trouble spots I observe."

A few months into his position, Jimmy transmitted an e-mail to every worker in the store, department supervisors included. The e-mail read in part: "Last evening during my late-night inspection, I noticed several deficiencies in the parking lot that I do not want to see repeated. I found several shopping carts scattered around the lot, instead of in their designated parking space. I found garbage on the ground. I saw two of our store associates puffing cigarettes outside the store.

"All of the above are totally unacceptable. Let me know by the end of your shift how you are going to fix the problem."

Toward the end of Jimmy's first year, the human resources department conducted its annual morale and job satisfaction survey using the company intranet. Participants were assured that all responses would be anonymous. As a result, participants were encouraged to be entirely candid. Several of the write-in comments about store manager Jimmy Badger were as follows:

- Our manager is energetic and eager to win. He is still learning about the home-improvement business, but I think his high standards will help us down the road.
- I heard that Jimmy was an officer on a submarine. Will somebody please tell Jimmy to not worry so much? One mistake by a store associate will not drown us.
- Our man Jimmy Badger is a good leader. But he needs to know that some of the yahoos we hire as store associates don't fix their mistakes with one dressing down.
- I like our store manager. But I think he thinks that our ship is sinking and his job is to pull off a rescue mission.

Questions

1. Which leadership characteristics of Jimmy Badger are revealed in this case?
2. Justify your conclusions.
3. To what extent should Jimmy modify his leadership approach?
4. What do you think of the home-improvement store's positive bias toward hiring former military officers for its management-training program?

ASSOCIATED ROLE PLAY

The Performance Review of Jimmy Badger

Today, district manager Lola Sanchez holds a performance review with store manager Jimmy Badger. One student plays the role of Lola, who is not looking forward to this review. She is pleased with Jimmy's results, but she is concerned that he is going too far in pushing for high standards of behavior and compliance with store rules. Lola worries that Jimmy's high standards of performance and behavior might create some unwanted turnover. Another student plays the role of Jimmy, who is expecting an outstanding performance evaluation because of his high standards of performance and behavior. Run the role play for about eight minutes, with observers providing some feedback after the role players have completed their task.

LEADERSHIP CASE PROBLEM B

Amy Touchstone Wants to Shape Up the Club

Amy Touchstone, 27, is feeling great these days, having just been promoted to director of operations at the East End Athletic Club. For two years previously, she worked as an administrator and receptionist at the club, which offers a wide range of fitness equipment; ten indoor tennis courts; six squash courts; one basketball court; and a variety of fitness programs, including massages.

Reporting to Touchstone is a staff of ten people, three of whom are full-time workers, and seven of whom are part-timers. Her main responsibilities are to ensure that the club is running smoothly outside of athletic programs and marketing. The billing office and custodial staff report to Touchstone.

When Touchstone asked her boss, the club manager, what she was supposed to accomplish as the director of operations, she was told, "East End isn't nearly as efficient, clean, and sharp as it should be for the rates we charge. So go fix it." Touchstone liked these general directives, but she thought that she would need to arrive at a few specific ideas for improvement.

Drawing from a technique she learned in a marketing course, Touchstone decided to dig into the responses in the club member suggestion box at the front desk. Amy dug back into three months of suggestions. The key themes for improving the club as revealed by these suggestions were as follows:

- The men's locker room is horrible because of the way the guests throw their towels on the floor. These guys have no respect for the club.
- Some of the staff don't seem interested in the members. Sometimes they are talking to each other when they should be paying attention to us. We are put on hold far too often when we call the club.
- Some of the people who work here act like they are doing us a favor to let us use the facilities.
- Stop charging us for everything, such as using the tennis courts, if we are already paying hefty monthly dues.

Amy reviewed the negative themes she found among the suggestions, and then discussed them with Joe Pellagrino, a fitness coach whom she had known for several years. Pellagrino said, "Don't worry about a handful of complainers. Only the people with a gripe bother to put something in the suggestion box."

Amy thought to herself, "Joe could have a point. Yet those suggestions seem pretty important. I should start taking action on improvements tomorrow. I have to think of a good way to approach the staff."

Questions

1. Which personal characteristics of a leader should Touchstone emphasize in bringing about improvements in the operation of the East End Athletic Club?
2. Which leadership roles (review Chapter 1) should Touchstone emphasize in bringing about improvements in the operation of the club?
3. What do you recommend that Touchstone do next to carry out her leadership responsibility of improving operations?

ASSOCIATED ROLE PLAY

One student plays the role of Amy, who is holding a meeting with her staff. Several other students play the role of staff members, who appear less concerned than Amy about dealing with the changes she thinks might be important. Amy will attempt to be appropriately self-confident and assertive in explaining the need for change. Amy wants to be an effective leader, but not abrasive. Run the role play for about ten minutes. Other class members will provide feedback about the effectiveness of the staff meeting at the athletic club.

LEADERSHIP SKILL-BUILDING EXERCISE 3-4

My Leadership Portfolio

For this addition to your leadership portfolio, first select five of the traits, motives, and characteristics described in this chapter that you think you have already exhibited. For each of these attributes, explain why you think you have it. An example would be as follows:

Insight into people and situations: As a restaurant manager, my job was to help hire an assistant manager who would share some of the responsibilities of running the restaurant. I invited a friend of mine, Laura, to apply for the position, even though she had never worked in a restaurant. I noticed that she was businesslike and also had a good touch with people. Laura was hired, and she proved to be a fantastic assistant manager. I obviously sized her up correctly.

Second, select several leadership traits, motives, or characteristics that you think you need to develop to enhance your leadership skills. Explain why you think you need this development and how you think you might obtain it. An example would be as follows:

Passion for the work and people: So far I am not particularly passionate about any aspect of work or any cause, so it is hard for me to get very excited about being a leader. I plan to read more about my field and then interview a couple of successful people in this field to find some aspect of it that would be a joy for me to get involved in.

LEADERSHIP SKILL-BUILDING EXERCISE 3-5

Analyzing the Traits, Motives, and Characteristics of a Well-Known Leader

Choose one or two well-known leaders as a topic for discussion. *Well-known* in this context refers to somebody whom the majority of the class has observed, either in person or through the media, including the Internet, newspapers, and on YouTube. Take a few class moments to agree on which leader or leaders will be analyzed. Possibilities include (a) your college president, (b) your country president or prime minister, or (c) a well-known NFL coach.

The next step is for the class to discuss this leader's traits, motives, and characteristics, using ideas from this chapter of the text. Look to see if you can find consensus about the leader's strongest and weakest personal attributes.

LEADERSHIP VIDEO CASE DISCUSSION QUESTIONS

To view the videos for this activity, you'll need access to the CourseMate that is available for this text. To get access, visit www.CengageBrain.com.

After watching "Numi's New Manager," answer the following questions.

1. What task-related personality trait does Danielle Oviedo possess that allowed her to successfully manage the turbulent environment at Numi Tea?
2. What general personality trait contributed most to Danielle's effectiveness as a leader?

How might this trait help Danielle's ability to lead?
3. How does Danielle ensure her knowledge of the business or group task? How does her emotional intelligence develop as she ensures knowledge of the group task?
4. In your opinion, does Danielle have the personalized power motive or the socialized power motive? Explain.

NOTES

1. A few observations in this story are from Donna Rawady, "Effective Leaders Need a Bird's Eye View," *Democrat and Chronicle Business* (Rochester, New York), July 27, 2010, p. 5B.
2. Stephen J. Zaccaro, "Trait Based Perspectives of Leadership," *American Psychologist*, January 2007, p. 6.
3. Timothy A. Judge, Ronald F. Picccolo, and Tomek Kosalka, "The Bright and Dark Sides of Leader Traits: A Review and Theoretical Extension of the Leader Trait Paradigm," *Leadership Quarterly*, December 2009, pp. 855–875; Zaccaro, "Trait Based Perspectives," p. 11.
4. George P. Hollenbeck and Douglas T. Hall, "Self-Confidence and Leader Performance," *Organizational Dynamics*, no. 3, 2004, p. 254.
5. Bernard M. Bass (with Ruth Bass), *The Bass Handbook of Leadership: Theory, Research, and Managerial Applications*, 4th ed. (New York: The Free Press, 2008), p. 189.
6. Quoted in Brian O'Keefe, "Battle-Tested: How a Decade of War Has Created a New Generation

of Elite Business Leaders," *Fortune*, March 22, 2010, p. 112.

7. "Sully's Landing: More Than Good Luck," *Executive Leadership*, March 2009, pp. 1–2.

8. Stephen G. Harrison, "Leadership and Hope Go Hand in Hand," *Executive Leadership*, June 2002, p. 8.

9. Jim Collins, "Level 5 Leadership: The Triumph of Humility and Fierce Resolve," *Harvard Business Review*, January 2001, p. 70.

10. Judge, Picccolo, and Kosalka, "The Bright and Dark Sides of Leader Traits," p. 866.

11. Gareth R. Jones and Jennifer M. George, "The Experience and Evolution of Trust: Implications for Cooperation and Teamwork," *Academy of Management Review*, July 1998, pp. 531–546.

12. Roy J. Lewicki, Daniel McAllister, and Robert J. Bies, "Trust and Distrust: New Relationships and Realities," *Academy of Management Review*, July 1998, p. 439.

13. Thomas A. Stewart, "Whom Can You Trust? It's Not So Easy to Tell," *Fortune*, June 12, 2000, p. 334; "4 Keys to Building Trust Quickly," *Manager's Edge*, March 2005, p. 4.

14. Kurt T. Kirks and Donald L. Ferrin, "Trust in Leadership: Meta-Analytic Findings and Implications for Research and Practice," *Journal of Applied Psychology*, August 2002, pp. 611–628.

15. Quy Huy and Christoph Zott, "Trust Me: For Entrepreneurs Looking to Gain Credibility, It's Often the Little Things That Count," *The Wall Street Journal*, November 30, 2009, p. R8.

16. Bill George, Peter Sims, Andrew N. McClean, and Diana Mayer, "Discovering Your Authentic Leadership," *Harvard Business Review*, February 2007, p. 130.

17. Ibid., pp. 129–138.

18. Fred O. Walumbwa, Peng Wang, Hui Wang, John Schaubroeck, and Bruce J. Avolio, "Psychological Processes Linking Authentic Leadership to Follower Behaviors," *Leadership Quarterly*, October 2010, pp. 901–914.

19. Timothy A. Judge, Joyce E. Bono, Remus Ilies, and Megan W. Gerhardt, "Personality and Leadership: A Qualitative and Quantitative Review," *Journal of Applied Psychology*, August 2002, pp. 765–780.

20. Researched reported in Judge, Picccolo, and Kosalka, "The Bright and Dark Sides of Leader Traits," p. 865.

21. Maurice Levi, Kai Li, and Feng Zhang, "Deal or No Deal: Hormones and Completion of Mergers and Acquisitions," *Journal of Management Science*, September 2010, pp. 1–36.

22. Robin Sidel, "Banga to Be MasterCard's Protector," *The Wall Street Journal*, May 29–30, 2010, p. B1.

23. Jared Sandberg, "The Office Pessimists May Not Be Lovable, But Are Often Right," *The Wall Street Journal*, November 27, 2007, p. B1.

24. Quoted in "Leadership Concepts," *Executive Strategies*, July 9, 1991, p. 1.

25. Eric J. Romeo and Kevin W. Cruthirds, "The Use of Humor in the Workplace," *Academy of Management Perspectives*, May 2006, 60, pp. 63–64.

26. Rick Weaver, "Five Essential Leadership Traits: The Story of Martha Stewart from Kmart to Macy's," *Ezine Articles* (http://ezinearticles.com), accessed January 2, 2001.

27. "Starbucks: More Than a Caffeine High," *Executive Leadership*, August 2006, p. 4.

28. Daniel Goleman, "What Makes a Leader?" *Harvard Business Review*, November–December 1998, p. 94.

29. Daniel Goleman, Richard Boyatzis, and Annie McKee, "Primal Leadership: The Hidden Driver of Great Performance," *Harvard Business Review*, December 2001, pp. 42–51.

30. Stéphane Côté, Paulo N. Lopes, Peter Salovey, and Christopher T. H. Miners, "Emotional Intelligence and Leadership Emergence in Small Groups," *Leadership Quarterly*, June 2010, pp. 496–508.

31. Joe Nocera, "Real Reason for Ousting H. P.'s Chief," *The New York Times* (www.nytimes.com), August 13, 2010, pp. 1–5; Ben Worthen and Joann S. Lublin, "Mark Hurd Neglected to Follow H-P Code," *The Wall Street Journal*, August 9, 2010, pp. B1, B5; James B. Stewart, "Hewlett-Packard Still Can't Handle the Truth," *The Wall Street Journal*, August 11, 2010, p. C4.

32. Lynette M. Loomis, "Use Emotions to Guide Thinking, Enhance Results," Rochester, New York, *Democrat and Chronicle*, October 21, 2007, p. 2E.

33. Goleman, Boyatzis, and McKee, "Primal Leadership," pp. 42–51.

34. Stefanie K. Johnson, "I Second That Emotion: Effects of Emotional Contagion and Affect at Work on Leader and Follower Outcomes," *Leadership Quarterly*, February 2008, pp. 1–19.

35. John Antonakis, Neal M. Ashkanasy, and Marie T. Dasborough, "Does Leadership Need Emotional Intelligence?" *Leadership Quarterly*, April 2009, pp. 247–261; Frank Walter, Michael S. Cole, and Ronald H. Humphrey, "Emotional Intelligence: Sine Qua Non of Leadership or Folderol?" *Academy of Management Perspectives*, February 2011, pp. 45–59.

36. Kathleen K. Reardon, "Courage as a Skill," *Harvard Business Review*, January 2007, p. 63.

37. David C. McClelland and Richard Boyatzis, "Leadership Motive Pattern and Long-Term Success in Management," *Journal of Applied Psychology*, December 1982, p. 727.

38. Locke and Associates, *The Essence of Leadership: The Four Keys to Leading Successfully* (New York, 1992), p. 22.

39. Quoted in Jeffrey Pfeffer, "The Courage to Rise Above," *Business 2.0*, May 2006, p. 86.

40. Locke and Associates, *The Essence of Leadership*, p. 22.

41. Peter Burrows, "Cisco's Extreme Ambitions," *Business Week*, November 30, 2009, pp. 026–027.

42. John B. Miner, Normal R. Smith, and Jeffrey S. Bracker, "Role of Entrepreneurial Task Motivation in the Growth of Technologically Innovative Firms," *Journal of Applied Psychology*, August 1989, p. 554.

43. Matthew Rand, "Medicine Man," *Forbes*, November 27, 2006, p. 152; Evelyn M. Rusli, "Stewart Rahr's Second Act," *DealBook* (http://dealbook.nytimes.com), November 19, 2010.

44. Timothy A. Judge, Amy E. Colbert, and Remus Ilies, "Intelligence and Leadership: A Quantitative Review and Test of Theoretical Propositions," *Journal of Applied Psychology*, June 2004, pp. 542–552.

45. Bass, *The Bass Handbook of Leadership*, p. 84.

46. Robert J. Sternberg, "The WICS Approach to Leadership: Stories of Leadership and the Structures and Processes that Support Them," *The Leadership Quarterly*, June 2008, pp. 360–371.

47. Amy Palanjian, "A Knack for Languages Evolves into a Career," *The Wall Street Journal*, April 28, 2009, p. D4.

48. Chuck Bartels, "Wal-Mart Names Chief Merchandising Officer," The Associated Press, January 28, 2011.

49. Quoted in Carol Hymowitz, "Leaders Must Produce Bold New Blueprints in Era of Architect CEO," *The Wall Street Journal*, April 17, 2006, p. B1.

50. From Jeffrey E. Garten, *The Mind of the C.E.O.* (Cambridge, Mass.: Perseus Publishing, 2001), as quoted in "Random Wisdom," *Executive Leadership*, April 4, 2002, p. 1.

51. James R. Hagerty, "'Lightning Bolt' Led Caterpillar to Look Outside," *The Wall Street Journal*, December 13, 2010, p. B5.

52. Jessica Shambora and Beth Kowitt, "The Queen of Pop," *Fortune*, September 28, 2009, p. 108.

53. "How Stanford Is Grooming Next Business Leaders," *The Wall Street Journal*, May 29, 2007, p. B6.

54. Research reported in Scott Shane, *Born Entrepreneurs. Born Leaders* (London: Oxford University Press, 2010).

55. Goleman, "What Makes a Leader?" p. 97.

56. Quoted in "Practice Makes Perfect for Leaders, Too," *HR Magazine*, December 2005, p. 14.

57. Kirkpatrick and Locke, "Leadership: Do Traits Matter?" p. 59.

58. Zacarro, "Trait-Based Perspectives," p. 14.

59. "Buff Up Your Emotional Intelligence," *Executive Leadership*, February 2009, p. 2.

The **Charismatic** and **Transformational** **Aspects** of **Leaders**

LEARNING OBJECTIVES

After studying this chapter and doing the exercises, you should be able to

- Describe many of the traits and behaviors of charismatic leaders.

- Explain the visionary component of charismatic leadership.

- Explain the communication style of charismatic leaders.

- Have an action plan for developing your charisma.

- Explain the nature of transformational leadership.

- Identify several of the impacts of charismatic and transformational leadership on performance and behavior.

- Describe the concerns about charismatic leadership from the scientific and moral standpoint.

CHAPTER OUTLINE

Business executives and financial analysts who have not met her before are surprised when Lynn Tilton, the CEO and principal of Patriarch Partners, strides into the meeting. The purpose of such a meeting is typically to discuss another buyout of a distressed manufacturer. Her attire for the occasion usually includes five-inch stiletto heels, a lavish diamond necklace, and a black leather jumpsuit or skirt. If the opportunity arises, Tilton will make a racy comment linked to the situation.

Fifty-three-year-old Tilton, who heads the $8 billion private equity firm Patriarch Partners, earned a B.A. with a major in American Studies from Yale University and an MBA with a concentration in finance from Columbia University. Her firm's mission is to invest in distressed companies and to partner with them to help them survive and prosper. Tilton contends that Patriarch Partners has saved over 250,000 jobs and 250 companies. She explains that she and her staff develop innovative financial solutions for troubled manufacturers and also assist with financial turnarounds. A report by *Forbes* published in 2011 stated that it is difficult to assess the true worth of both Tilton and Patriarch Partners because of the complicated financing methods involved, such as "structured finance vehicles," based on the debt of distressed companies.

Tilton lives a flashy lifestyle, including commuting to her New York City office by helicopter. She owns homes in Florida, Arizona, and Hawaii, as well as a villa in Italy. Her office decorations include whips and handcuffs sent to her by friends, New Age paintings, and a portrait of her draped across the hood of a black Mercedes.

Behind the flamboyant façade, Tilton is a sophisticated investor and manufacturing specialist who has become one of the richest self-made businesswomen in the United States. She and her company own or have a controlling interest in seventy-four companies whose total employment is about 120,000. She insists that the future of the United States depends on building a strong manufacturing base.

With an appearance similar to a rock singer, Tilton at first surprises workers at the many plants she visits. However, with her earthy sense of humor, good nature, and in-depth knowledge of manufacturing, she quickly wins their admiration and support.[1]

The words and actions of Lynn Tilton illustrate a couple of key points about charismatic and transformational leaders. They think big, and they are sometimes personally flamboyant (even if not as exaggeratedly so as Tilton). The study of charismatic and transformational leadership, an extension of the trait theory, has become an important way of understanding leadership. One of the many reasons that charisma is important is that it facilitates leaders in carrying out their roles. In the opinion of Jack and Suzy Welch, charisma makes the leader's job much easier. In today's fiercely competitive global economy, leaders need to energize their constituents more than ever. Helping people attain stretch goals and understand why change is necessary is done more quickly with charisma than relying solely on reasoning and logic.[2] (A stretch goal tests most of your capabilities but is not so difficult to attain that you are likely to fail.)

In this chapter, we examine the meaning and effects of charismatic leadership, the characteristics of charismatic leaders, how such leaders form visions, and how one develops charisma. We also describe the closely related and overlapping subject of transformational leadership. Finally, we look at the dark side of charismatic leadership.

THE MEANINGS OF CHARISMA

Charisma, like leadership itself, has been defined in various ways. Nevertheless, there is enough consistency among these definitions to make charisma a useful concept in understanding and practicing leadership. *Charisma* is a Greek word meaning "divinely inspired gift." In the study of leadership, **charisma** is a special quality of leaders whose purposes, powers, and extraordinary determination differentiate them from others.[3] In general use, the term *charismatic* means to have a charming and colorful personality, such as that shown by basketball star Carmelo Anthony or soccer star Mia Hamm.

The various definitions of charisma have a unifying theme. Charisma is a positive and compelling quality that makes many others want to be led by the person that has it. The phrase *many others* is chosen carefully. Few leaders are perceived as charismatic by *all* of their constituents. A case in point is the late Steve Jobs of Apple Inc., whose name surfaces frequently in discussions of charisma. Several years ago, he was nominated *Time* magazine person of the year by an entertainment executive, and given this accolade: "He is a true visionary who continues to lead the technological revolution. Year after year, Apple creates must-have products that shape how we live our lives. Jobs and Apple continue to lead us into a wonderful new technological future."[4] Two years later, *Fortune* magazine declared Jobs to be the CEO of the Decade in part because he has cheated death (overcome pancreatic cancer for a while), and changed our world.[5]

In contrast, a news reporter and novelist described Jobs as "a brilliant but short-tempered figure known for his outsized ego and penchant for control." He was also known to be stubborn and arrogant.[6] Such behavior is hardly characteristic of an inspiring leader.

Given that charisma is based on perceptions, an important element of charismatic leadership involves the *attributions* made by group members about the characteristics of leaders and the results they achieve. According to attribution theory, if people perceive a leader to have a certain characteristic, such as being visionary, the leader will more likely be perceived as charismatic. Attributions of charisma are important because they lead to other behavioral outcomes, such as commitment to leaders, self-sacrifice, and high performance.

A study of attributions and charisma found that the network a person belongs to influences the attributions he or she makes. The subjects in the study were police workers who rated the director of a police organization and students in an introductory business course who rated the charisma of their professors. The study found that network members influenced to some extent whether the study participants perceived their leader or professor to be charismatic and that perceptions of charisma were the closest among friends within networks.[7] What about you? Are your perceptions of the charisma of your professors influenced by the opinions of your network members?

Charisma: A Relationship Between the Leader, Group Members, and Other Stakeholders

A key dimension of charismatic leadership is that, like all leadership, it involves a relationship or interaction between the leader and the people being led.

Furthermore, the people accepting the leadership must attribute charismatic qualities to the leader. John Gardner believes that charisma applies to leader–constituent relationships in which the leader has an exceptional gift for inspiration and nonrational communication. At the same time the constituents' response is characterized by awe, reverence, devotion, or emotional dependence.[8] The late Sam Walton, founder of Walmart Stores, had this type of relationship with many of his employees. Walton's most avid supporters believed he was an inspired executive to whom they could trust their careers.

Charismatic leaders use impression management to deliberately cultivate a certain relationship with group members. In other words, they take steps to create a favorable, successful impression, recognizing that the perceptions of constituents determine whether they function as charismatic leaders.[9] Impression management seems to imply that these leaders are skillful actors in presenting a charismatic face to the world. But the behaviors and attitudes of truly charismatic leaders go well beyond superficial aspects of impression management, such as wearing fashionable clothing or speaking well. For example, a truly charismatic leader will work hard to create positive visions for group members.

A notable aspect of charismatic and transformational leaders is that their influence extends beyond the immediate work group and beyond reporting relationships. An example is that some consumers are influenced to purchase products from a company, and some suppliers want to do business with it, based partly on the charisma of a company leader.[10] Andrea Jung, the stylish chairperson of Avon, is a case in point. After seeing a story about Jung in a business magazine or seeing her interviewed on television, many consumers are willing to give Avon products a try.

Another way in which the highly charismatic leader influences external stakeholders is that he or she becomes the symbol of the organization. If the leader meets the stakeholders' (or followers') needs, such as wanting to identify with a powerful figure, the stakeholders will have favorable interactions with the organization. Visualize a teenage girl wanting to identify with a successful mother figure and who regards Jung as cool. She might then become a loyal Avon customer. Another example is that the owner of a distressed auto parts company might admire the personal qualities of Lynn Tilton so much that he wants to become part of the Patriarch group.

Charismatic leadership is possible under certain conditions. The constituents must share the leader's beliefs and must have unquestioning acceptance of and affection for the leader. The group members must willingly obey the leader, and they must be emotionally involved both in the mission of the charismatic leader and in their own goals. Finally, the constituents must have a strong desire to identify with the leader.[11]

The Effects of Charisma

The study of charisma grows in importance when its effects are recognized, such as whether by being charismatic a leader can enhance productivity, lower accidents, and enhance job satisfaction. Much of the impact of charisma is based on the positive affect (emotion) the charismatic leader triggers among the group members. A group of researchers conducted a study of firefighters and their leaders to explore how the emotional component of charisma affects the mood and happiness of subordinates.

The firefighter study followed a preliminary laboratory study with college students designed to explore how the leader's emotion might affect subordinate behavior. The field study involved 216 firefighters and 48 officers. Happiness, including positive affect and negative affect (unhappiness), was measured through a questionnaire. Leader charisma was measured by a questionnaire quite similar to one presented later in this chapter. The results suggested that firefighters under the command of a charismatic officer were happier than those under the command of a noncharismatic officer. Charismatic leaders who expressed positive emotion and thoughts tended to have an even stronger impact on the positive emotional state of firefighters. The positive affect of the officers also tended to reduce negative affect among the firefighters.

A conclusion of the study going beyond firefighters is that one of the ways by which charismatic leaders emotionally touch subordinates is through enhancing their positive affect. Furthermore, happier leaders spread their positive mood to group members.[12]

Another way of understanding the effects of charisma is to understand that top-level leaders sometimes lose their power and position because they are perceived as not being charismatic enough to get constituents to accomplish important goals. An example is Zoe Cruz, the former copresident and heir apparent at Morgan Stanley. Cruz had oversight over the part of the investment bank that suffered losses in the mortgage credit crisis of several years ago. It appeared she had escaped the bloodletting following the losses. But she also suffered from criticisms of her leadership style by many of her colleagues, who said that she lacked charisma and ease with people. Cruz may have been the victim of political infighting at Morgan Stanley.[13] Yet, if you are well liked, you are less likely to be a political victim.

The information just presented is useful for the aspiring charismatic leader. Using charisma and a positive mood to help workers become happy is valuable. Productivity might increase as stress might be reduced, resulting in less time lost to illness. Also, not being charismatic enough can sometimes make it difficult to hold on to a high-level leadership position.

TYPES OF CHARISMATIC LEADERS

The everyday use of the term *charisma* suggests that it is a straightforward and readily understood trait. As already explained, however, charisma has different meanings and dimensions. As a result, charismatic leaders can be categorized into five types: socialized charismatics, personalized charismatics, officeholder charismatics, personal charismatics, and divine charismatics.[14]

Following the distinction made for the power motive, some charismatic leaders use their power for the good of others. A **socialized charismatic** is a leader who restrains the use of power in order to benefit others. This type of leader also attempts to bring group members' values in line with his or her values. The socialized charismatic formulates and pursues goals that fulfill the needs of group members and provides intellectual stimulation to them. Followers of socialized charismatics are autonomous, empowered, and responsible. A study conducted in a health care organization indicated that direct reports of leaders perceived to be socialized charismatics are less likely to engage in workplace deviance (such as lying, stealing, and cheating). Part of the reason is that the socialized charismatic imparts positive values to group members.[15]

The effect of the socialized charismatic on followers provides more insight into this type of charismatic. In the socialized relationship, the followers have a clear sense of who they are and a clear set of values. The charismatic relationship gives them an opportunity to express their important values within the framework of being a group member, such as wanting to work together to preserve the planet. In a socialized relationship, the followers derive a sense of direction and self-expression not from identifying with the leader but from the leader's message.[16] The message of the socialized charismatic in this situation might be, "We want to make money but we want to contribute to a sustainable environment at the same time."

A second type of charismatic leader is the **personalized charismatic**. Such individuals serve primarily their own interests and so exercise few restraints on their use of power. Personalized charismatics impose self-serving goals on constituents, and they offer consideration and support to group members only when it facilitates their own goals. Followers of personalized charismatics are typically obedient, submissive, and dependent. They also identify more with the leader than the leader's message and therefore might follow the leader down an unethical path, such as granting homeowner loans that will most likely result in a high foreclosure rate.

Another type of charismatic leader is the *officeholder charismatic*. For this type of leader, charismatic leadership is more a property of the office occupied than of his or her personal characteristics. The chief executive officer of the Procter & Gamble Company, for example, might have considerable luster but would lose much of it immediately after leaving office. Officeholder charismatics attain high status by occupying a valuable role.

In contrast to officeholder charismatics, *personal charismatics* gain very high esteem through the faith others have in them. A personal charismatic exerts influence whether occupying a low- or high-status position because he or she has the right traits, characteristics, and behaviors. Former Secretary of State Colin H. Powell would qualify in the eyes of many as a personal charismatic. After retiring from his position as the top-ranking U.S. Army general, Powell was deluged with offers to serve on corporate boards and to make speaking appearances. He was eventually appointed as secretary of state in the George W. Bush administration and served during Bush's first term. Subsequently, he remained an influential figure on the world stage.

A historically important type of charismatic leader is the *divine charismatic*. Originally, charismatic leadership was a theological concept: A divine charismatic was someone endowed with a gift of divine grace. In 1924, Max Weber defined a charismatic leader as a mystical, narcissistic, and personally magnetic savior who would arise to lead people through a crisis. For millions of people, Joe Montana of Notre Dame and the San Francisco 49ers was the ultimate quarterback, and he also possessed a warm, magnetic personality. His expert power in football and his referent power as a person combined to help his post-football business, Joe Montana's Recipes, succeed. (Are you familiar with Comeback Kid Coleslaw or Overtime Oatmeal Cookies, among other tasty treats?)

The *celebrity charismatic* can be found in organizational life as well as in the political and entertainment realms. Charismatic people of this type may overlap with the other types such as being socialized and personal. Carly Fiorina, the former H-P CEO and one-time candidate for U.S. Senator, was perceived by many to be a celebrity charismatic. She was often accused of being more interested in personal fame than taking care of the internal operations of her Hewlett-Packard. Later, you will read about Mellody Hobson, a financial executive with high charisma. After she appears on a television show, there is an upward trend in inquiries about her company's mutual funds.

CHARACTERISTICS OF CHARISMATIC LEADERS

The outstanding characteristic of charismatic leaders is that they are charismatic, and therefore they can attract, motivate, or lead others. They also have other distinguishing characteristics. Because charisma is a key component of transformational leadership, many of these characteristics also apply to transformational leaders. A **transformational leader** is one who brings about positive, major changes in an organization. Many charismatic leaders, however, are not transformational. Although they inspire people, they may not bring about major organizational changes. As we look at the characteristics of charismatic leaders,[17] you will note that many of these characteristics apply to leaders in general.

First, charismatic leaders are *visionary* because they offer an exciting image of where the organization is headed and how to get there. A vision is more than a forecast; it describes an ideal version of the future of an entire organization or an organizational unit. The next section provides additional information about vision in leadership, including guidelines on how to develop a vision. Chapter 14, which discusses the leadership aspects of business strategy, also contains information about formulating visions.

Charismatic leaders also possess *masterful communication skills*. To inspire people, the charismatic leader uses colorful language and exciting metaphors and analogies. (More about the communication skills of charismatic leaders is presented later in this chapter.) Another key characteristic is the *ability to inspire trust*. Constituents believe so strongly in the integrity of charismatic leaders that they will risk their careers to pursue the chief's vision. Charismatic leaders are also *able to make group members feel capable*. Sometimes they do this by enabling group members to achieve success on relatively easy projects. They then praise the group members and give them more demanding assignments.

Charismatic people are typically tactful in social situations based partly on their ability to read other people's emotions (part of emotional intelligence). Related to reading emotions is the ability to connect with people, as in the now overdone phrase, "I feel your pain." For example, during a severe business downturn, a company leader might say, "I know a lot of you are worried about losing your jobs. Working with you as a team, we are fighting to avoid layoffs."

In addition, charismatic leaders demonstrate an *energy and action orientation*. Like entrepreneurs, most charismatic leaders are energetic and serve as role models for getting things done on time. *Emotional expressiveness and warmth* are also notable. A key characteristic of charismatic leaders is the ability to express feelings openly. A bank vice president claims that much of the charisma people attribute to her can be explained very simply: "I'm up front about expressing positive feelings. I praise people, I hug them, and I cheer if necessary. I also express my negative feelings, but to a lesser extent." Nonverbal emotional expressiveness, such as warm gestures and frequent (nonsexual) touching of group members, is also characteristic of charismatic leaders.

An example of a charismatic business executive who combines an action orientation with emotional expressiveness and warmth is Luis Manuel Ramirez, the CEO of the Industrial Solutions unit of GE. According to one observer, he "emits energy like one of GE's new WATT electric vehicle chargers. His hands are in perpetual motion, now orchestrating through the air, now reaching out to gently touch the wrist of the interviewer for emphasis."

The ability of Ramirez to adapt to multiple, global environments also enhances his charisma, including emotional expressiveness. As Ramirez explains:

> When they see my face in the Middle East, they think I am Middle Eastern. In India, they think I am Indian. In Europe, maybe I was born in southern Spain. People see that I am not the typical Anglo-American, and they ask me where I am from. It is like an icebreaker.[18]

Because emotional expressiveness is such an important part of being and becoming charismatic, you are invited to take Leadership Self-Assessment Quiz 4-1. It will help you think about a practical way of developing charismatic appeal.

Another trait of charismatic leaders is that they *romanticize risk*. They enjoy risk so much that they feel empty in its absence. Jim Barksdale, now a venture capitalist for online startup companies and former CEO of Netscape, says that the fear of failure is what increases your heart rate. As great opportunists, charismatic people yearn to accomplish activities others have never done before. Risk taking adds to a person's charisma because others admire such courage. In addition to treasuring risk, charismatic leaders use *unconventional strategies* to achieve success. The charismatic leader inspires others by formulating unusual strategies to achieve important goals. Anita Roddick, the late founder of the worldwide chain of cosmetic stores called The Body Shop, accomplished her goals unconventionally: She traveled around the world into native villages, searching out natural beauty products that in the manufacturing process would not harm the environment or animals.

LEADERSHIP SELF-ASSESSMENT QUIZ 4-1

The Emotional Expressiveness Scale

Instructions: Indicate how well each of the following statements describes you by circling the best answer: very inaccurately (VI), inaccurately (I), neutral (N), accurately (A), very accurately (VA).

		VI	I	N	A	VA
1.	While watching a movie, I sometimes shout in laughter or approval.	1	2	3	4	5
2.	During a group meeting, I have occasionally shouted my approval with a statement such as "Yes" or "Fantastic."	1	2	3	4	5
3.	During a group meeting, I have occasionally expressed disapproval by shouting an expression such as "Absolutely not" or "Horrible."	1	2	3	4	5
4.	Several times, while attending a meeting, someone has said to me, "You look bored."	5	4	3	2	1
5.	Several times while attending a social gathering, someone has said to me, "You look bored."	5	4	3	2	1
6.	Many times at social gatherings or business meetings, people have asked me, "Are you falling asleep?"	5	4	3	2	1
7.	I thank people profusely when they do me a favor.	1	2	3	4	5
8.	It is not unusual for me to cry at an event such as a wedding, graduation ceremony, or engagement party.	1	2	3	4	5
9.	Reading about or watching news events, such as an airplane crash, brings tears to my eyes.	1	2	3	4	5
10.	When I was younger, I got into more than my share of physical fights or shouting matches.	1	2	3	4	5
11.	I dread having to express anger toward a coworker.	5	4	3	2	1
12.	I have cried among friends more than once.	1	2	3	4	5
13.	Other people have told me that I am affectionate.	1	2	3	4	5
14.	Other people have told me that I am cold and distant.	5	4	3	2	1
15.	I get so excited watching a sporting event that my voice is hoarse the next day.	1	2	3	4	5
16.	It is difficult for me to express love toward another person.	5	4	3	2	1
17.	Even when alone, I will sometimes shout in joy or anguish.	1	2	3	4	5
18.	Many people have complimented me on my smile.	1	2	3	4	5
19.	People who know me well can easily tell what I am feeling by the expression on my face.	1	2	3	4	5
20.	More than once, people have said to me, "I don't know how to read you."	5	4	3	2	1

QUIZ 4-1 (continued)

Scoring and Interpretation: Add the numbers you circled, and use the following as a guide to your level of emotionality with respect to being charismatic and dynamic.

- **90–100:** Your level of emotionality could be interfering with your charisma. Many others interpret your behavior as being out of control.

- **70–89:** Your level of emotionality is about right for a charismatic individual. You are emotionally expressive, yet your level of emotional expression is not so intense as to be bothersome.

- **20–69:** Your level of emotionality is probably too low to enhance your charisma. To become more charismatic and dynamic, you must work hard at expressing your feelings.

If you believe that emotional expressiveness is a trait and behavior out of your reach or inclination, direct your efforts toward developing other traits and behaviors associated with charisma. For example, you could work on developing vision and taking risks.

Charismatic leaders often have a *self-promoting personality*. They frequently toot their own horn and allow others to know how important they are. Richard Branson, the colorful chairman of the Virgin Group, has relied on self-promotion to build his empire, a collection of about 200 companies with the Virgin trademark. Among his antics have been flying around the world in a balloon and sliding down the side of a silver ball attached to a New York City building. He also conducts much of his business electronically from his private island in the Virgin Islands.

Another characteristic observed in many charismatic leaders is that they challenge, prod, and poke. They test your courage and your self-confidence by asking questions like "Do your employees really need you?" Donald Trump regularly asks his builders why they cannot construct a part of a building to look better, yet at lower cost.

A final strategy for becoming more charismatic is really an amalgam of the ideas already introduced: being *dramatic and unique* in significant, positive ways is a major contributor to charisma. This quality stems from a combination of factors, such as being energetic, promoting yourself, romanticizing risk, and being emotionally expressive. Leadership scholar Warren G. Bennis contends that great leaders, particularly those in public life, are great actors. The effective leader sells people on a vision to elevate their spirits.[19] Richard Branson, mentioned earlier, is one of the most dramatic and unique business executives in the world. He appears at concerts such as his wearing a T-shirt in support of singer Willie Nelson, as well as plunging into a variety of markets, including a commercial airline, mobile phones, soda, vodka, and space tourism.[20]

THE VISION COMPONENT OF CHARISMATIC LEADERSHIP

A major buzzword in leadership and management is **vision**, the ability to imagine different and better future conditions and ways to achieve them. A vision is a lofty, long-term goal. An effective leader is supposed to have a vision, whereas an ineffective leader either lacks a vision or has an unclear one. Being a visionary is far from an ordinary task, and recent research in neuroscience suggests that visionary leaders use their brain differently than others.

Studies conducted at Arizona State University by Pierre Balthazard required participants to think about the future. Brain activity was measured through EEG technology. A key finding was that levels of brain activity differed significantly between those participants considered visionaries and non-visionaries. Classifying a business, academic, or political leader as "visionary" was based on interview observations. Visionaries showed much higher levels of brain activity in the areas of the brain associated with visual processing and the organization of information. For example, visionaries showed higher activity in the occipital lobe, which is associated with visual processing and procedural memory.[21]

Many people use the terms *vision* and *mission* interchangeably, yet management theorists see them differently. According to organizational change specialist Peter M. Senge, a mission is a purpose, and reason for being, whereas a vision is a picture or image of the future we seek to create.[22] A mission of a company that rents private warehouse space to consumers and small business might be, "To extend the living and working space of responsible people." The same company's vision might be, "To create a more comfortable, less cramped world for the decades ahead."

Creating a vision is one of the major tasks of top management, yet quite often vision statements fail to inspire constituents. According to Jim Collins, a vision statement is likely to be more inspirational when it combines three elements:

1. A reason for being beyond making money
2. Timeless, unchanging core values
3. Ambitious but achievable goals

Mechanisms should then be established that set the values into action.[23] At Google, for example, engineers have "20 percent time," in which they are free to pursue projects about which they are passionate.[24] This policy supports the company vision of being a world-class innovator. A vision is also considered an important part of strategy implementation. Implementing the vision (or ensuring that the vision is executed) is part of the leader's role. This is true despite the opinion that the leader creates the vision and the manager implements it.

Vision statements typically relate to the entire organization, yet a leader or manager responsible for an organizational unit can have a vision about what he or she is attempting to accomplish. An example is Laura Ipsen, the senior vice president and general manager of Smart Grid Cisco. Her big idea (vision) is to create the 21st century energy ecosystem—and take a big piece of what is forecasted to be a $100 billion smart-grid market.[25]

Visions have become so popular that some companies have them reproduced on wallet-size plastic cards, key rings, and coffee mugs. It has been said than an effective vision fits on a T-shirt. Here are several sample vision statements:

Google: To make nearly all information accessible to everyone all the time.
Microsoft Corporation: To enable people throughout the word to realize their potential.

Alcoa Corporation: At Alcoa, our vision is to become the best company in the world—in the eyes of our customers, shareholders, communities and people. We expect and demand the best we have to offer by always keeping Alcoa's values top of mind.

Blackstone Group LP: To become the pre-eminent global lodging company in the world.

Estée Lauder Companies: Bringing the best to everyone we touch.

Kraft Foods: Helping People Around the World Eat and Live Better.

Although many vision statements appear as if they could be formulated in fifteen minutes, managers invest considerable time in their preparation and often use many sources of data. To create a vision, obtain as much information from as many of the following sources as necessary:[26]

- Your own intuition about developments in your field, the market you serve, demographic trends in your region, and the preferences of your constituents. Think through what are the top industry standards.
- The work of futurists (specialists in making predictions about the future) as it relates to your type of work.
- A group discussion of what it takes to delight the people your group serves. Analyze carefully what your customers and organization need the most.
- Annual reports, management books, and business magazines to uncover the type of vision statements formulated by others.
- Group members and friends; speak to them individually and collectively to learn of their hopes and dreams for the future.
- For a vision of the organizational unit, support the organization's vision. You might get some ideas for matching your unit's vision with that of the organization.

Leadership Skill-Building Exercise 4-1 gives you an opportunity to practice vision formulation. Keep in mind that a critic of vision statements once said that it is often difficult to tell the difference between a vision and a hallucination.

LEADERSHIP SKILL-BUILDING EXERCISE 4-1

Formulating a Vision

Along with your teammates, assume the role of the top management group of an organization or organizational unit that is in need of revitalization. Your revitalization task is to create a vision for the organization. Express the vision in not more than twenty-five words, using the guidelines for developing a vision described in the text. Come to an agreement quickly on the organization or large organizational unit that needs a vision. Or choose one of the following:

- The manufacturer of an electric-powered automobile
- A distributor of paid-for online music
- A waste disposal company
- A chain of home-improvement and hardware stores
- A manufacturer of watches retailing for a minimum of $25,000

THE COMMUNICATION STYLE OF CHARISMATIC LEADERS

Charismatic and transformational leaders typically communicate their visions, goals, and directives in a colorful, imaginative, and expressive manner. In addition, they communicate openly with group members and create a comfortable communication climate. To set agendas that represent the interests of their constituents, charismatic leaders regularly solicit constituents' viewpoints on critical issues. They encourage two-way communication with team members while still promoting a sense of confidence.[27] Here we describe three related aspects of the communication style of charismatic leaders: management by inspiration, management by storytelling, and communication via social networking.

Management by Inspiration

According to Jay A. Conger, the era of managing by dictate is being replaced by an era of managing by inspiration. An important way to inspire others is to articulate a highly emotional message. An example would be the CEO explaining to her top-management team, "If we continue doing what we are doing these days, we will be bankrupt within twelve months." Conger has observed two major rhetorical techniques of inspirational leaders: the use of metaphors and analogies, and the ability to gear language to different audiences.[28]

Using Metaphors and Analogies   A well-chosen analogy or metaphor appeals to the intellect, to the imagination, and to values. The charismatic Mary Kay Ash (now deceased), founder of the cosmetics company Mary Kay, Inc., made frequent use of metaphors during her career. To inspire her associates to higher performance, she often said: "You see, a bee shouldn't be able to fly; its body is too heavy for its wings. But the bumblebee doesn't know that and it flies very well." Mary Kay explained the message of the bumblebee metaphor in these terms: "Women come to us not knowing they can fly. Finally, with help and encouragement, they find their wings—and then they fly very well indeed."[29]

Gearing Language to Different Audiences   Metaphors and analogies are inspiring, but effective leaders must also choose the level of language that will suit their audience. This is important because constituents vary widely in verbal sophistication. One day, for example, a CEO might be attempting to inspire a group of Wall Street financial analysts, and the next day she or he might be attempting to inspire first-level employees to keep working hard despite limited salary increases.

An executive's ability to speak on a colloquial level helps create appeal. A person with the high status of an executive is expected to use an elevated language style. When the person unexpectedly uses the everyday language of an operative employee, it may create a special positive response. One of the many reasons Donald Trump is so popular with construction workers and tradespeople is that he often speaks to them in a tough-guy language familiar to them.

Management by Storytelling

Another significant aspect of the communication style of charismatic and transformational leaders is that they make extensive use of memorable stories to get messages across. **Management by storytelling** is the technique of inspiring and instructing team members by telling fascinating stories. The technique is a major contributor to building a strong company culture. Storytelling also helps bring out the need for organizational change. Stephen Denning, a former manager at the World Bank, explains how storytelling helped him persuade leaders at the bank to adopt knowledge sharing as a key strategy:

> In June 1995, a health worker in a tiny town in Zambia went to the Centers for Disease Control and Prevention website and got the answer to a question about malaria treatment. Zambia is one of the poorest countries in the world—and this town is 375 miles from the capital city. But the most striking element in this picture, at least for us, was that the World Bank wasn't in it, despite its know-how on poverty. Imagine if it were. Think what an organization it could become.

This simple story prompted World Bank staff and managers to envision a different future and ultimately become a world leader in knowledge management.[30] (We do not have direct evidence, but it appears that Denning is charismatic.)

Storytelling as a leadership tool has been elevated to such a level that some companies hire corporate storytelling consultants to help their executives develop the art. Storytelling is regarded as a useful tool for getting people to embrace change, because a well-crafted story captures people's attention.

To get started developing the skill of management by storytelling, do Leadership Skill-Building Exercise 4-2.

Extensive Use of Social Networking

To help facilitate their interpersonal communication, charismatic leaders make extensive use of social networks—both in face-to-face interactions and through social media websites. The members of the network are basically contacts with whom the leader has some kind of relationship. The vast majority of managers and professionals also rely on social networking, yet charismatic leaders are particularly aware of its relevance for accomplishing their purposes.

LEADERSHIP SKILL-BUILDING EXERCISE 4-2

Charismatic Leadership by Storytelling

Instructions: Gather in a small problem-solving group to develop an inspiring anecdote about something that actually happened, or might have happened, at a current or former employer. Search for a scenario that illustrates an important value of the firm. For example, the CEO of a large international bank while on vacation discovered a company ATM that was not working properly. He immediately went inside the bank branch to investigate the problem and what could be done about it.

Share your stories with other members of the class, and discuss whether this exercise could make a contribution to leadership development.

Face-to-Face Networks   Charismatic leaders are aware of the importance of face-to-face interactions for establishing effective relationships with constituents. A charismatic leader is therefore likely to invest time in such activities as the following: having lunch with group members, visiting group members at their offices or cubicles, chatting with subordinates in the parking lot or cafeteria, dropping by break rooms to chat for a few moments, and attending as many company social functions as feasible.

In recognition of the importance of internal networks for building relationships and accomplishing goals, some large firms establish formal networking groups. An example is the GE Women's Network, which has 40,000 active members worldwide. The focus of the GE Network on leadership, advancement, and career-broadening opportunities has helped the company get to the point where women run businesses generating 20 percent of total company revenues. Women outside GE are invited to some of the key networking events, which helps the GE women strengthen their external as well as internal networks. Also, the company outsiders are key customers who might develop ties with the GE women that lead to a better working relationship and more sales.[31]

Social Networking Sites   The charismatic leader goes beyond the ordinary use of public social networking sites (such as Facebook, Twitter, and LinkedIn), and company-special social media sites. The ordinary use of these websites would be to post status reports, present due dates, ask questions, and perhaps post trivial personal information. A more charismatic use of social networking sites would be to post messages designed to inspire, motivate, and make group members feel good about themselves and the organization. A few examples of messages that might project charisma are as follows:

- I liked the cost-saving suggestion you made in this morning's meeting. I think it will result in cost-effective savings.
- Congratulations on having attained your certification as a professional office administrator. Our company can use more professionalism like that.
- I am so sorry that Taboo, your 15-year-old-cat, passed away. Yet it's wonderful to know that you had all the love and friendship for so long. (A charismatic leader will often show empathy.)

Related to communicating by social networking sites is the practice of leaders sending charismatic messages on YouTube or Hulu. Because the use of these popular video sites is still relatively infrequent, it has a dramatic touch. James Schiro, chief executive of Zurich Financial Services, regularly posts videos of approximately one-and-one-half minutes on YouTube so they can be viewed by all employees. Schiro says the videos are long enough to "articulate the strategy, tell them where we are going, what I want them to do, and what I'm hearing, good and bad in the organization."[32]

Despite the positive use of social networking sites to project charisma, the leader has to guard against posting sensitive information, such as an idea for a new product or service, or legal problems the company might be facing.

The accompanying Leader in Action insert illustrates a charismatic leader who emphasizes communicating to a wide audience.

LEADER IN ACTION

Mellody Hobson's official job title is president of Ariel Capital Management, LLC, a large mutual fund company based in Chicago. Hobson's primary responsibility as president is to help manage the firm, including strategic planning. She joined the firm after graduating from Princeton University in 1991, with a Bachelor of Arts degree in international relations and public policy.

Hobson is much better known for her work as a good-will ambassador for the firm, and a thought leader in encouraging members of the African-American community to invest in mutual funds. Hobson has become a nationally recognized authority on financial literacy and financial education. She was quoted in a magazine as saying, "My dream is of seeing black grandmothers in their bathing suits at the beach, retired comfortably. My dream is that the beach is their option."

She is a regular financial contributor to *Good Morning America,* and she makes numerous speaking appearances. Hobson is extremely well connected professionally, with people in her network including prominent business people, politicians, actors, and sports figures.

Hobson invests considerable time and effort into building these connections because they enable her to move smoothly across industry, ethnic, racial, and class settings. Among the many well-known people in her network are John Rogers Jr., the founder of Ariel; Diane Sawyer of *Good Morning America*; William Lauder, CEO of Estée Lauder; and Barack Obama, U.S. president.

A key lesson Hobson attempted to convey to her followers during the financial crisis of 2008 was not to panic, but instead to take the long-term approach typical of contrarian investors. She told investors that important lessons could be learned from the book *Deep Survival* by Laurence Gonzales: "When you are fighting for your life, you must hold on to your plan with a gentle grip and be willing to let go." Equally important, "Rigid people are dangerous people." Ariel adopted the tortoise as its company logo, symbolizing the patient, slow approach to accumulating wealth. Hobson decorates her office extensively with tortoise pictures and figurines.

Part of Hobson's public persona is to dress in high fashion, including dangling jewelry and brightly colored high heels. She exudes a warm smile and an optimistic, happy appearance and maintains physical fitness.

QUESTIONS

1. What evidence is presented in this vignette that Hobson is charismatic?
2. What evidence do you see that Hobson has a vision?
3. In what way might Hobson's celebrity status create conflict with her managerial responsibilities at Ariel?

Source: This story was created based on facts included in Jennifer Reingold, "The Unsinkable Mellody Hobson," *Fortune,* October 27, 2008, pp. 148–157; Mellody Hobson, "I Will Survive," *Black Enterprise,* April 2009, p. 26; "Mellody Hobson: Business Star," *www.npr.org,* March 22, 2007; "Mellody Hobson," *Gale Contemporary Black Biography* (as reprinted in *Answers.com* (www.answers.com/topic/mellody-hobson), accessed February 28, 2011.

THE DEVELOPMENT OF CHARISMA

A person can increase charisma by developing some of the traits, characteristics, and behaviors of charismatic people. Several of the charismatic characteristics described earlier in the chapter are capable of development. For example, most people can enhance their communication skills, become more emotionally expressive, take more risks, and become more self-promoting. In this section we examine several behaviors of charismatic people that can be developed through practice and self-discipline.

Techniques for Developing Charisma

Create Visions for Others Being able to create visions for others will be a major factor in your being perceived as charismatic. A vision uplifts and attracts others. To form a vision, use the guidelines presented previously in the chapter. The visionary person looks beyond the immediate future to create an image of what the organization or unit within is capable of becoming. A vision is designed to close the discrepancy between current and ideal conditions. The vision thus sees beyond current realities.

Another characteristic of an effective vision formulated by the leader is that it connects with the goals and dreams of constituents.[33] For example, the leader of a group that is manufacturing fuel cells for electric cars might listen to team members talk about their desires to help reduce pollution in the atmosphere and then base the vision statement on a "desire to save the planet" or "reduce global warming."

Be Enthusiastic, Optimistic, and Energetic A major behavior pattern of charismatic people is their combination of enthusiasm, optimism, and high energy. Without a great amount of all three characteristics, a person is unlikely to be perceived as charismatic by many people. A remarkable quality of charismatic people is that they maintain high enthusiasm, optimism, and energy throughout their entire workday and beyond. Elevating your energy level takes considerable work, but here are a few feasible suggestions:

1. Get ample rest at night, and sneak in a fifteen-minute nap during the day when possible. If you have a dinner meeting where you want to shine, take a shower and nap before the meeting.
2. Exercise every day for at least ten minutes, including walking. No excuses are allowed, such as being too busy or too tired or the weather being a handicap.
3. Switch to a healthy, energy-enhancing diet.
4. Keep chopping away at your To Do list so you do not have unfinished tasks on your mind—they will drain your energy.

An action orientation helps you be enthusiastic, optimistic, and energetic. "Let's do it" is the battle cry of the charismatic person. An action orientation also means that the charismatic person prefers not to agonize over dozens of facts and nuances before making a decision.

Be Sensibly Persistent Closely related to the high energy level of charismatics is their almost-never-accept-no attitude. I emphasize the word *almost* because outstanding leaders and individual contributors also know when to cut their losses. If an idea or a product will not work, the sensible charismatic absorbs the loss and moves in another, more profitable direction.

Remember People's Names Charismatic leaders, as well as other successful people, can usually remember the names of people they have seen only a few times. (Sorry, no charisma credits for remembering the names of everyday work associates.) This ability is partly due to the strong personal interest charismatic leaders take in other people.

The surest way to remember names, therefore, is to really care about people. Failing that, the best way to remember a name is to listen carefully to the name, repeat it immediately, and study the person's face. You can also use the many systems and gimmicks available for remembering names, such as associating a person's name with a visual image. For example, if you meet a woman named Betsy Applewhite, you can visualize her with a white apple (or a white personal computer) on her head. The best system of name retention remains to listen carefully to the name, repeat it immediately, and study the person's face.

Develop Synchrony with Others   A subtle, yet defining, aspect of a truly charismatic person is one who connects well with others. Psychology professor Frank Bernieri studies physical signals that people send to each other, and concludes that being in synch physically with other people is part of charisma. If someone is in synchrony with you, you tend to think he or she is charismatic. A practical method of being in synch with another person is to adjust your posture to conform to his or her posture. The other person stands up straight, and so do you; when he or she slouches, you do also. Charismatic people make these postural adjustments almost subconsciously, or at least without giving the process much thought. Highly skilled charismatic people through the timing of their breaths, gestures, and cadence can entrap listeners into synchrony to the point that they "breathe and sway in tune with the speaker."[34]

Develop a Personal Brand, Including Making an Impressive Appearance   A recent trend in career advancement is to build a personal brand. Understanding your basket of strengths forms the basis for developing your **personal brand** (or the *brand called you*). Your identity as shown on the Internet, including social networking sites such as Facebook, is also part of your personal brand. Your personal brand makes you unique, thereby distinguishing you from the competition.[35] Perhaps your brand will not reach the recognition of Nike or Rolex, but it will help develop your reputation. Your personal brand also helps you attract people to accept your leadership.

Another component of your personal brand is your appearance. By creating a polished appearance, a person can make slight gains in projecting a charismatic image. A few people can make great gains by looking good. Ralph Lauren, one of the most successful fashion designers in U.S. history, is a leader who has enhanced his charisma through his impeccable physical appearance. Given that he is in the fashion business, a "Ralph Lauren–like" appearance is important for his personal image as well as to help build a brand image.

In most cases, however, the effect of appearance depends on the context. If exquisite clothing and good looks alone made a person a charismatic leader, those impressive-looking store associates in upscale department stores would all be charismatic leaders. Therefore, in attempting to enhance your charisma through appearance, it is necessary to analyze your work environment to assess what type of appearance is impressive. Ralph Lauren, with his exquisite suits, cuff links, and pocket handkerchief, would create a negative image at a Silicon Valley firm: His carefully cultivated appearance would detract from his charisma. (Of course, Lauren could enhance his charisma by wearing clothing from his sporty Polo line.)

Despite these caveats, there is much you can do to enhance your appearance. In recent years, there has been a surge of image consultants who help businesspeople develop an appearance that is useful in influencing people and getting hired. These consultants perform such services as helping you shop for a new wardrobe, suggesting a new hairstyle, or helping you revamp your slouching posture.[36]

Be Candid Charismatic people, especially effective leaders, are remarkably candid with people. Although not insensitive, the charismatic person is typically explicit in giving his or her assessment of a situation, whether the assessment is positive or negative. Charismatic people speak directly rather than indirectly, so that people know where they stand. Instead of asking a worker, "Are you terribly busy this afternoon?" the charismatic leader will ask, "I need your help this afternoon. Are you available?"

John Chambers of Cisco Systems exemplifies the candor of many charismatic leaders. Although he is intensely proud of his company, he admits to the public when he sees a slowing down of revenues in the near future.[37] Although investors might think that Chambers's candor could hurt the price of Cisco stock, his candor enhances his reputation as a CEO.

Display an In-Your-Face Attitude The preferred route to being perceived as charismatic is to be a positive, warm, and humanistic person. Yet some people, including business and sports figures, earn their reputation for charisma by being tough and nasty. An in-your-face attitude may bring you some devoted supporters, although it will also bring you many detractors. The tough attitude is attractive to people who themselves would like to be mean and aggressive.

TRANSFORMATIONAL LEADERSHIP

Transformational leadership focuses on what the leader accomplishes, yet it still pays attention to the leader's personal characteristics and his or her relationship with group members. As mentioned previously, the transformational leader helps bring about major, positive changes by moving group members beyond their self-interests and toward the good of the group, organization, or society. The essence of transformational leadership is developing and transforming people.[38] As a result, the organization is transformed. In contrast, the *transactional* leader focuses on more routine transactions, rewarding group members for meeting standards (contingent reinforcement). Extensive research by Bernard M. Bass indicates that the transformational-versus-transactional distinction has been observed in a wide variety of organizations and cultures.[39]

The accompanying Leadership Self-Assessment Quiz 4-2 shows how transformational leadership is measured as perceived by subordinates.

So, who is a transformational leader? One example from the labor-union sector is Andrew L. Stern, who stepped down in 2010 as president of the Service Employees International Union (SEIU). During his fourteen-year reign, SEIU became the most rapidly-growing labor union, doubling in size to 2.2 million members. The union grew primarily by organizing service workers

LEADERSHIP SELF-ASSESSMENT QUIZ 4-2

The Dual-Level Transformational Leadership (TFL) Scale

Directions: Check which of the following statements are true or relatively true in relation to a specific manager or supervisor you work for now or in the past.

The Individual-Focused TFL Subscale

1. Encourages me to set high goals for myself.   ☐
2. Communicates high performance expectations to me.   ☐
3. Shows confidence in my ability to meet performance expectations.   ☐
4. Demonstrates total confidence in me.   ☐
5. Encourages me to live up to my potential.   ☐
6. Helps me develop my strengths.   ☐
7. Suggests training to improve my ability to carry out the job.   ☐
8. Provides me with developmental experiences.   ☐
9. Provides feedback to help me develop my abilities.   ☐
10. Provides coaching to help me improve my job performance.   ☐
11. Gets me to look at problems from many different angles.   ☐
12. Challenges me to think about old problems in new ways.   ☐
13. Challenges me to be innovative in my approach to work assignments.   ☐
14. Encourages me to be an independent thinker.   ☐
15. Commends me when I achieve my goals.   ☐
16. Gives me positive feedback when I perform well.   ☐
17. Gives me special recognition when my work is very good.   ☐
18. Acknowledges improvement in my quality of work.   ☐

The Group-Focused TFL Subscale

1. Encourages team members to take pride in our team.   ☐
2. Says things that make us feel proud to be members of the team.   ☐
3. Says positive things about the team.   ☐
4. Encourages others to place the interests of the team ahead of their own interests.   ☐
5. Emphasizes the uniqueness of the team.   ☐
6. Articulates a compelling vision of the future of our team.   ☐
7. Talks optimistically about the future of our team.   ☐
8. Talks enthusiastically about what needs to be accomplished by our team.   ☐
9. Communicates a clear direction of where our team is going.   ☐
10. Fosters collaboration among team members.   ☐
11. Encourages group members to be team players.   ☐
12. Develops a team attitude and spirit among team members.   ☐
13. Gets the team to work together for the same goal.   ☐
14. Resolves friction among team members in the interest of teamwork.   ☐

Scoring and interpretation: The Transformational Leadership Scale is a research instrument that subordinates respond to in relation to their manager. The greater the number of statements that apply to the manager, the more he or she is a transformational leader.

Source: Adapted from Xiao-Hua (Frank) Wang and Jane M. Howell, "Exploring the Dual Effects of Transformational Leadership on Followers," *Journal of Applied Psychology*, November 2010, p. 1144.

not previously represented by a labor union. Harley Shaiken, a labor professor at the University of California at Berkeley, said about Stern, "He transformed a whole class of jobs—from janitors to home health-care workers to nursing home workers—into middle-class jobs by helping them unionize and negotiate contracts."

Stern stood out among fellow union officials because he was an Ivy League graduate rather than a person who had worked his way up from an entry-level job in a factory. Stern recognized early in his union career what other union leaders were denying—that the AFL-CIO's membership was decreasing and aging. Stern fought hard to organize service workers as a way of replacing the labor movement's diminishing ranks.[40]

How Transformations Take Place

Leaders often encounter the need to transform organizations from low performance to acceptable performance or from acceptable performance to high performance. At other times, a leader is expected to move a firm from a crisis mode to high ground. To accomplish these lofty purposes, the transformational leader attempts to overhaul the organizational culture or subculture. His or her task can be as immense as the process of organizational change. To focus our discussion specifically on the leader's role, we look at several ways in which transformations take place.[41] (See also Figure 4-1.)

1. Raising people's awareness. The transformational leader makes group members aware of the importance and values of certain rewards and how to achieve them. He or she might point to the pride workers would experience should the firm become number one in its field. At the same time, the leader should point to the financial rewards accompanying such success.

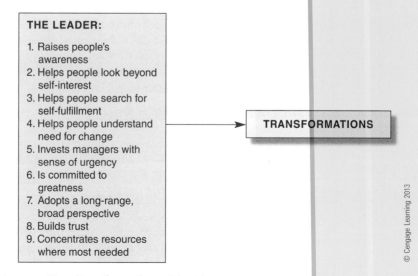

THE LEADER:

1. Raises people's awareness
2. Helps people look beyond self-interest
3. Helps people search for self-fulfillment
4. Helps people understand need for change
5. Invests managers with sense of urgency
6. Is committed to greatness
7. Adopts a long-range, broad perspective
8. Builds trust
9. Concentrates resources where most needed

TRANSFORMATIONS

© Cengage Learning 2013

FIGURE 4-1 How Transformations Take Place.

2. *Helping people look beyond self-interest.* The transformational leader helps group members look to the big picture for the sake of the team and the organization. The executive vice president of a bank told her staff members, "I know most of you dislike doing your own support work. Yet if we hire enough staff to make life more convenient for you, we'll be losing money. Then the government might force us to be taken over by a larger bank. Who knows how many management jobs would then have to be cut."

3. *Helping people search for self-fulfillment.* The transformational leader helps people go beyond a focus on minor satisfactions to a quest for self-fulfillment. The leader might explain, "I know that making sure you take every vacation day owed you is important. Yet if we get this proposal out on time, we might land a contract that will make us the envy of the industry." (Being the envy of the industry satisfies the need for self-fulfillment.)

4. *Helping people understand the need for change.* The transformational leader must help group members understand the need for change both emotionally and intellectually. The problem is that change involves dislocation and discomfort. An effective transformational leader recognizes this emotional component to resisting change and deals with it openly. Organizational change is much like a life transition. Endings must be successfully worked through before new beginnings are possible. People must become unhooked from their pasts.

Dealing with the emotional conflicts of large numbers of staffers is obviously an immense task. One approach taken by successful leaders is to conduct discussion groups in which managers and workers are free to discuss their feelings about the changes. This approach has been used quite effectively when firms are downsized. Many of the survivors feel guilty that they are still employed while many competent coworkers have lost their jobs. Clearly, conducting these sessions requires considerable listening skill on the manager's part.

Turnaround leader Greg Brenneman has led well-known consumer companies such as Continental Airlines, Burger King, and Quiznos. A key component of his turnaround strategy is to start spreading the word. At Quiznos each Friday, franchisees receive a voice mail, often from Brenneman, updating them on the business and pointing to needed changes.[42]

5. *Investing managers with a sense of urgency.* To create the transformation, the leader assembles a critical mass of managers and imbues in them the urgency of change. The managers must also share the top leader's vision of what is both necessary and achievable. To sell this vision of an improved organization, the transformational leader must capitalize on available opportunities.

6. *Committing to greatness.* Peter Koestenbaum argues that business can be an opportunity for individual and organizational greatness. By adopting this greatness attitude, leaders can ennoble human nature and strengthen societies. Greatness encompasses striving for business effectiveness such as profits and high stock value, as well as impeccable ethics. An emphasis on ethical leadership instills a desire for customer service and quality and fosters feelings of proprie-torship and involvement.[43] (A commitment to greatness is, of course, important for all leaders, not just those who are charismatic.)

7. *Adopting a long-range perspective and at the same time observing organi-zational issues from a broad rather than a narrow perspective.* Such think-ing on the part of the transformational leader encourages many group members to do likewise. Unless many people think with a future orientation, and broadly, an organization cannot be transformed.

8. *Building trust.* Another useful process for transforming a firm is to build trust between leaders and group members, particularly because distrust and suspicion are rampant during a company revival. Executive Carlos Ghosn found that building trust was an essential ingredient of his turnaround efforts at Nissan Motors in Japan. One component of building trust was to impose transparency on the entire organization. In this way everyone knew what every-one else was doing.[44]

9. *Concentrating resources on areas that need the most change.* The turn-around artist or transformational leader cannot take care of all problems at once in a troubled organization. A practical strategy is to get around limitations on funds, staff, or equipment by concentrating resources on problem areas that are most in need of change and have the biggest potential payoff. For example, when police chief Bill Bratton turned around the much-maligned New York Police Department in the mid-1990s, he concentrated resources on the narco-tics squad because so much crime is related to narcotics. During Brattons's ten-ure as the head of the NYPD, serious crime dropped by 33 percent and the murder rate decreased by 50 percent.[45]

Attributes of Transformational Leaders

Transformational leaders possess the personal characteristics of other effective leaders, especially charismatic leaders. In addition, a compilation of studies suggests that nine qualities are particularly helpful in enabling leaders to bring about transformations.[46] Our discussion of those nine qualities follows.

Above all, transformational leaders are *charismatic*. Two key personality fac-tors enhancing their charisma are agreeableness and extraversion, which com-bine to enhance their interpersonal relationships. Of these, extraversion had the biggest impact.[47] Included in the charisma of transformation leaders are their optimism and their openness to the viewpoints of others.

Unless they are the brutal slash-and-burn type of turnaround manager, trans-formational leaders have the respect, confidence, and loyalty of group mem-bers. One reason is that managers who use the transformational leadership style tend to score higher on *emotional intelligence*. A specific attribute here is that transformational leaders read emotions well.[48]

Charismatic, transformational leaders create a *vision*. By communicating a vision, they convey a set of values that guide and motivate employees. One such visionary is New York City Transportation Commissioner Janette Sadik-Kahn. Early on in her position she envisioned installing a 2.5-acre pedestrian plaza in Times Square, one of the most congested places in the United States. Sadik-Kahn commented, "This precolonial footpath has cut through the heart of New York's grid and created congestion for over 200 years." Her bold accomplishment attracted the attention of mayors and transportation officials around the world.[49]

Although transformational leaders are often greatly concerned with organizational survival, they also take the time to *encourage the personal development of their staff*. As group members develop, their performance is likely to increase. Transformational leaders also give *supportive leadership,* such as by giving positive feedback to group members and recognizing individual achievements. Supportive leadership also contributes to the development of group members.

Transformational leaders, like most effective leaders and managers, practice *empowerment* by involving team members in decision making. Empowerment is a key component of developing group members. *Innovative thinking,* another important characteristic, helps transformational leaders achieve their goals; for example, they might develop innovative ways to raise cash and cut costs quickly. Transformational leaders encourage their staff to think innovatively as well and give them challenging assignments. As with other effective leaders and managers, they also *lead by example*. During a period of cost-cutting, for example, a transformational leader might fly business coach and eat in the company cafeteria instead of having gourmet food catered to his or her office.

A study conducted with 132 managers and 407 subordinates indicated that managers who are perceived to be transformational score higher on a test of *moral reasoning* than do transactional leaders.[50] In contrast to the type of transformational leaders in the study just mentioned, those who specialize in rescuing failed corporations do not appear to score high in moral reasoning. Such actions include shutting down many company facilities, laying off much of the work force, and canceling contracts with various vendors.

Not every leader classified as transformational will have the nine characteristics just described. For example, some transformational leaders are brusque with people rather than agreeable. Furthermore, it is not always easy to determine whether a given leader can be accurately described as transformational. Sometimes situational forces contribute more heavily to the turnaround than do the leader's personal qualities. The director of an indoor-tennis club was complimented about how he transformed the club from one that was close to bankruptcy and short on membership. He replied, "It wasn't me. Two of our competitors closed down and we picked up a lot of their membership."

The Impact of Transformational and Charismatic Leadership on Performance and Behavior

Although the current discussion deals primarily with transformational leadership, it would be artificial to separate its impact on performance from that of charismatic leadership. An important reason is that charismatic leadership, as already discussed, is a component of transformational leadership. The general picture of the impact of transformational leadership is that, at its best, it can arouse followers to a higher level of thinking. Transformational leaders appeal to the ideals and values of their constituents, thereby enhancing commitment to a carefully crafted vision. Followers are inspired to develop new ways of thinking about problems. Group members become more responsible because they are inspired, and they engage in more constructive behavior such as organizational citizenship behavior—or helping out even without the promise of a reward.[51] Workers who report to transformational leaders are even more likely to have a positive mood throughout the workday.[52]

Here we look at several empirical studies about the effects of charismatic and transformational leadership in work settings. We review an overall analysis of the impact of transformational leadership and two specific studies. The studies summarized here are also useful in understanding how transformational leadership affects behavior.

Overall Validity of Transformational Leadership   Timothy A. Judge and Ronald F. Piccolo reviewed eighty-seven studies to examine the impact of transformational leadership on various measures of performance. The researchers also evaluated the impact of transactional leadership and laissez-faire leadership on performance. Laissez-faire leadership is a style that gives group members the freedom to do basically what they want with almost no direction. The three approaches to leadership were measured by questionnaires based on subordinates' perceptions.

Transformational leadership showed the highest overall relationships on six criteria: (a) follower job satisfaction, (b) follower leader satisfaction, (c) follower motivation, (d) leader job performance, (e) group or organization performance, and (f) rated leader effectiveness. Interestingly, transactional leadership was also shown to produce good results, and laissez-faire leadership was associated with negative results. Unlike previous studies, transactional leadership showed a strong positive relationship to transformational leadership. (Ordinarily, transformational leadership and transactional leadership are negatively related because transformational leaders are said not to engage in routine transactions with group members.) Transformational leadership was negatively related to laissez-faire leadership.[53] The explanation is most likely that transformational leaders are actively involved with group members.

Team Level Performance   Transformational and charismatic leadership also have positive effects on work teams. A study investigated the relationship between transformational leadership behavior and group performance in 218 financial service teams in U.S. and Hong Kong branches of a large bank. A branch supervisor being perceived as transformational indirectly improved team performance as measured by supervisory ratings of team effectiveness. Three examples of statements measuring transformational leadership were as follows: "Talks about the future in an enthusiastic, exciting way," "Will not settle for second best," and "Shows concern for me as a person."

The study demonstrated that transformational leadership, as perceived by team members, helped the team feel more *potent*. Team potency is the generalized beliefs of members about the capabilities of the team to perform well with a variety of tasks in different situations. Team potency, in turn, improved team performance.[54]

Organizational Level Performance   A group of researchers studied the impact of transformational CEOs on the performance of small firms and medium-size firms. A justification for studying less than large-size organizations is the large firms are so complex it can be difficult to measure the impact of the CEO's characteristics on company results. Transformational leadership was measured by a scale similar to the one presented in Leadership Assessment Quiz 4-2. Usable responses for the study were obtained from the CEOs of 158 firms and 431 of their top-management team members (who completed the transformational leadership survey about their CEO). The performance of the firm was measured in terms of sales growth and company performance as perceived by the CEO.

CEO transformational leadership was positively associated with both the objective and subjective measures of firm performance. The researchers concluded that their findings demonstrate the importance of transformational leadership at the firm level.[55] A study of this nature is much like a study demonstrating that physical exercise improves physical health: we know it to be true, but it is reassuring to have empirical evidence.

CONCERNS ABOUT CHARISMATIC LEADERSHIP

Up to this point, an optimistic picture has been painted of both the concept of charisma and charismatic leaders. For the sake of fairness and scientific integrity, contrary points of view must also be presented. The topic of charismatic leadership has been challenged from two major standpoints: the validity of the concept and the misdeeds of charismatic leaders.

Challenges to the Validity of Charismatic Leadership

Some leadership researchers doubt that charisma can be accurately defined or measured. Conducting research about charisma is akin to conducting research about high quality: You know it when you see it, but it is difficult to define in operational terms. Furthermore, even when one leader is deemed to be charismatic, that leader has many detractors. According to the concept of **leadership polarity**, leaders are often either revered or vastly unpopular. Martha Stewart is a prime example of a leader who experiences leadership polarity. Many of her fans are mesmerized by her personality and accomplishments. Many of her detractors detest her (perhaps based on envy) and were gleeful when Stewart was accused of insider trading and spent time in prison.

Another problem with the concept of charisma is that it may not be necessary for leadership effectiveness. Warren Bennis and Burt Nanus hypothesized that instead of charisma resulting in effective leadership, the reverse may be true: People who are outstanding leaders are granted charisma (perceived as charismatic) by their constituents as a result of their success.[56]

A study conducted with eighteen CEOs of major U.S. corporations and 770 top management team members supports the same idea. A major finding was that good organizational performance was associated with subsequent perceptions of the CEO being charismatic. In contrast, the perception that the CEO was charismatic was not associated with future performance of the firm.[57] The take-away lesson here is that if you are successful in attaining goals, it will enhance your charisma.

The Dark Side of Charismatic Leadership

Some people believe that charismatic leadership can be exercised for evil purposes. This argument was introduced previously in relation to personalized charismatic leaders. Forty-five years ago, Robert Tucker warned about the dark side of charisma, particularly with respect to political leaders:

> The magical message which mesmerizes the unthinking (and which can often be supplied by skilled phrase makers) promises that things will become not just better but perfect. Charismatic leaders are experts at promising Utopia. Since perfection is the end, often the most heinous actions can be tolerated as seemingly necessary means to that end.[58]

Some charismatic leaders are unethical and lead their organizations and outsiders toward illegal and immoral ends. People are willing to follow the charismatic leader down a quasi-legal path because of his or her personal magnetism. Perhaps the most widely publicized financial fraud in history was carried out by Bernard M. Madoff. Investors lost about $50 billion before approximately 10 percent of their money was recovered a few years later. Madoff, whose career included a term as the president of NASDAQ, a popular stock exchange, was well liked and considered by many to be warm and charismatic. His ability to defraud people depended somewhat on his ability to be well liked and entrusted.

Personality specialist Robert Hogan says that a potential problem with charismatic leaders is that some of them are narcissists (self-adoring to a fault). These leaders have the charisma attributes of being assertive, attractive, and powerful, but they often fail as leaders because they never admit mistakes. Charisma needs to be mixed with humility for full effectiveness.[59]

Boards of directors currently seek CEOs who do not overemphasize charisma and celebrity status at the expense of concentrating on running the business. In this way, the dark side of charisma can be minimized. Recognize that a true charismatic and transformational leader is highly concerned about human welfare and attaining outstanding organizational performance.

SUMMARY

Charisma is a special quality of leaders whose purposes, powers, and extraordinary determination differentiate them from others. It is also a positive and compelling quality of a person that makes many others want to be led by that person. An important element of charismatic leadership involves the attributions made by group members about the characteristics of leaders and the results they achieve. Social network members often influence a person's attributions of charisma. The relationship between group members and the leader is important because of these attributions. Charismatic leaders frequently manage their impressions to cultivate relationships with group members.

Much of the impact of charisma is based on the positive effect the charismatic leader triggers among group members. A study with firefighters showed that having a charismatic leader contributed to their happiness. In a top-level executive position, being perceived as not having enough charisma can lead to your downfall.

Charismatic leaders can be subdivided into five types: socialized, personalized (self-interested), officeholder, personal (outstanding characteristics), and divine. Charismatic leaders have characteristics that set them apart from noncharismatic leaders: they have a vision, masterful communication skills, the ability to inspire trust, and the ability to make group members feel capable. They are tactful; they have energy and an action orientation; they are emotionally expressive and warm; they romanticize risk; they use unconventional strategies; they have self-promoting personalities; and they emphasize being dramatic and unique.

The idea of vision is closely linked to charisma because charismatic leaders inspire others with an uplifting and attractive vision. Visionaries may have different levels of brain activities than non-visionaries in certain areas of the brain. A vision is more future-oriented than a mission. In formulating a vision, it is helpful to gather information from a variety of sources, including one's own intuition, futurists, and group members.

Charismatic and transformational leaders communicate their visions, goals, and directives in a colorful, imaginative, and expressive manner. Communication effectiveness allows for management by inspiration. One technique for inspiring others is to use metaphors, analogies, and organizational stories. Another is gearing language to different audiences. Charismatic and transformational leaders also extensively use memorable stories or anecdotes to get messages across. Social networking sites can be used to communicate the leader's charisma.

A person can increase his or her charisma by developing some of the traits, characteristics, and behaviors of charismatic people. The suggestions presented here include creating visions for others; being enthusiastic, optimistic, and energetic; being sensibly persistent; remembering people's names; developing a personal brand and making an impressive appearance; being candid; and displaying an in-your-face attitude.

To bring about change, the transformational leader attempts to overhaul the organizational culture or subculture. Specific change techniques include raising people's awareness of the importance of certain rewards and getting people to look beyond their self-interests for the sake of the team and the organization. Transformational leaders help people search for self-fulfillment and understand the need for change, and they invest managers with a sense of urgency. The transformational leader also commits to greatness, adopts a long-range perspective, builds trust, and concentrates resources where change is needed the most.

Transformational leaders have characteristics similar to those of other effective leaders. In addition, they are charismatic, extraverted, create a vision, encourage personal development of the staff, and give supportive leadership. Emphasis is also placed on empowerment, innovative thinking, and leading by example. Transformational leaders are likely to be strong on moral reasoning.

Transformational leadership can arouse followers to a higher level of thinking, and to engage in more constructive behavior. Transformational leadership is positively related to the criteria of follower job satisfaction, leader satisfaction, follower motivation, leader job performance, group or organization performance, and rated leader effectiveness. Transactional leadership attains the same results to a lesser degree, whereas laissez-faire leadership is negatively related to such criteria. Transformational and charismatic leadership also have positive effects on work teams. A study showed that being perceived as a transformational leader is related to the performance of small-size and medium-size firms.

One concern about charismatic and transformational leadership is that the concept is murky. Many noncharismatic leaders are effective. Another concern is that some charismatic leaders are unethical and devious, suggesting that being charismatic does not necessarily help the organization. A true charismatic and transformational leader is highly concerned about human welfare and attaining organizational goals.

KEY TERMS

charisma

socialized charismatic

personalized charismatic

transformational leader

vision

management by storytelling

personal brand

leadership polarity

✔ GUIDELINES FOR ACTION AND SKILL DEVELOPMENT

Following are suggestions to help a person act in a charismatic manner. All of them relate to well-accepted interpersonal skill techniques.

1. **Be sure to treat everyone you meet as the most important person you will meet that day.** For example, when at a company meeting, shake the hand of every person you meet.
2. **Multiply the effectiveness of your handshake.** Shake firmly without creating pain, and make enough eye contact to notice the color of the other person's eyes. When you take that much trouble, you project care and concern. Think a positive thought about the person whose hand you shake.
3. **Give sincere compliments.** Most people thrive on flattery, particularly when it is plausible. Attempt to compliment only those behaviors, thoughts, and attitudes you genuinely believe merit praise. At times you may have to dig to find something praiseworthy, but it will be a good investment of your time.
4. **Thank people frequently, especially your own group members.** Thanking others is still

so infrequently practiced that it gives you a charismatic edge.

5. **Smile frequently, even if you are not in a happy mood.** A warm smile seems to indicate a confident, caring person, which contributes to a perception of charisma. A smile generally says, "I like you. I trust you. I'm glad we're together."
6. **Maintain a childlike fascination for your world.** Express enthusiasm for and interest in the thoughts, actions, plans, dreams, and material objects of other people. Your enthusiasm directed toward others will engender enthusiasm in you.
7. **Be more animated than others.** People who are perceived to be more charismatic are simply more animated than others. They smile more frequently, speak faster, articulate better, and move their heads and bodies more often.[60]
8. **Think big.** If you want to become a charismatic and transformational leader, you must develop the capacity to spin beautiful, sweeping visions, and, in general, think big. It is so easy to

become preoccupied with small problems that face us daily, such as high prices at the gas pump or a smart-phone battery running low on power. Such problems require attention but can block visionary and charismatic thinking if they become preoccupying.

Discussion Questions and Activities

1. Identify a business, government, education, or sports leader whom you perceive to be charismatic. Explain the basis for your judgment.
2. Athletes and other celebrities who smile frequently and wave to the audience are often described as being charismatic. What is wrong or incomplete about this use of the term *charisma*?
3. Describe how a person might write e-mail messages to give an impression of being charismatic.
4. Explain why the presence of a charismatic leader tends to enhance the job satisfaction of group members.

5. A concern has been expressed that leaders who are charismatic are often incompetent. They simply get placed into key positions because they create such a good impression. What do you think of this argument?
6. To what extent do you think dressing expensively and fashionably really contributes to the charisma of a leader within an organization?
7. If a transformational leader is supposed to be so smart and visionary, why would he or she emphasize empowerment in his or her leadership approach?
8. Provide an example of an athletic coach who proved to be a transformational leader. Justify your opinion.
9. Do you think a true transformational leader should ever lay off thousands of workers to help make a company profitable?
10. What opportunities might a first-level supervisor or team leader have to be a transformational leader?

LEADERSHIP CASE PROBLEM A

Tim Puts His Charisma Online

Tim is the sales manager at a national auto parts supplier. Among the many accounts his company serves are small auto supply stores, service stations, repair shops, supermarkets, and small retailers. Tim has a staff of fifteen external sales representatives, as well as five internal sales specialists who deal with online and telephone sales.

The auto parts supply business is highly competitive, with most of the competition providing equally good parts and service. The personal touch therefore becomes quite important in gaining sales. Providing good service—such as refilling orders on frequently purchased parts and delivering on time—is essential. Tim also believes that inspiring the sales staff is vital in gaining a competitive edge. He notes, "If I inspire my sales reps, they will do a better job of building relationships with their customers. If I inspire the reps to sell more and better, they might inspire their customers to buy more parts and supplies from us."

Tim reasoned that his attempts to inspire and motivate the sales staff were working fairly well, but improvement was needed. When appropriate, he sees members of his staff in person, telephones them, and sends out frequent voice mails and texts messages. Yet Tim thought that he could do more: "I have been described as charismatic by my boss and several friends. Maybe I could get a bigger bang out of my charisma, if I made better use of the social media to inspire my staff."

Tim decided that for the next month he would post inspiring messages on the Facebook, Twitter, and LinkedIn pages of all the members of his sales staff, including the internal staff. Tim would also post the same messages on his own pages. Six of Tim's postings designed to project his charisma and inspire the staff were as follows:

- The only limits we have are those we impose on ourselves.

- If you are still breathing, maybe it's not such a bad day after all.
- I want to wake up the inner greatness in each and every one of you.
- If not you, who?
- Welcome every rejection. It means you are one step closer to a Yes.
- The harder you try, the luckier you get.

Tim received fewer responses than he anticipated, but a few sales representatives thanked him for the positive ideas.

Questions

1. How effective do you think Tim's posts are in terms of expressing his charisma?
2. How effective do you think Tim's posts are for purposes of inspiring the sales representatives to sell more auto parts and supplies?
3. What else do you recommend that Tim do to express his charisma via social networking websites?

LEADERSHIP CASE PROBLEM B

Time to Rebound at Willow Pond

Heather Osaka had worked ten years in the hospital administration field, at two hospitals, one HMO, and one nursing home. However, she had yet to hold a chief administrator position. One afternoon, she received a text message from Jake Wofford, a former classmate who was now in the executive recruiting business. "Maybe a great opportunity for you. Get back," said the message.

Osaka did get back to Wofford quickly. The opportunity to which he referred was a position as the director of Willow Pond, a medium-size assisted living home in the same city where Osaka now lived. "Assisted living" refers to helping older residents who are not quite able to care for themselves, yet do not require the level of care provided by a nursing home. Jake was frank in informing Heather that Willow Pond was troubled and that the previous director had been fired. Yet, the home still complied enough with state regulations to remain in operation.

The most recent problem at the home receiving publicity involved a man with a criminal record who walked into Willow Pond, sneaked into a resident's studio apartment, and sexually molested her. To gain entrance to the living area, the intruder donned a "Friends of Willow Pond" smock designated for volunteers. Wearing the smock facilitated his roaming the living area.

Before finally accepting the position, Heather spoke with the owners, who also operated several other homes for the elderly. She also consulted with a few of the supervisors and, with permission, interviewed four Willow Pond residents. The owners and Heather agreed that the following issues were among the most pressing:

- The residents and their families complain that the food is poor.
- Many of the residents are treated callously by the staff, and often told to "shut up" when they make a special demand, such as having a button sewn on, or ask for an off-menu item.
- The staff turnover is far higher than the industry average, with many young staffers just taking resident-care jobs as a last resort. Many of the people with experience in resident care who take a position at Willow Pond quickly leave for higher pay or for a more congenial atmosphere.
- Sanitation at the facility barely meets state requirements, and the building has a grungy, neglected appearance.
- Much of the equipment and furniture is old and shabby. Many of the TV sets produce blurry images.
- Willow Pond does not have high-speed Internet access for the residents, leaving those with computers in their rooms and apartments struggling to use the Internet.
- The physician and registered nurse service is not as reliable as at most assisted-care facilities.
- Willow Pond has shown a slight operating loss for three consecutive years.

The first day on the job, Heather thought to herself, "This looks like a job for Superwoman, or at least a great turnaround artist. So where do I begin making a difference?"

Questions

1. Why is this case included in a chapter about charismatic and transformational leadership?

2. What aspects of transformational leadership should Heather emphasize in her approach to rehabilitating Willow Pond?

3. How might emphasizing the charismatic aspects of her personality help Heather bring about the necessary changes?

4. Why might the job at Willow Pond prove to be a wonderful career opportunity for Heather Osaka?

ASSOCIATED ROLE PLAY

On the second day of her job Heather holds a staff meeting for the primary purpose of explaining to the staff that she will be working with them to make major changes in the operations of Willow Pond. She intends to mention some of the major changes will be needed as outlined in the case.

One student plays the role of Heather. Four other students play the role of supervisors attending the meeting. A couple of them are muttering to themselves, "Here's comes a new broom sweeping clean. We've heard about the need for changes before."

LEADERSHIP SKILL-BUILDING EXERCISE 4-3

My Leadership Portfolio

How much charisma, or how many charismatic behaviors, have you exhibited this week? Think back to all your interactions with people in this last week or two. What have you done that might have been interpreted as charismatic? Review the characteristics of a charismatic leader described in the text and in the Guidelines for Action and Skill Development. For example, did you smile warmly at someone, did you wave to a person you see infrequently and address him or her by name? Did you help your team, club, or group think seriously about its future? As part of this same exercise, record your charismatic behaviors for the upcoming week. Be alert to opportunities for displaying charisma.

LEADERSHIP SKILL-BUILDING EXERCISE 4-4

Exercise Related to Inspirational Messages on a Social Networking Site

The purpose of this exercise is to find a few inspiring messages on social media websites. For example, track down your followers on Twitter to see if you can find at least two inspirational messages such as those posted by Tim in the above case. Reflect on the effect these messages have on you. What impact do these messages have on your perception of the charisma of the sender? Compare your results to those of one or two other classmates.

▶❚❚ LEADERSHIP VIDEO CASE DISCUSSION QUESTIONS

To view the videos for this activity, you'll need access to the CourseMate that is available for this text. To get access, visit www.CengageBrain.com.

After watching "Leadership in Greensburg, KS," answer the following questions.

1. What is charisma? In your opinion, do Steve Hewitt, city administrator, and Lonnie McCollum, former mayor, possess charisma? Why or why not?

2. How does Steve Hewitt, city administrator of Greensburg, KS, utilize Halpert's dimensions of charisma?

3. What makes Steve Hewitt a transformational leader?

4. How does Steve make use of his self-promoting personality, which is a common element of charismatic leaders?

NOTES

1. This story is created from several facts in Jessica Pressler, "Private Equity CEO Lynn Tilton Whips Men, and Companies Into Shape, *Daily Intel* (http://nymag.com/daily/intel), January 11, 2011; Robert Frank, "Tilton Flaunts Her Style at Patriarch," *The Wall Street Journal*, January 8–9, 2011, pp. B1, B17; Forbes Staffers, "Femme Fatale: The Very Unconventional Story of Lynn Tilton," *Forbes*, May 9, 2011, p. 68; "Lynn Tilton, "CEO and Principal," *Patriarch Partners* (www.patriarch partners.com/our_team), January 11, 2011.

2. Jack and Suzy Welch, "It's Not about Empty Suits," *Businessweek*, October 16, 2006, p. 032.

3. Jay A. Conger and Rabindra N. Kanungo, *Charismatic Leadership in Organizations* (Thousand Oaks, Calif: Sage, 1998).

4. Comment by Hugh Hefner, founder and editor-in-chief of Playboy Enterprises, included in advertisement in *The Wall Street Journal*, December 13, 2007, p. C8.

5. Stephanie N. Mehta, "Why Him?" *Fortune*, November 23, 2009, pp. 89–90.

6. Daniel Lyons, "Digital Tools: Big Brother," *Forbes*, October 1, 2007, 51; Mehta, "Why Him?" p. 90.

7. Juan-Carlos Pastor, James R. Meindl, and Margarit C. Mayo, "A Network Effects Model of Charisma Attributions," *Academy of Management Journal*, April 2002, pp. 410–420.

8. Cited in Jay A. Conger, *The Charismatic Leader: Beyond the Mystique of Exceptional Leadership* (San Francisco: Jossey-Bass, 1989).

9. William L. Gardner and Bruce J. Avolio, "The Charismatic Relationship: A Dramaturgical Perspective," *Academy of Management Review*, January 1998, pp. 32–58.

10. Angelo Fanelli and Vilmos F. Misangyi, "Bringing Out Charisma: CEO Charisma and External Stakeholders," *Academy of Management Review*, October 2006, p. 1053.

11. Eugene Schmuckler, book review in *Personnel Psychology*, Winter 1989, p. 881.

12. Amir Erez, Vilmost Misangyi, Diane E, Johnson, Marcie A. LePine, and Kent C. Halverson, "Stirring the Hearts of Followers: Charismatic Leadership as the Transferal of Affect," *Journal of Applied Psychology*, May 2008, pp. 602–613.

13. Randall Smith and Ann Davis, "In Bloodletting on Street, Cruz Is Latest Casualty," *The Wall Street Journal*, November 30, 2007, p. C1.

14. Conger, Kanungo, and Associates, *Charismatic Leadership*; Bernard M. Bass with Ruth Bass, *The Bass Handbook of Leadership: Theory, Research, & Managerial Applications*, 4th ed. (New York: The Free Press, 1990), pp. 578–580.

15. Michael E. Brown and Linda K. Treviño, "Socialized Charismatic Leadership, Values Congruence, and Deviance in Work Groups," *Journal of Applied Psychology*, July 2006, pp. 954–962; Brown and Treviño, "Leader-Follower Values Congruence: Are Socialized Charismatics Better Able to Achieve It?" *Journal of Applied Psychology*, March 2009, pp. 478–490.

16. Jane M. Howell and Boas Shamir, "The Role of Followers in the Charismatic Leadership Process: Relationships and Their Consequences," *Academy of Management Review*, January 2005, p. 100.

17. Mark Greer, "The Science of Savoir Faire," *Monitor on Psychology*, January 2005, pp. 28–39; Jane M. Howell and Bruce Avolio, "The Ethics of Charismatic Leadership: Submission or Liberation?" *The Academy of Management Executive*, May 1992, pp. 43–52.

18. This quote and the preceding quote are from Stephen Barlas, "New Horizons for Growth at GE," *Hispanic Business*, January/February 2011, p. 25.

19. Warren Bennis, "Acting the Part of a Leader," *Businessweek*, September 19, 2009, p. 080.

20. Brad Stone, "Up in the Air: Will Richard Branson's Virgin America Fly?" *Bloomberg Business Week*, January 3-January 9, 2011, pp. 66–67.

21. Research reported in "This Is Your Brain on the Job," *The Wall Street Journal*, September 20, 2007, pp. B1, B6.

22. Cited in "Vision and Mission: Know the Difference," *Executive Leadership*, February 2006, p. 1.

23. Jim Collins, "Aligning Action and Values," Leader to Leader Institute, http://leadertoleader.org, as reported in "Actions: Louder Than Vision Statements," *Executive Leadership*, May 2004, p. 8.

24. Ed Frauenheim, "On the Clock but Off on Their Own Pet Project: Programs Set to Gain Wider Acceptance," *Workforce Management*, April 24, 2006, p. 40.

25. "Who's Next: Laura Ipsen: SVP and GM, Smart Grid Cisco," *Fast Company*, December 2010, January 2011, p. 39.

26. A couple of the ideas in the list are from "Nailing Down Your Vision: 8 Steps," *Executive Leadership*, September 2007, p. 2.

27. Howell and Avolio, "The Ethics of Charismatic Leadership," p. 46.

28. Jay A. Conger, "Inspiring Others: The Language of Leadership," *The Academy of Management Executive*, February 1991, p. 39.

29. Ibid.

30. Stephen Denning, "Stories in the Workplace," *HR Magazine*, September 2008, pp. 130–131.

31. Diane Brady and Jena McGregor, "What Works in Women's Networks," *Businessweek*, June 18, 2007, pp. 58–60.

32. Adam Bryant, "The C.E.O., Now Appearing on YouTube," *The New York Times* (www.nytimes.com), May 10, 2009.

33. Dennis A. Romig, *Side by Side Leadership: Achieving Outstanding Results Together* (Marietta, Ga.: Bard Press, 2001), p. 157.

34. Research cited in Greer, "The Science of Savoir Faire," p. 30.

35. Judy Martin, "Aligning Your Passion with Your Personal Brand," *San Francisco Examiner* (www.examiner.com), March 7, 2009.

36. Suzanne Hoppough, "Image Doctor," *Forbes*, February 26, 2007, p. 60.

37. Rolfe Winkler, "Cisco: The Too-Human Network," *The Wall Street Journal*, February 11, 2011, p. C8.

38. Marshall Sashkin and Molly G. Sashkin, *Leadership That Matters: The Critical Factors for Making a Difference in People's Lives and Organizations' Success* (San Francisco: Berrett-Kochler, 2003).

39. Bernard M. Bass, "Does the Transactional-Transformational Leadership Paradigm Transcend National Boundaries?" *American Psychologist*, February 1997, p. 130.

40. Holly Rosenkrantz, "What Andy Sterns Leaves Behind," *Bloomberg Business Week*, April 25, 2010, p. 23.

41. John J. Hater and Bernard M. Bass, "Superiors' Evaluations and Subordinates' Perceptions of Transformational and Transactional Leadership," *Journal of Applied Psychology*, November 1988, p. 65; Noel M. Tichy and Mary Anne Devanna, *The Transformational Leader* (New York: Wiley, 1990).

42. "Quiznos' Turnaround King," *Executive Leadership*, November 2008, p. 4.

43. Peter Koestenbaum, *Leadership: The Inner Side of Greatness* (San Francisco: Jossey-Bass, 1991).

44. Carlos Ghosn, "First Person: Saving the Business Without Losing the Company," *Harvard Business Review*, January 2002, p. 40.

45. W. Chan Kim and Renée Mauborgne, "Tipping Point Leadership," *Harvard Business Review*, April 2003, pp. 65–66; Susan Berfield. "Bill Bratton, Globocop," *Bloomberg Business Week*, April 12, 2010, p. 50.

46. Literature reviewed in Sally A. Carless, Alexander J. Wearing, and Leon Mann, "A Short Measure of Transformational Leadership," *Journal of Business and Psychology*, Spring 2000, pp. 389–405; Joyce E. Bono and Timothy A. Judge,

"Personality and Transformational and Transactional Leadership: A Meta-Analysis," *Journal of Applied Psychology*, October 2004, pp. 901–910; Taly Dvir, Dov Eden, Burce J. Avolio, and Boas Shamir, "Impact of Transformational Leadership on Follower Development and Performance: A Field Experiment," *Academy of Management Journal*, August 2002, pp. 735–744; Bass, *Bass's Handbook of Leadership*, pp. 633–636.

47. Timothy A. Judge and Joyce E. Bono, "Five-Factor Model of Personality and Transformational Leadership," *Journal of Applied Psychology*, October 2000, pp. 751–765; Bono and Judge, "Personality and Transformational and Transactional Leadership," pp. 901–910.

48. Robert S. Rubin, David C. Munz, and William H. Bommer, "Leading from Within: The Effects of Emotional Recognition and Personality on Transformational Leadership Behavior," *Academy of Management Journal*, October 2005, pp. 845–856.

49. Susan Adams, "Take Back the Streets," *Forbes*, October 5, 2009, pp. 34–36.

50. Nick Turner et al., "Transformational Leadership and Moral Reasoning," *Journal of Applied Psychology*, April 2002, pp. 304–311.

51. Ronald F. Piccolo and Jason A. Colquitt, "Transformational Leadership and Job Behaviors: The Mediating Role of Core Job Characteristics," *Academy of Management Journal*, April 2006, p. 327.

52. Joyce E. Bono, Hannah Jackson Foldes, Gregory Vinson, and John P. Muros, "Workplace Emotions: The Role of Supervision and Leadership," *Journal of Applied Psychology*, September 2007, pp. 1357–1367.

53. Timothy A. Judge and Ronald F. Piccolo, "Transformational and Transactional Leadership: A Meta-Analytic Test of Their Relative Validity," *Journal of Applied Psychology*, October 2004, pp. 755–768.

54. John Schaubroeck, Simon S. K. Lam, and Sandra E. Cha, "Embracing Transformational Leadership: Team Values and the Impact of Leader Behavior on Team Performance," *Journal of Applied Psychology*, July 2007, pp. 1020–1030.

55. Yan Ling, Zeki Simsek, Michael H. Lubatkin, and John Veiga, "The Impact of Transformational CEO on the Performance of Small- to Medium-Sized Firms: Does Organizational Context Matter?" *Journal of Applied Psychology*, July 2008, pp. 923–934.

56. Warren G. Bennis and Burt Nanus, *Leaders: Strategies for Taking Charge* (New York: Harper & Row, 1985), p. 223.

57. Bradley R. Agle, Nandu J. Nagarajan, Jeffrey A. Sonnefeld, and Dhinu Srinivasan, "Does CEO Charisma Matter? An Empirical Analysis of the Relationships Among Organizational Performance, Environmental Uncertainty, and Top Management Team Perceptions of CEO Charisma," *Academy of Management Journal*, February 2006, pp. 161–174.

58. Robert C. Tucker, "The Theory of Charismatic Leadership," *Daedalus*, Summer 1968, pp. 731–756.

59. Quoted in Greer, "The Science of Savoir Faire," p. 30.

60. The first six items on the list are from Roger Dawson, *Secrets of Power Persuasion: Everything You'll Need to Get Anything You'll Ever Want* (Upper Saddle River, N.J.: Prentice Hall, 1992), pp. 179–194; the seventh item is from James M. Kouzes and Barry Z. Posner, *The Leadership Challenge*, 3rd ed. (San Francisco: Jossey-Bass, 2002), p. 158.

The **Moral Aspects** of **Leadership**

LEARNING OBJECTIVES

After studying this chapter and doing the exercises, you should be able to

- Specify key principles of ethical and moral leadership.

- Apply a guide to ethical decision making.

- Present representative examples of unethical behavior by business leaders.

- Describe what leaders can do to foster an ethical and socially responsible organization.

- Explain the link between business ethics and organizational performance.

CHAPTER OUTLINE

Judy Chen, head of garment production at a clothing retailer for infants and children, was facing a dilemma caused by profit-margin squeezing pressures. Major increases in cotton and labor costs were making it much more expensive to produce garments without raising prices. Many other apparel company executives were upset by the increases in the cost of production because for a twenty-year period, production costs were stable or declining. The problem Chen and her counterparts in other companies faced was that budget-conscious consumers resisted higher prices.

Chen was familiar with the "deconstruction" approach several other apparel makers were taking to lower the price of producing a garment. The deconstruction approach involves some nipping and tucking to reduce the amount of fabric or buttons in a garment. In the manufacture of a pair of khaki pants that sold for about $34, the company could save about 50 cents per garment through such measures as eliminating cuffs, pleats, and coin pockets and replacing a metal hook and bar clasp with a button.

One day Chen was contemplating which cost-cutting steps to implement in order to save about $1 in the manufacture of two of the best-selling pants for children—"Khaki Prince" and "Khaki Princess." A deconstruction consultant suggested eliminating the coin pocket in the pants, reasoning that "What child or parent is going to notice the difference?" Chen thought about this particular cost savings of approximately 40 cents per garment, and she decided no. In her words, "First of all my own children, my nephews and nieces, and my neighbors' children love the small coin pockets. Just the other day, I found two little stones in the pocket, along with a small twig and a nickel. Then I did the public knowledge test, and I asked myself how I would feel if there were a Twitter post that said, 'Judy Chen saves company 40 cents per children's garment by eliminating coin pocket.' We'll find some other way to reduce manufacturing costs."[1]

In this chapter we examine leadership ethics and social responsibility from several major perspectives: principles of ethical and moral leadership, an ethical decision-making guide, examples of ethical violations, examples of how leaders develop an ethical and socially responsible culture, and the link between business ethics and organizational performance.

PRINCIPLES AND PRACTICES OF ETHICAL AND MORAL LEADERSHIP

Enough attention has been paid to what leaders at all levels *should* do that some principles of ethical and moral leadership have emerged. Because terms dealing with the ideal behavior of leaders are used so loosely, it is helpful to define what these terms have generally come to mean in the business community. **Ethics** is the study of moral obligations, or of separating right from wrong. *Ethics* can also be a plural noun meaning the accepted guidelines of behavior for groups or institutions.[2] In this sense it means much the same as **morals**, which are an individual's determination of what is right or wrong; morals are influenced by a person's values. Values are tied closely to ethics because ethics become the vehicle for converting values into action. A leader who values fairness will evaluate group members on the basis of their performance, not personal friendships. And a moral leader will practice good ethics.

Edwin H. Locke, the goal theorist, argues that ethics is at the center of leadership because the goal of a rational leader is to merge the interests of all parties so that everyone benefits and the organization prospers.[3] The ethics link is that if everyone benefits, all people are being treated ethically.

In this section, we present a sampling of ethical and moral behaviors, all centering on the idea that a leader should do the *right* thing, as perceived by a consensus of reasonable people. None of these terms can be pinned down with great precision. We also present a brief explanation of why the ethical and moral behavior of leaders differs so widely, and pay separate attention to the importance of an ethical mind. Before studying these principles, do Leadership Self-Assessment Quiz 5-1 to think through your work-related ethics and morality.

LEADERSHIP SELF-ASSESSMENT QUIZ 5-1

The Leadership Ethics Quiz

Directions: Circle the numbers to indicate how well each statement describes your current attitudes and behavior or how you would behave if placed in the situation suggested by the statement. Response choices: 1 = disagree strongly; 2 = disagree; 3 = agree somewhat; 4 = agree strongly.

1. A small bribe to make a sale is entirely reasonable.	1	2	3	4
2. As the manager, I would have no problem in taking credit for an innovative idea of a subordinate.	1	2	3	4
3. Supplying a customer with a prostitute to help win a big contract is justified.	1	2	3	4
4. I would be willing to use a video surveillance camera to see what my subordinates are doing when I am out of the office.	1	2	3	4
5. Cheating on your expense account up to about 10 percent of the total expenses is usually justifiable.	1	2	3	4
6. Honest guys and gals tend to finish last.	1	2	3	4
7. If I were fired, I would be willing to get revenge on my employer by taking away trade secrets.	1	2	3	4
8. I would avoid hiring someone into the work group who might become a competitor for my position.	1	2	3	4
9. Overcharging a government customer for goods or services is justified because most companies already pay too much in taxes.	1	2	3	4
10. All things being equal, I would give higher performance evaluations to people of my own ethnic group or race.	1	2	3	4
11. I deliberately give lower performance evaluations to subordinates who I dislike personally.	1	2	3	4
12. I typically play favorites within the group or team.	1	2	3	4
13. I am willing to fake productivity figures just to look good to upper management.	1	2	3	4

QUIZ 5-1 (continued)

14. I would not take time from writing an important report to coach a group member who needed help at the moment.	1	2	3	4
15. I exaggerate the mistakes a subordinate might make just so he or she does not become too self-confident.	1	2	3	4
16. I look for ways to get revenge on any group member who makes me look bad.	1	2	3	4
17. I rarely praise an employee without also finding a way to criticize something he or she has done.	1	2	3	4
18. If a subordinate wants me to do something I do not want to do, I blame upper management for not letting me do it.	1	2	3	4
19. I think it is justified to ask group members to run errands for me, such as getting my car repaired or shopping for me.	1	2	3	4
20. I will ignore an employee's request to help him or her with a problem just so I can spend some personal time on the Internet.	1	2	3	4

Scoring and interpretation: Add up your responses to the 20 statements. Recognize that people tend to perceive themselves as more ethical and honest than they really are, so your score could be positively biased.

- **20–25:** If you scored in this range, your self-image is that of a highly ethical and trustworthy leader or potential leader. Assuming that your answers are accurate, your ethics could be an asset to you as a leader.

- **26–45:** Scores in this range suggest the self-image of a leader or potential leader with an average level of ethics. There are probably times when you could behave more ethically.

- **46–80:** Scores in this range suggest the self-image of a highly unethical leader or potential leader. If your score is an accurate reflection of your behavior, you are (or would be) perceived as highly unethical and devious to the point that it could damage your career. You should study ethics seriously.

Four Ethical Leadership Behaviors

Be Honest and Trustworthy and Have Integrity in Dealing with Others   Reports of frauds and scandals in recent years have placed ethical behavior high on the priority list of many organizations. The problem is that ethical problems erode the trust of both leaders and organizations.[4] Despite the importance of leaders who are trustworthy, evidence suggests that trust in business leaders is now low. As part of an ongoing study of employee attitudes and opinions, the Ethics Resource Center surveyed 2,852 across a variety of industries. Among the unethical behaviors observed were as follows: lying to employees (19%), engaging in conflicts of interest (16%), lying to outside stakeholders (12%), and engaging in health and safety violations (11%).[5]

An ethical leader is honest and trustworthy and therefore has integrity. According to ethics researcher Thomas E. Becker, this quality goes beyond honesty and conscientiousness. **Integrity** refers to loyalty to rational principles;

it means practicing what one preaches regardless of emotional or social pressure.[6] For example, a leader with integrity would believe that employees should be treated fairly, and the pressure to cut costs would not prompt him or her to renege on a commitment to reimburse an employee for relocation expenses. As another example, a leader who preaches cultural diversity would assemble a diverse team.

Pay Attention to All Stakeholders   Ethical and moral leaders strive to treat fairly all interested parties affected by their decisions. To do otherwise creates winners and losers after many decisions are made. The widely held belief that a CEO's primary responsibility is to maximize shareholder wealth conflicts with the principle of paying attention to all stakeholders. A team of management scholars observes, "We used to recognize corporations as both economic and social institutions—as organizations that were designed to serve a balanced set of stakeholders, not just the narrow interests of the shareholder."[7] A leader interested in maximizing shareholder wealth might attempt to cut costs and increase profits in such ways as (1) laying off valuable employees to reduce payroll costs, (2) overstating profits to impress investors, (3) overcharging customers, and (4) reducing health benefits for retirees. Although these practices may be standard, they all violate the rights of stakeholders.

Jim Goodnight, the CEO of software company SAS, is among the business leaders who contend that there is a strong link between employee satisfaction and increased productivity and profits. He explains, "Because we put employee-oriented measures in place long ago, we have the benefit of years of experience to show that the long-term benefits far outweigh the short-term costs. Most companies don't know how to represent that kind of return in their annual reports."[8]

Another behavior of *authentic leaders* is to perceive their role to include having an ethical responsibility to all of their shareholders. The welfare of others takes precedence over their own personal welfare (as in servant leadership). Authentic leaders have a deep commitment to their personal growth as well as to the growth of other stakeholders.[9]

Build Community   A corollary of taking into account the needs of all stakeholders is that the leader helps people achieve a common goal. Leadership researcher Peter G. Northouse explains that leaders need to take into account their own and their followers' purposes and search for goals that are compatible to all.[10] When many people work toward the same constructive goal, they build community. A business leader who works with many people to help poor schoolchildren is an ideal example of someone who builds community.

The Global Compact, an initiative of the United Nations to ensure that business practices conform to human rights, labor, and environmental standards, seeks to build community on an international scale. The common goal is equitable treatment of workers. More than 8,700 corporate participants and other stakeholders from over 130 countries have joined. The pact has become the world's largest voluntary corporate citizenship group. Among the goals of the Global Compact is to get companies to make explicit statements about human rights in their policies.[11]

Respect the Individual Respecting individuals is a principle of ethical and moral leadership that incorporates other aspects of morality. If you tell the truth, you respect others well enough to be honest. If you keep promises, you also show respect. And if you treat others fairly, you show respect.[12] Showing respect for the individual also means that you recognize that everybody has some inner worth and should be treated with courtesy and kindness. An office supervisor demonstrated respect in front of his department when he asked a custodian who entered the office, "What can we do in this department to make your job easier?"

Factors Contributing to Ethical Differences

There are many reasons for differences in ethics and morality among leaders. One is the leader's *level of greed, gluttony, and avarice*. Many people seek to maximize personal returns, even at the expense of others. Former Federal Reserve chairman Alan Greenspan commented publicly on the problem of executive greed. He said that an infectious greed had contaminated the business community in the late 1990s, as one executive after another manipulated earnings or resorted to fraudulent accounting to capitalize on soaring stock prices.[13] The devastating stock market downturn in 2008 appeared to have a few similar causes. Table 5-1 presents a sampling of executive compensation that could be interpreted as signs of greed and avarice. Instead of taking so much money for themselves, how about sharing more of the money with employees and stockholders, and offering lower prices for customers? The counterargument is that supply and demand rules, with a limited supply of capable CEOs. So you have to pay talented executives loads of money to stay competitive, even if the compensation exceeds $100 million per year.

Timothy P. Flynn, chairman of the global accounting firm KPGM, has identified reasons why good people choose the wrong path. One reason is rationalization, which leads people to focus on the intent of the action rather than on the action itself. For example, people might say that they are doing something wrong (such as exaggerating profits) in order to help a client or that they are boosting the stock price to help investors. Another reason is implied permission—"Nobody is telling me to stop, so it must be OK."[14] For example,

TABLE 5-1 A Sampling of Extraordinary Compensation for Business Executives

EXECUTIVE AND COMPANY	RECENT ANNUAL SALARY, BONUS, AND STOCK OPTIONS
Lawrence Culp Jr., Dahaner Corp.	$141,000,000
Lawrence J. Ellison, Oracle Corp.	$114,000,000
Aubrey K. McClendon, Chesapeake Energy	$114,000,000
Ray R. Irani, Occidental Petroleum	$103,000,000
David C. Novak, Yum Brands	$ 76,000,000
Lawrence Ellison, Oracle	$ 68,600,000

Source: Table constructed from data presented in Scott DeCarlo, "What the Boss Makes," *Forbes.com*, April 28. 2010; Joann S. Lublin, "CEO Pay in 2010 Jumped 11%," *The Wall Street Journal*, May 9, 2011, p. B1.

managers might continue to place only personal friends and relatives in key jobs because they were not told to stop.

A fourth key contributor to a leader's ethics and morality is his or her *level of moral development*. Some leaders are morally advanced, whereas others are morally challenged—a mental condition that often develops early in life. People progress through three developmental levels in their moral reasoning. At the *preconventional level*, a person is concerned primarily with receiving external rewards and avoiding punishment. A leader at this level of development might falsify earnings statements for the primary purpose of gaining a large bonus. At the *conventional level*, people learn to conform to the expectations of good behavior as defined by key people in their environment and societal norms. A leader at this level might be moral enough just to look good, such as being fair with salary increases and encouraging contributions to the United Way campaign. At the *post-conventional level*, people are guided by an internalized set of universal principles that may even transcend the laws of a particular society. A leader at the post-conventional level of moral behavior would be concerned with doing the most good for the most people, without regard for whether such behavior brought him or her recognition and fortune.[15] The servant leader described later in Chapter 8 would be at this advanced level of moral development.

A fifth factor contributing to the moral excesses of business leaders is that many of them have developed a sense of **entitlement**. In the opinion of several psychiatrists and corporate governance experts, some CEOs lose their sense of reality and feel entitled to whatever they can get away with or steal. For example, Conrad Black, the CEO of Hollinger International, Inc., felt entitled to have the company pay for his personal servants. Also, many executives feel entitled to extraordinary compensation.[16] The average CEO pay at major corporations is currently 263 times higher than the lowest-paid employees.[17]

A sixth factor contributing to unethical and immoral leadership behavior is the *situation*, particularly the organizational culture. If leaders at the top of the organization take imprudent, quasi-legal risks, other leaders throughout the firm might be prompted to behave similarly. The imprudent risks in subprime mortgages taken with investor money by investment banks in recent years might also reflect an aggressive culture. Financial executives were pushed to maximize profits, sometimes not taking into account investor welfare.[18]

A person's character is a seventh factor that contributes to ethical differences. The higher the quality of a person's character, the more likely he or she will behave ethically and morally. For example, a leader who is honest and cooperative will tend to behave more ethically than a leader who is dishonest and uncooperative. Leadership Self-Assessment Quiz 5-2 digs into the behavioral specifics of good character as perceived by the U.S. Air Force.

A final factor to be considered here that contributes to unethical leadership behavior is *motivated blindness*, or seeing what we want to see and missing contradictory information. The result can be a conflict of interest, such as a compensation consultant being paid by the CEO to make recommendations about her financial compensation. Although the consultant is attempting to be honest, the desire to please the CEO leads him to recommend a pay package so generous that the CEO becomes overpaid. Another example of motivated

LEADERSHIP SELF-ASSESSMENT QUIZ 5-2

The Air Force Character Attributes Checklist

Instructions: Listed and defined next are character attributes the U.S. Air Force wants to see among the ranks of its leaders. For each attribute, note your standing as being high (H), average (A), or low (L). A checklist of this nature lends itself to self-serving bias, so work extra hard to be objective. When applicable, visualize an example of how you have exhibited, or have not exhibited, a particular character attribute.

FACTOR	DESCRIPTION	MY STANDING H	A	L
Integrity	Consistently adhering to a moral or ethical code or standard. A person who consistently chooses to do the right thing when faced with alternative choices.	☐	☐	☐
Honesty	Consistently being truthful with others.	☐	☐	☐
Loyalty	Being devoted and committed to one's organization, supervisors, coworkers, and subordinates.	☐	☐	☐
Selflessness	Genuine concern about the welfare of others and a willingness to sacrifice one's personal interests for others and the organization.	☐	☐	☐
Compassion	Concern for the suffering or welfare of others and providing aid or showing mercy for others.	☐	☐	☐
Competency	Capable of excelling at all tasks assigned. Is effective and efficient.	☐	☐	☐
Respectfulness	Shows esteem for and consideration and appreciation of other people.	☐	☐	☐
Fairness	Treats everyone in an equitable, impartial, and just manner.	☐	☐	☐
Responsibility and self-discipline	Can be depended on to make rational and logical decisions and to do tasks assigned. Can perform tasks assigned without supervision.	☐	☐	☐
Decisiveness	Capable of making logical and effective decisions in a timely manner. Makes good decisions promptly after considering data appropriate to the decision.	☐	☐	☐
Spiritual appreciation	Values the spiritual diversity among individuals with different backgrounds and cultures and respects all individuals' rights to differ from others in their beliefs.	☐	☐	☐
Cooperativeness	Willing to work or act together with others in accomplishing a task toward a common end or purpose.	☐	☐	☐

Interpretation: The more of the attributes you rated as *high*, the more likely it is that others perceive you as having good character. The list may provide some clues to leadership development. For example, if you are perceived to be low on integrity and cooperativeness, you are less likely to be able to influence others.

Note: Although competency and decisiveness are not ordinarily considered character traits, being competent and decisive contributes to having good character.

Source: U.S. Air Force, as reprinted in Cassie B. Barlow, Mark Jordan, and William H. Hendrix, "Character Assessment: An Examination of Leadership Levels," *Journal of Business and Psychology,* Summer 2003, 568.

blindness is that a manager who hires an individual may not notice the new hire's unethical behavior because the behavior would reflect an error in selecting the new hire.[19]

The Ethical Mind for Leaders

Cognitive and educational psychologist Howard Gardner believes that for a leader to stay ethical, he or she must develop an **ethical mind**, or a point of view that helps the individual aspire to good work that matters to their colleagues, companies, and society in general.[20] Developing an ethical mind begins with the belief that retaining an ethical compass is essential to the health of the organization. Early life influences, such as encouragement not to cheat on exams or plagiarize when writing papers, are a good start. Next, the leader must state his or her ethical beliefs and stick to them. (The ethical beliefs already mentioned in this chapter are relevant, such as being convinced that attention must be paid to all stakeholders.) The leader must also make a rigorous self-test to make sure values are being adhered to, such as checking to see if merit instead of favoritism is a key criterion for promotion. Taking the time to reflect on beliefs can help the leader stay focused on ethical behavior. Asking mentors to comment on the ethics of your behavior can be a useful reality check. Finally, to stay ethical, the leader should act quickly on strongly unethical behavior of others, such as confronting a colleague who is using the corporate jet for a family vacation.

So which leader has an ethical mind? You will probably find many of them as hard-working middle managers. A famous business leader with an ethical mind might be Warren Buffett, the investment sage. He has consistently been one of the world's richest people, yet he maintains high ethical standards for himself and his investment firm, Berkshire Hathaway. Buffett sends memos regularly to the companies owned by his firm, advising them to stay ethical. And he is widely quoted for stating that the rationale "everyone else is doing it" is not acceptable.[21]

GUIDELINES FOR EVALUATING THE ETHICS OF A DECISION

Several guidelines, or ethical screens, have been developed to help leaders or other influence agents decide whether a given act is ethical or unethical. The Center for Business Ethics at Bentley College has developed six questions to evaluate the ethics of a specific decision:[22]

- *Is it right?* This question is based on the deontological theory of ethics that states there are certainly universally accepted guiding principles of rightness and wrongness, such as "thou shalt not steal."
- *Is it fair?* This question is based on the deontological theory of justice that certain actions are inherently just or unjust. For example, it is unjust to fire a high-performing employee to make room for a less competent person who is a relative by marriage.
- *Who gets hurt?* This question is based on the utilitarian notion of attempting to do the greatest good for the greatest number of people.

- *Would you be comfortable if the details of your decision or actions were made public in the media or through email?* This question is based on the universalist principle of disclosure.
- *What would you tell your child, sibling, or young relative to do?* This question is based on the deontological principle of reversibility, which evaluates the ethics of a decision by reversing the decision maker.
- *How does it smell?* This question is based on a person's intuition and common sense. For example, counting a product inquiry over the Internet as a sale would smell bad to a sensible person.

Ethical issues that require a run through the guide are usually subtle rather than blatant, or a decision that falls into the gray zone. An example is the financial transactions of a small group of traders at the investment bank Goldman Sachs Group, Inc., during the subprime mortgage crisis. The group's gamble was that securities backed by risky home loans would fall in value generated nearly $4 billion in profits in a year. (This practice is referred to as *selling short*.) At the same time, subprime mortgages were being generated at a rapid pace and being sold to Goldman Sachs clients. So, the firm was making loads of money by hoping that investments sold to their own clients would lose value rapidly. The ethical question asked is why Goldman continued to sell collateral debt obligations to customers while its own traders were betting that the value of these investments would fall?[23] Also, should Goldman brokers have told clients that the smart money believed that they were being sold investments destined to decline in value rapidly? How would you like to purchase a house from a real estate broker who was making side bets that houses in the area were going to drop in value?

Leaders regularly face the necessity of running a contemplated decision through an ethics test. Leadership Skill-Building Exercise 5-1 provides an opportunity to think through the ethics of a decision facing an enterprise software and services firm.

LEADERSHIP SKILL-BUILDING EXERCISE 5-1

How Important Is This Contract?

A company that develops enterprise software and information technology services has been working diligently to close a sale to a government agency located near the Persian Gulf. The deal should bring in about $2 million for the first two years, with about $500,000 in service contracts for the following years. Business has not been good the last couple of years, and new revenue is badly needed. The sales representative working in the Persian Gulf region telephones one morning with an important message. She says that the government agency is ready to sign and to make a first payment of $1 million within the next few days. The representative then explains a pre-condition for the sale: "I am supposed to bring the agency head an athletic bag stuffed with $100,000 in U.S. dollars. He wants the money in different denominations including bills of $100, $50, and $20. The agency head claims the money will be used to provide shelter and food for homeless children."

Company leaders need to make a quick decision about whether to grant the precondition for the contract. Work in a small group to take their contemplated decision through the guidelines for evaluating the ethics of a decision. Be sure to make a decision!

A SAMPLING OF UNETHICAL LEADERSHIP BEHAVIORS

Earlier in this chapter, we have alluded to unethical behavior. Here we present a sampling of unethical behaviors from the past and present. A statement often made is that about 95 percent of business leaders are ethical and that the 5 percent of bad apples (mostly senior executives) get all the publicity. However, the impact of unethical leadership has been enormous. Unethical behavior has thrown companies into bankruptcy, led to the layoffs of thousands of workers, diminished trust in stock investments, and discouraged many talented young people from embarking on a business career.

Table 5-2 presents some unethical, immoral, and often illegal behaviors engaged in by business leaders whose acts have been publicly reported. Thousands of other unethical acts go unreported, such as a business owner who places a family member, friend, or lover on the payroll at an inflated salary for work of limited value to the firm.

TABLE 5-2 Examples of Unethical Behavior by Business Leaders

The sampling of behaviors presented here includes behaviors that resulted in criminal prosecutions, and those that result in only embarrassment and negative press.

LEADER AND COMPANY	OFFENSE AND OUTCOME
Bernard L. Madoff, former CEO of Bernard L. Madoff Investment Securities and also former chairman of Nasdaq (the stock exchange)	Convicted of defrauding investors out of about $50 billion over a period of years. Basically sold investors phantom investments, pocketed most of the money, and made some payments to new investors from money paid by earlier investors. Had worldwide network of brokers and other contacts sending him referrals. Sent to prison for 150 years for crimes including securities fraud, international money laundering, mail fraud, and wire fraud. At time of conviction, said he was sorry.
Angelo R. Mozilo, former CEO of Countrywide Financial (now a unit of Bank of America)	As CEO played major role in issuing mortgages to high-risk customers, then sold securities based on these mortgages, touting them as high-rated safe securities. Accused of knowing that many borrowers could not pay back their loans. Paid $67.5 million in penalties to settle civil fraud and insider-trading charges, but was not prosecuted. Later included as defendant in lawsuit by Allstate Corp., claiming that lax underwriting standards led to collapse of residential mortgage-based securities.
Martha Stewart, chairwoman and CEO of Martha Stewart Living Omnimedia	Charged with conspiracy and obstruction of justice and intentionally making false statements in connection with sale of ImClone stock. Convicted in 2004, and spent five months in prison and five months of house arrest including wearing an electronic ankle bracelet. Stewart returned to her company and television show after serving her sentence. Said that time in prison was well spent because of the friendships she developed, as well as chance for reflection.

(continued)

TABLE 5-2 continued

LEADER AND COMPANY	OFFENSE AND OUTCOME
Patricia Dunn, non-executive chairman of Hewlett-Packard	Spied on other board members to uncover who leaked sensitive information to the press. Nine reporters covering HP were also spied on. Spies were paid more than $325,000 to pose as journalists and board members (referred to as *pretexting*) to obtain phone records, and also used fake e-mail addresses and installed spyware on a board member's computer. Dunn resigned her post at HP. In 2007, the State of California dropped the criminal charges.
Paul Shinn Devine, Global Supply Manager at Apple Inc.	Accused in 2010 by a federal grand jury indictment of receiving more than $1 million in kickbacks from Apple suppliers in Asia. Devine was charged with offenses including wire fraud, money laundering, and unlawful monetary transactions. Apple also named Devine in a civil suit, with the company saying that it has zero tolerance for dishonest behavior.
Dennis Kozlowski, former CEO of Tyco International LTD	Did not pay back large sums of money borrowed form company; avoided paying sales tax on art; padded earnings growth. Sent to prison in 2004 for eight to twenty-five years, and paid $70 million in restitution. Federal judge later ruled that Kozlowski must forfeit all compensation earned between 1995 and 2002.

Source: The facts in the table have been widely circulated in the media. Representative sources for the facts include the following: "As If a Credit Tsunami Weren't Enough: The Case of Accused Ponzi Schemer Bernard L. Madoff," January 19, 2009, p. 61; David Benoit, "Allstate Sues Countrywide," *The Wall Street Journal*, December 29, 2010, p. C2; "High Profiles in Hot Water," *The Wall Street Journal*, June 28, 2002, p. B1; James S. Granelli, Kim Christensen and Jim Puzzanghera, "HP Spied on More Than Phone Calls," www.latimes.com/business, September 21, 2006; Barbara Kiviat, "The One that Got Away," *Time*, September 4, 2006, pp. 38–39; Yukari Iwatani Kane, "For Apple Suppliers, Pressure to Win." *The Wall Street Journal,* August 16, 2010, p. B3; "Executives on Trial," *The Wall Street Journal*, May 26, 2006, p. A9; Chad Bray, "Judge Orders Ex-Tyco CEO to Forfeit Compensation," *The Wall Street Journal*, December 3, 2010, p. B3.

LEADERSHIP, SOCIAL RESPONSIBILITY, AND CREATING AN ETHICAL ORGANIZATIONAL CULTURE

The idea of **corporate social responsibility** continues to evolve. It has recently been explained as the process by which managers within an organization think about and discuss relationships with stakeholders and how they will work toward attaining the common good. To analyze a firm's corporate social responsibility, it is therefore necessary to understand what it thinks, says, and tends to do in relation to others.[24] According to ethics professor R. Edward Freeman, corporate social responsibility is no longer an add-on, but is built into the core purpose of a business.[25] When corporate social responsibility generates value for shareholders and stakeholders, it is regarded as good business strategy.[26]

Being socially responsible fits into the Thou Shalt approach, or finding out better ways for leaders to make a positive contribution to society. In contrast, the Thou Shalt Not approach focuses on avoiding the kind of wrongdoing depicted in Table 5-2.[27] Our focus here is illustrative actions that leaders can

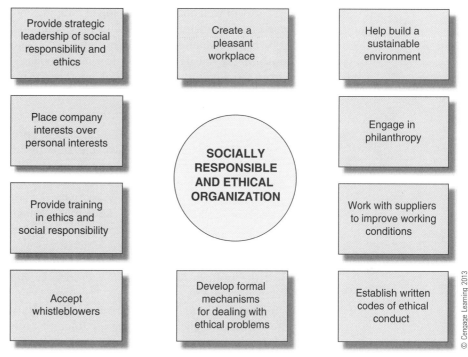

FIGURE 5-1 Initiatives for Achieving a Socially Responsible and Ethical Organization.

take to enhance social responsibility, as well as create an organizational culture that encourages ethical behavior, as outlined in Figure 5-1.

Providing Strategic Leadership of Ethics and Social Responsibility

The most effective route to an ethical and socially responsible organization is for senior management to provide strategic leadership in that direction. In this way, senior managers become ethics leaders: Their policies and actions set the ethical and social responsibility tone for the organization. If high ethics receive top priority, workers at all levels are more likely to behave ethically. Around 2008, an analysis of the troubles facing the banking industry suggested that lack of moral leadership was a contributing factor. Christina Rexrode, who follows the banking industry, wrote:

> Although the industry faces sweeping new rules and regulations imposed by Congress, legality isn't the same thing as morality. In some corridors of banking, people turned a blind eye to troubling practices—such as the issuance of subprime mortgages—as long as they were technically legal.[28]

Strategic leadership of ethics and social responsibility includes leading by example. If workers throughout the firm believe that behaving ethically is in and behaving unethically is out, ethical behavior will prevail. Ethical behavior that is rewarded is likely to endure. Linda Klebe Treviño and Michael E. Brown observe that ethical behavior can be rewarded by promoting and compensating people who perform well and have developed a reputation of integrity with managers, coworkers, and customers. In addition, workers who perform unethically should not be rewarded, and perhaps disciplined.[29] A sales manager who uses a 35-day month might not be rewarded for sales booked during those five days borrowed from the next month just to look good in the previous months.

Creating a Pleasant Workplace

Creating a comfortable, pleasant, and intellectually stimulating work environment is a social responsibility initiative that directly affects employees' well-being. Because many people invest about one-third of their time at work, a pleasant work environment increases the chances that their lives will be enriched. Robert Levering and Milton Moskowitz of the Great Place to Work® Institute, in cooperation with *Fortune*, have institutionalized the idea of being a "best company to work for." Employers nominate themselves, and two-thirds of the score is based on how randomly selected employees respond to the Great Place to Work Trust Index,© a survey measuring organizational culture. An evaluation of the Culture Audit by staff members at the Great Place to Work Institute determines the rest of the score. The focus is on employee satisfaction, yet the firms that fall into "the 100 best companies to work for" are also typically profitable. Among the benefits these companies offer are flexible working hours; on-site day care; concierge services, such as dry-cleaning pickup; domestic-partner benefits to same-sex couples; and fully paid sabbaticals. Following are the three of the most highly rated companies:[30]

> *SAS, Cary, N.C.:* This business analytics software and services firm took the top spot among Best Companies for two consecutive years and has been on the list for fourteen years. Notable perks include on-site health care, summer camp for employee children, car wash and interior cleaning service, a salon, and a massive gym on company premises. The company philosophy is "Treat employees like they make a difference and they will."

> *Google, Mountain View, California:* The company whose name has become a verb sets the standard for Silicon Valley. Among its perks are free gourmet meals, a swimming spa, and free medical services on-site. Engineers are empowered to spend 20 percent of their time on independent projects. Goggle employees are empowered to award one another $175 on-the-spot peer spot bonuses, and more than two-thirds of "Googlers" made the awards. Every employee received a 10 percent pay increase in a recent hear. Hiring standards are tough, emphasizing brilliance, good team-player skills, and diverse interests. Salary data are not made public, but many Google employees become wealthy through the exercise of legitimate stock options. Ninety percent of employees receive stock options.

> *Wegmans Food Markets, Inc., Rochester, New York:* The foundation belief of this privately held 71-store grocery chain is "Employees first, customers second." The Wegman family believes that when employees are happy, customers will be too. This private grocery chain receives thousands of letters every day from consumers who would like a Wegmans store in their neighborhood. During a recent year, 11,000 Wegmans employers participated in a challenge to eat five cups of fruit and vegetables and walk up to 10,000 steps per day for eight weeks.

The employee programs that qualify a company as a best place to work focus on employee benefits. However, the leaders of these companies also emphasize stimulating work.

Helping Build a Sustainable Environment

Socially responsible leaders influence others to sustain and preserve the external environment through a variety of actions that go beyond mandatory environmental controls such as managing toxic waste. Helping build a sustainable environment can involve hundreds of different actions such as making packaging smaller; making more extensive use of fluorescent lighting; and, when feasible, using energy from solar panels and wind turbines to replace burning of fossil fuels. Furthermore, many companies sponsor team-building events, in which participants build a playground or refurbish an old house in a declining neighborhood. Preserving an old building uses less energy than constructing a new one, and it enhances the aesthetics of the environment, as well.

A relatively new leadership position has been created in several firms, bearing a title such as chief sustainability officer. At Coca-Cola Co., the major role of chief sustainability officer Bea Perez is to work on sustainability issues in packaging and recycling, water, climate protection, and community.[31]

Three specific examples of representative leadership initiatives for helping create a sustainable environment follow:

- Several tire companies, including Bridgestone Corp. and Michelin SA, are manufacturing tires with less rolling resistance, or the force a tire must overcome to move a vehicle. Less fuel is consumed by a vehicle when it has less rolling resistance, yet there are concerns that the tire will not last as long and may have longer stopping distances on wet surfaces.[32]
- UPS has improved the fuel efficiency of its domestic delivery fleet by 10 percent in recent years. To improve another 10 percent, the company has added more alternative-fuel vehicles. UPS now has all-electric vehicles, hybrid-electric vehicles, vehicles that run on compressed natural gas, and those that run on liquid natural gas.[33]
- The cleaning products of Restore Products are substantially greener than their eco-friendly competitors. Customers are able to bring an empty bottle to a filling kiosk in one of twenty-two partner stores. A computer then reads the bar code, blends a new product, fills the bottle, and prints out a discount coupon.[34]

Whether or not you believe that the three examples just presented are publicity stunts to be perceived as an environmentally friendly company, the environment most likely benefits. Another way for a leader to help the environment is to be directly in the recycling business. Electronic recycling is particularly important because electronics are the fastest-growing solid waste stream in the world, and contain toxins such as mercury and chromium. A sizable company in this field is Electronic Recyclers International in Fresno, California. ERI chief executive John S. Shegerian takes performing a good deed for society one step further: One-third of the 200 full- and part-time employees are part of its second chance program, which includes primarily

LEADERSHIP SKILL-BUILDING EXERCISE 5-2

Conducting an Environmental Audit

To create an environmentally friendly workplace, somebody has to take the initiative to spot opportunities for change, thereby exercising leadership. Organize the class into groups of about five, with one person being appointed the team leader. You might have to do the work outside of class because your assignment is to do an environmental audit of a workplace, that might include nonprofit setting such as a place of worship, a school, or an athletic facility. If the audit is done during class time, evaluate a portion of the school, such as a classroom, an athletic facility, or the cafeteria. Your task is to conduct an environmental audit with respect to the energy efficiency and healthfulness of the workplace. Make judgments, perhaps on a 1-to-10 scale, plus comments about the following factors:

1. How energy efficient is the workplace in terms of such factors as building insulation, use of fluorescent lighting, heating and cooling, and use of solar panels?
2. How safe is the environment in terms of pollutants and steps to prevent physical accidents?
3. How aesthetic is the environment in terms of protecting against sight and sound pollution?

Summarize your findings and suggestions in a bulleted list of less than one page. Present your findings to classmates and perhaps to a manager of the workplace. Classmates might comment on whether your findings will really improve the planet from an ecological standpoint.

ex-cons and former addicts.[35] The social-good aspect is that being employed facilitates a person's not lapsing back into criminal behavior and drug addiction. Leadership Skill-Building Exercise 5-2 provides an opportunity for you to practice conducting an environmental audit.

Engaging in Philanthropy

A standard organizational leadership approach to social responsibility is to donate money to charity and various other causes. Most charities are heavily dependent on corporate support. Colleges, universities, and career schools also benefit from corporate donations. Many of the leading philanthropists donate money during their lifetime rather than giving through their estates. The most striking example is Bill and Melinda Gates of Microsoft, who formed their own foundation with the primary global aims of reducing extreme poverty, combatting AIDS, and vaccinating children against illnesses. Financier Warren Buffet is also a director of the foundation. In the United States, the focus is more on educational opportunities and access to information technology. In 2010, the foundation had an endowment of $24.5 billion, with Buffet having doubled the endowment in 2006. Furthermore, Bill Gates has called for a revision of capitalism in which poor people receive more benefits. Gates said he is troubled because advances in technology, health care, and education tend to help the rich and neglect the poor.[36]

Many corporate donors want their charitable investments to benefit the end consumer, not get lost in red tape and overhead, and show measurable results. The new breed of philanthropist studies each charitable cause as he or she would a potential business investment, seeking maximum return in terms of social impact. This philanthropist might also seek follow-up data, for example, on how many children were taught to read or by what percentage new cases of AIDS declined.

We ordinarily perceive philanthropists to be executives at major corporations or self-made millionaires and billionaires. In reality, many leaders of less recognition and wealth are philanthropists. A representative example is Bennie Fowler, the group vice president of Global Quality at Ford Motor Co. He founded the Powerstroke Athletic Club with the mission of developing positive characteristics and values in youth through hard work, discipline, education, and positive relationships. Fowler invests ten hours per week in teaching track and basketball at the club. Powerstroke is supported by fundraisers held twice a year, a minimum fee, and sponsors for children unable to pay the fee.[37]

Another approach to philanthropy is for a company representative to get physically, mentally, and emotionally involved in helping people in need. The accompanying Leader in Action illustrates this approach.

LEADER IN ACTION

Hattie Matthews, Store Manager at Lowes, Helps Build a Better World

"I've always felt it's an absolute honor and privilege to be able to participate in helping build someone's dream," beams Hattie Matthews, store manager for the home improvement company Lowe's in Buckeye, Arizona. Four years ago, Matthews, who formerly was a finish carpenter and licensed builder (a trade she learned in her family's construction business starting at age five), volunteered as instructor with Habitat for Humanity's Women Build program. The activity is a faction of the shelter relief organization that helps women develop the skills needed to participate on a Habitat worksite. It was an opening she pursued through Lowe's corporate partnership with the charitable group. Since then, she has participated in building twenty homes in Phoenix; Detroit; and Benton Harbor, Michigan.

Matthews often teaches basic construction skills at weekly Women Build clinics to help women overcome feelings of intimidation on the worksite. She believes that what women learn from the clinics is not only beneficial for completing tasks on Habitat worksites, but also helpful as they manage challenges in their lives. For instance, one single mother wanted to learn construction skills to repair her home. When the project was finished, the young woman, overwhelmed with emotion, looked at Matthews and cried; she never thought she would be able to complete a task like building a house. "You don't realize what the impact this has on someone's life" says Matthews.

In 2009, the mother of six will participated in Habitat's 2nd Annual National Women Build Week, a nationwide celebration of more than 6,000 women volunteers. Matthews continues to marvel at how a project that begins with nothing more than a slab can transform a life seven days later. She explains, "When you participate with Habitat, you always get back way more than you give and people are surprised by that."

QUESTIONS

1. In what ways is Hattie Matthews being socially responsible?
2. In what ways is management at Lowe's being socially responsible?
3. In what way or ways is Matthews exercising leadership?

Source: Black enterprise by SCOTT Copyright 2009. Reproduced with permission of BLACK ENTERPRISE MAGAZINE.

Working with Suppliers to Improve Working Conditions

An opportunity for practicing social responsibility is for company leaders to work with suppliers to improve physical and mental working conditions. Instead of refusing to deal with a supplier who operates a sweatshop, management might work with the supplier to improve plant working conditions. The justification for helping the supplier improve conditions is that the supplier's employees are often in dire need of a paying job. Almost any job is better than no job to a person facing extreme poverty or who is dependent on modest wages for food and shelter. Helping suppliers improve working conditions has been conceptualized as corporations being vehicles for positive social change—yet another way of demonstrating corporate social responsibility.[38]

Gap Inc., took a major initiative to begin improving working conditions at suppliers. Company leadership issued a report conceding that working conditions are far from perfect at many of the 3,000 factories worldwide that manufacture clothing for Gap. Among the working-condition violations were that between 10 and 25 percent of its Chinese factories used psychological coercion or verbal abuse. More than 50 percent of the factories visited in sub-Saharan Africa operated machinery without proper safety devices. Gap representatives now invest more time in training and helping factories develop programs for compliance with working-condition codes. The early initiative by Gap has evolved into membership in the Ethical Trading Initiative designed to improve the lives of workers making clothes for sale in Gap stores.[39]

Establishing Written Codes of Ethical Conduct

Many organizations use written codes of conduct as guidelines for ethical and socially responsible behavior. Such guidelines continue to grow in importance because workers in self-managing teams have less supervision than previously. Regardless of the industry, most codes deal with quite similar issues. Patricia Breeding, integrity compliance officer for Covenant Health, in Knoxville, Tennessee, says, "They all address conflicts of interest, gifts and things like vendor relationships. They use the word 'customer' in one and 'patient' in another but they're all about doing the right thing."[40]

Prohibition against bribery of government or corporate officials is being incorporated more frequently into ethical codes to combat potential major problems. For example, in 2011, U.S. regulators accused IBM of ten years of bribery in Asia, contending that employers handed over shopping bags filled with cash in South Korea. IBM allegedly also arranged junkets for government officials in China in exchange for millions of dollars in contracts. IBM agreed to pay $10 million to settle the civil charges in which more than 100 employees of IBM subsidiaries were involved in the bribes.[41] (This case is remarkable because IBM has a positive reputation for ethics and social responsibility.)

The Sarbanes-Oxley Act, triggered by the financial scandals around the year 2000, requires public companies to disclose whether they have adopted a code of ethics for senior financial officers. In some firms, such as Boeing Company, workers at all levels are required to sign the code of conduct. A written code of conduct is more likely to influence behavior when both formal and informal leaders throughout the firm refer to it frequently. Furthermore, adherence to the code must be rewarded, and violation of the code should be punished.

Developing Formal Mechanisms for Dealing with Ethical Problems

Many large employers have ethics programs of various types. Large organizations frequently establish ethics committees to help ensure ethical and socially responsible behavior. Top-level leadership participation in these formal mechanisms gives them more clout. Committee members include a top management representative, plus other managers throughout the organization. An ethics and social responsibility specialist from the human resources department might also join the group. The committee establishes policies for ethics and social responsibility and may conduct an ethical audit of the firm's activities. In addition, committee members might review complaints about ethical problems.

The U.S. federal government includes a unit called the Pentagon's Standards of Conduct Office for dealing with ethical problems. Its most potent weapon is an Encyclopedia of Ethical Failure, a listing of ethical failures within the government that is published on the Internet by Pentagon lawyer Stephen Epstein. Brief case histories are presented of shenanigans and shockingly poor judgment that have derailed the careers of public servants in various governmental bureaus. One example is that an Army official was caught channeling bogus business to himself and his girlfriend's daughter. Epstein reported the episode under the headline, "One Happy Family Spends Time Together in Jail."[42]

The takeaway point here is that unethical behavior within a large organization might be made public, resulting in considerable embarrassment and a career setback for the accused.

Accepting Whistleblowers

A **whistleblower** is an employee who discloses organizational wrongdoing to parties who can take action. It was a whistleblower who began the process of exposing the scandalous financial practices at Enron Corporation, such as hiding losses. Sherron Watkins, a vice president, wrote a one-page anonymous letter exposing unsound, if not dishonest, financial reporting: Enron had booked profits for two entities that had no assets. She dropped the letter off at company headquarters the next day.

Whistleblowers often go directly to a federal government bureau to report what they consider to be fraud and poor ethics by their employer. The single largest settlement so far was $920 million against Tenet Healthcare Corp., the nation's second-largest hospital chain. Following allegations by six whistleblowers, prosecutors accused Tenet of overbilling the government by $806 million in Medicare payments and paying $49 million in kickbacks to physicians who referred patients to the health care organization.[43] The Dodd-Frank financial reform law passed in July, 2010, may lead to larger settlements in the future.

Whistleblowers are often ostracized and humiliated by the companies they hope to improve. For example, they may receive no further promotions or poor performance evaluations. Also, many whistleblowers are fired or demoted, even for high-profile tips that proved true.[44] The Sarbanes-Oxley Act includes some protection for whistleblowers. Employees who report fraud related to corporate accounting, internal accounting controls, and auditing have a way of gaining reinstatement, as well as back pay and legal expenses. More than half of the pleas of whistleblowers are ignored.

Harry Markopolos, a derivatives analyst from Boston who suspected that Bernard Madoff's investment business was a fraud, is a prime example of a whistleblower who was ignored. Through intuition and analytical detective work, Markopolos demonstrated that Madoff could not be earning the consistent returns he claimed. Markopolos blew the whistle by informing the Securities and Exchange Commission, but his pleas were not taken seriously and the matter was dropped.[45] Because the pleas of whistleblowers are often dismissed, it is important for leaders at all levels to create a comfortable climate for legitimate whistleblowing. The leader needs to sort out the difference between a troublemaker and a true whistleblower.

Being a whistleblower requires a small act of leadership, in the sense of taking the initiative to bring about change. However, leaders of the organization that is turned in might not perceive the change as constructive.

Providing Training in Ethics and Social Responsibility

Forms of ethics training include messages about ethics and social responsibility from company leadership, classes on ethics at colleges, and exercises in ethics. These training programs reinforce the idea that ethically and socially responsible behavior is both morally right and good for business. Much of the content of this chapter reflects the type of information communicated in such programs. Training programs in ethics and social responsibility are most likely to be effective when the organizational culture encourages ethical behavior.

Caterpillar, the manufacturer of construction and mining equipment, exemplifies a modern approach to training in ethics. During the annual training, all 95,000 employees ponder a series of questions presented to them either via the Internet or on paper. The scenarios, written in-house, encourage workers to consider the best way to behave in a particular situation. Employees are able to consult the code of ethics as they reflect on the scenarios. One scenario involves a plant-floor employee adding a cleansing agent used by other employees to the agent the employee is presently using. One of the alternatives is "Check with an environmental health and safety group to ensure the combination is safe."[46]

To help develop future ethical leaders some business schools have taken to hiring former white-collar felons to speak to students about corporate crime. The point is to scare MBA students straight. One such ex-felon is Walter A. Pavlo Jr., who was engaged in a $6 million money laundering scheme at MCI,

LEADERSHIP SKILL-BUILDING EXERCISE 5-3

Getting More Bang for the Buck with Layoffs

Your assignment as mid-level leaders in a large company is to develop a list of workers to lay off for purposes of company downsizing. The CEO says that she wants you to develop a list of fifty employees to lay off. She says that the more money you save the company, the better, but that you should still pay some attention to retaining high-producing workers. As you and your team start poring over employee salaries, you notice that the older employees are often the most highly paid because they have received salary increases for many years. These high-paid workers are

a mix of outstanding, average, and below-average performers based on the results of performance evaluations. You also notice that some of the younger employees who are not necessarily outstanding performers are relatively low paid.

Your job is to develop criteria for choosing fifty employees to lay off, taking into account both financial and ethical factors. You want to practice ethically and socially responsible leadership, but you also want the lay off to save the company a lot of money, thereby keeping your CEO happy.

and later served a two-year sentence in federal prison. As you might suspect, paying convicted criminals for talking about their crimes is controversial.[47]

Leadership Skill-Building Exercise 5-3 gives you the opportunity to engage in a small amount of ethics training.

Placing Company Interests over Personal Interests

Many ethical violations, such as senior managers' voting themselves outrageous compensation, stem from managers' placing their personal interests over the welfare of the company and other employees. Jonathan M. Tish, the chairman and CEO of Loews Hotels, says that success in today's interdependent world demands *We* leaders, or people who look beyond self-interest to build partnerships in pursuit of a greater good. We leaders unify rather than divide, collaborate rather than compete, and believe that it is possible to do *well* and do *good* at the same time. A major requirement for building a partnership is fairness. Everyone must benefit from a partnership.[48]

According to the research and theorizing of management professors Craig L. Pearce, Charles C. Manz, and Henry P. Sims Jr., executives are more likely to be less corrupt (and therefore placing company interests first) when leadership is shared. The researchers reason that power can corrupt and absolute power can be an especially toxic influence. Shared leadership can provide a robust system of checks and balances, thereby reducing the possibility of some unethical and criminal behavior by business executives.[49] Nevertheless, we still have to be realistic. Criminal business leaders such as Bernie Madoff probably enlisted the cooperation of a few other executives (thereby engaging shared leadership) to pull off their massive swindles.

Leadership Skill-Building Exercise 5-3 gives you an opportunity to work through issues of ethics and social responsibility.

ETHICAL AND SOCIALLY RESPONSIBLE BEHAVIOR
AND ORGANIZATIONAL PERFORMANCE

High ethics and social responsibility are sometimes related to good financial performance. A current model of the relationship between corporate social performance and profits emphasizes the role of supply and demand. The model states that when demand for social responsibility investments increases, value-maximizing managers will find it in their self-interest to make these investments even if cash flow is reduced. Also, despite spending money, the market value of the firm might increase when the demand for these investment opportunities is greater than the supply. An example might be that investing in programs to improve literacy among poor children might have a payoff because there is a big demand for this type of investment.[50] However, investing money to help preserve reptiles in the Arizona desert might not have a good return because of low demand.

The relationship between social responsibility and profits can also work in two directions: More profitable firms can better afford to invest in social responsibility initiatives, and these initiatives can lead to more profits. In a pioneering study, Sandra A. Waddock and Samuel B. Graves analyzed the relationship between corporate social performance and corporate financial performance for 469 firms, spanning thirteen industries, for a two-year period. They used many different measures of social and financial performance. An example of social performance would be helping to redevelop a poor community.

The researchers found that financial success creates enough money left over to invest in corporate social performance. The study also found that good corporate social performance contributes to improved financial performance as measured by return on assets and return on sales. Waddock and Graves concluded that the relationship between social and financial performance may be a **virtuous circle**, meaning that corporate social performance and corporate financial performance feed and reinforce each other.[51]

According to a study conducted by the Ethics Resource Center, employees who work in an ethical environment tend to be better motivated. The study concluded that the chance to contribute to something larger than themselves and be recognized for it is a strong incentive to employees for delivering superior performance.[52] Using this approach, it is helpful if company leaders explain why the work is larger than oneself, such as a cement manufacturer explaining to employees that the cement is vital for building infrastructure that serves the needs of many people.

Being ethical also helps avoid the costs of paying huge fines for being unethical, including charges of discrimination and class-action lawsuits because of improper financial reporting. The fine imposed on IBM, as mentioned earlier, illustrates the potential cost of being unethical. Being accused of unethical and illegal behavior can also result in a sudden drop in customers and clients, as well as extreme difficulty in obtaining new customers and clients.

In short, a leader who is successful at establishing a climate of high ethics and social responsibility can earn and save the company a lot of money.

Yet there are times when being socially responsible can eat into profits. A small company called Earth Mama Angel Baby uses recycled materials for packaging its organic, preservative-free lotions, shampoos, and other products for pre- and postnatal women and infants. Owner Melinda Olsen says that her ideals come at a high price, with the cost of organic ingredients lowering her gross margins to about 13 percent in comparison to the competition.[53] Yet, as a leader, she places a higher value on her ideals than she does on maximizing profit.

SUMMARY

Principles of ethical and moral leadership all center on the idea that a leader should do the right thing, as perceived by a consensus of reasonable people. Key principles of ethical and moral leadership are as follows: (1) be honest and trustworthy and have integrity in dealing with others, (2) pay attention to all stakeholders, (3) build community, and (4) respect the individual.

Differences in ethics and morality can be traced to seven factors: (1) the leader's level of greed, gluttony, and avarice; (2) rationalization; (3) implied permission to engage in unethical acts; (4) the leader's level of moral development; (5) a sense of entitlement; (6) situational influences; and (7) a person's character. It has been proposed that to stay ethical a leader must develop an ethical mind focused on good work.

Before reaching a decision about an issue that is not obviously ethical or blatantly unethical, a leader or manager should seek answers to questions such as: Is it right? Is it fair? Who gets hurt? Unethical behavior has brought companies into bankruptcy, led to layoffs of thousands of workers, diminished trust in stock investments, and discouraged many talented young people from embarking on a business career.

Another way a leader can be ethical and moral is to spearhead the firm, or a unit within it, toward doing good deeds—toward being socially responsible and creating an ethical organizational culture. Among the many possible socially responsible and ethical acts are (1) providing strategic leadership of social responsibility and ethics, (2) creating a pleasant workplace, (3) helping build a sustainable environment, (4) engaging in philanthropy, (5) working with suppliers to improve working conditions, (6) establishing written codes of conduct, (7) developing formal mechanisms for dealing with ethical problems, (8) accepting whistleblowers, (9) providing training in ethics, and (10) placing company interests over personal interests.

High ethics and social responsibility are sometimes related to good financial performance, according to research evidence and opinion. Causes in big demand are more likely to have a financial payoff. More profitable firms have the funds to invest in good social programs. Being ethical helps avoid big fines for being unethical, and ethical organizations attract more employees. Socially responsible behavior can be cost-effective. However, being socially responsible can sometimes lower profit margins, yet the leader's ideals are important.

KEY TERMS

ethics

morals

integrity

entitlement

ethical mind

corporate social responsibility

whistleblower

virtuous circle

✔ GUIDELINES FOR ACTION AND SKILL DEVELOPMENT

A solid foundation for developing a leadership career is to establish a personal ethical code. An ethical code determines what behavior is right or wrong, good or bad, based on values. The values stem from cultural upbringing, religious teachings, peer influences, and professional or industry standards. A code of professional ethics helps a leader deal with such issues as accepting bribes, backstabbing coworkers, and sexually harassing a work associate.

A provocative explanation of the causes of unethical behavior emphasizes the strength of relationships among people. Assume that two people have close ties to each other—they may have worked together for a long time or have known each other both on and off the job. As a consequence, they are likely to behave ethically toward one another on the job. In contrast, if a weak relationship exists between two individuals, either party is more likely to treat the other badly. In the work environment, the people involved may be your work associates, your contacts, or your internal and external customers.[54] The message is for you as a leader to build strong relationships with others in order to increase the frequency of ethical behavior.

Discussion Questions and Activities

1. If reputable companies such as IBM and Apple have been charged with using bribes to obtain sales, why should you worry about being ethical?
2. The majority of business executives accused of unethical behavior have studied ethics either as a subject in a business course or as an entire course. So what do you think went wrong?
3. Suppose you had inside information that your employer was thinking about declaring bankruptcy, and you find out that a family member was about to purchase $20,000 in the stock of your employer. To what extent would it be unethical for you to dissuade the family member from making the investment?
4. What role should company leadership have in assuring that employees do not make nasty posts about the competition on social media websites?
5. How can consumers use the Internet to help control the ethical behavior of business leaders?
6. In what ways are many retail customers quite unethical?
7. What is your position on the ethics of a business leader's receiving $100 million or more in annual compensation?
8. Should leaders of companies that produce fattening food that can lead to cardiac problems and obesity be targeted for being socially irresponsible?
9. A study by Liberty Mutual Research Institute found that approximately 2,600 deaths, 330,000 injuries, and 1.5 million instances of property damage annually in the United States stem from using mobile phones while driving. What social responsibility obligations should mobile phone manufacturers and mobile phone service providers have for dealing with this problem?
10. Explain whether you would be willing to accept a 10 percent smaller salary increase or bonus so that your employer could invest in a socially responsible cause, such as providing shelter for homeless people or Internet access for poor children.

LEADERSHIP CASE PROBLEM A

The Extreme Craft Brew

It is banned in thirteen states, and it sure doesn't come in a six-pack. The maker of Samuel Adams beer has released an updated version of its biennial beer Utopias, the highest-alcohol-content beer on the market. At 25.5% alcohol by volume and $150 a bottle, the limited release of the brandy-colored Utopias comes as more brewers take advantage of improvements in science to increase potency and enhance taste.

"Just part of trying to push the envelope," said Jim Koch, founder and owner of Boston Beer Co., the maker of Sam Adams. "I'm pushing it beyond what the laws of these 13 states ever contemplated when they passed these laws decades ago."

Since the 1990s, craft brewers like Boston Beer Co. and the Delaware-based Dogfish Head have produced a number of extreme beers that challenge old notions of beer and the decades-old laws that have governed them.

Paul Gatza, director of the national Brewers Association, Boulder, Colorado, said new yeast research allowed brewers to experiment with the emerging science that pushed the traditional cap of 14% alcohol by volume for beer. "As a result, these new beers, like Utopias, balance sweetness, higher alcohol content, and more ingredients," Gatza said.

A few states also have moved to adapt their laws to allow for the emerging craft-brew market. For example, Alabama and West Virginia recently passed laws to allow higher alcohol content in the beer. Lawmakers in Iowa and Mississippi are considering similar legislation. Gatza said consumers are also pushing for changes. That's what sparked a brew battle between Boston Beer Co. and Dogfish Head.

In 1993, Koch set a new bar by creating Triple Bock, a beverage with 18% alcohol by volume. In the early 2000s, Dogfish Head responded with beers of their own that went to 22%. But the latest Utopias alcohol volume gives Koch and Boston Beer Co. the clear title of having the strongest beer, said Sam Calagione, president and founder of Dogfish Head.

"I must bow before him for Utopias," Calagione said. "I don't think we'll be brewing a beer that strong for a while."

Questions

1. Considering that the average beer is 5% alcohol by volume, what are some of the ethical issues in producing a beer with 25.5% alcohol by volume?
2. Although few consumers may be willing to pay $150 for a bottle of beer, how socially responsible is it for the executives at Boston Beer Co. to gain publicity for high-alcohol-content beer?
3. Putting on your marketing hat for a moment, which demographic group would be interested in purchasing a bottle of Utopias?

Source: "Not for Joe Six-Pack, But Beer Packs Punch?" Associated Press, December 2, 2009.

ASSOCIATED ROLE PLAY

Enhancing Social Responsibility at Boston Beer

One student plays the role of a middle manager at the Boston Beer Co. The middle manager has a meeting today with Jim Koch, the company CEO. The middle manager wants Koch to think through the ethical and social responsibility issues involved in Boston Beer producing Utopias. Koch is more concerned about gaining publicity for the company, and believes that the company is quite ethical and socially responsible. Observers will key in on whether the middle manager and Koch have a good grasp of some the issues relating to ethics and social responsibility.

LEADERSHIP CASE PROBLEM B

Let's Go Green

Monica is the CEO of a regional chain of hospitals and clinics that includes several thousand employees. The medical facilities continue to grow as insurance companies are eager to form partnerships with relatively low-cost suppliers and the population ages. Monica has been thinking lately that medical facilities have not been as aggressive as manufacturing companies in pushing for environmental sustainability. In her words, "Medical facilities could be a lot greener than they are. Obviously we don't throw contaminated bandages and body parts into the river, but we could still do a lot more. I think that we need to get more of our leaders and regular employees thinking green."

The following week, Monica worked with her administrative assistant, Hillary, to come up with a list of suggestions that hospital and clinic managers, supervisors, and employees could implement to help create a greener environment. Monica believes strongly that only collective action can create a sustainable environment, meaning that all employees can help make medical facilities more environmentally friendly. She then sent an e-mail to every employee with a work e-mail address making suggestions for creating a greener environment. Monica also explained that the hospital had established a central budget to help fund some of the green initiatives. Her suggestions for helping the hospitals and clinics contribute to a sustainable environment contained 25 suggestions, including the following six:

- Conserve energy by adjusting thermostats to keep working areas cooler during cold months, and warmer during warm months.

- Encourage patients to conserve on the use of towels because laundering towels consumes so much energy.
- Encourage visitors to hospitals and clinics to not waste so much gas circling around the parking lots to find a spot close to the medical facility. Our patients and their family members are spewing too much carbon dioxide into their air because they want to minimize walking.
- Encourage employee use of mass transportation in any locations where it is feasible.
- Use mugs instead of Styrofoam, and set up bins to recycle aluminum cans and plastic bottles.
- Create signs that say "Think Before You Print" and post them near office printers and copy machines. At the same time include under your e-mail signature a line that encourages people not to print e-mails unless absolutely necessary.

Among the first replies from her mass-distributed e-mail were, "Thanks. If we follow your advice we will soon be one of the greenest health care chains in the country," and "Nice idea, but our staff is already so overworked I doubt we can work on the environment."

Questions

1. What do you think of the effectiveness of Monica's leadership in sending an e-mail message to encourage environmental sustainability?
2. What other leadership technique might Monica use to help prompt the hospitals and clinics toward sustainability?
3. Help CEO Monica by stating a vision to cover her efforts toward sustainability.

ASSOCIATED ROLE PLAY

Assemble in a small group to play the role of supervisors in one of the hospitals in the chain headed by CEO Monica. Your group decides to brainstorm some ideas for helping the hospital contribute to a sustainable environment. Spend about 15 minutes on the group brainstorming session. Edit the list down to about six useful suggestions. Send them to Monica to demonstrate that your group wants to exercise leadership in going green.

LEADERSHIP SKILL-BUILDING EXERCISE 5-4

My Leadership Portfolio

For this chapter's entry into your leadership journal, reflect on any scenario you have encountered recently that would have given you the opportunity to practice ethical or socially responsible behavior. The scenario could have taken place in relation to employment, an interaction with fellow students, or being a customer of some type. Write down the scenario, and how you responded to it. Indicate what you learned about yourself. An example follows:

I had been thinking of purchasing advanced software to manage and edit photos on my computer. The software I needed would cost several hundred dollars. The other day, while going through my e-mail, I came upon an advertisement offering the exact photo software I wanted for $50. At first, I thought this would be a real money saver. After thinking through the ethical issues, I came to realize that the person selling this software was probably a pirate. If I purchased from this character, I would be supporting a software pirate. Besides, buying stolen goods might even be a crime. I learned from this incident that there are many opportunities in everyday life to practice good—or bad—ethics. I want to become a moral leader, so practicing good ethics will help me.

P.S.: By being ethical, I probably avoided buying virus-infected software that could have played havoc with my computer.

LEADERSHIP SKILL-BUILDING EXERCISE 5-5

Company Policy for Employee Recycling of Electronic Products

Assume that you are in a leadership position within your company. You and several other managers are concerned about the physical environment becoming cluttered with discarded electronic products, including personal computers, laptop computers, smart phones, and television sets. You know that there are appropriate channels for discarding and recycling these products responsibly, yet these channels are often neglected. Your company has environmentally conscious procedures for getting rid of electronic devices. You are concerned, however, that employees are not doing enough at home to safely discard used electronic products.

Work individually or with other students to develop a company policy that will facilitate employees being socially responsible when discarding electronic devices no longer in use. Recognize that the company has limited direct control over who employees conduct their personal life. A suggested guideline is to create a company policy about 100 words long.

LEADERSHIP VIDEO CASE DISCUSSION QUESTIONS

To view the videos for this activity, you'll need access to the CourseMate that is available for this text. To get access, visit www.CengageBrain.com.

After watching "Numi Teas," answer the following questions.

1. How do Brian Durkee, director of operations at Numi Organic Teas, and other Numi managers ensure the integrity of the company? Explain.
2. Do you believe Numi Organic Teas is a socially responsible company? Explain.
3. In today's economic climate, do you think it is wise for managers at Numi, such as Brian Durkee, to spend money to improve fair-trade and other socially responsible practices? Explain.

NOTES

1. A couple of facts about the clothing industry in this story are from Chris Burritt, "Why 'Less Is More' Rules Fashion," *Bloomberg Business Week*, May 30–June 5, 2011, pp. 18–19.
2. James G. Clawson, *Level Three Leadership: Getting Below the Surface*, 2nd ed. (Upper Saddle River, N.J.: Prentice Hall, 2002), p. 54.
3. Cited in Joanne B. Ciulla, ed., *Ethics: The Heart of Leadership*, 2nd ed. (Westport, CT.: Praeger, 2004), p. 119.
4. Karianne Kalshoven, Deanne N. Den Hartog, and Annebel H. B. De Hoogh, "Ethical Leadership at Work Questionnaire (ELW): Development and Validation of a Multidimensional Measure," *Leadership Quarterly*, February 2001, p. 51.
5. *National Business Ethics Survey*, Ethics Resource Center, Arlington, VA, 2009 survey (www.ethics.org).
6. Thomas E. Becker, "Integrity in Organizations: Beyond Honesty and Conscientiousness," *Academy of Management Review*, January 1998, pp. 154–161.
7. Robert Simons, Henry Mintzberg, and Kunal Basu, "Memo to CEOs Re Five Half-Truths of Business," *Fast Company*, June 2002, p. 118.
8. Tricia Bisoux, "Corporate Counter Culture," *BizEd*, November/December 2004, p. 18.
9. Douglas R. May, Adrian Y. L. Chan, Timothy D. Hodges, and Bruce J. Avolio, "Developing the Moral Component of Authentic Leadership," *Organizational Dynamics*, no. 3, 2003, p. 248.
10. Peter G. Northouse, *Leadership: Theory and Practice*, 2nd ed. (Thousand Oaks, Calif.: Sage, 2001), p. 263.
11. Pete Engardio, "Global Compact Strengthens Efforts to Promote Human Rights in Business," www.unglobalcompact.org, December 10, 2007; "Overview of the UN Global Compact." www.unglobalcompact.org., November 23, 2010.
12. Clawson, *Level Three Leadership*, p. 57.
13. "Fed Chief Points to Cautious Recovery," Gannett News Service, July 17, 2002.
14. "KPMG's Timothy Flynn: Restoring Credibility and Not Looking Back," *Knowledge @ Wharton*, December 12, 2007, p. 1.
15. Lawrence Kohlberg, *Essays on Moral Development* (New York: Harper & Row, 1984).
16. Susan Chandler, "Why Do Rich CEOs Steal? Entitlement," Knight Ridder News Service, September 19, 2004.
17. "Trends in CEO Pay," www.aflcio.org/corporatewatch, 2011.
18. Aaron Lucchetti and Monica Langley, "Perform-or-Die Culture Leaves Thin Talent Pool for Top Wall Street Jobs," *The Wall Street Journal*, November 5, 2007, p. A1.
19. Max H. Bazerman and Ann E. Tenbrunsel, "Ethical Breakdowns," *Harvard Business Review*, April 2011, pp. 61–62.
20. "The Ethical Mind: A Conversation with Psychologist Howard Gardner," *Harvard Business Review*, March 2007, pp. 51–56.
21. Timberly Ross, "Buffet Warns Execs to Avoid Temptation," The Associated Press, October 10, 2006.
22. James L. Bowditch and Anthony F. Buono, *A Primer on Organizational Behavior*, 5th ed. (New York: Wiley, 2001), p. 4.
23. Kate Kelly, "How Goldman Won Big on Mortgage Meltdown," *The Wall Street Journal*, December 14, 2007, pp. A1, A18.
24. Kunal Basu and Guido Palazzo, "Corporate Responsibility: A Process Model of Sensemaking," *Academy of Management Review*, January 2008, p. 124.
25. R. Edward Freeman, "From the Boardroom to the Classroom: An Ethics Revolution," *The Wall Street Journal*, December 10, 2007, p. A15.
26. Christine Arena, "'Corporate Social Responsibility': A Wobbly Concept," *The Christian Science Monitor* (CSMonitor.com), October 22, 2010, p. 2.
27. Richard L. Schmalensee, "The 'Thou Shalt' School of Business," *The Wall Street Journal*, December 30, 2003, p. B4.
28. Christina Rexrode, "Ringing Silence on Topic of Ethics, Banking," *The Charlotte Observer*, December 25, 2010.
29. Linda Klebe Treviño and Michael E. Brown, "Managing to Be Ethical: Debunking Five Business Ethics Myths," *Academy of Management Executive*, May 2004, p. 79.
30. Milton Moskowitz, Robert Levering & Christopher Tkaczyk, "100 Best Companies to Work For," *Fortune*, February 7, 2011, pp. 91–98;

Robert Levering and Milton Moskowitz, "The 2008 List," *Fortune*, February 4, 2008, p. 75.

31. The Colvin Interview, "Linda Fisher: Chief Sustainability Officer, DuPont," *Fortune*, November 23, 2009, pp. 45–46; Jeremiah McWilliams, "Coca-Cola Names Bea Perez Chief Sustainability Officer" *The Atlanta Journal-Constitution* (www.ajc.com), May 19, 2011, p. 1.

32. Stephen Power, "Green Push Hits Tire Makers," *The Wall Street Journal*, December 11, 2007, p. A18.

33. Geoff Colvin, "The UPS Green Dream," *Fortune*, December 27, 2010, pp. 49–50.

34. Stacy Perman, "Save the World, Inc." *Businessweek SmallBiz*, April/May 2009, p. 54.

35. Erika Brown, "Rehab, Reuse, Recycle," *Forbes*, April 21, 2008, pp. 71, 72.

36. For details, see www.gatesfoundation.org.

37. Brittany Hutson, "A Passion for Giving," *Black Enterprise*, May 2009, p. 70.

38. Robert J. Bies, Jean M. Bartunek, Timothy L. Fort, and Mayer N. Zald, "Corporations as Social Change Agents: Individual, Interpersonal, Institutional, and Environmental Dynamics," *Academy of Management Review*, July 2007, pp. 788–793.

39. Amy Merrick, "Gap Offers Unusual Look at Factory Conditions," *The Wall Street Journal*, May 12, 2004, pp. A1, A12; "Tara and Stacey Meet Gap," *Ethical Trading Initiative* (www.ethicaltrade.org), June 5, 2009.

40. Quoted in Joanne Lozar Glenn, "Making Sense of Ethics," *Business Education Forum*, October 2004, p. 10.

41. Jessica Holzer and Shayndi Raice, "IBM Settles Bribery Charges," *The Wall Street Journal*, March 19–20, 2011, p. B1.

42. Jonathan Karp, "At the Pentagon, An 'Encyclopedia of Ethical Failure,'" *The Wall Street Journal*, May 14, 2007, p. A15.

43. Lara Lakes Jordan, "Whistle-Blowers Identified $1.3 in Fraud over Year," The Associated Press, November 22, 2006.

44. "A Tip for Whistleblowers: Don't," *Mother Jones*, June 2007, reprinted in *The Wall Street Journal*, May 31, 2007, p. B6.

45. Harry Markopolos, *No One Would Listen* (New York: Wiley, 2010).

46. Jean Thilmany, "Supporting Ethical Employees," *HR Magazine*, September 2007, p. 108.

47. Jane Porter, "Using Ex-Cons to Scare MBAs Straight," *Business Week*, May 5, 2008, p. 058.

48. Jonathan M. Tisch, "From 'Me' Leadership to 'We' Leadership," *The Wall Street Journal*, October 26, 2004, p. B2.

49. Craig L. Pearse, Charles C. Manz, and Henry P. Sims Jr., "The Roles of Vertical and Shared Leadership in the Enactment of Executive Corruption: Implications for Research and Practice," *Leadership Quarterly*, June 2008, pp. 353–359.

50. Alison Mackey, Tyson B. Mackey, and Jay B. Barney, "Corporate Social Responsibility and Firm Performance: Investor Preferences and Corporate Strategies," *Academy of Management Review*, July 2007, p. 833.

51. Sandra A. Waddock and Samuel B. Graves, "The Corporate Social Performance–Financial Performance Link," *Strategic Management Journal*, Spring 1997, pp. 303–319.

52. "Employees Who Work in an Ethical Environment Are More Inclined to Go the Extra Mile for the Boss," *Ethics Resource Center* (www.ethics.org), July 8, 2010.

53. Anne Field, "Mission Possible," *Businessweek SmallBiz*, December 2007–January 2008, pp. 41–42.

54. Daniel J. Brass, Kenneth D. Butterfield, and Bruce C. Skaggs, "Relationships and Unethical Behavior: A Social Network Perspective," *Academy of Management Review*, January 1998, pp. 14–31.

Enhancing Teamwork within the Group

LEARNING OBJECTIVES

After studying this chapter and doing the exercises, you should be able to

- Understand the leader's role in a team-based organization.
- Describe leader actions that foster teamwork.
- Explain the potential contribution of outdoor training to the development of team leadership.
- Describe how the leader–member exchange model contributes to an understanding of leadership.

CHAPTER OUTLINE

D arryl is the manager of a sales group that sells wind turbines (big windmills) to communities and companies. Selling a wind turbine is a long and complicated activity that requires the cooperation and careful teamwork of at least five people in the group. Today, Darryl is interviewing Kate, a candidate for a cost estimator position. Kate has already made it through a telephone interview. If she is successful in today's interview, she will be moved to the next step—being interviewed by several members of the team simultaneously. At the moment, Darryl is attempting to gauge whether Kate has already developed good teamwork skills.

Darryl: I see that you did quite well in college. How much of your studies required collective effort and cooperative learning?

Kate: At least ten of my courses required group and team projects, especially my business courses. For one course project, our group played the role of business consultants that helped a local pottery shop expand its business.

Darryl: How did you like that experience?

Kate: It was terrific. Our group actually helped the pottery shop boost sales. What a great group we had.

Darryl: Sounds good, but I notice that you played on the college tennis team. That's not really a team sport is it?

Kate: It is true that tennis is not a team sport like hockey or soccer. But our coach emphasized teamwork. We helped each other by working on areas for improvement in practice. We planned our strategy for the individual matches in a group. And we hung out together a lot as a team.

Darryl: What other teamwork experience have you had?

Kate: For about four years, part-time, I worked at an upscale restaurant. The owner believed strongly that the success of a restaurant depends on everybody pulling together, and helping out each other. If we all gave good service, there would be more customers and more tips. We received a small bonus each month based on the total success of the restaurant. The serve staff working as a team was an awesome idea.

The anecdote about the wind turbine sales manager illustrates the importance business firms attach to building better teamwork. Part of this strategy includes hiring workers who are oriented toward being team players. Developing teamwork is such an important leadership role that team building is said to differentiate successful from unsuccessful leaders.[1] Furthermore, leaders with a reputation as teamwork builders are often in demand, such as Tim Cook, the new CEO of Apple Inc. His ability to work smoothly with managers from different disciplines at the company has contributed to him being chosen as the CEO of Apple to replace Steve Jobs.

A difficulty in understanding teams is that the words *teams* and *teamwork* are often overused and applied loosely. For some people, *team* is simply another term for *group*. As used here, a **team** is a work group that must rely on collaboration if each member is to experience the optimum success and achievement.[2] **Teamwork** is work done with an understanding and commitment to group goals on the part of all team members.

All teams are groups, but not all groups are teams. Jon R. Katzenbach and Douglas K. Smith, on the basis of extensive research in the workplace, make a clear differentiation between teams and groups.[3] A team is characterized by a common commitment, whereas the commitment within a group might not be as strong. A team accomplishes many collective work products, whereas group members sometimes work slightly more independently. A team has shared leadership roles, whereas members of a group have a strong leader.

Although the distinction between a group and a team may be valid, it is difficult to cast aside the practice of using the terms *group* and *team* interchangeably. For example, a customer service team is still a team even if its teamwork is poor.

The central focus of this chapter is a description of specific leader actions that foster teamwork. We also describe outdoor training, a widely used method of teamwork development. In addition, we summarize a leadership theory that provides insight into how teamwork emerges within a work group.

To evaluate how well any work team or group familiar to you is functioning as a team, do Leadership Self-Assessment Quiz 6-1. The quiz will help sensitize you to important dimensions of team effectiveness.

LEADERSHIP SELF-ASSESSMENT QUIZ 6-1

The Teamwork Checklist

Instructions: This checklist serves as an informal guide to diagnosing teamwork. Base your answers on the experiences you have in leading a team, at work or outside work. Indicate whether your team has (or had) the following characteristics:

	MOSTLY YES	MOSTLY NO
1. Definite goals each member knows and understands	_____	_____
2. Clearly established roles and responsibilities	_____	_____
3. Members who work together very well without strong egos or personalities that create problems	_____	_____
4. Well-documented guidelines for behavior and ground rules	_____	_____
5. After a consensus is reached, support from every team member	_____	_____
6. Awareness of team members that they have achieved success	_____	_____
7. Open communication in an atmosphere of trust	_____	_____
8. Continuous learning and training in appropriate skills	_____	_____
9. Flexible, open-minded, and dependable team members	_____	_____
10. Patient and supportive higher management	_____	_____
11. Individual member pride in own work	_____	_____
12. Rewards tied to individual as well as team results	_____	_____
13. Team members who automatically provide backup and support for one another without the team leader stepping in	_____	_____
14. Frequent sharing of information such as e-mail messages, text messages, and social media postings	_____	_____
15. Socializing with others, such as during coffee breaks, lunches, and sometimes after hours	_____	_____

Scoring and Interpretation: The more statements are answered "mostly yes," the more likely it is that good teamwork is present. The answers will serve as discussion points among team members for improving teamwork and group effectiveness. Negative responses to the statements can be used as suggestions for taking action to improve teamwork in your group.

Source: Most of the statements are based on material gathered from Mark Kelly, *The Adventures of a Self-Managing Team* (San Diego, CA: Pfeiffer, 1991); "Team Leadership: How to Inspire Commitment, Teamwork and Cooperation," brochure, Seminars International, Olathe, Kansas, 1996.

THE LEADER'S ROLE IN THE TEAM-BASED ORGANIZATION

Although an important goal of a team-based organization is for group members to participate in leadership and management activities, leaders still play an important role. In fact, they learn to lead in new ways. Team-based organizations need leaders who are knowledgeable in the team process and can help with the interpersonal demands of teams, for example, by giving feedback and resolving conflict. Quite often the leader is a facilitator who works with two or three teams at a time. He or she helps them stay focused when personality and work-style differences create problems. Without effective leadership, teams can get off course, go too far or not far enough, lose sight of their mission, and become blocked by interpersonal conflict. Effective leadership is particularly important early in the history of a group to help it reach its potential. Key roles of a leader in a team-based organization include the following:

- Building trust and inspiring teamwork
- Coaching team members and group members toward higher levels of performance
- Facilitating and supporting the team's decisions
- Expanding the team's capabilities
- Creating a team identity
- Anticipating and influencing change
- Inspiring the team toward higher levels of performance
- Enabling and empowering group members to accomplish their work
- Encouraging team members to eliminate low-value work[4]

Several of these roles have already been noted in this book, and several others, such as building trust and coaching, are described later. All of these roles contribute to effective leadership in general. The enabling role, for example, centers on empowerment. Yet properly motivating team members also enables, or facilitates, work accomplishment. The empowering processes that will be discussed in Chapter 11 are a major part of enabling. Group members who are empowered are enabled to accomplish their work. The leader behavior and attitudes that foster teamwork, described in the next section, might also be interpreted as part of the leader's role in a team-based organization.

We emphasize again that an important role for the leader in a team-based organization is often to lead a group of people who do not report directly to him or her.[5] As a consequence, many of the teamwork development tactics described in this chapter become all the more important for accomplishing results.

When the leader is not a member of the team, he or she is classified as an *external leader*. A study conducted in three different industrial workplaces with self-managing teams offers some understanding of the external leader's role. (A self-managing team has considerable autonomy.) It was found that under ordinary work conditions, when the leaders were too actively involved in coaching the team and in sense making, satisfaction with leadership declined. *Sense making* refers to identifying important environmental events, and offering interpretations of these events to the team. An example would be identifying increases in the price of natural gas, and then explaining to the facilities maintenance team how price increases will affect their work. When the team faced disruptive conditions, such as an unusually heavy work overload or a rapid change in technology, coaching and sense making by the leader increased satisfaction with leadership.[6]

LEADER ACTIONS THAT FOSTER TEAMWORK

Fostering teamwork is well worth the leader's attention because teamwork is a major contributor to team success. Based on a study of 130 offshore operations in India, two researchers found that what really determines success versus failure is not the ease with which knowledge can be transferred from one location to another. Instead, the major success factor is managing teamwork, or helping onshore and offshore workers to coordinate their linked work effectively. Projects that attended to managing coordination performed close to four times as well as their less successful counterparts.[7]

Sometimes a leader's inspiring personality alone can foster teamwork. An experiment with Dutch business students showed that leaders who were perceived as charismatic and fair facilitated cooperation among group members.[8] Yet inspirational leaders, as well as less charismatic ones, can also encourage teamwork through their attitudes and what they do. Table 6-1 lists the teamwork-enhancing actions that are described in the following pages. For convenience, the actions

TABLE 6-1 Leader Actions That Foster Teamwork

ACTIONS LEADERS CAN TAKE USING THEIR OWN RESOURCES	ACTIONS GENERALLY REQUIRING ORGANIZATION STRUCTURE OR POLICY
1. Defining the team's mission and tasks	1. Designing physical structures that facilitate communication
2. Establishing a climate of trust	2. Emphasizing group recognition and rewards
3. Developing a norm of teamwork, including emotional intelligence	3. Initiating ritual and ceremony
4. Emphasizing pride in being outstanding	4. Practicing open-book management
5. Serving as a model of teamwork, including power sharing	5. Selecting team-oriented members
6. Using a consensus leadership style	6. Using technology that facilitates teamwork including social media
7. Establishing urgency, demanding performance standards, and providing direction	7. Blending representatives from the domestic company and foreign nationals on the team
8. Encouraging competition with another group	
9. Encouraging the use of jargon	
10. Minimizing micromanagement	
11. Practicing e-leadership for virtual teams	

are divided into two types: actions that leaders can take using their own resources (informal techniques) and actions that generally require organization structure or policy (formal techniques).

Actions Leaders Can Take Using Their Own Resources

Defining the Team's Mission   A starting point in developing teamwork is to specify the team's mission. Commitment to a clear mission is a key practice of a highly effective team. The mission statement for the group helps answer the questions, "Why are we doing this?" and "What are we trying to accomplish?" To answer these questions, the mission statement should set out a specific goal, purpose, and philosophical tone. Any goal contained within the mission statement should be congruent with organizational objectives. If a team wants to cut back on its number of suppliers, the organization should have the same intent as well. Here are two examples of team mission statements:

- To plan and implement new manufacturing approaches to enhance our high-performance image and bolster our competitive edge.
- To enhance our website development capability so we can provide decision makers throughout the organization with assistance in developing websites that exceed the state of the art.

The leader can specify the mission when the team is formed or at any other time. Developing a mission for a long-standing team breathes new life into its activities. Being committed to a mission improves teamwork, as does the process of formulating a mission. The dialogue necessary for developing a clearly articulated mission establishes a climate in which team members can express feelings, ideas, and opinions. Participative leadership is required in developing a mission, as in most other ways of enhancing teamwork.

To help implement the mission, it is quite helpful for the leader to define the team tasks, or to work with the group in defining these tasks. Team members can then identify the subtasks for which each member has responsibility.[9] For example, a dental office might want to understand why so many patients have left the practice. One team member might be assigned the task of contacting former patients, and another team member might be assigned the task of asking current patients if they are experiencing any problems with the dental practice.

Establishing a Climate of Trust   If team members do not trust each other or the leader, it is unlikely that they will work cooperatively together. Trust is at the heart of collaboration. Unless team members trust each other, they will not be dependent on each other and therefore will not work well as a team.[10] A starting point in establishing a climate of trust is for the leader to be credible and engage in the many other trustworthy behaviors described in Chapter 3. Encouraging open communication about problems and sharing information are two specific ways the leader can help promote a climate of trust. Being open about problems facing the group and being candid in expressing opinions is often referred to as the leader being *transparent*.

Developing a Norm of Teamwork, Including Emotional Intelligence   A major strategy of teamwork development is to promote the attitude among group members that working together effectively is expected. Developing a norm of teamwork is difficult for a leader when a strong culture of individualism exists within a firm. Nokia, Inc., the telecommunications firm based in Finland, illustrates the teamwork type of organizational culture. Part of the culture of collegiality can be traced to the Finnish character. It is natural for Nokia employees to work together and iron out differences of opinion. Nokia is almost as interested in the personalities of job candidates as their technical credentials. Company leaders look for new employees whose personality would contribute to the teamwork and creative spirit of Nokia.[11]

Cooperation Theory   A belief in cooperation and collaboration rather than competitiveness as a strategy for building teamwork has been referred to as **cooperation theory**.[12] Individuals who are accustomed to competing with one another for recognition, salary increases, and resources must now collaborate. Despite the challenge of making a culture shift, the leader can make progress toward establishing a teamwork norm by doing the following:

- Encourage team members to treat one another as if they were customers, thus fostering cooperative behavior and politeness.
- Explicitly state the desirability of teamwork on a regular basis both orally and in writing.
- Communicate the norm of teamwork by frequently using words and phrases that support teamwork. Emphasizing the words *team members* or *teammate* and deemphasizing the words *subordinates* and *employees* helps communicate the norm of teamwork.
- Work with the group to establish a code of conduct that everyone agrees to follow. Aspects of the code might include "never abandon a teammate," "never humiliate anyone," and "keep all agreements."

Normative statements about teamwork by influential team members are also useful in reinforcing the norm of teamwork. A team member might assume a leadership role by saying to coworkers: "I'm glad this project is a joint effort. I know that's what earns us merit points here."

Group Emotional Intelligence   The leader's role in developing teamwork can also be described as helping the group develop emotional intelligence. The leader contributes to the group's emotional intelligence by creating norms that establish mutual trust among members. It is also important for members to have a sense of group identity as defined in their mission statement. Group efficacy, or feeling competent to complete the group task, also contributes to emotional intelligence. Ensuring that the group has the right skills can enhance such efficacy. These three conditions—mutual trust, group identity, and group efficacy—are the foundation of cooperation and collaboration.

The leader can also promote group emotional intelligence by bringing emotions to the surface in both group and one-on-one meetings. The leader then discusses how these emotions might be affecting the group's work.[13] For example, team members might discuss how they feel about their perceived importance to the organization. One maintenance group said that they felt entirely unappreciated until a key piece of equipment broke down, and this under-appreciation was adversely affecting their morale. The team leader helped the group develop an internal public relations campaign about their contribution to productivity.

Another example of dealing with emotions is encouraging group members to speak up when they feel the group is being either unproductive or highly productive. Expressing positive emotion can be an energizer.

Emphasizing Pride in Being Outstanding   A standard way to build team spirit, if not teamwork, is to help the group realize why it should be proud of its accomplishments. Most groups are particularly good at some task. The leader should help the group identify that task or characteristic and promote it as a key strength. A shipping department, for example, might have the best on-time shipping record in the region. Or a claims-processing unit might have the fewest overpayments in an insurance company.

To try your hand at being part of an outstanding team, do Leadership Skill-Building Exercise 6-1.

Serving as a Model of Teamwork, Including Power Sharing   A powerful way for a leader to foster teamwork is to be a positive model of team play. And one way to exemplify teamwork is to reveal important information about ideas and attitudes relevant to the group's work. As a result of this behavior, team members may follow suit. A leader's self-disclosure fosters teamwork because it leads to shared perceptions and concerns.[14] Self-disclosure is an element of leader transparency.

Interacting extensively with team members serves as a model of teamwork because it illustrates the mechanism by which team development takes place—frequent informal communication. While interacting with team members, the team leader can emphasize that he or she is a team member. For example, the

LEADERSHIP SKILL-BUILDING EXERCISE 6-1

Shelters for the Homeless

This exercise should take about thirty-five minutes; it can be done inside or outside class. Organize the class into teams of about six people. Each team takes on the assignment of formulating plans for building temporary shelters for the homeless. The dwellings you plan to build, for example, might be two-room cottages with electricity and indoor plumbing. During the time allotted to the task, formulate plans for going ahead with Shelters for the Homeless. Consider dividing up work by assigning certain roles to each team member. Sketch out tentative answers to the following questions: (1) How will you obtain funding for your venture?

(2) Which homeless people will you help? (3) Where will your shelters be? (4) Who will do the construction?

After your plan is completed, evaluate the quality of the teamwork that took place within the group. Review the chapter for techniques you might have used to improve it.

The same kind of teamwork skills you use in this exercise can be readily applied to most teamwork assignments on the job. Note carefully that although some types of teams call for members to be generalists, dividing up the tasks is still a basic principle of collective effort.

team leader might say, "Remember the deadline. We must all have the proposal in the mail by Thursday." A less team-member-oriented statement would be, "Remember the deadline. I need the proposals in the mail by Thursday."[15]

Another way of being a model of teamwork is to share power with group members because a good team player avoids hogging power and making all of the decisions. As each team member takes the opportunity to exert power, he or she feels more like a major contributor to team effort. Peter Pronovost, an anesthesiologist and critical-care specialist at Johns Hopkins Hospital, believes that hospitals would be safer for patients with more power sharing among physicians and other medical personnel. (The mistakes in hospitals he refers to include ordering the wrong drug or operating on the wrong limb.) Pronovost believes that nurses should have the power to challenge doctors, and members of the medical team need to work like flight crews in terms of power sharing to help minimize medical mistakes.[16]

To be a model of team play as a leader, you need the attitudes of a team player. Leadership Self-Assessment Quiz 6-2 gives you an opportunity to measure such attitudes.

LEADERSHIP SELF-ASSESSMENT QUIZ 6-2

Team Player Attitudes

Instructions: Describe how well you agree with each of the following statements, using the following scale: disagree strongly (DS); disagree (D); neutral (N); agree (A); agree strongly (AS).

	DS	D	N	A	AS
1. I am at my best when working alone.	5	4	3	2	1
2. I have belonged to clubs and teams since I was a child.	1	2	3	4	5
3. It takes far too long to get work accomplished with a group.	5	4	3	2	1
4. I like the friendship of working in a group.	1	2	3	4	5
5. I would prefer to run a one-person business than to be a member of a large firm.	5	4	3	2	1
6. It is difficult to trust others in the group on key assignments.	5	4	3	2	1
7. Encouraging others comes to me naturally.	1	2	3	4	5
8. I like the give-and-take of ideas that is possible in a group.	1	2	3	4	5
9. It is fun to share responsibility with others in the group.	1	2	3	4	5
10. Much more can be accomplished by a team than by the same number of people working alone.	1	2	3	4	5
11. I will often poke fun at my other members of my work group through a social media post.	5	4	3	2	1
12. I would pay a deserving compliment to a team member through a social media post.	1	2	3	4	5

Total score: _____

Scoring and Interpretation: Add the numbers you circled to obtain your total score.

- **46–60:** You have strong positive attitudes toward being a team member and working cooperatively with other members.
- **35–46:** You have moderately favorable attitudes toward being a team member and working cooperatively with other members.
- **15–34:** You much prefer working by yourself to being a team member. To work effectively in a company that emphasizes teamwork, you may need to develop more positive attitudes toward working jointly with others.

Using a Consensus Leadership Style   Teamwork is enhanced when a leader practices consensus decision making. Contributing to important decisions helps group members feel that they are valuable to the team. Consensus decision making also leads to an exchange of ideas within the group, with group members supporting and refining each other's suggestions. As a result, the feeling of working jointly on problems is enhanced. Generation X managers (born between 1965 and 1980) and Generation Y managers (born between 1981 and 2002) are likely to practice consensus leadership. Of course, it is the older members of Generation Y who would hold managerial positions. Part of the reason is that many of these people have taken leadership courses. Bonnie Stedt, an independent human resources professional, made this analysis of Generation X managers that still holds today and that would also apply to Generation Y managers:

> I look at them as a very promising generation. They bring so much to the work force especially as managers. Xers tend to be flexible, good at collaboration and consensus building and mature beyond their years. They are also capable of multitasking. Gen-X managers are very team oriented, and they absolutely want everyone on the team to get credit.[17]

Striving for consensus does not mean that all conflict is submerged to make people agree. Disagreements over issues are healthy, and team members are more likely to be committed to the consensus decision if their voice has been heard. When voices are heard, some power is shared. An example of a conflict over an issue would be the marketing team of an automotive company debating whether dealer discounts improve sales in the long run.

Establishing Urgency, Demanding Performance Standards, and Providing Direction   Team members need to believe that the team has urgent, constructive purposes. They also want a list of explicit expectations. The more urgent and relevant the rationale is, the more likely it is that the team will achieve its potential. A customer service team was told that further growth for the corporation would be impossible without major improvements in providing service to customers. Energized by this information, the team met the challenge.

To help establish urgency, it is helpful for the leader to challenge the group regularly. Teamwork is enhanced when the leader provides the team valid facts and information that motivate them to work together to modify the status quo. New information prompts the team to redefine and enrich its understanding of the challenge it is facing. As a result, the team is likely to focus on a common purpose, set clearer goals, and work together more smoothly.[18]

Encouraging Competition with Another Group   One of the best-known methods of encouraging teamwork is rallying the support of the group against a real or imagined threat from the outside. Beating the competition makes more sense when the competition is outside your organization. When the enemy is within, the team spirit within may become detrimental to the overall organization, and we-they problems may arise. While encouraging competition with another group, the leader should encourage rivalry, not intense competition that might lead to unethical business practices, such as making false charges against them. An example of ethical competition against another group would be a product development group at Research In Motion (producer of the BlackBerry) competing to produce a tablet computer to compete against the iPad of Apple Inc.

Encouraging the Use of Jargon   Lee G. Bolman and Terrence E. Deal contend that the symbolic and ritualistic framework of a group contributes heavily to teamwork. An important part of this framework is a specialized language that fosters cohesion and commitment. In essence, this specialized language is in-group jargon that creates a bond among team members; sets the group apart from outsiders; reinforces unique values and beliefs, thus contributing to corporate culture; and allows team members to communicate easily, with few misunderstandings.[19] Examples of in-group jargon at Microsoft Corporation are to label an intelligent person as having "bandwidth," and a serious person as being "hardcore."

Minimizing Micromanagement   A strategic perspective on encouraging teamwork is for the leader to minimize **micromanagement**, the close monitoring of most aspects of group member activities (as will be discussed in Chapter 8 in relation to leadership behaviors). To be a good team leader, the manager must give group members ample opportunity to manage their own activities. Avoiding micromanagement is a core ingredient of employee empowerment because empowered workers are given considerable latitude to manage their own activities. Not stepping in to make suggestions or corrections helps team members develop, and the feeling of growing professionally will often translate into workers developing a stronger team spirit.

A micromanager is also referred to as a *control freak*, because he or she wants to maintain so much control. Mickey Drexler, formerly of Gap, and now CEO of J. Crew, is by his own admission a control freak. His job satisfaction is the highest when he is involved in every facet of merchandising, even button selection. He also personally responds to shopper e-mails and telephone calls. Drexler is an acknowledged merchandising talent, and also the CEO and part owner of J. Crew, so his micromanaging is tolerated. At the team level, a micromanager might be perceived as more of an annoyance.[20]

The contingency leader recognizes the fine line between avoiding micromanagement and not providing the guidance and accountability that team members may need to function well as a unit. Consultant Bruce Tulgan reports, "When we asked employees what they want from the people above them, the first thing they mention is never a raise. It's always more coaching, more guidance, clearer goals, more constructive criticism, and more recognition for achievement."[21] An implication is that a manager tinged with a little micromanagement is likely to engage in these constructive behaviors.

Practicing E-Leadership for Virtual Teams   The heavy presence of communication technology has had a significant impact on team leadership, especially when team members do not work in the same physical location.

If team leader Jennifer, based in Seattle, sends a note of congratulations to team member Surinda, based in Mumbai, she is practicing e-leadership. Jennifer and Surinda are part of a virtual team: They work with each other, yet they do not share the same physical facility. **E-leadership** is a form of leadership practiced in a context where work is mediated by information technology. The leadership focus shifts from individuals to networks of relationships because the Internet facilitates connecting so many people.[22] E-leadership could, therefore, encompass any activity undertaken by a leader when the Internet connects people. Our concern here is how e-leadership facilitates building teamwork, especially in a virtual team.

When team members are geographically dispersed, a leader's communication with team members takes place using information technology, including the dissemination of information needed for task accomplishment. A participative leader may establish chat rooms to solicit opinions from members of a crossborder virtual team before reaching a final decision. The leader might also conduct an electronic poll to attain consensus on a controversial issue and have all team members share their reactions on an intranet or social media site.

The leader can foster team spirit (and therefore teamwork) by sending congratulatory e-mail messages for a job well done. In short, the e-leader improves teamwork by staying connected electronically to team members—although not to the point of blitzing them with so many messages that he or she becomes an annoyance.

Based on observations, interviews, and survey data, two intensive studies have identified leadership practices of effective leaders of virtual teams. The purpose of these practices is to overcome the unique challenges of managing virtual teams, such as not being able to see in-person when the team needs focus and direction. The conclusions of the researchers along with a few other studies dealing mostly with building teamwork are presented next.[23]

1. *When building a virtual team, solicit volunteers when feasible.* As the experiences at Wikipedia and Linux have shown, virtual teams appear to thrive when they include volunteers with valuable skills. A team of volunteers has an elite status that contributes to team spirit. In addition to being volunteers, it is helpful for the virtual team to include members who already know each other. In this way a component of camaraderie already exists.

2. *Ensure that the task is meaningful to the team and the company.* Ideally, the team task should resonate with the values of each member and the team collectively. Team members working on a relevant task are more likely to be spirited and co-operative. A case in point is when Alcoa, Inc., wanted to improve knowledge transfer and innovation in its Global Primary Products division. To most members of a technical team, knowledge sharing and innovation are highly worthwhile because these workers tend to be intellectually curious. The company created a web of global virtual teams that operate outside and across the traditional lines of authority.

The virtual teams are credited with generating substantial increases in production output and saving millions of dollars in operating costs. People assigned to the teams were required to do extra work beyond their regular responsibilities. To help cope with this problem of work overload, the professionals were assigned technically challenging tasks of interest to them. Of significance, virtual team members had some leeway in choosing which tasks to tackle.[24]

3. *Establish and maintain trust through the use of communication technology.* A major hurdle in working with a virtual team is deciding on what information gets communicated and to whom. In some instances, a norm might be established that restricts members from conveying negative information to anyone outside the team. It is also useful to ensure that all team members are equally inconvenienced by time zone differences, such as having a meeting at 3 A.M. their time. Meeting times would be rotated so team members in one time zone would not suffer.

4. *Ensure that diversity in the team is understood, appreciated, and leveraged.* Diversity within the team can take many forms, such as experiences, skills, and interests. To ensure that diversity is understood and appreciated, leaders frequently develop an *expertise directory* when the team first forms. The directory can include a photo of each member along with details about his or her training, experience, and previous assignments. A skills matrix of team members can serve the same purpose.

5. *Maintain frequent communications, including virtual meetings.* The majority of team leaders in the study reported that regular audio-conferences involving all members were the lifeblood of the team, even when tasks were distributed among the team members. The virtual meetings are used to keep members engaged, excited about the work, and aligned with each other. At the beginning of the meeting, it is helpful to have the team member reconnect with the human side of each team member. Exchanging personal stories helps build closeness.

Other forms of communication besides audio-conferences can serve the function of developing teamwork. At Nokia, for example, the favored communication tool is text messaging, while at other companies e-mail or voice mail was more effective. A growing number of companies are using internal social media websites to encourage frequent shared interaction among team members. Most importantly, communication should be frequent and rapid.

An example of a virtual team keeping in close touch is the Pantone Color Institute team that searches around the world to forecast which colors are likely to be hot for consumer purposes. While the team is scattered across the country and makes international trips, they are in frequent contact by phone, e-mail, or in-person meetings to share and interpret their findings. Team leader Leatrice Eiseman says, "Forecasting is a marriage of trend directions. It's about how many places I'm seeing a color—if it's popping up in graphics and products. Not just on the runway."[25] (Notice that the team has to work together smoothly to blend their findings.)

6. *Monitor team progress through the use of technology.* An example of monitoring would be checking to see who is using the team's online knowledge repository regularly and who is not. The leader can also check to see if some members are not doing their fair share of work, and then coach the underperformer. This approach might improve teamwork because loafers drag down a team.

7. *Enhance external visibility of the team and its members.* Virtual team members may have at least two bosses (the virtual team leader and the on-site boss) so it is important that the work of the virtual team gets reported externally. A virtual team in the electronics testing industry was required to report the team's results to a steering committee. The link to teamwork is that receiving rewards and recognition helps build team spirit.

8. *Ensure that individuals benefit from participating in virtual teams.* Even if the members are good team players, they need personal benefits to experience team spirit. One approach is to have virtual reward ceremonies, such as having gifts delivered to each team member and then having a virtual party. (No need for designated drivers here because the party takes place at the homes of team members!) The team leader can also encourage executives at the team members' work environment to thank the team members. Offering opportunities for personal growth, such as mini-lectures by an expert, can also be helpful.

9. *To maintain a high touch environment, conduct one or two face-to-face meetings per year.* According to Richard Lepsinger, president of OnPoint Consulting, electronic technology is not a perfect substitute for human interaction. Lack of attention during virtual meetings is a warning sign to look for. Virtual teams that invest in one or two face-to-face meetings annually tend to perform better than those who skip such meetings.[26] Even the use of the most advanced videoconferencing equipment or Skype lacks the feel of interacting with a colleague face to face.

10. *Recognize and reward above-average individual and team performance.* As with other types of teams, the rewards given to virtual teams should be linked to individual and team goals and they should be rewarded frequently.

You will observe that the ten suggestions for leading virtual teams include both actions leaders can take on their own, plus the use of company technology.

Actions Generally Requiring Organization Structure or Policy

Designing Physical Structures That Facilitate Communication   Group cohesiveness, and therefore teamwork, is fostered when team members are located close together and can interact frequently and easily. In contrast, people who spend most of their time in their private offices or cubicles are less likely to interact. Frequent interaction often leads to camaraderie and a feeling of belongingness. A useful tactic for achieving physical proximity is to establish a shared physical facility, such as a conference room, research library, or beverage lounge. This area should be decorated differently from other areas in the building, and a few amenities should be added, such as a coffeepot, microwave oven, and refrigerator. Team members can then use this area for refreshments and group interaction.

Recognizing the contribution of a shared physical facility to promoting teamwork, many organizations have incorporated more open working space into the workplace, often eliminating private offices. Many people express dissatisfaction with this lack of privacy, but it is difficult to assess the productivity loss and morale problems stemming from limited opportunity for quiet reflection on the job.

Emphasizing Group Recognition and Rewards Giving rewards for group accomplishment reinforces teamwork because people receive rewards for what they have achieved collaboratively. Also, much of work that is accomplished in organizations requires collaboration, so group rewards are justifiable and sensible. The recognition accompanying the reward should emphasize the team's value to the organization rather than that of the individual. Recognition promotes team identity by enabling the team to take pride in its contributions and progress. The following are examples of team recognition:

- A display wall for team activities such as certificates of accomplishment, schedules, and miscellaneous announcements
- Team logos on items such as identifying T-shirts, athletic caps, mugs, jackets, key rings, and business cards
- Celebrations to mark milestones such as first-time activities, cost savings, and safety records
- Equipment painted in team colors
- Athletic team events such as softball, volleyball, and bowling
- Team-of-the-Month award, with gifts from the organization to team members or to the entire team

A warning is that many employees may view switching to a team-based pay plan that places much of their pay at risk as an unnerving proposition.

Initiating Ritual and Ceremony Another way to enhance teamwork is to initiate ritual and ceremony.[27] Ritual and ceremony afford opportunities for reinforcing values, revitalizing spirit, and bonding workers to one another and to the team. An example is holding a team dinner whenever the group achieves a major milestone, such as making a winning bid on a major contract. Another formal ritual is to send a team on a retreat to develop its mission and goals and to build camaraderie. When the team is working and socializing closely together during the retreat—even one long day—teamwork is reinforced.

Practicing Open-Book Management A method of getting the company working together as a team is to share information about company finances and strategy with large numbers of employees. In **open-book management** every employee is trained, empowered, and motivated to understand and pursue the company's business goals. In this way employees become business partners and perceive themselves to be members of the same team.

In a full form of open-book management, workers share strategic and financial information as well as responsibility. The company also shares risks and rewards based on results, so workers are likely to pull together as a team so that the company can succeed.[28] The idea is to have a well-informed, partner-oriented, high-performance company. Part of keeping workers well informed is for company leaders to host roundtable discussions about company financial information. Another approach is to regularly disseminate, by e-mail, information about the company's financial progress.

Selecting Team-Oriented Members   A foundation strategy for achieving good teamwork is to select members for the team with aptitude, skill, and interest in teamwork. (Selecting team-oriented members is often a company policy, but it is also an action managers can take operating on their own.) A starting point is self-selection. It is best for the team leader to choose workers who ask to be members of a team. A person's record of past team activity can also help one determine whether that person is an effective team player (as suggested in the opening case to this chapter). Many managers believe that those who participate in team sports now or in the past are likely to be good team players on the job.

At times, workers will be assigned to the team rather than selected by the team leader or team members, so selecting team-oriented members is not possible. Among the key criteria for selecting teamwork-oriented members would be teamwork experience, prior success as a team player, and favorable personality traits such as agreeableness and extraversion.

Todd Carlisle, the Google staffing manager, looks carefully for teamwork preferences and skills when selecting new employees for the company. One of Carlisle's criteria is simply how likeable the candidates are: "You have to want to take them to lunch after the interview. It's important to hire leaders who play well with others, so ask about their experiences working on a team. Their bragging that they convinced everybody else that they were right or taking credit for everything are red flags."[29]

Using Technology That Enhances Teamwork   Workers can collaborate better when they use information technology that fosters collaboration, often referred to as *groupware*. For example, the straightforward act of exchanging frequent e-mail messages and instant messages can facilitate cooperation. Electronic brainstorming is another example of groupware. Virtual teams by their nature rely on information technology to enhance teamwork.

Advances in videoconferencing facilitate teamwork because of the ease in which geographically separated workers can participate in a virtual conference and exchange ideas *almost* as effectively as in a face-to-face meeting. An example is that Cisco Systems relies extensively on TelePresence, an advanced conferencing system installed in its own offices, customer offices, and in the homes of company executives. Meetings can be called spontaneously and group decisions made rapidly without traveling.[30]

Social networking might be regarded as the most far-reaching technology for enhancing teamwork because so many workers can exchange information with each other and thereby collaborate more extensively. Also, when groups of people can readily see what information others are exchanging, a spirit of cooperation might develop. Even the exchange of jokes and interesting YouTube and Hulu videos might improve team spirit.

David Eisert, associate director of emerging technologies at the Kelley School of Business, Indiana University, says, "When you've got people in the network engaged, sharing information and openly communicating, that's where the meat of knowledge transfer comes from."[31] When the knowledge transfer leads to more collaboration, teamwork is enhanced. Merely glancing over posted information and doing nothing about it has no positive impact on teamwork.

The accompanying Leader in Action insert illustrates how leaders are using social networking websites to develop teamwork.

LEADER IN ACTION

Kevin Kaplan of Long Realty Builds Teamwork with Internal Social Networking

Agents from Long Realty in Tucson, Arizona were eager to find a safe place to discuss the complexities of the real estate market after the housing bubble burst a few years ago. Some of the agents began exchanging information on Facebook, but anyone could read their comments including clients and bankers.

Having that conversation on Facebook wasn't the appropriate venue, said Kevin Kaplan, vice president of marketing and technology at Long Realty.

As a result, Long Realty launched a revolutionary new agent-to-agent social media networking platform called Long Connects that enables their agents to connect to other Long Realty professionals in a safe, online environment. This is yet another way Long Realty is taking the industry lead to help their real estate professionals work smarter and more efficiently to provide the highest level of service.

For several years, real estate agents have been using social media for marketing purposes. By using photo and video sharing to make listings more attractive, many agents have been able to attract more buyers.

An example would be presenting a story about an unusual home for sale. Real estate veterans also use professional networking sites to hone their sales skills. Yet using social networking to enhance teamwork within a real estate company is a recent development.

Long Realty is one of the first real estate companies to implement this type of internal social media network. It is an entirely new way for their agents to interact, network, and accomplish their work. By implementing this new online agent community, Long Realty is setting the technological standard to help further extend cooperation and teamwork among their agents.

Agents can network with each other and share information more efficiently to help match buyers and sellers. Long Realty agents can also use this new platform to learn from each other and from the company by keeping one another up to date with the latest industry developments, newest marketing and technology trends, and best business practices.

Rosey Koberlein, CEO of the Long Companies, says: "Long Connects uses the latest Enterprise 2.0 technology to empower our team of real estate professionals to provide the best service possible while increasing their knowledge and level of productivity."

"Long Connects uses a powerful social media technology suite in a secure intranet environment to connect our sales associates, Core Services teams and employees," states Kaplan. The features that enable the real estate professionals to connect with each other Include online forums, media galleries, micro blogging, and community groups. Long has taken a giant step forward integrating social media into Its everyday business practice.

Long Connects is making it possible for Long Realty agents to develop their professional relationships, advance their real estate skills, and grow their business into a robust business model that could help shape the future of real estate.

QUESTIONS

1. How does the internal social networking site Long Connects facilitate teamwork?

2. Why might Long Connects be better for enhancing cooperation among agents than old fashioned methods such as making phone calls or having lunch together?

3. What type of leadership is Kevin Kaplan exercising?

Source: Debbie Goodman-Butler, "Long Realty Launches New Social Media Platform to Help Agents Connect," *www.thesmarterwaytosell. com/LongConnects.asp*, © 2001–2011 Long Realty Company. A HomeServices of America Inc. company; Susan Ladika, "Socially Evolved," *Workforce Management*, September 2010, pp. 18–19; Lauren Beale, "More Real Estate Agents Turning to Social Media," *Los Angeles Times*, June 16, 2011 (http://articles.latimes.com/2011); Erica Swallow, "How Real Estate Pros are Using Social Media for Real Results,"*http://mashable.com*, June 28, 2010, pp. 1–2.

Blending Representatives from the Domestic Company and Foreign Nationals on the Team   Cross-cultural considerations enter into enhancing teamwork, as well as in most aspects of leadership. The fact of working with people from your own country, as well as a representative from the country of company headquarters often enhances teamwork. Perhaps having a representative from the parent company, yet still respecting local talent, creates a spirit of cooperation. Also, blending cultural differences is appealing to some workers and might make them more interested in performing as a team.

A case in point is the experience of Jessica C. Isaacs, senior vice president of field operations for a reinsurance division of AIG. She notes: "Every time we've opened in a new country, instead of shipping expats in we've seen a transition from that and we've started to hire more local talent. My best performing teams are teams where I have lots of local talent sprinkled with some expat or foreign talent. Having the balance really optimizes everyone's skill set and opens new opportunities."[32]

OFFSITE TRAINING AND TEAM DEVELOPMENT

Cognitive information about strategies and tactics for improving teamwork is potentially valuable. People reading such information can selectively apply the concepts, observe the consequences, and then fine-tune an approach. Another approach to developing teamwork is to participate in experiential activities (several are presented throughout this text).

The most popular experiential approach to building teamwork and leadership skills is offsite outdoor training, also referred to as outdoor training. Wilderness training is closely associated with outdoor training, except that the setting is likely to be much rougher—perhaps in the frozen plains of northernmost Minnesota. Some forms of outdoor training take place in city parks, as well as in the city itself in order to rehabilitate or build a house.

Both outdoor and wilderness training are forms of learning by doing. Participants are supposed to acquire leadership and teamwork skills by confronting physical challenges and exceeding their self-imposed limitations. The goals of outdoor training are reasonably consistent across different training groups. The Big Rock Creek Camp, which offers team building and leadership training, specifies these representative goals:

- Discover your strengths and weaknesses.
- Test your limits (they are far broader than you imagine).
- Work together as a team.
- Have fun.
- Face the essence of who you are and what you are made of.

Features of Outdoor and Offsite Training Programs

Program participants are placed in a demanding outdoor environment, where they rely on skills they did not realize they had and on one another to complete the program. The emphasis is on building not only teamwork but also self-confidence for leadership. Sometimes lectures on leadership, self-confidence, and teamwork precede the activity. The list of what constitutes a team-building activity continues to grow and now includes tightrope walking, gourmet cooking as a team, paintballing, and scavenger hunts. Building or repairing houses for people in need is popular, as described in one of the cases in the end of this chapter. Another novel approach is for participants to work with horses in a stable to simulate the role of the boss and employee (played by the horse). In one of these team-building activities, blindfolded individuals mount the horses and rely on coworkers to guide them through an obstacle course.[33]

Outward Bound is the best-known and largest outdoor training program. It offers more than 500 courses in wilderness areas in twenty states and provinces. The courses typically run from three days to four weeks. Worldwide, Outward Bound runs about forty-eight schools on five continents. The Outward Bound Professional Development Program, geared toward organizational leaders, emphasizes teamwork, leadership, and risk taking. The wilderness is the classroom, and the instructors draw analogies between each outdoor activity and the workplace. Among the courses offered are dog-sledding, skiing and winter camping, desert backpacking, canoe expeditions, sailing, sea kayaking, alpine mountaineering, mountain backpacking and horse-trailing, and cycling.

Rope activities are typical of outdoor training. Participants are attached to a secure pulley with ropes; then they climb up a ladder and jump off to another spot. Sometimes the rope is extended between two trees. Another activity is a trust fall, in which each person takes a turn standing on a platform and falling backward into the arms of coworkers. The trust fall can also be done on ground level. Many readers of this book have already participated in a trust fall. Leadership Skill-Building Exercises 6-2 and 6-3 present representative offsite activities.

LEADERSHIP SKILL-BUILDING EXERCISE 6-2

The Newspaper Shelter

The objective of this exercise is to allow for observation of team interaction while exploring communication skills, co-operation, planning, and having fun. Organize the class into teams of about seven to ten people. The materials required are newspapers and masking tape or duct tape.

Imagine that you are stuck in the desert or on a deserted island. Your assignment is to build a structure that is free-standing and will protect the entire group from the sun. (If weather and time permit, this activity might be conducted outdoors.) You have about fifteen minutes to plan how you are going to build the structure. After the fifteen minutes, you will have twenty minutes to build the structure, but you are not allowed to talk to each other during the building phase.

After the activity is completed, answer the following questions about team process:

1. What worked during the process? What hindered the process?
2. How did the planning take place?
3. Did everyone have an active role?
4. How did it feel to not be able to talk during the building phase?
5. Did you work as a team? How did you know?
6. What did you learn about yourself and your team-mates during this exercise?

Source: Adapted from the Leadership Center at Washington State University.

LEADERSHIP SKILL-BUILDING EXERCISE 6-3

Trust Me

Part of trusting team members is to trust them with your physical safety. The trust builder described here has been incorporated into many team-building programs. Proceed as follows:

- *Step 1:* Each group member takes a turn being blindfolded, perhaps using a bandanna.
- *Step 2:* The remaining team members arrange between five and eight chairs into a formation of their choosing, using a different formation for each blindfolded member.
- *Step 3:* At the appropriate signal from a team member, the blindfolded person starts to walk. The rest of the team gives instructions that will enable

the blindfolded person to get past the formation of chairs without a collision.
- *Step 4:* At the end of the blindfolded person's experience, he or she immediately answers the following questions: (a) How did you feel when blindfolded in this exercise? (b) Explain why you either trusted or did not trust your team members. (c) What did you need from your team members while you were blindfolded?
- *Step 5:* After each person has taken a turn, discuss in your team (a) the impact of this exercise on the development of trust in teams and (b) what you learned about teamwork from the exercise.

Outdoor training enhances teamwork by helping participants examine the process of getting things done through working with people. Participants practice their communication skills in exercises such as rappelling down a cliff by issuing precise instructions to one another about how to scale the cliff safely. At the same time, they have to learn to trust one another because their survival appears to depend on trust.

One of the most intensive and extensive examples of team building through outdoor training is conducted annually at Seagate Technology, the leading manufacturer of hard drives. About 200 employees from around the world spend a week in Queenstown, New Zealand, located at the bottom of the world. The activities include hiking, kayaking, adventure racing, and breaking boards with the goal of building a more collaborative, team-oriented company. (Adventure racing is about running and biking through an unfamiliar course, such as at the bottom of a glacier.) Participants frequently shout to each other, "You're awesome," throughout many of the activities. A major rationale for the extensive team-building activity is that when people are placed in unfamiliar situations, especially when fatigued, they are more likely to ask for help and work as a team.[34]

Evaluation of Outdoor Training for Team Development

Many outdoor trainers and participants believe strongly that they derive substantial personal benefits from outdoor training. Among the most important are greater self-confidence, appreciating hidden strengths, and learning to work better with others. Strong proponents of outdoor training believe that those who do not appreciate the training simply do not understand it. Many training directors also have positive attitudes toward outdoor training. They believe that a work team that experiences outdoor training will work more cooperatively back at the office. For example, Ron Roberts, the president of Action Centered Training, points out that paintball may have little to do with a job but it can have a powerful effect. Winning demands teamwork, including forceful communication. Roberts says, "If they don't work as a team, they get shot and experience pain. It's not for everybody. But the principles of communication, teamwork, leadership and strategic planning are there."[35]

Many people have legitimate reservations about outdoor training, however. Although outdoor trainers claim that almost no accidents occur, a threat to health and life does exist, and groin injuries are frequent. (To help minimize casualties, participants usually need medical clearance.) Another concern is that the teamwork learned in outdoor training does not spill over into the job environment. Based on his research, management professor Chris Neck concludes that there is little compelling evidence of long-term benefits for entire teams, but there is evidence that individuals' attitudes and teamwork skills improve immediately after the exercises.[36]

A major concern about offsite training is that some participants or potential participants find it repellent. Not every worker wants to play games, climb rocks, or prepare a gourmet meal with coworkers after hours. They would prefer a more natural, relaxing environment in which to build teamwork, such as doing volunteer work or having a family day at the workplace.[37]

One way to facilitate the transfer of training from outdoors to the office is to hold debriefing and follow-up sessions. Debriefing takes place at the end of outdoor training. The participants review what they learned and discuss how they will apply their lessons to the job. Follow-up sessions can then be held periodically to describe progress in applying the insights learned during outdoor training.

THE LEADER–MEMBER EXCHANGE MODEL AND TEAMWORK

Research and theory about the development of teamwork lag research and theory about many other aspects of leadership. Nevertheless, the leader–member exchange model, developed by George Graen and associates, helps explain why one subgroup in a unit is part of a cohesive team but another group is excluded.[38] The theory, already mentioned several times in this text, deals with the relationship between a leader and a team member. However, the same theory tells us a lot about teamwork.

The **leader–member exchange model (LMX)** proposes that leaders develop unique working relationships with group members. One subset of employees, the in-group, is given additional rewards, responsibility, and trust in exchange for their loyalty and performance. The in-group becomes part of a smoothly functioning team headed by the formal leader. In contrast, the out-group employees are treated in accordance with a more formal understanding of leader–group member relations. Out-group members are less likely to experience good teamwork.

Figure 6-1 depicts the major concept of the leader–member exchange model. Here we look at several aspects of LMX as it relates most closely to teamwork. Leader–member exchange has also been researched in relationship to many other aspects of workplace behavior, and published research about LMX continues to expand.

Different-Quality Relationships

Leaders do not typically use the same leadership style in dealing with all group members. Instead, they treat each member somewhat differently. The linkages (relationships) that exist between the leader and each individual team member

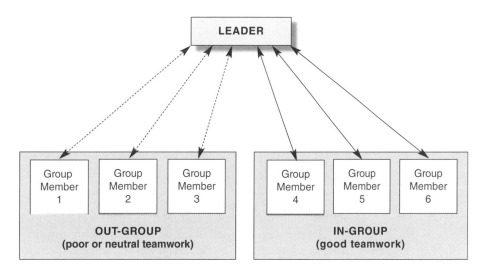

FIGURE 6-1 The Leader–Member Exchange Model.

Source: From Gregory Moorhead and Ricky W. Griffin, *Organizational Behavior: Managing People and Organizations*, 4th ed., 314. Copyright © 1995 by Houghton Mifflin Company. Reprinted by permission of Houghton Mifflin Company.

probably differ in quality. In theory, the differences lie on a continuum of low quality to high quality. With group members on the top half of the continuum, the leader has a good relationship; with those on the lower half of the continuum, the leader has a poor relationship. Each of these pairs of relationships, or dyads, must be judged in terms of whether a group member is in or out with the leader. The positive regard that leaders and members have for each other is a major contributor to the quality of their relationship.[39]

A note of caution about leader-member exchanges is that evidence suggests that the leader and the group members may perceive the quality of the exchange differently.[40] For example, the leader might think the exchange is positive, whereas the subordinate might think the exchange is neutral or negative. Because of this difference in perception, the leader should look carefully for evidence of the quality of a relationship with a given subordinate.

Treatment of In-Group versus Out-Group Members   In-group members are invited to participate in important decision making, are given added responsibility, and are privy to interesting gossip. Members of the out-group are managed according to the requirements of their employment contract. They receive little warmth, inspiration, or encouragement. In-group members tend to achieve a higher level of performance, commitment, and satisfaction than do out-group members. Furthermore, they are less likely to quit. A study conducted in a retail setting found that when the quality of the leader–member exchange is high, group members are more strongly committed to company goals.[41] In turn, this commitment leads to stronger teamwork because the workers pull together to pursue goals.

Reciprocity between Leader and Members   The in-group versus out-group status also includes an element of reciprocity or exchange. The leader grants more favors to the in-group member, who in response works harder to please the leader, a contributor to being a good team player. Two studies provide more specific information about the consequences of a positive exchange between a supervisor and group members. In a hospital setting, positive exchanges involved group members' engaging in increased good citizenship behavior and in-group role behaviors such as putting extra effort into performing their duties.[42] As a result, the leader would feel justified in granting the in-group members more resources, such as a larger salary increase or a larger budget.

Extra-Role Behavior   A study conducted in diverse industrial settings also found that high-quality exchanges between supervisors and employees contribute to employees' engaging in extra-role behavior, or being cooperative in ways that were not expected of them. Supervisory ratings of employee altruism were used to measure helping behaviors, as when an accountant helps a sales representative prepare a sales forecast. The researchers concluded that through the development of high-quality relationships with group members, supervisors are able to motivate the group members and enable them to engage in helping behaviors that benefit them as well as their coworkers.[43]

Safety Performance   Another contribution of positive LMXs is that they facilitate good safety performance, an important aspect of teamwork in many work environments. Sixty-four group leaders in a manufacturing plant participated in a study. A major finding of the study was that positive leader–member exchanges were associated with more communication about safety. The enhanced communication led to more commitment to safety, which in turn led to fewer accidents on the job.[44]

Transformational Effects   Another of the many consequences of positive leader–member exchanges is that they may facilitate the leader having a transformational effect. A study of 283 individuals from a broad cross-section of job types indicated that transformational relationships were significantly stronger for followers who perceived high-quality relationships with their supervisors. An example of a transformational relationship would be inspiring the subordinate to seek different perspectives when solving problems or bringing about change.[45] Transformational effects also tie in with teamwork because the workers become energized to jointly accomplish goals.

Leader Status   When group members perceive leaders to have high status, it is easier for the leader to form the type of high-quality relationships that contribute to good teamwork. A study of 184 bank employees and 42 managers found that leaders who were perceived to have higher quality relationships with their bosses and who were strongly connected to network members were regarded as having relatively high status. As a result, the leaders were able to have higher quality exchanges with their subordinates.[46]

First Impressions

The leader's first impression of a group member's competency plays an important role in placing the group member in the in-group or the out-group. Another key linking factor is whether the leader and team member have positive or negative chemistry. We can assume that group members who make effective use of influence and political tactics increase their chances of becoming members of the in-group.

A field study seems to confirm that first impressions make a difference. The researchers gathered ratings of six aspects of the manager–group member dyad. Results showed that the initial leader expectations of members and member expectations of the leader were good predictors of the leader–member exchanges at two weeks and at six weeks. Member expectations of the leader also accurately predicted member assessments of the quality of the leader–member exchange at six months. An important interpretation of these results is that the leader–member exchange is formed in the first days of the relationship.[47] As the adage states, "You have only one chance to make a good first impression."

In summary, the leader–member exchange model provides a partial explanation of teamwork development. Members of the in-group work smoothly together and with the leader because they feel privileged. Being a member of the out-group may not diminish teamwork, but it certainly does not make a positive contribution.

SUMMARY

Leaders are required to build teamwork because it is needed for such key activities as group problem solving and achieving high quality. Teamwork is an understanding of and commitment to group goals on the part of all group members.

Leaders still play an important role in a team-based organization, such as being expert in the team process, being facilitators, building trust and inspiring teamwork, and enabling and empowering group members to accomplish their work. The enabling role centers on empowerment. The external leader of a self-managing team plays a key role when the team faces disruptive conditions.

A wide range of leader actions fosters teamwork. Measures leaders can take using their own resources include (1) defining the team's mission and tasks; (2) establishing a climate of trust; (3) developing a norm of teamwork, including emotional intelligence; (4) emphasizing pride in being outstanding; (5) serving as a model of teamwork, including power sharing; (6) using a consensus leadership style; (7) establishing urgency, demanding performance standards, and providing direction; (8) encouraging competition with another group; (9) encouraging the use of jargon; (10) minimizing micromanagement; and (11) practicing e-leadership for virtual teams.

Techniques to foster teamwork that require relying on organization structure or policy include the following: (1) designing physical structures that facilitate communication; (2) emphasizing group recognition and rewards; (3) initiating ritual and ceremony; (4) practicing open-book management; (5) selecting team-oriented members; (6) using technology that facilitates teamwork including social media; and (7) blending representatives from the domestic company and foreign nationals on the team.

In outdoor (or off-site) training, a popular experiential approach to building teamwork and leadership skills, building self-confidence is the focus. Outdoor training enhances teamwork by helping participants examine the process of collaboration. The Outward Bound Professional Development Program is geared toward organization leaders. Opinion about the effectiveness of outdoor training for developing teamwork and leadership skills is mixed. Concern has been expressed that the skills learned in the field do not carry over to the workplace.

The leader–exchange model helps explain why one subgroup in a work unit is part of a cohesive team and another unit is excluded. According to the model, leaders develop unique working relationships with subordinates. As a result, in-groups and out-groups are created. Members of the in-group tend to perform better, have higher satisfaction, and exhibit more teamwork than members of the out-group. The leader's first impression of a group member's competency plays an important role in placing that person into the in-group or the out-group.

KEY TERMS

team

teamwork

cooperation theory

micromanagement

e-leadership

open-book management

leader–member exchange model (LMX)

✔ GUIDELINES FOR ACTION AND SKILL DEVELOPMENT

When attempting to develop teamwork, the leader would ordinarily be thinking of coaching individual team members to be more effective team players. Some research, however, suggests that teamwork is more likely to be enhanced when the team leader coaches the team as an entity.[48] For example, the team leader might meet with the group physically or through an internal website, and say, "I don't notice you folks offering each other enough constructive feedback. In an effective team, the members learn from each other."

Improving teamwork through the design of offices is receiving considerable attention. Texas Professional Training Associates explains how to customize your (you being the leader/manager) space to promote teamwork:

1. **Create common areas.** Have ample space, accessible from throughout your office, for the team to meet formally and informally. Leave your team-meeting tools—flip charts, whiteboards—in place even when the team is not meeting. One such building enables employees to collaborate more in a single, one-story space designed to encourage creative interaction and teamwork.

2. **Put yourself in the center.** Instead of reserving the back office, try to put yourself in the middle. You can be close to day-to-day action and more accessible to your team.

3. **Set up multipurpose rooms.** The back office can be used as a well-equipped workroom or library whenever team members—individually or in groups—feel they would be more productive away from their desks.

4. **Insert activity generators.** Lively activity depends on having generators to draw traffic and bring people together. In your office, this could be the coffeepot, the mailboxes, or the reception desk. Turn these areas into places for team members to gather and interact comfortably and productively.[49]

Discussion Questions and Activities

1. What would be the potential disadvantages of selecting a team leader who is highly charismatic and visionary?

2. How could you be a team leader, yet the team members are not really your subordinates?

3. To what extent do you think teamwork is required of members of the executive group of a business or not-for-profit organization?

4. Imagine yourself as the team leader, and the gang invites you to join them for an after-hours drink at a bar. From the standpoint of enhancing teamwork, explain whether joining the team would be effective.

5. Is there a role for independent-thinking, decisive, and creative leaders in a team-based organization? Explain.

6. What forces for and against being a good team player are embedded in U.S. culture?

7. As the team leader, should you dress in about the same fashion as the rest of the team? Or should you dress a little fancier? Explain your reasoning.

8. What is your opinion of the value of experience in team sports for becoming a good team player in the workplace?

9. Why would the team-building activity of preparing a gourmet meal lead to enhanced teamwork back on the job?

10. How can political skill help a person avoid being adversely affected by the leader–member exchange model?

LEADERSHIP CASE PROBLEM A

The Global Insurance Tag Team

Calvin is the director of disaster insurance at a global insurance company. He has a large department of his own in New York, but he is also the team leader of ten different representatives around the world. Each team member is responsible for encouraging the sales representatives in offices around the globe to sell disaster insurance to cover such risks as floods, hurricanes, earthquakes, and terrorist attacks.

As Calvin describes it, "I wear two major hats. One hat is the leader of my own group of professionals in the disaster insurance field. My other major hat is that of a team leader and product manager who is trying to get team members around the worlds to facilitate the sale of disaster insurance. What makes this hat so difficult is that the team members do not really report to me. To complicate matters further, the reps who actually sell the insurance do not actually report to the members of my team."

When asked how the disaster insurance team was performing, Calvin replied, "Not as well as I would like. I have to keep chasing after the team members to remind them of their roles in helping the company cover disaster risks. Hillary, my team leader in Great Britain, told me that I need to trigger an earthquake in Europe to get clients interested in more disaster insurance. She asked me to start a major flood as a second possibility."

"Another problem I'm facing," said Calvin, "is that I don't see much integrated effort among the team members. I do see a few e-mails sent to the group discussing common concerns, but I don't see much coordinated effort.

"We held a videoconference early this year, attempting to get everybody on board pulling together. One problem was that we couldn't get full participation because of the difficulty in finding a time to meet because of the wide spread in time zones. We had a few laughs, with Tom from Australia saying that his wife thought he was headed out to the pub, not really attending a late-night meeting.

"Another hurdle I need to conquer is that there seem to be some cross-cultural differences in the importance businesspeople attach to disaster insurance. Sophie, our team member in Columbia, told me that executives in South American countries worry less about potential disasters than do Americans. As a result, she said it is difficult for her to be as heavily committed to selling disaster insurance as some of the other team members."

"One of my biggest agenda items for the year," concluded Calvin, "is to get my disaster insurance team coordinating their efforts better."

Questions

1. Identify the teamwork problems you think Calvin might be facing.
2. What steps do you recommend Calvin take to enhance teamwork in his global disaster insurance team?
3. What might Calvin do to provide stronger leadership to his global team?

ASSOCIATED ROLE PLAY

One student plays the role of Calvin who is conducting a transnational videoconference to encourage better teamwork in selling disaster insurance. Four or five other students play the roles of team members across the globe, not all of whom are so convinced that disaster insurance will sell well in their country.

Home Rehab Day at Tymco

Fifteen years ago, Maria Cortez was working as a freelance writer of technical manuals for a variety of companies. The manuals supported a number of products, including household appliances, alarm systems, lawnmowers, and tractors. Soon, Cortez's freelance activity became more than she could handle, so she subcontracted work to one other freelancer, and then another, and then another. Two years later, Cortez founded Tymco, and the firm has grown steadily. The company now provides technical manuals, training and development, and foreign language translation and interpreting.

Tymco now employs seventy-five full-time employees, as well as about forty-five freelancers who help the company with peak loads and specialized services. For example, one freelancer translates software into Japanese. Another freelancer specializes in preparing user guides for digital cameras and digital video cameras.

Cortez recently became concerned that the unit heads and other key personnel in the company were not working particularly well as a team. She explained to Tim Atkins, a training specialist on the staff, "We all work for a company called Tymco, yet we function like independent units and freelancers. I notice that our staff members hardly ever have lunch together. I've arranged a couple of group dinners, and we have a nice meal, but no team spirit seems to develop.

"I think that if we had better teamwork, our units could help each other. We might even be able to cross-sell better. I'll give you an example. A person in the technical manual group might have an assignment to prepare a manual for an appliance. He or she should immediately mention that Tymco has another group that could do the foreign language translations for the manual. A lot of manuals for U.S. distribution are written in English, Spanish, and French."

Atkins replied, "Look, I've been eager to run a team development activity that has worked well for dozens of companies. It is so simple. We first designate who you think should be included in the group that requires the most development as a team. You choose one work day for the team-building activity. It involves targeting an old house badly in need of repair in a poor neighborhood. Abandoned houses don't count. We need a house with a family living in it. Working with churches in the neighborhood, it's easy to find a suitable house and a family willing to be helped.

"About a week before the team-building date, a handyperson and I visit the house to get some idea of the type of work that needs to be done. We then purchase paint, roofing shingles, wood, and other needed supplies. We also round up the ladders, paintbrushes, and tools. Our team arrives at the house about 7:00 A.M. the morning of the rehabilitation.

"On team building day, the group arrives at the house and starts the rehab process. Two days is usually needed. If we start the job on Friday, it could be finished on Saturday. In this way, the group would receive one day off from work and the members would contribute one day of their time."

Maria was so enthusiastic about Atkins' idea that she agreed on the spot that Friday, May 19th, would be the team-building day. She suggested that the day be called Tymco Home Rehab. Cortez made up a list of ten key employees, including herself, to participate in the team-building activity.

Friday morning, five cars and trucks arrived at 47 Blodgett Street, filled with Tymco staff members, ladders, tools, and home-building supplies. Teena Jones, supervisor of technical manuals, shouted to the group, "We can't get anywhere until we start getting rid of the debris around the house and in the hallway. So let's get shovelling. The dumpster is on the way."

"Grab a few people, and do what you want," said Larry Boudreau, supervisor of technical documentation. "If we don't patch up that roof first, nothing else will matter. I need two warm bodies who aren't acrophobic [afraid of heights] to help me." Two staffers agreed to work with Larry while the seven other staff members including Cortez formed the clean-up brigade.

"Carpentry is my thing," said Mary Benito from translations services. "Let's get out the hammers, saws, nails, and screws and start repairing this broken porch first. I want us to be ready for painting the house by noon tomorrow."

"Do what you want, Mary," said Dale Jenkins, a technical training team leader. "I'm good at home plumbing, and the toilets and sinks here are leaking more than the Titanic. I need a skilled pair of hands to help me. Anyone care to volunteer?"

Maria said, "While you folks are shovelling debris and fixing, I'll run out and get us the food for snacks and lunch, and I'll order pizza for a supper break."

"That's the most sensible idea I've heard today," commented Larry.

The Tymco team-building participants had supper together at 5:00 P.M. that evening and went home at 8:00 P.M., planning to return at 7:00 A.M. the next morning. By 1:00 P.M. Saturday, painting had begun, with all ten people on the team participating. By 7:30 P.M., the house at 47 Blodgett Street was painted. The family, who were staying with neighbors, came by to cheer and weep with joy.

The Tymco team members exchanged smiles, high fives, and hugs. "We can all go home now feeling that we've accomplished something really important as a team. And we can come back to the office on Monday morning knowing that we can work well as a team despite a few bumps and bruises."

"Good comment, Mary," said Ian Graham from the technical manual group. "Yet, I'm not so sure that replacing shingles on an old roof has made me a better team player."

Case Questions

1. What evidence was presented in this case that the staff members from different units at Tymco might have become better acquainted?
2. What should Maria do next to improve the chances that the home rehab day results in genuine team development?
3. What evidence is presented in this case that the home rehab day did give a boost to team spirit?
4. How valid is Ian's comment about replacing shingles having no particular impact on becoming a better team player?

ASSOCIATED ROLE PLAY

The Team Building Debriefing

One student plays the role of Maria who decides to hold a debriefing session four days after the home rehab day. She wants to help the Tymco team members appreciate how valuable that day was in terms of developing teamwork. Several other students play the roles of the Tymco team members who participate in the meeting. At least one student plays the role of a skeptic about the team-building value of the home rehab day. Observers will provide feedback about Maria's effectiveness in conducting the debriefing session, including her leadership skills.

 ## LEADERSHIP SKILL-BUILDING EXERCISE 6-4

My Leadership Portfolio

Now that you have studied a basketful of ideas about enhancing teamwork, you can add to your skill repertoire by implementing a few of these tactics. The next time you are involved in group activity, as either the leader or a group member, attempt to enhance cooperation and teamwork within the group. Make specific use of at least two of the recommended tactics for improving teamwork. Make an entry in your journal after your first attempts to enhance teamwork. Here is an example:

I am the head of the Hispanic Business Club at our college. Attendance hasn't been too great in recent meetings, and the club seems headed nowhere. So at our last meeting, I suggested that we devote the entire meeting to building a mission statement. I explained that if we knew what our purpose was, maybe we would pull together better. We are still working on the mission, but so far it has to do with enhancing the impact and reputation of Hispanic business leaders. I also suggested that we invest in T-shirts with a logo we could be proud of. This idea may sound hokey, but the group really rallied around the idea of building unity through new T-shirts.

 LEADERSHIP SKILL-BUILDING **EXERCISE 6-5**

The Trust Fall

Perhaps the most widely used team-building activity is the trust fall, which may be familiar to many readers. Nevertheless, each application of this exercise is likely to produce new and informative results. The class organizes itself into teams. In each team, each willing member stands on a chair and falls back into the arms of teammates. A less frightening alternative to falling off a chair is to simply fall backward standing up. Team members who, for whatever physical or mental reason, would prefer not to fall back into others or participate in catching others are unconditionally excluded. However, they can serve as observers. After the trust falls have been completed, a team leader gathers answers to the following questions and then shares the answers with the rest of the class.

1. How does this exercise develop teamwork?
2. How does the exercise develop leadership skills?
3. What did the participants learn about themselves?

▶❚❚ **LEADERSHIP** VIDEO **CASE** DISCUSSION **QUESTIONS**

To view the videos for this activity, you'll need access to the CourseMate that is available for this text. To get access, visit www.CengageBrain.com.

After watching "Leading Teams at Evogear," answer the following questions.

1. What is the difference between a group leader and a team leader? Are Evogear employees more of a group or a team? Explain.

2. How might Bryce Phillips, a founder of Evogear, and Nathan Decker emphasize group recognition and rewards? What is the benefit in doing so?

3. What role does Nathan Decker play in the team-based organization?

NOTES

1. Edwin A. Locke and Associates, *The Essence of Leadership: The Four Keys to Leading Successfully* (New York: Lexington/Macmillan, 1991), p. 94.

2. W. Dyer, *Team Building: Issues and Alternatives* (Reading, Mass.: Addison-Wesley, 1977), as cited in Lynn R. Offerman and Rebecca K. Spiros, "The Science and Practice of Team Development: Improving the Link," *Academy of Management Journal*, April 2001, p. 380.

3. Jon R. Katzenbach and Douglas K. Smith, "The Discipline of Teams," *Harvard Business Review*, March–April 1993, p. 112.

4. Shari Caudron, "Teamwork Takes Work," *Personnel Journal*, February 1994, p. 45; Andrew J. DuBrin, *The Reengineering Survival Guide: Managing and Succeeding in the Changing Workplace* (Mason, OH.: Thomson Executive Press, 1996), pp. 129–144.

5. Alan Murray, *The Wall Street Journal Essential Guide to Management* (New York: Harper Business, 2010), p. 89.

6. Frederick P. Morgeson, "The External Leadership of Self-Managing Teams: Intervening in the Context of Novel and Disruptive Events," *Journal of Applied Psychology*, May 2005, pp. 497–508.

7. Kannan Srikanth and Phanish Puranam, "Advice for Outsourcers: Think Bigger," *The Wall Street Journal*, January 25, 2010, p. R7.

8. David De Cremer and Daan van Knippenberg, "How Do Leaders Promote Cooperation? The Effects of Charisma and Procedural Fairness," *Journal of Applied Psychology*, October 2002, pp. 858–866.

9. "Clarify Team Roles to Ensure Success," *Manager's Edge*, August 2005, p. 6.

10. James M. Kouzes and Barry Z. Posner, *The Leadership Challenge*, 3rd ed. (San Francisco: Jossey-Bass, 2002), p. 244.

11. John Blau, "At Nokia Temperament Is a Core Competence, *Research Technology Management*, July/August 2003, p. 6; Stephen Baker, "Nokia: Can CEO Ollila Keep the Cellular Superstar Flying High?" *Businessweek*, August 10, 1998, p. 056.

12. Dean Tjosvold and Mary M. Tjosvold, *The Emerging Leader: Ways to a Stronger Team* (New York: Lexington Books, 1993); "Improve Teamwork with a 'Code of Conduct,'" *Manager's Edge*, February 2005, p. 1.

13. Vanessa Urch Druskat and Steven B. Wolff, "Building the Emotional Intelligence of Groups," *Harvard Business Review*, March 2001, pp. 80–90.

14. Paul S. George, "Teamwork Without Tears," *Personnel Journal*, November 1987, p. 129.

15. Clive Goodworth, "Some Thoughts on Creating a Team," in Michel Syrett and Clare Hogg, eds., *Frontiers of Leadership* (Oxford, England: Blackwell Publishers, 1992), p. 472.

16. Peter Pronovost and Eric Vohr, *Safe Patients, Smart Hospitals* (New York: Hudson Street Press, 2010).

17. Quoted in Nancy Hatch Woodward, "The Coming of the X Managers," *HR Magazine*, March 1999, pp. 75, 76. Updated at LinkedIn, April 12, 2011.

18. Katzenbach and Smith, "The Discipline of Teams," pp. 118–119.

19. Lee G. Bolman and Terrence E. Deal, "What Makes a Team Work?" *Organizational Dynamics*, Autumn 1992, p. 6.

20. John Brodie, "King of Cool," *Fortune*, September 1, 2008, p. 52; Tina Gaudoin, "Mickey Drexler: Retail Therapist," *The Wall Street Journal* (http://magazine.wsj.com), June 10, 2010, p. 3.

21. Anne Fisher, "In Praise of Micromanaging," *Fortune*, August 23, 2004, p. 40.

22. Bruce J. Avolio and Surinder S. Kahai, "Adding 'E' to E-Leadership: How It May Impact Your Leadership," *Organizational Dynamics*, vol. 31, no. 4, 2003, p. 325.

23. Arvind Malhotra, Ann Majchzak, and Benson Rosen, "Leading Virtual Teams," *Academy of Management Perspectives*, February 2007, pp. 60–70, study reported in Lynda Gratton, "Working Together … When Apart," *The Wall Street Journal*, June 16–17, 2007, p. R4; Bill Leonard, "Managing Virtual Teams," *HR Magazine*, June 2011, pp. 38–42.

24. John Cordery, Christine Soo, Bradley Kirkman, Benson Rosen, and John Mathieu, "Leading Parallel Global Virtual Teams: Lessons from Alcoa," *Organizational Dynamics*, July–September 2009, pp. 204–216.

25. "Teamwork: The Color Committee Gets to Work," *Fortune*, October 26, 2009, p. 37.

26. Richard Lepsinger, "Virtual Team Failure: Six Common Missteps that Threaten Your Team's Success," *Communication Briefings*, February 2011, p. 6.

27. Bolman and Deal, "What Makes a Team Work?" pp. 41–42.

28. Thomas J. McCoy, *Creating an "Open Book" Organization…Where Employees Think and Act Like Business Partners* (New York: AMACOM, 1999); John Case, "HR Learns How to Open the Books," *HR Magazine*, May 1998, pp. 71–76.

29. Jennifer Wang, "Unbeatable," *Entrepreneur*, February 2011, p. 16.

30. John Chambers, "Cisco Sees the Future," *Harvard Business Review*, November 2008, p. 55.

31. Quoted in Todd Henemann, "Firms Making Friends with Social Media," *Workforce Management*, April 2010, p. 4.

32. Quoted in Sonia Alleyne, "Rallying the Troops," *Black Enterprise*, February 2011, p. 75.

33. Joyce Gannon, "Horses Help People Learn to Work Better with Others," *Pittsburgh Post-Gazette*, June 4, 2004.

34. Jeffrey M. O'Brien, "Team Building in Paradise," *Fortune*, May 26, 2008, pp. 112–116.

35. Quoted in Jeffrey M. O'Brien, "Team Building in Paradise," *Fortune*, May 26, 2008, pp. 112–116.

36. Cited in Michael P. Regan, "Radical Steps to Help Build Teamwork," Associated Press, February 20, 2004.

37. "Avoid 'Cringe Factor' in Team Building," *Manager's Edge*, May 2009, p. 8.

38. George Graen and J. E. Cashman, "A Role-Making Model of Leadership in Formal Organizations: A Developmental Approach," in J. G. Hunt and L. L. Larson, eds., *Leadership Frontiers* (Kent, O.: Kent State University Press, 1975), pp. 143–165; Robert P. Vecchio, "Leader–Member Exchange, Objective Performance, Employment Duration, and Supervisor Ratings: Testing for Moderation and Mediation," *Journal of Business and Psychology*, Spring 1998, p. 328.

39. Elaine M. Engle and Robert G. Lord, "Implicit Theories, Self-Schemas, and Leader–Member Exchange," *Academy of Management Journal*, August 1997, pp. 988–1010.

40. Xiaohua (Tracy) Zhou and Chester A. Schriesheim, "Supervisor-Subordinate Convergence in Descriptions of Leader-Member Exchange (LMX) Quality: Review and Testable Propositions," *The Leadership Quarterly*, December 2009, pp. 920–932.

41. Howard J. Klein and Jay S. Kim, "A Field Study of the Influences of Situational Constraints, Leader–Member Exchange, and Goal Commitment on Performance," *Academy of Management Journal*, February 1998, pp. 88–95.

42. Randall P. Settoon, Nathan Bennett, and Robert C. Liden, "Social Exchange in Organizations: Perceived Organizational Support, Leader–Member Exchange, and Employee Reciprocity," *Journal of Applied Psychology*, June 1995, pp. 219–227.

43. Pamela Tierney and Talya N. Bauer, "A Longitudinal Assessment of LMX on Extra-Role Behavior," *Academy of Management Best Papers Proceedings*, 1996, pp. 298–302.

44. David A. Hofman and Frederick P. Morgeson, "Safety-Related Behavior as a Social Exchange: The Role of Perceived Organizational Support and Leader–Member Exchange," *Journal of Applied Psychology*, April 1999, pp. 286–296.

45. Ronald F. Piccolo and Jason A. Colquitt, "Transformational Leadership and Job Behaviors: The Mediating Role of Core Job Characteristics," *Academy of Management Journal*, April 2006, pp. 327–340.

46. Vijaya Venkataramani, Stephen G. Green, and Deidra J. Schleicher, "Well-Connected Leaders: The Impact of Leaders' Social Network Ties on LMX and Members' Work Attitudes," *Journal of Applied Psychology*, November 2010, pp. 1071–1084.

47. Robert C. Liden, Sandy J. Wayne, and Deal Stilwell, "A Longitudinal Study on the Early Development of Leader–Member Exchanges," *Journal of Applied Psychology*, August 1993, pp. 662–674.

48. Ruth Wageman, Colin M. Fisher, and J. Richard Hackman, "Leading Teams When the Time is Right: Finding the Best Moments to Act," *Organizational Dynamics*, July–September 2009, p. 193.

49. "Promote Teamwork by Rearranging the Office," *people@work*, sample issue, 1999, published by Texas Professional Training Associates, Inc.; Diana Louise Carter, "Global Crossing Fuses Staff," Rochester, New York, *Democrat and Chronicle*, January 18, 2008, pp. 6D, 5D.

The **Leader** as a **Motivator** and **Coach**

teve Ballmer has been CEO of Microsoft Corp since 2001, after serving as the number two person behind company cofounder Bill Gates for many years. Ballmer and his future boss Gates hit it off quite well when they met as Harvard University students in 1973. Ballmer was an outgoing person, involved in several student leadership roles, whereas Gates was much more introverted. Gates dropped out of college to work fulltime at Microsoft. Ballmer stayed at Harvard to earn a degree in applied math and economics.

Ballmer began his career at Procter and Gamble, and in 1980 he was recruited by his college buddy Gates to join Microsoft. Ballmer is often credited with having created the marketing and sales strategy that catapulted Microsoft into its dominant position in software. Many observers believe that the impact of Microsoft is on the decline, but it remains a highly profitable company with a dominant market share for many of its software products.

Ballmer is an exceptionally intelligent strategic thinker, but he is recognized even more for his extraordinary enthusiasm for Microsoft as a company—its products and employees. Ballmer can be extreme in expressing enthusiasm. His vocal cords required surgery after he screamed "Windows, Windows, Windows" continuously at a company meeting in Japan in 1991. In recent years, his emotional displays have been captured on YouTube videos. In the "Monkey Dance" he lurches on the stage doing a wild solo dance. His screaming and shouting are also shown on YouTube clips called "Going Crazy," and "I Love This Company."

During Microsoft's 25th-anniversary celebration, Ballmer popped out of a giant anniversary cake to surprise the audience. At a developers conference a few days later, a sweat-soaked Ballmer screamed "developers" about fourteen times in front of a bewildered audience (also shown on a YouTube video).

Ballmer has been described by *Fortune* magazine as "a relentless salesman as persistent as a piston striking steel." He believes that his extraordinary enthusiasm has been a key force in motivating Microsoft sales as well as technical staff. Some people perceive Ballmer to be Microsoft's key motivator and coach. His passion for the company is thought to be contagious. (Yet some people are critical of his motivational style, perceiving it to be excessive).[1]

This story about a well-known business executive illustrates how a motivational leader can help move an organization forward. Some people might think that prancing around in a sweat-soaked frenzy is a little hokey, but the technique does have the effect of showing that the CEO cares about revving up performance. Effective leaders are outstanding motivators and coaches. They influence others in many of the ways previously described. In addition, they often use specific motivational and coaching skills. These techniques are important because not all leaders can influence others through formal authority or charisma and inspirational leadership alone. Face-to-face, day-by-day motivational skills are also important. Good coaching is a related essential feature of management because motivating workers is an important part of coaching them. During a coaching session, the leader will often attempt to motivate the person being coached.

In this chapter, we approach motivation and coaching skills from various perspectives. First, we take an overview of motivation by explaining the leader's role in employee engagement. We then examine first how leaders make effective use of expectancy theory, recognition, goal setting, and equity theory to motivate group members. Second, we describe coaching, including a description of specific coaching skills and the role of the executive coach. Most readers of this book have already studied motivation, so here we describe how it is possible to apply a few popular motivation theories rather than repeat a discussion of theories you have already studied, such as reinforcement theory or Maslow's need hierarchy.

Before reading about several approaches to worker motivation, you are invited to take Leadership Self-Assessment Quiz 7-1, which deals with your understanding of motivation.

LEADERSHIP SELF-ASSESSMENT QUIZ 7-1

My Approach to Motivating Others

Instructions: Describe how often you act or think in the way indicated by the following statements when you are attempting to motivate another person. Scale: very infrequently (VI); infrequently (I); sometimes (S); frequently (F); very frequently (VF).

	VI	I	S	F	VF
1. I ask the other person what he or she is hoping to achieve in the situation.	1	2	3	4	5
2. I attempt to figure out if the person has the ability to do what I need done.	1	2	3	4	5
3. When another person is not working hard, it usually means he or she is lazy.	5	4	3	2	1
4. I explain exactly what I want to the person I am trying to motivate.	1	2	3	4	5
5. I like to give the other person a reward up front so he or she will be motivated.	5	4	3	2	1
6. I give lots of feedback when another person is performing a task for me.	1	2	3	4	5
7. The only sensible way to motivate a worker is to offer that person more money for a job well done.	5	4	3	2	1
8. I make sure that the other person feels fairly treated.	1	2	3	4	5
9. I figure that if I explain how hard I work, I can get the other person to work as hard as I do.	5	4	3	2	1
10. I attempt to get what I need done by instilling fear in the other person.	5	4	3	2	1
11. I specify exactly what needs to be accomplished, but I give the other person some room to choose the best method.	1	2	3	4	5
12. I generously praise people who help me get my work accomplished.	1	2	3	4	5
13. A job well done is its own reward. I therefore keep praise to a minimum.	5	4	3	2	1
14. I make sure to let people know how well they have done in meeting my expectations on a task.	1	2	3	4	5
15. To be fair, I attempt to reward people similarly no matter how well they have performed.	5	4	3	2	1
16. When somebody doing work for me performs well, I recognize his or her accomplishments promptly.	1	2	3	4	5
17. Before giving somebody a reward, I attempt to find out what would appeal to that person.	1	2	3	4	5
18. I make it a policy not to thank somebody for doing a job he or she is paid to do.	5	4	3	2	1
19. If people do not know how to perform a task, motivation will suffer.	1	2	3	4	5
20. If properly laid out, many jobs can be self-rewarding.	1	2	3	4	5

Total score: _____

Scoring and Interpretation: Add the circled numbers to obtain your total score.

- **90–100:** You have advanced knowledge and skill with respect to motivating others in a work environment. Continue to build on the solid base you have established.
- **50–89:** You have average knowledge and skill with respect to motivating others. With additional study and experience, you will probably develop advanced motivational skills.
- **20–49:** To effectively motivate others in a work environment, you will need to greatly expand your knowledge of motivation theory and techniques.

Source: The general idea for this quiz but not the contents comes from David Whetton and Kim Cameron, *Developing Management* Skills, 5th ed. (Upper Saddle River, N.J.: Prentice Hall, 2002), pp. 302–303.

LEADERSHIP AND EMPLOYEE ENGAGEMENT

A broad purpose of leaders applying motivation and coaching techniques is to get employees involved in their work and excited about working for the organization. **Engagement** is the current buzz word for the commitment workers make to their employer. According to Jim Harter, a Gallup research scientist, engagement—or the lack of it—has substantial implications for how well business organizations achieve their goals.[2] Engagement is reflected in employee willingness to stay with the firm and go beyond the call of duty. Gaining employee commitment is especially important in the current era because several studies have found that most American workers are not fully engaged in their work.[3] They do what is expected of them but do not contribute extra mental and physical effort to be outstanding.

Quantitative evidence points toward the impact of employee engagement. A Gallup Organization study involving approximately 32,400 business units found that those in the top quartile on engagement had 18 percent higher productivity; 16 percent higher profitability, and 29 percent fewer accidents than companies in the bottom quartile on engagement.[4] Engagement was measured by a questionnaire.

A key link between leadership, motivation and coaching techniques, and engagement is that leaders need to use motivation and coaching techniques to help keep employees engaged. An example of the value of a coaching technique is that a survey of 1,000 employees revealed that leaders who give positive feedback to employees foster engagement. Furthermore, giving mostly negative feedback is better than no feedback or being ignored. Here are the specific numbers:

- 61% of employees were engaged who believed that supervisors focused on their strengths (37% of employees fell into this category)

- 45% of employees were engaged who believed that supervisors focused on their weaknesses (11% of employees fell into this category)
- 2% of employees were engaged who believed that supervisors ignored them (25% of employees fell into this category)[5]

Looking at the leader's role in enhancing motivation more broadly, Jean Houston, an Atlanta-based human resources consultant, says that managers can engage their workers by seeing them as whole people and having the courageous conversations that will build trust and see what is really going on. Houston also encourages managers to learn and use soft skills such as communication, recognition, mentoring, and caring because soft skills can have a hard impact.[6] (Such is the thrust of this chapter and this book.)

According to a recent survey conducted by BlessingWhite Inc., 20 percent of respondents cited career advancement as a key driver of engagement. A specific technique for leaders to engage employees is therefore to initiate career discussions.[7]

EXPECTANCY THEORY AND MOTIVATIONAL SKILLS

Expectancy theory is a good starting point in learning how leaders can apply systematic explanations of motivation, for two major reasons. First, the theory is comprehensive: It incorporates and integrates features of other motivation theories, including goal theory and behavior modification. Second, it offers the leader many guidelines for triggering and sustaining constructive effort from group members. Although not much research is conducted about expectancy theory nowadays, it remains a stable approach to understanding work motivation.

The **expectancy theory** of motivation is based on the premise that the amount of effort people expend depends on how much reward they expect to get in return. In addition to being broad, the theory deals with cognition and process. Expectancy theory is cognitive because it emphasizes the thoughts, judgments, and desires of the person being motivated. It is a process theory because it attempts to explain how motivation takes place.

The theory is really a group of theories based on a rational, economic view of people.[8] In any given situation, people want to maximize gain and minimize loss. The theory assumes that they choose among alternatives by selecting one they think they have the best chance of attaining. Furthermore, they choose the alternative that appears to have the biggest personal payoff. Given a choice, people will select the assignment they think they can handle the best and will benefit them the most.

Basic Components of Expectancy Theory

Expectancy theory contains three basic components: valence, instrumentality, and expectancy. Because of these three components, the theory is often referred to as VIE theory. Figure 7-1 presents a basic version of expectancy

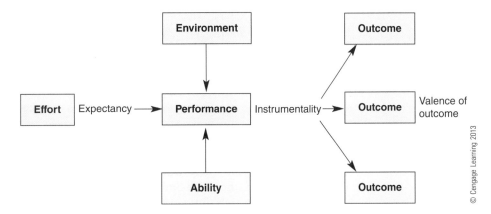

FIGURE 7-1 The Expectancy Theory of Motivation.

theory. All three elements must be present for motivation to take place. To be motivated, people must value the reward, think they can perform, and have reasonable assurance that their performance will lead to a reward.

Valence   The worth or attractiveness of an outcome is referred to as **valence**. As shown in Figure 7-1, each work situation has multiple outcomes. An **outcome** is anything that might stem from performance, such as a reward. Each outcome has a valence of its own. And each outcome can lead to other outcomes or consequences, referred to as *second-level outcomes*. A person who receives an outstanding performance evaluation (a first-level outcome) becomes eligible for a promotion (a second-level outcome). Second-level outcomes also have valences. The sum of all the valences must be positive if the person is to work hard. If the sum of all of the valences is negative, the person might work hard to avoid the outcome.

Valences range from −100 to +100 in the version of expectancy theory presented here. (The usual method of placing valences on a −1.00 to +1.00 scale does not do justice to the true differences in preferences.) A valence of 100 means that a person intensely desires an outcome. A valence of −100 means that a person is strongly motivated to avoid an outcome such as being fired or declaring bankruptcy. A valence of zero signifies indifference to an outcome and is therefore of no use as a motivator.

An example of using negative and positive valence at the same time would be for the CEO to use data to point out how bleak the company will become if it does not change, and how wonderful the company will become if it does change.

Instrumentality   An individual's assessment of the probability that performance will lead to certain outcomes is referred to as **instrumentality**. (An instrumentality is also referred to as a *performance-to-outcome expectancy* because it relates to the outcome people expect from performing in a certain way.) When people engage in a particular behavior, they do so with the intention of achieving a desired outcome or reward. Instrumentalities range from 0 to 1.0, where 0 is no chance of receiving the desired reward and 1.0 is a belief that the reward is certain to follow. For example, an hourly worker might say, "I know for sure that if I work overtime, I will receive overtime pay."

Expectancy   An individual's assessment of the probability that effort will lead to correct performance of the task is referred to as **expectancy**. (The same concept is also referred to as *effort-to-performance expectancy*.) An important question people ask themselves before putting forth effort to accomplish a task is, "If I put in all this work, will I really get the job done properly?" Expectancies range from 0 to 1.0, where 0 is no expectation of performing the tasks correctly, and 1.0 signifies absolute faith in being able to perform the task properly. Expectancies thus influence whether a person will even strive to earn a reward. Self-confident people have higher expectancies than do less self-confident people. Being well trained increases a person's subjective sense that he or she can perform the task.

The importance of having high expectancies for motivation meshes well with the contribution of **self-efficacy**, the confidence in your ability to carry out a specific task. If you have high self-efficacy about the task, your motivation will be high. Low self-efficacy leads to low motivation. Some people are poorly motivated to skydive because they doubt they will be able to pull the rip cord while free-falling at 120 mph.

In short, if you are confident about your task-related skills, you will get your act together to do the task. This is one reason that you should give people the skills and confidence they need to put forth effort.

An apparent contradiction in expectancy theory requires explanation. Some people will engage in behaviors with low expectancies, such as trying to invent a successful new product or become the CEO of a major corporation. The compensating factor is the large valences attached to the second-level outcomes associated with these accomplishments. The payoffs from introducing a successful new product or becoming a CEO are so great that people are willing to take a long shot.

A Brief Look at the Evidence   The application of expectancy theory to work motivation had been the subject of research for close to forty years (1964–2004). Two researchers performed a meta-analysis of seventy-seven studies examining how well various aspects of expectancy theory related to workplace criteria, such as performance and effort. Although the results were not consistent, the general conclusion reached was that the three components of expectancy theory related positively to workplace criteria. For example, job performance showed a positive correlation with valence, instrumentality, expectancy, and the total VIE model. The total VIE model typically refers to a multiplication of the values for valence, instrumentality, and expectancy. In another finding, effort expended on the job was positively correlated with valence, instrumentality, expectancy, the VIE model, and performance.[9] The last correlation helps verify the justification for leaders' and managers' concern about motivating employees: People who try harder perform better.

Leadership Skills and Behaviors Associated with Expectancy Theory

Expectancy theory has many implications for leaders and managers with respect to motivating others.[10] Some of these implications also stem from other motivational theories, and they fit good management practice in general. As you read each implication, reflect on how you might apply the skill or behavior during a leadership assignment.

1. *Determine what levels and kinds of performance are needed to achieve organizational goals.* Motivating others proceeds best when workers have a clear understanding of what needs to be accomplished. At the same time, the leader should make sure that the desired levels of performance are possible. For example, sales quotas might be set too high because the market is already saturated with a particular product or service.

2. *Make the performance level attainable by the individuals being motivated.* If the group members believe that they are being asked to perform extraordinarily difficult tasks, most of them will suffer from low motivation. A task must generally be perceived as attainable to be motivational.

3. *Train and encourage people.* Leaders should give group members the necessary training and encouragement to be confident they can perform the required task. Some group members who appear to be poorly motivated simply lack the right skills and self-confidence.

4. *Make explicit the link between rewards and performance.* Group members should be reassured that if they perform the job to standard, they will receive the promised reward.

5. *Make sure the rewards are large enough.* Some rewards that are the right kind fail to motivate people because they are not in the right amount. The promise of a large salary increase might be motivational, but a 1 percent increase will probably have little motivational thrust for most workers.

6. *Analyze what factors work in opposition to the effectiveness of the reward.* Conflicts between the leader's package of rewards and other influences in the work group may require the leader to modify the reward. For example, if the work group favors the status quo, a large reward may be required to encourage innovative thinking.

7. *Explain the meaning and implications of second-level outcomes.* It is helpful for employees to understand the value of certain outcomes, such as receiving a favorable performance evaluation. (For example, it could lead to a salary increase, assignment to a high-status task force, or promotion.)

8. *Understand individual differences in valences.* To motivate group members effectively, leaders must recognize individual differences or preferences for rewards. An attempt should be made to offer workers rewards to which they attach a high valence. One employee might value a high-adventure assignment; another might attach a high valence to a routine, tranquil assignment. Cross-cultural differences in valences may also occur. For example, many (but not all) Asian workers prefer not to be singled out for recognition in front of the group. According to their cultural values, receiving recognition in front of the group is insensitive and embarrassing. Another example is that gift certificates for stores might have more valence in the United States than in Italy, where workers may prefer a small fashion boutique. Leadership Skill-Building Exercise 7-1 deals with the challenge of estimating valences.

LEADERSHIP SKILL-BUILDING EXERCISE 7-1

Estimating Valences for Applying Expectancy Theory

Instructions: A major challenge in applying expectancy theory is estimating what valence attaches to possible outcomes. A leader or manager also has to be aware of the potential rewards or punishment in a given work situation. Listed are a group of rewards and punishments, along with a space for rating the reward or punishment on a scale of −100 to +100. Work with about six teammates, with each person rating all of the rewards and punishments.

POTENTIAL OUTCOME	RATING (−100 TO +100)
1. Promotion to vice president	_____
2. One-step promotion	_____
3. Above-average performance evaluation	_____
4. Top-category performance evaluation	_____
5. $8,000 performance bonus	_____
6. $4,000 performance bonus	_____
7. $150 gift certificate	_____
8. Employee-of-the-month plaque	_____
9. Note of appreciation sent by e-mail or posted on social media website, and placed in file	_____
10. Lunch with boss at good restaurant	_____
11. Lunch with boss in company cafeteria	_____
12. Challenging new assignment	_____
13. Allowed to accumulate frequent flyer miles for own use	_____
14. Allowed to purchase latest tablet computer for own use	_____
15. Assigned latest smart phone for own use	_____
16. Private corner office with great view	_____
17. Assigned a full-time administrative assistant	_____
18. Documentation of poor performance	_____
19. Being fired	_____
20. Being fired and put on industry bad list	_____
21. Demoted one step	_____
22. Demoted to entry-level position	_____
23. Being ridiculed in front of others	_____
24. Being suspended without pay	_____
25. Being transferred to undesirable geographic location	_____

EXERCISE 7-1 (continued)

After completing the ratings, discuss the following issues:

1. Which rewards and punishments received the most varied ratings?
2. Which rewards and punishments received similar ratings?

Another analytical approach would be to compute the means and standard deviations of the valences for each outcome. Each class member could then compare his or her own valence ratings with the class norm. To add to the database, each student might bring back two sets of ratings from employed people who are not in the class.

To apply this technique to the job, modify this form to fit the outcomes available in your situation. Explain to team members that you are attempting to do a better job of rewarding and disciplining and that you need their thoughts. The ratings made by team members might provide fruitful discussion for a staff meeting.

9. *Recognize that when workers are in a positive mood, high valences, instrumentalities, and expectancies are more likely to lead to good performance.* An experiment with college students indicated that participants in a positive mood performed better, were more persistent, tried harder, and reported higher levels of motivation than those in a neutral mood. The positive affect made awards appear more attractive (higher valence). Being in a good mood also strengthened the link between performance and outcome (instrumentality), as well as between effort and performance (expectancy).[11] A note of caution is that the mood elevator in this experiment was a bag of candy. A manager might need more sustainable methods of increasing positive affect. Being able to keep employees in a good mood is an advanced application of emotional intelligence.

GOAL THEORY

Goal setting is a basic process that is directly or indirectly part of all major theories of work motivation. Leaders and managers widely accept goal setting as a means to improve and sustain performance. A vision, for example, is really an exalted goal. To inspire his workers, Doug Ducey, the founder of the ice cream chain Cold Stone Creamery, formulated the vision "The world will know us as the ultimate ice cream experience." Ducey believes that the vision helped his company grow from 74 stores to 1,000 stores during a five-year period.[12]

The core finding of goal theory is that individuals who are provided with specific hard goals perform better than those who are given easy, nonspecific, "do your best" goals or no goals. At the same time, however, the individuals must have sufficient ability, accept the goals, and receive feedback related to the task.[13] Our overview of goal theory elaborates on this basic finding.

Basic Findings of Goal Theory

The premise underlying goal theory (or goal-setting theory) is that behavior is regulated by values and goals. A **goal** is what a person is trying to accomplish. Our values create within us a desire to behave in a way that is consistent with them. For example, a leader who values honesty will establish a goal of hiring only honest employees. The leader would therefore have to make extensive use of reference checks and honesty testing. Edwin A. Locke and Gary P. Latham have incorporated hundreds of studies about goals into a theory of goal setting and task performance.[14] Figure 7-2 summarizes some of the more consistent findings, and the information that follows describes them. A leader should keep these points in mind when motivating people through goal setting.

To begin, remember that *specific goals lead to higher performance than do generalized goals*. Telling someone, "Do your best" is a generalized goal. A specific goal would be, "Increase the number of new hires to our management training program to fifteen for this summer." Another key point is that *performance generally improves in direct proportion to goal difficulty*. The harder one's goal is, the more one accomplishes. An important exception is that when goals are too difficult, they may lower performance. Difficulty in reaching the goal leads to frustration, which in turn leads to lowered performance (as explained in relation to expectancy theory).

The finding about effective goals being realistic has an important exception for the accomplishment of high-level complex tasks. Effective leaders often inspire constituents by framing goals in terms of a noble cause or something heroic. The manager of a group that made photo printers, for example, might explain that making high-quality printers enables people to preserve their memories.[15] Here are two suggestions for developing noble powerful goals:

- Create a big, comprehensive goal: an ideal accomplishment for your group.
- Break the goal down into smaller steps, such as hiring two top-notch workers for the group. Regard each step (or sub-goal) as a project designed to get you to your destination.[16] The same approach has been referred to as "running sprints rather than marathons."

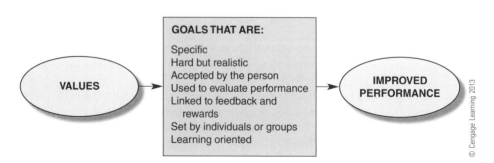

FIGURE 7-2 Goal Theory.

commissions, many investment bankers sold investor toxic securities—such as those based on subprime mortgages—to investors unaware of the risks. (The giant investment banking firm Goldman Sachs has often been accused of this type of unethical behavior.) We emphasize, however, that financial incentives alone are not the villain. Not monitoring the method used to earn the financial reward is a major part of the problem.

A heavy emphasis on goals can also create such problems as workers focusing so much on attaining their goals that they neglect emergencies and new opportunities. For example, a recruiter might ignore an inquiry from an excellent prospect because he or she had to finish a quota of processing job inquiries to the company website.

The potential pitfalls of over-reliance on goals have been humorously condensed by group of researchers suggesting the following "warning label" for setting goals:[21]

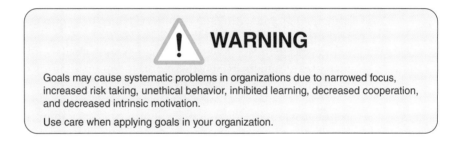

! **WARNING**

Goals may cause systematic problems in organizations due to narrowed focus, increased risk taking, unethical behavior, inhibited learning, decreased cooperation, and decreased intrinsic motivation.

Use care when applying goals in your organization.

Goal setting is widely practiced by leaders and managers, but they typically do not give careful consideration to goal theory. Leadership Skill-Building Exercise 7-2 gives you an opportunity to apply what you have learned about goal setting.

LEADERSHIP SKILL-BUILDING EXERCISE 7-2

The Application of Goal Theory

In a group of about five to six people, visualize your group as a task force whose mission is to make and implement suggestions for making your company more environmentally sustainable (greener). The company manufactures sports clothing, such as athletic shoes, swimsuits, and soccer outfits. One of the group members plays the role of the task-force leader. The leader must help the group establish goals that are likely to be motivational, following the principles of goal theory.

The goal of today's meeting is to establish four goals that are likely to lead to a greener company but not be excessive in cost. After each team has established its goals, present them to other class members. Students listening to the goals of the other groups should be willing to offer constructive feedback.

Practice in setting effective goals is useful because leaders and managers are frequently expected to set goals. When the goal follows at least some of the major findings of goal theory, there is a greater likelihood that productivity will increase.

For goals to improve performance, the group member must accept them. If a group member rejects a goal, he or she will not incorporate it into planning. This is why it is often helpful to discuss goals with group members rather than impose goals on them. More recent research, however, suggests that the importance of goal commitment may be overrated. Goals appeared to improve performance whether or not people participating in the studies felt committed to them.[17] Despite these recent findings, many managers and leaders think employee commitment to goals is important.

Participating in goal setting has no major effect on the level of job performance except when it improves goal acceptance. Yet the leader should recognize that participation is valuable because it can lead to higher satisfaction with the goal-setting process. *Goals are more effective when they are used to evaluate performance.* When workers know that their performance will be evaluated in terms of how well they attain their goals, the impact of goals increases.

Keep in mind the key principle that *goals should be linked to feedback and rewards*. Rewarding people for reaching goals is the most widely accepted principle of management. Another goal-setting principle is that *group goal setting is as important as individual goal setting*. Having employees work as teams with a specific team goal, rather than as individuals with only individual goals, increases productivity. Furthermore, a combination of compatible group and individual goals is more effective than either individual or group goals alone.

A final goal-setting principle is that a *learning goal orientation* improves performance more than a *performance goal orientation* does. A person with a learning (or mastery) goal orientation wants to develop competence by acquiring new skills and mastering new situations. In contrast, the person with a performance goal orientation wants to demonstrate and validate his or her competence by seeking favorable judgments and avoiding negative judgments. In support of the distinction being made, a study with medical supply sales representatives found that a learning goal orientation had a positive relationship with sales performance. In contrast, a performance goal orientation was unrelated to sales performance.[18]

The Importance of How Goals Are Attained and Other Concerns

A major concern about using goals to motivate performance is that leaders, as well as other workers, will take unethical and dysfunctional shortcuts to attain their goals. For example, a CEO might drastically reduce investment in research and development and lay off too many valuable workers to meet a profit goal such as earnings per share. Also, managers have been known to engage in unethical behavior such as shipping unfinished products to reach sales goals.[19] To implement goal setting without creating dysfunctions, it is therefore essential to specify *how* the goals will be attained with a particular focus on ethical behavior.

The use of financial incentives for attaining goals often encourages unethical behavior. One analysis conducted at the Wharton School of the University of Pennsylvania, suggests that excessive reliance on financial incentives facilitated the major financial scandals in recent history.[20] A case in point is the Wall Street financial scandals that triggered the Great Recession. To attain huge

USING RECOGNITION AND PRIDE TO MOTIVATE OTHERS

Motivating others by giving them recognition and praise can be considered a direct application of positive reinforcement, that is, reinforcing the right behavior by giving a reward. Nevertheless, recognition is such a potentially powerful motivator that it merits separate attention. Also, recognition programs to reward and motivate employees are a standard practice in business and non-profit firms. An example is rewarding high-performing employees with a crystal vase inscribed with the company logo or designating them as employee of the month. Pride, as described next, is related to recognition. People who are proud of their work want to be recognized for their good deeds.

Recognition is a strong motivator because it is a normal human need. To think through the strength of your own need for recognition, take Leadership Self-Assessment Quiz 7-2. Recognition is also effective because most workers feel they do not receive enough recognition. Deanna Baker, VP of employee development and human resources for Intelispend Prepaid Solutions, says, "One of the best ways to drive employee engagement is through a creative

---

LEADERSHIP SELF-ASSESSMENT QUIZ 7-2

How Much Do I Crave Recognition?

Instructions: Respond to the following statements on the following scale: disagree strongly (DS), disagree (D), neutral (N), agree (A), and agree strongly (AS).

	DS	D	N	A	AS
1. I keep (or would keep) almost every plaque, medal, or trophy I have ever received on display in my living quarters.	1	2	3	4	5
2. I feel a nice warm glow each time somebody praises my efforts.	1	2	3	4	5
3. When somebody tells me "nice job," it makes my day.	1	2	3	4	5
4. When I compliment someone, I am really looking for a compliment in return.	1	2	3	4	5
5. I would rather win an employee-of-the-month award than receive a $100 bonus for my good work.	1	2	3	4	5
6. If I had the resources to make a large donation to charity, I would never make the donation anonymously.	1	2	3	4	5
7. Thinking back to my childhood, I adored receiving a gold star or similar acknowledgment from my teacher for my good work.	1	2	3	4	5
8. I would rather be designated as *Time* magazine's Person of the Year than be one of the world's richest people.	1	2	3	4	5
9. I love to see my name in print or electronically.	1	2	3	4	5
10. I do not receive all the respect I deserve.	1	2	3	4	5
11. I regularly check to see how many times my name shows up on an Internet search (such as Google or Bing).	1	2	3	4	5

Total score: _____

QUIZ 7-2 (continued)

Scoring and Interpretation: Add the circled numbers to obtain your total score.

- **50–55:** You have an above-average recognition need. Recognition is therefore a strong motivator for you. You will be happiest in a job where you can be recognized for your good deeds.
- **30–49:** You have an average need for recognition and do not require constant reminders that you have done a good job.
- **11–29:** You have a below-average need for recognition and like to have your good deeds speak for themselves. When you do receive recognition, you would prefer that it be quite specific to what you have done, and not too lavish. You would feel comfortable in a work setting with mostly technical people.

rewards and recognition program."[22] However, managers do not need a formal company program to dispense recognition.

Several studies conducted over a fifty-five-year time span have indicated that employees welcome praise for a job well done as much as they welcome a regular paycheck. For example, in one study it was found that 66 percent of employees named appreciation as their most important motivator.[23] This finding should not be interpreted to mean that praise is an adequate substitute for salary. Employees tend to regard compensation as an entitlement, whereas recognition is perceived as a gift.[24] Workers, including your coworkers, want to know that their output is useful to somebody.

Appealing to the Recognition Need of Others

To appeal to the recognition need of others, identify a meritorious behavior, and then recognize that behavior with an oral, written, or material reward. Two examples of using recognition to sustain desired behavior (a key aspect of motivation) follow:

- As the team leader, you receive a glowing letter from a customer about Kate, one of your team members, who solved the customer's problem. You have the letter laminated and present it as a gift to Kate. (The behavior you are reinforcing is good customer service.)
- One member of your department, Jason, is a mechanical engineer. At a department lunch taking place during National Engineers Week, you stand up and say, "I want to toast Jason in celebration of National Engineers Week. I certainly would not want to be sitting in this office building today if a mechanical engineer had not assisted in its construction." (Here, the only behavior you are reinforcing is the goodwill of Jason, so your motivational approach is general, not specific.)

An outstanding advantage of recognition, including praise, as a motivator is that it is no cost or low cost yet powerful. Reward expert Bob Nelson reminds us that while money is important to employees, thoughtful recognition motivates them to elevate their performance.[25] Recognition thus has an enormous return on investment in comparison to a cash bonus. Following are a few suggestions for the motivational use of recognition and praise:

1. To maximize its motivational impact, recognition should be linked to corporate values and should also help workers attain personal goals. Visualize a security guard whose outside passion is sustaining the environment who becomes recognized with the new title of Security and Energy Conservation Monitor. The title combines his interest in saving energy with the company's interest in keeping outside doors closed and unusual lights turned off.[26]

2. Inform others in the group and organization about the meritorious behavior, such as via a mention in a staff meeting or a posting on the intranet. Also, praise related to specific tasks is usually more effective than general praise. Workers may appreciate praise, but they also prefer to know what specifically they are being praised for, such as, "Your forecast for the sale of our cutting gear to factories in Poland was right on target. Congratulations."

3. Do not use praise to set employees in competition against one another. Praise the employee who merits the praise, but do not suggest that other employees are less praiseworthy, such as: "Great job, José. I wish the rest of the group had put in the same kind of effort."[27]

4. Take into account the individual's preference for the type of praise. A challenge in using recognition effectively is that not everyone responds well to the same form of recognition. An example is that highly technical people tend not to like general praise like "Great job" or "Awesome, baby." Instead, they prefer a laid-back, factual statement of how their work made a contribution. According to one study, the more highly a person sees himself or herself as having a technical orientation, the more the person wants praise to be quite specific and task oriented.[28] The tech center worker who just conquered a virus on your desktop would prefer a compliment such as, "I appreciated you having disabled the virus and restored my computer to full functioning." This type of compliment would be preferable to, "Fantastic, you are a world-class virus fighter."

Appealing to Pride

Wanting to feel proud motivates many workers, and giving recognition for a job well done helps satisfy this desire to feel proud. Being proud of what you accomplish is more of an internal (intrinsic) motivator than an external (extrinsic) motivator such as receiving a gift. Giving workers an opportunity to experience pride can therefore be a strong internal motivator yet they simultaneously receive recognition.

Imagine that you are the assistant service manager at a company that customizes recreational vehicles to meet the requirements of individual clients. Your manager asks you to prepare a PowerPoint presentation of trends in customization for people who live most of the year in their RVs. You make your presentation to top management, the group applauds, executives shake your hand, and later you receive several congratulatory e-mail messages. One of the many emotions you experience is likely to be pride in having performed well. You are motivated to keep up the good work.

Workers can also experience pride in relation to recognition symbols. For example, a worker might receive a floor clock for having saved the company thousands of dollars in shipping costs. The clock might be more valuable to the worker as a symbol of accomplishment than as a household decoration. The feeling of pride stems from having accomplished a worthwhile activity (saving the company money) rather than from being awarded a floor clock.

According to consultant Jon R. Katzenbach, managers and leaders can take steps to motivate through pride. A key tactic is for the manager to set his or her compass on pride, not money. It is more important for workers to be proud of what they are doing day by day than for them to be proud of reaching a major goal. The manager should celebrate steps (or attaining small goals) equally as much as landings (major goals). The most effective pride builders are masters at identifying and recognizing the small achievements that will instill pride in their people.[29]

EQUITY THEORY AND SOCIAL COMPARISON

Expectancy theory, as described earlier, emphasizes the rational and thinking side of people. Similarly, another theory focuses on how fairly people think they are being treated in comparison to certain reference groups. According to **equity theory**, employee satisfaction and motivation depend on how fairly the employees believe they are treated in comparison to peers. The theory contends that employees hold certain beliefs about the outcomes they receive from their jobs, as well as the inputs they invest to obtain these outcomes.

The outcomes of employment include pay, benefits, status, recognition, intrinsic job factors, and anything else stemming from the job that workers perceive as useful. The inputs include all the factors that employees perceive as being their investment in the job or anything of value that they bring to the job. These inputs include job qualifications, skills, education level, effort, trust in the company, support of coworkers, and cooperative behavior.

The core of equity theory is that employees compare their inputs and outcomes (making social comparisons) with others in the workplace.[30] If employees believe that they receive equitable outcomes in relation to their inputs, they are generally satisfied and motivated. When workers believe that they are being treated equitably, they are more willing to work hard. Conversely, when employees believe that they give too much as compared to what they receive from the organization, a state of tension, dissatisfaction, and demotivation ensues. The people used for reference are those whom the employee perceives as relevant for comparison. For example, an industrial sales representative would make comparisons with other industrial sales reps in the same industry about whom he has information.

There are two kinds of comparisons. People consider their own inputs in relation to outcomes received, and they also evaluate what others receive for the same inputs. Equity is said to exist when an individual concludes that his or her own outcome/input ratio is equal to that of other people. Inequity exists if the person's ratio is not the same as that of other people. All these comparisons are similar to those judgments made by people according to expectancy theory—they are subjective hunches that may or may not be valid. Inequity can be in either direction and of varying magnitude. The equity ratio is often expressed as follows:

$$\frac{\text{Outcomes of Individual}}{\text{Inputs of Individual}} \quad \text{compared to} \quad \frac{\text{Outcomes of Others}}{\text{Inputs of Others}}$$

According to equity theory, the highest level of motivation occurs when a person has ratios equal to those of the comparison person. When people perceive an inequity, they are likely to engage in one or more of the three following actions that lead to a negative outcome for the employer.

1. *Alter the outcome.* The person who feels mistreated might ask for more salary or for a bonus, promotional opportunities, or more vacation time. Some people might even steal from the company to obtain the money they feel they deserve. Others might attempt to convince management to give less to others.

2. *Alter the input.* A person who feels treated inequitably might decrease effort or time devoted to work. The person who feels underpaid might engage in such self-defeating behavior by faking sick days to take care of personal business. Another extreme would be to encourage others to decrease their inputs so they will earn less money.

3. *Leave the situation.* As an extreme move, the person who feels treated inequitably might quit a job. He or she would then be free to pursue greater equity in another position.

A practical implication of equity theory, as well as expectancy theory, for leaders and manager is to not give everybody the same salary increase or bonus. The problem is that the workers who think they have provided the highest inputs will think they are treated unjustly. According to Jack and Suzy Welch, under these conditions, "top performers inevitably head for the door."[31]

Equity theory has several direct implications for the leader who is attempting to motivate subordinates. First, no matter how well designed a program of productivity or cost-cutting might be, it must still provide equitable pay. Otherwise, the negative perceptions of workers might lead to less effort to accomplish the goals of management. Second, the leader should attempt to see that subordinates perceive themselves to be getting a fair deal in terms of what they are giving to and receiving from the company. For example, a discussion with a given worker might reveal that the worker feels underused in terms of his or her education, training, and experience. Giving the worker a new, challenging assignment might lead to higher motivation on the part of the worker.

Another approach to enhancing motivation would be to place the worker in a job with a higher pay grade, so he or she would feel more equitably treated. (Of course, there are often constraints on how much a leader can manipulate pay and job assignments.)

Leadership Skill-Building Exercise 7-3 will help you personalize equity theory.

LEADERSHIP SKILL-BUILDING EXERCISE 7-3

The Application of Equity Theory

The object of this skill-building exercise is to apply equity theory to yourself, so you can then apply the theory to motivating others. The focus of the exercise is to search for values for the two ratios.

1. *Outcomes of Individual/Inputs of Individual*

   Reflect on a job you hold now or held in the past. First, list all the outcomes you received or are receiving on that job. Information in the text will give you some ideas. List factors such as salary, bonuses, friendships with coworkers, vacations, and new learning. Next, list all your inputs, such as education, prior training, money invested in education, and cooperative behavior.

2. *Outcomes of Others/Inputs of Others*

   To obtain data for this ratio, you will have to do some research. Perhaps you can send e-mails to current or past coworkers. To find out what others doing this type of work are earning, you might consult www. salary.com or similar websites. Reach any conclusion you can about whether you were, or are, being treated equitably.

   Next, reflect on how your evaluation of equity might affect your past or current motivation. Ask several of your classmates about their results for this exercise. Based on your analysis, does it appear that equity theory offers any promise as a motivational theory for leaders to apply?

COACHING AS AN APPROACH TO MOTIVATION

Effective leaders are good coaches, and good coaches are effective motivators. The coaching demands are much less rigorous for leaders who have little face-to-face contact with organization members, such as financial deal makers, CEOs, and chairpersons of the board. Nevertheless, there is a coaching component at all levels of leadership. David Novak, the chief executive of Yum Brands, Inc., sees himself more as a coach and cheerleader than as The Boss. Part of his being a coach includes careful listening to the ideas of staff members.[32]

Coaching is a way of enabling others to act and build on their strengths. To coach is to care enough about people to invest time in building personal relationships with them. The organization also benefits from coaching because of the elevated productivity of many of the workers who are coached. Coaching is also seen as a key vehicle for engaging (or motivating) workers. James Harter, chief scientist for Gallup's international management practice, contends that the majority of engaged employees work for managers who devote substantial time to helping their subordinates succeed.[33]

Key Characteristics of Coaching

Coaching in the workplace might ordinarily be explained as the art of management. Because a coaching relationship is unique, the person being coached is better motivated to accomplish goals for the good of the organization. Coaching is an interaction between two people, usually the manager and an employee. The purpose of the interaction is to help the employee learn from the job in order to help his or her development.[34] The interaction of the two personalities influences the coaching outcome. Some leaders, for example, can successfully coach certain people but not others.

Coaching requires a moderate degree of interpersonal risk and trust on the part of both people in the relationship. The coach might give the person being coached wrong advice. Or the person being coached might reject the coach's encouragement. Think of the risk involved when a basketball player asks the coach for advice on how to correct a shot that is not working well. As a result of the coaching, the player might shoot more poorly, to the embarrassment of both. Similarly, an organizational leader might coach a team member in a direction that backfires—for example, that results in even fewer sales than before.

Research at the Center for Creative Leadership found that managers too often perceive coaching as simply telling people what to do. Effective coaching focuses on the growth and development of individuals rather than telling direct reports what to do in a given situation. To help subordinates grow and develop, the leader as coach should give subordinates the resources they need to make their own decisions. The people being coached should be challenged to find the right solution, and then should be provided feedback on how well they have performed.[35]

Assume that a manager wants the accident rate on the construction of skyscrapers reduced substantially. Instead of telling a direct report exactly how to accomplish this goal, the manager might point to new sources of help for accident reduction. In the process, the direct report might find solutions the manager did not already know about.

A key advantage of coaching is that it generates new possibilities for action and facilitates breakthroughs in performance. A vice president might say to a lower-ranking manager, "Have you thought of getting your people more involved in setting objectives? If you did, you might find greater commitment and follow-through." The middle manager begins to involve managers more in setting objectives, and performance increases. Coaching in this situation has achieved substantial results.

At its best, coaching offers concrete contributions, including higher motivation. An effective coach keeps spirits up and offers praise and recognition frequently. Good coaching also leads to personal development. Group members are encouraged to cross-train and serve as backups for each other. Good coaching also improves group performance. The effective coach makes team members aware of one another's skills and how these skills can contribute to attaining the group's goals.[36]

Fallacies About Coaching

Another approach to understanding the coaching function of leadership is to examine certain common misperceptions about coaching, as explained by Ian Cunningham and Linda Honold.[37] One false belief is that *coaching applies only in one-to-one work*. In reality, the team or other group can also be coached. As a team leader, you might make a suggestion to the group, such as, "Why are you rushing through such an important issue?" A major misperception is that *coaching is mostly about providing new knowledge and skills*. The truth is that people often need more help with underlying habits than with knowledge and skills. A good example is coaching another person about work habits and time management. You can provide the individual with loads of useful knowledge and techniques; however, if the person is a procrastinator, he or she must reduce procrastination before time-management skills will help.

Another stereotype deals with an important ethical issue: *if coaches go beyond giving instruction in knowledge and skills, they are in danger of getting into psychotherapy*. The counterargument is that coaches should simply follow the model of effective parents: listening to the other person, attempting to understand his or her real concerns, and offering support and encouragement. Another stereotype particularly resistant to extinction is that *coaches need to be expert in something in order to coach*. To use a sports analogy, a good coach does not have to be or have been an outstanding athlete. An important role for the coach is to ask pertinent questions and listen. Questioning and listening can help the other person set realistic learning goals.

An understandable stereotype is that *coaching has to be done face-to-face*. The face-to-face approach facilitates coaching. Nevertheless, telephone, e-mail, and text messaging are useful alternatives when time and distance create barriers. A worker on a field trip, for example, might send his manager an e-mail similar to this one: "The customer says that if I make a mistake with this installation, he'll never do business with us again. Any suggestions?"

The accompanying Leader in Action profile illustrates how effective coaching might contribute to an organization

LEADER IN ACTION

Tammy the Kindly Coach

Tammy is the administrative vice president of Quality Components, a manufacturer and distributor of automated manufacturing systems. The company makes such specialty machines as leak-testing equipment for vehicle radiators. At a luncheon in honor of her twenty-five years of service to the company, Tammy was asked to briefly address the gathering. Her comments included the following:

"Our CEO, Brad, asked me to tell you what I am most proud of during my first quarter of a century with Quality Components. My job title has stayed essentially the same for ten years, but that is OK with me. The way I see it, a company leader at my level should be more concerned about the development of company employees than getting promoted. We sometimes forget that a manager is a teacher and a coach as well as a businessperson.

"What I am most proud of, without a doubt, is having spent a lot of time with my staff giving them whatever guidance and encourage I could. My happiest days at Quality have been when I gave somebody advice and he or she became more effective because of that advice."

After Tammy set down to cheers, Terry, an office supervisor, stood up and said, "Tammy is so right, she has helped so many of us. I remember joining the company a few years back, nervous and unsure if I could be successful at Quality Components. Tammy was wonderful. She coached me; she gave me constructive feedback when I made an error. She helped me believe in myself. So here's to Tammy—a great coach and a great leader."

QUESTIONS

1. What does this brief description tell you about the importance of coaching subordinates?
2. What is Tammy implying about the possible conflict between getting promoted and being a good coach.

Source: The facts for this story were collected in Fairfax, Virginia, April 2011, from a source who chooses to remain anonymous.

COACHING SKILLS AND TECHNIQUES

Leaders and managers have varied aptitudes for coaching. One way to acquire coaching skill is to study basic principles and suggestions and then practice them. Another is to attend a training program for coaching that involves modeling (learning by imitation) and role playing. Here we examine a number of suggestions for coaching, all of which might also apply to coaching a group or a team as well as an individual. The typical scenario for a leader to coach a team would take place in a meeting with all or most of the group. If implemented with skill, the suggestions will improve the chances that coaching will lead to improved performance of individuals and groups.

1. *Communicate clear expectations to group members.* For people to perform well and to continue to learn and grow, they need a clear perception of what is expected of them. The expectations of a position become the standards by which performance will be judged, thus serving as a base point for coaching. If a team member is supposed to contribute three new ideas each month for improving operations, coaching is justified when an average of only one idea per month is forthcoming.

2. *Build relationships.* Effective coaches build personal relationships with team members and work to improve their interpersonal skills.[38] Having established rapport with team members facilitates entering into a coaching relationship with them. The suggestions that follow about active listening and giving emotional support are part of relationship building.

3. *Give feedback on areas that require specific improvement.* To coach a group member toward higher levels of performance, the leader pinpoints what specific behavior, attitude, or skills require improvement. An effective coach might say, "I read the product-expansion proposal you submitted. It's OK, but it falls short of your usual level of creativity. Our competitors are already carrying each product you mentioned. Have you thought about … ?" Another important factor in giving specific feedback is to avoid generalities and exaggerations, such as, "You never come up with a good product idea" or "You are the most unimaginative product development specialist I have ever known." To give good feedback, the leader or manager has to observe performance and behavior directly and frequently, such as by watching a supervisor dealing with a safety problem.

To make the feedback process less intimidating, it is helpful to ask permission before you start coaching, indicate your purposes, and explain your positive intentions: for example, "Jack, do you have a few minutes for me to share my thoughts with you?" (permission); "I'd like to talk to you about the presentation you just made to the venture capitalists" (purpose); "I liked your creativity, yet I have some ideas you might use in your next presentation" (positive intentions).[39] Feedback is also likely to be less intimidating when the coach explains which behaviors should decrease and which should increase. This approach is a variation of combining compliments with criticism to avoid insulting the person being coached. You might say, "Tanya, I need you to place more emphasis on quality and less on speed."

Feedback can also be made less intimidating when the coach begins with a question, such as "How do you think you're doing?" The question helps give the person being coached joint ownership of the problem, and helps him or her feel included rather than excluded.[40]

Should the coach be dealing with a person who is highly sensitive to criticism, it can be helpful to convert the criticism into a positive suggestion to avoid intimidating the person being coached. Replace "A few of your facts were way off in your last report" with "You could improve your accuracy by double checking your facts."[41]

4. *Listen actively.* Listening is an essential ingredient in any coaching session. An active listener tries to grasp both facts and feelings. Observing the group member's nonverbal communication is another part of active listening. The leader must also be patient and not poised for a rebuttal of any difference of opinion between him or her and the group member. Beginning each coaching session with a question helps set the stage for active listening. The question will also spark the employee's thinking and frame the discussion: for example, "How might we use the new database of customers who have purchased similar products help our staff generate more sales?"

Part of being a good listener is encouraging the person being coached to talk about his or her performance. Asking open-ended questions facilitates a flow of conversation: for example, ask, "How did you feel about the way you handled conflict with the marketing group yesterday?" A close-ended question covering the same issue would be, "Do you think you could have done a better job of handling conflict with the marketing group yesterday?"

5. *Help remove obstacles.* To perform at anywhere near top capacity, individuals may need help in removing obstacles such as a maze of rules and regulations and rigid budgeting. An important role for the leader of an organizational unit is thus to be a barrier buster. A leader or manager is often in a better position than a group member to gain approval from a higher-level manager, find money from another budget line, expedite a purchase order, or authorize hiring a temporary worker to provide assistance. Yet if the coach is too quick to remove obstacles for the group member, the latter may not develop enough self-reliance.

6. *Give emotional support and empathy.* By being helpful and constructive, the leader provides much-needed emotional support to the group member who is not performing at his or her best. A coaching session should not be an interrogation. An effective way of giving emotional support is to use positive rather than negative motivators. For example, the leader might say, "I liked some things you did yesterday, and I have a few suggestions that might bring you closer to peak performance."

Displaying empathy is an effective way to give emotional support. Indicate with words that you understand the challenge the group member faces with a statement such as, "I understand that working with a reduced staff has placed you under heavy time pressures." The genuine concern you show will help establish the rapport useful in working out the problem together.

7. *Reflect content or meaning.* An effective way of reflecting meaning is to rephrase and summarize concisely what the group member is saying. A substandard performer might say, "The reason I've fallen so far behind is that our company has turned into a bureaucratic nightmare. We're being hit right and left with forms to fill out for customer satisfaction. I have fifty e-mail messages that I haven't read yet." You might respond, "You're falling so far behind because you have so many forms and messages that require attention." The group member might then respond with something like, "That's exactly what I mean. I'm glad you understand my problem." (Notice that the leader is also giving the group member an opportunity to express the feelings behind his or her problem.)

8. *Give some gentle advice and guidance.* Too much advice giving interferes with two-way communication, yet some advice can elevate performance. Also, workers being coached usually expect to receive some advice. The manager should assist the group member in answering the question "What can I do about this problem?" Advice in the form of a question or suppositional statement is often effective. One example is, "Could the root of your problem be insufficient planning?" A direct statement such as, "The root of your problem is obviously insufficient planning," often makes people resentful and defensive. By responding to a question, the person being coached is likely to feel more involved in making improvements.

Part of giving gentle guidance for improvement is to use the word *could* instead of *should*. To say, "You should do this," implies that the person is currently doing something wrong, which can trigger defensiveness. Saying, "You could do this," leaves the person with a choice: accept or reject your input and weigh the consequences.[42] (You *could* accept this advice to become a better coach!)

9. *Allow for modeling of desired performance and behavior.* An effective coaching technique is to show the group member by example what constitutes the desired behavior. Assume that a manager has been making statements to customers that stretch the truth, such as falsely saying that the product met a zero-defects standard. In coaching him, the manager's boss might allow the manager to observe how she handles a similar situation with a customer. The manager's boss might telephone a customer and say, "You have been inquiring about whether we have adopted a zero-defects standard for our laser printers. Right now, we are doing our best to produce error-free products. Yet so far we do not have a formal zero-defects program. We stand by our printers and will fix any defect at no cost to you."

10. *Gain a commitment to change.* Unless the leader receives a commitment from the team member to carry through with the proposed solution to a problem, the team member may not attain higher performance. An experienced manager develops an intuitive sense for when employees are serious about performance improvement. Two clues that commitment to change is lacking are (1) over-agreeing about the need for change and (2) agreeing to change without display of emotion.

11. *Applaud good results.* Effective coaches on the playing field and in the workplace are cheerleaders. They give encouragement and positive reinforcement by applauding good results. Some effective coaches shout with joy when an individual or team achieves outstanding results; others applaud.

Leadership Self-Assessment Quiz 7-3 will help you think through the development you need to be an effective coach. If you are already an effective coach, look for ways to improve. Leadership Skill-Building Exercise 7-4 gives you a chance to practice coaching.

LEADERSHIP SELF-ASSESSMENT QUIZ 7-3

Characteristics of an Effective Coach

Instructions: Following is a list of traits, attitudes, and behaviors characteristic of effective coaches. Place a check mark next to each trait, attitude, or behavior that you need to develop along those lines (for example, whether you need to become more patient). On a separate sheet of paper, design an action plan for improvement for each trait, attitude, or behavior that you need to develop. An example of an action plan for improving patience might be, "I'll ask people to tell me when I appear too impatient. I'll also try to develop self-control about my impatience."

TRAIT, ATTITUDE, OR BEHAVIOR	
1. Empathy (putting self in other person's shoes)	☐
2. Listening skill	☐
3. Insight into people	☐
4. Diplomacy and tact	☐
5. Patience toward people	☐
6. Concern for welfare of people	☐
7. Low hostility toward people	☐
8. Self-confidence and emotional security	☐
9. Non-competitiveness with group members	☐
10. Enthusiasm for people	☐
11. Satisfaction in helping others grow	☐
12. Interest in development of group members	☐
13. High expectations for each group member	☐
14. Ability to give authentic feedback	☐
15. Interest in people's potential	☐
16. Honesty and integrity (or trustworthiness)	☐
17. Friendliness	☐
18. Develops trust and respect	☐

Source: Items 11–15 gathered from information in William D. Hitt, *The Leader–Manager: Guidelines for Action* (Columbus, OH.: Battelle Press, 1988), pp. 183–186.

LEADERSHIP SKILL-BUILDING EXERCISE 7-4

Coaching for Improved Performance

Clayton is a financial consultant (stockbroker) at a branch office of an established financial services firm. His manager, Marlene, is concerned that Clayton is 25 percent below quota in sales of a new gold mutual fund offered by the company. Marlene schedules a late-afternoon meeting in her office to attempt to help Clayton make quota. She has told Clayton, "I want to talk about your sales performance on the new gold fund and see if I can be helpful." Clayton is concerned that the meeting might be a discipline session in disguise.

Have one member of the class assume the role of Marlene and another the role of Clayton. Marlene will attempt to implement recommended coaching techniques. Other class members will watch and then provide constructive feedback.

This exercise is a key skill builder because so much of face-to-face leadership involves working out performance problems with group members. If every employee were an outstanding, independent performer, we would have less need for managers and leaders.

EXECUTIVE COACHING AND LEADERSHIP EFFECTIVENESS

A form of coaching in vogue is for managers to consult professional coaches to help them become more effective leaders and to guide them in their careers. **Executive coaching** is "A one-on-one development process formally contracted between a coach and a management-level client to help achieve goals related to professional development and/or business performance."[43]

In the past, management psychologists were typically hired as outside coaches to help managers become more effective leaders. Today, people from a wide variety of backgrounds become executive coaches, as well as career coaches and life coaches. Many executive coaches are former executives themselves.

Specific Forms of Assistance Provided by Executive Coaches

Executive coaches help managers become more effective leaders by helping them in a variety of ways. A survey of 140 leading executive coaches revealed that the three top reasons coaches are engaged are (1) develop high potentials or facilitate transition (48%); (2) act as a sounding board (26%); and (3) address derailing, or failing, behavior (12%).[44] A variety of reasons for hiring coaches are described next. However, it is unlikely that one coach would provide all these services, or that one manager would want or need all of them.

- Helping corporate stars attain peak performance, similar to an athletic coach working with an outstanding athlete. One approach to heightened performance is to help the leader uncover personal assets and strengths he or she may not have known existed. An example would be discovering that the leader has untapped creativity and imagination.[45]
- Counseling the leader about weaknesses that could interfere with effectiveness, such as being too hostile and impatient. The coach will also solicit

feedback by interviewing coworkers and subordinates, and then distilling the feedback to help the executive. One coaching client provided this description of how the coach's comments provided a critical moment for him: "It was when my coach directly challenged me to be bolder and give more of myself as a management team member. I had been reflecting on this for a while, and his challenge was what was needed. The timing was right."[46]

- Serving as a sounding board when the leader faces a complex decision about strategy, operations, or human resource issues. Closely related to being a sounding board is a coach's ability to ask tough questions, such as asking why the executive is pursuing a particular strategy.[47]
- Making specific suggestions about self-promotion and image enhancement, including suggestions about appearance and mannerisms.
- Helping the leader achieve a better balance between work and family life, thereby having more focused energy for the leadership role.
- Serving as a trusted confidante to discuss issues the leader might feel uncomfortable talking about with others: for example, talking about feeling insecure in his or her position.
- Giving advice about career management, such as developing a career path.
- Strengthening the executive's strategic decision-making skills by helping him or her think more broadly about issues and appreciate how his or her actions will affect the organizational system. The coach might point out a blind spot in the leader's decision making, such as neglecting part of the human consequences of a decision.
- Assisting an executive in selecting direct reports by looking for compatibility between the candidate and the executive, as well as reviewing other qualifications.[48]

Note that the coach works as an adviser about behavior but does not explicitly help the leader with functional details of the job, such as how to develop a new product strategy or design an organization.

The leader/manager's employer usually hires the executive coach. The purpose of engaging the coach could be to accelerate the development of a star player or assist an executive who is having soft-skill problems. For example, the direct reports of a manager at a consulting firm referred to her as a "weed whacker," so an executive coach was hired to help the executive develop more emotional intelligence. The executive soon learned that employees perceived in her tone and body language that she was attacking them. Coaching helped her soften her approach and work better with others.[49]

A refinement of individual coaching is for the coach to work with both the individual and his or her work associates. The coach solicits feedback from the group members and involves them in helping the manager improve. For example, the coach might tell team members to assert their rights when the manager throws a temper tantrum or makes unreasonable demands. The coach might also work with the superiors or peers of the person being coached. Coach Marshall Goldsmith says, "My success rate as a coach has improved dramatically, as I've realized that people's getting better is not a function of me; it's a function of the person and the people around the person."[50]

Contributions of and Concerns About Executive Coaching

Executive coaching may frequently accomplish several of the ends specified in the previous list. Executive coaching, however, has some potential drawbacks for the leader. A major problem is that a coach may give advice that backfires because he or she does not understand the particular work setting. One outside coach told a manager in an information technology firm that she should become more decisive in her decision making and less dependent on consensus. The advice backfired because the culture of the firm emphasized consensus decision making. Furthermore, many people who present themselves as executive coaches may not be professionally qualified or may not have much knowledge about business.[51]

An ethical problem is that many coaches delve into personal and emotional issues that should be reserved for mental health professionals. Psychotherapist Steven Berglas contends that executive coaches can make a bad situation worse when they ignore psychological problems they do not understand.[52] The leader who is performing poorly because of a deep-rooted problem such as hostility toward others is given superficial advice about making nice. (The opposite ethical problem occurs when a relationship coach offer business advice, without having the experience or qualifications to offer such advice.) Another potential ethical problem is that the leader/manager may become too dependent on the coach, checking with him or her before making any consequential decision.[53]

SUMMARY

Effective leaders are outstanding motivators and coaches, and the role of the leader and manager today emphasizes coaching. A broad purpose of leaders applying motivation and coaching techniques is getting employees involved in their work and excited about working for the organization. Engagement is reflected in employee willingness to stay with the firm and go beyond the call of duty. Leaders use motivation and coaching techniques to help keep employees engaged.

The expectancy theory of motivation is useful for developing motivational skills because it is comprehensive, building on other explanations of motivation.

Expectancy theory has three major components: valence, instrumentality, and expectancy. *Valence* is the worth or attractiveness of an outcome. Each work situation has multiple outcomes, and each outcome has a valence of its own. Valences range from -100 to $+100$ in the version of expectancy theory presented here. Zero valences reflect indifference and therefore are not motivational. Very high valences help explain why some people persist in efforts despite a low probability of payoff. *Instrumentality* is the individual's assessment of the probability that performance will lead to certain outcomes. (An outcome is anything that might stem from performance, such as a reward.) *Expectancy* is an individual's assessment of the probability that effort will lead to performing the task correctly.

Expectancy theory has implications and provides guidelines for leaders, including the following: (1) determine necessary performance levels; (2) make the performance level attainable; (3) train and encourage people; (4) make explicit the link between rewards and performance; (5) make sure the rewards are large enough; (6) analyze factors that oppose the effectiveness of the reward; (7) explain the meaning and implications of second-level outcomes; (8) understand individual differences in valences; and (9) recognize that when workers are in a good mood, valences, instrumentalities, and expectancies will more likely enhance performance.

Goal setting is a basic process that is directly or indirectly part of all major theories of motivation. Goal theory includes the following ideas: (1) specific and difficult goals result in high performance (yet outrageous goals can inspire); (2) goals must be accepted by group members; (3) goals are more effective when they are linked to feedback and rewards; (4) the combination of individual and group goals is very effective; and (5) a learning goal orientation is more effective than a performance goal orientation.

A major concern about using goals to motivate performance is that leaders, as well as other workers, will take unethical and dysfunctional shortcuts to attain their goals.

Motivating others by giving them recognition and praise can be considered a direct application of positive reinforcement. Recognition programs to reward and motivate employees are standard practice. Recognition is a strong motivator because it is a normal human need to crave recognition, and workers often do not feel they receive enough recognition. To appeal to the recognition need, identify a meritorious behavior and then recognize that behavior with an oral, written, or material reward. To maximize its motivational impact, recognition should be linked to corporate values and personal goals. Recognition and praise are no-cost or low-cost motivators that are powerful.

Giving workers an opportunity to experience pride can be a strong internal motivator, yet workers still receive recognition. To motivate through pride, it is best for the manager to set the compass on pride, not money, and for workers to be proud of daily accomplishments.

Equity theory can be applied to employee motivation. The core of the theory is that employees compare their inputs and outcomes with others in the workplace. When employees believe that they are being treated equitably, they are more willing to work hard. Then the leader should attempt to see that subordinates see themselves as getting a fair deal in terms of what they are giving to and getting from the company.

A major purpose of coaching is to achieve enthusiasm and high performance in a team setting. Several characteristics of coaching contribute to its close relationship with leadership. Coaching is a two-way process, suggesting that being a great coach requires having a talented team. Coaching requires a high degree of interpersonal risk and trust on the part of both sides in the relationship. Effective coaching focuses on the growth and development of people rather than telling them how to deal with a given situation.

The coaching function can also be understood by recognizing several common misperceptions: (1) coaching applies only to one-on-one work; (2) coaching is mostly about providing new knowledge and skills; (3) coaching easily falls into psychotherapy; (4) coaches need to be experts in what they are coaching; and (5) coaching has to be done face-to-face.

Suggestions for improving coaching are as follows: (1) communicate clear expectations, (2) build relationships, (3) give feedback on areas that require specific improvement, (4) listen actively, (5) help remove obstacles, (6) give emotional support including empathy, (7) reflect content or meaning, (8) give gentle advice and guidance, (9) allow for modeling of desired performance and behavior, (10) gain a commitment to change, and (11) applaud good results.

Managers frequently consult executive coaches to help them be more effective leaders. Such coaches provide a variety of services, including helping attain peak performance, counseling about weaknesses, helping achieve balance in life, helping the leader uncover hidden assets, and giving career advice. Executive coaching often achieves its purposes, yet there are potential problems: executive coaches can give bad advice, the coach might be unqualified in general or to deal with mental health issues and the leader may become too dependent on the coach.

KEY TERMS

engagement	instrumentality	equity theory
expectancy theory	expectancy	executive coaching
valence	self-efficacy	
outcome	goal	

✔ GUIDELINES FOR ACTION AND SKILL DEVELOPMENT

It is worth repeating that a major way goal-setting can backfire as a motivational strategy is when there is not careful agreement about the ethical means by which the goal will be pursued. For example, the manager of a trucking fleet might be assigned a goal of reducing costs by 10 percent. An unethical means would be to reduce truck safety by delaying tire and brake replacements.

Given that recognition can be such a relatively low-cost yet highly effective motivator, the leader/ manager should keep in mind available forms of recognition. In addition to considering those in the following list, use your imagination to think of other forms of recognition. For the recognition technique to work well, it should have high valence for the person or group under consideration.

- Compliments, such as "You help us accomplish our mission," or "Our customers love what you are doing for them"
- Encouragement for a job well done
- Comradeship with the boss
- A pat on the back or a handshake
- Public expression of appreciation such as on an intranet or social media website (company exclusive or public)
- A meeting of appreciation with the executive
- Team uniforms, hats, T-shirts, or mugs
- A note of thanks to the individual (handwritten, e-mail, or text message)
- A flattering letter from a customer distributed over e-mail
- Employee-of-month award
- A special commendation placed in employee file

- A gift from the company recognition program, such as a watch, a clock, or a pin

Approaches to recognition may pack an extra punch when they do not take the same form every time. For a job well done, the worker might receive a warm e-mail one week, a gift certificate the next, and perhaps an employee-of-the month designation in the future.

Discussion Questions and Activities

1. Why do many people think that motivation is the most important part of a leader's job?
2. Describe any two actions a leader might take to bring about employee engagement.
3. Identify several outcomes you expect from occupying a leadership position. What valences do you attach to them?
4. How can the influence exerted by a charismatic leader tie in with expectancy theory?
5. What is an example of a noble cause a leader at Domino's Pizza might use to motivate a store manager? What about a noble cause for workers in the Electrolux division of Whirlpool? (The best-known Electrolux product is vacuum cleaners.)
6. In what way might giving team members frequent recognition contribute to a leader's being perceived as charismatic?
7. For purposes of recognition, many companies give out watches, clocks, and sport shirts with a company log embedded. What do you think of the effectiveness of this form of recognition?

8. How would a leader/manager be aware of a given group member's input/output ratio so the leader/manager could apply equity theory?

9. How might a leader use coaching to help increase ethical behavior among group members?

10. Ask a manager or coach to describe the amount of coaching he or she does on the job. Be prepared to bring your findings back to class.

LEADERSHIP CASE PROBLEM A

Justin Salisbury Tries a Little Recognition

Justin Salisbury is a super-franchiser for a large chain of soup-and-sandwich shops. He owns twelve shops in the same region, having invested $2 million to own these stores. One-half the investment in the stores came from inheritance and investments Justin had made prior to becoming a franchiser. The other half of the money was borrowed, so Justin feels considerable pressure to earn enough gross profit from the stores to make his debt payments and earn a living.

Justin concluded that he needed to increase revenues from his stores about 15 percent in order to net enough profit for a comfortable living. He believed that his business processes were good enough to make a profit, and that the company was giving his franchise operations enough marketing and advertising support. Justin also thought that his managers were running efficient operations. He was concerned, however, that they weren't trying hard enough to achieve good customer service by encouraging the order takers at the stores to pay more attention to customers. For example, when Justin visited the stores (or sent a family member in his place), the order takers didn't smile enough or ask frequently enough, "What else would you like with your order?"

Justin decided that he shouldn't micromanage by telling the store managers how to motivate their staffs. Yet he decided to discuss with his managers what he wanted—more profit by doing a better job of motivating the order takers and cashiers. He also pointed out to his twelve store managers that he would be rewarding and recognizing their accomplishments in boosting store revenues. After consulting with the managers, Justin established the goal of a 15 percent increases in revenues within twelve months.

Two weeks after the goal-setting discussions with the twelve store managers, Justin announced that he would be recognizing and rewarding attaining a 15 percent or better increase in revenue with two of the following forms of recognition:

- A wall plaque designating the manager as a "Store Manager of the Year"
- A year's membership in an athletic club for the manager and a spouse or partner
- A bonus equivalent to 2 percent of annual salary
- Choice of an iPad or an iPod
- An expense-paid trip for the manager and his or her family to one day at an amusement park or theme park

Justin waited for responses from his managers to the proposed recognition plan. He received several e-mail messages acknowledging an appreciation of his program, yet no burst of enthusiasm. Justin thought to himself, "I guess the managers don't understand yet how great it feels to be recognized for making a tough financial target. I think that when they earn their recognition awards, I will see a lot more enthusiasm."

Questions

1. What advice can you give Justin Salisbury about the most likely motivational consequences of his recognition program?

2. What other form of recognition should Justin offer the store managers?

3. Would it be better for Justin to have a recognition program aimed directly at the order takers and cashiers than at their managers? Explain your reasoning.

ASSOCIATED ROLE PLAY

One student plays the role of Justin, who is filled with enthusiasm about his recognition program and wants to understand why the response from store managers so far has been lukewarm. Justin decides to have a face-to-face meeting with a store manager to diagnose what might be wrong with his proposed recognition program. Another student plays the role of a store manager who thinks that the recognition program might be a waste of time.

After all, the manager reasons, good results speak for themselves and should be rewarded with money. Yet the store manager wants to maintain a good relationship with Justin.

Observers will look to see how well Justin conveys enthusiasm for his program, and how well he listens to the store manager. Observers will also see how well the store manager gets across his or her point, as well as being tactful.

LEADERSHIP CASE PROBLEM B

Coach Sally Gorman

Sally Gorman is the manager of the mortgage department of a suburban bank branch. She has six direct reports, including three mortgage consultants. Although the consultants work full-time at the bank, they are considered subcontractors who work only on commission—without any salary and benefits. A consequence of this compensation arrangement is that the mortgage consultants are under considerable pressure to sell home mortgages to bank customers. Until a mortgage is approved, the consultant receives zero financial compensation.

Tony Costello, a 28-year-old mortgage consultant, asked for an appointment to speak to Sally about his recent problems in nailing down mortgages. Sally was eager to meet with Tony because she was also under pressure for the mortgage department to place more mortgages. A partial transcript of their meeting follows:

Tony: Sally, I've come to you for help. For several months, I haven't been closing enough mortgages to make a living. My wife and I have two children, and we can't make ends meet on her salary alone. Is there any way the bank can put me on salary? Or maybe give me a few months' advance? I've been a great producer in the past.

Sally: Grow up, Tony. When you took this job, you knew it did not include a salary and that the bank does not allow advances. We need you to produce,

but we can't change the bank rules. We are not a mom-and-pop operation.

Tony: Do you know how brutal it is out there? Home sales are down 20 percent in our area. I don't have enough warm leads coming into the bank to shop for a mortgage. Besides that, our approval committee has been shooting down too many deals on me lately.

Sally: Wake up, Tony. The mortgage business has changed recently. We can't add any more high-risk loans to our portfolio. It's very difficult to resell those mortgages to other institutions.

Tony: Okay, then, what do you propose I do to generate more mortgage applications that the mortgage committee will approve?

Sally: Do what you do best. You're a professional. Just bear down harder on good mortgage possibilities who visit your desk. Be persuasive. Turn up the heat. Do something good or be gone.

Tony: I am trying. I want my commissions as much as the bank wants its mortgages.

Sally: Just keep trying harder, and get back to me with results, not excuses.

Tony: I guess that the bank and I are in the same boat. I'll talk to you later, Sally.

Questions

1. What advice can you offer Sally Gorman to do a better job of coaching Tony Costello?
2. What advice can you offer Tony Costello to get more out of the coaching session?
3. What is the most positive thing Sally did as a coach?
4. What is the most negative thing Sally did as a coach?

ASSOCIATED ROLE PLAY

One student plays the role of Sally Gorman, who may seem heartless, but perhaps the role player can make her a little more encouraging. Another person plays the role of Tony Costello, who is discouraged about his sales performance but wants to do better. Observers will look to see if the coaching session offers any promise of picking up Tony's spirits and pointing him toward improved performance. About eight minutes should suffice for this role play.

 ## LEADERSHIP SKILL-BUILDING EXERCISE 7-5

My Leadership Portfolio

One of the easiest and most powerful ways of motivating people is to recognize their efforts, as described in this chapter. Like any other interpersonal skill, being effective at giving recognition takes practice. During the next week, find three people to recognize, and observe how they react to your recognition. For example, if a server gives you fine service, explain after the meal how much you enjoyed the service and leave a larger-than-average tip. If your hair stylist does a fine job, similarly provide a compliment and a good tip. Or find some helper to recognize with a compliment but without a tip. Observe the responses of these people—both their facial expressions and what they say. Of even more importance, observe if any of these people appear eager to serve you the next time you interact with them.

As with other parts of your leadership portfolio, keep a written record of what happened to you and how much skill you think you have developed.

 ## LEADERSHIP SKILL-BUILDING EXERCISE 7-6

Position Paper on Motivation

Write a position paper on the topic of whether or not a leader/manager should have to invest time motivating workers. The general argument for a leader needing to spend time motivating subordinates is that it is part of human nature to not work very hard unless an external force provides some motivation. The general argument against a leader needing to spend time motivating subordinates is that people are expected to work hard, especially because they are financially compensated.

▶❚❚ LEADERSHIP VIDEO CASE DISCUSSION QUESTIONS

To view the videos for this activity, you'll need access to the CourseMate that is available for this text. To get access, visit www.CengageBrain.com.

After watching "Bright Horizons," answer the following questions.

1. Do you think expectancy theory is used at Bright Horizons? Explain.
2. How has Linda Mason, chair and founder of Bright Horizons Family Solutions, appealed to employees' sense of purpose?
3. How is recognition used at Bright Horizons to motivate employees? In addition, how has Bright Horizons been recognized?
4. What are some of the extrinsic motivators that Bright Horizons offers employees? Would you be motivated by these extrinsic rewards?

NOTES

1. Story created based on facts from a variety of the following sources: Gary Rivlin, "The Problem with Microsoft," *Fortune*, April 11, 2001, pp. 45–52; Peter Burrows, "Microsoft Defends Its Empire," *Business Week*, July 6, 2009, pp. 028–033; "Ballmer, Steve," *Novelguide.com* (1999 by Gale Research (accessed April 1, 2001); Jeff Atwood, "Steve Ballmer: Sweatiest Billionaire Ever," *Coding Horror* (www.codinghorror.com), July 27, 2005, pp. 1–5.
2. Cited in Gary Kranz, "Employees Want Feedback, Even if It's Negative," *Workforce Management*, February 2010, p. 11.
3. Ed Frauenheim, "Downturn Puts New Emphasis on Engagement," *Workforce Management*, July 20, 2009, p. 8.
4. Ed Frauenheim, "Commitment Issues," *Workforce Management*, November 16, 2009, p. 20.
5. Garry Kranz, "Employees Want Feedback—Even If It's Negative," *Workforce Management*, February 2010, pp. 10–11.
6. Cited in Laura Raines, "Re-engaging Workers Is a Big Hurdle for HR," *AJC* (www.ajc.com/jobs), March 17, 2011, p. 2.
7. Survey cited in "Special Report: Employee Engagement," *Workforce Management*, July 2011, p. 26.
8. Thad Green, *Motivation Management: Fueling Performance by Discovering What People Believe About Themselves and Their Organizations* (Palo Alto, CA: Davies-Black Publishing, 2000). An original version of expectancy theory applied to work motivation is Victor H. Vroom, *Work and Motivation* (New York: Wiley, 1964).
9. Wendelien Van Eerde and Hank Thierry, "Vroom's Expectancy Models and Work-Related Criteria: A Meta-Analysis," *Journal of Applied Psychology*, October 1996, pp. 548–556.
10. David A. Nadler and Edward E. Lawler III, "Motivation: A Diagnostic Approach," in Richard Hackman, Edward E. Lawler III, and Lyman W. Porter, eds., *Perspectives on Behavior in Organizations*, 2nd ed. (New York: McGraw-Hill, 1983), pp. 67–78; James A. F. Stoner and R. Edward Freeman, *Management*, 4th ed. (Upper Saddle River, N.J.: Prentice Hall, 1989), p. 448.
11. Amir Erez and Alice M. Isen, "The Influence of Positive Affect on the Components of Expectancy Motivation," *Journal of Applied Psychology*, December 2002, pp. 1055–1067.
12. "The Secret to Meeting Your Goals," *Manager's Edge*, Special Issue, 2008, p. 3.
13. Literature reviewed in Gerard H. Seitjts, Gary P. Latham, Kevin Tasa, and Bradon W. Latham, "Goal Setting and Goal Orientation: An Integration of 'Two Different Yet Related Literatures,'" *Academy of Management Journal*, April 2004, pp. 227–228.
14. Edwin A. Locke and Gary P. Latham, *A Theory of Goal Setting and Task Performance* (Upper Saddle River, N.J.: Prentice Hall, 1990); Latham, *Work Motivation: History, Theory, Research, and Practice* (Thousand Oaks, CA: Sage, 2007).

15. "Motivate Staff with Noble Cause," *Manager's Edge*, June 2005, p. 1.

16. Cited in "Set Outrageous Goals," *Executive Leadership*, June 2001, p. 7.

17. John J. Donavan and David J. Radosevich, "The Moderating Role of Goal Commitment on the Goal Difficulty–Performance Relationship: A Meta-Analytic Review and Critical Reanalysis," *Journal of Applied Psychology*, April 1998, pp. 308–315.

18. Don VandeWalle, Steven P. Brown, William L. Cron, and John W. Slocum Jr., "The Influence of Goal Orientation and Self-Regulation Tactics on Sales Performance: A Longitudinal Field Test," *Journal of Applied Psychology*, April 1999, pp. 249–259.

19. Maurcie E. Schweitzer, Lisa Ordoñez, and Bambi Douma, "Goal Setting as a Moderator of Unethical Behavior," *The Academy of Management Journal*, June 2004, p. 430.

20. The Problem with Financial Incentives—And What to Do About It," *Knowledge @Wharton* (http://knowledge.wharton.upenn.edu), March 30, 2011, pp. 1–4.

21. Lisa D. Ordóñez, Maurice E. Schweitzer, Adam D. Galinksy, and Max H. Bazerman, "Goals Gone Wild: The Systematic Side Effects of Overprescribing Goal Setting," *Academy of Management Perspective*, February 2009, p. 14.

22. Quoted in Julie Bos, "Beating the Burnout: Six Top Strategies for Effective Employee Rewards and Recognition," *Workforce Management*, October 2010, p. 40.

23. Study cited in Adrian Gostick and Chester Elton, *The Carrot Principle: How the Best Managers Use Recognition to Engage Their People, Retain Talent, and Accelerate Performance* (New York: The Free Press, 2007).

24. Jennifer Laabs, "Satisfy Them with More Than Money," *Workforce*, November 1998, p. 43.

25. Leslie Gross Klaff, "Getting Happy with the Rewards King," *Workforce*, April 2003, p. 47.

26. Gostick and Elton, *The Carrot Principle*.

27. "Raise Workplace Morale without Spending a Dime," *Communication Briefings*, April 2010, p. 5.

28. Andrew J. DuBrin, "Self-Perceived Technical Orientation and Attitudes Toward Being Flattered," *Psychological Reports*, 96, 2005, pp. 852–854.

29. Cited in John A. Byrne, "How to Lead Now," *Fast Company*, August 2003, p. 66.

30. J. Stacy Adams, "Toward an Understanding of Inequality," *Journal of Abnormal and Social Psychology*, 67, 1963, pp. 422–436; M. R. Carrell and J. E. Dettrick, "Equity Theory: The Recent Literature, Methodological Considerations, and New Directions," *Academy of Management Review*, April 1978, pp. 202–210.

31. Jack and Suzy Welch, "Give Till It Doesn't Hurt," *Businessweek*, February 11, 2008, p. 092.

32. David Novak with John Boswell, *The Education of an Accidental CEO* (New York: Crown Business, 2007).

33. Cited in Carol Hymowitz, "Managers Lose Talent When They Neglect to Coach Their Staffs," *The Wall Street Journal*, March 19, 2007, p. B1.

34. James M. Hunt and Joseph R. Weintraub, *The Coaching Manager: Developing Top Talent in Business* (Thousand Oaks, CA.: Sage, 2002).

35. Douglas Riddle, "Prepping Tomorrow's Leaders Today," *Leading Effectively*, www.ccl.org, September 2006.

36. Robert D. Evered and James E. Selman, "Coaching and the Art of Management," *Organizational Dynamics*, Autumn 1989, p. 15.

37. Ian Cunningham and Linda Honold, "Everyone Can Be a Coach," *HR Magazine*, June 1998, pp. 63–66.

38. "Coaching—One Solution to a Tight Training Budget," *HRfocus*, August 2002, p. 7.

39. "Request Permission to Coach," *Manager's Edge*, June 2003, p. 5.

40. Karen Wright, "A Chic Critique," *Psychology Today*, March/April 2011, p. 59.

41. "Tips of the Month," *Communication Briefings*, October 2010, p. 1.

42. "Fast Tips for Savvy Managers," *Executive Strategies*, April 1998, p. 1.

43. Anna Marie Valerio and Robert J. Lee, *Executive Coaching: A Guide for the HR Professional* (San Francisco: Pfeiffer, 2005).

44. Diane Coutu and Carol Kauffman, "What Can Coaches Do for You?" *Harvard Business Review*, January 2009, p. 92.

45. Douglas P. Shuit, "Huddling with the Coach," *Workforce Management*, February 2005, pp. 53–57.

46. Erik De Haan, Colin Bertie, Andrew Say, and Charlotte Sills, "Clients' Critical Moments of Coaching: Toward a 'Client Model' of Executive Coaching," *Academy of Management Learning & Education*, December 2011, p. 612.

47. Diane Brady, "The Unknown Guru," *Bloomberg Business Week*, November 29–December 5, 2010, p. 86.

48. This last item is from Joann S. Lublin, "Now, Add One More to the Hiring Process: The Boss's Coach," *The Wall Street Journal*, April 3, 2007, p. B1.

49. Amy Joyce, "Career Coaches Nurture Executives," *Washington Post* syndicated story, August 16, 2004.

50. Interview by Bob Rosner, "'Team Players' Expect Real Choices," *Workforce*, May 2001, p. 63.

51. Stratford Sherman and Alyssa Freas, "The Wild West of Executive Coaching," *Harvard Business Review*, November 2004, pp. 86–88; Brady, "The Unknown Guru," *Bloomberg Business Week*, November 29, 2010, p. 84.

52. Steve Berglas, "The Very Real Dangers of Executive Coaching," *Harvard Business Review*, June 2002, pp. 86–92.

53. Michael Maccoby, "The Dangers of Dependence on Coaches," *Harvard Business Review*, January 2009, p. 95.

CHAPTER 8

Leadership Actions, Attitudes, and Styles

LEARNING OBJECTIVES

After studying this chapter and doing the exercises, you should be able to

- Explain the key leadership dimensions of initiating structure and consideration.

- Describe at least five task-oriented leadership behaviors and attitudes.

- Describe at least five relationship-oriented attitudes and behaviors.

- Explain how leaders use 360-degree feedback to improve their performance.

- Describe the autocratic and participative leadership styles.

- Present the case for the entrepreneurial style of leadership and for gender differences in leadership style.

- Determine how to choose the most appropriate leadership style.

CHAPTER OUTLINE

Lori Greeley is the CEO for Victoria's Secret, the $5 billion intimate apparel retailer with more than 1,000 stores across the United States and abroad. Business was in the blood of her family. Her grandfather owned the local lumberyard. Her father, not wanting to follow in his father's footsteps, started an excavation and construction business. The lumberyard became Greeley's childhood playground: Her father's name-emblazoned trucks were a reminder of her family's status in the community. "I saw my family name almost in lights," she noted. It was "a subliminal reinforcement for really going after your dreams."

Greeley graduated as high-school valedictorian and won a full scholarship to play field hockey at Bucknell University. She received a bachelor's degree in psychology in 1982. Later, she entered the retailing field. "I started to understand that what I loved about retail was that you got a report card every day," she said. "You either made your sales plan or you didn't. It was really kind of a high if you're someone who likes to take risks and likes to place bets." After successful experiences working for two other retailers, Greeley was recruited to join Victoria's Secret as an associate buyer in 1989.

As the CEO, Greeley says she tried to engage others and create an environment open to risk taking. In meetings, she looks for what she calls "thought bubbles" over people's heads—indications that they have ideas but aren't expressing them. She encourages them to open up. "It's always really important to be a great listener," she noted. "People don't always need to have their ideas adopted, but they like to know they were heard."

Greeley recounted a story of one product launch that fell flat—a line of lingerie made of 100 percent fair-trade organic cotton sourced from female farmers in Africa. Victoria's Secret had partnered with the women hoping the products would be popular with socially minded consumers. But the price of the products proved to be too high. "It would have been easy for this idea to go away," Greeley said, but a Victoria's Secret employee who worked on the project wanted to continue collaborating with the women cotton farmers. So the company found a way to use a small amount of the organic cotton in all lines of cotton panties. "The majority of cotton panties are now incorporating the cotton crops of these women," Greeley said. "It costs a bit more, but we didn't pass it along to our customers, and we're not marketing it to them."

Greeley's career advice is to follow your heart and do what you love. "Be really good at what you do."[1]

The story about the successful retailing CEO illustrates how leaders' behaviors can influence their effectiveness. Among these behaviors are welcoming feedback, taking risks, and listening carefully to staff members. This chapter describes a number of key behaviors and attitudes that help a manager function as a leader. We also describe the closely related topic of leadership styles.

Frequent reference is made in this chapter, and at other places in the text, to leadership effectiveness. A working definition of an **effective leader** is one who helps group members attain productivity, including high quality and customer satisfaction, as well as job satisfaction. Leadership effectiveness is typically measured by two key criteria.

The first criterion relates to objective data, such as those dealing with sales, production, safety, number of patents produced by the group, cost cutting, or staying within budget. Measures of job satisfaction and turnover are also used to measure leadership effectiveness. The second criterion focuses on judgments by others about the leader's effectiveness, such as a plant manager rating a supervisor or the board rating a CEO. Most of the research reported throughout this text includes measures of leadership effectiveness in the study design.

THE CLASSIC DIMENSIONS OF CONSIDERATION AND INITIATING STRUCTURE

Studies conducted at Ohio State University in the 1950s identified 1,800 specific examples of leadership behavior that were reduced to 150 questionnaire items on leadership functions.[2] The functions are also referred to as *dimensions of leadership behavior*. This research became the foundation for most future research about leadership behavior, attitudes, and styles. The researchers asked team members to describe their supervisors by responding to the questionnaires. Leaders were also asked to rate themselves on leadership dimensions. Two leadership dimensions accounted for 85 percent of the descriptions of leadership behavior: *consideration* and *initiating structure.*

Consideration is the degree to which the leader creates an environment of emotional support, warmth, friendliness, and trust. The leader creates this environment by being friendly and approachable, looking out for the personal welfare of the group, keeping the group abreast of new developments, and doing small favors for the group.

Leaders who score high on the consideration factor typically are friendly and trustful, earn respect, and have a warm relationship with team members. Leaders with low scores on the consideration factor typically are authoritarian and impersonal in their relationships with group members. Three questionnaire items measuring the consideration factor are as follows:

1. Do personal favors for people in the work group.
2. Treat all people in the work group as your equal.
3. Do little things to make it pleasant to be a member of the staff.

The relationship-oriented behaviors described later in this chapter are specific aspects of consideration. Another key example of consideration is *making connections* with people. Julia Stewart, chief executive of DineEquity, believes that making connections is one of her most essential leadership functions. Back in her days at Applebee's (now a division of DineEquity), she spent about five minutes every day checking in with each of the nine managers who directly reported to her. They talked about such social topics as where they ate over the weekend (even if it was not Applebee's). Stewart says that leaders cannot afford *not* to take time to chitchat. "I worry about the bosses who are in the crisis mode 80 or 90 percent of the time. By spending the first couple of minutes each day with the employees, I have more of an understanding of what makes them tick."[3]

Being soft-spoken is a leadership style element that contributes to consideration because workers feel respected when the leader does not attempt to dominate the discussion. Marc Bolland is a successful retailing CEO in England. His latest position is head of the illustrious British store Marks & Spencer. Part of his recognized turnaround skill is his being soft-spoken and willing to listen to the suggestions of work associates.[4]

Initiating structure means organizing and defining relationships in the group by engaging in such activities as assigning specific tasks, specifying procedures to be followed, scheduling work, and clarifying expectations for team members. A team leader who helped group members establish realistic goals would be engaged in initiating structure. Other concepts that refer to the same idea include *production emphasis*, *task orientation*, and *task motivation*. The task-related leadership behaviors and attitudes described later in this chapter are specific aspects of initiating structure.

Leaders who score high on this dimension define the relationship between themselves and their staff members, as well as the role that they expect each staff member to assume. Such leaders also endeavor to establish well-defined channels of communication and ways of getting the job done. Three self-assessment items measuring initiating structure are as follows:

1. Try out your own new ideas in the work group.
2. Emphasize meeting deadlines.
3. See to it that people in the work group are working up to capacity.

A positive example of a leader who emphasizes initiating structure is Yahoo CEO Carol Bartz (she was the Leader in Action for Chapter 3). For example, Bartz considers herself to be an operations person, and she is quite active in designing company organization structure.[5]

Leaders have been categorized with respect to how much emphasis they place on consideration and initiating structure. As implied by Figure 8-1, the two dimensions are not mutually exclusive. A leader can achieve high or low status on both. For example, an effective leader might contribute to high productivity and still place considerable emphasis on warm human relationships. The four-cell grid of Figure 8-1 is a key component of several approaches to describing leadership style. We return to this topic later in this chapter and in Chapter 9.

A study of the validity of consideration and initiating structure indicates that these classic dimensions do indeed contribute to an understanding of leadership because they are related to leadership outcomes. A meta-analysis

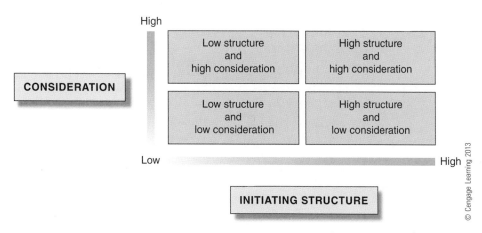

FIGURE 8-1 Four Combinations of Initiating Structure and Consideration.

showed that consideration is strongly related to the job satisfaction of group members, satisfaction with the leader, worker motivation, and leader effectiveness. Initiating structure was slightly more strongly related to job performance, group performance, and organization performance. However, initiating structure was also associated with satisfaction and performance.[6] These results are encouraging because they reinforce the importance of this pioneering research.

TASK-RELATED ATTITUDES AND BEHAVIORS

The task-related versus relationship-related classification remains a useful framework for understanding leadership attitudes, behaviors, and practices. This section identifies and describes task-related attitudes and behaviors that are characteristic of effective leaders, as outlined in Table 8-1. *Task-related* in this context means that the behavior, attitude, or skill focuses more on the task to be performed than on the interpersonal aspect of leadership.

1. *Adaptability to the situation.* Effective leaders adapt to the situation. Adaptability reflects the contingency viewpoint: A tactic is chosen based on the unique circumstances at hand. A leader who is responsible for psychologically immature group members will find it necessary to supervise them closely. If the group members are mature and self-reliant, the leader will use less supervision. The adaptive leader also selects an organization structure that is best suited to the demands of the situation, such as choosing between a brainstorming group and a committee.

2. *Direction setting.* Given that a major responsibility of leadership is to produce change, the leader must set the direction of that change. Direction setting is part of creating a vision and a component of strategy. The strategy describes a feasible way of achieving the vision. Former GE executive turned business author Larry Bossidy believes that it is part of a business leader's job to communicate clearly where the business is going, why, and how the company will benefit if goals are achieved.[7]

TABLE 8-1 Task-Related Leadership Attitudes and Behaviors

1. Adaptability to the situation
2. Direction setting
3. High performance standards
4. Concentrating on strengths of group members
5. Risk taking and execution of plans
6. Hands-on guidance and feedback
7. Ability to ask tough questions
8. Organizing for collaboration

3. *High performance standards.* Effective leaders consistently hold group members to high standards of performance. Jeff Immelt, CEO and chairman of GE says, "The ability to demand high performance without being heartless has been part of GE for a long time."[8] High performance standards can also take the form of challenging the thinking of others. General Motors CEO Daniel Akerson has been known to press executives in meetings to justify their plans and initiatives. Furthermore, he does not back down when told that matters were complicated. Akerson would reply that issues should not be complicated; instead, they should be simplified.[9]

When performance is measured against high standards, productivity is likely to increase, since people tend to live up to the expectations of their superiors. This is called the **Pygmalion effect**, and it works in a subtle, almost unconscious way. When a managerial leader believes that a group member will succeed, the manager communicates this belief without realizing it. Conversely, when a leader expects a group member to fail, that person will not disappoint the manager. The manager's expectation of success or failure becomes a self-fulfilling prophecy because the perceptions contribute to success or failure.

4. *Concentrating on the strengths of group members.* An axiom of effective leadership and management is to make good use of the strengths of group members rather than concentrating effort on patching up areas for improvement. The effective leader helps people improve, yet still capitalizes on strengths. A team member might have excellent interpersonal skills, yet poor technical skills. It would be best to assign that person a role that emphasizes interpersonal skills, while at the same time helping him or her improve technical skills. Marcus Buckingham emphasizes that capitalizing on each person's unique pattern of skills saves time because group members are not laboring at tasks outside their capability and interest. The manager might even develop a job description that best fits each employee's uniqueness.[10] Suppose you are the manager of a call center, and one staffer is great at calming down angry customers. Other call center members are then asked to refer customers who have gone ballistic to your team member who can handle customer rage well.

5. *Risk taking and execution of plans.* To bring about constructive change, the leader must take risks and be willing to implement those risky decisions. Larry Bossidy says about the importance of execution: "I'm an impatient person, and I get more satisfaction from seeing things get done than I do about philosophizing or building sand castles. Many people regard execution as detail work that's beneath the dignity of a business leader. That's wrong. It's a leader's most important job."[11]

Mike Duke, CEO of Walmart, operates the way Bossidy suggests. Duke's mode of operation is to study a problem quickly, then take action. When he was the head of Walmart International, one of his first acts was to shut down the company's German division, which had been a problem for Walmart for many years.[12]

6. *Hands-on guidance and feedback.* You will recall that technical competence and knowledge of the business are important leadership characteristics. They enable the leader to provide group members with hands-on guidance about how to accomplish important work. The leader who provides such guidance helps the group accomplish important tasks; at the same time, group members learn important skills. Too much guidance of this nature, however, can be a symptom of poor delegation and micromanagement (managing too closely). Too little guidance, and macromanagement is the result, in which the manager gives too little or no direction to group members. Henry Mintzberg observes that the leader's strategy might suffer because he or she does not understand the operations of the business.[13]

To improve their hands-on management skills, about 150 officials of Loews Hotels are required to spend a day every year in an entry-level job at one of its eighteen U.S. and Canadian hotels. They share impressions with employees in their temporary departments and solicit ideas for making these jobs easier. One result was the installation of handlebars on room-service carts so they are easier for waiters to push.[14]

Closely related to guidance is giving frequent feedback on performance. The leader can rarely influence the actions of group members without appropriate performance feedback. This feedback tells group members how well they are doing so that they can take corrective action if needed. It also serves as reinforcement that prompts group members to continue favorable activities. Leadership Skill-Building Exercise 8-1 provides practice in developing feedback skills.

The accompanying Leader in Action profile illustrates how the CEO of an international vehicle manufacturer chooses to get involved in the details of operations.

LEADERSHIP SKILL-BUILDING EXERCISE 8-1

Feedback Skills

After small groups have completed an assignment such as answering the case questions or discussion questions, hold a performance feedback session. Also use observations you have made in previous problem-solving activities as the basis for your feedback. Each group member provides some feedback to each other member about how well he or she thinks the other person performed. Use only volunteers, because this type of feedback may be uncomfortable and disturbing to some individuals. Students not receiving feedback can serve as observers and later present their views on what took place during the exercise. To increase the probability of benefiting from this experience, feedback recipients must listen actively. Refer to the section in Chapter 7 on coaching skills and techniques for more information on feedback and active listening.

A convenient way to do this exercise is for everyone to sit in a circle. Choose one feedback recipient to begin. Going clockwise around the circle, each group member gives that person feedback. After all people have spoken, the feedback recipient gives his or her reactions. The person to the left of the first recipient is the next one to get feedback.

After everyone has had a turn receiving performance feedback, hold a general discussion. Be sure to discuss three key issues:

1. How helpful was the feedback?
2. What was the relative effectiveness of positive versus negative feedback?
3. Were some group members better than others in giving feedback?

LEADER IN ACTION

Sergio Marchionne, CEO of Fiat and Chrysler

Sergio Marchionne, the CEO of Fiat S.p.A. (Italian Automobile Factory of Turin) since 2004, and the chief executive of Chrysler Group LLC since 2009, has a large table in his office lined with toy cars, trucks, and earth-moving equipment. All of the vehicles are replicas of Fiat and Chrysler products.

Marchionne's formal education is in law and accounting, yet in recent years he became a specialist in turning around car companies. He is a citizen of both Italy and Canada. Marchionne's business hero is Steve Jobs because of the way Jobs transformed Apple from a struggling computer company into a world-class standard for cool consumer products.

A major focus of Marchionne's early efforts at Chrysler was to reposition the company from making large automobiles that consumed considerable gas into a manufacturer of energy-efficient vehicles. An exception is that, under Marchionne's direction, Chrysler intensified its production and marketing of the Jeep Cherokee, a robust-size sports utility vehicle (SUV). As part of implementing this thrust, Marchionne announced a product strategy in 2010 to modify a Fiat compact to meet U.S. standards and distribute the vehicle through Chrysler dealers.

In the early days of his Chrysler turnaround, Marchionne said he wanted to work closely with the engineers and managers making daily decisions. "It shows me he's going to be very hands-on," said a person who works with senior Chrysler executives. Marchionne involves himself heavily in organizational design issues. He has invested considerable time in integrating business operations between Fiat and Chrysler to increase operations and reduce costs.

One day, Marchionne was informed that the door handle on the Dodge Charger had a small leak, allowing water to enter the latch and disrupt the electronics. Marchionne assigned engineers the task of working relentlessly on the problem. While in another meeting, a message flashed on one of Marchionne's smart phones that the nature of the problem was discovered—an uneven fit between two plastic parts. Marchionne was relieved, and he explained his concern in these words: "…Some of the issues that we are dealing with now and cause me apoplexy would have probably been swept under the carpet 10 years ago. But if you really want to run the business, you need to get involved at this level."

Despite Marchionne's penchant for details of his operation, he does not perceive himself to be a micromanager. "My job as CEO is not to make decisions about the business but to set stretch objectives and help our managers work out how to reach them," he wrote. Also, Marchionne has told employees that he was establishing a culture in which everyone is expected to lead.

QUESTIONS

1. Based on the evidence presented in this story, to what extent does it appear that Marchionne is more of a micromanager than he thinks?
2. How reasonable does it seem to you for the CEO of essentially two auto companies to be concerned about a door handle that is not water-tight?
3. How might Marchionne's being a dual citizen of Italy and Canada be an asset in his role as CEO of the combination of Fiat and Chrysler?

Note: Full disclosure here is that your author has proudly owned Chrysler products, including Jeeps, for many years.

Source: This case is created based on facts found in Jeff Bennett, "Chrysler Narrows Loss, Sees Profit," *The Wall Street Journal, The Wall Street Journal*, February 1, 2011, p. B4; March 2, 2011, pp. 1–4; Peter Gumbel, "The Turnaround Artista," *Time*, June 29, 2009, pp. 42–43; Neal E. Boudette, "Fiat CEO Sets New Tone at Chrysler," *The Wall Street Journal*, June 19, 2009, p. B1; Paul Ingrassia, "The Weekend Interview with Sergio Marchionne: Resurrecting Chrysler," *The Wall Street Journal*, July 3–4, 2010, p. A9.

7. *Ability to ask tough questions.* Often, leaders can be effective by asking tough questions rather than providing answers. A **tough question** is one that makes a person or group stop and think about why they are doing or not doing something. (A tough question might also be considered the *right* question.) In this way, group members are forced to think about the effectiveness of their activities. They might ask themselves, "Why didn't I think of that? It seems so obvious." Asking questions is important because quite often group members may have the solutions to difficult problems facing the organization.

When Alan R. Mulally was the newly appointed CEO at Ford Motor Co., he was told that the company loses close to $3,000 every time a customer buys a Focus compact. He asked, "Why haven't you figured out a way to make a profit?" Given a few excuses, Mulally hammered away again: "I want to know why no one figured a way to build this car at a profit, whether it has to be built in Michigan or China or India, if that's what it takes."[15]

8. *Organizing for collaboration.* A leadership behavior on the borderline between a task-orientation and a relationship orientation is to demand that workers collaborate with each other. The task focus is that the information sharing takes place, whereas the relationship focus is that group members must work collaboratively with each other. Web 2.0 (or Enterprise 2.0) technologies are often implemented to foster collaboration. The Corporate Executive Board, a research and advisory service company, recommends three steps for the leader who wants more collaboration:

- First, identify the high-value business outcomes desired, such as accelerating new-product development, before selecting collaboration technologies.
- Second, identify collaboration hot spots. Speak with employees to understand their communication patterns and workflows. (A specialist might be required here to help map workflows, such as who is interacting with whom. More will be said about this topic in Chapter 12.)
- Select technologies that will improve or speed up existing workflows. For example, a search engine dedicated to in-company practices might be effective. Most leaders would have to work with an IT consultant to find a technology most likely to increase collaboration.[16]

Now that you have studied various components of task-oriented attitudes and behaviors, do Leadership Self-Assessment Quiz 8-1. It will further sensitize you to the task activities of leaders and managers.

RELATIONSHIP-ORIENTED ATTITUDES AND BEHAVIORS

Leadership involves influencing people, so it follows that many effective leadership attitudes, behaviors, and practices deal with interpersonal relationships. Randy Komisar, who helps launch start-up technology firms, was asked how he sweeps into companies and manages employees effectively. He replied: "I rely

LEADERSHIP SELF-ASSESSMENT QUIZ 8-1

Task-Oriented Attitudes and Behaviors

Instructions: Indicate whether you mostly agree or mostly disagree with the following statements. Relate the statements to any work situation—including sports, community activities, and school activities—in which you have been responsible for others' work. If a work situation does not come to mind, imagine how you would act or think.

	MOSTLY AGREE	MOSTLY DISAGREE
1. I keep close tabs on productivity figures and interpret them to the group.	☐	☐
2. I send frequent e-mail and text messages to group members, giving them information about work procedures.	☐	☐
3. I clearly specify the quality goals our group needs to achieve.	☐	☐
4. I maintain clear-cut standards of performance.	☐	☐
5. When I conduct a meeting, the participants can count on a clear-cut agenda.	☐	☐
6. I feel good about my workweek only if our team has met or exceeded its productivity goals.	☐	☐
7. Workers should not access e-mail, text messages, or the Internet during working hours unless the activity is actually increasing productivity.	☐	☐
8. I freely criticize work that does not meet standards.	☐	☐
9. I spend at least 5 percent of my workweek either planning myself or helping team members with their planning.	☐	☐
10. I spend a good deal of time solving technical or business problems myself, or helping group members do the same.	☐	☐

Interpretation: If you responded "mostly agree" to eight, nine, or ten of these statements, you have a strong task orientation. If you responded "mostly disagree" to four or more of the statements, you have below-average task-oriented behaviors and attitudes.

Skill Development: A task orientation is important because it can lead directly to goal attainment and productivity. Nevertheless, a task orientation must be balanced with a strong people orientation and interpersonal skills for maximum effectiveness.

on relationship power, not traditional position power that comes from my title. I find that building relationships with people and inspiring them are the keys to my leadership. That's how I think any manager becomes a leader."[17]

Table 8-2 lists the seven relationship-oriented attitudes and behaviors that we will discuss next. (Most other parts of this book describe the interpersonal skill aspects of leadership.)

TABLE 8-2 Relationship-Oriented Attitudes and Behaviors

1. Aligning people
2. Openness to worker opinions
3. Creating inspiration and visibility
4. Satisfying higher-level needs
5. Giving emotional support and encouragement
6. Promoting principles and values
7. Being a servant leader

© Cengage Learning 2013

1. *Aligning people.* Getting people pulling in the same direction and collaborating smoothly is a major interpersonal challenge. To get people pulling together, it is necessary to speak to many people. The target population can involve many different stakeholders. Among them are managers and team leaders, higher-ups, peers, and workers in other parts of the organization, as well as suppliers, government officials, and customers. Anyone who can implement the vision and strategies or who can block implementation must be aligned.[18] After being aligned, organizational members can pull together toward a higher purpose. Alignment also incorporates getting the group working together smoothly.

A focus on getting people to pull together is evident in the leadership strategy of Dennis Ratner, the founder and CEO of Ratner Cos., the largest family-owned and operated chain of hair salons in the United States, including the Hair Cuttery. Ratner says that he has a vision of a company of happy people who understand their tasks and have shared accountability.[19]

2. *Openness to worker opinions.* A major part of relationship-oriented leadership is to engage in **management openness**, or a set of leader behaviors particularly relevant to subordinates' motivation to voice their opinion.[20] When the leader is open in this way, subordinates perceive that their boss listens to them, is interested in their ideas, and gives fair consideration to suggestions. Being open to worker opinions is part of the consideration dimension, and it is also central to participative leadership.

3. *Creating inspiration and visibility.* As described in the discussion of charismatic and transformational leadership, inspiring others is an essential leadership practice. Inspiring people usually involves appealing to their emotions and values, such as when the head of a snowmobile business unit encourages workers to believe that they are making winters more enjoyable for people who live in regions that accumulate snow.

Because human contact and connections reinforce inspiration, another part of being inspirational is being visible and available. One of the many ways in which Sam Palmisano, the CEO of IBM, inspires people is through his visibility. He frequently interacts face-to-face with workers at all levels in the company. His ability to chat with almost anybody he meets makes him approachable to employees and customers.[21]

4. *Satisfying higher-level needs.* To inspire people, effective leaders motivate them by satisfying higher-level needs, such as needs for achievement, personal growth, a sense of belonging, recognition, self-esteem, and a feeling of control over one's life. Many leaders in organizations express an awareness of the importance of need satisfaction for building good relationships with workers. A robust method of satisfying workers' higher-level needs is to help them grow professionally. Star executive W. James McNerney, now the Boeing Company chairman, president, and CEO, says that he has been a successful executive at three major companies primarily through helping people perform better. McNerney contends that people who grow are open to change, have the courage to do so, work hard, and are good team players. In his words, "What I do is figure out how to unlock that in people, because most people have that inside of them. But they often get trapped in a bureaucratic environment where they've been beaten about the head and shoulders."[22]

5. *Giving emotional support and encouragement.* Supportive behavior toward team members usually increases leadership effectiveness. A supportive leader gives frequent encouragement and praise and also displays caring and kindness even about non-work-related matters such as the health of a worker's ill family member. Keep in mind that encouragement means to fill with courage.[23] One of the many work-related ways of encouraging people is to allow them to participate in decision making. Emotional support generally improves morale and sometimes improves productivity. In the long term, emotional support and encouragement may bolster a person's self-esteem. Being emotionally supportive comes naturally to the leader who is empathetic and warm.

Michael Mathieu, the CEO of YuMe, an online video advertising team, believes that part of the reason he landed his job was his personality, which includes the willingness to encourage workers. He says that his employees can talk to him about anything with absolutely no fear of being told their idea is stupid.[24]

6. *Promoting principles and values.* A major part of a top leader's role is to help promote values and principles that contribute to the welfare of individuals and organizations. This promotion can be classified as relationship-oriented because it deals directly with the emotions and attitudes of people, and indirectly with the task. Stephen Covey, who is widely quoted for his uplifting messages, advises that an organization's mission statement must be for all good causes.[25] Leaders who believe in these good causes will then espouse principles and values that lead people toward good deeds in the workplace. To encourage managers and all other employees to conduct their work affairs at a high moral level, many companies put their values in written form. The values might be placed in employee handbooks, on company intranets, or on company websites.

What constitutes the right values depends on the leader's core beliefs. Bill George, the former chairman and CEO of Medtronic, Inc., and now Harvard Business School professor, has inspired many managers with his thoughts about authentic leadership. Such leaders place the welfare of customers and employees above those of shareholders in the corporate hierarchy. Another key value of an authentic leader is to help employees achieve a fair balance between work and family life.[26] In his book *True North*, George says that authentic leaders lead with their hearts, as well as their heads, enabling them to have passion. One example is Howard Schultz, the founder of Starbucks, who wanted to develop an enterprise his father would be proud of. Another authentic leader is Andrea Jung of Avon, who joined the company so she could help women achieve self-sufficiency. In general, authentic leaders stay true to their values, even under pressure. Furthermore, they keep in mind that employees want meaning and significance in their work, not only money.[27]

Another value that often helps an enterprise is a strong focus on the welfare of employees. A notable example is the leadership of Rich Snyder, CEO of the successful fast-food chain, In-N-Out Burger. Wages and benefits are relatively high, and managers who meet their goals are eligible for company-paid luxury vacations. As a result, In-N-Out Burger boasts one of the lowest turnover rates in the industry.[28]

Providing moral leadership begins with understanding one's own values. Leadership Skill-Building Exercise 8-2 gives you an opportunity to think through your work-related values so that you can better provide moral leadership to others.

7. *Being a servant leader.* Your desire to help others is another important workplace value. A **servant leader** serves constituents by working on their behalf to help them achieve their goals, not the leader's own goals. The idea behind servant leadership, as formulated by Robert K. Greenleaf, is that leadership derives naturally from a commitment to service.[29] Serving others, including employees, customers, and community, is the primary motivation for the servant leader. And true leadership emerges from a deep desire to help others. A servant leader is therefore a moral leader. Servant leadership has been accomplished when group members become wiser, healthier, and more autonomous. The following are key aspects of servant leadership.[30]

- *Place service before self-interest*. A servant leader is more concerned with helping others than with acquiring power, prestige, financial reward, and status. The servant leader seeks to do what is morally right, even if it is not financially rewarding. He or she is conscious of the needs of others and is driven by a desire to satisfy them. (You will recall that wanting to satisfy the needs of others is a basic relationship behavior.)
- *Listen first to express confidence in others*. The servant leader makes a deep commitment to listening in order to get to know the concerns, requirements, and problems of group members. Instead of attempting to impose his or her will on others, the servant leader listens carefully to understand what course of action will help others accomplish their goals. After understanding others, the best course of action can be chosen. Through listening, for example, a servant leader might learn that the group is more concerned about team spirit and harmony than striving for companywide recognition. The leader would then concentrate more on

LEADERSHIP SKILL-BUILDING EXERCISE 8-2

Clarifying Your Interpersonal Work Values

Instructions: To provide effective value leadership, it is essential that you first understand your own values with respect to dealing with others. Rank from 1 to 15 the importance of the following values to you as a person. The most important value on the list receives a rank of 1; the least important, a rank of 15. Use the space next to "Other" if we have left out an important value related to interpersonal relations on the job.

_____ Having respect for the dignity of others

_____ Ensuring that others have interesting work to perform

_____ Earning the trust of others

_____ Earning the respect of others

_____ Impressing others with how well my group performs

_____ Giving others proper credit for their work

_____ Inspiring continuous learning on the part of each member in our group, myself included

_____ Holding myself and others accountable for delivering on commitments

_____ Helping others grow and develop

_____ Inspiring others to achieve high productivity and quality

_____ Developing the reputation of being a trustworthy person

_____ Being in contact regularly with work associates using social networking sites

_____ Contributing to the job satisfaction of work associates

_____ Avoiding creating intense job dissatisfaction for any work associate

_____ Other

1. Compare your ranking of these values with that of the person next to you, and discuss.
2. Perhaps your class, assisted by your instructor, might arrive at a class average on each of these values. How does your ranking compare to the class ranking?
3. Look back at your own ranking. Does your ranking surprise you?
4. Are there any surprises in the class ranking? Which values did you think would be highest and lowest?

Clarifying your values for leadership is far more than a pleasant exercise. Many business leaders have fallen into disgrace and brought their companies into bankruptcy because of values that are unacceptable to employees, stockholders, outside investigators, and the legal system. For example, a CEO who valued "developing the reputation of being a trustworthy person" would not borrow $400 million from the company while paying thousands of employees close to the minimum wage.

building teamwork than searching for ways to increase the visibility of the team.

- *Inspire trust by being trustworthy*. Being trustworthy is a foundation behavior of the servant leader. He or she is scrupulously honest with others, gives up control, and focuses on the well-being of others. Usually such leaders do not have to work hard at being trustworthy because they are already moral. In support of this principle, a survey found that most employees want a boss who is a trusted leader, not a pal.[31]
- *Focus on what is feasible to accomplish*. Even though the servant leader is idealistic, he or she recognizes that one individual cannot accomplish everything. Therefore, the leader listens carefully to the array of problems facing

group members and then concentrates on a few. The servant leader thus systematically neglects certain problems. A labor union official might carefully listen to all the concerns and complaints of the constituents and then proceed to work on the most pressing issue.

- *Lend a hand.* A servant leader looks for opportunities to play the Good Samaritan. As a supermarket manager, he or she might help out by bagging groceries during a busy period. Or a servant leader might help clean out mud in the company lobby after a hurricane.
- *Provide emotional healing.* A servant leader shows sensitivity to the personal concerns of group members, such as a worker being worried about taking care of a disabled parent. At clothing retailer Men's Warehouse, Inc., servant leadership is in style. A district manager at the Warehouse may want to go home and be with his family, but he will tell a store manager that he will stay and cover the store, so the store manager can spend time with *his* or *her* family at a child's baseball game. The underlying idea is for managers to give top priority to helping others.[32]

In addition to being logically sound, research with 182 workers indicates that servant leadership has a positive relationship with organizational citizenship behavior, job performance, and staying with the organization.[33] A study with seven multinational companies in Kenya suggested that servant leadership sets up a positive climate (company atmosphere) that in turn encourages employees to be good organizational citizens.[34]

Leadership Skill-Building Exercise 8-3 provides an opportunity for you to practice relationship-oriented and task-oriented behaviors. Combined, these are sometimes referred to as the nuts and bolts of leadership.

LEADERSHIP SKILL-BUILDING EXERCISE 8-3

Applying Relationship-Oriented and Task-Oriented Attitudes and Behaviors

About six role players who can tolerate brutal outdoor conditions are needed for this exercise. The setting is an oil drilling rig in the Arctic Circle, where deep-underground oil reserves have been discovered, and energy companies are now digging. Today the wind-chill factor is –40 degrees Fahrenheit. The crew of five is uncomfortable and a little confused about how to get the drilling started this morning. The leadership task of the supervisor is to help the crew get the digging accomplished.

Supervisor A attempts to engage in relationship-oriented attitudes and behavior with the group. He or she will use several of the behaviors mentioned in the text. The other five or so role players will react to his or her leadership. Work the role play for about ten minutes.

After the first scenario is complete, Supervisor B will engage in task-oriented attitudes and behaviors, using several of the behaviors mentioned in the text. The other five or so role players will react to this leadership. Continue the role play for about ten minutes.

Class members not thrown into the frozen tundra will observe the interactions of the supervisor with the workers. Provide feedback as to (a) how well the leadership attitudes and behaviors were carried out, and (b) how likely these attitudes and behaviors were helpful in accomplishing the task of getting the drilling started.

360-DEGREE FEEDBACK FOR FINE-TUNING A LEADERSHIP APPROACH

In most large organizations, leaders not only provide feedback to group members, but they also receive feedback that gives them insight into the effects of their attitudes and behaviors. This feedback is systematically derived from a full sampling of parties who interact with the leader. In particular, **360-degree feedback** is a formal evaluation of superiors based on input from people who work for and with them, sometimes including customers and suppliers. It is also referred to as multisource feedback or multirater feedback. The process is also called 360-degree survey because the input stems from a survey of a handful of people. The multiple input becomes another way of measuring leadership effectiveness. The particular 360-degree form is often customized to a particular firm's needs, but standardized (off-the-shelf) forms are used by about 25 percent of firms using the method.

Specialists in the field view 360-degree feedback as more suited for its original purpose of development for a manager or leader than for administrative purposes, such as performance evaluation and salary administration. When used for development, 360-degree feedback should emphasize qualitative comments rather than strictly quantitative ratings.[35] For example, being told, "You do not maintain eye contact with me during meetings," is more helpful than simply receiving a low rating on "Makes others feel comfortable." The feedback is communicated to the leader (as well as others receiving 360-degree feedback) and interpreted with the assistance of a human resources professional or an external consultant.

The data from the survey can be used to help leaders fine-tune their attitudes and behavior. For example, if all the interested parties gave the leader low ratings on "empathy toward others," the leader might be prompted to improve his or her ability to empathize, such as by reading about empathy, attending a seminar, or simply making a conscious attempt to empathize when involved in a conflict of opinion with another person.

An example of a 360-degree feedback form is shown in Figure 8-2. The example shows the gaps between the leader's self-perceptions and the group's perceptions. When such gaps occur, professionally trained counselors or business coaches should be involved in 360-degree feedback. Some people feel emotionally crushed when they find a wide discrepancy between their self-perception on an interpersonal skill dimension and the perception of others. A middle manager involved in a 360-degree evaluation prided herself on how well she was liked by others. The feedback that emerged, however, depicted her as intimidating, hostile, and manipulative. Upon receiving the feedback, the woman went into a rage (proving the feedback true!) and then into despondency. Professional counseling can sometimes help a person benefit from critical feedback and place it in perspective.

For best results, it is extremely important that 360-degree surveys reflect those behaviors and attitudes that the organization values most highly. Care should also be taken that the dimensions measured reflect important aspects of leadership functioning. Following are some suggestions for making better use of 360-degree surveys.[36]

- Focus on business goals and strategy. Feedback should provide leaders and managers with insight into the skills they need to help the organization meet its goals.

Manager evaluated: *Jeremy Blackstone*

Ratings *(10 is highest)*

Behavior or Attitude	Self-Rating	Average Group Rating	Gap
1. Gives right amount of structure and guidance	9	6.5	-2.5
2. Gives right amount of useful feedback	9	6.5	-2.5
3. Considerate of the feelings of people	10	6.2	-3.8
4. Sets a direction for group effort	8	5.9	-2.1
5. Sets high performance standards	7	9.0	+2.0
6. Coaches team members as needed	10	6.3	-3.7
7. Gets people working together as a team	9	5.1	-3.9
8. Inspires team members	10	2.8	-7.2
9. Gives emotional support when needed	8	3.7	-4.3
10. Is a strategic thinker	9	8.5	-0.5

© Cengage Learning 2013

FIGURE 8-2 A 360-Degree Feedback Chart.

Note: A negative gap means you rate yourself higher on the behavior or attitude than does your group. A positive gap means the group rates you higher than you rate yourself.

- Ensure that the feedback dimensions reflect important aspects of leadership functioning.
- Train workers in giving and receiving feedback. Giving constructive feedback takes coaching, training, and practice.
- Create an action plan for improvement for each leader based on the feedback. For example, a leader rated low on interpersonal skills might benefit from training in emotional intelligence.
- Ensure that the managers rated have full ownership of the feedback information so that they will perceive the feedback as being geared toward personal development rather than administrative control.

A potential problem with 360-degree feedback is its anonymity. Much like people who post nasty comments about people on social media websites, an angry subordinate can write an insulting and crushing comment about a manager on the 360-degree feedback form. The criticism might be without merit.

LEADERSHIP STYLES

A leader's combination of attitudes and behaviors leads to a certain regularity and predictability in dealing with group members. **Leadership style** is the relatively consistent pattern of behavior that characterizes a leader. Studying leadership style is an extension of understanding leadership behaviors and attitudes. Most classifications of leadership style are based on the dimensions of consideration and initiating structure. Comments such as "He's a real command-and-control-type" and "She's a consensus leader" have become commonplace.

Here we describe the participative leadership style, the autocratic leadership style, the Leadership Grid™, the entrepreneurial leadership style, gender differences in leadership style, and choosing the best style. Chapter 9 continues the exploration of leadership styles by presenting several contingency leadership theories.

Participative Leadership

Sharing decision making with group members and working with them side by side has become the generally accepted leadership approach in the modern organization. **Participative leaders** share decision making with group members. The terms *shared leadership*, *collaborative leadership*, and *team leadership* all refer to the same idea as participative leadership. Participative leadership encompasses so many behaviors that it can be divided into three subtypes: consultative, consensus, and democratic.

Consultative leaders confer with group members before making a decision. However, they retain the final authority to make decisions. **Consensus leaders** strive for consensus. They encourage group discussion about an issue and then make a decision that reflects general agreement and that group members will support. All workers who will be involved in the consequences of a decision have an opportunity to provide input. A decision is not considered final until it appears that all parties involved will at least support the decision. **Democratic leaders** confer final authority on the group. They function as collectors of group opinion and take a vote before making a decision.

The participative style is based on management openness because the leader accepts suggestions for managing the operation from group members. Welcoming ideas from below is considered crucial because as technology evolves and organizations decentralize, front-line workers have more independence and responsibility. These workers are closer to the market, closer to seeing how the product is used, and closer to many human resource problems. Front-line knowledge can provide useful input to leaders for such purposes as developing marketing strategy and retaining employees.

The participative style encompasses the teamwork approach. Predominant behaviors of participative leaders include coaching team members, negotiating their demands, and collaborating with others. Often, the team member who has the most relevant knowledge for the task at hand slips into a leadership role. Research indicates that poor-performing teams are often dominated by the team leader, whereas high-performing teams are characterized by shared leadership.[37]

The participative style is well suited to managing competent people who are eager to assume responsibility. Such people want to get involved in making decisions and giving feedback to management. Because most graduates from business and professional programs expect to be involved in decision making, participative leadership works well with the new breed of managers and professionals.

Ricardo Semler, the CEO of the Brazilian equipment supplier Semco, makes extreme use of participative leadership and management. The company continues to grow substantially and be profitable. Of the 3,000 employee votes,

Semler is allotted only one. Working with an educator, Clovis da Silva Boiji-kian, Semler took radical steps, including the following:

- Hearing frequent complaints about the company cafeteria, he asked the employees to help improve it and eventually turned it over to them.
- He empowered employees to set their own compensation. An analyst helped benchmark pay across positions and companies, setting average wage scales, adding 10 percent to make Semco more competitive, and then made salary levels public information.[38]

Participative leadership does have some problems. It often results in extensive and time-consuming team meetings and committee work. Also, consensus and democratic leaders are sometimes accused of providing too little direction, or being *macromanagers*. Sometimes, participative leadership is carried to extremes. Team members are consulted about trivial things that management could easily handle independently. Another problem is that many managers still believe that sharing decision making with members reduces their power.

If democratic leadership goes one step further, the result is extreme macromanagement, which is referred to as the laissez-faire leadership style. A study conducted with 4,500 Norwegian employees found that employees managed by a laissez-faire leader experienced role ambiguity. The ambiguity led them to anxiously guess what criteria their supervisor would follow when evaluating their performance, and also guess about which tasks should receive the highest priority.[39]

A practical problem with participative leadership, especially the consensus subtype, is that it consumes so much time, particularly in the form of so many meetings to make decisions. At Google, three top executives had been equally involved in decision making for years. In 2011, one of the reasons the management structure was simplified was to speed up decision making.[40]

Autocratic Leadership

In contrast to participative leaders are **autocratic leaders**, who retain most of the authority. They make decisions confidently, assume that group members will comply, and are not overly concerned with group members' attitudes toward a decision. Autocratic leaders are considered task-oriented because they place heavy emphasis on getting tasks accomplished. Typical autocratic behaviors include telling people what to do, asserting authority, and serving as a model for team members.

In some situations, and in some organizational cultures, autocratic leadership is called for. Dan Ackerman became the CEO at General Motors in 2010, a time when quick results were needed. He had served GM for a year previously as a financial officer. Ackerman was a former naval officer with a reputation for being tough-minded in seeking results and quite decisive. Also, as a private equity fund manager, he had led companies in turnaround situations where clear goals must be attained quickly. As with other effective autocratic leaders, Ackerman moves quickly in making many decisions but does seek some input from trusted advisors.[41] To be described as *autocratic* does not necessarily mean the leader is impulsive or stubborn.

Part of your skill development as a leader involves gaining insight into your own leadership style or potential style. To this end, do Leadership Self-Assessment Quiz 8-2.

LEADERSHIP SELF-ASSESSMENT QUIZ 8-2

What Style of Leader Are You or Would You Be?

Instructions: Answer the following statement, keeping in mind what you have done, or think you would do, in the scenarios and attitudes described.

	MOSTLY TRUE	MOSTLY FALSE
1. I am more likely to take care of a high-impact assignment myself than turn it over to a group member.	☐	☐
2. I would prefer the analytical aspects of a manager's job to working directly with group members.	☐	☐
3. An important part of my approach to managing a group is to keep the members informed almost daily of any information that could affect their work.	☐	☐
4. It is a good idea to give two people in the group the same problem and then choose what appears to be the best solution.	☐	☐
5. I like to have updates a few times a day on the work progress of subordinates, even if the update is simply a text message or instant message.	☐	☐
6. I look for opportunities to obtain group input before making a decision, even on straightforward issues.	☐	☐
7. I would reverse a decision if several of the group members presented evidence that I was wrong.	☐	☐
8. Differences of opinion in the work group are healthy.	☐	☐
9. I think that activities to build team spirit, like fixing up a poor family's house on a Saturday, are an excellent investment of time.	☐	☐
10. If my group were hiring a new member, I would like the person to be interviewed by the entire group.	☐	☐
11. An effective team leader today uses e-mail or other digital media for about 98 percent of communication with team members.	☐	☐
12. Some of the best ideas are likely to come from the group members rather than from the manager.	☐	☐
13. If our group were going to have a banquet, I would get input from each member on what type of food should be served.	☐	☐
14. I have never seen a statue of a committee in a museum or park, so why bother making decisions by committee if you want to be recognized?	☐	☐
15. I dislike it intensely when a group member challenges my position on an issue.	☐	☐
16. I typically explain to group members how (what method) they should use to accomplish an assigned task.	☐	☐
17. If I were out of the office for a week, most of the important work in the department would get accomplished anyway.	☐	☐
18. Delegation of important tasks is something that would be (or is) very difficult for me.	☐	☐
19. When a group member comes to me with a problem, I tend to jump right in with a proposed solution.	☐	☐
20. When a group member comes to me with a problem, I typically ask that person something like, "What alternative solutions have you thought of so far?"	☐	☐

QUIZ 8-2 (continued)

Scoring and Interpretation: The answers for a participative leader are as follows:

1. Mostly false	8. Mostly true	15. Mostly false
2. Mostly false	9. Mostly true	16. Mostly false
3. Mostly true	10. Mostly true	17. Mostly true
4. Mostly false	11. Mostly false	18. Mostly false
5. Mostly false	12. Mostly true	19. Mostly false
6. Mostly true	13. Mostly true	20. Mostly true
7. Mostly true	14. Mostly false	

If your score is 15 or higher, you are most likely (or would be) a participative leader. If your score is 5 or lower, you are most likely (or would be) an authoritarian leader.

Skill Development: The quiz you just completed is also an opportunity for skill development. Review the twenty statements and look for implied suggestions for engaging in participative leadership. For example, statement 20 suggests that you encourage group members to work through their own solutions to problems. If your goal is to become an authoritarian leader, the statements can also serve as useful guidelines. For example, statement 19 suggests that an authoritarian leader first looks to solve problems for group members.

Leadership Grid™ Styles

A classic method of classifying leadership styles suggests that the best way to achieve effective leadership is to integrate the task and relationship orientations. The **Leadership Grid™** is a framework for specifying the extent of a leader's concern for production and people.[42]

Concern for production is rated on the grid's horizontal axis. Concern for production includes results, bottom line, performance, profits, and mission. Concern for people is rated on the vertical axis, and it includes concern for group members and coworkers. Both concerns are leadership attitudes or ways of thinking about leadership. Each of these concerns (or dimensions) exists in varying degrees along a continuum from 1 to 9. A manager's standing on one concern is not supposed to influence his or her standing on the other. As shown in Figure 8-3, the Grid encompasses seven leadership styles. If you are already familiar with the Grid, you will notice that the names of the styles have been changed in this version.

The creators of the Grid argue strongly for the value of 9, 9 Sound (contribute and commit). According to their research, the sound management approach pays off. It results in improved performance, low absenteeism and turnover, and high morale. Sound (9, 9) management relies on trust and respect, which combine to bring about good results.

An example of a manager who might qualify as a 9,9 leader is Sallie Krawcheck, the president of the Bank of America Corp. Global Wealth and Investment Management division. Perhaps the most powerful woman on

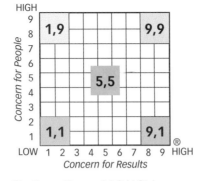

The Seven Managerial Grid Styles

9,1 Controlling (Direct & Dominate)

- I expect results and take control by clearly stating a course of action. I enforce rules that sustain high results and do not permit deviation.

1,9 Accommodating (Yield & Comply)

- I support results that establish and reinforce harmony. I generate enthusiasm by focusing on positive and pleasing aspects of work.

5,5 Status Quo (Balance & Compromise)

- I endorse results that are popular but caution against taking unnecessary risk. I test my opinions with others involved to assure ongoing acceptability.

1,1 Indifferent (Evade & Elude)

- I distance myself from taking active responsibility for results to avoid getting entangled in problems. If forced, I take a passive or supportive position.

PAT Paternalistic (Prescribe & Guide)

- I provide leadership by defining initiatives for myself and others. I offer praise and appreciation for support, and discourage challenges to my thinking.

OPP Opportunistic (Exploit & Manipulate)

- I persuade others to support results that offer me private benefit. If they also benefit, that's even better in gaining support. I rely on whatever approach is needed to secure an advantage.

9,9 Sound (Contribute & Commit)

- I initiate team action in a way that invites involvement and commitment. I explore all facts and alternative views to reach a shared understanding of the best solution.

FIGURE 8-3 The Leadership Grid.™

The Managerial Grid (or the Leadership Grid) is a very simple framework that elegantly defines seven basic styles that characterize workplace behavior and the resulting relationships. The seven Managerial Grid styles are based on how two fundamental concerns (concern for people and concern for results) are manifested at varying levels whenever people interact.

Source: © Copyright 2004–2006 Grid International, Inc. (All rights reserved.)

Wall Street, her group is one of the best performers inside Bank of America (a production emphasis). At the same time, Krawcheck maintains a soft human touch (a people emphasis). In a previous position at Citibank, she attempted to get reimbursements for clients who had purchased securities based on subprime loans that plunged in value. When Merrill Lynch was merged into Bank of America, she worked hard to win over brokers with personal visits.[43]

Entrepreneurial Leadership

Many entrepreneurs use a similar leadership style that stems from their personality characteristics and circumstances. Although there are different types and definitions of entrepreneurs, in general an entrepreneur is a person who founds and operates an innovative business. Not all business owners, including franchise operators, are therefore entrepreneurial leaders. The general picture that emerges of an entrepreneur is a task-oriented and charismatic person. Entrepreneurs drive themselves and others relentlessly, yet their personalities also inspire others.

This entrepreneurial leadership style often incorporates the behaviors described in the following paragraphs.[44] However, authorities disagree about whether an entrepreneurial personality exists.

1. ***Strong achievement drive and sensible risk taking.*** Entrepreneurs have stronger achievement motives than most leaders (see Chapter 3). Building a business is an excellent vehicle for accomplishment and risk taking. To accomplish what they think needs to be accomplished, entrepreneurs are willing to work extraordinary hours, with twelve-hour days, seven days a week not being unusual. Because entrepreneurs take sensible risks, many do not perceive themselves as being risk takers—just as many tightrope walkers believe they are not taking risks because they perceive themselves to be in control. Leadership Self-Assessment Quiz 8-3 gives you the opportunity to think about your risk-taking tendencies.

2. ***High degree of enthusiasm and creativity.*** Entrepreneurs are highly enthusiastic, partially because they are so excited about their achievements. As *Entrepreneur* magazine puts it, "Something about being an entrepreneur is, for them, a five-star, butt-kicking, rocket-boosting blast." Entrepreneurs' enthusiasm, in turn, makes them persuasive. As a result, they are often perceived as charismatic. Some entrepreneurs are so emotional that they are regarded as eccentric.

The enthusiasm of entrepreneurs often develops into passion. The late Anna Roddick, who founded the Body Shop, asserted that "to succeed you have to believe in something with such a passion that it becomes a reality." A theoretical analysis of entrepreneurial passion suggests that is invested in three roles. First is the inventor role of recognizing an opportunity such as seeing the need for a product or service. Second is the founder role of creating the venture, with all its

LEADERSHIP SELF-ASSESSMENT QUIZ 8-3

What Is Your Propensity for Taking Risks?

Instructions: Indicate how well each of the following statements reflects your attitudes or behavior, using this scale: very inaccurately (VI); inaccurately (I); moderately well (MW); accurately (A); very accurately (VA).

	VI	I	MW	A	VA
1. If I had the opportunity I would take a helicopter ride on vacation, such as flying over the Grand Canyon.	1	2	3	4	5
2. I invest (or would invest) much more money in bonds or CDs (certificates of deposit) than in stocks.	5	4	3	2	1
3. The thought of starting my own business appeals to me.	1	2	3	4	5
4. I am (or was) willing to go on blind dates frequently.	1	2	3	4	5
5. My career advice to young people is to pursue a well-established occupation with a high demand for newcomers to the field.	5	4	3	2	1
6. I would be willing to relocate to a city where I had no family or friends.	1	2	3	4	5
7. During the last few years, I have taken up a new sport, dance, or foreign language on my own.	1	2	3	4	5
8. My preference is to have at least 90 percent of my compensation based on guaranteed salary.	5	4	3	2	1
9. I have no problem posting my telephone number and address on a social networking website.	1	2	3	4	5
10. The idea of piloting my own single-engine plane over the ocean appeals to me.	1	2	3	4	5

Total score: _____

Scoring and Interpretation: Obtain your score by adding the numbers you have circled.

- **56–60:** You are a heavy risk taker, bordering on reckless at times. You are most likely not assessing risk carefully enough before proceeding.

- **48–55:** You probably are a sensible risk taker and an adventuresome person in a way that enhances your leadership appeal to others.

- **15–47:** You have a propensity to avoid risks. Your conservatism in this regard could detract from an entrepreneurial leadership style.

Risk taking is important for leadership because both charismatic and entrepreneurial leaders are noted for their risk taking. In addition, it is difficult to bring about change (a vital leadership function) if you are averse to taking risks.

associated managerial and leadership responsibilities. Third is the developer role of growing the venture, such as expanding into the global market.[45]

3. *Tendency to act quickly when opportunity arises.* Entrepreneurs are noted for seizing upon opportunity. When a deal is on the horizon, they push themselves and those around them extra hard.

4. *Constant hurry combined with impatience.* Entrepreneurs are always in a hurry. While engaged in one meeting, their minds typically begin to focus on the next meeting. Their flurry of activity rubs off on group members and those around them. Entrepreneurs often adopt a simple dress style in order to save time, and they typically allow little slack time between appointments.

5. *Visionary perspective combined with tenacity.* Entrepreneurs, at their best, are visionaries. As with other types of effective leaders, they see opportunities others fail to observe. Specifically, they have the ability to identify a problem and arrive at a solution. Ted Turner of CNN is a legendary example of an entrepreneurial visionary. Turner picked up on a trend that people wanted—an all-news cable channel that they could access anytime. Not only is CNN a commercial success, but it also revolutionized the way people get their news all over the globe. After the vision is established, the entrepreneur tenaciously implements the vision, working an eighty-hour week if need be.

For many entrepreneurs, just growing their businesses requires tenacity. A relevant example is none other than Mark Zuckerberg, who in his early twenties became one of the best-known entrepreneurs of all time. During the Great Recession, he sank money and time into developing Facebook, and grew its engineering ranks by 50 percent. "What 2009 was about for us was making the site better and growing users," says Zuckerberg.[46]

6. *Dislike of hierarchy and bureaucracy.* Entrepreneurs are not ideally suited by temperament to working within the mainstream of a bureaucracy. Many successful entrepreneurs are people who were frustrated by the constraints of a bureaucratic system. The implication for leadership style is that entrepreneurs deemphasize rules and regulations when managing people.

7. *Preference for dealing with external customers.* One reason that entrepreneurs have difficulty with bureaucracy is that they focus their energies on products, services, and customers, rather than on employees. Some entrepreneurs are gracious to customers and moneylenders but brusque with company insiders. A blind spot many entrepreneurs have is that they cannot understand why their employees do not share their passion for work and customer focus. As a result, they may be curt with employees who do not share their dedication to the firm.

8. *Eye on the future.* Entrepreneurs have the pronounced characteristic of thinking about future deals and business opportunities even before a current business is running smoothly. "Where is my next deal coming from?" is the mantra of the true entrepreneur. Even after accumulating great wealth from a current business activity, the entrepreneurial leader looks toward future opportunities. A good example is Richard Branson, whose empire contains about 250

LEADERSHIP SKILL-BUILDING EXERCISE 8-4

Entrepreneurial Leadership

An important part of the entrepreneurial role is convincing others of the merit of your idea so that they will invest in your company or lend you money. Two students play the role of a team of entrepreneurs who have a new product or service and want to launch a business. (The two entrepreneurs choose the product or service.) About five other students play the role of a group of venture capitalists or bankers listening to the presentation to decide whether to invest or lend money. The entrepreneurs will communicate excitement and commitment about their product, along with a good business plan. (You might want to quickly review the material about persuasive communication in Chapter 12.) The students who are not participating will evaluate how well the two entrepreneurs displayed aspects of the entrepreneurial leadership style.

companies with the Virgin label, yet he continues to look for the next company to start or acquire.

The entrepreneurial personality, if carried to an extreme, can lead to addictive behavior, including substance abuse. To practice one aspect of entrepreneurial leadership, do Leadership Skill-Building Exercise 8-4.

Gender Differences in Leadership Style

Controversy over whether men and women have different leadership styles continues. Several researchers and observers argue that women have certain acquired traits and behaviors that suit them for relations-oriented leadership. Consequently, women leaders frequently exhibit a cooperative, empowering style that includes nurturing team members. According to this same perspective, men are inclined toward a command-and-control, militaristic leadership style. Women find participative management more natural than do men because they appear to feel more comfortable interacting with people. Furthermore, it is argued that women's natural sensitivity to people gives them an edge over men in encouraging group members to participate in decision making. Here we look briefly at some of the evidence and reasoning whether gender differences exist in leadership style.

As many researchers use the term, *gender* refers to perceptions about the differences among males and females. An example would be to believe that women managers tend to be better listeners than their male peers. Gender differences refer to roles that men and women occupy. Sex differences, however, refer to actual (objective and quantitative) differences, such as the fact that the mean height of men exceeds that of women. Nevertheless, the terms *gender* and *sex* are still used interchangeably in general usage and to some extent in scholarly writings.

The Argument for Male–Female Differences in Leadership Style Judy Rosener, specialist in workplace gender issues, concluded that men and women do tend toward opposite styles. Based on self-reports, she found that men tended toward a command-and-control style. In contrast, women tended toward a transformational style, relying heavily on interpersonal skills.[47] As corporate managers, women tend to place greater emphasis on forming caring, nurturing relationships with employees. Women are also more likely than men to praise group members. And when an employee falls short of expectations, women are more likely to buffer criticism by finding something praiseworthy.[48]

Fundamental differences in the biological and psychological makeup of men and women have also been used as evidence that the two sexes are likely to manifest different leadership styles. Brain researchers Raquel Gur and Ruben Gur uncovered one such set of differences. They found that women may be far more sensitive to emotional cues and verbal nuances than men are. Women leaders would therefore be more suited to responding to the feelings of group members and understanding what they really mean by certain statements.[49]

Gender differences in communication also are reflected in leadership style. Above all, women are more likely than men to use spoken communication for building relationships and giving emotional support.[50] Men focus more on disseminating information and demonstrating competence. Women are therefore more likely to choose a relationship-oriented leadership style.

The Argument against Gender Differences in Leadership Style   Based on a literature review, Jan Grant concluded that there are apparently few, if any, personality or behavioral differences between men and women managers. Also, as women move up the corporate ladder, their identification with the male model of managerial success becomes important; they consequently reject even the few managerial feminine traits they may have earlier endorsed.[51]

To what extent the stereotypes of men and women leaders are true is difficult to judge. Even if male and female differences in leadership style do exist, they must be placed in proper perspective. Both men and women leaders differ among themselves in leadership style. Plenty of male leaders are relationship oriented, and plenty of women practice command and control (the extreme task orientation). Many women believe that women managers can be more hostile and vindictive than men managers.

Carol Meyrowitz, the chief executive of the retailer TJX Cos., makes this forceful statement about gender differences in leadership: "Good leadership and good performance are not about any one thing, but a host of factors and circumstances."[52]

Perhaps the best approach to leadership takes advantage of the positive traits of both men and women. To compete in the global marketplace, companies need a diverse leadership team including men and women. Not recognizing that both male and female styles are needed can lead to confusion for women managers. Alice H. Eagly and Linda L. Carli write that female leaders often struggle to cultivate an appropriate and effective leadership style—one that reconciles the communal qualities preferred in women with the harsher qualities many people think are needed to succeed.[53]

Selecting the Best Leadership Style

An underlying theme of our discussion of leadership styles in this and the next chapter is that there is no one best or most effective leadership style. A study of 3,000 executives revealed that leaders who get the best results do not rely on one style. Instead, they use several different styles in one week, such as being autocratic in some situations and democratic in others.[54] Another consideration is the national culture in which the leadership takes place. An effective leadership style for most German workers would be a high performance (task) orientation and a modest amount of compassion (consideration).[55] However, Scandinavian workers respond best to a democratic leadership style.

The organizational culture also influences which leadership style will be tolerated and effective. A friendly, collaborative culture calls for more of a consensus style of leadership. In contrast, in a perform-or-perish culture, a more directive or autocratic leadership style will be effective.

At several places in this book we will mention the leader-member exchange (LMX) theory. A key point of the theory is that the leader establishes different quality relationships with each group member.[56] Part of establishing a high-quality relationship would be for the leader to vary his or her style to meet the needs of each subordinate. For example, Randy might need more guidance, and Suzanne might want to work more independently.

Forty years ago, pioneering researcher Ralph Stogdill made a statement about selecting a leadership style that still holds today: "The most effective leaders appear to exhibit a degree of versatility and flexibility that enables them to adapt their behavior to the changing and contradictory demands made on them."[57]

Before moving on to the end-of-chapter activities, do Leadership Skill-Building Exercise 8-5 which deals with flexibility.

LEADERSHIP SKILL-BUILDING EXERCISE 8-5

Contrasting Leadership Styles

One student plays the role of a new associate working for a financial services firm that sells life insurance and other investments. The associate has completed a six-week training program and is now working full-time. Four weeks have passed, and the associate still has not made a sale. The associate's boss is going to meet this associate today to discuss progress. Another student plays the role of a task-oriented leader. The two people participate in the review session.

Before playing (or assuming) the role of the associate or the boss, think for a few minutes how you would behave if you were placed in that role in real life. Empathize with the frustrated associate or the task-oriented leader. A good role player is both a scriptwriter and an actor.

Another two students repeat the same scenario, except that this time the manager is a strongly relationship-oriented leader. Two more pairs of students then have their turn at acting out the task-oriented and relationship-oriented performance reviews. Another variation of this role play is for one person to play the roles of both the task-oriented and the relationship-oriented boss. Other class members observe and provide feedback on the effectiveness of the two styles of leadership.

SUMMARY

Effective leadership requires the right behaviors, skills, and attitudes, as emphasized in the classic Ohio State University studies. Two major dimensions of leadership behavior were identified: consideration and initiating structure. Consideration is the degree to which the leader creates an environment of emotional support, warmth, friendliness, and trust. Making connections with people is a current aspect of consideration. Initiating structure is the degree to which the leader organizes and defines relationships in the group by such activities as assigning tasks and specifying procedures. Both consideration and initiating structure are related to important leadership outcomes such as job satisfaction and performance.

Many task-related attitudes and behaviors of effective leaders have been identified. Among them are (1) adaptability to the situation, (2) direction setting, (3) high performance standards, (4) concentrating on strengths of group members, (5) risk taking and execution of plans, (6) hands-on guidance and feedback, (7) ability to ask tough questions, and (8) organizing for collaboration.

Many relationship-oriented attitudes and behaviors of leaders have also been identified. Among them are (1) aligning people, (2) openness to workers' opinions, (3) creating inspiration and visibility, (4) satisfying higher-level needs, (5) giving emotional support and encouragement, (6) promoting principles and values, and (7) being a servant leader.

Servant leaders are committed to serving others rather than achieving their own goals. Aspects of servant leadership include placing service before self-interest, listening to others, inspiring trust by being trustworthy, focusing on what is feasible to accomplish, lending a hand, and emotional healing.

Many leaders receive extensive feedback on their behaviors and attitudes in the form of 360-degree feedback, whereby people who work for or with the leader provide feedback on the leader's performance. Such feedback is likely to be useful when the feedback relates to business goals and

strategy and to important aspects of leadership, when training is provided in giving and receiving feedback, when action plans are developed, and when managers own the feedback evaluation. The anonymous comments in 360-degree feedback can be a problem.

Understanding leadership style is an extension of understanding leadership attitudes and behavior. Participative leaders share decision making with group members. The participative style can be subdivided into consultative, consensus, and democratic leadership. The participative style is well suited to managing competent people who are eager to assume responsibility. Yet the process can be time-consuming, and some managers perceive it to be a threat to their power. Autocratic leaders retain most of the authority for themselves. The Leadership Grid™ classifies leaders according to their concern for both production (task accomplishment) and people.

Another important style of leader is the entrepreneur. The entrepreneurial style stems from the leader's personal characteristics and the circumstances of self-employment. It includes a strong achievement drive and sensible risk taking; a high degree of enthusiasm (including passion) and creativity; the tendency to act quickly on opportunities; hurriedness and impatience; a visionary perspective; a dislike of hierarchy and bureaucracy; a preference for dealing with external customers; and an eye on the future.

Male–female differences in leadership style have been observed. Women have a tendency toward relationship-oriented leadership, whereas men tend toward command and control. Some people argue that male–female differences in leadership are inconsistent and not significant.

Rather than searching for the one best style of leadership, managers are advised to diagnose the situation and then choose an appropriate leadership style to match. To be effective, a leader must be able to adapt style to circumstance.

KEY TERMS

effective leader	management openness	consultative leaders
consideration	servant leader	consensus leaders
initiating structure	360-degree feedback	democratic leaders
Pygmalion effect	leadership style	autocratic leaders
tough question	participative leaders	Leadership Grid™

✔ GUIDELINES FOR ACTION AND SKILL DEVELOPMENT

A major consideration about choosing a leadership style is that you may have to modify your style to fit the occasion. For example, your group members may need close direction at one point, and at other times they may require less direction (as explained in several of the leadership theories presented in this chapter).

Most leadership-style classifications are based on the directive (task-oriented) dimension versus the nondirective (relationship-oriented) dimension. In deciding which of these two styles is best, consider the following questions:

1. **What is the structure of your organization and the nature of your work?** You might decide, for example, that stricter control is necessary for some types of work, such as dealing with proprietary information.
2. **Which style suits you best?** Your personality, values, and beliefs influence how readily you can turn over responsibility to others.
3. **Which style suits your boss and the organization culture?** For example, a boss who is highly directive may perceive you as weak if you are too nondirective. In a tough-minded, perform-or-perish culture, you might want to use a highly directive leadership style.
4. **Is there high potential for conflict in the work unit?** A directive leadership style can trigger conflict with independent, strong-willed people. A more nondirective style allows for more freedom of discussion, which defuses conflict.[58]

Discussion Questions and Activities

1. How would good cognitive skills help a leader be effective at initiating structure?
2. Give an example of a high-consideration behavior that a supervisor of yours showed on your behalf. What was your reaction to his or her behavior?
3. Why is direction setting still an important leadership behavior in an era of empowerment and shared leadership?
4. Why is an effective leader supposed to provide emotional support to team members even when they are mature adults?
5. Which type of leader would be the opposite of a servant leader?
6. How might a manager use e-mail and text messaging to help carry out both task-oriented and relationship-oriented behaviors?
7. Visualize yourself in a leadership position in a field of interest to you. How would you feel about being described as a hands-on leader by the members of your team?
8. How would you characterize the leadership style of your favorite executive, athletic coach, or television character who plays a boss?
9. Why is the consensus leadership style widely recommended for providing leadership to workers under age 35?
10. Several people have commented that this chapter deals with the "nuts and bolts of leadership." What makes them say that?

LEADERSHIP CASE PROBLEM A

Frank Won't Accept "We Can't" for an Answer

Frank is the business development manager at a small firm that provides business process improvement solutions to federal, state, and local governments. His firm's organization structure includes four project managers who are both managers of projects and also solicit for new business. Up until last year, the company had enough contracts to be profitable. This year, a few big government contracts have expired and have not yet been renewed. As a result, the company could lose money and perhaps be forced to lay off one-third of the staff.

Frank is particularly worried. He calls a meeting with his four project managers to discuss the need for more sales. A couple of minutes into the meeting, Frank informs his four direct reports, "The time for excuses is over. We need at least $1 million worth of new contracts to stay afloat. I haven't heard about even a warm lead for a new contract from any of you in about a year. We need new business, and we need it now."

Project manager Jennifer responded: "Frank, I hear you. The other project managers hear you. But government spending has tightened up. It's not possible to squeeze a contract out of a government agency if they don't have money in the budget."

Oliver, another project manager, responded, "Frank, I have to agree with Jenny. There is no way to coax a contract out of a government agency when the well is dry. You know as well as we do that government funding is way down for everything but national defense. Help us by pointing us in a new direction for obtaining contracts. Do you have any contacts in private industry that we might pursue?"

Shaking his head in discouragement, Frank said: "I've heard enough excuses. I know you are trying, but get out there and try harder. I don't care which one of you pulls it off, but I want one new pending contract for my approval within six months.

"I will do what I can to find new business for the firm also. But I am not here to do your job. Get back to me when you have made some progress."

Questions

1. Based on the limited evidence, how would you characterize Frank's leadership style?
2. What leadership behaviors and attitudes is Frank displaying?
3. How else might Frank approach his project managers about developing new business?

ASSOCIATED ROLE PLAY

One student plays the role of Frank who wants to use an effective leadership approach to encourage his project managers/account managers to bring in a few new accounts. He knows that this is a tough leadership task. Four other students play the roles of the project manager who will react to Frank's leadership initiatives. Class members providing feedback should be particularly observant of Frank's leadership approach.

LEADERSHIP CASE PROBLEM B

Is Margo Too Macro?

Margo Santelli is the director of the municipal bond group of a financial services firm. Santelli has four managers reporting to her, each of whom supervises a unit of the group, including retail sales, institutional sales, customer service, and internal administration.

Laura Gordon, the branch director and company vice president, heard rumblings that the group was not receiving enough supervision, so she decided to investigate. During a dinner meeting requested by Laura, she asked Margo about her approach to leading the group. Margo replied:

"I am leading my four managers as if they are all responsible professionals. I believe in management by exception. Unless I am aware of a problem, I am hesitant to get involved in how my managers conduct their work. Don't forget that as the head of the municipal bond group, I have some responsibility for spending time with major customers as well as meeting with you and other senior executives.

"I do hold a weekly meeting, and conduct my annual performance reviews as required."

Laura thanked Margo for having attended the dinner, and said that the meeting was informative. With Margo's permission, Laura said that she would be visiting the municipal bond group to have a few casual conversations with the four managers.

When asked about Margo's leadership, the first manager said his nickname for Santelli was Macro Margo because, instead of being a micromanager, she went to the other extreme and was a macromanager who maintained minimal contact with the group. He added that at times Margo didn't even seem to care what was happening. The manager said, "I recently

asked Margo's advice about finding a good contact who could introduce me to the pension fund manager of a hospital. Margo told me that a big part of my job was to develop contacts on my own."

The second manager Laura spoke to said that she enjoyed working with Margo because she was a nice person who didn't get in her hair. "I don't need a boss to remind me to attain my goals or get my work done on time. A little smile of encouragement here and there is all I need," the manager said.

The third manager said to Laura, "I think Margo would be a great manager for me a few years down the road. But right now, I do not want to feel so much on my own. Margo is a talented person who I could learn from. Yet she is more involved with customers and higher-level management than she is her managers. I'm new in the field, so I could use more of a coaching style of manager."

The fourth manager said, "I remember meeting Margo a few times, but I don't remember much about her. You said she is my manager? I don't care if my comments get back, because I'm joining a competitor next month."

Questions

1. To what extent has Margo Santelli chosen the right approach to leading the managers in her unit of the financial services firm?
2. What advice can you offer Margo to be a more effective leader?
3. What advice can you offer Laura to help Margo be a more effective leader?
4. Explain whether or not you think Laura was justified in asking Margo's direct reports about Margo's approach to leadership.

ASSOCIATED ROLE PLAY

One student plays the role of Margo, who will be holding a brief face-to-face meeting with a manager reporting to her who is having a problem. Another student plays the role of the manager facing the

problem of having difficulty selling a relatively new financial product—an indexed annuity. The annuity is supposed to pay dividends that are in line with a chosen stock market index. However, this type of investment is being criticized as very complex to understand, and perhaps of questionable ethics. As a result the sales representatives are having considerable difficult selling the product. Margo is her usual macromanaging self, much to the frustration of the manager with whom she is meeting. Class members who provide feedback will be particularly observant of (a) how well Margo carries out the macromanager role, and (b) how well the manager reporting to her deals with the situation.

LEADERSHIP SKILL-BUILDING EXERCISE 8-6

My Leadership Portfolio

For this addition to your leadership portfolio, identify four leadership task-oriented behaviors or relationship-oriented behaviors that you have demonstrated this week. Your list can comprise any combination of the two sets of behaviors. Also jot down the result you achieved by exercising these behaviors. Here is an example:

"Thursday night, I applied *direction setting* and it really worked. We have a group assignment in our marketing class with each group consisting of about five people. Our assignment is to analyze how well employee self-service is working in supermarkets and home-improvement stores. The group was hitting a wall because in their Internet searches they were finding mostly advertisements for Home Depot and the like. I suggested that we each visit a supermarket or home-improvement store and make firsthand observations of the customers who were using the automated checkout system. I also suggested we ask a couple of questions of the store associate supervising the activity. The group loved my idea, and the project was a big success. We supplemented written articles with a firsthand field study. I set the group in the right direction."

LEADERSHIP SKILL-BUILDING EXERCISE 8-7

The Entrepreneurial Leadership Style

Work in a small group to write an essay about an entrepreneurial leader. First, agree on an entrepreneur for whom there is likely to be considerable information available in magazines and newspapers, including Internet access to this material. Prepare an essay of about 400 words, concentrating on the person's entrepreneurial traits and behaviors. Refer back to the chapter section about entrepreneurial leadership to gather some ideas for categories, such as "high degree of enthusiasm and creativity." Also, look to see if you can identify traits or behaviors not mentioned in the text. Remember that an entrepreneur is somebody who founds and develops a business based on a creative idea, such as Mark Zuckerberg of Facebook.

▶❚❚ LEADERSHIP VIDEO CASE DISCUSSION QUESTIONS

To view the videos for this activity, you'll need access to the CourseMate that is available for this text. To get access, visit www.CengageBrain.com.

After watching "Gold & Williams," answer the following questions.

1. Do Mitchell Gold and Bob Williams exhibit task-related behaviors? If so, which ones?

2. What were some relationship-oriented attitudes and behaviors that Mitchell and Bob engaged in?

3. Do Mitchell and Bob create an environment of consideration? Explain.

4. What makes Mitchell and Bob participative leaders? Explain.

NOTES

1. Excerpted from "From Soup to Negligee: Success According to Victoria's Secret's Lori Greeley and Campbell Soup's Denise Morrison," *Knowledge@Wharton* (http://knowledge. wharton.upenn.edu), March 02, 2011, pp. 1–5.

2. Ralph M. Stogdill and Alvin E. Coons, eds., *Leader Behavior: Its Description and Measurement* (Columbus, OH.: The Ohio State University Bureau of Business Research, 1957); Carroll L. Shartle, *Executive Performance and Leadership* (Upper Saddle River, N.J.: Prentice Hall, 1956).

3. Margaret Littman, "Best Bosses Tell All," *Working Woman*, October 2000, p. 50; Jeff Bailey, "Reinventing Applebee's," *Forbes.com*, December 2, 2009, pp. 1–3.

4. Cecilie Robwedder, "Marks & Spencer Plucks New CEO from Rival," *The Wall Street Journal*, November 19, 2009, p. B12.

5. "The World's Most Powerful Women," *Forbes*, September 7, 2009, pp. 84–88.

6. Timothy A. Judge, Ronald F. Piccolo, and Remus Ilies, "The Forgotten Ones? The Validity of Consideration and Initiating Structure in Leadership Research," *Journal of Applied Psychology*, February 2004, pp. 36–51.

7. Larry Bossidy, "What Your Leader Expects of You, and What You Should Expect in Return," *Harvard Business Review*, April 2007, p. 64.

8. Geoffrey Colvin, "What Makes GE Great?" *Fortune*, March 6, 2006, p. 96.

9. Sharon Terlep and Joann S. Lublin, "New GM CEO: Brash, Blunt, and Demanding," *The Wall Street Journal*, August 16, 2010, p. B2.

10. Marcus Buckingham, "What Great Managers Do," *Harvard Business Review*, March 2005, pp. 70–79.

11. Desa Philadelphia, "Q&A: Larry Bossidy on Execution." *Time Global Business*, July 2002, p. B5.

12. Brian O'Keefe, "Meet the CEO of the Biggest Company on Earth," *Fortune*, September 27, 2010, pp. 83, 84.

13. Henry Mintzberg, *Managing* (San Francisco: Berrett-Koehler, 2009), p. 88.

14. Joann S. Lublin, "Top Brass Try Life in the Trenches," *The Wall Street Journal*, June 25, 2007, p. B1.

15. Quoted in David Kiley, "The New Heat on Ford," *BusinessWeek*, June 4, 2007, p. 035.

16. Mitch Betts, "Hot Job: Corporate Anthropologist to Boost Collaboration," *Computerworld*, October 25, 2010 (www.computerworld.com).

17. "A CEO on the Go: Randy Komisar on the Art of Snap Leadership," *Executive Strategies*, July 2000, p. 3.

18. John P. Kotter, "What Leaders Really Do," *Harvard Business Review*, May–June 1990, pp. 105–106.

19. Nancy Dahlberg, "Hair Cuttery Founder: 'Just a Regular Guy' with a Big Vision," *The Miami Herald* (www.miamiherald.com), February 23, 2001, pp. 1–3.

20. James R. Detert and Ethan R. Burris, "Leadership Behavior and Employee Voice: Is the Door Really Open?" *Academy of Management Journal*, August 2007, p. 871.

21. David Kirkpatrick, "Inside Sam's $100 Billion Growth Machine," *Fortune*, June 14, 2004, p. 88.

22. Geoffrey Colvin, "How One CEO Learned to Fly," *Fortune*, October 30, 2006, p. 98.

23. "Carrot and Stick Failing? Try Encouragement," *Executive Leadership*, July 2007, p. 4.

24. Cited in Adam Bryant, "Want the Job? Tell Him the Meaning of Life," *The New York Times* (www.nytimes.com), June 18, 2010, p. 3.

25. "Covey Proposes Principle-Based Leadership," *Management Review*, September 1995, p. 21.

26. Bill George, *Authentic Leadership* (San Francisco: Jossey-Bass, 2003).

27. Erin White, "'Authentic' Ways of Leading," *The Wall Street Journal*, December 3, 2007, p. B3.

28. Stacy Perlman, "The Secret Sauce at In-N-Out Burger," (Book Excerpt), *Businessweek*, April 20, 2009, pp. 068–069.

29. Robert K. Greenleaf, *The Power of Servant Leadership* (San Francisco: Berrett-Koehler, 1998).

30. Based on Robert K. Greenleaf, *Servant Leadership: A Journey into the Nature of Legitimate Power and Greatness* (Mahwah, N.J.: Paulist Press, 1997); Robert C. Liden, Sandy J. Wayne, Hao Zhao, and David Henderson, "Servant Leadership: Development of a Multidimensional Measure and Multi-Level Assessment," *The Leadership Quarterly*, April 2008, pp. 161–177.

31. "Be a Leader, Not a Pal," *Manager's Edge*, March 2007, p. 3.

32. "The Essence of Servant Leadership," *Manager's Edge*, January 2004, p. 3.

33. Liden et al., "Servant Leadership: Development of a Multidimensional Measure," p. 172.

34. Fred O. Walumbwa, Chad A. Hartnell, and Adegoke Oke, "Servant Leadership, Procedural Justice Climate, Service Climate, Employee Attitudes, and Organizational Citizenship Behavior," *Journal of Applied Psychology*, May 2010, pp. 517–529.

35. D. Scott DeRue, Jennifer D. Nahrgang, Ned Wellman, and Stephen E. Humphrey, "Trait and Behavioral Theories of Leadership: An Integration and Meta-Analytic Test of Their Relative Validity," *Personnel Psychology*, Number 1, 2011, pp. 7–52.

36. Bruce Pfau and Ira Kay, "Does 360-Degree Feedback Negatively Affect Company Performance?" *HR Magazine*, June 2002, pp. 58–59; Richard Lepsinger and Anntoinette D. Lucia, *The Art and Science of 360 Degree Feedback*, 2nd ed. (San Francisco: Pfeiffer, 2009).

37. Craig L. Pearse, "The Future of Leadership: Combining Vertical and Shared Leadership to Transform Knowledge Work," *Academy of Management Executive*, February 2004, pp. 47–57.

38. "Ricardo Semler's Huge Leap of Faith," *Executive Leadership*, April 2006, p. 6.

39. Anders Skogstad et al., "The Destructiveness of Laissez-faire Leadership Behavior," *Journal of Occupational Health Psychology*, no. 1, 2007, pp. 80–92.

40. Cited in Martin Peers, "Google Turns the Page on Schmidt," *The Wall Street Journal*, January 21, 2011, p. C10.

41. "GM Boss-to-Be Has Hard-Nosed Reputation," *Detroit Free Press*, August 14, 2010.

42. Robert R. Blake and Anne Adams McCanse, *Leadership Dilemmas—Grid Solutions* (Houston, TX: Gulf Publishing, 1991); http://www.gridinternational .com/gridtheory.html, 2007.

43. "Sallie Krawcheck: Bring on the Indies," *Investment News* (www.investmentnews.com) March 4, 2011, pp. 1–7; Dan Fitzpatrick, "B of A Sees Sharp Cut in Merrill Exits," *The Wall Street Journal*, January 15, 2010, p. C3.

44. J. Robert Baum and Edwin A. Locke, "The Relationship of Entrepreneurial Traits, Skill, and Motivation to Subsequent Venture Growth," *Journal of Applied Psychology*, August 2004, pp. 587–598; Gayle Sato Stodder,

"Goodbye Mom and Pop: The Neighborhood's Not Big Enough for Today's Entrepreneur. Only the World Will Do," *Entrepreneur*, May 1999, pp. 145–151.

45. Melissa S. Cardon, Joakim Wincent, Jagdip Singh, and Mateja Dronovsek, "The Nature and Experience of Entrepreneurial Passion," *Academy of Management Review*, July 2009, pp. 511–532. The Roddick quote is also from this source, p. 511.

46. Quoted in "The World's 50 Most Innovative Companies," *Fast Company*, March 2010, p. 67.

47. Judy Rosener, "Ways Women Lead," *Harvard Business Review*, November–December 1990, pp. 119–125.

48. Debra Phillips, "The Gender Gap," *Entrepreneur*, May 1995, pp. 110, 111.

49. Research reported in Michael Schrage, "Why Can't a Woman Be More Like a Man?" *Fortune*, August 16, 1999, p. 184.

50. Much of the research on this topic is summarized in Mary Crawford, *Talking Difference: On Gender and Language* (London: Sage, 1995).

51. Jan Grant, "Women Managers: What Can They Offer Organizations?" *Organizational Dynamics*, Winter 1988, pp. 56–63.

52. Quoted in Del Jones, "Female CEOs Taking Charge Firmly," *USA Today*, December 31, 2009.

53. Alice H. Eagly and Linda L. Carli, "Women and the Labyrinth of Leadership," *Harvard Business Review*, September 2007, p. 66.

54. Daniel Goleman, "Leadership That Gets Results," *Harvard Business Review*, March–April 2000, pp. 78–90.

55. Felix Brodbeck, Michael Frese, and Mansour Havidan, "Leadership Made in Germany: Low on Compassion, High on Performance," *Academy of Management Executive*, February 2002, pp. 16–30.

56. David J. Henderson, Robert C. Liden, Brian C. Glibkowski, and Anjali Chaudhry, "LMX Differentiation: A Multilevel Review and Examination of its Antecedents and Outcomes," *Leadership Quarterly*, August 2009, pp. 517–534.

57. Ralph M. Stogdill, "Historical Trends in Leadership Theory and Research," *Journal of Contemporary Business*, Autumn 1974, p. 7.

58. "Directive Management or Not?" *Working SMART*, December 1992, p. 3.

How Leaders Respond
to the **Situation** at **Hand**

LEARNING OBJECTIVES

After studying this chapter and doing the exercises, you should be able to

- Describe how the situation influences the choice of leadership objectives.
- Present an overview of the contingency theory of leadership effectiveness.
- Explain the path-goal theory of leadership effectiveness.
- Explain Situational Leadership® II (SLII).

- Use the normative decision model to determine the most appropriate decision-making style in a given situation.
- Explain the basics of leadership during a crisis.
- Explain how evidence-based leadership can contribute to contingency and situational leadership.

CHAPTER OUTLINE

wo years after his appointment as emergency financial manager for the Detroit Public Schools, Robert Bobb was still struggling to resolve a crisis. The district had fallen into a deeper crisis than when he arrived. Bobb's hope was that sterner deficit-reduction plans would help resolve the problems. He believed that the budget cuts he had made were preventing the school district from falling into a $500 million deficit.

When Bobb's appointment was extended for a second year in 2010, Michigan Governor Jennifer Granholm called Bobb fearless in his approach. She also said that his zero-tolerance approach was exactly what the doctor ordered for Detroit Public Schools. "Having completed negotiations with Governor Jennifer Granholm, I am pleased to say to Detroit that I'm in," Bobb said. "The words of my grandmother came to mind at this point, especially when she said that one should finish what they [meaning he or she] start."

Bobb said that fixing the finances is just one part of the massive job he is tackling. "We learn more with each passing day that what we have is not only a financial emergency, but an academic emergency as well. We also have a reading emergency. And as facts become clearer, just as we early on restated the financial deficit, we gain new insights into the many emergencies that must be addressed before our work is complete.

"We have an attendance emergency for both adults and children. And in some cases we have a parenting emergency. We continue to confront ways to respond to what has too often been an emergency of safety and security."[1]

The story about the emergency financial manager in a troubled school system illustrates an increasingly important leadership task: leading people through a crisis. Leadership of this type is a special case of the general subject of this chapter—adjusting one's approach to the situation. Contingency and situational leadership further expand the study of leadership styles by adding more specific guidelines about which style to use under which circumstance.

In this chapter, we present an overview of the situational perspective on leadership. We then summarize four classic contingency theories of leadership: Fiedler's contingency theory, path-goal theory, the situational leadership model, and the normative decision model. We also explain how a more contemporary theory, the leader-member exchange, contributes to understanding the contingency perspective. In addition, we describe crisis leadership because leading others through a crisis has become a frequent challenge in recent years. Finally, we describe how evidence-based leadership and management contribute to the contingency approach.

SITUATIONAL INFLUENCES ON EFFECTIVE LEADERSHIP BEHAVIOR

The situation can influence the leadership behavior or style a leader emphasizes. The essence of a **contingency approach to leadership** is that leaders are most effective when they make their behavior contingent on situational forces, including group member characteristics. Both the internal and the external environment have a significant impact on leader effectiveness. For example, the quality of the workforce and the competitiveness of the environment can influence which behaviors the leader emphasizes. A manager who supervises competent employees might be able to practice consensus leadership readily. And a manager who faces a competitive environment might find it easier to align people to pursue a new vision.

A useful perspective on implementing contingency leadership is that the manager must be flexible enough to avoid clinging to old ideas that no longer fit the current circumstances.[2] Being stubborn about what will work in a given situation and clinging to old ideas can result in ineffective leadership. The effective leader adapts to changing circumstances. For example, at one point, offering employees generous benefits might not have been motivational. In reality, with many employers having cut back on benefits such as health insurance, these benefits can actually be helpful in attracting and retaining workers.

As mentioned in several places in this textbook, the leader needs to take into account the major situational variable of organizational culture when choosing which approach to leadership will lead to favorable outcomes. A command-and-control leadership style may not be effective in a company with a collaborative, friendly organizational culture. If the culture seems at odds with what a highly placed leader wants to accomplish, the leader may attempt to change the culture.

Victor H. Vroom and Arthur G. Jago have identified three conclusions about the role of situations in leadership, and these findings support the model of leadership presented in Figure 1-2, Chapter 1. The conclusions are geared to support the idea that leadership involves motivating others to work collaboratively in the pursuit of a common goal.[3]

1. *Organizational effectiveness is affected by situational factors not under leader control.* The leader might be able to influence the situation, yet some situational factors are beyond the leader's complete control. The manager of a prosperous, independent coffee shop might be running her business and leading her employees successfully for ten years. Suddenly, a Starbucks opens across the street, thereby seriously affecting her ability to lead a successful enterprise. She might be smart enough to have a contingency plan of offering services Starbucks cannot match, yet staying in business will be a struggle.

2. *Situations shape how leaders behave.* Contingency theorists believe that forces in the situation are three times as strong as the leader's personal characteristics in shaping his or her behavior. How the leader behaves is therefore substantially influenced by environmental forces. In the face of competition from Starbucks, our coffee shop owner might now act with a greater sense of urgency, be much more directive in telling her workers what to do, and become much less warm and friendly. Her normal level of enthusiasm might also diminish.

3. *Situations influence the consequences of leader behavior.* Popular books about management and leadership assume that certain types of leader behavior work in every situation. Situational theorists disagree strongly with this position. Instead, a specific type of leadership behavior might have different outcomes in different situations. The leader behavior of empowerment illustrates this idea. Perhaps empowerment will work for our coffee shop owner because she has a group of dedicated workers who want their jobs and her enterprise to endure. However, empowering incompetent workers with a weak work ethic is likely to backfire because the workers will most likely resist additional responsibility.

Relatively recent work of Mintzberg has identified the form of organization as a key situational variable influencing which approach to leadership is likely to be most effective. Two examples will suffice here. In an *entrepreneurial organization*, the key leader will engage in considerable doing and dealing as well as creating visions. In a *machine organization*, or classic bureaucracy, the leader will engage in a considerable amount of controlling.[4]

In this chapter, as well as throughout the book, possible situational factors are mentioned that should be taken into consideration in leading others. A general approach to being aware of all these factors is for the leader to be *mindful* of events in the environment. If you are mindful you are sensitive to what is happening around you. According to stress researcher Jon Kabat-Zinn, you learn to pay attention on purpose to the present moment, in a nonjudgmental way, to whatever arises in your leadership situation.[5]

FIEDLER'S CONTINGENCY THEORY OF LEADERSHIP EFFECTIVENESS

Fred E. Fiedler developed a widely researched and quoted contingency model more than forty years ago that holds that the best style of leadership is determined by the situation in which the leader is working.[6] Here we examine how the style and situation are evaluated, the overall findings of the theory, and how leaders can modify situations to their advantage.

Measuring Leadership Style: The Least Preferred Coworker (LPC) Scale

Fiedler's theory classifies a manager's leadership style as relationship motivated or task motivated. Style is therefore based on the extent to which the leader is relationship motivated or task motivated. According to Fiedler, leadership style is a relatively permanent aspect of behavior and thus difficult to modify. Leaders are regarded as having a consistent style of task or relations orientation. Fiedler reasons that once leaders understand their particular leadership style, they should work in situations that match that style. Similarly, the organization should help managers match leadership styles and situations.

The least preferred coworker (LPC) scale measures the degree to which a leader describes favorably or unfavorably his or her least preferred coworker— that is, an employee with whom he or she could work the *least well*. A leader who describes the LPC in relatively favorable terms tends to be relationship motivated. In contrast, a person who describes this coworker in an unfavorable manner tends to be task motivated. The coworker is described by rating him or her on a series of eighteen polar-opposite adjectives, such as the following:

Pleasant	8	7	6	5	4	3	2	1	Unpleasant
Tense	1	2	3	4	5	6	7	8	Relaxed

The leadership style measure presented in Leadership Self-Assessment Quiz 8-1 is a more direct and less abstract way of measuring your style. To repeat, the general idea of the LPC approach is that if you have a positive, charitable attitude toward people you had a difficult time working with, you are probably relationship oriented. In contrast, if you take a dim view of people who gave you a hard time, you are probably task oriented. The message here is that a relationship-oriented leader should be able to work well with a variety of personalities.

Measuring the Leadership Situation

Fiedler's contingency theory classifies situations as high, moderate, and low control. The more control that the leader exercises, the more favorable the situation is for the leader. The control classifications are determined by rating the situation on its three dimensions: (1) *leader–member relations* measure how well the group and the leader get along; (2) *task structure* measures how clearly the procedures, goals, and evaluation of the job are defined; and (3) *position power* measures the leader's authority to hire, fire, discipline, and grant salary increases to group members.

Leader–member relations contribute as much to situation favorability as do task structure and position power combined. The leader therefore has the most control in a situation in which relationships with members are the best.

Overall Findings

The key points of Fiedler's contingency theory are summarized and simplified in Figure 9-1. The original theory is much more complex. Leadership effectiveness depends on matching leaders to situations in which they can exercise more control. A leader should therefore be placed in a situation that is favorable to, or matches, his or her style. If this cannot be accomplished, the situation might be modified to match the leader's style by manipulating one or more of the three following situational variables.

The theory states that task-motivated leaders perform the best in situations of both high control and low control. Relationship-motivated leaders perform

Task-motivated leaders perform best when they have the most control (highly favorable). *High*	Relationship-motivated leaders perform best when they have moderate control (moderately favorable). *Moderate*	Task-motivated leaders perform best when they have low control (highly unfavorable). *Low*

← AMOUNT OF SITUATIONAL CONTROL BY LEADER →

a. Leader-member relations are good. b. Task is well structured. c. Leader has high position power.	Both favorable and unfavorable factors are present.	a. Leader-member relations are poor. b. Task is poorly structured. c. Leader has low position power.

FIGURE 9-1 Summary of Findings from Fiedler's Contingency Theory.

Situational Characteristics

Situation (Octant) Number →	1	2	3	4	5	6	7	8
Leader–Member Relations	Good	Good	Good	Good	Poor	Poor	Poor	Poor
Task Structure	High	High	Low	Low	High	High	Low	Low
Position Power	Strong	Weak	Strong	Weak	Strong	Weak	Strong	Weak

© Cengage Learning 2013

FIGURE 9-2 The Eight Different Situations in Fiedler's Contingency Theory.

the best in situations of moderate control. The results of many studies indicated that the relationship-motivated leader outperformed the task-motivated leader in three of the eight situations but that the reverse was true in the other five situations. The eight situations result from each of the three situational variables being classified in one of two ways (good or poor, high or low, or strong or weak), as shown in Figure 9-2.

Task-motivated leaders perform better in situations that are highly favorable for exercising control because they do not have to be concerned with the task. Instead, they can work on relationships. In moderately favorable situations, the relationship-motivated leader achieves higher group productivity because he or she can work on relationships and not get involved in overmanaging. In very-low-control situations, the task-motivated leader is able to structure and make sense out of confusion, whereas the relationship-motivated leader wants to give emotional support to group members or call a meeting.

Making the Situation More Favorable for the Leader

A practical implication of contingency theory is that leaders should modify situations to match their leadership style, thereby enhancing their chances of being effective. Consider a group of leaders who are task motivated and decide that they need to exercise more control over the situation to achieve higher work-unit productivity. To increase control over the situation, they can do one or more of the following:

- Improve leader–member relations through displaying an interest in the personal welfare of group members, having meals with them, actively listening to their concerns, telling anecdotes, and in general being a nice person.
- Increase task structure by engaging in behaviors related to initiating structure, such as being more specific about expectations, providing deadlines, showing samples of acceptable work, and providing written instructions.
- Exercise more position power by requesting more formal authority from higher management. For example, the leader might let it be known that he or she has the authority to grant bonuses and make strong recommendations for promotion.

Now imagine a relationship-motivated leader who wants to create a situation of moderate favorability so that his or her interests in being needed by the group could be satisfied. The leader might give the group tasks of low structure and deemphasize his or her position power.

Evaluation of Fiedler's Contingency Theory

A major contribution of Fiedler's work is that it has prompted others to conduct studies about the contingency nature of leadership. Fiedler's theory has been one of the most widely researched theories in industrial/organizational psychology, and at one time it was used extensively as the basis for leadership training programs. The model has also alerted leaders to the importance of sizing up the situation to gain control. At the same time, Fielder pioneered in taking into account both traits and the situation to better understand leadership.[7]

Despite its potential advantages, however, the contingency theory is too complicated to have much of an impact on most leaders. A major problem centers on matching the situation to the leader. In most situations, the amount of control the leader exercises varies from time to time. For example, if a relationship-motivated leader were to find the situation becoming too favorable for exercising control, it is doubtful that he or she would be transferred to a less favorable situation or attempt to make the situation less favorable.

THE PATH-GOAL THEORY OF LEADERSHIP EFFECTIVENESS

The **path-goal theory** of leadership effectiveness, as developed by Robert House, specifies what a leader must do to achieve high productivity and morale in a given situation. In general, a leader attempts to clarify the path to a goal for a group member so that the group member receives personal payoffs. At the same time, this group member's job satisfaction and performance increase.[8] Like the expectancy theory of motivation on which it is based, path-goal theory is multifaceted and has several versions. Its key features are summarized in Figure 9-3.

The theory is so complex that it is helpful to consider an overview before studying more of the details. The major proposition of path-goal theory is that the manager should choose a leadership style that takes into account the characteristics of the group members and the demands of the task. Furthermore, initiating structure will be effective in situations with a low degree of subordinate task structure, but ineffective in highly structured task situations. The rationale is that in the first situation, subordinates welcome initiating structure because it helps to provide structure to their somewhat ambiguous tasks. Instead of just flailing around, the leader provides guidance. In the situation of highly structured tasks, more structure is seen as unnecessary and associated with overly close supervision.[9]

In his reformulated version of path-goal theory, House offered a meta-proposition, which provides a capsule summary of a dizzying amount of studies and theorizing in relation to the theory. Understanding this meta-proposition would be a good take-away from the theory: For leaders to be

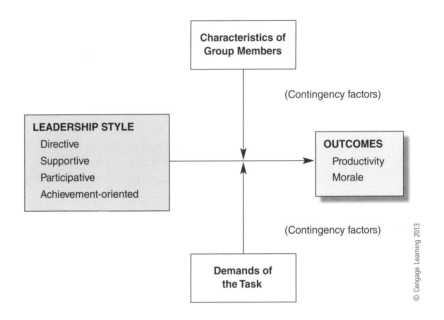

FIGURE 9-3 **The Path-Goal Theory of Leadership.**
To achieve the outcomes of productivity and morale, the manager chooses one of four leadership styles, depending on (a) the characteristics of the situation and (b) the demands of the task.

effective, they should engage in behaviors that complement subordinates' environments and abilities. They should engage in these behaviors in a manner that compensates for deficiencies and that enhances subordinate satisfactions as well as individual and work-unit performance.[10] For example, if our coffee shop owner found that one of her workers was fearful of losing his job because of Starbucks competition, she would give him lots of encouragement and explain the survival plan of the coffee shop in detail.

Two key aspects of this theory will be discussed: matching the leadership style to the situation and steps the leader can take to influence performance and satisfaction.

Matching the Leadership Style to the Situation

Path-goal theory emphasizes that the leader should choose among four leadership styles to achieve optimum results in a given situation. Two important sets of contingency factors are the type of subordinates and the tasks they perform (a key environmental factor). The type of subordinates is determined by how much control they think they have over the environment (locus of control) and by how well they think they can do the assigned task.

Environmental contingency factors are those that are not within the control of group members but influence satisfaction and task accomplishment. Three broad classifications of contingency factors in the environment are (1) the group members' tasks, (2) the authority system within the organization, and (3) the work group.

To use path-goal theory, the leader must first assess the relevant variables in the environment. Then she or he selects the one of the four styles listed next that fits those contingency factors best:

1. *Directive style.* The leader who is directive (similar to task motivated) emphasizes formal activities such as planning, organizing, and controlling. When the task is unclear, the directive style improves morale.

2. *Supportive style.* The leader who is supportive (similar to relationship motivated) displays concern for group members' well-being and creates an emotionally supportive climate. The supportive leader enhances morale when group members work on dissatisfying, stressful, or frustrating tasks. Group members who are unsure of themselves prefer the supportive leadership style.

3. *Participative style.* The leader who is participative consults with group members to gather their suggestions, and then considers these suggestions seriously when making a decision. The participative leader is best suited for improving the morale of well-motivated employees who perform non-repetitive tasks.

4. *Achievement-oriented style.* The leader who is achievement oriented sets challenging goals, pushes for work improvement, and sets high expectations for team members, who are also expected to assume responsibility. This leadership style works well with achievement-oriented team members and with those working on ambiguous and non-repetitive tasks.

A leader can sometimes successfully combine more than one of the four styles, although this possibility is not specified in path-goal theory. For example, during a crisis, such as a major product recall, the marketing manager might need to be directive to help the group take fast action. After the initial emergency actions have been taken, the leader, recognizing how stressed the workers must be, might shift to a supportive mode.

Steps Leaders Can Take to Influence Performance and Satisfaction

In addition to recommending the leadership style to fit the situation, the path-goal theory offers other suggestions to leaders. Most of them relate to motivation and satisfaction, including the following:

1. Recognize or activate group members' needs over which the leader has control.

2. Increase the personal payoffs to team members for attaining work goals. The leader might give high-performing employees special recognition.

3. Make the paths to payoffs (rewards) easier by coaching and providing direction. For instance, a manager might help a team member be selected for a high-level project.

4. Help group members clarify their expectations of how effort will lead to good performance and how performance will lead to a reward. The leader might

say, "Anyone who has gone through this training in the past came away knowing how to implement an ISO 9000 (quality standards) program. And most people who learn how to meet these standards wind up getting a good raise."

5. Reduce frustrating barriers to reaching goals. For example, the leader might hire a temporary worker to help a group member catch up on paperwork and e-mail.

6. Increase opportunities for personal satisfaction if the group member performs effectively. The *if* is important because it reflects contingent behavior on the leader's part.

7. Be careful not to irritate people by giving them instructions on things they already can do well.

8. To obtain high performance and satisfaction, the leader must provide structure if it is missing and supply rewards contingent on adequate performance. To accomplish this, leaders must clarify the desirability of goals for the group members.[11]

As a leader, you can derive specific benefit from path-goal theory by applying these eight methods of influencing performance. Although research interest in path-goal theory has almost disappeared in recent years, the basic tenets of the theory are on target. Any comprehensive theory of leadership must include the idea that the leader's actions have a major impact on the motivation and satisfaction of group members.[12] Despite the potential contributions of path-goal theory, it contains so many nuances and complexities that it has attracted little interest from managers.

SITUATIONAL LEADERSHIP® II (SLII)

The two contingency approaches to leadership presented so far take into account collectively the task, the authority of the leader, and the nature of the subordinates. Another explanation of contingency leadership places its primary emphasis on the characteristics of group members. **Situational Leadership II (SLII)**, developed by Kenneth H. Blanchard and his colleagues, explains how to match leadership style to the capabilities of group members on a given task.[13] The SLII model presented here is a newer version of the older Hersey-Blanchard Situational Leadership Theory (SLT). For example, you might need less guidance from a supervisor when you are skilled in a task than when you are performing a new task. The situational model is particularly applicable to front-line leaders such as supervisors and team leaders.

SLII is designed to increase the frequency and quality of conversations about performance and professional development between managers and group members so that competence is developed, commitment takes place, and turnover among talented workers is reduced. Leaders are taught to use the leadership style that matches or responds to the needs of the situation.

Before delving further into the situational leadership model, do Leadership Self-Assessment Quiz 9-1. It will help alert you to the specific behaviors involved in regarding the characteristics of group members as key contingency variables in choosing the most effective leadership style.

LEADERSHIP SELF-ASSESSMENT QUIZ 9-1

Measuring Your Situational Perspective

Instructions: Indicate how well you agree with the following statements, using the following scale: DS = disagree strongly; D = disagree; N = neutral; A = agree; AS = agree strongly. Circle the most accurate answer.

1.	Workers need to be carefully trained before you can place high expectations on them.	DS	D	N	A	AS
2.	Workers who are more knowledgeable have less need of small, day-by-day goals.	DS	D	N	A	AS
3.	Workers who are self-confident and intelligent require less supervision and guidance than do other workers.	DS	D	N	A	AS
4.	Workers who are anxious usually need a lot of reassurance.	DS	D	N	A	AS
5.	Most workers learn at about the same pace, so the manager can give about the same amount of instruction to each worker.	DS	D	N	A	AS
6.	The same well-delivered pep talk will usually appeal to workers at all levels.	DS	D	N	A	AS
7.	A manager will usually need to provide clear directions during a crisis.	DS	D	N	A	AS
8.	As a manager, I would invest the least amount of time supervising the most competent workers.	DS	D	N	A	AS
9.	An effective approach to supervising emotionally immature workers is to grant them a lot of freedom.	DS	D	N	A	AS
10.	It is best not to put much effort into supervising unenthusiastic staff members.	DS	D	N	A	AS
11.	An effective leader delegates equal types and amounts of work to group members.	DS	D	N	A	AS
12.	If I noticed that a team member appeared to be insecure and anxious, I would give him or her especially clear instructions and guidance.	DS	D	N	A	AS
13.	Many competent workers get to the point where they require relatively little leadership and supervision.	DS	D	N	A	AS
14.	Whether a person is a young adult or old adult often influences the best approach to leading him or her.	DS	D	N	A	AS
15.	A person's cultural background usually has no significance in providing him or her appropriate leadership.	DS	D	N	A	AS

QUIZ 9-1 (continued)

Scoring and Interpretation

1. DS = 1, D = 2, N = 3, A = 4, AS = 5
2. DS = 1, D = 2, N = 3, A = 4, AS = 5
3. DS = 1, D = 2, N = 3, A = 4, AS = 5
4. DS = 1, D = 2, N = 3, A = 4, AS = 5
5. DS = 5, D = 4, N = 3, A = 2, AS = 1
6. DS = 5, D = 4, N = 3, A = 2, AS = 1
7. DS = 1, D = 2, N = 3, A = 4, AS = 5
8. DS = 1, D = 2, N = 3, A = 4, AS = 5
9. DS = 5, D = 4, N = 3, A = 2, AS = 1
10. DS = 5, D = 4, N = 3, A = 2, AS = 1
11. DS = 5, D = 4, N = 3, A = 2, AS = 1
12. DS = 1, D = 2,N = 3, A = 4, AS = 5
13. DS = 1, D = 2, N = 3, A = 2, AS = 1
14. DS = 1, D = 2. N = 3, A = 4, AS = 5
15. DS = 5, D = 4, N = 3, A = 2, AS = 1

- **46–75 points:** You have (or would have) a strong situational perspective as a leader and manager.
- **31–45 points:** You have (or would have) an average situational perspective as a leader and manager.
- **15–30 points:** You rarely take (or would take) a situational perspective as a leader and manager.

Skill Development: For the vast majority of leadership and management assignments, it pays to sharpen your situational perspective. If you scored lower than you want, sharpen your insights into situations by asking yourself, "What are the key factors in this situation that will influence my effectiveness as a leader-manager?" Study both the people and the task in the situation.

Basics of SLII

Situational Leadership II stems from the original situational model. The major premise of SLII is that the basis for effective leadership is managing the relationship between a leader and a subordinate on a given task. The major concepts of the SLII model are presented in Figure 9-4. According to SLII, effective leaders adapt their behavior to the level of *commitment* and *competence* of a particular subordinate to complete a given task. For example, team member Tanya might be committed to renting some empty office space by year-end and also highly skilled at such an activity. Or she might feel that the task is drudgery and not have much skill in selling office space. The combination of the subordinate's commitment and competence determines his or her *developmental level*, as follows:

D1—Enthusiastic Beginner. The learner has low competence but high commitment.

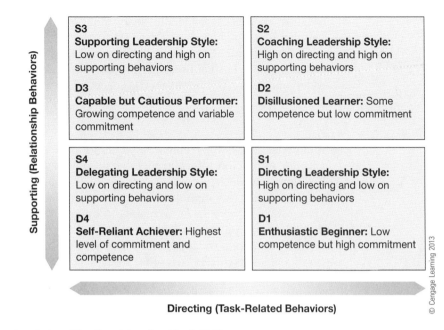

FIGURE 9-4 Situational Leadership II (SLII).

D2—Disillusioned Learner. The individual has gained some competence but has been disappointed after having experienced several setbacks. Commitment at this stage is low.

D3—Capable but Cautious Performer. The learner has growing competence, yet commitment is variable.

D4—Self-Reliant Achiever. The learner has high competence and commitment.

SLII explains that effective leadership depends on two independent behaviors: *supporting* and *directing*. (By now, you have read about this dichotomy several times in this chapter as well as in Chapter 8.) Supporting refers to relationship behaviors such as the leader's listening, giving recognition, communicating, and encouraging. Directing refers to task-related behaviors such as the leader's giving careful directions and controlling.

As shown in Figure 9-4, the four basic styles are:

S1—Directing. High directive behavior/low supportive behavior.
S2—Coaching. High directive behavior/high supportive behavior.
S3—Supporting. Low directive behavior/high supportive behavior.
S4—Delegating. Low directive behavior/low supportive behavior.

For best results on a given task, the leader is required to match his or her style to the developmental level of the group member. Each quadrant in Figure 9-4 indicates the desired match between leader style and subordinate development level.

A key point of SLII is that no single style is best: An effective leader uses all four styles depending on the subordinate's developmental level on a given task.

The most appropriate leadership style among S1 to S4 corresponds to the subordinate developmental levels of D1 to D4, respectively: Enthusiastic beginners (D1) require a directing (S1) leader; disillusioned learners (D2) need a coaching (S2) leader; capable but cautious performers (D3) need a supporting (S3) style of leader; and self-reliant achievers (D4) need a delegating (S4) style of leader.

Evaluation of SLII

Situational leadership represents a consensus of thinking about leadership behavior in relation to group members: Competent people require less specific direction than do less competent people. The model is also useful because it builds on other explanations of leadership that emphasize the role of task and relationship behaviors. As a result, it has proved to be useful as the basis for leadership training. At least 3 million managers have been trained in situational leadership, covering various stages of the model, so we can assume that situational leadership makes sense to managers and companies. The situational model also corroborates common sense and is therefore intuitively appealing. You can benefit from this model by attempting to diagnose the readiness of group members before choosing the right leadership style.

A challenge in applying SLII is that the leader has to stay tuned into which task a group member is performing at a given time and then implement the correct style. Because assignments can change rapidly and group members are often working on more than one task in a day, the leader may have to keep shifting styles.

SLII presents categories and guidelines so precisely that it gives the impression of infallibility. In reality, leadership situations are less clear-cut than the four quadrants suggest. Also, the prescriptions for leadership will work only some of the time. For example, many supervisors use a coaching style (S2) with a disillusioned learner (D2) and still achieve poor results. A major concern is that there are few leadership situations in which a high-task, high-relationship orientation does not produce the best results.

Leadership Skill-Building Exercise 9-1 provides you with the opportunity to practice implementing the situational leadership model. The same exercise also supports other contingency and situational models.

LEADERSHIP SKILL-BUILDING EXERCISE 9-1

Applying Situational Leadership II

You are playing the role of a team leader whose team has been given the responsibility of improving customer service at a consumer electronics megastore. Before jumping into this task, you decide to use SLII. Today, you are going to meet with three team members individually to estimate their developmental level with respect to performing the customer-service-improvement task. You will want to estimate both their *competence* and *commitment* to perform the task. (Three different people will play the role of group members whose readiness is being assessed.) After the brief interviews (about five minutes) are conducted, you will announce which leadership style you intend to use with each of the people you interviewed. Class members not directly involved in the role play will offer feedback on how well you assessed the team members' readiness.

THE NORMATIVE DECISION MODEL

Another contingency viewpoint is that leaders must choose a style that elicits the correct degree of group participation when making decisions. Since many of a leader's interactions with group members involve decision making, this perspective is sensible. The **normative decision model** views leadership as a decision-making process in which the leader examines certain factors within the situation to determine which decision-making style will be the most effective. Here we present the latest version of the model that has evolved from the work of Victor Vroom and his associates over thirty years, based on research with more than 100,000 managers.[14] The models have changed but they all include the basic idea of matching decision-making style to situational factors.

Decision-Making Styles

The normative model (formerly known as the leader-participation model) identifies five decision-making styles, each reflecting a different degree of participation by group members:

1. *Decide.* The leader makes the decision alone and either announces or sells it to the group. The leader might use expertise in collecting information from the group or from others who appear to have information relevant to the problem.
2. *Consult (Individually).* The leader presents the problem to the group members individually, gathers their suggestions, and then makes the decision.
3. *Consult (Group).* The leader presents the problem to group members in a meeting, gathers their suggestions, and then makes the decision.
4. *Facilitate.* The leader presents the problem and then acts as a facilitator, defining the problem to be solved and the boundaries in which the decision must be made. The leader wants concurrence and avoids having his or her ideas receive more weight based on position power.
5. *Delegate.* The leader permits the group to make the decision within prescribed limits. Although the leader does not directly intervene in the group's deliberations unless explicitly asked, he or she works behind the scenes, providing resources and encouragement.

Contingency Factors and Application of the Model

The leader diagnoses the situation in terms of seven variables, or contingency factors, that contribute to selecting the most appropriate decision-making style. Based on answers to those variables, the leader or manager follows the path through decision matrices to choose one of five decision-making styles. The model has two versions: one when time is critical, and one when a more important consideration is developing group members' decision-making capabilities. When development of group members receives higher priority, the leader or

model a contingency approach. The decision-making style chosen depends on these factors, which are defined as follows:

Decision Significance: The significance of the decision to the success of the project or organization (significance deals with decision quality).

Importance of Commitment: The importance of team members' commitment to the decision (commitment deals with decision acceptance).

Leader Expertise: Your knowledge or expertise in relation to the problem.

Likelihood of Commitment: The likelihood that the team will commit itself to a decision you might make on your own.

Group Support: The degree to which the team supports the organization's objectives at stake in the problem.

Group Expertise: Team members' knowledge or expertise in relation to the problem.

Team Competence: The ability of the team members to work together in solving problems.

Accurate answers to these seven situational factors can be challenging to obtain. The leader may have to rely heavily on intuition and also minimize distorted thinking, such as believing he or she has some expertise but in fact does not.

To apply the model, visualize yourself as the division head of a medical supplies company. A decision you face is whether to globally outsource the manufacture of knee braces. The industry is booming because so many people twist or severely damage their knees in sports. Competition is increasing, however, so manufacturing costs must be reduced. The problem statement for the group is "Shall we outsource the manufacture of our knee braces to a medical supply company in Malaysia?" The company in mind has a fine reputation for its manufacture of other medical products such as crutches and prosthetic devices. You proceed as follows:

1. Begin at the left side of the matrix in Figure 9-5, at the "Problem Statement." At the top of the matrix are the seven situational factors, each of which may be present (H for high) or absent (L for low) in that problem. Keep in mind that you are not allowed to cross a horizontal line as you proceed through the matrix.

2. Ascertaining if the decision is significant, or has a high impact on the success of the project, you select H.

3. Moving to the right, you answer the second question about the importance of commitment. You would certainly need the key members of the team to be committed to an activity as complex as the manufacture of knee braces, so you select H.

4. You move to the right again, this time answering the question about leader experience. You conclude that you don't have much relevant experience about globally outsourcing (or offshoring) a medical product, so you answer L.

5. You move to the right again without crossing a horizontal line, and answer the question of likelihood of commitment. You decide that it is unlikely that the team will commit itself to a decision you might make on your own, so you go answer L.

6. Moving to the right, and again not crossing the horizontal line, you answer the question about group support. You think that the group does support the organization's objective of lowering costs on the knee brace, so you answer H.

7. You move to the right, don't cross the line, and answer the question about group expertise. You decide that the group can acquire expertise about outsourcing knee braces, so you answer H.

8. Still moving to the right and heading toward the end of the matrix, you answer the question about the team members' ability to work together in solving problems. You know that your team is strong in group problem solving, so you answer H.

9. A little shift to the right, and you reach the shaded box labeled "Facilitate." So you use the decision-making style Number 4, Facilitate, and you will act as a facilitator in coming to a decision about whether to outsource the manufacture of knee braces to Malaysia.

If you make a few practice decisions with the model in Figure 9-5, it becomes much easier to do. If you continue the process without crossing any horizontal line on the matrix, you will arrive at one of the five recommended decision styles. Sometimes a conclusive determination can be made based on two factors, such as L, L. Others require three (such as L, H, H), four (such as H, H, H, H), or as many as seven factors (such as H, H, L, L, H, H, H).

Different people giving different answers to the situational factors will arrive at different conclusions about the recommended decision style in the situation. The leader needs sufficient information to answer each of seven questions accurately. Leadership Skill-Building Exercise 9-2 presents a

---

LEADERSHIP SKILL-BUILDING EXERCISE 9-2

Applying the Time-Driven Model

The exercise presented here can be done individually or in small groups.

The bank examiners have just left, having insisted that many of your commercial real estate loans be written off, which will deplete your already low capital. Along with the many other banks in your region, your bank is in serious danger of being closed by the regulators. As the financial problems surfaced, many of the top executives left to pursue other interests, but fortunately you were able to replace them with three highly competent younger managers. Although they had no prior acquaintance with one another, each is a product of a fine training program with one of the money center banks, in which they rotated through positions in all of the banking functions.

Your extensive experience in the industry leads you to the inevitable conclusion that the only hope is a two-pronged approach involving the reduction of all but

the most critical expenses and the sale of assets to other banks. The task must be accomplished quickly because further deterioration of the quality of the loan portfolio could result in a negative capital position and force regulators to close the bank.

The strategy is clear to you, but many details will need to be worked out. You believe that you know what information will be needed to get the bank on a course for future prosperity. You are fortunate in having three young executives to help you. Although they have had little or no experience in working together, you know that each is dedicated to the survival of the bank. Like you, they know what needs to be done and how to do it.

The suggested path is found in the References section for Chapter 9.

Source: Victor H. Vroom's Time-Driven Model, reproduced from *A Model of Leadership Style*. Copyright 1998. Reprinted by permission of the author.

scenario that Vroom developed to give you another opportunity to apply the model.

The normative model provides a valuable service to practicing managers and leaders. It prompts them to ask questions about contingency variables in decision-making situations. It has been found that for previous versions of the model, managers who follow its procedures are likely to increase their decision-making effectiveness. Furthermore, managers who make decisions consistent with the model (again based on previous versions) are more likely to be perceived as effective.[15]

LEADER-MEMBER EXCHANGE (LMX)
AND CONTINGENCY THEORY

Another perspective on the contingency approach is suggested by the leader-member exchange theory. Leaders who adapt their style to different individuals within the group, or have different quality relationships with individual group members, are essentially practicing contingency leadership. Hundreds of studies have been conducted about LMX theory. One of the many questionnaires used to measure the quality of the relationship between the leader and the group member is presented in Leadership Self-Assessment Quiz 9-2. Here we present several conclusions from LMX research that suggest a contingency approach to leadership.

1. Leaders tend to give members of their in-group more favorable performance ratings than they give to out-group members, even when their objective performance is the same. This finding reflects the idea that the leader might be kinder toward group members he or she likes.

2. Leaders do not always develop entirely different relationships with each group member, but may respond the same way to a few members of the group. For example, the leader might show equal care and trust for three members of an eight-person team.[16]

3. In larger groups, there tends to be more differences with respect to leader-member exchanges. As a result, the leader of a large group is more likely to use a slightly different style with various group members, such as being more authoritarian with several of the group members.

4. A manager is more likely to act as a servant leader toward subordinates with whom he or she has high-quality exchanges.[17] As a consequence, in-group members are likely to perceive that they have a leader who is working on their behalf.

5. Leaders are more likely to empower group members with whom they have a high-quality exchange (or good relationship) because they are more likely to trust those members. Research suggests, however, that better

LEADERSHIP SELF-ASSESSMENT QUIZ 9-2

Quality of Leader-Member Relations

Instructions: Indicate whether you agree or disagree with each of the following statements in reference to a specific present or former supervisor.

STATEMENT	AGREE	DISAGREE
1. I like my supervisor very much as a person.	☐	☐
2. I respect my supervisor's knowledge and competence on the job.	☐	☐
3. My supervisor would defend me to others in the organization if I made a mistake.	☐	☐
4. I am impressed with my supervisor's knowledge of his/her job.	☐	☐
5. My supervisor is the kind of person one would like to have as a friend.	☐	☐
6. My supervisor is a lot of fun to work with.	☐	☐
7. I do not mind working my hardest for my supervisor.	☐	☐
8. I admire my supervisor's professional skills.	☐	☐
9. My supervisor would come to my defense if I were "attacked" by others.	☐	☐
10. I am willing to apply extra efforts, beyond those normally required to meet my supervisor's work goals.	☐	☐
11. My supervisor defends my work actions to a superior, even without complete knowledge of the issue in question.	☐	☐
12. I do my work for my supervisor that goes beyond what is specified in my job description.	☐	☐

Scoring and Interpretation: The more of the above statements you agree with, the higher the quality of your leader-member exchange. Agreeing with 9 or more statements suggests a high-quality leader-member exchange. Agreeing with 3 or fewer suggest a poor-quality leader-member exchange. Agreeing with between 4 and 8 statements suggests an average quality leader-member exchange.

Source: Robert Eisenberger et al., "Leader-Member Exchange and Affective Organizational Commitment: The Contribution of Supervisor's Organizational Embodiment," *Journal of Applied Psychology*, November 2010, p. 1091.

results for the organization will be attained if leaders attempt to have high-quality relationships with more group members and empower them at the same time.[18]

The Leader in Action profile describes a key industrial leader who adapts well to different situations, including getting an organization through a crisis.

LEADER IN ACTION

Alan Mulally, the CEO of Ford Motor Co., has become one of the world's most admired business executives for his accomplishments in recapturing some of the past glory of Ford, as well as U.S. manufacturing. Mulally has played a key role in two different industries. As the president of the commercial airplane business at Boeing in the late 1990s, he revitalized the company including a major thrust into digital technology. He also helped the company survive the aftermath of the terrorist attack of September 11, 2001, which heavily set back the aerospace industry.

Mulally was hired as CEO of Ford in 2006, to help turn around the company, at a time when Ford was on the verge of collapse. One of Mulally's first giant moves was to borrow $23 billion by putting up Ford's assets as collateral. The purpose of the loan was to give the company enough cash to survive until its cash-flow position improved. The huge loan enabled the company to avoid bankruptcy and a federal government bailout. As a result goodwill improved, and consumers were attracted to the brand in increasing numbers. A few years later, Mulally bought back $10 billion of the debt at a large discount. By 2010 it appeared that Ford was once again a stable, profitable company.

As part of the revitalization of Ford, Mulally had to call for some drastic action. He laid off about one-half the company workforce, and then reduced the compensation—both pay and benefits—for the survivors. Another key part of the turnaround plan was to create global heads of manufacturing, marketing, and product development, thereby contributing to a consolidation labeled "One Ford." Related to creating One Ford was the sale of luxury brands that did not carry the Ford nameplate—Land Rover, Jaguar, and Volvo. The Ford Mercury was discontinued as part of the simplification of the company. On the growth side, Mulally spearheaded the move to restore the Ford Taurus model.

Mulally's problem-solving approach includes analyzing massive amounts of data, then reducing the data to a simplified and clear plan. He presents the entire Ford strategy, including its products and operating plan, on about one-and-one half pages. The plan includes four goals or expected behaviors: (1) Foster functional and technical excellence, (2) own working together, (3) role model Ford values, and (4) deliver results. Each goal is explained in more detail; for example, a sub-goal under (1) is "know and have a passion for our business and our customers."

As part of Mulally's disciplined thinking, he does not allow distractions in meetings such as side conversations or the use of smart phones. In reference to behavior in a meeting, Mulally says, "If somebody starts to talk or they don't respect each other, the meeting stops."

Despite his good-natured demeanor, Mulally can be confrontational, particularly for the purpose of stimulating the thinking of others. During the formulation of turnaround plans, Mulally pored over the Ford profit-and-loss statement, and said to his team, "You know, you guys lost $14 billion last year. Is there anything not going well here?"

QUESTIONS

1. What evidence do you observe that Alan Mulally can adapt to the situation?
2. What crisis did Mulally lead Ford through?
3. To what extent does Mulally make use of his cognitive skills as a leader?

Source: The story about Alan Mulally is created from various facts in Alex Taylor III, "2010's Top People in Business," *Fortune*, December 6, 2010, p. 136; Keith Naughton, "The Happiest Man in Detroit," *Bloomberg Business Week*, February 7–February 13, 2011, pp. 66–71; David Kiley, "Ford's Savior?" *Business Week*, March 16, 2009, pp. 030–034; Alex Taylor III, "Fixing Up Ford," *Fortune*, pp. 44–51; Steve Ballmer," Alan Mulally," *Time*, May 11, 2009, p. 74; Bill Saporito, "How to Make Cars and Make Money Too," *Time*, August 8, 2010, pp. 36–39.

LEADERSHIP DURING A CRISIS

Among the potential crises facing organizations are a drastic revenue decline; pending bankruptcy; homicide in the workplace; scandalous or criminal behavior by executives; natural disasters, such as hurricanes, floods, or earthquakes; nuclear radiation spills; and bombings and other terrorist attacks. Leading during a crisis can be regarded as contingency leadership because the situation demands that the leader emphasize certain behaviors, attitudes, and traits. **Crisis leadership** is the process of leading group members through a sudden and largely unanticipated, intensely negative, and emotionally draining circumstance. Here we describe eight leadership attributes and behaviors associated with successfully leading an organization or organizational unit through a crisis.

Be Decisive   The best-accepted principle of crisis leadership is that the leader should take decisive action to remedy the situation. The graver the crisis, the less time the leader has to consult a wide array of people. After the plan is formulated, it should be widely communicated to help reassure group members that something concrete is being done about the predicament. After their physical facilities were destroyed in the terrorist attacks on the World Trade Center on September 11, 2001, several leaders announced the next day that their firms would move to nearby backup locations. Communicating plans helps reduce uncertainty about what is happening to the firm and the people in it. A leader who takes highly visible action to deal with a crisis is likely to be viewed as competent.[19]

A corollary of being decisive during a crisis is not to be indecisive or to hide from the crisis in its midst. The first phase of crisis leadership is to stabilize the emergency situation and buy time.[20] Suppose, for example, that five key managers leave the company at the same time to join a competitor, and only one in-house replacement is available. To deal with the emergency, the CEO might hire four managers from an employment agency that specializes in providing temporary managers and professionals. The next step would be to prepare other company personnel to replace managers who quit in the near future.

Being decisive in response to a crisis also includes communicating widely the plans for resolving the problems that created the crisis, assuming that the organization had some responsibility for the crisis. In 2010, the McNeil Consumer HealthCare Unit of Johnson & Johnson had a series of recalls of over-the-counter medicines, a dreadful crisis for a pharmaceutical company. Chief executive William Weldon responded by sketching out for employees his plans for fixing the manufacturing problems that created the necessity for the recalls and prompted a criminal investigation of the company.[21] Announcing these plans appeared to give many employees hope for better times ahead.

Another component of decisiveness is to avoid the fear of failure that can prevent taking the necessary action to exit the crisis. Chris Warner and Don Schmincke, authors of *High Altitude Leadership*, advise leaders that fear is the ultimate strategy killer. "It stops staff from making great decisions, stops change agents from disrupting the status quo, and stops leaders from leading."[22] The decision of Alan Mullaly at Ford to bring back the defunct Taurus model is a good example of avoiding the fear of failure. Ford officials had discontinued the Taurus because of declining sales, but Mullaly thought the former popularity of the model warranted bringing it back to the public.

Lead with Compassion   Displaying compassion with the concerns, anxieties, and frustrations of group members is a key interpersonal skill for crisis leadership. The type of compassionate leadership that brings about organizational healing involves taking some form of public action that eases pain and inspires others to act as well. Compassionate leadership encompasses two related sets of actions. The first is to create an environment in which affected workers can freely discuss how they feel, such as a group meeting to talk about the crisis or disaster. The second is to create an environment in which the workers who experience or witness pain can find a method to alleviate their own suffering and that of others. The leader might establish a special fund to help the families of workers who were victims of the disaster or give workers the opportunity to receive grief counseling.

Another way to display compassion is for the leader to make personal sacrifices before asking others to make sacrifices to get through the crisis.[23] During a financial crisis facing an organization, many leaders have voluntarily taken a pay cut before mandating a salary reduction for others. An extreme approach is for the CEO of a troubled company to ask the board for an annual salary of $1.00 until the company is again profitable. (Skeptics will point out that executives who take the $1.00 annual salary usually receive generous stock options.)

Reestablish the Usual Work Routine   A temporary drop in performance and productivity is almost inevitable for most workers after disaster strikes, such as an earthquake or terrorist attack—even if the organization was not directly affected.

Although it may appear callous and counterintuitive, the leader should emphasize the temporary nature of the performance decline. An effective way of helping people deal with a workplace crisis is to encourage them to return to their regular work. It is important for workers to express their feelings about the crisis before refocusing on work, but once they have, returning to work helps ground them in reality and restores purpose to their lives. Randall Marshall, director of trauma studies for the New York State Office of Mental Health, said after 9/11, "A healthy response to this type of situation is to get back into a routine."[24]

Avoid a Circle-the-Wagons Mentality   One of the worst ways to lead a group through a crisis is to strongly defend yourself against your critics or deny wrongdoing. The same denial approach is referred to as maintaining a bunker mentality or stonewalling the problem. Instead of cooperating with other stakeholders in the crisis, the leader takes a defensive posture. A case in point is how U.S. Interior Secretary Ken Salazar dealt with one aspect of the disastrous BP oil spill in the Gulf of Mexico in 2009. Part of the problem had been attributed to a too-friendly relationship between the Minerals Management Service and oil companies which might have resulted in non-rigorous inspections of oil drilling. Instead of denying that problems existed at the Minerals Management Service, Salazar quickly reorganized the government unit with a new name: Bureau of Ocean Energy Management, Regulation, and Enforcement. Stricter ethical standards were also imposed to show that the new agency would act more independently in inspecting oil-drilling equipment and processes.[25]

Display Optimism   Pessimists abound in every crisis, so an optimistic leader can help energize group members to overcome the bad times. The effective crisis leader draws action plans that give people hope for a better future. Barbara Baker Clark contends that the role of a leader during a crisis is to encourage hopefulness. She states:

> I'm not saying that you have to plaster a stupid grin on your face even if the bottom line is tanking or people are dying in battle. I am saying don't wallow in pessimism. Believe it or not, it matters to your employees that you remain reasonably optimistic. It will reduce anxiety and keep everyone motivated. That's the power of leadership.[26]

Prevent the Crisis through Disaster Planning   The ideal form of crisis leadership is to prevent a crisis through disaster planning. A key part of planning for a physical disaster, for example, is to anticipate where you would go, how you would get in touch with employees, and where you might set up a temporary workplace. Having a list of backup vendors in case they are hit by a physical disaster is also important. Small business owners should be networking with other business owners and agree to assist each other if a crisis strikes. Arranging in advance for support groups, such as grief counselors, is another key element of disaster planning. Even the fact of letting employees know that a disaster plan is in place can be an effective leadership act because it may lower worker anxiety. Also, the leader might communicate that the company has purchased disaster insurance.

The Deepwater Horizon oil-spill disaster was attributed in part to inadequate disaster plans. Former BP executive Tony Hayward said it was probably true that the company didn't do enough planning in advance of the disaster. He said that "There are some capabilities that we could have available to deploy instantly rather than creating as we go." Apparently BP was not prepared for the long-term, round-the-clock process of coping with a deep-sea spill.[27]

Provide Stable Performance   Effective leaders are steady performers, even under heavy workloads and uncertain conditions. Remaining steady under crisis conditions contributes to effectiveness because it helps team members cope with the situation. When the leader remains calm, group members are reassured that things will work out. Stability also helps the managerial leader appear professional and cool under pressure. A representative example is James Kennedy, the CEO of investment firm T. Rowe Price, who kept up the confidence of employees and investors during the financial disasters of 2008, including the collapse of Lehman Brothers. Kennedy maintained a calm demeanor including making time for personal life. In addition, Kennedy spearheaded preemptive cost cutting which helped T. Rowe Price weather the financial storm.[28]

Be a Transformational Leader   During times of large and enduring crisis, transformational leadership may be the intervention of choice. The transformational leader can often lead the organization out of its misery. Transformational leadership is likely to benefit the troubled organization both in dealing with the immediate crisis and in performing better in the long run. David Novak, the CEO of Yum Brands (which includes KFC, Taco Bell, Pizza Hut, and Long John Silver's), has seen his share of crisis, including vermin infestation in a restaurant that was broadcast on television and YouTube. He says that honesty, consistency, and continuity of communication is the key to managing through these issues and that the transformation may take six to nine months.[29]

Another way a transformational leader helps a company or work unit cope with crisis is to establish a climate of trust long before a crisis strikes.[30] If workers and other shareholders trust the leader, they will take more seriously his or her directives during the crisis. Leadership at both Walmart and McDonald's did a notable job of holding their work force together after Hurricane Katrina. Executives and store managers alike scrambled to get in touch with employees to assure them that they would all have their jobs back as soon as operations were up and running. In general, workers in the Gulf Coast area had trusted leadership at the two companies.

EVIDENCE-BASED LEADERSHIP FOR THE CONTINGENCY AND SITUATIONAL APPROACH

A leading-edge way for a person to practice contingency leadership would be to look for research-based evidence about the best way to deal with a given situation. Before taking action, the leader would ask, "What does the research literature tell me is most likely to work in this situation?" **Evidence-based leadership or management** is an approach whereby managers translate principles based on best evidence into organizational practices.[31] Quite often the best evidence is empirical (based on experience) and recent. Yet at times old principles can still be useful. For example, it has been known for at least a century that when a manager has too many subordinates, coordinating the work of subordinates is difficult. The alternative to evidence-based leadership is to rely heavily on common sense and adopting practices used by other companies, whether or not they fit a particular situation. Many of the principles and suggestions presented throughout this text would help a manager practice evidence-based leadership.

An example of using evidence-based leadership follows: Research indicates that empowerment is more likely to succeed with group members whose cultural values favor a manager or leader sharing power. In contrast, empowerment is less likely to succeed when the group members expect the leader to retain most of the power. (See Chapter 2 for the evidence.) In this example, a *principle* (empowerment works best when cultural values are compatible) is translated into *practice* (using empowerment to motivate and satisfy workers when the cultural values of the workers are compatible with empowerment).

An example of using evidence-based leadership stemming from the experience of managers is to regularly express thanks for a job well done.[32] The thank-you can be expressed orally or in writing and should focus on something specific the person has accomplished such as, "Your tracking down of potential candidates for our opening by using the social media produced four good prospects. Thanks so much for lending your expertise."

Evidence-based leadership and management is not yet widely practiced, but taking the study of leadership and management seriously will move managers and organizations toward basing their practices and decisions on valid evidence. The result is likely to be more precise contingency leadership.

SUMMARY

Theories of contingency and situational leadership build on the study of leadership style by adding more specific guidelines about which style to use under which circumstances. Leaders are most effective when they make their behavior contingent on situational forces, including group member characteristics. Organizational effectiveness is affected by situational factors not under the leader's control. Situations shape how leaders behave, and they also influence the consequences of leader behavior.

Fiedler's contingency theory states that the best style of leadership is determined by the leader's work situation. Style, in Fiedler's theory, is measured by the least preferred coworker (LPC) scale. If you have a reasonably positive attitude toward your least preferred coworker, you are relationship motivated. You are task motivated if your attitude is negative. Situational control, or favorability, is measured by a combination of the quality of leader-member relations, the degree of task structure, and the leader's position power.

The key proposition of Fiedler's theory is that in situations of high control or low control, leaders with a task-motivated style are more effective. In a situation of moderate control, a relationship-motivated style works better. Leaders can improve situational control by modifying leader-member relations, task structure, and position power.

The path-goal theory of leadership effectiveness specifies what the leader must do to achieve high productivity and morale in a given situation. The major proposition of the theory is that the manager should choose a leadership style that takes into account the characteristics of the group members and the demands of the task. Initiating structure by the leader works best when the group faces an ambiguous task. Effective leaders clarify the paths to attaining goals, help group members progress along these paths, and remove barriers to goal attainment. Leaders must choose a style that best fits the two sets of contingency factors—the characteristics of the subordinates and the tasks. The four styles in path-goal theory are directive, supportive, participative, and achievement oriented.

Situational Leadership II (SLII), developed by Blanchard, explains how to match leadership style to the capabilities of group members on a given task. The combination of the subordinate's commitment and competence determines the four developmental levels: enthusiastic beginner, disillusioned learner, capable but cautious performer, and self-reliant achiever. The model classifies leadership style according to the relative amounts of supporting and directing the leader engages in. The four styles are different combinations of task and relationship behavior, both rated as high versus low: directing, coaching, supporting, and delegating. The most appropriate leadership style corresponds to the subordinate developmental levels. For example, enthusiastic beginners require a directing leader.

The normative decision model explains that leadership is a decision-making process. A leader examines certain contingency factors in the situation to determine which decision-making style will be the most effective in either a time-driven or developmental situation. The model defines five decision-making styles: two individual styles and three group styles. By answering a series of seven diagnostic questions in a matrix, the manager follows the path to a recommended decision style.

Leader-member exchange theory provides some insights into contingency leadership. LMX influences such factors as the favorability of performance ratings, which group member receives servant leadership, and extent of empowerment.

Leading others through a crisis can be considered a form of contingency leadership because the leader adapts his or her style to the situation. In a crisis, leaders should (a) be decisive, (b) lead with compassion, (c) reestablish the usual work routine, (d) avoid a circle-the-wagons mentality, (e) display optimism, (f) prevent the crisis through disaster planning, (g) provide stable performance, and (h) be a transformational leader.

A leading-edge way for a person to practice contingency leadership would be to look for research-based evidence about the best way to deal with a given situation. This approach means using evidence-based leadership or management.

KEY TERMS

contingency approach to leadership	Situational Leadership II (SLII)	crisis leadership
path-goal theory	normative decision model	evidence-based leadership or management

✔ GUIDELINES FOR ACTION AND SKILL DEVELOPMENT

1. A major contingency factor for a team or group leader is the talent and motivation of the individual being led. Although talented and well-motivated workers may not require close monitoring of their efforts, they still require encouragement and recognition to sustain high performance. Otherwise, the leader has very little impact on their performance or their intention to stay a member of the team or group.

2. Consider four factors as a shortcut to deciding whether a decision is best made by a group, thereby practicing participative leadership. The stronger the need for *buy-in* or *commitment,* the more important group participation is. When a *creative solution* is important, group input is valuable because varied viewpoints ordinarily enhance creativity. When *time is scarce,* it is better for the leader to make the decision. When a decision is needed that *reflects the bigger picture,* the leader is often in the best position to make it.

3. When practicing the leader-member exchange theory of leadership by forming unique relationships with members of the group, it is important to minimize the potential unintended negative consequences of this type of leadership. For morale purposes, it is important to avoid establishing favorites or pets in the group, and having only superficial, mechanical relationships with other group members.

4. A subtle way of practicing contingency leadership is to adapt to times that may have changed in terms of the demands of your leadership position.[32] You have to fine-tune your leadership approach to meet the new circumstances. Assume that hospital administrator Maggie has held her position for ten years. According to her perception of her role, the focus of her leadership would be to inspire her staff toward doing what is best for patient care. Yet her role has now changed. Focusing on what is good for patients still receives high priority, yet

Maggie has to emotionally accept the reality that finding ways to inspire her group to reduce the cost of operating the hospital has become a key part of her leadership and management role.

Discussion Questions and Activities

1. Visualize yourself preparing a job résumé with the intent of finding a leadership position in business. Explain whether or not you would include on your résumé the fact that you practice contingency leadership.
2. Describe how it might be possible for a manager to be charismatic yet also practice contingency leadership.
3. Identify a personality trait you think would help a manager function as a contingency leader. Also identify a trait you think might detract from a manager's ability to function as a contingency leader.
4. How might a leader modify the clothing he or she wore to different work situations to help practice contingency leadership?
5. How would a manager know which variables in a given situation should influence which approach to leadership he or she should take?
6. Which of the four path-goal styles do you think would be the best for managing a professional football or professional soccer team? Justify your answer.
7. To what extent do you think that battlefield experience would help a person become an effective crisis leader in a business situation?
8. Why might a transformational leader be helpful in a crisis?
9. To what extent do you think most business leaders will ever use experience-based leadership or management?
10. In what way do effective teachers practice contingency leadership?

LEADERSHIP CASE PROBLEM A

Supervisory Styles at the Red Rascal

Jessica Perez is the manager of a thriving Red Rascal Restaurant, a chain of several hundred moderately priced restaurants throughout the country. Jessica recently returned from a regional conference in which she was informed about a new program of recruiting several developmentally disabled workers to work at each restaurant. The restaurants would work closely with local institutions that provided vocational training for individuals who are intellectually challenged. In many of the communities these institutions coordinate their effort with both psychology and special education departments at local colleges.

The developmentally disabled workers would be hired into basic positions that fit their capabilities, such as salad chefs, bakers, dishwashing-machine attendants, and custodial workers. Restaurant (store) managers would receive training into how to optimize the capabilities of developmentally disabled workers, as well as how to motivate or discipline the workers as needed.

Three months after the program was launched, Jessica's branch had hired three developmentally disabled young adults, all assigned jobs within the kitchen. Jessica spent a little time coaching her kitchen supervisors about supervising developmentally disabled workers. She emphasized the importance of providing clear, uncomplicated directions, and not overwhelming these workers by changing their assignments frequently. As instructed at regional headquarters, Jessica also explained the need to provide positive feedback and encouragement to the intellectually challenged recruits.

The program of hiring a few developmentally disabled kitchen workers appeared to be going generally well at the Red Rascal. No particular problems with the food prepared by the new workers were found, food preparation was not delayed, and their attendance was satisfactory. Yet as Jessica listened to several of the restaurant associates, the wait staff and kitchen staff included, she heard some grumbling. Head chef Tammy expressed her concerns in these terms: "I'm not exactly sure why this is happening, but these days my supervisor is treating me like I'm 10 years old. She's so condescending, and she tells me what she wants done in tiny details. I asked Mindy (the supervisor) to taste a new salad dressing I prepared. She told me, 'Tammy, I'm so proud of you. You did a great job.' I mean, she's acting like I'm stupid or something."

Kurt, the host, made a similar comment about Jessica. He said, "All of a sudden you're treating me as if I'm a little slow. You made such a fuss just because my shoes were shined and my shirt was

wrinkle free. Are you forgetting that I'm not developmentally challenged?"

Mindy began to think that maybe there were some supervisory style problems at the Red Rascal.

Questions

1. What does the restaurant scenario presented above have to do with contingency leadership?
2. In what ways might Jessica and the supervisors modify their leadership styles to adapt to the differences in intellectual levels of the Red Rascal staff?
3. What's the problem with the kitchen staff and wait staff at the Red Rascal? Shouldn't all workers receive careful instructions, feedback, and encouragement?

ASSOCIATED ROLE PLAY

Getting Started with the New Salad Chef

One student plays the role of a supervisor whose responsibility it is to show a developmentally challenged recruit how to prepare a salad in a giant bowl, that will then be divided into single-portion salads as needed.

Another student plays the role of the 20-year-old recruit who has never previously prepared food. Observers should be particularly cognizant if the supervisor is using an effective leadership style.

LEADERSHIP CASE PROBLEM B

How Do I Decide about Tweets?

Brian Casey is the CEO of Builder Electro, a medium size company that manufactures and sells electronic products to the construction industry. Some of Builder Electro's products are sold in home improvement and hardware stores. The most successful product is a quartz heater that builders use when working in an unheated area, such as a garage or house under construction. Another successful product line is battery-operated drills and screwdrivers.

Casey has recently noticed some disturbing mentions of the company and its personnel on social networking sites, particularly Twitter. Some of the postings are favorable in reference to the company,

such as "Had another great day doing my best for Builder Electro." Some of the unfavorable tweets are offensive to the company, and are potentially offensive to its reputation. Two examples: "Frostbite can result from using a Builder Electro space heater," and "Meet the Worst Boss of the Year at Builder Electro." Most of the offensive tweets appear to have been posted by company employees.

Brian Casey is convinced that action needs to be taken to stop the negative postings about Builder Electro. Yet he is also concerned about creating an environment in which dissent and free speech are suppressed. Casey's first thought was to consult with the company's legal counsel and then announce a company policy about Internet postings by employees that are derogatory toward the company. Many companies have such policies so an effective policy could be basically taken off the shelf. Casey thought that the entire issue of negative postings about the company could then be settled in a few days.

Casey then sent an e-mail to Naomi Colbert, the director of human resources, explaining his decision about how to curb negative tweets about Builder Electro. Naomi responded that Brian should wait before making such a big decision. She suggested specifically, "Brian, I think you should hold a series of meetings with all the vice presidents and directors before establishing a policy about these negative posts. We are talking about a complicated issue."

Brian was perplexed. He thought he could establish a policy about negative tweets quite quickly. Now he wondered if he should involve the entire executive team in making the decision.

Questions

1. Advise Brian Casey as to whether he should decide on a policy by himself with respect to employee social media postings that are derogatory toward Builder Electro.
2. Suggest a leadership theory that might help Casey decide whether he should make an individual or a group decision with respect to employee Internet postings.
3. To what extent is Casey attempting to block an employee's right to freedom of speech?

ASSOCIATED ROLE PLAY

Group Decision Making about a Social Media Policy

One student plays the role of Brian, who decides that perhaps he should receive input from his four key managers about developing a company policy about posting negative comments on social media, particularly on Twitter. But Brian thinks that working with the attorney to use an off-the-shelf policy is really the answer to the problem. Four other students play the role of the managers who are being consulted about the social media policy. All are eager to provide valuable input to this decision. Observers will provide feedback about the type of decision-making style that Brian is really using.

 LEADERSHIP SKILL-BUILDING **EXERCISE 9-3**

My Leadership Portfolio

For this chapter entry in your leadership portfolio, visualize two different leadership scenarios that you witnessed directly, read about, or saw on television or in a movie. Think through how you would have used a different leadership approach for each one if you had been the leader. To illustrate, suppose you had passed a construction site for a skyscraper and noticed that the crane operator seemed confident and competent. You might conclude, "In this situation, I would have used a *delegating* style of leadership with the crane operator because she was so self-sufficient. Yet I would still have given her some recognition for a job well done at the end of her shift."

Another scenario might be that you witnessed a bloody fight at a professional hockey match. You might conclude, "In this situation, I would be as directive as possible. I would suspend and fine the players, with no room for negotiation. Decisive action must be taken to quell violence in professional sports."

LEADERSHIP SKILL-BUILDING **EXERCISE 9-4**

Crisis Leadership

Working in a small group, find a crisis that a business or not-for-profit organization is facing these days. Examples would include a pharmaceutical firm needing to recall an over-the-counter medicine that has triggered illnesses in hundreds of consumers, or an investment banking firm in which several key executives have been accused of insider trading. After agreeing on which crisis to tackle, develop a list of suggestions on how the CEO should deal with the situation. Use several ideas from the section about crisis leadership presented in this chapter to help you develop an action plan.

LEADERSHIP VIDEO **CASE** DISCUSSION **QUESTIONS**

To view the videos for this activity, you'll need access to the CourseMate that is available for this text. To get access, visit www.CengageBrain.com.

After watching "Preserve by Recycline," answer the following questions.

1. Do you believe Eric Hudson, founder and president of Recycline, uses the contingency approach to leadership? Explain.
2. How does C.A. Webb, marketing director, use the contingency approach to leadership?
3. How is the external environment of Recycline changing? Explain.

NOTES

1. The first sentence of facts is based on Matthew Dolan, "Crisis Mode Persists For Detroit Schools," *The Wall Street Journal*, February 11, 2011, p. A5. The rest of the information is excerpted and adapted from "Office of the Emergency Financial Manager," http://detroit12.org/azdmin/finance/manager/, p. 17. Accessed March 14, 2011, p. 17.
2. "Surprising and Effective Cure for Today's Biggest Workplace Crisis," *Executive Focus*, September 2004, p. 21.
3. Victor H. Vroom and Arthur G. Jago, "The Role of the Situation in Leadership," *American Psychologist*, January 2007, pp. 6–16.
4. Henry Mintzberg, *Managing* (San Francisco: Berrett-Koehler, 2009), pp. 106–107.
5. Cited in Karen Barrow, "Mindfulness Lets Leaders See More Possibilities," *Democrat and Chronicle* (Rochester, New York), January 18, 2009, p. 2E.
6. For a synthesis of contingency theory by one of its key researchers, see Martin M. Chemers, *An Integrative Theory of Leadership* (Mahwah, N.J.:

Erlbaum, 1997), pp. 28–38. See also Bernard M. Bass with Ruth Bass, *The Bass Handbook of Leadership: Theory, Research, & Managerial Applications*, 4th edition (New York: The Free Press, 2008), pp. 522–527.
7. Vroom and Jago, "The Role of the Situation," p. 20.
8. Robert J. House, "A Path-Goal Theory of Leader Effectiveness," *Administrative Science Quarterly*, September 1971, pp. 321–328; Robert T. Keller, "A Test of the Path-Goal Theory with Need for Clarity as a Moderator in Research and Development Organizations," *Journal of Applied Psychology*, April 1989, pp. 208–212; Robert J. House and Terence R. Mitchell, "Path-Goal Theory of Leadership," *Journal of Contemporary Business*, Autumn 1974, pp. 81–97.
9. Vroom and Jago, "The Role of the Situation," p. 20.
10. Robert House, "Path-Goal Theory of Leadership: Lessons, Legacy, and a Reformulated Theory," *Leadership Quarterly*, no. 3, 1996, p. 348.

11. House and Mitchell, "Path-Goal Theory," p. 84; Bass, *The Bass Handbook of Leadership*, pp. 804–811.

12. Chemers, *An Integrative Theory of Leadership*, p. 48.

13. Kenneth H. Blanchard, David Zigarmi, and Robert Nelson, "Situational Leadership After 25 Years: A Retrospective," *Journal of Leadership Studies*, vol. 1, 1993, pp. 22–26; Kenneth Blanchard and Robert Nelson, "Recognition and Reward," *Executive Excellence*, no. 4, 1997, p. 15; "Building Materials Leader Builds Better Leaders," kenblanchard.com/casestudies/certainteed.pdf, accessed November 26, 2004.

14. Victor H. Vroom, "Leadership and the Decision-Making Process," *Organizational Dynamics*, Spring 2000, pp. 82–93; Vroom, "Educating Managers in Decision Making and Leadership," *Management Decision*, vol. 10, 2003, pp. 968–978.

15. Richard H. G. Field and Robert J. House, "A Test of the Vroom–Yetton Model Using Manager and Subordinate Reports," *Journal of Applied Psychology*, June 1990, pp. 362–366.

16. The first two statements are based on Li Ma and Qing Qu, "Differentiation in Leader-Member Exchange: A Hierarchical Linear Modeling Approach," *Leadership Quarterly*, October 2010, pp. 733–744.

17. The second two statements are based David J. Henderson, Robert C/ Liden, Brian C. Glibkowski, and Anjali Chaudrhy, "LMX Differentiation: A Multilevel Review and Examination of Its Antecedents," *Leadership Quarterly*, August 2009, pp. 517–534.

18. Kenneth J. Harris, Anthony R. Wheeler, and K. Michele Kacmar, "Leader-Member Exchange and Empowerment: Direct and Interactive Effects on Job Satisfaction, Turnover Intentions, and Performance," *Leadership Quarterly*, June 2009, p. 399.

19. Research cited in Gary Yukl, *Leadership in Organizations*, 5th ed. (Upper Saddle River, N.J.: Prentice Hall, 2002), p. 344.

20. Ronald Heifetz, Alexander Grashow, and Marty Linsky, "Leadership in a (Permanent) Crisis," *Harvard Business Review*, July–August 2009, p. 64.

21. Joann S. Lublin and Jonathan D. Rockoff, "J&J Chief Tends Corporate Wounds," *The Wall Street Journal*, August 30, 2010, p. B3.

22. Chris Warner and Don Schmincke, *High Altitude Leadership: What the World's Forbidding Techniques Teach Us About Success* (San Francisco: Jossey-Bass, 2009), p. 6.

23. Observation of Bill George reported in Alan Murray, *The Wall Street Journal Essential Guide to Management* (New York: Harper Business, 2010), p. 18.

24. Suzanne Koudsi, "How to Cope with Tragedy," *Fortune*, October 1, 2001, p. 34.

25. Neil Simon, "Crisis Management: Department of Interior, Department of Labor," *Hispanic Business*, October 2010, p. 43.

26. Barbara Baker Clark, "Leadership During a Crisis," *Executive Leadership*, December 2001, p. 8.

27. Quoted in Ben Casselman and Guy Chazan, "Disaster Plans Lacking at Deep Rigs." *The Wall Street Journal*, May 18, 2010, p. 1A.

28. Douglas MacMillan, "Survivor: CEO Edition," *Bloomberg BusinessWeek*, March 1, 2010, p. 36.

29. Jia Lynn Yang, "A Recipe for Consistency," *Fortune*, October 29, 2007, p. 58.

30. Erika Hayes James and Lynn Perry Wooten, "How to Display Competence in Times of Crisis," *Organizational Dynamics*, vol. 34, no. 2, 2005, p. 146.

31. Demis M. Rousseau, "Presidential Address: Is There Such a Thing as 'Evidence-Based Management'?" *The Academy of Management Review*, April 2006, pp. 256–269; Wayne F. Cascio, "Evidence-Based Management and the Marketplace for Ideas," *Academy of Management Journal*, October 2007, pp. 1009–1012.

32. Quint Studer, "Evidence-Based Leadership," *StuderGroup* (www.studergroup.com), January 14, 2008.

Suggested path for Leadership Skill-Building Exercise 9-2: Applying the Time-Driven Model: H H H L H H L CONSULT GROUP.

manager relies more on the group to make a decision even if the process is time consuming.

Figure 9-5 depicts the matrix for time-driven group problems, a situation in which a decision must be reached rapidly. The situational factors, or problem variables, are listed at the top of the matrix. Specifying these factors makes the

Instructions: The matrix operates like a funnel. You start at the left with a specific decision problem in mind. The column headings denote situational factors which may or may not be present in that problem. You progress by selecting High or Low (H or L) for each relevant situational factor. Proceed down from the funnel, judging only those situational factors for which a judgment is called for, until you reach the recommended process.

PROBLEM STATEMENT

Decision Significance	Importance of Commitment	Leader Expertise	Likelihood of Commitment	Group Support	Group Expertise	Team Competence	
H	H	H	H	–	–	–	Decide
H	H	H	L	H	H	H	Delegate
H	H	H	L	H	H	L	Consult (Group)
H	H	H	L	H	L	–	Consult (Group)
H	H	H	L	L	–	–	Consult (Group)
H	H	L	H	H	H	H	Facilitate
H	H	L	H	H	H	L	Consult (Individually)
H	H	L	H	H	L	–	Consult (Individually)
H	H	L	H	L	–	–	Consult (Individually)
H	H	L	L	H	H	H	Facilitate
H	H	L	L	H	H	L	Consult (Group)
H	H	L	L	H	L	–	Consult (Group)
H	H	L	L	L	–	–	Consult (Group)
H	L	H	–	–	–	–	Decide
H	L	L	–	H	H	H	Facilitate
H	L	L	–	H	H	L	Consult (Individually)
H	L	L	–	H	L	–	Consult (Individually)
H	L	L	–	L	–	–	Consult (Individually)
L	H	–	H	–	–	–	Decide
L	H	–	L	–	–	H	Delegate
L	H	–	L	–	–	L	Facilitate
L	L	–	–	–	–	–	Decide

FIGURE 9-5 The Time-Driven Model for Choosing a Decision-Making Style.

Source: Victor H. Vroom's Time-Driven Model, reproduced from *A Model of Leadership Style*. Copyright 1998. Reprinted by permission of the author.

How Leaders Exert Influence

n September 2010, Elizabeth Warren, a Harvard Law professor, was appointed as special adviser for the Consumer Financial Protection Bureau, so she could help set it up. Warren had originally proposed the idea of the agency. She thought it could be a defense of what she describes as the "tricks and traps" that banks slide into credit-card agreements and home mortgages.

In the early part of Warren's career, she became a consumer activist, including giving financial advice to young families during an appearance on the TV show *Dr. Phil.* With her daughter, she wrote a general-audience book, entitled *The Two-Income Trap.* When she was part of a panel overlooking the Troubled Asset Relief Program (TARP), Warren would hound the U. S. Treasury Department, demanding more information. At the same time, she wanted better investment returns from the banks that were bailed out and increased efforts to help borrowers.

Warren emphasized in an address to the U.S. Chamber of Commerce that she and the members of that group have one important belief in common: She said, "I know this won't come as a shock to you but the Chamber and I have not always seen eye to eye on issues. But I do not consider myself in hostile territory right now because I believe we share a point of principle: Competitive markets are good for consumers and business. The important question is how to ensure that markets are competitive."

Warren also said: "A cop on the beat looking out for consumers does not reduce the freedom or effectiveness of the markets; rather, it permits honest competition to flourish. If you are one of the guys who don't use steroids when you play ball, then you don't want to compete against those who are juicing. Competition only flourishes when rules are consistently enforced."

Previous to her address, some members of Congress had called the Consumer Protection Bureau superfluous and a burden to business that will trap them in red tape. Warren persisted in her attempts to influence members of Congress and the financial community about the importance of the Bureau. Opposition to her plans was strong from most Republicans, some moderate Democrats, and Wall Street representatives. In July 2011, Warren stepped down from her administration advisor position, and was replaced as de facto acting director by a top aide.[1]

In her leadership role, Elizabeth Warren was working hard to influence a group who was inclined to resist her efforts. She appealed to logic, and she also brought considerable expertise to the table. Without effective influence tactics, a leader is similar to a soccer player who has not learned to kick a soccer ball, or a newscaster who is unable to speak. Leadership, as oft repeated, is an influence process.

To become an effective leader, a person must be aware of the specific tactics leaders use to influence others. Here we discuss a number of specific influence tactics, but other aspects of leadership also concern influence. Being charismatic, as described in Chapter 4, influences many people. Leaders influence others through power and politics, as will be described in Chapter 11. Furthermore, motivating and coaching skills, as described in Chapter 7, involve influencing others toward worthwhile ends.

The terms *influence* and *power* are sometimes used interchangeably, whereas at other times power is said to create influence and vice versa. In this book, we distinguish between power and influence as follows: **Influence** is the ability to affect the behavior of others in a particular direction,[2] whereas **power** is the potential or capacity to influence. Leaders are influential only when they exercise power. A leader, therefore, must acquire power in order to influence others.

Influence tactics have grown in importance because so often a leader or corporate professional has to influence others without having formal authority over them. An example is that a vice president at Google needed to lobby Gmail engineers who did not work for him to modify software for potential corporate customers. He likens his efforts to a Peace Corps mission: all heart but with little power to enforce his will.[3]

Another factor contributing to the importance of influence tactics is that employees often doubt that the leader, particularly a CEO, will be around for long. As a result, employees will wait out the boss rather than comply with unpopular orders. Therefore the most reliable way for managers to be effective is to get employees on their side.[4]

This chapter presents a model of power and influence, a description and explanation of influence tactics (both ethical and less ethical), a description of how leaders influence large-scale change, and a summary of the research about the relative effectiveness and sequencing of influence tactics. We also present a theory about the characteristics group members expect in a leader in order to be influenced by him or her.

A MODEL OF POWER AND INFLUENCE

The model shown in Figure 10-1 illustrates that the end results of a leader's influence (the outcomes) are a function of the tactics he or she uses. The influence tactics are in turn moderated, or affected by, the leader's traits, the leader's behaviors, and the situation.

Looking at the right side of the model, the three possible outcomes are commitment, compliance, and resistance. **Commitment** is the most successful outcome: the target of the influence attempt is enthusiastic about carrying out the request and makes a full effort. Commitment is particularly important for complex, difficult tasks because these require full concentration and effort. If you were influencing a technician to upgrade your operating system software, you would need his or her commitment. **Compliance** means that the influence

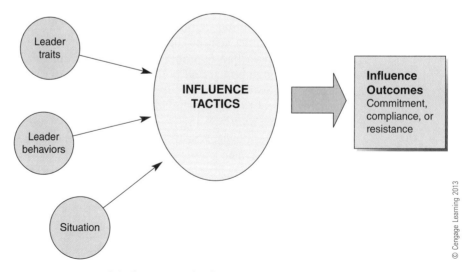

FIGURE 10-1 A Model of Power and Influence.

attempt is partially successful: the target person is apathetic (not overjoyed) about carrying out the request and makes only a modest effort. The influence agent has changed the person's behavior but not his or her attitude. A long-distance truck driver might comply with demands that he sleep certain hours between hauls, but he is not enthusiastic about losing road time. Compliance for routine tasks—such as wearing a hard hat on a construction site—is usually good enough. Resistance is an unsuccessful influence attempt: the target is opposed to carrying out the request and finds ways to either not comply or do a poor job. **Resistance** includes making excuses for why the task cannot be carried out, procrastinating, and outright refusing to do the task.[5]

Going to the left side of the model, the leader's personality traits affect the outcome of influence tactics. An extroverted and warm leader who has charisma can more readily use some influence tactics than a leader who is introverted and cold. For example, he or she can make an inspirational appeal. A highly intelligent leader would be able to influence others because he or she has built a reputation as a subject matter expert. Whichever influence tactics leaders choose, the goal is to get group members on their side.

The leader's behaviors also affect the outcome of influence tactics in a variety of ways, particularly because influence tactics *are* actions or behaviors. For example, setting high standards facilitates making an inspirational appeal. Additionally, leaders who perform well consistently are better able to lead by example because they are good role models.

Finally, the situation partly determines which influence tactic will be effective. The organizational culture or subculture is one such key situational factor. For example, in a high-technology environment, inspirational appeal and emotional display are less likely to be effective than rational persuasion and being a subject matter expert, because high-tech workers are more likely to be impressed by facts than by feeling.

The rest of this chapter identifies and describes influence tactics, including some mention of situational variables. Leader traits and power have been described in previous chapters. Leadership Self-Assessment Quiz 10-1 will give you an opportunity to think about which influence tactics you tend to use.

DESCRIPTION AND EXPLANATION OF INFLUENCE TACTICS

Influence tactics are often viewed from an ethical perspective. Following this perspective, the influence tactics described here are classified into three categories: (a) those that are essentially ethical and honest, (b) those that are essentially neutral with respect to ethics and honesty, and (c) those that are essentially manipulative and dishonest. The categorization presented here is far from absolute. Except for the extremes, most of the tactics could conceivably be placed in any of the three categories, depending on how they are used. For example, one can use the tactic "joking and kidding" in either a well-meaning or mean-spirited way. Joking and kidding could therefore be classified as "essentially ethical," "essentially neutral," or "essentially dishonest and unethical."

LEADERSHIP SELF-ASSESSMENT QUIZ 10-1

Survey of Influence Tactics

Instructions: Indicate how frequently you use the influence tactics listed here: VI = very infrequently or never; I = infrequently; S = sometimes; F = frequently; VF = very frequently. The VI to VF categories correspond to a 1-to-5 scale.

	1 VI	2 I	3 S	4 F	5 VF
1. I lead by demonstrating the right behavior myself.	☐	☐	☐	☐	☐
2. I rely on facts and logic to persuade others.	☐	☐	☐	☐	☐
3. People often listen to me because of my expertise.	☐	☐	☐	☐	☐
4. If I want something done, I stand ready to do a favor in return.	☐	☐	☐	☐	☐
5. I enjoy negotiating a price or an offer.	☐	☐	☐	☐	☐
6. I am assertive (open and forthright in my demands).	☐	☐	☐	☐	☐
7. I joke with or kid other people to make a point.	☐	☐	☐	☐	☐
8. I will sometimes get quite emotional to make a point.	☐	☐	☐	☐	☐
9. I promise to reward the person to get what I want.	☐	☐	☐	☐	☐
10. I attempt to get other people on my side in order to win my point.	☐	☐	☐	☐	☐
11. I cooperate with others in order to influence them.	☐	☐	☐	☐	☐
12. As a leader, I participate heavily in the task of the group.	☐	☐	☐	☐	☐
13. I form an alliance with the other person.	☐	☐	☐	☐	☐
14. I threaten to go over the person's head to the boss.	☐	☐	☐	☐	☐
15. I compliment the other person.	☐	☐	☐	☐	☐
16. I use as much charm as possible to get my way.	☐	☐	☐	☐	☐
17. I will post a positive comment about a work associate on the Internet, such as Facebook, if he or she has done something I particularly like.	☐	☐	☐	☐	☐
18. I will make a comment pointing out that I am not much good at what I want the other person to do.	☐	☐	☐	☐	☐
19. I would bring the person a little gift, such as a beverage he or she likes or an attractive ballpoint pen.	☐	☐	☐	☐	☐
20. I refer to the importance of doing a particular task for the overall good of the organization.	☐	☐	☐	☐	☐

Scoring and Interpretation: The more of these tactics you use frequently or very frequently, the more influential you probably are. Experience is a factor because you could be potentially influential but have not yet had the opportunity to use many of these tactics.

Skill Development: The Survey of Influence Tactics might give you some clues for development. Look for influence tactics that appear to represent a good idea, but where you need skill development. Next, take the opportunity to practice the tactic. For example, take statement 15, "I compliment the other person." Perhaps you neglect to compliment others when you want to influence them. Use the guidelines for flattery given in the next chapter practice to compliment another person when you want to influence him or her.

TABLE 10-1 Essentially Ethical and Honest Influence Tactics

1. Leading by example and respect
2. Using rational persuasion
3. Apprising the target
4. Making a personal appeal
5. Developing a reputation as a subject matter expert
6. Exchanging favors and bargaining
7. Legitimating a request
8. Making an inspirational appeal, being charming, and emotional display
9. Consultation with others
10. Forming coalitions
11. Being a team player
12. Practicing hands-on leadership

© Cengage Learning 2013

Essentially Ethical and Honest Tactics

This section describes essentially ethical and honest tactics and strategies for influencing others, as outlined in Table 10-1. Used with tact, diplomacy, and good intent, these strategies can help you get others to join you in accomplishing a worthwhile objective. Because these influence tactics vary in complexity, they also vary with respect to how much time is required to develop them.

Leading by Example and Respect   A simple but effective way of influencing group members is by **leading by example**, or acting as a positive role model. The ideal approach is to be a "do as I say and do" manager—that is, one whose actions and words are consistent. Actions and words confirm, support, and often clarify each other. Being respected facilitates leading by example because group members are more likely to follow the example of leaders they respect.

Leading by example is often interpreted to mean that the leader works long and hard, and expects others to do the same, with this type of behavior being prevalent among entrepreneurs who hire a staff. A case in point is Steven A. Cohen, who built a highly successful financial services and hedge fund firm, SAC Capital. He spends weekends working at his trading desk.[6]

Using Rational Persuasion   Rational persuasion is an important tactic for influencing people. It involves using logical arguments and factual evidence to convince another person that a proposal or request is workable and likely to achieve the goal. Assertiveness combined with careful research is necessary to make rational persuasion an effective tactic. It is likely to be most effective with people who are intelligent and rational. Chief executive officers typically use rational persuasion to convince their boards that an undertaking, such as product diversification, is mandatory. A major moderating variable in rational persuasion is the credibility of the influence agent. Credibility helps an individual be more persuasive in two ways. First, it makes a person more convincing.

Second, it contributes to a person's perceived power, and the more power one is perceived to have, the more targets will be influenced.[7]

The following two statements are samples of how rational persuasion is measured as perceived by subordinates in research about influence processes.

- Explains clearly why a request or proposed change is necessary to attain a task objective.
- Provides information or evidence to show that a proposed activity or change is likely to be successful.[8]

Leaders who emphasize the rational decision-making model favor rational persuasion. For example, a leader favoring this model might say, "Don't tell me what you feel, give me the facts," in response to a subordinate who said, "I have the feeling that morale is down." Leaders at Google heavily emphasize such data-based decision making. A Google professional in a meeting would be rejected if he or she said, "I think there are too many random photos appearing in Google Images." In contrast, he or she would be accepted if the statement were, "I sampled 100 Google Images, and found that eight of them had random images."

Appraising the Target   A strongly effective way of influencing another person is to explain what's in it for him or her if that individual honors your request. **Appraising** means that the influence agent explains how carrying out a request or supporting a proposal will benefit the target personally, including advancing the target's career.[9] An example of appraising would be for the manager to tell a subordinate, "Perhaps two weeks helping out for one month on the company's oil rig in the Arctic Circle may seem like a tough assignment. But you will seem like a hero to top management, and you will make great contacts."

Two appraising behaviors on the part of the leader are as follows:

- Describes benefits you could gain from doing a task or activity (e.g., learn new skills, meet important people, enhance your reputation).
- Explains how the task he/she wants you to do could help your career.

Making a Personal Appeal   A personal appeal in the context of influence theory is the same as it is in everyday life. The agent asks the target to implement a request or support a proposal out of friendship.[10] Another form of personal appeal is to ask for a personal favor before specifying the nature of the favor, as in "How would you like to do something important for me?" Asking for a favor without specifying its nature would likely be interpreted as unprofessional in a work environment. Two behaviors reflecting a personal appeal by a leader are as follows:

- Appeals to your friendship when asking you to do something.
- Asks for your help as a personal favor.

Developing a Reputation as a Subject Matter Expert   Becoming a subject matter expert (SME) on a topic of importance to the organization is an effective strategy for gaining influence. Being an SME can be considered a subset of rational persuasion. Managers who possess expert knowledge in a relevant field and who continually build on that knowledge can get others to help them get work accomplished. Many of the leaders described throughout this text use expert knowledge to influence others. The leaders of Internet and social media companies such as Google and Foursquare are usually subject-matter experts.

Small-business owners, in particular, rely on being subject matter experts because they founded the business on the basis of their product or technical knowledge. (Also, the major high-tech companies usually began small.) For example, the leader of a software company is usually an expert in software development.

Exchanging Favors and Bargaining   Offering to exchange favors if another person will help you achieve a work goal is another standard influence tactic. By making an exchange, you strike a bargain with the other party. The exchange often translates into being willing to reciprocate at a later date. It might also be promising a share of the benefits if the other person helps you accomplish a task. For example, you might promise to place a person's name on a report to top management if that person will help you analyze the data and prepare the tables.

A recommended approach to asking for a favor is to give the other person as much time as feasible to accomplish the task, such as by saying, "Could you find ten minutes between now and the end of the month to help me?" Not pressing for immediate assistance will tend to lower resistance to the request. Giving a menu of options for different levels of assistance also helps lower resistance. For example, you might ask another manager if you can borrow a technician for a one-month assignment; then, as a second option, you might ask if the technician could work ten hours per week on the project.[11] To ensure that the request is perceived as an exchange, you might explain what reciprocity you have in mind: that you will mention your coworker's helpfulness to his or her manager.

Two behavior specifics for exchanging favors and bargaining are as follows:

- Offers to do a specific task for you in return for your help and support.
- Offers to do something for you in the future for your help now.

Legitimating a Request   To legitimate is to verify that an influence attempt is within your scope of authority. Another aspect of legitimating is showing that your request is consistent with the organizational policies, practices, and expectations of professional people. Making legitimate requests is an effective influence tactic because most workers are willing to comply with regulations. A team leader can thus exert influence with a statement such as this one: "Top management wants a 25 percent reduction in customer complaints by next year. I'm therefore urging everybody to patch up any customer problems he or she can find."

Legitimating sometimes takes the form of subtle organizational politics. A worker might push for the acceptance of his or her initiative because it conforms to the philosophy or strategy of higher management. At Wal-Mart, for example, it is well known that Chairman Mike Duke is green in the sense of wanting to preserve the external environment. A store manager might then encourage workers to put all plastic bottles in recycling bins because "It's something Mike would want us to do."

Two leadership behaviors that reflect legitimating are as follows:

* Says that his/her request is consistent with official rules and policies.
* Verifies that a request is legitimate by referring to a document such as a work order, policy manual, charter, bylaws, or formal contract.

Making an Inspirational Appeal, Being Charming, and Emotional Display A leader is supposed to inspire others, so it follows that making an inspirational appeal is an important influence tactic. As Jeffrey Pfeffer notes, "Executives and others seeking to exercise influence in organizations often develop skill in displaying, or not displaying, their feelings in a strategic fashion."[12] An inspirational appeal usually involves displaying emotion and appealing to group members' emotions. A moderating variable in the effectiveness of an inspirational appeal or emotional display is the influence agent's **personal magnetism**, or the quality of being captivating, charming, and charismatic. Possessing personal magnetism makes it easier for the leader to inspire people.

A useful component of inspirational appeal for leaders is to provide meaning to the work, showing that it has significance to the entire organization or the outside world. Most people like to be involved with projects that matter, and sometimes the leader might have to explain why the work matters.[13] For example, the leader of a company that specializes in subprime mortgages might have to explain, "Without our type of work, loads of people with modest incomes would not be able to become homeowners."

Powerful people sometimes combine personal magnetism, including charm, with having tougher qualities. Stephen A. Schwarzman is the CEO of the giant investment and advisory firm, The Blackstone Group. A business reporter noted, "With personal riches estimated at more than $3 billion and undisputed control over Wall Street's hottest firm, Schwarzman can afford to be soft-spoken, even charming, despite his reputation as one of the Street's most aggressive, demanding bosses."[14]

Two recorded behaviors of leaders who make an inspirational appeal are as follows:

* Says a proposed activity or change is an opportunity to do something really exciting and worthwhile.
* Makes an inspiring speech or presentation to arouse enthusiasm for a proposed activity or change.

Consultation with Others Consultation with others before making a decision is both a leadership style and an influence technique. The influence target becomes more motivated to follow the agent's request because the target is involved in the decision-making process. Consultation is most effective as an influence tactic when the objectives of the person being influenced are consistent with those of the leader.[15] An example of such goal congruity took place in a major corporation. The company had decided to shrink its pool of suppliers to form closer partnerships with a smaller number of high-quality vendors. As a way of influencing others to follow this direction, a manufacturing vice president told his staff, "Our strategy is to reduce dealing with so many suppliers to improve quality and reduce costs. Let me know how we should implement this strategy." The vice president's influence attempt met with excellent reception, partially because the staff members also wanted a more streamlined set of vendor relationships. Two specific leadership behaviors reflecting consultation are as follows:

- Asks you to suggest things you could do to help him or her achieve a task objective or resolve a problem.
- Invites you to suggest ways to improve a preliminary plan or proposal that he or she wants you to support or help implement.

Forming Coalitions   At times, it is difficult to influence an individual or group by acting alone. A leader will then have to form coalitions, or alliances, with others to create the necessary clout. A **coalition** is a specific arrangement of parties working together to combine their power. Coalition formation works as an influence tactic because, to quote an old adage, "there is power in numbers." Coalitions in business are a numbers game—the more people you can get on your side, the better. However, the more powerful leaders are, the less they need to create a coalition.

Having a network of powerful people facilitates forming a coalition. If you need something done, you can get these other influential people to agree that it is a good idea. An example of getting something done might be getting permission to erect an office building close to a park.

One of the best connected and therefore one of the most powerful people in business is Richard D. Parsons, now the chair of Citigroup. His A-list of contacts include Presidents Barack Obama and George W. Bush; Timothy Geithner, U.S. Treasury Secretary; Jeff Bewkes, Time Warner CEO; Lynn de Rothschild, CEO of E. L. Rothschild; and Michael Bloomberg, New York City mayor and owner of several business information services.

Being well connected to powerful people has helped Parsons become a specialist in fixing companies in trouble. The reverse is also true: Being a specialist in fixing companies has helped him become connected to powerful people. The three companies Parsons has helped survive are Dime Savings Bank, Time Warner, and the Citigroup. Parsons is regarded as an old-fashion fixer who works the system with his interpersonal skills and political connections. For example, in helping rescue the Citigroup, Parsons spent a lot of time with bank regulators and the policymakers in Washington.[16] (Working with Washington policymakers is an example of how Parsons' network facilitated a coalition between his organization and an outside force.)

Two specific leadership behaviors that reflect coalition formation are as follows:

- Mentions the names of other people who endorse a proposal when asking you to support it.
- Brings someone along for support when meeting with you to make a request or proposal.

Being a Team Player   Influencing others by being a good team player is an important strategy for getting work accomplished. A leader might be a team player by doing such things as pitching in during peak workloads. An example would be an information technology team leader working through the night with team members to combat a virus attack on the company's computer network.

Being a team player is a more effective influence tactic in an organizational culture that emphasizes collaboration than one in which being tough-minded and decisive is more in vogue. A study of CEO leadership profiles among buy-out firms found that teamwork was less associated with success than traits such as persistence and efficiency. Leaders in buyout firms are strongly financially oriented and are much more concerned with making deals than building relationships.[17]

Practicing Hands-On Leadership A **hands-on leader** is one who gets directly involved in the details and processes of operations. Such a leader has expertise, is task oriented, and leads by example. By getting directly involved in the group's work activities, the leader influences subordinates to hold certain beliefs and to follow certain procedures and processes. For example, managers who get directly involved in fixing customer problems demonstrate to other workers how they think such problems should be resolved.

Hands-on leadership is usually expected at levels below the executive suite, yet many high-level executives are also hands-on leaders. A strong example is Sergio Marchionne, the Chrysler and Fiat CEO described in Chapter 8, who intervenes in such matters as a leaking car door handle. The downside of being a hands-on leader is that if you do it to excess, you become a micromanager.

Essentially Neutral Influence Tactics

The four influence tactics described in this section and listed in Table 10-2 might best be regarded as neutral with respect to ethics and honesty. If implemented with good intent, they tend to be positive, but if implemented with the intent of duping another person, they tend to be negative.

Ingratiation When ingratiation takes the form of well-deserved flattery or compliments, it is a positive tactic. Yet, getting somebody else to like you can be considered a mildly manipulative influence tactic if you do not like the other person.

Ingratiation is often directed upward, in the sense of a subordinate attempting to get the superior to like him or her, as in organizational politics. Ingratiation

TABLE 10-2 Essentially Neutral Influence Tactics

1. Ingratiation
2. Joking and kidding
3. Upward appeal
4. Co-opting antagonists

also works in a downward direction, when leaders attempt to get their subordinates to like them. Typical ingratiating techniques directed toward subordinates include luncheon invitations, compliments, giving a plum work assignment, and feeding a subordinate's hobby, such as contributing a rare stamp to an employee's collection.

Leaders who ordinarily are quite the opposite of ingratiating will sometimes go out of their way to be humble and agreeable to fit an important purpose. A case in point is Bill Gates, who is often sarcastic and cutting. At one time when Gates was with Microsoft Corp., the company was being sued by the U.S. Department of Justice for possible monopolistic practices. Gates went on a goodwill tour, an events-packed trip around San Francisco and Silicon Valley. During his meetings with the public, Gates was modest and at times self-deprecating, even praising the competition. He shook hands, signed autographs, and smiled frequently. Gates was so convincing that a schoolgirl said, "You can tell he's not in it for the money. He wants to make software better."[18] (Later on in life, Gates and his wife became major philanthropists, helping poor children throughout the world, so maybe the schoolgirl was insightful!)

Ingratiating tactics identified in a study about influence tactics included the following:

- Says you have the special skills or knowledge needed to carry out a request.
- Praises your skill or knowledge when asking you to do something.

Leadership Self-Assessment Quiz 10-2 provides you an opportunity to measure your own ingratiating tendencies and to think through further what ingratiating yourself to your boss means in practice. Remember that being liked helps you get promoted, receive more compensation, and avoid being downsized, yet you should avoid being dishonest.

Joking and Kidding   Good-natured kidding is especially effective when a straightforward statement might be interpreted as harsh criticism. Joking or kidding can thus get the message across and lower the risk that the influence target will be angry with the influence agent. Joking and kidding might be interpreted either as dishonest or as extraordinarily tactful because the criticizer softens the full blow of the criticism. A small-business owner successfully used joking and kidding to help the receptionist wear clothing more appropriate for the position. As the owner entered the office, he noticed that the receptionist was wearing a tank top and very large hoop earrings. The owner said, "Melissa, you look great, but I think you have your dates confused. You are dressed for the company picnic, and it takes place tomorrow." Melissa smiled, and then dressed more professionally in the future.

Upward Appeal   In **upward appeal**, the leader exerts influence on a team member by getting a person with more formal authority to do the influencing. Some managers and researchers regard upward appeal as an ethical and standard practice, yet it does contain an element of manipulation and heavy-handedness. An example: "I sent the guy to my boss when he wouldn't

LEADERSHIP SELF-ASSESSMENT QUIZ 10-2

Measure of Ingratiating Behavior in Organizational Settings (MIBOS)

Instructions: Indicate how frequently you use (or would use) the tactics for pleasing your boss listed here.
N = never do it; S = seldom do it; Oc = occasionally do it; Of = often do it; A = almost always do it.
The N-to-A categories correspond to a 1-to-5 scale.

	1 N	2 S	3 OC	4 OF	5 A
1. Impress upon your supervisor that only he or she can help you in a given situation mainly to make him or her feel good.	☐	☐	☐	☐	☐
2. Show your supervisor that you share enthusiasm about his or her new idea even when you may not actually like it.	☐	☐	☐	☐	☐
3. Try to let your supervisor know that you have a reputation for being liked.	☐	☐	☐	☐	☐
4. Try to make sure that your supervisor is aware of your success.	☐	☐	☐	☐	☐
5. Highlight the achievements made under your supervisor's leadership in a meeting he or she does not attend.	☐	☐	☐	☐	☐
6. Give frequent smiles to express enthusiasm and interest about something your supervisor is interested in even if you do not like it.	☐	☐	☐	☐	☐
7. Express work attitudes that are similar to your supervisor's as a way of letting him or her know that the two of you are alike.	☐	☐	☐	☐	☐
8. Tell your supervisor that you can learn a lot from his or her experience.	☐	☐	☐	☐	☐
9. Exaggerate your supervisor's admirable qualities to convey the impression that you think highly of him or her.	☐	☐	☐	☐	☐
10. Disagree on trivial or unimportant issues but agree on those issues in which he or she expects support from you.	☐	☐	☐	☐	☐
11. Try to imitate such work behaviors of your supervisor as working late or occasionally working on weekends.	☐	☐	☐	☐	☐
12. Look for opportunities to let your supervisor know your virtues and strengths.	☐	☐	☐	☐	☐
13. Ask your supervisor for advice in areas in which he or she thinks he or she is smart to let him or her feel that you admire his or her talent.	☐	☐	☐	☐	☐
14. Try to do things for your supervisor that show your selfless generosity.	☐	☐	☐	☐	☐
15. Look out for opportunities to admire your supervisor.	☐	☐	☐	☐	☐
16. Let your supervisor know the attitudes you share with him or her.	☐	☐	☐	☐	☐
17. Compliment your supervisor on his or her achievement, however it may appeal to you personally.	☐	☐	☐	☐	☐
18. Laugh heartily at your supervisor's jokes even when they are really not funny.	☐	☐	☐	☐	☐
19. Go out of your way to run an errand for your supervisor.	☐	☐	☐	☐	☐
20. Offer to help your supervisor by using your personal contacts.	☐	☐	☐	☐	☐
21. Try to persuasively present your own qualities when attempting to convince your supervisor about your abilities.	☐	☐	☐	☐	☐
22. Volunteer to be of help to your supervisor in matters like locating a good apartment, finding a good insurance agent, etc.	☐	☐	☐	☐	☐
23. Spend time listening to your supervisor's personal problems even if you have no interest in them.	☐	☐	☐	☐	☐
24. Volunteer to help your supervisor in his or her work even if it means extra work for you.	☐	☐	☐	☐	☐

Scoring and Interpretation: The more of these ingratiating behaviors you use frequently or almost always, the more ingratiating you are. A score of 40 or less suggests that you do not put much effort into pleasing your manager, and you may need to be a little more ingratiating to achieve a good relationship with your supervisor. A score between 41 and 99 suggests a moderate degree of ingratiating behavior. A score of 100 or more suggests that you are too ingratiating and might be perceived as being too political or insincere. So some honesty is called for, providing you are tactful.

Skill Development: Leaders or future leaders should remember that a moderate amount of ingratiating behavior is the norm in relationships with superiors. Ingratiating yourself to people who report to you can also be a useful influence tactic.

Source: Adapted from Kamalesh Kumar and Michael Beyerlein, "Construction and Validation of an Instrument for Measuring Ingratiatory Behaviors in Organizational Settings," *Journal of Applied Psychology*, October 1991, p. 623. Copyright © by the American Psychological Association. Adapted with permission.

listen to me. That fixed him." More than occasional use of upward appeal weakens the leader's stature in the eyes of group members and superiors, eroding effectiveness. Leaders can apply upward appeal in other ways. A leader might attempt to persuade another staff member that higher management approved his or her request. The target of the influence event is thus supposed to grant acceptance automatically. Or the leader can request higher management's assistance in gaining another person's compliance with the request. The influence target thus feels pressured.[19]

Co-Opting Antagonists   A potentially effective influence tactic, as well as a method of conflict resolution, is to find a clever way to get the other person or group of persons to join forces with you. In this sense, to **co-opt** is to win over opponents by making them part of your team or giving them a stake in the system.[20] Assume that the director of human resources is receiving considerable opposition to some of her initiatives from the chief financial officer. For example, the CFO is opposed to her proposed program of cross-cultural training. To soften the opposition, and perhaps even make him an ally, the director of human resources invites the CFO to become a member of the "human resources advisory board" composed of company executives and distinguished citizens from the community.

Essentially Dishonest and Unethical Tactics

The tactics described in this section are less than forthright and ethical, yet they vary in intensity with respect to dishonesty. Most people would consider the first two strategies presented here as unethical and devious, yet they might regard the second two tactics as still within the bounds of acceptable ethics, even though less than fully candid. The tactics in question are outlined in Table 10-3.

TABLE 10-3 Essentially Dishonest and Unethical Influence Tactics

1. Deliberate Machiavellianism
2. Gentle manipulation of people and situations
3. Undue pressure
4. Debasement

© Cengage Learning 2013

Deliberate Machiavellianism   Niccolò Machiavelli advised that princes must be strong, ruthless, and cynical leaders because people are self-centered and self-serving. People in the workplace who ruthlessly manipulate others have therefore come to be called **Machiavellians**. They tend to initiate actions with others and control the interactions. Machiavellians regularly practice deception, bluffing, and other manipulative tactics.[21] A modern example of deliberate Machiavellianism is the practice of forcing managerial and professional employees into working many extra hours of uncompensated overtime. The employees are told that if they refuse to work extra hours, they will not be considered worthy of promotion or as good team players. Even when positions in other companies are readily available, most career-minded people will stay because they want to preserve a good reputation.

Gentle Manipulation of People and Situations   Some people who attempt to influence others are manipulative, but to a lesser extent than an outright Machiavellian. They gain the compliance of another person by making untrue statements or faking certain behaviors. For example, a leader might imply that if a colleague supports his position in an intergroup conflict, the person might be recommended for promotion. Another manipulative approach is to imply dire consequences to innocent people if the influence target does not comply with demands of the influence agent, such as, "Even if you don't want to put in extra effort for me, think of the people with families who will be laid off if we don't make our targets."

A widely used manipulative approach is the **bandwagon technique**, in which one does something simply because others are doing likewise. An example is a manager who informs the vice president that she wants an enlarged budget for attendance at the latest social networking seminars because "all other companies are doing it."

The bandwagon technique can be combined with peer pressure to influence a group member. If one person is not stepping forward to work well as a team member, the manager will say, "Bob, everyone in the department is committed to developing a team atmosphere, and we'd like you to be a part of it."[22]

Undue Pressure   Effective leaders regularly use motivational techniques such as rewards and mild punishments. Yet when rewards become bribes for compliance and threats of punishment become severe, the target person is subjected to undue pressure or coercion. An example of a bribe by a manager might be, "If you can work eighty hours on this project this week,

I'll recommend you for the highest pay grade." Another approach to pressure is for the manager to scream and swear at the subordinate as a form of intimidation. As one manager under pressure of his own, shouted to a subordinate: "Get some of these _____ receivables paid by the end of the week or find another job."

Two specific behaviors labeled pressure in a research study were as follows:

- Uses threats or warnings when trying to get you to do something.
- Tries to pressure you to carry out a request.

Debasement   A subtle manipulative tactic is **debasement**, demeaning or insulting oneself to control the behavior of another person. Richard Parsons, mentioned above, uses debasement to disarm people. A long-time friend says of Parsons, "Richard's ability to get people to underestimate him is a great skill. If you are obvious, they know where to hit you. Who wins between the bull and matador?"[23] Specific debasing tactics revealed by research include the following: "I lower myself so she'll do it," and "I act humble so she'll do it."[24]

In studying the most severe unethical influence (and political) tactics, it is important to recognize that the use of these influence approaches can bring about human suffering. For example, bullying and intimidating tactics may not be illegal, but they are unethical. Cruelty in the organization creates many problems. As one observer notes, "Cruelty is blatantly unethical and erodes the organizational character through intellectual, emotional, moral, and social vices that reduce the readiness of groups to act ethically."[25] Examples of cruelty include insulting a group member's physical appearance or belittling him or her.

Leadership Skill-Building Exercise 10-1 gives you an opportunity to practice influence tactics in a high-stakes business situation.

Leadership Skill-Building Exercise 10-2 will help you recognize several of the influence tactics described in this chapter. Another tactic mentioned in the exercise, assertiveness, was described in Chapter 3.

LEADERSHIP SKILL-BUILDING **EXERCISE 10-1**

Ethical Influence Tactics

One student plays the role of an Air Force procurement officer. Another student plays the role of an aerospace company chief financial officer. The two are discussing at lunch a possible $23 billion deal for the aerospace company. The chief financial officer desperately wants the contract for the aerospace company, and the Air Force procurement officer sees this as an opportunity to gain some personal advantage from the deal: She might advance her career and help her daughter's boyfriend get a job at the aerospace company. But despite the procurement officer's hints about gaining some personal advantage, the company financial officer decides to use ethical influence tactics to win the contract. The two role players conduct the interview for about ten minutes. Later, the class observers will provide feedback about the effectiveness of the influence tactics used by both players.

LEADERSHIP SKILL-BUILDING **EXERCISE 10-2**

Identifying Influence Tactics

Instructions: After reading each tactic listed here, label it as being mostly an example of one of the following: I = ingratiation; E = exchange of favors; R = rational persuasion; C = forming coalitions; U = upward appeal.

	TACTIC CODE
1. I sympathized with the person about the added problems that my request caused.	_____
2. I offered to help if the person would do what I wanted.	_____
3. I obtained support and encouragement for my proposal from the most senior member of our team.	_____
4. I obtained the informal support of higher-ups.	_____
5. I used logic to convince him or her.	_____
6. I made a formal appeal to higher levels to back up my request.	_____
7. I enlisted the cooperation of several people in another department to support my proposal.	_____
8. I offered to make a personal sacrifice if the person would do what I wanted (for example, work late or harder).	_____
9. I made him or her feel good about me before making my request.	_____
10. I explained the reasons for my request.	_____

Answers:

1. I	**5.** R	**9.** I
2. E	**6.** U	**10.** R
3. C	**7.** C	
4. U	**8.** E	

Skill Development: Being able to identify influence tactics raises your awareness of how to influence others and which tactics others are using to influence you.

Source: Based on information in Chester A. Schriescheim and Timothy R. Hinkin, "Influence Tactics Used by Subordinates: A Theoretical and Empirical Analysis and Refinement of the Kipnis, Schmidt, and Wilkinson Subscales," *Journal of Applied Psychology*, June 1990, p. 246. Copyright © 1990 American Psychological Association. Adapted with permission.

LEADERSHIP INFLUENCE FOR ORGANIZATIONAL CHANGE

Most of the discussion so far relates to the leader/manager influencing people one at a time or in small groups. Top-level leaders exert many of their influence attempts in the direction of bringing about changes throughout the entire organization, often by attempting to overhaul the organizational culture. One such change would be attempting to influence a culture that was too collaborative to make decisions more quickly and independently, or the reverse. Another change would be to make the culture more focused on products the market wanted, and less focused on innovation for its own sake. Yet another cultural change facing a CEO would be to make a risk-averse workforce more entrepreneurial and risk taking.

Before plunging ahead with attempts at massive cultural change, the leader needs to study the old culture and understand why it contributed to the prosperity and growth of the organization. For example, when Leo Apotheker was appointed as CEO of Hewlett Packard in 2010, his predecessor Mark Hurd was embroiled in an expense account scandal. Before Hurd, CEO Carly Fiorina was ousted from her position as HP CEO. Apotheker moved cautiously and slowly before proposing changes partly because HP was still a great technology company with a long tradition of excellence. Apotheker walked around the company, absorbing what he could about the culture. In his words, "I learned about the issues: what doesn't work, what needs to be improved, and what needs to be improve really fast. I was impressed by the employees."[26] Within one year, however, Apothecker did make some key changes. He eliminated the administrative officer position, and had more executives reporting directly to him with the hopes of having more accountability in the company. He had more executives reporting directly to him, and moved HP more into computer services. The board did not like all of Apotheker's changes and fired him after eleven months as CEO.

After a new CEO is appointed, the person typically makes a public statement to the effect that: "My number-one job is to change the culture." A leader might do the following to bring about change as well ensuring that a healthy corporate culture is maintained.

- Serve as a role model for the desired attitudes and behaviors. Leaders must behave in ways consistent with the values and practices they wish to see imitated throughout the organization. If the change the leader wants is a stronger focus on customer service, leaders must treat employees as customers, thereby acting as role models for the way customers should be treated. The leaders must also talk in positive terms about customer service, with a statement such as, "The real joy in our work is helping customers solve their problems." Another frequently used method of bringing about change by acting as a role model is for the newly appointed leader to be frugal to encourage frugality throughout the organization. The frugal CEO, for example, might fly on commercial airlines and not by corporate jet, have one instead of several administrative assistants, and eat lunch in the company cafeteria.
- Impose a new approach through executive edict. From the time he started his position as chairman and CEO of General Electric, Jeff Immelt was on a mission to transform the hard-driving process-oriented company into an organization steeped in creativity and wired for business growth. In addition to outstanding efficiency in operations, Immelt presented new imperatives for risk taking, sophisticated marketing, and, of utmost importance, innovation.[27]
- Establish a reward system that reinforces the culture, such as giving huge suggestion awards to promote an innovative culture. At Boeing Co., CEO W. James McNerney Jr. wanted to create a common culture and work toward a shared goal. So, to discourage negative internal competition and the hoarding of information, he based part of executive compensation on how well managers share information with other units across the company.[28]

- Select candidates for positions at all levels whose values mesh with the values of the desired culture. Many firms hire only those candidates whose work and school experience suggest that they might be good team players—a cultural value.
- Sponsor new training and development programs that support the desired cultural values. Among many examples, top management might sponsor diversity training to support the importance of cultural diversity, or training in quality to support the value of quality.

A leader who exhibited all of these behaviors would qualify as a transformational leader because of all the positive changes. The accompanying Leader in Action profile below describes a CEO who is attempting to bring about some changes you will be able to experience with the investment of the price of a latte.

LEADER IN ACTION

Starbucks CEO Howard Schultz Stirs Up His Coffee Chain

The roots of Starbucks trace back to 1971, from a single roaster and retailer of whole bean and ground coffee in Seattle, Washington. Forty years later, Starbucks had over 17,000 stores worldwide in 50 countries, with about 11,000 stores in the United States. Despite the size of the operation, when Starbucks managers are about to initiate an idea, they might say, "What would Uncle Howie think?" The uncle in question is CEO Howard Schultz, who bought the company when it was a six-store coffee chain. He still contributes heavily to decisions about matters such as how frequently coffee beans should be roasted in a store and the look of the Starbucks logo.

Despite the growth of Starbucks into one of the world's most recognizable brands, the company has faced a few rough patches. The company experienced a substantial sales decline during the Great Recession. Outside analysts said that consumers were shifting their restaurant coffee purchases to lower priced alternatives, particularly Dunkin' Donuts, McDonalds, 7-Eleven, and Tim Horton. Schultz insisted that many Starbuck customers were simply buying less coffee outside, not shifting to the competition.

To help the company rebound, Schultz who had been serving as chairman only for eight years, returned to his CEO post. Schultz was concerned that Starbucks had lost its way: It had become too big, too bureaucratic, and stores had lost of some of their ambience.

Schultz wanted to take the company back to its roots and to be loved again. One of his first steps was to modify work processes to assure that customers could hear the whir of grinders and smell the aroma of coffee all day. Schultz was concerned that the switch to pre-ground coffee had taken the romance and theater out of a visit to Starbucks. He wanted Starbuck partners to put their feet in the shoes of customers and enhance the customer experience.

Although Schultz did not want to be like other business corporations, he took major steps toward profit improvement. He shuttered 800 stores in the United States and laid off approximately 8,000 employees. Schultz also spearheaded efficiencies in coffee preparation. For example, it was discovered that baristas were pouring millions of dollars of leftover milk down the drain. To help solve this problem, etched lines were placed in the steaming pitchers so the baristas would know precisely how much milk to use for each size drink. Schultz, who makes heavy use of stories and metaphors to inspire his partners (a.k.a. employees) said, "The celebration of that line in the halls of Starbuck has become a metaphor. How many other lines can we find?"

An important part of the Starbucks comeback has been through heavy participation in the social media. Schultz heavily endorsed social media presence as a way of rebuilding trust in the company and communicating company values. At one point, Starbucks had 20 million Facebook connections and 1.4 million Twitter followers.

Schultz took great pride in how well the company had implemented the changes he proposed and how well it rebounded from the Great Recession. He told his partners in 2011, "We're sitting today with record revenue, record profit, and a stock price at a five-year high. This isn't an accident."

QUESTIONS

1. Which influence tactics is Schultz attempting to use to rejuvenate Starbucks?
2. Write a bulleted memo to Howard Schultz telling him what changes you think Starbucks should make to enhance the company success even further.

3. Think back to a recent time when you visited a Starbucks coffee shop. Did you experience "romance and theater"? If you are not a Starbucks patron, ask the same question of somebody who is.

Source: This story is created based on facts and observations from the following sources: Julie Jargon, "Coffee Talk: Starbucks Chief on Prices, McDonald's Rivalry," *The Wall Street Journal*, March 7, 2001, p. B6; Howard Schultz, *Onward* (New York: Rodale, 2011); Heather Caliendo, "Leadership and Accountability: Howard Schultz, CEO of Starbucks," *360 Feedback: A Leadership Blog* (http://360degreefeedback.blogspot.com), October 5, 2010, pp. 1–3; Burt Helm and Jena McGregor, "Howard Schultz's Grande Challenge," *Business Week*, January 21, 2008, p. 028; Sarah Skidmore, "Starbucks: New Logo, New Plan," Associated Press, January 6, 2011; Julie Jargon, "At Starbucks, It's Back to the Grind," *The Wall Street Journal*, June 17, 2009, pp. B1, B2; Susan Berfield, "Howard Schultz versus Howard Schultz," *Business Week*, August 17, 2009, pp. 028–033; "Recession Forces Starbucks to Think Lean," *MSN Money*, August 6, 2009, pp. 1–4; "Starbucks Company Profile," www.starbucks.com (accessed April 1, 2011).

RELATIVE EFFECTIVENESS AND SEQUENCING OF INFLUENCE TACTICS

Although we have described influence tactics separately, they must also be understood in relation to one another. Two ways of comparing influence tactics are to examine their relative effectiveness and to study the order in which they might be used to achieve the best result.

Relative Effectiveness of Influence Tactics

Since influence tactics are a major component of leadership, research about their relative effectiveness is worth noting. A study by Gary Yukl and J. Bruce Tracey provides insights into the relative effectiveness of influence tactics.[29] One hundred and twenty managers participated in the study, along with 526 subordinates, 543 peers, and 128 superiors, who also rated the managers' use of influence tactics. Half the managers worked for manufacturing companies, and half worked for service companies.

The people who worked with the managers completed a questionnaire to identify which of nine influence tactics the managers used. As defined for the participants, the tactics were as follows: (1) rational persuasion, (2) inspirational appeal, (3) consultation, (4) ingratiation, (5) exchange, (6) personal appeal, (7) coalition, (8) legitimating, and (9) pressure.

Another question asked how many influence attempts by the agent resulted in complete commitment by the target respondent. Respondents were also asked to rate the overall effectiveness of the manager in carrying out managerial job responsibilities. The item had nine response choices, ranging from "the least effective manager I have ever known" to "the most effective manager."

The results suggested that the most effective tactics were rational persuasion, inspirational appeal, and consultation. (An effective tactic was one that led to task commitment and that was used by managers who were perceived to be effective by the various raters.) In contrast, the least effective were pressure, coalition, and appealing to legitimate authority (legitimating). Ingratiation and exchange were moderately effective for influencing team members and peers. The same tactics, however, were not effective for influencing superiors. A related interpretation of the data would be that noncoercive tactics that provide a rational and justifiable basis for attitude change are more effective in gaining compliance than are threatening or manipulative attempts.[30]

Inspirational appeal, ingratiation, and pressure were used primarily in a downward direction, that is, toward a lower-ranking person. Personal appeal, exchange, and legitimating were used primarily in a lateral direction. It was also found that coalitions were used most in lateral and upward directions and that rational persuasion was used most in an upward direction.

The researchers concluded that some tactics are more likely to be successful than others. Yet they caution that the results do not imply that these tactics will always result in task commitment. The outcome of a specific influence attempt is also determined by other factors, such as the target's motivation and the organizational culture. Also, any tactic can trigger target resistance if it is not appropriate for the situation or if it is applied unskillfully. Tact, diplomacy, and insight are required for effective application of influence tactics.

Which influence tactic a manager might consider effective, and therefore choose, depends to some extent on how much group members are trusted. When we distrust people, we are likely to attempt to control their actions. Carole V. Wells and David Kipnis conducted a survey about trust involving 275 managers and 267 employees. The managers answered questions about subordinates, and subordinates answered questions about their managers. The two groups, however, were not describing each other. A key finding was that both managers and employees used strong tactics of influence when they distrusted the other party—either a manager or a subordinate. The strong influence tactics studied were appeals to higher authority, assertiveness, coalition building, and sanctions.[31]

Another perspective on the relative effectiveness of influence tactics comes from a study of territory managers and their service-center managers who worked for a distribution company. A major finding was that the quality of the relationship with the leader (leader–member exchange, or LMX) had an impact on the effectiveness of influence tactics. When group members perceived a poor relationship with their leader, the leader's use of inspirational appeal and exchange resulted in less helping of coworkers by members. However, the leaders' consultation tactics were positively associated with the members helping work associates. When group members perceived their relationship with the leader as positive, exchange tactics by the leaders positively related to helping behavior.

An interpretation offered for these interactions has a lesson for leaders. Members in low-quality relationships may interpret appeals to their values, goals, and aspirations or exchange offers as empty. As a result, the members did not engage in more helping behaviors based on inspirational appeals. Yet consultation is more effective and may prompt members to become more helpful.[32]

Sequencing of Influence Tactics

Another important consideration in using influence tactics is the sequence or order in which they should be applied. In general, you should begin with the most positive, or least abrasive, tactic. If you do not gain the advantage you seek, proceed to a stronger tactic. For example, if you want a larger salary increase than that initially assigned you, try rational persuasion. If persuasion does not work, move on to exchanging favors. Use a more abrasive tactic such as upward appeal only as a last resort. The reason is that abrasive tactics trigger revenge and retaliation. Many people who have taken their complaints to an outside agency such as a governmental office have found themselves with a limited future in their organization. Although the appeal is legally justified, it is politically unwise.

The sequencing of tactics can also be considered in terms of cost and risk. A sensible approach is to begin with low-cost, low-risk tactics. If the outcome is important enough to the influence agent, he or she can then proceed to higher-cost and higher-risk influence tactics. An example of a low-cost, low-risk tactic would be joking and kidding. An accounting manager who was disappointed with the budget offered her group might say to her boss, "Does the new budget mean that our group will have to pay for our own print cartridges and green eyeshades?" It would be much more costly in terms of time and potential retaliation to form a coalition with another under-budgeted group to ask for an enlarged budget.

In addition to the sequencing of tactics, the influence agent must also consider the direction of the influence attempt as a contingency factor. In general, the more position power an individual exerts over another, the less the need for being cautious in the use of influence tactics. For example, a vice president can more readily use undue pressure against a supervisor than vice versa. When you have more power, there are likely to be fewer negative consequences from using more powerful tactics.

Leadership Skill-Building Exercise 10-3 provides an opportunity to practice implementing various influence tactics. As with any other skill, influence skills need to be practiced under field conditions.

LEADERSHIP SKILL-BUILDING EXERCISE 10-3

Applying Influence Tactics

Divide the class into small teams. Each group assigns one leadership influence tactic to each team member. During the next week or so, each team member takes the opportunity to practice the assigned influence tactic in a work or personal setting. Hold a group discussion with the same class teams after the influence attempts have been practiced. Report the following information: (1) under what circumstances the influence tactic was attempted;

(2) how the influence target reacted; and (3) what results, both positive and negative, were achieved.

Practicing influence tactics directly contributes to your leadership effectiveness because leadership centers on influence. If you want to exert leadership as a non-manager, you will have to be particularly adept at using influence tactics because your formal authority will be quite limited.

IMPLICIT LEADERSHIP THEORIES AND LEADERSHIP INFLUENCE

A final perspective on influence tactics is that people are more likely to be influenced by leaders who match their expectations of what a leader should be. **Implicit leadership theories** are personal assumptions about the traits and abilities that characterize an ideal organizational leader. These assumptions, both stated and unstated, develop through socialization and past experiences with leaders. The assumptions are stored in memory and activated when group members interact with a person in a leadership position. Our assumptions about leaders help us make sense of what takes place on the job. Assume that Reggie was raised in a household and neighborhood in which business leaders are highly respected and thought to be dedicated and intelligent. When Reggie later works in a full-time professional job, he is most likely to be influenced by a supervisor he perceives to be dedicated and intelligent because this person fits Reggie's preconceived notion of how a leader should behave.

According to implicit leadership theory, as part of making assumptions and expectations of leader traits and behaviors, people develop leadership prototypes and antiprototypes. *Prototypes* are positive characterizations of a leader, whereas *antiprototypes* are traits and behaviors people do not want to see in a leader. People have different expectations of what they want in a leader, yet research conducted with 939 subordinates in two different samples in British companies shows there is some consistency in implicit leadership theories. The study showed that these theories are consistent across different employee groups and are also stable, trait-based stereotypes of leadership.[33] Another study in England showed that if the leader matches employee assumptions about having the right traits, the leader-member exchange (LMX) will be more positive. In turn, the group member will be more readily influenced by the leader.[34]

Table 10-4 lists the six traits group members want to see in a leader (prototypes), as well as the two traits they do not want to see in a leader (antiprototypes). Your study of leadership traits in Chapters 3 and 4 will reinforce

TABLE 10-4 Implicit Leadership Theory Dimensions

LEADERSHIP PROTOTYPE	LEADERSHIP ANTIPROTOTYPE
1. Sensitivity (compassion, sensitive)	**1.** Tyranny (dominant, selfish, manipulative)
2. Intelligence (intelligent, clever)	**2.** Masculinity (male, masculine)
3. Dedication (dedicated, motivated)	
4. Charisma (charismatic, dynamic)	
5. Strength (strong, bold)	
6. Attractiveness (well dressed, classy)	

Source: Gathered from information in Olga Epitropaki and Robin Martin, "Implicit Leadership Theories in Applied Settings: Factor Structure, Generalizability, and Stability over Time," *Journal of Applied Psychology*, April 2004, 297–299.

these leadership attributes. The antiprototype of *masculinity* suggests that followers prefer a compassionate and relationship-oriented leader to a command-and-control leader. An implication of these data is that a leader who fits group members' prototypes is more likely to influence them than a leader who fits their antiprototype.

SUMMARY

To become an effective leader, a person must be aware of specific influence tactics. Influence is the ability to affect the behaviors of others in a particular direction. Power, in contrast, is the potential or capacity to influence. A model presented here indicates that a leader's influence outcomes are a function of the influence tactics he or she uses. The influence tactics are, in turn, moderated, or affected by, the leader's traits and behaviors and also by the situation. The outcomes of influence attempts are commitment, compliance, or resistance, all of which influence end results such as group success or failure.

Influence tactics are often viewed from an ethical perspective. Some tactics are clearly ethical, some are neutral, but others are clearly unethical. Used with tact, diplomacy, and good intent, ethical influence tactics can be quite effective. The essentially ethical tactics described here are leading by example and respect, using rational persuasion, apprising, personal appeal, being a subject matter expert, exchanging favors and bargaining, legitimating a request, making an inspirational appeal and emotional display, consulting, forming coalitions, being a team player, and practicing hands-on leadership.

Influence tactics essentially neutral with respect to ethics are ingratiation, joking and kidding, upward appeal, and co-opting antagonists. Essentially dishonest and unethical tactics presented here were deliberate Machiavellianism, gentle manipulation of people and situations, undue pressure, and debasement.

Top-level leaders exert many of their influence attempts toward bringing about changes throughout the entire organization, often by attempting to overhaul the organizational culture. The leader should first study the old culture to search for its merits. Tactics for cultural change by the leader include serving as a role model, executive edict, giving rewards to reinforce the culture, selecting candidates who fit the culture, and establishing training and development programs to support the culture.

A study of influence tactics concluded that the most effective were rational persuasion, inspirational appeal, and consultation. The least effective were pressure, coalition, and appealing to legitimate authority. The quality of the leader–member (LMX) relationship has an impact on the effectiveness of influence tactics, with a poor relationship lowering the effectiveness of inspirational appeal and exchange.

Certain tactics are more effective for exerting influence upward, whereas others are better suited for downward influence. For example, inspirational appeal, ingratiation, and exchange are moderately effective for influencing subordinates and peers. Yet the same tactics are not effective for influencing superiors. When we distrust people, we tend to think that stronger influence tactics, such as an appeal to higher authority, will be effective.

Sequencing of influence tactics is another important consideration. In general, begin with the most positive, or least abrasive, tactic. If you do not gain the advantage you seek, proceed to a stronger tactic. Also, begin with low-cost, low-risk tactics.

Implicit leadership theories are personal assumptions about the traits and abilities that characterize an ideal organizational leader. Prototypes are positive characterizations of a leader, whereas anti-prototypes are negative. Subordinates are more likely to be influenced by leaders who fit their prototype, and do not fit their antiprototype, of a leader.

KEY TERMS

influence	apprising	Machiavellians
power	personal magnetism	bandwagon technique
commitment	coalition	debasement
compliance	hands-on leader	implicit leadership theories
resistance	upward appeal	
leading by example	co-opt	

✓ GUIDELINES FOR ACTION AND SKILL DEVELOPMENT

A field study provides some clues as to the circumstances in which more heavy-handed influence tactics will work with a subordinate. Managers tended to use hard (tough) follow-up tactics when a subordinate's refusal is related to work expected in his or her role, and when the subordinate was seen as malingering. (An example here would be saying to a specialist in accounts receivable, "You've been goofing off too long. If you don't chase after those customers overdue on their accounts, you might not get a raise for next year.") Harder tactics were also used more frequently when exchanges between the leader and member were not positive. Managers withdrew their request when the request was seen as outside the subordinate's role, or the request was ambiguous. When the leader–member exchange was less positive, managers were also more likely to withdraw the request.[35]

Discussion Questions and Activities

1. Explain the following analogy: Influence is to leadership as eggs are to an omelet.
2. Which influence tactic described in this chapter do you think would work the best for you? Why?
3. How might a manager use leading by example to help develop ethical behavior in his or her unit?
4. Assume that you work for a large employer, and that the CEO decides that the company needs to reduce costs by 5 percent. To get this message across, the CEO sends every employee a tweet explaining the goal. Explain how effective you think this message might be.
5. Identify two exchanges of favor you have seen or can envision on the job.
6. In what way is being a subject matter expert (SME) a source of power as well as an influence tactic?

7. Why is developing a reputation as a subject matter expert important for a leader if leadership deals so heavily with interpersonal skills?

8. How might a business owner use the band-wagon technique to get his or her employees to lead a healthier lifestyle?

9. Why should a top-level executive worry about respecting the existing organizational culture when trying to influence an organization to change in a particular direction?

10. Get the opinion of an experienced leader as to the most effective influence tactics. Share your findings with class members.

LEADERSHIP CASE PROBLEM A

Be Fit or Be Out of Favor at CFI Westgate

Central Florida Investments has become the largest privately held corporation in the Central Florida region. CFI operates dozens of businesses including hotels, insurance, magazines, real estate, travel services, oil, cattle, and Internet companies. Employees at CFI Westgate Resorts, an Orlando, Florida–based vacation properties company, have an incentive to get healthy. If they join in the company-wide weight-loss contest and succeed in reaching their goals, they could win cash prizes or a luxury vacation.

Inspiration for the contest came from CEO David Siegel, who himself lost more than 20 pounds a few years ago. "He put it on the radar," says Mark Waltrip, chief operating office at Westgate, adding that in the contest's first year, some employees lost up to 60 pounds.

Westgate was one of the first companies to take a hard line on smoking several years ago. Peter Cappelli, director of the Center for Human Resources at Wharton, was asked to comment on the anti-smoking campaign. He said that crackdowns on employees who smoke on or off the job were the "thin edge of a wedge... It has become socially acceptable to attack smoking and smokers. Will we see the same thing concerning obesity? The time is probably ripe for that."

In 2002, Siegel announced that all Westgate employees would have one year to quit smoking completely or else face termination. The company offered smoking cessation classes, nicotine patches, and other support, according to Waltrip, who said Siegel decided on the policy after a close friend died of lung cancer—and after he learned that Florida state law does not protect smokers. Another concern was the fact that smokers drive up health care premiums.

"If someone wants to smoke, that is their [he means his or her] choice, but when their choices impact their employer and fellow employees, then, frankly, we're not going to take it," says Waltrip. Since the ban on smoking was finally enacted in 2003, health premiums have increased at an average of 5 percent at Westgate, much lower than increases at other companies.

Siegel found himself at the center of controversy when he told a Florida TV station that Westgate would take every legal step to insist on healthy employees. "If you are an alcoholic, and we have the right to fire you, we will do that, too," he said. Bloggers and online commentators attacked Siegel for discriminating unfairly against overweight people and stepping too far into employees' private lives. A pregnant woman said, "Last time I was pregnant, I gained 40 pounds. How much time would I have to lose that weight before getting canned?"

According to Waltrip, however, Westgate is approaching the obesity issue more gingerly than Siegel's comment would imply. "Weight [he means being overweight] is complicated—it can be caused by disease—so before we go down that path of penalizing employees who are overweight, we need to understand and build a consensus around it." He says the company does not currently penalize overweight or obese workers.

Questions

1. Which influence tactics does David Siegel appear to be using in his attempt to combat employee smoking and obesity?
2. What suggestions might you offer Siegel to help him be more successful in his attempts at influencing employee weight control?
3. What is your evaluation of the ethics of a CEO attempting to influence employees to avoid obesity?

Source: Adapted and excerpted from "From Incentives to Penalties: How Far Should Employers Go to Reduce Workplace Obesity?" *Knowledge@Wharton* http://knowledge.wharton.upenn), January 9, 2008; A few additional facts are from "Westgate Resorts," *www.westgateresorts.com.*, 1998–2011.

ASSOCIATED ROLE PLAY

You guessed it! One student plays the role of a telephone reservations agent at Westgate who is 120 pounds above average weight for a person of his or her height. The employee is also known to smoke one pack of cigarettes per day. Another student plays the role of CEO Siegel, who has heard of this employee and calls for a personal meeting to influence the agent to lose weight and stop smoking—in a hurry. The reservations agent is quite sensitive about having his or her civil liberties violated. Observers will look to see which influence tactics Siegel uses and how effective he appears to be in executing the tactics.

LEADERSHIP CASE PROBLEM B

Maya the Manipulator

Maya is the director of sales for United Events, a company that organizes events, such as trade shows and exhibitions for other companies. In addition to lining up the hotel or convention hall space, United Events sets up booths as well as the communication technology for the events. The company has done well in recent years, partly because the activity of organizing events has become too complicated to do in-house.

Maya is regarded by most clients and staff as mentally sharp and charming. Yet several members of the sales representatives are concerned about how she treats them. A leadership coach found out the following in speaking to two sales representatives:

Ivan, a sales rep in the New Jersey area, said, "Maya shows a little disconnect between what she hints she will do and what she actually does. Six months ago I had a good prospect lined up for us to organize an annual meeting for them. The problem was that I would have to invest an enormous amount of time in bagging the contract. The company wanted to go over endless details. Plus they wanted documentation of a couple of annual meetings we had organized for other companies.

"I told Maya that his pinning down this contract might not be cost effective because of all the time it would take that I could be spending on other prospects. Maya told me to keep trying because the CEO might be very pleased with the contract, to the point that I *could* be eligible for a double bonus.

"Well, I finally did get us the contract even though the deal took a ridiculous amount of time away from my personal life. I did get an ordinary bonus, but no double bonus. When I asked Maya about the size of the bonus, she said she told me that I could be eligible but that did not imply a guarantee."

Courtney, a sales representative in the Chicago region, said that she was having the best year last year among her five years with the company. During an in-person meeting with Maya, Courtney was asked if she would mind crediting Maya with her biggest individual sale. Maya said to her, "You have had a great year, and my personal accounts are a little below average this year. If I receive full credit for the last big sale, you will still have had a great year. And don't forget that as your leader, I gave you suggestions for bringing the deal home."

When Courtney expressed some hesitancy in transferring credit for the big sale to Maya, the latter said, "Courtney, please remember that I am your ally. Remember how I let you off the hook last year on that little expense account irregularity? If I do get

credit for the sale, I will not change my mind about overlooking the irregularity."

Questions

1. In what specific ways is Maya being a manipulator?
2. To what extent do you think Maya's behavior is justifiable?
3. How should Ivan and Courtney have handled the situation?
4. What suggestions might you offer Maya for being a more effective leader?

ASSOCIATED ROLE PLAY

You guessed it! One student plays the role of a telephone reservations agent at Westgate who is known to smoke a pack of cigarettes a day and drink heavily on the weekends. Another student plays the role of CEO Siegel, who has heard of this employee and calls for a personal meeting to influence the agent to stop smoking and drinking excessively—in a hurry. The reservations agent is quite sensitive about having his or her civil liberties violated. Observers will look to see which influence tactics Siegel uses and how effective he appears to be in executing the tactics.

LEADERSHIP SKILL-BUILDING EXERCISE 10-4

My Leadership Portfolio

Influence is to leadership as an egg is to an omelet, so you need to practice your influence tactics to enhance your leadership effectiveness. In this chapter's entry to your leadership journal, describe any influence tactic you implemented recently. Describe what you did and how the influence target reacted. Comment on how you might use the tactic differently in your next influence attempt. Also describe which influence tactic or combination of tactics you plan to use in the upcoming week. Here is a possible example:

> I coach a youth basketball team called the West Side Chiefs. The kids are great, and I am enjoying the experience. Yet the name Chiefs really bothers

me because it is so behind the times, and a lot of people think using the term *Chief* for sport is racist. So I tried to influence the league director that we needed a name change. I presented my argument using a bunch of facts about how Chief has become passé for sports teams. (My technique was rational persuasion.) I did get a listen, but I didn't get approval for the name change. So next, I combined my logical argument with an inspirational appeal. I asked the league directors how they would like it if our team were called The West Side Chinese or the West Side Jews. Finally, my influence tactics worked, and for next season my team will be the West Side Rattlers.

LEADERSHIP SKILL-BUILDING **EXERCISE 10-5**

A Leadership Essay

Now that you have studied leadership power and influence in this chapter, it is your turn to write something about leadership. Work alone, or collaboratively in a small group, to write about an article on the subject of "How to Become a Powerful and Influential Leader." Your article should be about 400 words long, and will be published in a print or online magazine. Several individuals or groups might share their article with other class members. Look for similarities and differences among the articles.

►II **LEADERSHIP** VIDEO **CASE** DISCUSSION **QUESTIONS**

To view the videos for this activity, you'll need access to the CourseMate that is available for this text. To get access, visit www.CengageBrain.com.

After watching "Recycline," answer the following questions.

1. What is influence? What sort of ethical and honest tactics does Eric Hudson, Recycline founder and president, use to influence the behavior of Recycline employees?

2. What are implicit leadership theories? In your opinion, what sort of prototypes does Eric Hudson have?

3. How do Recycline use marketing efforts to influence consumer and retail partner behavior?

4. How might the bandwagon technique be used to get consumers to purchase Recycline products? What is a potential problem with using this technique?

NOTES

1. This story is created from facts and observations found in the following sources: David Vladek, "About the Bureau of Consumer Protection," *Federal Trade Commission*, *www.ftc.giv/bep/about.shtm* June 16, 2009; Maya Jackson Randall, "Warren Defends Watchdog Agency," *The Wall Street Journal*, March 17, 2011, p. C9; Jennifer Liberto, "Elizabeth Warren's Olive Branch to Big Business," *CNNMoney.com* (http://money.cnn.com), March 30, 2011, pp. 1–2; Edward Wyatt, "Obama Adviser on Consumer Agency to Address Business Leaders," *The New York Times* (www.nytimes.com), March 30, 2011, pp. 1–2; Michael Scherer, "The New Sheriffs of Wall Street,: *Time*, May 24, 2010, pp. 25–26; Carter Doughtery and Robert Schmidt, "Time's Nearly Up for Elizabeth Warren," *Bloomberg Businessweek*, April 18–April 24, 2011. pp. 29–30; Jim Puzzanghera, "Elizabeth Warren to Step Down from Consumer Agency Monday,"

Los Angeles Times (http: latimesblogs.latimes.com/money), July 218, 2011, p. 1.
2. Allan R. Cohen, Stephen L. Fink, Herman Gadon, and Robin D. Willits, *Effective Behavior in Organizations: Cases, Concepts, and Student Experiences*, 5th ed. (Homewood, Ill.: Irwin, 1992), p. 139.
3. Cited in Adam Lashinsky, "Where Does Google Go Next?" *Fortune*, May 26, 2008, p. 108.
4. Geoff Colvin, "Power: A Cooling Trend," *Fortune*, December 10, 2007, p. 114.
5. Gary Yukl, *Leadership in Organizations*, 5th ed. (Upper Saddle River, NJ: Prentice Hall, 2002), p. 143.
6. "Steven Cohen: Speaking Softly but Carrying a Big Hedge Fund," *Time*, May 14, 2007, p. 165.
7. Mitchell S. Nesler, Herman Aguinis, Brian M. Quigley, and James T. Tedeschi, "The Effect of Credibility on Perceived Power," *Journal of Applied Social Psychology*, 1993, vol. 23, no. 17, pp. 1407–1425.

8. The sample statements indicating the influence tactic in question here and at the other places in the chapter where they are presented are from Gary Yukl, Charles F. Seifert, and Carolyn Chavez, "Validation of the Extended Influence Behavior Questionnaire," *The Leadership Quarterly*, October 2008, pp. 618–620 (© Gary Yukl).

9. Yukl, Seifert, and Chavez, "Validation of the Extended Influence Behavior Questionnaire," p. 610.

10. Yukl, Seifert, and Chavez, "Validation of the Extended Influence Behavior Questionnaire," p. 610. (For both endnotes 9 and 10 the definitions are credited as Copyright © 2001 by Gary Yukl.

11. "You Scratch My Back … Tips on Winning Your Colleague's Cooperation," *Working Smart*, October 1999, p. 1.

12. Jeffrey Pfeffer, *Managing with Power: Power and Influence in Organizations* (Boston: Harvard Business School Press, 1992), p. 224.

13. Alan Murray, *The Wall Street Journal Essential Guide to Management* (New York: Harper Business, 2010), p. 90.

14. Nelson D. Schwartz, "Wall Street's Man of the Moment," *Fortune*, March 5, 2007, p. 76.

15. Gary Yukl, *Skills for Managers and Leaders: Text, Cases, and Exercises* (Upper Saddle River, NJ: Prentice Hall, 1990), p. 65.

16. Devon Leonard, "Company on Fire? Light a Cigar," *Bloomberg Businessweek*, March 28–April 3, 2011, pp. 84–90.

17. George Anders, "Tough CEOs Often Most Successful, a Study Finds," *The Wall Street Journal*, November 19, 2007, p. B3.

18. Amy Cortese, "I'm Humble, I'm Respectful," *BusinessWeek*, February 9, 1998, p. 40.

19. Gary Yukl and Cecilia M. Falbe, "Influence Tactics and Objectives in Upward, Downward, and Lateral Influence Attempts," *Journal of Applied Psychology*, April 1990, p. 133.

20. Jeffrey Pfeffer, "Power Play," *Harvard Business Review*, July-August 2010, p. 90.

21. Bernhard M. Bass (with Ruth Bass), *The Bass Handbook of Leadership: Theory, Research, & Managerial Applications*, 4th ed. (New York: The Free Press, 2008), p. 160.

22. "Create an Arsenal of Influence Strategies," *Manager's Edge*, March 2003, p. 1.

23. Anthony Bianco and Tom Lowry, "Can Dick Parsons Rescue AOL Time Warner?" *Businessweek*, May 19, 2003, p. 89.

24. David M. Buss, Mary Gomes, Dolly S. Higgins, and Karen Lauterbach, "Tactics of Manipulation," *Journal of Personality and Social Psychology*, December 1987, p. 1222.

25. Comment contributed anonymously to author by a professor of organizational behavior.

26. Jordan Robertson, "CEO Interview: New HP CEO on Taking the Helm," Associated Press, March 22, 2011.

27. Diane Brady, "The Immelt Revolution: He's Turning GE's Culture Upside Down, Demanding Far More Risk and Innovation," *Businessweek*, March 28, 2005, pp. 64–66, 71–73.

28. Stanley Holmes, "Cleaning Up Boeing," *Businessweek*, March 13, 2006, p. 64.

29. Gary Yukl and J. Bruce Tracey, "Consequences of Influence Tactics Used with Subordinates, Peers, and the Boss," *Journal of Applied Psychology*, August 1992, pp. 525–535.

30. Martin M. Chemers, *An Integrative Theory of Leadership* (Mahwah, NJ: Lawrence Erlbaum Associates, 1997), p. 76.

31. Carole V. Wells and David Kipnis, "Trust, Dependency, and Control in the Contemporary Organization," *Journal of Business and Psychology*, Summer 2001, pp. 593–603.

32. Raymond T. Sparrowe, Budi W. Soetjipto, and Maria L. Kraimer, "Do Leaders' Influence Tactics Relate to Members' Helping Behavior? It Depends on the Quality of the Relationship," *Academy of Management Journal*, December 2006, pp. 1194–1208.

33. Olga Epitropaki and Robin Martin, "Implicit Leadership Theories in Applied Settings: Factor Structure, Generalizability, and Stability over Time," *Journal of Applied Psychology*, April 2004, pp. 297–299.

34. Epitropaki and Martin, "From Real to Ideal: A Longitudinal Study of Implicit Leadership Theories in Leader–Member Exchanges and Employee Outcomes," *Journal of Applied Psychology*, July 2005, pp. 659–676.

35. Study described in Chester A. Schriesheim and Linda L. Neider, eds., *Power and Influence in Organizations: New Empirical and Theoretical Perspectives* (Greenwich, Conn.: IAP, 2006), Chapter 1.

How Leaders Attain and Maintain Power

LEARNING OBJECTIVES

After studying this chapter and doing the exercises, you should be able to

- Recognize the various types of power.
- Identify tactics used for becoming an empowering leader.
- Know how to use delegation to support empowerment.

- Pinpoint factors contributing to organizational politics.
- Describe both ethical and unethical political behaviors.
- Explain how a leader can control dysfunctional politics.

CHAPTER OUTLINE

Sheryl Sandberg is one of the most powerful and influential leaders in Silicon Valley, although she is less well known than her boss, Mark Zuckerberg, the founder of Facebook. Born in 1969, Sandberg's formal title at her company is chief operating officer. The functions reporting directly to Sandberg include sales, marketing, business development, human resources, public policy, and communications.

Prior to joining Facebook, Sandberg's positions included president of global online sales at operations at Google, and chief of staff for the United States Treasury Department under President Bill Clinton. Sandberg's departure from Google was seen as a loss by the company because she was a highly regarded executive. She was influential in building the online operations of two programs that accounted for the vast majority of Google's revenue for several years. Her department grew from four employees to thousands of employees in a couple of years, and Sandberg became a multimillionaire while at Google. When hired by Facebook, Sandberg said, "The opportunity to help another young company to grow into a global leader is the opportunity of a lifetime."

Earlier in her career, Sandberg was a management consultant for the prestigious McKinsey & Company, and an economist for the World Bank. Her formal education includes an undergraduate degree in economics from Harvard, as well as an MBA. Sandberg has been cited by *Fortune* magazine on its list of its 50 Most Powerful Women in business.

In addition to her sharp intellect and business decision-making skills, Sandberg has developed a reputation for outstanding interpersonal skills, including her gregariousness. She and Zuckerman meet twice weekly, and she gives him advice and feedback on his business decisions and leadership skills. Sandberg has built close business relationships with some of the world's largest advertisers, which has helped generate revenue for Facebook—a company that was originally more effective at growing users than revenue.

Pedram Keani, the leader of a team that builds the tools to handle complaints and requests from Facebook users, commented about Sandberg: "She operates at every level. She's good at strategy and dives deep and understands how teams work together." Although Sandberg is well regarded by Facebook employees, she does not come to work dressed in jeans and running shoes as do other employees. Instead, she dresses in high style, thereby retaining her individuality.[1]

This powerful and influential Internet executive's story illustrates several sources of power held by leaders, including expertise and the ability to form high-quality relationships. This chapter covers the nature of power, the ways leaders acquire power and empower others, and the use and control of organizational politics.

SOURCES AND TYPES OF POWER

To exercise influence, a leader must have **power**, the potential or ability to influence decisions and control resources. Organizational power can be derived from many sources. How people obtain power depends to a large extent on the type of power they seek. Therefore, to understand the mechanics of acquiring power, one must also understand what types of power exist and the sources and origins of these types of power. Seven types of power, including some of their subtypes, are described in the following sections.

Position Power

Power is frequently classified according to whether it stems from the organization or the individual.[2] Four bases of power—legitimate power, reward power, coercive power, and information power—stem from the person's position in the organization.

Legitimate Power   The lawful right to make a decision and expect compliance is called **legitimate power**. People at the highest levels in the organization have more power than do people below them. However, organizational culture helps establish the limits to anyone's power. Newly appointed executives, for example, are often frustrated with how long it takes to effect major change. A chief financial officer (CFO) recruited to improve the profitability of a telecommunications firm noted, "The company has been downsizing for three years. We have more office space and manufacturing capacity than we need. Yet whenever I introduce the topic of selling off real estate to cut costs, I get a cold reception."

At the top of the organization, a leader's legitimate power is strengthened when he or she carries the titles of both chief executive officer and chairman or chairwoman. For example, Jeffrey R. Immelt is both the chairman and chief executive at General Electric Co. Adding to his legitimate power, in 2011, he was appointed by President Barack Obama as the next top outside economic adviser to the White House.

In contrast to strengthening legitimate power, some organizations set up an arrangement whereby position power is shared between two people, such as the practice of having co-CEOs. The power sharing can also take place below the level of the CEO position. A few years ago, the giant bank J. P. Morgan Chase & Co. promoted the head of its telecommunications investment banking group in order for him to jointly run its technology, media, and telecommunications team. Kurt Simon, the person promoted, then shared power with Jennifer Nason who was formerly the head of the group. The purpose of the power sharing was to bring more expertise to the position.[3]

Reward Power   The authority to give employees rewards for compliance is **reward power**. If a vice president of operations can directly reward supervisors with cash bonuses for achieving productivity targets, this manager will exert considerable power. Almost any leader occupying a formal position has some reward power. Even the ability to give a subordinate a positive performance evaluation is a form of reward power.

Coercive Power   **Coercive power** is the power to punish for noncompliance; it is based on fear. A common coercive tactic is for an executive to demote a subordinate manager who does not comply with the executive's plans for change. Coercive power is limited, in that punishment and fear achieve mixed results as motivators. The leader who relies heavily on coercive power runs the constant threat of being ousted from power. Nevertheless, coercive power is widely practiced. The former chief executive of Merrill Lynch & Co., E. Stanley O'Neal, exercised considerable coercive power. He presided over one of the most intense restructurings in Wall Street history, eliminating more than 23,000 jobs, closing more than 300 offices, and ousting 19 senior executives. In the process, he purged an entire generation of key people to strengthen his own power grip. Several years later, when the firm lost billions of dollars on investments linked to subprime mortgages, O'Neal was ousted immediately.[4]

Information Power   **Information power** is power stemming from formal control over the information people need to do their work. A sales manager who controls the leads from customer inquiries holds considerable power. As the branch manager of a real estate agency put it: "Ever since the leads were sent directly to me, I get oodles of cooperation from my agents. Before that, they would treat me as if I were simply the office manager." The World Wide Web has weakened information as a source of power to some extent because more people have access to more information, especially in a field such as real estate. Within an organization, computerized databases also detract from information power because so many people have access to the information they need, providing they have the necessary skills to find what they want.

Personal Power

Three sources of power stem from characteristics or behaviors of the power actor: expert power, referent power, and prestige power. All are classified as **personal power** because they are derived from the person rather than the organization. Expert power and referent power contribute to charisma. Referent power is the ability to influence others through one's desirable traits and characteristics (see Chapter 4). Expert power is the ability to influence others through specialized knowledge, skills, or abilities. An example of a leader with substantial expert power is Mike Duke, the CEO of Wal-Mart. One aspect of his expertise is navigating international markets. Prior to becoming CEO, Duke led Wal-Mart through a rapid period of international expansion. Another of Duke's expertise areas is merchandising, such as understanding which products appeal the most to the company's target demographic groups.[5]

Another important form of personal power is **prestige power**, the power stemming from a person's status and reputation.[6] A manager who has accumulated important business successes acquires prestige power. Managers acquire visibility based on their reputation—for example, a middle manager who has been successful at reducing turnover in the restaurant or hotel industry. Integrity is another contributor to prestige power because it enhances a leader's reputation. Executive recruiters identify executives who can readily be placed in senior positions because of their excellent track records (or prestige).

Manager Assessment Quiz 11-1 provides a sampling of the specific behaviors associated with five of the sources of power—three kinds of position power and two kinds of personal power.

Power Stemming from Ownership

Executive leaders accrue power in their capacity as agents acting on behalf of shareholders. The strength of ownership power depends on how closely the leader is linked to shareholders and board members. A leader's ownership power is also associated with how much money he or she has invested in the

MANAGEMENT ASSESSMENT QUIZ 11-1

Rating a Manager's Power

Instructions: If you currently have a supervisor or can clearly recall one from the past, rate that supervisor. Circle the appropriate number of your answer, using the following scale: 5 = strongly agree; 4 = agree; 3 = neither agree nor disagree; 2 = disagree; 1 = strongly disagree. (The actual scale presents the items in random order. They are classified here according to the power source for your convenience.)

	STRONGLY AGREE				STRONGLY DISAGREE
My manager can (or former manager could) …					
Reward Power					
1. increase my pay level.	5	4	3	2	1
2. influence my getting a pay raise.	5	4	3	2	1
3. provide me with specific benefits.	5	4	3	2	1
4. influence my getting a promotion.	5	4	3	2	1
Coercive Power					
5. give me undesirable job assignments.	5	4	3	2	1
6. make my work difficult for me.	5	4	3	2	1
7. make things unpleasant here.	5	4	3	2	1
8. make being at work distasteful.	5	4	3	2	1
Legitimate Power					
9. make me feel that I have commitments to meet.	5	4	3	2	1
10. make me feel like I should satisfy my job requirements.	5	4	3	2	1
11. make me feel I have responsibilities to fulfill.	5	4	3	2	1
12. make me recognize that I have tasks to accomplish.	5	4	3	2	1
Expert Power					
13. give me good technical suggestions.	5	4	3	2	1
14. share with me his or her considerable experience and/or training.	5	4	3	2	1
15. provide me with sound job-related advice.	5	4	3	2	1
16. provide me with needed technical knowledge.	5	4	3	2	1
Referent Power					
17. make me feel valued.	5	4	3	2	1
18. make me feel that he or she approves of me.	5	4	3	2	1
19. make me feel personally accepted.	5	4	3	2	1
20. make me feel important.	5	4	3	2	1

Total score: _____

QUIZ 11-1 (continued)

Scoring and Interpretation: Add all the circled numbers to calculate your total score. You can make a tentative interpretation of the score as follows:

- **90+:** High power
- **70–89:** Moderate power
- **below 70:** Low power

Also, notice whether you rated your manager significantly higher in one category.

Skill Development: This skill development rating can help you as a leader because it points to specific behaviors you can use to be perceived as high or low on a type of power. For example, a behavior specific for establishing referent power is to "make people feel important" (No. 20).

Source: Adapted from "Development and Application of New Scales to Measure the French and Raven (1959) Bases of Social Power," by Timothy R. Hinkin and Chester A. Schriescheim, *Journal of Applied Psychology*, August 1989, p. 567. Copyright © 1989 by the American Psychological Association. Adapted with permission of the American Psychological Association and Timothy R. Hinkin.

firm.[7] An executive who is a major shareholder is much less likely to be fired by the board than one without an equity stake. The CEOs of high-technology firms are typically company founders who later convert the firm into a publicly held company by selling stock. After the public offering, many of these CEOs own several hundred million dollars' worth of stock, making their position quite secure. Should Facebook go public, as is often rumored, founder Mark Zuckerberg would most likely become one of the world's richest people. The New Golden Rule applies: The person who holds the gold rules.

Power Stemming from Dependencies

According to the **dependence perspective**, people accrue power when others are dependent on them for things of value. Figure 11-1 depicts this basic model of sources of power. Because the things valued could be physical resources or a personal relationship, dependence power can be positional or personal. Richard M. Emerson noted that power resides implicitly in the other's dependence.[8] A leader–group member example would be that the group member who needs considerable recognition to survive becomes dependent on the leader, who is a regular source of such recognition. An organizational example is that the health care system in the United States is becoming more dependent on information technology to help streamline the system. Health care information technology specialists therefore have more power.

An extension of the dependence theory is the **resource dependence perspective**. According to this perspective, the organization requires a continuing flow of human resources, money, customers and clients, technological inputs, and materials to continue to function. Organizational subunits or individuals who can provide these key resources accrue power.[9]

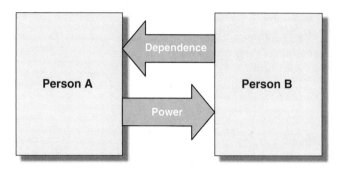

FIGURE 11-1 The Dependence Theory of Power.

Source: Adapted from Wilf H. Ratsburg, "Power Defined," www.geocities.com/Athens/Forum/1650/htmlpower.html, accessed January 4, 2008.

When leaders start losing their power to control resources, their power declines. A case in point is Donald Trump. When his vast holdings were generating a positive cash flow and his image was one of extraordinary power, he found many willing investors. The name *Trump* on a property escalated its value. As his cash-flow position worsened, however, Trump found it difficult to find investment groups willing to buy his properties close to the asking price. However, by mid-1993, Trump's cash-flow position had improved again, and investors showed renewed interest.

A few years later Trump had regained all of his power to control resources, and money from investors flowed freely in his direction. In 2004, the Trump casino business filed for bankruptcy, mostly to refinance debt. Trump Entertainment Resorts, Inc., filed for Chapter 11 protection again in 2009, and the value (power) of the Trump brand was a subject of debate the following year. Trump was trying to retain control of three of his Atlantic City Casinos, in opposition to investor Carl Icahn, who was trying to take control. Trump insisted his brand was still powerful.

Yet Trump has so much equity built into the Trump name that it is a resource that makes many developers dependent on him. Many condominium developers, for example, give "The Donald" an equity stake in the business just because the Trump name is on the business. Trump, after all, claims that he is "the hottest brand on the planet."[10] (The point of this seemingly contradictory example is that when you lose control of resources your power might decline, but, if you are super-powerful, you will recover quickly. Furthermore, having accumulated power in the past makes it difficult for others to take it away from you.)

Power Derived from Capitalizing on Opportunity

Power can be derived from being in the right place at the right time and taking the appropriate action. It pays to be where the action is. For example, the best opportunities in a diversified company lie in one of its growth divisions. Also, many small recycling firms moved from junkyard status to ecology firms as the interest in environmental sustainability surged in the late 2000s. A person or a firm also needs to have the right resources to capitalize on an opportunity, such as having the capacity to recycle on a larger scale.

Another ecology-related example of capitalizing on opportunity took place at outdoor clothing manufacturer Patagonia. For years, founder Yvon Chouinard had led campaigns to use eco-friendly materials and fabrics in its clothing. Patagonia had also pioneered sustainable manufacturing practices. During the Great Recession, Patagonia enjoyed its two best years ever. The opportunity capitalized on had two aspects: First, despite the recession many upscale consumers still want to purchase eco-friendly products.[11] Second, during a recession many consumers want to purchase durable, multiple-use clothing—such as using the same jacket for hiking, skiing, and shopping.

Power Stemming from Managing Critical Problems

The **strategic contingency theory** of power suggests that units best able to cope with the firm's critical problems and uncertainties acquire relatively large amounts of power.[12] The theory implies, for example, that when an organization faces substantial lawsuits, the legal department will gain power and influence over organizational decisions. Another important aspect of the strategic contingency theory concerns the power a subunit acquires by virtue of its centrality. Recall the chapter-opening story about Sheryl Sandberg. Some of her initial power at Facebook stemmed from helping the company make money from (monetize) its incredible popularity.

Centrality is the extent to which a unit's activities are linked into the system of organizational activities. A unit has high centrality when it is an important and integral part of the work done by another unit. The second unit is therefore dependent on the first subunit. A sales department would have high centrality, whereas an employee credit union would have low centrality.

Power Stemming from Being Close to Power

The closer a person is to power, the greater the power he or she exerts. Likewise, the higher a unit reports in a firm's hierarchy, the more power it possesses. In practice, this means that a leader in charge of a department reporting to the CEO has more power than one in charge of a department reporting to a vice president. Leaders in search of more power typically maneuver toward a higher-reporting position in the organization.

Historian Robert A. Caro reminds us that acquiring power alone does not make for great leadership. It takes an ambitious person to acquire power, and sometimes the approach to acquiring power may not be highly ethical, such as hoarding vital information or making others dependent on you. The person who then uses the accumulated power to create and implement a useful vision qualifies as an excellent leader.[13] The concept of who is an excellent leader could be based on a person's values, but two leaders already described in this book might qualify: Mellody Hobson of Ariel Capital Management and Alan Mullaly of Ford Motor Co.

LEADER IN ACTION

Adam Gryglak, Ford's Diesel King

If you reach Adam Gryglak, chief diesel engineer at Ford Motor Co. on the phone, you will hear a one-word greeting: "Diesel." His greeting reflects his enthusiasm for what he and his team were accomplishing, the development of a turbocharged diesel engine (the Power Stroke) for the 2011 Ford Super Duty. "The bar was raised for this new diesel and the Power Stroke team did a fantastic job meeting performance and durability targets," Gryglak said. His team, located offsite, included engineering, design, manufacturing, and purchasing which helped get the job done quickly. Grylak's can-do attitude impresses both members of his team and visitors to his project.

To build team spirit, Gryglak code-named the diesel Scorpion, after his favorite rock band. The team logo, a mechanical scorpion designed from engine components, was inserted on internal reports. Spirit at Team Scorpion reached such a high level that team members played jokes on each other, including building a full-size snowman decorated with machine parts and placed on the desks of team members. The team organized a Pinewood Derby competition, but milled cars out of aluminum instead of pinewood. A few of the miniature vehicles had remote controls and electric motors.

In building the new engine, Gryglak spearheaded the risk of using a lighter material that would add to fuel efficiency. (The risk was that the engine would not work properly.) The Super Duty truck developed with the Power Stroke diesel engine was the first of its kind to use the state of the art antipollution technology that meets current federal regulations. The fuel economy is well above average and the truck will require only routine maintenance for the first 300,000 miles.

Tony Hudson, a Project Scorpion engineer, was quite enthused about Grylak's leadership as well as the team effort. He said that the team accomplished what initially had seemed impossible. "That will give us license to do it again."

QUESTIONS

1. What types of power did team leader Adam Gryglak use to accomplish his mission?
2. Why was team spirit important to accomplishing the mission of building a new truck engine?
3. Why should a person studying leadership care about the activities of a diesel chief engineer at the truck division of a vehicle manufacturer?

Source: Story created from facts presented in "Adam Gryglak: Providing 'Stinging' Inspiration for All-New Ford Power Stroke Diesel Engine," *www.media.ford.com*, August 3, 2010, pp. 1–2; "Ford Motor Company Team Organizes a Team Pinewood Derby," *www.fastpinewoodderbytips.com* (accessed March 25, 2011), pp. 1–4; David Kiley, "Putting Ford on Fast Forward," *BusinessWeek*, October 26, 2009, pp. 056–057; Keith Griffin, "Interesting Profile of the Man Behind the New Ford Power Stroke Diesel Engine," *Hartford Autos Examiner*, August 31, 2009, pp. 1–4.

The accompanying Leader in Action profile provides a brief description of a leader who uses several types of power described so far to accomplish his mission.

TACTICS FOR BECOMING AN EMPOWERING LEADER

A leader's power and influence increase when he or she shares power with others. Empowerment is therefore the basic component of shared or distributed leadership. As team members receive more power, they can accomplish more—they become more productive. And because managers share credit for their accomplishments, they become more powerful. A truly powerful leader empowers team members to accomplish tasks on their own.

A similar rationale for empowerment is that in a competitive environment that is increasingly dependent on knowledge, judgment, and information, the most successful organizations will be those that effectively use the talents of all players on the team.[14] As Stephen Covey notes, empowerment and leadership distribution are happening among progressive companies throughout the world. Also, the more trusting the culture is, the more likely it is that employees will be empowered.[15]

From a cost perspective, empowering workers to assume more managerial responsibility enables the organization to get by with fewer bosses. Research in Europe suggests that a manager's span of control (number of direct reports) can be more than thirty employees, in part because of using technology to communicate and help monitor work. The leader/manager who empowers workers can focus less on controlling them and more on helping them overcome obstacles or capitalize on opportunities, such as pursuing innovative ideas.[16]

Here we look briefly at the nature of empowerment before discussing a number of practices and two cautions about empowerment.

The Nature of Empowerment

In its basic meaning, **empowerment** refers to passing decision-making authority and responsibility from managers to group members. Almost any form of participative management, shared decision making, and delegation can be regarded as empowerment. Gretchen M. Spreitzer conducted research in several work settings to develop a psychological definition of empowerment.[17] Four components were identified: meaning, competence, self-determination, and impact. Full-fledged empowerment includes all four dimensions, along with a fifth one, internal commitment.

Meaning is the value of a work goal, evaluated in relation to a person's ideals or standards. Work has meaning when there is a fit between the requirements of a work role and a person's beliefs, values, and behaviors. A person who is doing meaningful work is likely to feel empowered. *Competence,* or *self-efficacy,* is an individual's belief in his or her capability to perform a particular task well. People who feel competent believe that they have the capability to meet performance requirements in a given situation, such as a credit analyst saying, "I've been given the authority to evaluate credit risks up to $10,000 and I know I can do it well." A newer model of empowerment also features the key roles of self-efficacy and competence in helping a fellow group member feel that he or she has gained power.[18]

Self-determination is an individual's sense of having a choice in initiating and regulating actions. A high-level form of self-determination occurs when workers feel that they can choose the best method to solve a particular problem. Self-determination also involves such considerations as choosing the work pace and work site. A highly empowered worker might choose to perform the required work while on a cruise rather than remain in the office. *Impact* is the degree to which the worker can influence strategic, administrative, or operating outcomes on the job. Instead of feeling there is no choice but to follow the company's course, a worker might have a say in the future of the company. A middle manager might say, "Here's an opportunity for recruiting minority employees that we should exploit. And here's my action plan for doing so."

Another dimension of true empowerment is for the group member to develop an *internal commitment* toward work goals. Internal commitment takes place when workers are committed to a particular project, person, or program for individual motives. An example would be a production technician in a lawn mower plant who believes he or she is helping create a more beautiful world.

The focus of empowerment, then, is on the changes taking place within the individual. However, groups can also be empowered in such a way that the group climate contributes to these attitudes and feelings. An example of a statement reflecting an empowering climate would be "People in our organization get information about the organization's performance in a timely fashion."[19] Being part of an empowered group can help a member commit to achieving shared goals.

Empowering Practices

The practices that foster empowerment supplement the standard approaches to participative management, such as conferring with team members before reaching a decision. The practices, as outlined in Figure 11-2, are based on direct observations of successful leaders and experimental evidence. Before reading about these practices, do Leadership Self-Assessment Quiz 11-1.

Foster Initiative and Responsibility   A leader can empower team members simply by fostering greater initiative and responsibility in their assignments. For example, a manufacturer of battery-powered construction tools might inform an information technology enthusiast in the company, "From now on, you are

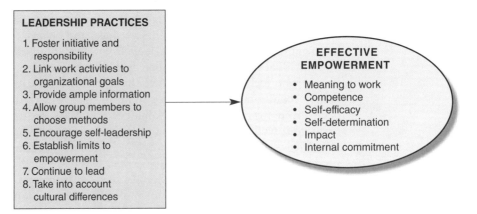

FIGURE 11-2 Effective Empowering Practices.

Certain leadership and managerial practices lead to effective empowerment, which in turn often leads to higher motivation and productivity.

● LEADERSHIP SELF-ASSESSMENT QUIZ 11-1

Empowering Attitudes and Beliefs

Instructions: To empower employees successfully, the leader has to convey appropriate attitudes and have certain beliefs. To the best of your ability, indicate which attitudes you now have and which ones require further development.

Empowering Attitude or Belief	HAVE NOW	WOULD NEED TO DEVELOP
1. Most workers have considerable unused talent that could be put to good use.	_____	_____
2. Instead of demanding immediate results, the leader should give group members the time to develop the needed information or skill.	_____	_____
3. It is productive for the leader to ask team members questions to help them develop a new perspective on problems.	_____	_____
4. Responsible workers usually know what needs to be done without too much direction from the boss.	_____	_____
5. It is ideal to let a professional worker figure out the best method for accomplishing a task.	_____	_____
6. Even if workers are empowered, a little inspiration and encouragement from the leader is still useful.	_____	_____
7. Feedback to workers is still useful even if they have considerable responsibility for a task or project.	_____	_____
8. Quite frequently, workers have more knowledge of how to solve a particular problem than does the boss.	_____	_____
9. I urge (or would urge) subordinates to think of problems as opportunities rather than problems.	_____	_____
10. Good results come about when workers are encouraged to search for solutions without supervision.	_____	_____

Skill Development: If, as a leader or manager, you already have most of these attitudes and have engaged in most of these behaviors, you will be good at empowerment. Most of these attitudes and practices can be developed without transforming your personality.

Source: Statements 9 and 10 are adapted from Robert P. Vecchio, Joseph E. Justin, and Craig L. Pearse, "Empowering Leadership: An Examination of Mediating Mechanisms within a Hierarchical Structure," *Leadership Quarterly*, June 2010, p. 540.

responsible for online sales. You have the product knowledge and the IT smarts. I don't. The job is your baby."

Henry Mintzberg reminds us that many professional workers already have considerable initiative and responsibility. In his words: "Truly empowered workers, such as doctors in a hospital, even bees in a hive, do not await gifts from their managerial gods; they know what they are there to do, and just do it."[20] The workers assigned to the Scorpion Team who were developing the truck diesel engine (described in the Leader in Action) most likely fit the same category. If they did not have considerable initiative, they would not have volunteered to join the team.

Link Work Activities to Organizational Goals Empowerment works better when the empowered activities are aligned with the strategic goals of the organization. Empowered workers who have responsibility to carry out activities that support the major goals of the organization will identify more with the company. At the same time, they will develop a feeling of being a partner in the business.[21] Imagine a scenario in which a company auditor is authorized to spend large sums of travel money to accomplish her job. She is given this authority because a strategic goal of top-level management is to become a company admired for its honest business practices.

Provide Ample Information For empowerment to be effective, employees should have ample information about everything that affects their work. Especially important is for workers to fully understand the impact of their actions on the company's costs and profits. Armed with such information, employees are more likely to make decisions that have a positive influence on the bottom line. And they are more likely to use empowerment to make decisions that contribute to business success. For example, an empowered sales representative, armed with cost information, is less likely to grant discounts that lose money for the company.

Allow Group Members to Choose Methods Under ideal conditions, the leader or manager explains to the individual or group what needs to be done (sets a direction) and lets the people involved choose the method. Explaining why the tasks need to be performed is also important. One of the roles of a true professional is to choose the method for accomplishing a task, such as a tax consultant deciding how to prepare the taxes for a business owner. Allowing people to determine the most efficient work technique is the essence of empowerment.[22]

Encourage Self-Leadership Encouraging team members to lead themselves is the heart of empowerment. The basic idea of **self-leadership** is that all organizational members are capable of leading themselves at least to some extent. Complete self-leadership would involve workers deciding what should be done, why it should be done, and how to accomplish the task. A trigger to self-leadership would be to give a handful of talented employees the general instructions, "Why not spend a few hours per week dreaming up something that can make us money?"

When employees practice self-leadership, they feel empowered. At W. L. Gore & Associates, Inc., a manufacturer of insulated material, including GORE-TEX,® there are no bosses or managers, but many leaders. Every employee is regarded as a knowledge worker who has the ability to identify profitable new products.[23]

Establish Limits to Empowerment   One of the major situations in which empowerment creates disharmony and dysfunction is when workers lack a clear perception of the boundaries of empowerment. Empowered group members may feel that they can now make decisions unilaterally, without conferring with managers, team leaders, or other team members.[24] Limits to empowerment might mean explaining to employees that they have more authority than before, but still they cannot engage in such activities as the following:

- Set their own wages and those of top management
- Make downsizing decisions
- Hire mostly friends and relatives
- Work fewer than forty hours for full pay

Many employees justify dysfunctional actions by saying, "I'm empowered to do what I want." It is management's responsibility to guide employment activities that support the organization.

Continue to Lead   Although leaders empower group members, they should still provide guidance, emotional support, and recognition. Mark Samuel helps companies organize into teams to enhance accountability for results, yet at the same time he emphasizes the leader's role: "Empowerment often becomes an abdication of leadership. In other words, if I empower you, I don't have to guide you. People need guidance. Leadership cannot abdicate the role of providing guidance."[25] Because employees are empowered does not mean that they should be abandoned.

The general manager of the JW Marriott Marquis Miami, Florencia Tabeni, provides a realistic example of finding the right balance between empowering the staff, yet continuing to lead. She explains: "I like to give empowerment to the staff. I am much more flexible, more patient now than before. My staff knows they can count on me and I'm always available, but they appreciate empowerment."[26]

Take into Account Cultural Differences   All empowering practices can be influenced by cross-cultural factors. A group member's cultural values might lead to either an easy acceptance of empowerment or reluctance to be empowered. Americans are stereotyped as individualists. Nevertheless, they are so accustomed to working in teams (sports included) that being part of an empowered team would seem natural.

But not all cultures support empowerment. In one study, data from employees of a single firm with operations in the United States, Mexico, Poland, and India were used to test the fit of empowerment and continuous improvement practices with national culture. The company was engaged in light manufacturing, and data were collected from about forty sites. Empowerment was negatively associated with job satisfaction in the Indian plants, but positively associated in the other three samples. The underlying cultural reason is that Indians (at least those working in India) expect the leader or manager to make most of the decisions.[27] Continuous improvement was positively related to satisfaction in all four samples.

Empowerment is an integral part of leadership and management, and therefore presumed to contribute to individual and organizational effectiveness. A study of management teams in 102 hotel properties demonstrated that empowerment is beneficial, yet works indirectly. Empowering leadership was positively related to workers sharing knowledge and team efficacy. The latter refers to self-confidence about attaining goals, measured by such perceptions as "We are confident of achieving the occupancy goal of our hotel." Both knowledge sharing and efficacy were positively associated with team performance, as measured by the hotel's occupancy rate.[28] A study with M.B.A. students engaged in consulting projects showed that when leadership was shared between team leaders and group members, clients tended to rate the consulting teams more favorably. Business faculty advisers were the team leaders. The tie-in with empowerment is that shared leadership is a form of empowerment.[29]

Effective Delegation and Empowerment

A major contributor to empowerment is **delegation**, the assignment of formal authority and responsibility for accomplishing a specific task to another person. Without delegation, effective leadership and management cannot take place. Delegation becomes more important as more tasks need to be done, and those tasks are complex. To lead is to inspire and persuade others to accomplish tasks, not to accomplish everything by working alone.

Delegation is narrower than empowerment because it deals with a specific task, whereas empowerment covers a broad range of activities and a mental set about assuming more responsibility. Delegation, like empowerment, is motivational because it gives group members a chance to develop their skills and demonstrate their competence. Instead of delegation being simply a method for the manager or leader to lighten the personal workload, it becomes a developmental opportunity for the recipient of the delegated task.

When delegation is poor, conflict often erupts between the individual who thought he or she was responsible for a task and the delegator. A classic example of this type of conflict took place during the brief reign of William Perez as CEO of Nike, reporting to founder Phil Knight. Perez thought he had been delegated considerable responsibility from chairman Knight, but in fact the delegation was limited. For example, Perez thought he would have free rein to revamp marketing strategy. He proposed increasing direct sales to consumers through Web and Nike stores. However, Knight jumped in and favored the existing practice of selling through third-party retailers. Perez lasted only fourteen months in the position.[30]

You are invited to gain some practice in the realities of empowerment by doing Leadership Skill-Building Exercise 11-1. Keep in mind the importance of delegation when doing the exercise.

LEADERSHIP SKILL-BUILDING EXERCISE 11-1

Conducting an Empowerment Session

If you are already a manager, the description of empowering practices has given you some useful ideas about empowering others. The role-playing exercise described here gives you a chance to practice your empowering skills. One person plays the role of a leader, and six other people play the role of group members. You are meeting with your group today to get them started on the road toward empowerment. You will need to engage in dialogue with the group to begin the process. The following scenarios should be staffed by different groups of students:

Information Technology Customer-Service Center

You are in charge of an information technology call center whose primary activity is to respond to telephone inquiries from around the country from customers who are having problems using the company's software. The workers who answer the phone are full-time professionals, many of whom are recent college graduates. A major goal of yours is to empower your workers to do as much as they can to satisfy callers' demands. You want your staff to take more personal responsibility for customer problems.

Debt-Collection Specialists

You are the manager of a regional office of a large debt-collection service. Most of your clients are business firms owed money by other firms. Your office is 25 percent below is target for debt collection so far this fiscal year, with five months remaining. The standard methods of debt collection prescribed by the company do not appear to be effective enough. You meet with your staff today to empower them to go beyond the standard methods of debt collection, such as a series of letters and phone calls.

Doing this exercise is useful because it helps you develop the right mental set for a leader who empowers group members. Another advantage is that it sensitizes you to the importance of looking for signs of hesitation and ambivalence when you attempt to empower group members.

FACTORS THAT CONTRIBUTE TO ORGANIZATIONAL POLITICS

As used here, the term **organizational politics** refers to informal approaches to gaining power through means other than merit or luck. Politics are played to achieve power, either directly or indirectly. For example, a person seeking to enhance his or her legitimate power might use a variety of tactics to be favorably perceived by top-level decision makers in the company. Power may be achieved in such diverse ways as by being promoted, by receiving a larger budget or other resources, by obtaining more resources for one's work group, or by being exempt from undesirable assignments. The meaning of *organizational politics* continues to shift in a positive, constructive direction. A group of researchers concluded: "Political skill is an interpersonal style that combines social awareness with the ability to communicate well."[31] Leaders need political skill for such purposes as building alliances and gaining resources for their constituents. Nevertheless, many writers still regard organizational politics as emphasizing self-interest at the expense of others, engaging in mysterious activities, or kissing up.

People want power for many different reasons, which is why political behavior is so widespread in organizations. By definition, politics is used to acquire power. A number of individual and organizational factors contribute to political behavior, as described next.

Pyramid-Shaped Organization Structure

The very shape of large organizations is the most fundamental reason why organizational members are motivated toward political behavior. A pyramid concentrates power at the top. Only so much power is therefore available to distribute among the many people who would like more of it. Each successive layer on the organization chart wields less power than the layer above. At the very bottom of the organization, workers have limited power except for their legal rights. Also, an entry-level worker with a valuable skill in a tight labor market has some usable power. Since most organizations today have fewer layers than they previously had, the competition for power has become more intense. Although empowerment may be motivational for many workers, it is unlikely to satisfy the quest to hold a formal position of power. Workers still struggle to obtain a corner office or even a corner cubicle.

Subjective Standards of Performance

People often resort to organizational politics because they do not believe that the organization has an objective and fair way of judging their performance and suitability for promotion. Similarly, when managers have no objective way of differentiating effective people from less effective, they will resort to favoritism. The adage "It's not what you know but who you know" applies to organizations that lack clear-cut standards of performance.

Environmental Uncertainty and Turbulence

When people operate in an unstable and unpredictable environment, they tend to behave politically. They rely on organizational politics to create a favorable impression because uncertainty makes it difficult to determine what they should really be accomplishing.

The uncertainty, turbulence, and insecurity created by corporate downsizings are a major contributor to office politics. Many people believe intuitively that favoritism plays a major role in deciding who will survive the downsizing. In response to this perception, organizational members attempt to ingratiate themselves with influential people.

Emotional Insecurity

Some people resort to political maneuvers to ingratiate themselves with superiors because they lack confidence in their own talents and skills. A pension fund manager who has directed the firm toward investments with an annualized 15 percent return does not have to be overly political because he or she will have confidence in being capable. A person's choice of political strategy may indicate emotional insecurity. For instance, an insecure person might laugh loudly at every humorous comment the boss makes.

Machiavellian Tendencies

Some people engage in political behavior because they want to manipulate others, sometimes for their own personal advantage. The term *Machiavellianism* traces back to Niccolò Machiavelli (1469–1527), an Italian political philosopher and statesman. His most famous work, *The Prince*, describes how a leader may acquire and maintain power. Machiavelli's ideal prince was an amoral, manipulating tyrant who would restore the Italian city-state of Florence to its former glory. Three hundred and sixty years later, a study by Gerald Biberman showed a positive relationship between Machiavellianism and political behavior, based on questionnaires that measured these two tendencies.[32]

Encouraging Admiration from Subordinates

Most organizational leaders say they do not encourage kissing up and that they prefer honest feedback from subordinates. Yet, without meaning to, these same managers and leaders encourage flattery and servile praise. Managers, as well as other workers, send out subtle signals that they want to be praised, such as smiling after receiving a compliment and frowning when receiving negative feedback. Also, admirers are more likely to receive good assignments and high performance evaluations. Executive coach Marshall Goldsmith explains that, without meaning to, many managers create an environment where people learn to reward others with accolades that are not completely warranted. People generally see this tendency in others but not in themselves.[33]

Communication technology, including social media, facilitates the admiration of superiors. A subordinate who might feel uncomfortable complimenting a superior in-person, or by phone can easily post a compliment online. For example, a status update on Facebook or a tweet might state: "Just received some dynamite feedback from Shana. She pointed me in right direction."

POLITICAL TACTICS AND STRATEGIES

To make effective use of organizational politics, leaders must be aware of specific political tactics and strategies. To identify and explain the majority of political tactics would require years of study and observation. Leaders so frequently need support for their programs that they search for innovative types of political behaviors. Furthermore, new tactics continue to emerge as the workplace becomes increasingly competitive. Here we look at a representative group of political tactics and strategies categorized as to whether they are ethical or unethical. (Several of the influence tactics described in Chapter 10, such as ingratiation, might also be considered political behaviors.)

Ethical Political Tactics and Strategies

So far, we have discussed organizational politics without pinpointing specific tactics and strategies. This section describes a sampling of ethical political behaviors, divided into three related groups: tactics and strategies aimed at (1) gaining power, (2) building relationships with superiors and coworkers, and (3) avoiding political blunders. All of these political approaches help the leader gain or retain power. Using them can also help the leader succeed in and manage stressful work environments. As defined by a group of researchers, political skill is a constructive force. It is an interpersonal style that manifests itself in being socially astute and engaging in behaviors that lead to feelings of confidence, trust, and sincerity.[34] For example, a middle manager with political skill might be able to defend his or her group against an angry CEO looking for a scapegoat.

Leadership Self-Assessment Quiz 11-2 gives you an opportunity to measure your tendencies toward engaging in positive political tactics and strategies.

LEADERSHIP SELF-ASSESSMENT **QUIZ 11-2**

The Positive Organizational Politics Questionnaire

Answer each question "mostly agree" or "mostly disagree," even if it is difficult for you to decide which alternative best describes your opinion.

	MOSTLY AGREE	MOSTLY DISAGREE
1. Pleasing my boss is a major goal of mine.	_____	_____
2. I go out of my way to flatter important people.	_____	_____
3. I am most likely to do favors for people who can help me in return.	_____	_____
4. I intend to, or already have, cultivated friendships with powerful people.	_____	_____
5. I will compliment a coworker even if I have to think hard about what might be praiseworthy.	_____	_____
6. If I thought my boss needed the help, and I had the expertise, I would show him or her how to use an electronic gadget for personal life.	_____	_____
7. I laugh heartily at my boss's humor, so long as I think he or she is at least a little funny.	_____	_____
8. I would not be too concerned about following a company dress code, so long as I looked neat.	_____	_____
9. If a customer sent me a compliment through e-mail, I would forward a copy to my boss and another influential person.	_____	_____
10. I smile only at people in the workplace whom I genuinely like.	_____	_____
11. An effective way to impress people is to tell them what they want to hear.	_____	_____
12. I would never publicly correct mistakes made by the boss.	_____	_____

QUIZ 11-2 (continued)

	MOSTLY AGREE	MOSTLY DISAGREE
13. I would be willing to use my personal contacts to gain a promotion or desirable transfer.	_____	_____
14. I think it is a good idea to send a congratulatory note to someone in the company who receives a promotion to an executive position.	_____	_____
15. I think office politics is only for people who cannot succeed based on their talents.	_____	_____
16. I have already started to develop a network of useful contacts.	_____	_____
17. I am quite willing to make negative comments about my company on social media websites if the comments are deserved.	_____	_____
18. I don't care if there are silly photos of me posted on the Internet because private life is separate from one's career.	_____	_____
19. I have posted positive comments about my boss on the Internet.	_____	_____
20. I have posted positive comments about my employer on the Internet.	_____	_____

Scoring and interpretation: Give yourself a plus 1 for each answer that matches the answer key. Each question that receives a score of plus 1 shows a tendency toward playing positive organizational politics. The scoring key is as follows:

1. Mostly agree	8. Mostly disagree	15. Mostly disagree
2. Mostly agree	9. Mostly agree	16. Mostly agree
3. Mostly agree	10. Mostly disagree	17. Mostly disagree
4. Mostly agree	11. Mostly agree	18. Mostly disagree
5. Mostly agree	12. Mostly agree	19. Mostly agree
6. Mostly agree	13. Mostly agree	20. Mostly agree
7. Mostly agree	14. Mostly agree	

- 1–9: Below-average tendency to play office politics
- 10–14: Average tendency to play office politics
- 15 and above: Above-average tendency to play office politics; strong need for power

Skill Development: Thinking about your political tendencies in the workplace is important for your career because most successful leaders are moderately political. The ability to use politics effectively and ethically increases with importance in the executive suite. Most top players are effective office politicians. Yet being overly and blatantly political can lead to distrust, thereby damaging your career.

Strategies Aimed at Gaining Power All political tactics are aimed at acquiring and maintaining power, even the power to avoid a difficult assignment. Tom Peters says that although power can often be abused, it can also be used to bene-fit many people. "And as a career building tool, the slow and steady (and subtle) amassing of power is the surest road to success."[35] Here are eleven techniques aimed directly at gaining power.

1. *Develop power contacts.* Cultivating friendly, cooperative relationships with powerful organizational members and outsiders can make the leader's cause much easier to advance. Developing power contacts is a focused type of social networking. These contacts can benefit a person by supporting his or her ideas in meetings and other public forums. One way to develop these contacts is to be more social, for example, by throwing parties and inviting powerful people and their guests. Some organizations and some bosses frown on social familiarity, however. And power holders receive many invitations, so they might not be available.

Considerable networking for the development of power contacts now takes place through social networking websites geared toward professionals, such as LinkedIn, and specialty sites such as those geared toward special industry groups, such as sales and marketing, and information technology. Business writer Denise Campbell notes that the social media websites have become to business professionals and entrepreneurs what golf is to C-suite occupants—an opportunity to strategically network and execute business transactions. Also, social media can level the playing field by allowing more people access without restrictions on time, location, or social status.[36]

A key aspect of networking is to find some way of reciprocating when a network member provides you a useful contact or helps you in some other way. Leadership Skill-Building Exercise 11-2 provides some insight into reciprocity when networking.

2. *Have a compelling vision.* Jeffrey Pfeffer, a noted professor of organizational behavior at Stanford University, writes that a compelling vision helps the leader exercise power. A compelling vision in this context is a socially valuable objective. A leader within a school system will often recommend a particular initiative, such as establishing rewards for good teachers, because it

---

LEADERSHIP SKILL-BUILDING EXERCISE 11-2

Paying Back Favors from Network Members

Most readers are aware that effective networkers find some way to pay back those people in their network who have done them favors. For example, if a store owner refers you to a contact that leads to a job interview you might refer a customer to his or her store. However, finding useful ways to reciprocate favors by network members is not so easy. Your assignment is to brainstorm in groups to develop alternative solutions to the problem, "How can we reciprocate when a network member does us a favor?" The network members can be those developed offline as well as those you have developed virtually, such as Facebook members. Aim for at least a dozen suggestions. After first compiling the suggestions, refine the list for duplication and precision. Perhaps reduce your list to the six most effective suggestions. If feasible, a team leader from each group presents the suggestions to the rest of the class.

Class members might then discuss answers to these questions: (1) Which several suggestions were the most frequently offered across the groups? (2) Which suggestions do I think are good enough to use now or in the future?

is in the best interests of the children. In a business organization, a leader might propose an initiative, such as acquiring another company, because it serves the interests of shareholders.[37]

3. *Control vital information.* Power accrues to those who control vital information, as indicated in the discussion of personal power. Many former government or military officials have found power niches for themselves in industry after leaving the public payroll. Frequently, such an individual will be hired as the Washington representative of a firm that does business with the government. They control the vital information of knowing whom to contact in order to sidestep some of the roadblocks to getting government contracts approved.

Although the reflex answer for obtaining information is now "Google it," personal contacts are still important for non-recorded information. To facilitate controlling vital information, it is politically important to stay informed. Successful leaders develop a pipeline to help them keep abreast, or even ahead, of developments within the firm. For this reason, a politically astute individual befriends the president's assistant. No other source offers the potential for obtaining as much information as the executive administrative assistant.

4. *Control lines of communication.* Related to controlling information is controlling the lines of communication, particularly access to key people. Administrative assistants and staff assistants frequently control an executive's calendar. Both insiders and outsiders must curry favor with the conduit in order to see an important executive. Although many people attempt to contact executives directly through e-mail, some executives delegate the responsibility of screening e-mail messages to an assistant. The assistant will also screen telephone calls, thus being selective about who can communicate directly with the executive.

5. *Do what the political environment demands.* A high-level political strategy is to do whatever the political environment demands to attain your goals. In this way, you gain the support of decision makers. Ralph D. Crosby is chairman of EADS North America—the U.S. defense arm of the giant European Aeronautic Defence & Space Co., whose divisions include Airbus. A few years ago, when Crosby was the company CEO, one of his first moves to facilitate obtaining orders from the U.S. government was establishing stateside final production factories for helicopters. The move brought 645 high-paying assembly jobs to Texas, Mississippi, and Alabama. Crosby also partnered with big U.S. contractors to help cultivate senators who make defense-spending decisions.[38]

6. *Bring in outside experts.* To help legitimize their positions, executives will often hire a consultant to conduct a study or cast an opinion. Consciously or unconsciously, many consultants are hesitant to bite the hand that feeds them. A consultant will therefore often support the executive's position. In turn, the executive will use the consultant's findings to prove that he or she is right. This tactic might be considered ethical because the executive believes he or she is obtaining an objective opinion.

7. *Make a quick showing.* A display of dramatic results can help gain acceptance for one's efforts or those of the group. Once a person has impressed management with his or her ability to solve that first problem, that person can look forward to working on problems that will bring greater power. A staff professional might volunteer to spruce up a company website to make it more appealing. After accomplishing that feat, the person might be invited to join the e-commerce team.

8. *Remember that everyone expects to be paid back.* According to the Law of Reciprocity, everybody in the world expects to be paid back.[39] If you do not find some way to reimburse people for the good deeds they have done for you, your supply of people to perform good deeds will run short. Because many of these good deeds bring you power, such as by supporting your initiative, your power base will soon erode. As a way of paying back the person who supported your initiative, you might mention publicly how the person in question provided you with expert advice on the technical aspects of your proposal.

Leadership Skill-Building Exercise 11-2 gives you an opportunity to develop practical solutions to the challenge of reciprocating for favors granted you by network members.

9. *Be politically correct.* Political correctness involves being careful not to offend or slight anyone, and being extra civil and respectful.[40] The politically correct person therefore avoids creating some enemies. An effective use of political correctness would be to say that "We need a ladder in our department because we have workers of different heights who need access to the top shelves." It would be politically incorrect to say, "We need ladders because we have some short workers who cannot reach the top shelves."

10. *Be the first to accept reasonable changes.* A natural inclination for most people is to resist change, so the person who steps forward first to accept reasonable changes will acquire some political capital. The team member who welcomes the changes exerts a positive influence on group members who may be dragging their heels about the change. An example might be that the company is attempting to shift to an online system of performance evaluation, thereby eliminating paper filing. It is politically wise to be an early adopter of the new system.

11. *Develop positive psychological capital.* A comprehensive strategy for both gaining power, as well as building relationships, is to develop **positive psychological capital**. The term refers to an individual's positive psychological state of development, characterized by four psychological resources: self-efficacy, hope, optimism, and resilience. (Self-efficacy refers to confidence to take on and invest the necessary effort to succeed at challenging tasks.) Although a complex aspect of behavior, positive psychological capital can be developed over time, particularly if the individual focuses on one of the four resources at a time. A person with considerable positive psychological capital tends to be powerful.

A study conducted with 79 police leaders and 264 sergeants indicated that leaders' psychological capital was positively related to the job performance of their team members. Performance was measured in terms of a straightforward scale developed for the study, with one of the items being, "How would you judge the overall competence of this individual?"[41] The link to power in this study is that strong job performance by subordinates accrues power to the leader.

Strategies and Tactics Aimed at Building Relationships   You would probably not be studying leadership if you did not think building relationships was a key part of success in the workplace. To reinforce this point, here is what Stephen I. Sadove, the chairman and chief executive of Saks, Inc., said were his biggest leadership lessons:

> I used opportunities to get involved and develop relationships with a diverse set of people, as opposed to the narrow group of people I was dealing with day-to-day, and that made a huge difference. It shaped my philosophy in terms of the importance of relationship building. It really underlies my entire philosophy of how to run a business.[42]

The lion's share of organizational politics involves building positive relationships with network members who can be helpful now or later. This network includes superiors, subordinates, other lower-ranking people, coworkers, external customers, and suppliers. Following are several representative strategies and tactics:

1. *Display loyalty.* A loyal worker is valued because organizations prosper more with loyal than with disloyal employees. Blind loyalty—the belief that the organization cannot make a mistake—is not called for; most rational organizations welcome constructive criticism. A clear form of loyalty to the organization is longevity. Although job-hopping is more acceptable today than in the past, tenure with the company is still an asset for promotion. Tenure tends to contribute more to eligibility for promotion in a traditional industry, such as food processing, than in high-technology firms.

2. *Manage your impression.* Impression management includes behaviors directed at enhancing one's image by drawing attention to oneself. Often the attention of others is directed toward superficial aspects of the self, such as clothing and grooming. Yet impression management also deals with deeper aspects of behavior, such as speaking well and presenting one's ideas coherently. Bad speech habits are recognized as a deterrent to advancement in organizations.[43]

Another part of impression management is telling people about your success or implying that you are an insider. E-mail is used extensively today to send messages to others for the purpose of impressing them with one's good deeds. Displaying good business etiquette has received renewed attention as a key part of impression management, with companies sending staff members to etiquette classes to learn how to create favorable impressions on key people. Etiquette training for professionals and managers is in high demand because so many people have neglected to learn about etiquette earlier in life, and civility in the workplace has declined.[44] Many management scholars take a dim view of impression management, yet the topic has been carefully researched.[45]

3. *Ask satisfied customers to contact your boss.* A favorable comment by a customer receives considerable weight because customer satisfaction is a top corporate priority. If a customer says something nice, the comment will carry more weight than one from a coworker or subordinate. The reason is that co-workers and subordinates might praise a person for political reasons. Customers' motivation is assumed to be pure because they have little concern about pleasing suppliers.

4. *Be courteous, pleasant, and positive.* Courteous, pleasant, and positive people are the first to be hired and the last to be fired (assuming they also have other important qualifications). Polite behavior provides an advantage because many people believe that civility has become a rare quality.

5. *Ask advice*. Asking advice on work-related topics builds relationships with other employees. Asking another person for advice—someone whose job does not require giving it—will usually be perceived as a compliment. Asking advice transmits a message of trust in the other person's judgment.

6. *Send thank-you notes to large numbers of people.* One of the most basic political tactics, sending thank-you notes profusely, is simply an application of sound human relations. Many successful people take the time to send hand-written notes to employees and customers to help create a bond with those people. Handwritten notes have gained in currency because they are a refreshing change from electronic communication.

7. *Flatter others sensibly.* Flattery in the form of sincere praise can be an effective relationship builder. By being judicious in your praise, you can lower the defenses of work associates and make them more receptive to your ideas. A survey of 760 directors found that ingratiatory behavior toward the chief executive plays a bigger role in receiving a board appointment than does having attended an elite school or having elite social connections. James D. Westphal and Ithai Stern concluded that the most efficient way to get more board appointments is to engage in ingratiating behavior (a form of politics). The type of political behavior focused on flattery. Providing advice and information to CEOs frequently was advantageous. Furthermore, not monitoring the strategic decisions of board members too closely was also effective in receiving nominations to other boards. Caucasian males appeared to gain more advantage from ingratiating themselves to peer directors than did ethnic minorities and women.[46]

An effective, general-purpose piece of flattery is to tell another person that you are impressed by something he or she has accomplished. Leadership Skill-Building Exercise 11-3 will help you enhance your skills in flattery.

An example of the research evidence about the contribution of political skill to relationship building comes from a study with 179 employees conducted in a retail service organization. Employees who scored higher on a test of political skill tended to overcome a challenging aspect of leader-member exchanges. Prior research had suggested that superiors and subordinates who were of the same race typically had better quality leader-member exchanges (or quality of the relationship). Correspondingly, racial dissimilarity was associated with a poorer quality leader-member exchange. The results of the study under consideration indicated that subordinates with good political skill were able to develop better relationships with superiors who were of a different race.[47]

LEADERSHIP SKILL-BUILDING EXERCISE 11-3

Flattery Role Play

One student plays the role of a team leader who wants to build alliances with important people in the organization. The company is a major player in consumer electronics, including HDTV and smart phones. One day, the team leader is waiting in line to board an airplane, and he or she figures the wait will be about ten minutes. Another student plays the role of the corporate vice president of marketing, who unexpectedly is standing next to the team leader in the boarding line.

The marketing vice president is middle age, a family person, and has been with the company for twenty-five years. The alliance-building team leader figures he or she has about seven minutes available to make an initial contact with the senior executive and perhaps start a good working relationship. So the team leader decides to engage in appropriate flattery. The marketing vice president seems at least willing to converse with the team leader. Run the scenario for about six minutes in front of the class. The rest of the class members will observe and provide some feedback on the effectiveness of the flattery techniques.

The potential contribution of this exercise is that it may help raise your awareness of the opportunity to engage in constructive political behavior. Recognizing opportunities to gain political advantage can be helpful to a leader's career.

Strategies Aimed at Avoiding Political Blunders   A strategy for retaining power is to refrain from making power-eroding blunders. Committing these politically insensitive acts can also prevent one from attaining power. Several leading blunders are described next.

1. *Criticizing the boss in a public forum.* The oldest saw in human relations is to "praise in public and criticize in private." Yet in the passion of the moment, we may still surrender to an irresistible impulse to criticize the boss publicly. Also, hundreds of people have lost their jobs because they make a vindictive statement about their boss on a social media website, particularly Facebook.[48]

2. *Bypassing the boss.* Protocol is still highly valued in a hierarchical organization. Going around the boss to resolve a problem is therefore hazardous. You might be able to accomplish the bypass, but your career could be damaged and your recourses limited. Except in cases of outrageous misconduct such as blatant sexual harassment or criminal misconduct, your boss's boss will probably side with your boss.

3. *Declining an offer from top management.* Turning down top management, especially more than once, is a political blunder. You thus have to balance sensibly managing your time against the blunder of refusing a request from top management. Today, an increasing number of managers and corporate professionals decline opportunities for promotion when the new job requires geographic relocation. For these people, family and lifestyle preferences are more important than gaining political advantage on the job.

4. *Putting your foot in your mouth (being needlessly tactless).* To avoid hurting your career, it is important to avoid—or at least minimize—being blatantly tactless toward influential people. An example would be telling the CEO that

he or she should delegate speech making to another person because he or she is such a poor speaker. "You don't get to be a senior person if you are repeatedly tactless," advises the head of a New York recruiting firm.[49] When you feel you are on the verge of being critical, delay your response, and perhaps reword it for later delivery. Use your emotional intelligence! If you are needlessly tactless, compensate the best you can by offering a full apology later.

Putting your foot in your mouth can also take the form of making a public statement that many people interpret to have a negative meaning or to reflect callousness. The Deepwater Horizon oil rig explosion in 2010 spewed hundreds of millions of gallons of oil into the Gulf of Mexico and killed eleven workers. BP Chief Executive at the time, Tony Hayward, made a series of public appearances explaining the company's recovery efforts. During one appearance, Hayward said he wanted his "life back," which angered many people because they thought he had not suffered much in comparison to the many victims of the disaster. This gaffe contributed to his inability to elicit much empathy from the U.S. public, and he was dismissed shortly thereafter.[50]

5. *Not conforming to the company dress code.* Although some degree of independence and free thinking is welcome in many organizations, violating the dress code can block you from acquiring more power. Conforming to the dress code suggests that you are part of the team and you understand what is expected. Dress codes can be violated by dressing too informally *or* formally, and by wearing clothing that symbolizes a cultural identity.[51]

6. *Writing embarrassing or incriminating e-mail messages.* A political blunder committed frequently is to use company e-mail to send messages that if discovered would embarrass you or place you at risk for being fired. Hundreds of workers have sent messages to the effect, "The CEO is an idiot," only to be confronted with the evidence later. (Almost any e-mail message can be retrieved by IT specialists.) As mentioned previously, inappropriate Internet postings can be political blunders.

Unethical Political Tactics and Strategies

Any technique of gaining power can be devious if practiced in the extreme. A person who supports a boss by feeding him or her insider information that could affect the price of company stock is being devious. Some approaches are unequivocally unethical, such as those described next. In the long run they erode a leader's effectiveness by lowering credibility. Devious tactics might even result in lawsuits against the leader, the organization, or both.

Backstabbing   The ubiquitous back stab requires that you pretend to be nice but all the while plan someone's demise. A frequent form of backstabbing is to initiate a conversation with a rival about the weaknesses of a common boss, encouraging negative commentary and making careful mental notes of what the person says. When these comments are passed along to the boss, the rival appears disloyal and foolish. E-mail has become a medium for the back stab. The sender of the message documents a mistake made by another individual and includes key people on the distribution list. A sample message sent by one manager to a rival began as follows, "Hi, Ted. I'm sorry you couldn't make our important meeting. I guess you had some other important priorities. But we need your input on the following major agenda item we tackled...."

Embrace or Demolish   The ancient strategy of "embrace or demolish" suggests that you remove from the premises rivals who suffered past hurts through your efforts; otherwise, the wounded rivals might retaliate at a vulnerable moment. This kind of strategy is common after a hostile takeover; many executives lose their jobs because they opposed the takeover. A variation of embrace or demolish is to terminate managers from the acquired organization who oppose adapting to the culture of the new firm. For example, a free-wheeling manager who opposes the bureaucratic culture of the acquiring firm might be terminated as "not able to identify with our mission."

Setting a Person Up for Failure   The object of a setup is to place a person in a position where he or she will either fail outright or look ineffective. For example, an executive whom the CEO dislikes might be given responsibility for a troubled division whose market is rapidly collapsing. The newly assigned division president cannot stop the decline and is then fired for poor performance.

Divide and Rule   An ancient military and governmental strategy, this tactic is sometimes used in business. The object is to have subordinates fight among themselves, therefore yielding the balance of power to another person. If team members are not aligned with one another, there is an improved chance that they will align with a common superior. One way of getting subordinates to fight with one another is to place them in intense competition for resources. An example would be asking them to prove data explaining why their budget is more worthy than the budget requested by rivals.

Playing Territorial Games   Also referred to as turf wars, **territorial games** involve protecting and hoarding resources that give one power, such as information, relationships, and decision-making authority. Territorial behavior, according to Annette Simmons, is based on a hidden force that limits peoples' desire to give full cooperation. People are biologically programmed to be greedy for whatever they think it takes to survive in the corporate environment.

The purpose of territorial games is to vie for the three kinds of *territory* in the modern corporate survival game: information, relationships, or authority. A relationship is hoarded through such tactics as discouraging others from visiting a key customer or blocking a high performer from getting a promotion or transfer.[52] For example, the manager might tell others that his star performer is mediocre to prevent the person from being considered for a valuable transfer possibility. Other examples of territorial games include monopolizing time with clients, scheduling meetings so someone cannot attend, and shutting out coworkers from joining you on an important assignment.

A review of research and theory suggests that territoriality can sometimes help the organization by increasing the commitment of workers and reducing conflict. Commitment might increase because workers might feel a sense of ownership, such as feeling at home in a personally decorated cubicle. Conflict might be reduced because people stay out of each other's territory. However, a major negative consequence of territoriality is that employees become self-focused, which detracts from their ability to focus on the organization. Territoriality can create isolation among workers, leading to less connectedness with others in the organization.[53] As one marketing manager said, "Why do we bother inviting finance types to our meetings?"

Creating and Then Resolving a False Catastrophe   An advanced devious tactic is for a manager to pretend a catastrophe exists and then proceed to "rescue" others from the catastrophe, thereby appearing to be a superhero.[54] The political player rushes in and declares that everything is a mess and the situation is almost hopeless; shortly thereafter, he or she resolves the problem. An example would be for a newly appointed information technology manager to inform top management that the system he inherited is antiquated and approaching the point of severely damaging the company's operations. One week later, he claims to have miraculously overhauled the information system, such as by ordering new equipment and hiring a few key personnel.

Abusing Power   Abusing power might be conceptualized as an unethical political tactic because the abuse often relates to behavior outside of formal responsibility. (Formal ways of abusing power might be for a CEO to close a plant overseen by a manager he or she disliked, or to use company funds to build an exorbitantly luxurious personal office.) Political abuse of power includes such acts as shouting and swearing at subordinates, sexually harassing them, and humiliating them in meetings. As one example, Sumner Redstone, the chair of Viacom, Inc., is notorious for expressing rage toward subordinates. Several surveys have suggested that most of rude and inappropriate behavior, such as the shouting of profanities, stem from those people with the most formal authority.[55]

EXERCISING CONTROL OVER DYSFUNCTIONAL POLITICS

Carried to excess, organizational politics can hurt an organization and its members. Too much politicking can result in wasted time and effort, thereby lowering productivity. A group of researchers conducted a meta-analysis of available studies of the relationship between the perception of organizational politics and certain important outcomes. The perception of political behavior refers to the recognition that organizational politics is present, as in "I can't take all the politics around here." The major outcomes related to the perception of politics were as follows: (1) more strain, or adverse effects of stress, (2) more intentions to quit, (3) less job satisfaction, (4) less emotional commitment to the employer, (5) lower task performance, and (6) less organizational citizenship behavior.[56]

In short, when a high degree of political behavior is perceived to exist, it can damage individuals and the organization. To avoid these negative consequences, leaders are advised to combat political behavior when it is excessive and dysfunctional. Table 11-1 presents some symptoms of dysfunctional office politics.

TABLE 11-1 Symptoms of Dysfunctional Office Politics (the DOOP Scale)

The ten statements that follow concern ethics in interpersonal relationships on the job. The more frequently any of these actions occur, the more likely the organization or organizational unit is beset with dysfunctional office politics.

1. A conflict between two or more persons or groups was resolved on the basis of who held the most power rather than on what would have made sense and would have worked better.
2. A person or group got even in some way with another person or group.
3. Information about what was going on at work was withheld from a person or group.
4. Information was reported about a person or group that was intentionally exaggerated, misconstrued, and/or made mostly untrue by some other person or group.
5. A person or group was led to believe one thing, when the other was clearly true.
6. A person or group agreed with another person or group solely to keep the boat from rocking.
7. A person or group's worthwhile efforts or initiatives were intentionally undermined.
8. A person reported confidential or unfavorable information about a person or group in order to gain a special advantage.
9. A person or group who looked at things differently and had different points of view was punished and/or silenced by another person or group.
10. An organizational decision was based on self-interest rather than on what made sense and would have worked better.

Source: From Thomas P. Anderson, "Creating Measures of Dysfunctional Office and Organizational Politics: The DOOP and Short Form DEEP Scales," *Psychology: A Journal of Human Behavior,* vol. 31, no. 2, 1994, 34. Reprinted by permission of the author.

In a comprehensive strategy to control politics, *organizational leaders must be aware of its causes and techniques.* For example, during a downsizing, the CEO can be on the alert for instances of backstabbing and transparent attempts to please. Open communication also can constrain the impact of political behavior. For instance, open communication can let everyone know the basis for allocating resources, thus reducing the amount of politicking. If people know in advance how resources are allocated, the effectiveness of attempting to curry favor with the boss will be reduced. When communication is open, it also makes it more difficult for some people to control information and pass along gossip as a political weapon.

Avoiding favoritism and cronyism—avoiding giving the best rewards to the group members you like the best or to old friends—is a potent way of minimizing politics within a work group. If group members believe that getting the boss to like them is much less important than good job performance in obtaining rewards, they will kiss up to the boss less frequently. In an attempt to minimize favoritism, managers must reward workers who impress them through task-related activities.

Setting good examples at the top of the organization can help reduce the frequency and intensity of organizational politics. When leaders are nonpolitical in their actions, they demonstrate in subtle ways that political behavior is not welcome. It may be helpful for the leader to announce during a staff meeting that devious political behavior is undesirable and unprofessional.

LEADERSHIP SKILL-BUILDING **EXERCISE 11-4**

Controlling Office Politics

One student plays the role of a corporate executive visiting one of the key divisions. Six other students play the roles of managers within the division, each of whom wants to impress the boss during their meeting. The corporate executive gets the meeting started by asking the managers in turn to discuss their recent activities and accomplishments. Each division-level manager will attempt to create a very positive impression on the corporate executive. After about nine minutes of observing them fawning over him or her, the executive decides to take action against such excessive politicking. Review the information on political tactics and their control before carrying out this role-assuming exercise.

Another way of reducing the extent of political behavior is for *individuals and the organization to share the same goals,* a situation described as *goal congruence.* If political behavior will interfere with the company and individuals achieving their goals, workers with goal congruence are less likely to play office politics excessively. A project leader is less likely to falsely declare that the boss's idea is good just to please the boss if the project leader wants the company to succeed.

Politics can sometimes be constrained by a *threat to discuss questionable information in a public forum.* People who practice devious politics usually want to operate secretly and privately. They are willing to drop hints and innuendoes and make direct derogatory comments about someone else, provided they will not be identified as the source. An effective way of stopping the discrediting of others is to offer to discuss the topic publicly.[57] The person attempting to pass on the questionable information will usually back down and make a statement closer to the truth.

Finally, *hiring people with integrity* will help reduce the number of dysfunctional political players. References should be checked carefully with respect to the candidate's integrity and honesty.[58] Say to the reference, "Tell me about _____'s approach to playing politics." Leadership Skill-Building Exercise 11-4 provides an opportunity to practice the subtle art of discouraging excessive political behavior on the job.

SUMMARY

Organizational power is derived from many sources, including position power (legitimate, reward, coercive, and information) and personal power (expert, reference, and prestige). Power also stems from ownership, dependencies, capitalizing on opportunity, managing critical problems, and being close to power.

Full-fledged empowerment includes the dimensions of meaning, self-determination, competence, impact, and internal commitment. Actions that can be taken to become an empowering leader include the following: foster initiative and responsibility, link work activities to the goals of the organization, provide ample information, allow group members to choose methods, encourage self-leadership, establish limits to empowerment, and continue to lead. Also, take into account cultural differences in how empowerment is accepted. Delegation is another important part of empowerment.

To acquire and retain power, a leader must skillfully use organizational politics. The meaning of *politics* continues to shift in a positive, constructive

direction. Contributing factors to organizational politics include the pyramidal shape of organizations, subjective performance standards, environmental uncertainty, emotional insecurity, Machiavellian tendencies, and encouraging admiration from subordinates.

To make effective use of organizational politics, leaders must be aware of specific political tactics and strategies. Ethical methods can be divided into those aimed directly at gaining power, those aimed at building relationships, and those aimed at avoiding political blunders. Unethical and devious tactics, such as the embrace or demolish strategy, constitute another category of political behavior.

Carried to extremes, organizational politics can hurt an organization and its members. Being aware of the causes and types of political behavior can help leaders deal with the problem. Setting good examples of nonpolitical behavior is helpful, as is achieving goal congruence and threatening to publicly expose devious politicking. It is also good to hire people who have integrity.

KEY TERMS

power	prestige power	empowerment
legitimate power	dependence perspective	self-leadership
reward power	resource dependence perspective	delegation
coercive power		organizational politics
information power	strategic contingency theory	positive psychological capital
personal power	centrality	territorial games

✔ GUIDELINES FOR ACTION AND SKILL DEVELOPMENT

A striking advantage of gaining power is that it helps you control your environment, which in turn leads to less stress and better physical and mental health—and therefore prolongs your life. In contrast, having so little power that you cannot control your job and your environment creates stress, leading to poorer physical and mental health, and quite often a shorter life.[59]

Finding ways to increase your power is therefore a vital life skill.

So much has been said and written about the importance of building your in-person and virtual network that it seems as if the more contacts you have the better. It is usually better to have a smaller network of useful, high-quality contacts. British anthropologist Robin Dunbar claims the average human can maintain only 150 close social connections. With information technology, that number can be stretched a bit, but mental capacity and available time set limits to the size of a useful network.[60]

Discussion Questions and Activities

1. How might an employee working for a large company such as GE or Honda have considerable power even though the employee did not hold a position with an executive title?
2. How can a leader occupy a top-level executive position and still have relatively little power?
3. Contrary to popular opinion, CEOs of major U.S. companies come from a wide variety of private universities and state universities, not just a handful of well-publicized M.B.A. programs. What does this fact tell you about sources of power and organizational politics?
4. What can you do this week to enhance your power?

5. To what extent do you think wearing the right type of clothing and accessories can really make a person appear more powerful?
6. Many business leaders say something to the effect of, "We practice empowerment because we don't expect our employees to leave their brains at the door." What are these leaders talking about?
7. Empowerment has been criticized because it leaves no one in particular accountable for results. What is your opinion of this criticism?
8. Many people have asked the question "Isn't office politics just for incompetents?" What is your answer to this question?
9. Give an example of a political blunder you or anybody in your network has witnessed. What were the consequences to the individual stemming from having committed this blunder?
10. Ask an experienced worker to give you an example of the successful application of organizational politics. Which tactic was used, and what was the outcome?

LEADERSHIP CASE PROBLEM A

Yo-Yo Empowerment at Direct Mail, Inc.

Business has been great for Direct Mail, Inc., a company that designs a variety of direct marketing campaigns for its customers. Despite the increase in online advertising, direct mail has been a growth industry in recent years. Among the services of Direct Mail are personalized advertising flyers gearing products to the interests of the recipients, with flyers being mailed to both homes and offices. For example, a person who had ordered fine wines online or by telephone might receive a brochure about wine racks or wine storage cabinets. Another service Direct Mail offers is transactional promotions, or bills that arrive with advertising on the same page.

Dennis Parker, the founder and CEO of Direct Mail, says that he is astonished by the growth of his industry. When he started his company, Parker was warned that going into the junk mail business was a high-risk venture. Yet recently, advertisers have come to realize that people act on flyers directed to

their interest at a higher rate than they respond to Internet advertising or general advertisements in newspapers and magazines.

Parker says that he is passionate about his business for many reasons. He enjoys keeping up with the technology of digital presses, and seeing so much new business coming to Direct Mail based on its reputation. Parker says also that he enjoys the leadership and management challenge of running a growing business. "I'm especially good at motivating my workers through empowerment," he says.

Audrey Valentine, the director of marketing, was having a dinner meeting with Parker at her initiative to talk about his empowering style of leadership. With a gentle laugh, Valentine said to Parker, "I'm not telling you anything this evening I haven't hinted at least six times before. The management team knows you are a sharp businessperson, and a kind manager, but you are also a *yo-yo delegator*."

"What do you mean, I'm a yo-yo delegator?" asked Parker.

"I'll explain what I mean, Dennis. You do the same thing to me, the head of finance, and our operations guy. Remember when you told me something like, 'We haven't done much business yet in the home furnishing field. Why don't you see what new business you can generate in that field?' I put my best effort into drumming up a lead with a home furnishing executive. When I told you of my progress, you asked me to turn over the lead to you so you could wrap up the deal. The yo-yo here is that you give me something to do, and then you take it back when it looks good. What you send out comes back quickly to you."

After listening to Valentine's feedback about the yo-yo delegation, Parker calmly explained: "In this business, high-level contacts and relationships are important. Empowerment can only go so far. A big customer would prefer to deal directly with the CEO, so that's why I step in to help you."

Questions

1. What advice can you offer Parker about his approach to empowerment?
2. To what extent is Valentine committing a political blunder in telling her boss that he is a yo-yo delegator?
3. What is your evaluation of the corporate social responsibility of a direct mail business, considering that probably over 95 percent of recipients of the mailings throw them away immediately?

ASSOCIATED ROLE PLAY

Complaining about Yo-Yo Delegation

CEO Dennis sends director of marketing, Audrey, a text message this morning, stating, "Didn't like being called a yo-yo delegator. Let's meet in my office." Audrey sends back a text message, "Sorry you're ticked off. When to meet?" Toward the end of the day, Dennis and Audrey meet to discuss his discontent with his style of delegation on key products. One student plays the role of Dennis, who believes he has the power to delegate in the manner he wants. Another student plays the role of Audrey, who believes that she is right, but still wants to preserve a good working relationship with Dennis.

Observers will pay special attention to the political skill of Audrey in attempting to win her point, yet not make a bad political mistake.

LEADERSHIP CASE PROBLEM B

Brenda the Tweeting Leader

Brenda is the director of claims processing in a business process outsourcing company that specializes in taking care of the payroll and benefits administration for small- and mid-size companies. Her manager, the CEO, has told Brenda that her leadership skills are satisfactory, but it would be better if she had a bigger impact on the employees in her area of responsibility. "Touch their lives more; be a bigger influence," the CEO told Brenda. "It's up to you to figure out how."

In thinking about potential tactics, Brenda thought of having a bigger impact on her direct reports, as well as other members of the company, by sending them encouraging tweets. Brenda reflected, "Using Twitter, I can spend about thirty minutes per night developing the type of positive relationships it would take days and hours to do with lunch and coffee breaks."

Two days later, Brenda began her Twitter campaign. Much to her comfort, she found that most people in her target group had accounts. Some of Brenda's tweets were as follows:

"You're doing great. It's a pleasure to work for the same employer as you." [Sent to everybody on her list of company employees with Twitter accounts.]

"Carpal tunnel syndrome can cure itself. Sweat it out." [Sent to input clerk on medical leave with carpal tunnel syndrome.]

"You are simply the best leader. Can learn from you." [Sent to company CEO.]

"You are a ray of sunshine on a cloudy day." [Sent to all four mailroom workers.]

"Love ya baby, but put on some speed." [Sent to her administrative assistant.]

"Can't live without you. Wouldn't want to." [Sent to a member of the tech support staff.]

One of the tweet recipients said to another, "Brenda is so cool these days. She's leading by tweet." Another one of these tweet recipients said to another, "Have you seen what Brenda is doing with her Twitter account? She's given me another good reason not to check Twitter every day."

Questions

1. What impact do you think Brenda's tweeting will have on her leadership effectiveness?
2. What do you think of the political effectiveness of sending the same tweet to several workers?
3. What suggestions might you offer Brenda for making even more effective use of Twitter as a leadership tool?

ASSOCIATED ROLE PLAY

Tweet Damage Control

One student plays the role of a worker who reports to Brenda. The worker receives yet another tweet from Brenda, this one stating, "I know that today is going to be a winner for all of us." The worker is having a bad day at home and work. As a result, the worker perceives Brenda's tweet to be annoying, and sends the following e-mail to a few coworkers: "Did Brenda's tweet of the day sicken you also?" The worker then receives a tweet from Brenda, saying, "I just heard that my latest tweet sickened you. What's your problem?" Another student plays the role of Brenda who perceives the counter-tweet to reflect poor judgment, and decides to express her discontent to the worker.

 ## LEADERSHIP SKILL-BUILDING EXERCISE 11-5

My Leadership Portfolio

For this insert into your leadership portfolio, think through all the recent opportunities you might have had to use political tactics. How did you deal with the situation? Did you capitalize on any opportunities? Did you use an ethical approach? Did you use any unethical tactics? Did you commit any political blunders? Here would be an example:

> I saw a flyer indicating that our Business Management Association was having a guest speaker, an executive from Merrill Lynch. I had been pretty

busy with studies, my job, and social life, yet I decided to invest the time and attend. As it worked out, the meeting was a wonderful opportunity to make a couple of good contacts. After the talk, I spoke to the speaker and complimented her. We had a brief conversation about how I was looking for a career in investment banking, and she gave me her business card. I sent her an e-mail message the next day, thanking her for the time she gave me. I also met a couple of important people at the meeting and got their cards also.

LEADERSHIP SKILL-BUILDING **EXERCISE 11-6**

Dealing with a Political Blunder

One student plays the role of a middle manager at Microsoft Corp. who receives an e-mail message from CEO Steve Ballmer stating that several employees in the manager's unit have been spotted using iPhones. Ballmer is adamant that loyal Microsoft employees should not use iPhones—particularly on company premises—because iPhones are manufactured by heated rival, Apple Inc. The middle manager knows that several of his workers are emotionally attached to their iPhones and iPads and do not want to part with them. The middle manager, however, knows that pleasing Ballmer is important because Ballmer is so strong willed and opinionated. Another person plays the role of the volatile Steve Ballmer, who is really upset about these sightings of Microsoft employees using iPhones and iPads, so he calls for an in-person meeting with the middle manager. The goal of the middle manager at the meeting is to maintain political peace with Ballmer, yet still preserve his or her stature with subordinates as a strong leader.

Observers will focus on the political skill of the middle manager in dealing with the situation.

Source: The hypothetical scenario for this exercise was suggested by facts presented in Nick Wingfield, "Forbidden Fruit: Microsoft Workers Hide their iPhones," *The Wall Street Journal*, March 13–14, 2010, pp. A1, A10.

▶❙❙ **LEADERSHIP** VIDEO **CASE** DISCUSSION **QUESTIONS**

To view the videos for this activity, you'll need access to the CourseMate that is available for this text. To get access, visit www.CengageBrain.com.

After watching "Numi Teas," answer the following questions.

1. How do managers use different types of position power at Numi? Provide examples.

2. What sort of empowering practices does Ahmed Rahim use at Numi?

3. What is the Law of Reciprocity? How is it used at Numi?

NOTES

1. Story created from facts found in the following sources: "Sheryl Sandberg, Chief Operating Officer," www.facebook.com/press/info, accessed March 25, 2011; Marshall Kirkpatrick, "Facebook Exec: All Media Will Be Personalized in 3 to 5 Years," *ReadWriteWeb* (www.read writeweb), September 29, 2010, pp. 1–3; Brad Stone and Miguel Helft, "Facebook Hires a Google Executive as No. 2," *New York Times* (www.nytimes.com), March 5, 2008, pp. 1–3; Miguel Helft, "Mark Zuckerberg's Most Valuable Friend," *The New York Times* (www. nytimes.com), October 2, 2010, pp. 1–6; Evan Hessel, "The World's Most Powerful Women," *Forbes*, September 7, 2009, pp. 78–83.

2. John R. French and Bertram Raven, "The Basis of Social Power," in Dorwin Cartwright, ed., *Studies in Social Power* (Ann Arbor, Mich.: Institute for Social Research, 1969); Timothy R. Hinkin and Chester A. Schriescheim, "Power and Influence: The View from Below," *Personnel*, May 1988, pp. 47–50.

3. Jeffrey McCracken, "J. P. Morgan Taps Simon to C-Lead Tech Team," *The Wall Street Journal*, October 13, 2009, p. C3.

4. Ann Davis and Randall Smith, "Merrill Switch: Popular Veteran Is In, Not Out," *The Wall Street Journal*, August 13, 2003, p. C1; Landon Thomas Jr., "Dismantling a Wall Street Club," www. nytimes.com, November 2, 2003; George Anders,

"Is There a Second Act for O'Neal After Merrill?" *The Wall Street Journal*, October 31, 2007, p. A2.

5. Brian O'Keefe, "Meet the CEO of the Biggest Company on Earth," *Fortune*, September 27, 2010, pp. 80–94.

6. Sydney Finkelstein, "Power in Top Management Teams: Dimensions, Measurement, and Validation," *Academy of Management Journal*, August 1992, p. 510.

7. Finkelstein, "Power in Top Management Teams," p. 510.

8. Richard M. Emerson, "Power-Dependence Relations," *American Sociological Review*, vol. 27, 1962, p. 32.

9. Jeffrey Pfeffer, *Managing with Power: Power and Influence in Organizations* (Boston: Harvard Business School Press, 1992), pp. 100–101.

10. Alexandria Berzon and Christina S. N. Lewis, "Debating the Value of the Trump Name," *The Wall Street* Journal, February 26, 2010, pp. B1, B2; Diane Brady, "It's All Donald, All the Time," *BusinessWeek*, January 22, 2007, p. 051; "The Forbes 400 Landlords," *Forbes*, October 9, 2006, p. 110.

11. Jennifer Wang, "Patagonia, from the Ground Up," *Entrepreneur*, June 2010, pp. 26–28.

12. C. R. Hinings, D. J. Hickson, C. A. Lee, R. E. Schenck, and J. W. Pennings, "Strategic Contingencies Theory of Intraorganizational Power," *Administrative Science Quarterly*, 1971, pp. 216–229.

13. "Lessons in Power: Lyndon Johnson Revealed: A Conversation with Historian Robert A. Caro," *Harvard Business Review*, April 2006, pp. 47–52.

14. Gregory G. Dess and Joseph Picken, "Changing Roles: Leadership in the 21st Century," *Organizational Dynamics*, Winter 2000, p. 22.

15. "The Secrets of His Success," *Fortune*, November 29, 2004, p. 158.

16. George Anders, "Overseeing More Employees— With Fewer Managers," *The Wall Street Journal*, March 24, 2008, p. B6.

17. Gretchen M. Spreitzer, "Psychological Empowerment in the Workplace: Dimensions, Measurement, and Validation," *Academy of Management Journal*, October 1995, pp. 1442–1465.

18. Lauren Bennett Cattaneo and Aliya R. Chapman, "The Process of Empowerment: A Model for Use

in Research and Practice," *American Psychologist*, October 2010, pp. 646–659.

19. Scott E. Seibert, Seth R. Silver, and W. Alan Randolph, "Taking Empowerment to the Next Level: A Multiple-Level Model of Empowerment, Performance, and Satisfaction," *Academy of Management Journal*, June 2004, pp. 332–349.

20. Henry Mintzberg, *Managing* (San Francisco: Berrett-Koehler, 2009), p. 64.

21. Barbara Ettorre, "The Empowerment Gap: Hype vs. Reality," *HRfocus*, July 1997, p. 5.

22. Phillip M. Perry, "Seven Errors to Avoid When Empowering Your Staff," *Success Workshop* (a supplement to *Manager's Edge*), March 1999, p. 3.

23. Craig L. Pearce and Charles C. Manz, "The New Silver Bullets of Leadership: The Importance of Self- and Shared-Leadership in Knowledge Work," *Organizational Dynamics*, no. 2, 2005, pp. 130–140.

24. Kyle Dover, "Avoiding Empowerment Traps," *Management Review*, January 1999, p. 52.

25. Dimitry Elias Léger, "Tell Me Your Problem, and I'll Tell You Mine," *Fortune*, October 6, 2000, p. 408.

26. Quoted in "Hotel Executive's Mantra: 'You Can Do It'," *The Miami Herald* (www.miamiherald.com), November 1, 2010, p. 2.

27. Christopher Robert et al., "Empowerment and Continuous Improvement in the United States, Mexico, Poland, and India: Predicting Fit on the Basis of the Dimensions of Power Distance and Individualism," *Journal of Applied Psychology*, October 2000, pp. 751–765.

28. Abhishek Srivastava, Kathryn M. Bartol, and Edwin A. Locke, "Empowering Leadership in Management Teams: Effects on Knowledge Sharing, Efficacy, and Performance," *Academy of Management Journal*, December 2006, pp. 1239–1251.

29. Jay B. Carson, Paul E. Telsuk, and Jennifer A. Marrone, "Shared Leadership in Teams: An Investigation of Antecedent Conditions and Performance," *Academy of Management Journal*, October 2007, pp. 1217–1234.

30. Stanley Holmes, "Inside the Coup at Nike," *Businessweek*, February 6, 2006, pp. 034–037.

31. Gerald R. Ferris et al., "Political Skill at Work," *Organizational Dynamics*, Spring 2000, p. 25.

32. Gerald Biberman, "Personality Characteristics and Work Attitudes of Persons with High,

Moderate, and Low Political Tendencies," *Psychological Reports*, vol. 57, 1985, p. 1309.

33. Marshall Goldsmith, "All of Us Are Stuck on Suck-Ups," *Fast Company*, December 2003, p. 117.

34. Pamela L. Perrewé et al., "Political Skill: An Antidote for Workplace Stressors," *Academy of Management Executive*, August 2000, p. 115.

35. Tom Peters, "Power," *Success*, November 1994, p. 34.

36. Denise Campbell, "What's Your Social Media Strategy?" November 2010, p. 75.

37. Stanley Holmes, "EADS' Unlikely American Ascent," *BusinessWeek*, April 9, 2007, p. 068.

38. Jeffrey Pfeffer, "Power Play," *Harvard Business Review*, July-August 2010, p. 92.

39. Michael Warshaw, "The Good Guy's (and Gal's) Guide to Office Politics," *Fast Company*, April 1998, p. 160.

40. Robin J. Ely, Debra Meyerson, and Martin N. Davidson, "Rethinking Political Correctness," *Harvard Business Review*, September 2006, p. 80.

41. The definition of psychological capital and the research findings are from Fred O. Walumbwa, Suzanne J. Peterson, Bruce J. Avolio, and "An Investigation of the Relationships Among Leader and Follower Psychological Capital, Service Climate, and Job Performance," *Personnel Psychology*, Winter 2010, pp. 937–963.

42. Cited in Adam Bryant, "For the Chief of Saks, It's Culture That Drives Results," *The New York Times* (www.nytimes.com), May 28, 2010.

43. Joann S. Lublin, "To Win Advancement, You Need to Clean Up Any Bad Speech Habits," *The Wall Street Journal*, October 3, 2004, p. B1.

44. "Etiquette School," *Bloomberg Businessweek*, October 16–Ocrtober 24, 2010, pp. 89–91.

45. Much of the scholarly impression management research is reviewed in Andrew J. DuBrin, *Impression Management in the Workplace: Research, Theory, and Practice* (New York and London: Routledge, 2011).

46. James D. Westphal and Ithai Stern, "Flattery Will Get You Everywhere (Especially If You Are a Male Caucasian): How Ingratiation, Boardroom Behavior, and Demographic Minority Status Affect Additional Board Appointments at U. S. Companies," *Academy of Management Journal*, April 2007, pp. 267–288.

47. Robyn L. Brouer, Allison Duke, Darren C. Treadway, and Gerald R. Ferris, "The Moderating Effect of Political Skill on the Demographic Dissimilarity—Leader-Member Exchange Quality Relationship," *Leadership Quarterly*, April 2009, pp. 61–69.

48. "Etiquette School," *Bloomberg Businessweek*, p. 90.

49. Quoted in Joann S. Lublin, "Did I Just Say That?! How You Can Recover from Foot-in-Mouth," *The Wall Street Journal*, June 18, 2002, p. B1.

50. Paul Sonne, "Hayward Fell Short of Modern CEO Demands," *The Wall Street Journal*, July 26, 2010, p. A7.

51. Tracy Minor, "Office Politics: Master the Game by Making Connections," *Monster: Diversity & Inclusion*, October 30, 2002 (monster.com).

52. Annette Simmons, *Territorial Games: Understanding & Ending Turf Wars at Work* (New York: AMACOM, 1998); Robert J. Herbold, *The Fiefdom Syndrome* (New York: Currency Doubleday, 2004).

53. Graham Brown, Thomas B. Lawrence, and Sandra L.Robinson, "Territoriality in Organizations," *Academy of Management Review*, July 2005, pp. 577–594.

54. Jared Sandberg, "Office Superheroes: Saving the Rest of Us from Unseen Dangers," *The Wall Street Journal*, December 10, 2003, p. B1.

55. Jonah Lehr, "The Power Trip," *The Wall Street Journal*, August 14–15, 2010, p. W1; Anne Kreamer, "Go Ahead—Cry at Work," *Time*, April 4, 2011, p. 52.

56. Chu-Hsiang Chang, Christopher C.Rosen, and Paul E. Levy, "The Relationship between Perceptions of Organizational Politics and Employee Attitudes, Strain, and Behavior: A Meta-Analytic Examination," *Academy of Management Journal*, August 2009, pp. 779–801.

57. Robert P. Vecchio, *Organizational Behavior*, 4th ed. (Fort Worth, Tex.: The Dryden Press, 2000), p. 136.

58. "Throw Politics Out of Your Office," *Manager's Edge*, July 2001, p. 8.

59. Research synthesized in Pfeffer, "Power Play, p. 90.

60. Research cited in Chris Brogan, "The Network Is Everything," *Entrepreneur*, October 2010, p. 56.

Communicating with Others and Resolving Conflict

LEARNING OBJECTIVES

After studying this chapter and doing the exercises, you should be able to

- Describe how leaders use communication networks to accomplish their tasks.

- Describe the basics of inspirational and emotion-provoking communication.

- Describe key features of a power-oriented linguistic style.

- Describe the six basic principles of persuasion.

- Describe the challenge of selective listening, and the basics of making the rounds.

- Be sensitive to the importance of overcoming cross-cultural barriers to communication.

- Identify basic approaches to resolving conflict and negotiating.

CHAPTER OUTLINE

In early 2010, Steven Freiberg became CEO of E*Trade, the financial services company known primarily as an online stock brokerage. The financial aspect of Freiberg's career began with a bachelor's degree in banking and finance and an MBA from the Frank Garb School of Business at Hofstra University in Hempstead, New York. He then spent thirty years with Citigroup, retiring in 2009.

The executive leadership positions he held at Citigroup included Co-Chairman and CEO of the Global Consumer Group, Chairman and CEO of Citicards, and Chairman and CEO of Citicorp Investment Group. His biggest accomplishment at Citigroup was assuming responsibility for the company's struggling branch network in the late 1990s and making it profitable within two years. Freiberg developed the reputation of an exceptional senior financial services executive in the consumer side of the business.

Many of Freiberg's successes as a business leader appear to have been facilitated by his willingness to communicate with employees, with a particular emphasis on listening. Based on his careful listening, he has sometimes been referred to as introverted. At the same time he has a reputation for fixing problems and attaining organizational efficiency.

When Freiberg first joined E*Trade, he said that a high priority for him was to discuss the troubled company's direction and operations with a large sampling of employees. Rumors had been circulating that because E*Trade had lost so much money betting on mortgage-backed securities, the company would be put up for sale. Freiberg listened to the argument, and said that a sale was one alternative for enhancing value, but that his primary goal was to improve the company's business.[1]

The executive leader just described acts on an obvious truth that many leaders ignore—open communication between company leaders and group members helps an organization overcome problems and attain success. Effective managers and leaders listen to employees, and open communications contribute to leadership effectiveness. John Hamm notes that effective communication is a leader's most essential tool for executing the essential job of leadership: inspiring organizational members to take responsibility for creating a better future.[2]

Effective communication skills contribute to inspirational leadership. Chapter 4 describes how charismatic leaders are masterful oral communicators. This chapter expands on this theme and also covers the contribution of nonverbal, written, and supportive communication. In addition, this chapter describes the leadership use of communication networks, how the ability to overcome cross-cultural communication barriers enhances leadership effectiveness. Finally, because leaders spend a substantial amount of time resolving conflicts, the chapter also discusses conflict resolution and negotiating skills.

To focus your thinking on your communication effectiveness, complete Leadership Self-Assessment Quiz 12-1.

LEADERSHIP SELF-ASSESSMENT QUIZ 12-1

A Self-Portrait of My Communication Effectiveness

Instructions: The following statements relate to various aspects of communication effectiveness. Indicate whether each of the statements is mostly true or mostly false, even if the most accurate answer would depend somewhat on the situation. Asking another person who is familiar with your communication behavior to help you answer the questions may improve the accuracy of your answers.

	MOSTLY TRUE	MOSTLY FALSE
1. When I begin to speak in a group, most people stop talking, turn toward me, and listen.	☐	☐
2. I receive compliments on the quality of my writing, including my e-mail messages and social media postings.	☐	☐
3. The reaction to the outgoing message on my voice mail has been favorable.	☐	☐
4. I welcome the opportunity to speak in front of a group.	☐	☐
5. I have published something, including a letter to the editor, an article for the school newspaper, or a comment in a company newsletter.	☐	☐
6. I have my own website, and have received at least two compliments about its effectiveness.	☐	☐
7. The vast majority of my written projects in school have received a grade of B or A.	☐	☐
8. People generally laugh when I tell a joke or make what I think is a witty comment.	☐	☐
9. I stay informed by reading newspapers, watching news on television, or reading news websites.	☐	☐
10. I have heard such terms as enthusiastic, animated, colorful, or dynamic applied to me.	☐	☐
11. The text messages I send look a little better in terms of spelling and grammar than most of the text messages I receive.	☐	☐

Total score: _____

Scoring and Interpretation: If eight or more of these statements are true in relation to you, it is most likely that you are an effective communicator. If three or fewer statements are true, you may need substantial improvement in your communication skills. Your scores are probably highly correlated with charisma.

Skill Development: The behaviors indicated by the ten statements in the self-assessment exercise are significant for leaders because much of a leader's impact is determined by his or her communication style. Although effective leaders vary considerably in their communication style, they usually create a positive impact if they can communicate well. Observe some current business leaders on CNBC news or a similar channel to develop a feel for the communication style of successful business leaders.

COMMUNICATION NETWORKS FOR LEADERS

A major feature of communication by leaders is to rely on networks of contacts both in-person and electronically. Without being connected to other people, leaders would find it almost impossible to carry out their various roles.

Communication researchers Bruce Hoppe and Claire Reinelt note that leadership networks are a response to a rapidly changing world in which interconnectedness is important because it facilitates learning and solving complex problems. Networks provide resources and support for leaders. With networks, leaders have more impact because they influence more people.[3]

Many of these contacts are within the organization, but many are also external. Peter Whatnell, an information technology executive at Sunoco, cogently explains the importance of networking with colleagues in the industry:

> It's where a lot of ideas come from. It doesn't even have to be in your industry. You could hear someone from a health system talking about how they use mobile devices to enable doctors to access medical information and you think, "I could use that same approach to help engineers who are working on a refinery site."[4]

Here we describe briefly how organizational leaders use face-to-face (or in-person) as well as social media networks to communicate. Recognize, however, that the categories often overlap. A leader might be chatting with a colleague from another department in the company cafeteria, and then continue the communication that evening by tweeting the network member.

Face-to-Face Communication Networks

Developing networks of live interpersonal contacts remains an essential method for a leader building relationships, motivating others, and attaining collaboration. Even the most Blackberry-obsessed executives who carry several mobile devices with them at the same time supplement their electronic messages with some personal contacts.

Various types of leadership networks have been identified, with four of these types being particularly relevant. First is the *peer leadership network* that is a system of social ties among leaders who are connected through shared interests and commitments, as well as shared work. Network members share information, provide advice and support, engage in mutual learning, and sometimes collaborate together. Members of the leader's network are perceived as providing resources that can be trusted.[5] (The Sunoco IT executive mentioned above appears to have been referring to a peer leadership network.)

The *operational network* is aimed at doing one's assigned task more effectively. It involves cultivating stronger relationships with coworkers whose membership in the network is clear. Some of these relationships may be part of the formal structure, such as getting cost data from a member of the finance department. *Personal networks* engage cooperative people from outside the organization in a person's effort to develop personally and advance. This type of networking might involve being mentored on how to deal with a challenge, such as dealing with the problem of sexual harassment by a senior manager. (The personal network has much in common with the peer network, except that it might include people who are not peers.)

Strategic networks focus networking on attaining business goals directly. At this level, the manager creates a network that will help identify and capitalize on new opportunities for the company, such as breaking into the African market.[6] Even when the manager's own company has good resources for identifying business opportunities, speaking to external people can provide a fresh and useful perspective.

Social Media Networks

An important use of the social media is for the leader to build and maintain a professional network, much like being a member of LinkedIn. The productive leader is more likely to focus on contacts of relevance or *density* rather than focus on accumulating hundreds of superficial network members. The websites used for networking can be external (or public) as well as internal. Most consulting and management services firms, such as Accenture, have widely internal social media websites.

The *strength-of-ties* perspective explains the difference between strong and weak ties.[7] The quality of a contact in the network is particularly important for social media networks because so many contacts can be of dubious value. A key part of the theory is that there are different densities in different parts of the network. A high-density network consists of close friends or associates linked together, such as CEOs in the same industry exchanging information. In contrast, a low-density network consists of acquaintances linked together.

The relationships among the different actors in a network can be broadly classified into two major types: strong versus weak ties and direct versus indirect ties. An acquaintance would be a weak tie, whereas a close friend would be a strong tie. Strength of ties would ordinarily be measured by frequency of contact, yet some contact could be relatively superficial and others might be more emotional and intimate. Melissa might ask Trevor for status reports on his prediction about currency fluctuation, whereas she talks to Sylvie about her career and her relationship with her boss. (The conversation about the relationship with the boss would probably only take place on a social media website if it could not be observed by others.)

Direct versus indirect ties relate to whether you are directly connected to a person because of a contact you developed, or indirectly, such as a friend of a friend. Your direct contact might be Mike, but Mike is connected to Sally, so Sally is an indirect contact.

A caution about internal social networking sites such as Yammer and Chatter is that the leader or other worker will communicate in the same brash, insulting, and overly-casual manner often found on public social networking sites. The result is that the leader or other worker will appear unprofessional, thereby detracting from his or her leadership image. Noshir Contractor, a professor of behavioral sciences at Northwestern University, warns that people can fall into the trap of being too informal on internal social media sites. "When you're considered for a promotion … anything you said on Yammer will be used in some case to determine if you're qualified," said Contractor.[8]

The accompanying Leader in Action illustrates how a leader and a company can make productive use of a social business network (or an internal social media website). Notice that this application is not aimed at building a personal network, but instead to improve operational efficiency by communicating with a wide audience.

LEADER IN ACTION

EMC Leaders Use Social Business Network to Solicit Employee Input

EMC Corp.'s social business network, called EMC/One, had been in place about a year when the company turned sour. The developer of information infrastructure products was about to learn the value of a Facebook-like platform for use within the company.

As the company spiraled downward in 2008, EMC's chief financial offer began issuing missives about things employees could not do or have in order to reduce annual operating expenses by $450 million. As grumbling in the ranks grew, one contributor to the social business network already used by several thousand of EMC's 40,000 employees started a forum for workers to share and discuss ideas for cutting costs.

According to Polly Pearson, then EMC's vice president for employment brand and strategy engagement, employees offered ideas such as turning down the temperature by two degrees in winter. When the CFO got wind of the forum, he read the postings and decided to adopt many of the ideas. Throughout 2009, the forum was the site of a collaborative exercise among thousands of employees across the globe to understand the reductions and to help meet the $450 million cost-cutting goal. Without a social business network, such an exercise would have been impossible.

"EMC/One was important in driving faster adoption and more broad-based understanding of the cost-cutting actions among our employees in a short period of time," says Lesley Ogrodnick, a company spokeswoman. It is not possible to quantify the exact contribution of the EMC/One to this cost-cutting effort, she says, but it was instrumental in EMC's ability to be more aggressive with the company's cost-transformation program.

Pearson, who left the company to form her own venture and continues to consult with EMC, sees the social business network as the latest—and most effective—variant of the networked organization. "It used to be two guys having lunch. Then it was e-mail," she says. "Business gets done through networking, and these internal social networks are the widest and most inclusive way of doing that."

QUESTIONS

1. What has this story got to do with leadership?
2. What leadership error might have the CFO been making that prompted an employee to start a forum?
3. To what extent do you think a social business networking website will really replace "two guys having lunch"?

Source: HRNews by SOCIETY FOR HUMAN RESOURCE MANAGEMENT (U.S.) Copyright 2010. Reproduced with permission of SOCIETY FOR HUMAN RESOURCE MANAGEMENT.

INSPIRATIONAL AND POWERFUL COMMUNICATION

Information about communicating persuasively and effectively is extensive. Here we focus on suggestions for creating the high-impact communication that contributes to effective leadership. Effective communication is frequently a criterion for being promoted to a leadership position. In this section, suggestions for becoming an inspirational and emotion-provoking communicator are divided into the following two categories: (1) speaking and writing, and (2) nonverbal communication. We also discuss six basic principles of persuasion.

Speaking and Writing

You are already familiar with the basics of effective spoken and written communication. Yet the basics—such as writing and speaking clearly, maintaining eye contact, and not mumbling—are only starting points. The majority of effective leaders have an extra snap or panache in their communication style, both in day-by-day conversations and when addressing a group. The same energy and excitement is reflected in both speaking and writing. Suggestions for dynamic and persuasive oral and written communication are presented next and outlined in Table 12-1.

Be Credible   Attempts at persuasion, including inspirational speaking and writing, begin with the credibility of the message sender. If the speaker is perceived as highly credible, the attempt at persuasive communication is more likely to be successful. The perception of credibility is influenced by many factors, including those covered in this entire section. Being trustworthy heavily influences being perceived as credible. A leader with a reputation for lying will have a difficult time convincing people about the merits of a new initiative such as outsourcing. Being perceived as intelligent and knowledgeable is another major factor contributing to credibility.

Research conducted by two accounting professors at Stanford University suggests that business leaders who lie during earnings conference calls with the finance community display tell-tale signs. (Lying was measured by later having to revise their books.) Consistent clues about hiding the truth included seldom referring to themselves or their companies in the first person. Instead, "I" and "we" were avoided in favor of "the team" and "the company." Another clue to misrepresentation of facts was making short statements with minimum hesitation, presumably because they had carefully rehearsed the misrepresentations in advance. These indicators of untrue statements proved to make accurate predictions between 50 percent and 65 percent of the time.[9]

Gear Your Message to the Listener   An axiom of persuasive communication is that a speaker must adapt the message to the listener's interests and motivations. The company CEO visiting a manufacturing plant will receive careful

TABLE 12-1 Suggestions for Inspirational Speaking and Writing

---

A. A Variety of Inspirational Tactics

1. Be credible.

2. Gear your message to the listener.

3. Sell group members on the benefits of your suggestions.

4. Use heavy-impact and emotion-provoking words.

5. Use anecdotes to communicate meaning.

6. Back up conclusions with data (to a point).

7. Minimize language errors, junk words, and vocalized pauses.

8. Write crisp, clear memos, letters, and reports, including a front-loaded message.

9. Use business jargon in appropriate doses.

B. The Power-Oriented Linguistic Style

Included here are a variety of factors such as downplaying uncertainty, emphasizing direct rather than indirect talk, and choosing an effective communication frame.

attention—and build support—when he says that jobs will not be outsourced to another country. The same CEO will receive the support of stockholders when he emphasizes how cost reductions will boost earnings per share and enlarge dividends. The average intelligence level of the group is a key contingency factor in designing a persuasive message. People with high intelligence tend to be more influenced by messages based on strong, logical arguments. Bright people are also more likely to reject messages based on flawed logic.[10]

Sell Group Members on the Benefits of Your Suggestions   A leader is constrained by the willingness of group members to take action on the leader's suggestions and initiatives. As a consequence, the leader must explain to group members how they can benefit from what he or she proposes. For example, a plant manager attempting to sell employees on the benefits of recycling supplies as much as possible might say, "If we can cut down enough on the cost of supplies, we might be able to save one or two jobs." Jesse Thomas, chairman, president, and CEO of Molina Healthcare of Michigan, says that part of communication technique for selling ideas is "always about the money."[11]

Use Heavy-Impact and Emotion-Provoking Words   Certain words used in the proper context give power and force to your speech. Used comfortably, naturally, and sincerely, these words will project the image of a self-confident person with leadership ability or potential. Two examples of heavy-impact phrases are "We will be outsourcing those portions of our knowledge work that are not mission critical," and "We will be innovational in both product development and business processes." However, too much of this type of language will make the leader appear that he or she is imitating a Dilbert cartoon (a long-running cartoon satire about managers and businesspeople).

Closely related to heavy-impact language is the use of emotion-provoking words. An expert persuasive tactic is to sprinkle your speech with emotion-provoking—and therefore inspiring—words. Emotion-provoking words bring forth images of exciting events. Examples of emotion-provoking and powerful words include "*outclassing* the competition," "*bonding* with customers," "*surpassing* previous profits," "*capturing* customer loyalty," and "*rebounding* from a downturn."

Communications specialist Frank Lunt found that five words resonate in the current business world: consequences, impact, reliability, mission, and commitment. A leader who incorporated these words into his or her business vocabulary would therefore be influential.[12] It also helps to use words and phrases that connote being modern. Those now in vogue include *virtual organization*, *transparent organization*, and *seamless organization*.

A large vocabulary assists using both heavy-impact and emotion-provoking words. When you need to persuade somebody on the spot, it is difficult to search for the right words in a dictionary or thesaurus—even if you access the Internet with your smart phone. Also, you need to practice a word a few times to use it comfortably for an important occasion.

Use Anecdotes to Communicate Meaning   Anecdotes are a powerful part of a leader's kit of persuasive and influence tactics, as already mentioned in this chapter and in Chapter 4 about charismatic leadership. Although storytelling is an ancient art, it is more in vogue than ever as a method for leaders to influence and inspire others.[13] A carefully chosen anecdote is also useful in persuading group members about the importance of organizational values. So long as the anecdote is not repeated too frequently, it can communicate an important message.

Zippo is a consumer-products company that has hundreds of anecdotes to share about how those sturdy steel cigarette lighters saved somebody's life by deflecting a bullet. It seems that the stories originated in World War II but have continued into modern times, such as how a Zippo in the pocket of a police worker prevented a criminal's bullet from killing the officer. Zippo leaders can inspire workers with such heroic tales starring the Zippo lighter. In recent years, Zippo has shifted into many non-smoking-related products, but the anecdotes are still inspiring for the non-smoker.

Back Up Conclusions with Data You will be more persuasive if you support your spoken and written presentations with solid data. One approach to obtaining data is to collect them yourself—for example, by conducting an online survey of your customers or group members. Published sources also provide convincing data for arguments. Supporting data for hundreds of arguments can be found in the business pages of newspapers, in business magazines and newspapers, and on the Internet. The Statistical Abstract of the United States, published annually, is an inexpensive yet trusted reference for thousands of arguments.

Relying too much on research has a potential disadvantage, however. Being too dependent on data could suggest that you have little faith in your own intuition. For example, you might convey a impression of weakness if, when asked your opinion, you respond, "I can't answer until I collect some data." Leaders are generally decisive. An important issue, then, is for the leader to find the right balance between relying on data and using intuition alone when communicating an important point.

Minimize Language Errors, Junk Words, and Vocalized Pauses Using colorful, powerful words enhances the perception that you are self-confident and have leadership qualities. Also, minimize the use of words and phrases that dilute the impact of your speech, such as "like," "y know," "you know what I mean," "he goes" (to mean "he says"), and "uh." Such junk words and vocalized pauses convey the impression of low self-confidence, especially in a professional setting, and detract from a sharp communication image.

An effective way to decrease the use of these extraneous words is to video-record your side of a phone conversation and then play it back. Many people are not aware that they use extraneous words until they hear recordings of their speech.

A good leader should be sure always to write and speak with grammatical precision to give the impression of being articulate and well informed, thereby enhancing his or her leadership stature. Here are two examples of common language errors: "Just between you and I" is wrong; "just between you and me" is correct. "Him and I," or "her and I," are incorrect phrases despite how frequently they creep into social and business language. "He and I" and "she and I" are correct when used as the subjects of a sentence. "Him and me" or "Her and me" are correct when used as the objects of a sentence. For example, "She and I greeted the client" and "The client greeted her and me" are both correct.

Another very common error is using the plural pronoun *they* to refer to a singular antecedent. For example, "The systems analyst said that *they* cannot help us" is incorrect. "The systems analyst said *she* cannot help us" is correct. Using *they* to refer to a singular antecedent has become so common in the English language that many people no longer make the distinction between singular and plural. For example, nowadays most people say, "Everyone placed their order," when actually "Everyone placed his (or her) order" is the grammatically correct statement. Staff at Facebook systematically confuse singular and plural with such statements as "What does Jessica do in *their* spare time?" Some of these errors are subtle and are made so frequently that many people do not realize they are wrong; but again, avoiding grammatical errors may enhance a person's leadership stature.

Perhaps the most common language error business leaders make is to convert hundreds of nouns into verbs. Many nouns do become legitimate verbs, such as using the noun *phone* for a verb, such as "I will phone you later." The leader has to set a limit, and perhaps not use such verb-to-noun conversions such as, "Facebook me tonight," "Focus-group this problem," and "Skype me a message." Yet, the hip leader will correctly use nouns that have been recently been converted into dual use as a verb and noun, such as "Google some potential customers for this product." Judgment is called for with respect to which nouns should be used as verbs to avoid sounding silly, and therefore weak.

When in doubt about a potential language error, consult a respected dictionary. An authoritative guide for the leader (and anyone else) who chooses to use English accurately is *The Elements of Style* by William Strunk Jr. and E. B. White.[14]

Use Business Jargon in Appropriate Doses   Business and government executives and professionals make frequent use of jargon. Often the jargon is used automatically without deliberate thought, and at other times jargon words and phrases are chosen to help establish rapport with the receiver. A vastly overused phrase these days is "at the end of the day," with "buckets" fighting for second place. "The end of the day" has come to replace "in the final analysis," and "buckets" replace "categories." Many businesspeople say "at the end of the day" twice in the same few sentences.

A subtle use of jargon is to make a product or service sound more sophisticated and appealing. Ingersoll-Rand PLC now describes itself as "world leader in creating safe, comfortable and efficient environments." The company product line includes locks, air-conditioning equipment, and battery-operated golf carts. Among the products of Parker Hannifin Corp. are pumps and valves, yet it styles itself as "the global leader in motion and control technologies."[15]

Sprinkling business talk with jargon does indeed help establish rapport, and adds to a person's popularity. But too much jargon makes a person seem stereotyped in thinking, and perhaps even unwilling to express an original thought—and therefore lacking power.

Write Crisp and Clear Memos, Letters, and Reports that Include a Front-Loaded Message   Business leaders characteristically write easy-to-read, well-organized messages, both in e-mail and in more formal reports. Writing, in addition to speaking, is more persuasive when key ideas are placed at the beginning of a conversation, e-mail message, paragraph, or sentence.[16] Front-loaded messages (those placed at the beginning of a sentence) are particularly important for leaders because people expect leaders to be forceful communicators. A front-loaded and powerful message might be "Cost reduction must be our immediate priority," which emphasizes that cost reduction is the major subject. It is clearly much more to the point than, for example, "All of us must reduce costs immediately."

One way to make sure messages are front-loaded is to use the active voice, making sure the subject of the sentence is doing the acting, not being acted upon. Compare the active (and front-loaded) message "Loyal workers should not take vacations during a company crisis" to the passive (not front-loaded) message "Vacations should not be taken by loyal workers during a company crisis." Recognize, however, that less emphasis is placed on the active voice today than several years ago.

Suggestions for effective business writing continue to evolve, and many of these tips are worthy of a leader or potential leader's attention. Claudia Coplon, co-founder of Executive Speak/Write Inc., recommends that you skip beginning business letters or addresses with "Thank you for ..." Instead indicate what impressed you about the experience.[17] A statement of appreciation to the group might begin, "Without question, you have improved productivity by 25% and have thereby contributed to company profits."

Use a Power-Oriented Linguistic Style   A major part of being persuasive involves choosing the correct **linguistic style**, a person's characteristic speaking pattern. According to Deborah Tannen, linguistic style involves such aspects as amount of directness, pacing and pausing, word choice, and the use of such communication devices as jokes, figures of speech, anecdotes, questions, and apologies.[18]

Linguistic style is complex because it includes the culturally learned signals by which people communicate what they mean, along with how they interpret what others say and how they evaluate others. The complexity of linguistic style makes it difficult to offer specific prescriptions for using one that is power oriented. Many of the elements of a power-oriented linguistic style are included in other suggestions made in this section of the chapter, including using heavy-impact words. Nevertheless, here are several components of a linguistic style that would give power and authority to the message sender in many situations, as observed by Deborah Tannen and other language specialists:[19]

* Speak loudly enough to be heard by the majority of people with at least average hearing ability. Speaking too softly projects an image of low self-confidence.

- Use the pronoun *I* to receive more credit for your ideas. (Of course, this could backfire in a team-based organization.)
- Minimize self-deprecation with phrases such as "This will probably sound stupid, but ..." Apologize infrequently, and particularly minimize saying, "I'm sorry."
- Make your point quickly. You know you are taking too long to reach a conclusion when others look bored or finish your sentences for you.
- Emphasize direct rather than indirect talk: say, "I need your report by noon tomorrow," rather than, "I'm wondering if your report will be available by noon tomorrow."
- Weed out wimpy words. Speak up without qualifying or giving other indices of uncertainty. It is better to give dates for the completion of a project rather than say "I'll get it to you soon" or "It shouldn't be a problem." Instead, make a statement like "I will have my portion of the strategic plan shortly before Thanksgiving. I need to collect input from my team and sift through the information."
- Know exactly what you want. Your chances of selling an idea increase to the extent that you have clarified the idea in your own mind. The clearer and more committed you are at the outset of a session, the stronger you are as a persuader and the more powerful your language becomes.
- Speak at length, set the agenda for a conversation, make jokes, and laugh. Be ready to offer solutions to problems, as well as to suggest a program or plan. All of these points are more likely to create a sense of confidence in listeners.
- Strive to be bold in your statements. As a rule of thumb, be bold about ideas, but tentative about people. If you say something like "I have a plan that I think will solve these problems," you are presenting an idea, not attacking a person.
- Frame your comments in a way that increases your listener's receptivity. The *frame* is built around the best context for responding to the needs of others. An example would be to use the frame, "Let's dig a little deeper," when the other people present know something is wrong but cannot pinpoint the problem. Your purpose is to enlist the help of others in finding the underlying nature of the problem.

Despite these suggestions for having a power-oriented linguistic style, Tannen cautions that there is no one best way to communicate. How you project your power and authority is often dependent on the people involved, the organizational culture, the relative rank of the speakers, and other situational factors. The power-oriented linguistic style should be interpreted as a general guideline.

The Six Basic Principles of Persuasion

Persuasion is a major form of influence, so it has gained in importance in the modern organization because of the reason described in Chapter 10: Managers must often influence people for whom they have no formal responsibility. The trend stems from leaner corporate hierarchies and the breaking down of division walls. Managers must persuade peers in situations where lines of authority are unclear or do not exist. One way to be persuasive is to capitalize on scientific evidence about how to persuade people. Robert B. Cialdini has synthesized knowledge from experimental and social psychology about methods for getting people to concede, comply, or change. These principles can also be framed as influence principles, but with a focus on persuasion.[20] The six principles described next have accompanying tactics that can be used to supplement the other approaches to persuasion described in this chapter.

1. *Liking: People like those who like them.* As a leader, you have a better chance of persuading and influencing group members who like you. Emphasizing similarities between you and the other person and offering praise are the two most reliable techniques for getting another person to like you. The leader should therefore emphasize similarities, such as common interests with group members. Praising others is a powerful influence technique and can be used effectively even when the leader finds something relatively small to compliment. Genuine praise is the most effective.

2. *Reciprocity: People repay in kind.* Managers can often influence group members to behave in a particular way by displaying the behavior first. The leader might therefore serve as a model of trust, good ethics, or strong commitment to company goals. In short, give what you want to receive.

3. *Social proof: People follow the lead of similar others*. Persuasion can have high impact when it comes from peers. If you as the leader want to influence a group to convert to a new procedure, such as virtually eliminating paper records in the office, ask a believer to speak up in a meeting or send his or her statement of support via e-mail. (But do not send around paper documents.)

4. *Consistency: People align with their clear commitments*. People need to feel committed to what you want them to do. After people take a stand or go on record in favor of a position, they prefer to stay with that commitment. Suppose you are the team leader and you want team members to become more active in the community as a way of creating a favorable image for the firm. If the team members talk about their plans to get involved and also put their plans in writing, they are more likely to follow through. If the people involved read their action plans to each other, the commitment will be even stronger.

5. *Authority: People defer to experts*. The action plan here is to make constituents aware of your expertise to enhance the probability that your plan will persuade them. A leader might mention certification in the technical area that is the subject of influence. For example, a leader attempting to persuade team members to use statistical data to improve quality might mention that he or she is certified in the quality process Six Sigma (is a Six Sigma Black Belt).

6. *Scarcity: People want more of what they can have less of.* An application of this principle is that the leader can persuade group members to act in a particular direction if the members believe that the resource at issue is shrinking rapidly. They might be influenced to enroll in a course in outsourcing knowledge work, for example, if they are told that the course may not be offered

again for a long time. Another way to apply this principle is to persuade group members by using information not readily available to others. The leader might say, "I have some preliminary sales data. If we can increase our sales by just 10 percent in the last month of this quarter, we could be the highest performing unit in the company."

The developer of these principles explains that they should be applied in combination to multiply their impact. For example, while establishing your expertise you might simultaneously praise people for their accomplishments. It is also important to be ethical, such as by not fabricating data to influence others.[21]

Nonverbal Communication Including Videoconferencing and Telepresence

Effective leaders are masterful nonverbal as well as verbal communicators. Nonverbal communication is important because leadership involves emotion, which words alone cannot communicate convincingly. A major component of the emotional impact of a message is communicated nonverbally.

A self-confident leader not only speaks and writes with assurance but also projects confidence through body position, gestures, and manner of speech. Not everybody interprets the same body language and other nonverbal signals in the same way, but some aspects of nonverbal behavior project a self-confident leadership image in many situations.[22]

- Using an erect posture when walking, standing, or sitting. Slouching and slumping are almost universally interpreted as an indicator of low self-confidence.
- Standing up straight during a confrontation. Cowering is interpreted as a sign of low self-confidence and poor leadership qualities.
- Patting other people on the back while nodding slightly.
- Standing with toes pointing outward rather than inward. Outward-pointing toes are usually perceived as indicators of superior status, whereas inward-pointing toes are perceived to indicate inferiority.
- Speaking at a moderate pace, with a loud, confident tone. People lacking in self-confidence tend to speak too rapidly or very slowly.
- Smiling frequently in a relaxed, natural-appearing manner.
- Maintaining eye contact with those around you.
- Gesturing in a relaxed, non-mechanical way, including pointing toward others in a way that welcomes rather than accuses, such as using a gesture to indicate, "You're right," or "It's your turn to comment."

A general approach to using nonverbal behavior that projects confidence is to have a goal of appearing self-confident and powerful. This type of autosuggestion makes many of the behaviors seem automatic. For example, if you say, "I am going to display leadership qualities in this meeting," you will have taken an important step toward appearing confident.

Your external image also plays an important role in communicating messages to others. People pay more respect and grant more privileges to those they perceive as being well dressed and neatly groomed. Even on casual dress days, most effective leaders will choose clothing that gives them an edge over others. Appearance includes more than the choice of clothing. Self-confidence is projected by such small items as the following:

- Neatly pressed and sparkling clean clothing
- Freshly polished shoes
- Impeccable fingernails
- Clean jewelry in mint condition
- Well-maintained hair
- Good-looking teeth with a white or antique-white (or off-white) color

What constitutes a powerful and self-confident external image is often influenced by the organizational culture. At a software development company, for example, powerful people might dress more casually than at an investment banking firm. Leadership at many law firms is moving back toward formal business attire for the professional staff. Your verbal behavior and the forms of nonverbal behavior previously discussed contribute more to your leadership image than your clothing, providing you dress acceptably.

Videoconferencing places extra demands on the nonverbal communication skills of leaders, managers, and other participants. A recent advance in videoconferencing, referred to as *telepresence*, places even more demands on nonverbal communication skills because it appears closer to human presence. For example, the illumination highlights the facial features of the people sitting in the telepresence studio. Some telepresence systems are custom-built meeting rooms equipped with a bank of high-definition screens and cameras. Other systems take the form of humanoid robots that are used outside of meeting rooms. With the robots placed at different physical locations, leaders can take virtual coffee breaks with geographically dispersed workers.[23]

Jeffrey Schwartz, chief executive officer of an industrial real estate investment trust, explains that videoconferences represent a powerful tool for far-flung managers to make a name for themselves back at corporate headquarters.[24] The opposite is also true: if your verbal and nonverbal communication skills are poor, you will create a poor impression. The camera magnifies everything you do, including scratching your head, biting your lip, inserting your finger in your ear, and checking your mobile device. Etiquette tips for making a strong nonverbal presence during a videoconference include the following (and are similar to nonverbal communication suggestions in general):

- Choose what you wear carefully, remembering that busy (confusing and complex) patterns look poor on video. Also do not wear formal attire mixed with running shoes because you might move into full camera view.
- Speak in crisp conversational tones and pay attention. (The tone and paying attention are the nonverbal aspects of communication.)
- Never forget the video camera's powerful reach, such as catching you rolling your eyes when you disagree with a subordinate.
- Avoid culturally insensitive gestures including large hand and body gestures that make many Asians feel uncomfortable. Asians believe that you should have long-term relationships before being demonstrative.[25]

LEADERSHIP SKILL-BUILDING EXERCISE 12-1

Feedback on Verbal and Nonverbal Behavior

Ten volunteers have one week to prepare a three-minute presentation on a course-related subject of their choice. The topics of these presentations could be as far-reaching as "The Importance of the North American Free Trade Agreement" or "My Goals and Dreams." The class members who observe the presentations prepare feedback slips on 3 × 5 cards, describing how well the speakers communicated powerfully and inspirationally. One card per speaker is usually sufficient. Notations should be made for both verbal and nonverbal feedback.

Emphasis should be placed on positive feedback and constructive suggestions. Students pass the feedback cards along to the speakers. The cards can be anonymous to encourage frankness, but they should not be mean-spirited.

Persuading and inspiring others is one of the main vehicles for practicing leadership. Knowing how others perceive you helps you polish and refine your impact.

An effective way of sharpening your videoconferencing and telepresence nonverbal skills, as well as other nonverbal skills, is to be videotaped several times. Make adjustments for anything you don't like, and repeat what you do like. Feedback on your behavior from another observer can be quite helpful.

Now that you have refreshed your thoughts on effective verbal and nonverbal communication, do Leadership Skill-Building Exercise 12-1.

LISTENING AS A LEADERSHIP SKILL

Listening is a fundamental management and leadership skill. Listening also provides the opportunity for dialogue, in which people understand each other better by taking turns having their point of view understood. For a leader to support and encourage a subordinate, active listening (as described in the discussion of coaching) is required. Also, effective leader–member exchanges require that each party listen to one another. The relationship between two parties cannot be enhanced unless each one listens to the other. Furthermore, leaders cannot identify problems unless they listen carefully to group members. Multitasking is a major deterrent to listening carefully to subordinates because the leader who is involved in another task at the moment, such as glancing at a tablet computer, is not paying full attention to the speaker.

According to Richard M. Harris, in today's complex, fast-paced organization, effective communication—including listening—is essential. But all too frequently, messages are misinterpreted, ignored, or missed altogether. As a result, creativity is stifled, morale is lowered, and goals may go unmet.[26]

Two major impediments face the leader who wants to be an effective listener. First, the leader is so often overloaded with responsibilities, including analytical work, that it is difficult to take the time to carefully listen to subordinates. Second is the speed difference between speaking and listening.

The average rate of speaking is between 110 and 200 words per minute, yet people can listen in the range of 400 to 3,000 words per minute. So the leader, as well as anybody else, will often let his or her mind wander.

Here we look at two leadership aspects of listening to supplement your general knowledge of listening, acquired most likely in other courses: selective listening to problems and making the rounds.

Selective Listening to Problems

Organizational leaders are so often bombarded with demands and information that it is difficult to be attentive to a full range of problems. So the leader makes an intentional or unintentional decision to listen to just certain problems. Erika H. James notes that despite how our brains ordinarily work, success is dependent on staying open to all incoming information.[27] The busy leader must avoid listening to limited categories of information such as good news, bad news, or financial news. A CEO with a propensity to listen only to financial results might ignore any word of problems so long as the company is earning a profit.

Making the Rounds

A robust communication channel for the leader/manager is to engage in face-to-face communication with direct reports and others, with an emphasis on listening. **Making the rounds** refers to the leader casually dropping by constituents to listen to their accomplishments, concerns, and problems and to share information. *Rounding* is a well-established concept from health care in which the physician talks to patients and other health care workers to observe problems and progress firsthand.[28] Through rounding, vital information is gathered if the physician or manager listens carefully. Making the rounds is also referred to as *management by walking around*, yet *rounding* seems more focused and systematic.

From the perspective of listening, the leader stays alert to potential problems. Assume that a subordinate is asked, "How are things going?" and she replies, "Not too terrible." This response begs a little digging, such as, "What is happening that is a little terrible?"

A leader who makes the rounds can often enhance morale, particularly when the organization is going through a difficult period. During a recession, the face-to-face contact with workers increases in importance. A representative example is the experience of Bart Cleveland, a partner in an advertising firm in Albuquerque, New Mexico. During the Great Recession, he observed that staff members at the agency were overly stressed. Leadership at the agency chose to communicate more frequently with their employees about their concerns. Cleveland recognized the need for more face time with the boss, and then proceeded to walk around the office and talk with them daily. His approach appeared to lower stress and boost morale.[29]

Leadership Skill-Building Exercise 12-2 gives you an opportunity to try out the fundamental leadership skill of communication.

LEADERSHIP SKILL-BUILDING EXERCISE 12-2

Leadership Listening

Six or seven students gather for a team meeting to discuss an important operational problem, such as finding new ways to reduce the cycle time required to complete their tasks, or deciding how to convince top management to expand the team budget. One person plays the role of the team leader. All of the group members take turns at making both useful and apparently not useful suggestions. The team leader, along with team members, displays careful listening whenever ideas surface. Students not directly involved in the group role play will take note of the listening skills they observe so that they can provide feedback later. Be particularly observant of selective listening. If class time allows, another team of six or seven students can repeat the group role play.

OVERCOMING CROSS-CULTURAL COMMUNICATION BARRIERS

Another communication challenge facing leaders and managers is overcoming communication barriers created by dealing with people from different cultures and subcultures. Leaders typically communicate with people from other countries and with a more diverse group of people in their own country. Because of this workplace diversity, leaders who can manage a multicultural and cross-cultural work force are in strong demand. Here we give some guidelines for overcoming a variety of cross-cultural communication barriers. Implementing these guidelines will help overcome and prevent many communication problems. A useful starting point here is to take Leadership Self-Assessment Quiz 12-2 to help you think through your cross-cultural skills and attitudes.

LEADERSHIP SELF-ASSESSMENT QUIZ 12-2

Cross-Cultural Skills and Attitudes

Instructions: Listed here are various skills and attitudes that various employers and cross-cultural experts think are important for relating effectively to coworkers in a culturally diverse environment. Indicate whether or not each statement applies to you.

	APPLIES TO ME NOW	NOT THERE YET
1. I have spent some time in another country.	☐	☐
2. At least one of my friends is deaf, blind, or uses a wheelchair.	☐	☐
3. I have an approximate idea of how much the U.S. dollar is worth in comparison to the euro.	☐	☐
4. I have tried eating food from a culture much different than my own—aside from eating in a Chinese or Italian restaurant.	☐	☐
5. I can speak in a language other than my own.	☐	☐
6. I can read and write in a language other than my own.	☐	☐

QUIZ 12-2 (continued)

	APPLIES TO ME NOW	NOT THERE YET
7. I can understand people speaking in a language other than my own.	☐	☐
8. I use my second language at least once a week.	☐	☐
9. My friends include people of races different from my own.	☐	☐
10. My friends include people of different ages.	☐	☐
11. I feel (or would feel) comfortable having a friend with a sexual orientation different from mine.	☐	☐
12. My attitude is that although another culture may be very different from mine, that culture is equally good.	☐	☐
13. I would be willing to (or already do) hang art from different countries in my home.	☐	☐
14. I would accept (or have already accepted) a work assignment of more than several months in another country.	☐	☐
15. I have a passport.	☐	☐

Scoring and Interpretation: If you answered "Applies to Me Now" to 10 or more questions, you most likely function well in a multicultural work environment. If you answered "Not There Yet" to 10 or more questions, you need to develop more cross-cultural awareness and skills to work effectively in a multicultural work environment. You will notice that being bilingual gives you at least 4 points on this quiz.

Source: Several ideas for statements on this quiz are derived from Ruthann Dirks and Janet Buzzard, "What CEOs Expect of Employees Hired for International Work," *Business Education Forum,* April 1997, pp. 3–7; Gunnar Beeth, "Multicultural Managers Wanted," *Management Review,* May 1997, pp. 17–21.

1. *Be sensitive to the fact that cross-cultural communication barriers exist.* Awareness of these potential barriers is the first step in dealing with them. When dealing with a person of a different cultural background, solicit feedback to minimize cross-cultural barriers to communication. For example, investigate which types of praise or other rewards might be ineffective for a particular cultural group. In many instances, Asians newly arrived in the United States feel uncomfortable being praised in front of others because in Asian cultures group performance is valued more than individual performance.

Being alert to cultural differences in values, attitudes, and etiquette will help you communicate more effectively with people from different cultures. Observe carefully the cultural mistakes listed in Table 12-2. At the same time, recognize that these *mistakes* are based on cultural stereotypes and reflect typical or average behavior of members of a particular cultural group.

2. *Challenge your cultural assumptions.* The assumptions we make about cultural groups can create communication barriers. The assumption you make about another group may not necessarily be incorrect, but stopping to challenge the assumptions may facilitate communication. A U.S. leader, for

TABLE 12-2 Cultural Mistakes to Avoid with Selected Cultural Groups

Europe

Great Britain	• Asking personal questions. The British protect their privacy.
	• Thinking that a businessperson from England is unenthusiastic when he or she says, "Not bad at all." English people understate positive emotion.
	• Gossiping about royalty.
France	• Expecting to complete work during the French two-hour lunch.
	• Attempting to conduct significant business during August—*les vacances* (vacation time).
	• Greeting a French person for the first time and not using a title such as *sir* or *madam* (or *monsieur*, *madame*, or *mademoiselle*).
Italy	• Eating too much pasta, as it is not the main course.
	• Handing out business cards freely. Italians use them infrequently.
Spain	• Expecting punctuality. Your appointments will usually arrive twenty to thirty minutes late.
	• Making the U.S. sign for "OK" with your thumb and forefinger. In Spain (and many other countries) this is vulgar.
Scandinavia (Denmark, Sweden, Norway)	• Being overly rank-conscious in these countries. Scandinavians pay relatively little attention to a person's place in the hierarchy.

Asia

All Asian Countries	• Pressuring an Asian job applicant or employee to brag about his or her accomplishments. Asians feel self-conscious when boasting about individual accomplishments and prefer to let the record speak for itself. In addition, they prefer to talk about group rather than individual accomplishment.
Japan	• Shaking hands or hugging Japanese (as well as other Asians) in public. Japanese consider the practices offensive.
	• Not interpreting "We'll consider it" as a "no" when spoken by a Japanese businessperson. Japanese negotiators mean "no" when they say, "We'll consider it."
	• Not giving small gifts to Japanese when conducting business. Japanese are offended by not receiving these gifts.
	• Giving your business card to a Japanese businessperson more than once. Japanese prefer to give and receive business cards only once.
China	• Using black borders on stationery and business cards. Black is associated with death.
	• Giving small gifts to Chinese when conducting business. Chinese are offended by these gifts.
	• Making cold calls on Chinese business executives. An appropriate introduction is required for a first-time meeting with a Chinese official.
Korea	• Saying "no." Koreans feel it is important to have visitors leave with good feelings.
India	• Telling Indians you prefer not to eat with your hands. If the Indians are not using cutlery when eating, they expect you to do likewise.

Mexico and Latin America

Mexico	• Flying into a Mexican city in the morning and expecting to close a deal by lunch. Mexicans build business relationships slowly.
Brazil	• Attempting to impress Brazilians by speaking a few words of Spanish. Portuguese is the official language of Brazil.
Most Latin American Countries	• Wearing elegant and expensive jewelry during a business meeting. Most Latin Americans think Americans should appear more conservative during a business meeting.

Source: A cultural mistake for Americans to avoid when conducting business in most countries outside the United States and Canada is to insist on getting down to business too quickly. North Americans in small towns also like to build a relationship before getting down to business. Also, the entire world is becoming more informal, as evidenced by people from different cultures addressing others by their first name upon first meeting.

example, might assume that the norms of independence and autonomy are valued by all groups in the workplace. Trudy Milburn notes that even the concept of equality can be phrased to alienate cultural groups. A sentence from the Johnson & Johnson mission statement reads, "Everyone must be considered as an individual." However, the word *individual* does not have positive connotations for all groups. Among many Latino cultural groups, the term *individual* is derogatory because it may connote the separation of one person from the rest of the community.[30]

3. *Show respect for all workers.* The same behavior that promotes good cross-cultural relations in general helps overcome communication barriers. A widely used comment that implies disrespect is to say to a person from another culture, "You have a funny accent." Should you be transposed to that person's culture, you too might have a "funny accent." The attitude of highest respect is to communicate your belief that although another person's culture is different from yours, it is not inferior to your culture. Showing respect for another culture can be more important than being bilingual in overcoming communication barriers.[31]

4. *Use straightforward language, and speak slowly and clearly.* When working with people who do not speak your language fluently, speak in an easy-to-understand manner. Minimize the use of idioms and analogies specific to your language. A systems analyst from New Delhi, India, left confused after a performance review with her manager. The manager said, "I will be giving you more important assignments because I notice some good chemistry between us." The woman did not understand that *good chemistry* means *rapport*, and she did not ask for clarification because she did not want to appear uninformed.

Speaking slowly is also important because even people who read and write a second language at an expert level may have difficulty catching some nuances of conversation. Facing the person from another culture directly also improves communication because your facial expressions and lips contribute to comprehension. And remember, there is no need to speak much louder.

5. *Look for signs of misunderstanding when your language is not the listener's native language.* Signs of misunderstanding may include nods and smiles not directly connected to what you are saying, a lack of questions, inappropriate laughter, and a blank expression. If these signs are present, work harder to apply the suggestions in point 4.[32]

6. *When the situation is appropriate, speak in the language of the people from another culture.* Americans who can speak another language are at a competitive advantage when dealing with businesspeople who speak that language. The language skill, however, must be more advanced than speaking a few basic words and phrases. Speaking the local language will often bring a person more insight and prevent misunderstandings. Equally important, being bilingual helps bring a person the respect that a leader needs to be fully credible.[33]

A frustration the native English speaker who is using another language is that so many people around the world capitalize on an opportunity to speak English. So the leader who speaks another language to establish rapport might be rebuffed. Despite this problem, speaking another language in the workplace is likely to have a positive net effect.

As more deaf people have been integrated into the work force, knowing American Sign Language can be a real advantage to a leader when some of his or her constituents are deaf.

7. *Observe cross-cultural differences in etiquette.* Violating rules of etiquette without explanation can erect immediate communication barriers. A major rule of business etiquette in most countries is that the participants conducting serious business together should first share a meal. So if you are invited to a banquet that takes place the night before discussions about a major business deal, regard the banquet as a major opportunity to build a relationship. To avoid the banquet is a serious faux pas.

8. *Do not be diverted by style, accent, grammar, or personal appearance.* Although these superficial factors are all related to business success, they are difficult to interpret when judging a person from another culture. It is therefore better to judge the merits of the statement or behavior. A highly intelligent worker from another culture may still be learning English and thus make basic mistakes. He or she might also not yet have developed a sensitivity to dress style in your culture, for example.

9. *Avoid racial or ethnic identification except when it is essential to communication.* Using a person's race or ethnicity as an adjective or other descriptor often suggests a negative stereotype.[34] For example, suppose a leader says, "I am proud of André. He is a very responsible (*member of his race*) customer service rep." One possible interpretation of this statement is that most customer service reps of André's race are not so responsible. Or, a leader might say, "We are happy to have Martha on our team. She is an easy-to-get-along-with (*mention of ethnicity*) lady." A possible implication is that women from Martha's particular country are usually not too easy to work with.

10. *Be sensitive to differences in nonverbal communication.* A person from another culture may misinterpret nonverbal signals. To use positive reinforcement, some managers will give a sideways hug to an employee or will touch the employee's arm. People from some cultures resent touching from workmates and will be offended. Koreans in particular dislike being touched or touching others in a work setting.

11. *Be attentive to individual differences in appearance.* A major cross-cultural insult is to confuse the identity of people because they are members of the same race or ethnic group. An older economics professor reared in China and teaching in the United States had difficulty communicating with students because he was unable to learn their names. The professor's defense was that "so many of these Americans look alike to me." A study suggests that people have difficulty seeing individual differences among people of another race because they see so-called racial differences first; they might think, "He has the nose of a Chinese person." However, people can learn to search for more distinguishing features, such as a dimple or eye color, and expression (serious or not so serious).[35]

THE LEADER'S ROLE IN RESOLVING CONFLICT AND NEGOTIATING

Leaders and managers spend considerable time resolving conflicts and negotiating. A frequent estimate is that they devote about 20 percent of their time to dealing with conflict including negotiation. Conflict arises frequently among top executives, and it can have enormous consequences for the organization. An example of such competition would be two business units competing for resources.

Departmental competition has been regarded as the ugly underbelly of all sizes of companies, often resulting in product delays, increased costs, and dwindling market shares as departments fight each other for domination behind the scenes. Frequent conflict is found also between off-line and online units.[36] Until conflict between or among the groups is resolved, collaboration is unlikely.[37] For example, if the operations group is in conflict with the human resources group, it will be difficult for the two groups to collaborate on a diversity training program.

Leaders are sometimes involved in conflict with groups outside their organization, and such conflict may need to be resolved. An example is that state governments have begun demanding sales taxes from online merchants who claimed that they were exempt from such taxation. In April 2011, Amazon.com closed its suburban distribution center because the Texas comptroller's office demanded $269 million in uncollected sales tax. The dispute went into litigation.[38]

An extensive description of conflict resolution is more appropriate for the study of managerial skills than for the study of leadership skills. The reason is because conflict resolution has more to do with establishing equilibrium than with helping the firm or organizational unit reach new heights. Here we focus on a basic framework for understanding conflict resolution styles, resolving conflict between two group members, and a few suggestions for negotiating and bargaining.

Conflict Management Styles

As shown in Figure 12-1, Kenneth W. Thomas has identified five major styles of conflict management: competitive, accommodative, sharing, collaborative, and avoidant. Each style is based on a combination of satisfying one's own concerns (assertiveness) and satisfying the concerns of others (cooperativeness).[39] Leadership Self-Assessment Quiz 12-3 gives you an opportunity to think about your conflict management style.

Competitive Style   The competitive style is a desire to achieve one's own goals at the expense of the other party, or to dominate. A person with a competitive orientation is likely to engage in win–lose power struggles.

Accommodative Style   The accommodative style favors appeasement, or satisfying the other's concerns without taking care of one's own. People with this orientation may be generous or self-sacrificing just to maintain a relationship. An irate customer might be accommodated with a full refund, "just to shut

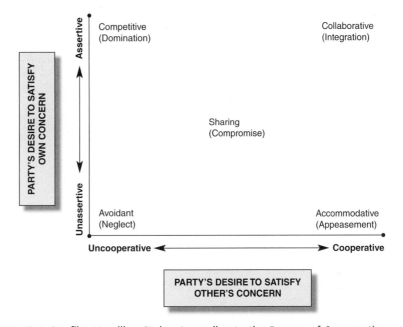

FIGURE 12-1 Conflict-Handling Styles According to the Degree of Cooperation and Assertiveness.

Source: Kenneth W. Thomas, "Organizational Conflict," in Marvin D. Dunnette, ed., *Handbook of Industrial and Organizational Psychology*, p. 900 (Rand McNally). Copyright © 1976, Marvin D. Dunnette. Used by permission of Marvin D. Dunnette.

him (or her) up." The intent of such accommodation might also be to retain the customer's loyalty.

Sharing Style   The sharing style is halfway between domination and appeasement. Sharers prefer moderate but incomplete satisfaction for both parties, which results in a compromise. The term *splitting the difference* reflects this orientation, which is commonly used in such activities as purchasing a house or car.

Collaborative Style   In contrast to the other styles, the collaborative style reflects a desire to fully satisfy the desires of both parties. It is based on the underlying philosophy of the **win–win approach to conflict resolution**, the belief that after conflict has been resolved, both sides should gain something of value. The user of win–win approaches is genuinely concerned about arriving at a settlement that meets the needs of both parties, or at least does not badly damage the welfare of the other side. When collaborative approaches to resolving conflict are used, the relationships among the parties are built on and improved.

The collaborative style of conflict management has many variations, one of which is to agree with the person criticizing you. When you agree with a critic, you show that you seek a solution, not a way to demonstrate that you are right.

LEADERSHIP SELF-ASSESSMENT QUIZ 12-3

My Conflict Resolution Style

Instructions: Answer each of the following statements "mostly true" or "mostly false" with respect to how you have dealt with the situation, would deal with the situation, or how much you agree with the attitude expressed.

	MOSTLY TRUE	MOSTLY FALSE
1. I see myself as a hard-hitting, smash-mouth negotiator.	☐	☐
2. The best way to resolve conflict is to overwhelm the other side.	☐	☐
3. When negotiating a price, I like to make sure that the other side walks away with at least some profit.	☐	☐
4. When negotiating a price, I like to start with an outrageous demand or offer so I can eventually get the price I really wanted.	☐	☐
5. After a successful negotiation, one side wins and one side loses.	☐	☐
6. After a successful negotiation, both sides walk away with something of value.	☐	☐
7. When I am in conflict with somebody else, I try to listen carefully to understand his or her point of view.	☐	☐
8. Face it: Business is war, so why grant concessions when in a dispute?	☐	☐
9. When working out a disagreement with a workmate, I keep in mind the fact that we will have to work together in the future.	☐	☐
10. Nice people finish last when it comes to resolving disputes.	☐	☐

Total score: _____

Scoring and Interpretation: Give yourself a score of 1 for each answer that matches the scoring key:

1. Mostly false	**5.** Mostly false	**9.** Mostly true
2. Mostly false	**6.** Mostly true	**10.** Mostly false
3. Mostly false	**7.** Mostly true	
4. Mostly true	**8.** Mostly false	

If your score is 8, 9, or 10, you most likely use the collaborative (win–win) approach to resolving conflict and negotiating. If your score is 7 or less, you most likely use the competitive (win–lose) approach to resolving conflict and negotiating. The collaborative approach is more likely to enhance your leadership effectiveness in the long run.

If you agree with the substance of the criticism, you show that you are aware of the situation and ready to do what is best to solve the problem.

To illustrate, if a group member criticizes you for having been too harsh in your evaluation of him or her, you might say: "I agree that my evaluation was harsh, but I was harsh for a purpose. I want to be candid with you so you will be motivated to make what I think are necessary improvements." Your agreement is likely to spark further discussion about how the group member can improve. The collaborative style is the approach an effective leader is most likely to use because the outcome leads to increased productivity and satisfaction.

Another form of agreeing with criticism is for leaders to apologize when they have truly made a mistake. An apology often reduces conflict because the other side becomes less hostile, and the scene is set for cooperation. Visualize a scenario in which members of the executive team vote themselves large financial bonuses during a period of financial losses to the company and layoffs of employees. Saying, "We're sorry, and we goofed" to the union and/or employees can help soften the sting. Giving back some of the bonuses would be even more helpful. In general, a good apology must be perceived as genuine, with an honest appeal for forgiveness.[40]

Avoidant Style   Avoiders combine lack of cooperation and unassertiveness. They are indifferent to the concerns of either party. The person may actually be withdrawing from the conflict or be relying upon fate. An example of an avoider is a manager who stays out of a conflict between two team members, leaving them to resolve their own differences. The decision of Amazon.com to remove its distribution center from Texas might be described as avoidant because the company did not attempt to work out a mutually favorable solution to the tax conflict.

People engaged in conflict resolution typically combine several of the five resolution styles to accomplish their purpose. For example, a generally effective approach to resolving conflict is to be competitive with regard to a cost that is important to oneself but unimportant to the opponent, and at the same time use accommodation for a cost that is unimportant to oneself but important to the opponent.[41]

Deciding which mode or modes of conflict handling to use depends upon a number of variables. The major contingency factors are the importance of the conflict issue and the relative power of the opposing parties. An issue may be so important to a leader, such as preventing his or her organizational unit from being outsourced, that domination may be the most effective mode. At other times, a leader may use the accommodating mode of conflict management when the opposing side has much more power, and he or she may want to save domination for a more important issue in the future.

Resolving Conflict between Two Group Members

A high-level managerial skill is to help two or more group members resolve conflict between or among them. Much of the time a manager or leader invests in conflict resolution is geared toward assisting others to resolve their conflict. Often, the conflict is between the heads of two different departments or divisions. The most useful approach is to get the parties in conflict to engage in confrontation and problem solving. (*Confrontation* refers to discussing the true problem, and *problem solving* refers to finding a way to resolve the conflict.) The manager sits down with the two sides and encourages them to talk to each other about the problem (rather than to the manager). This approach is preferable to inviting each side to speak with the manager or leader alone, because then each side might attempt to convince the manager that he or she is right. An abbreviated example follows:

Leader: I've brought you two together to see if you can overcome the problems you have about sharing the workload during a period in which one of you is overloaded.

Stephanie: I'm glad you did. Josh never wants to help me, even when I'm drowning in customer requests.

Josh: I would be glad to help Stephanie if she ever agreed to help me. If she has any downtime, she runs to the break room so she can chat on her cell phone.

Stephanie: Look who's talking. I have seen you napping in your SUV when you have a little downtime.

Leader: I'm beginning to see what's going on here. Both of you are antagonistic toward each other, and you look for little faults to pick. With a little more respect on both sides, I think you would be more willing to help each other out.

Josh: Actually, Stephanie's not too bad. And I know she can perform well when she wants to. Next time I see her needing help, I'll pitch in.

Stephanie: I know that the name "Josh" is related to joking around, but our Josh really has a warm heart. I'm open to starting with a fresh slate. Maybe Josh can ask me politely the next time he needs help.

Conflict specialist Patrick S. Nugent believes that being able to intervene in the conflicts of group members is a management skill that grows in importance. Such competencies are useful in an emerging form of management based less on traditional hierarchy and more on developing self-managing subordinates and teams. When the conflict is between two different groups, such as online versus off-line marketing, a major goal of conflict resolution is to get the two sides to see the company's big picture.[42]

Negotiating and Bargaining

As mentioned in Chapter 1, negotiation is a basic leadership role. In support of this idea, Michael Watkins says it is not enough for leaders to be visionaries; they also need to be capable negotiators. One reason is that younger people are less prone to accept power and authority. Another reason is that the trend toward flatter organizations and the use of matrix structures require leaders to be negotiating continuously. (A matrix structure is a project team superimposed on a functional structure.) People often accept orders only after negotiation.[43]

Conflicts can be considered situations that call for negotiating and bargaining, or conferring with another person to resolve a problem. When you are trying to negotiate a fair price for relocating an office, you are simultaneously trying to resolve a conflict. At first, the demands of the two parties may seem incompatible, but through negotiation a salary may emerge that satisfies both parties. Here we review a handful of practical negotiating tactics a leader will find helpful. The approaches to negotiation presented here emphasize a strategy of integration or collaboration, with a philosophy of win–win.

Listen First to Investigate What the Other Side Wants   An advanced negotiating technique is to begin by soliciting the other person's or group's point of view. You can use this information to shape the objectives of the negotiation, and figure out how you will be able to attain them.[44] For example, a business unit leader might be negotiating with executives from headquarters about outsourcing the manufacture of a product. The unit head might attempt to analyze why the headquarters group really wants to outsource. Are they attempting to reduce operating costs? Are they concerned mostly about increasing quality? Are they concerned mostly about enhancing profits?

Listening skills are essential for seeing the big picture. Bobby Covie says, "There's a saying among negotiators that whoever talks the most during a negotiation loses." Being the first to listen helps establish trust. Listening also involves paying attention to what the other side is saying.[45] A person might begin a negotiating session claiming to want a bigger share of the division budget. Yet careful listening might indicate that he really is looking for his department to receive more respect and attention. So the issue is not financial.

As shown in the example just presented, listening helps the negotiator dig for information as to why the other side wants what it does.[46] If the other side wants a bigger budget just to have more respect, there are less expensive ways to grant respect than grant a bigger share of the budget. Perhaps the leader can give the person a classier job title, rename the department, or appoint the person to head a task force. For example, the head of marketing is renamed "chief of brands," and her department, "brand development."

Begin with a Plausible Demand or Offer   Most people believe that compromise and allowing room for negotiation include beginning with an extreme demand or offer. The theory is that the final compromise will be closer to the true demand or offer than if the negotiation were opened more realistically. But a plausible demand is better because it reflects good-faith bargaining. Also, if a third party has to resolve the conflict, a plausible demand or offer will receive more sympathy than an implausible one.

When it appears that the negotiation requires compromise to reach a satisfactory solution, it is usually time to *brainstorm and barter*. Brainstorming is helpful when a negotiation has hit a wall, and when no middle ground seems possible. According to negotiation researcher Nadine Kaslow, it may be helpful for both sides to consider multiple, mutual solutions. All parties should come up with at least ten options.[47] For example, both sides might search for ten ways of increasing an employee pension fund without damaging profits or lowering the stock price.

In bartering, the parties exchange one set of goods and services for another, in a way that pleases both sides. Bartering, however, may not be applicable to many types of negotiation. A possible example is that a leader of an information technology services company might be willing to provide a construction company a couple of years of cloud computing in exchange for a lower price on a new building.

Focus on Interests, Not Positions   Rather than clinging to specific negotiating points, one should keep overall interests in mind and try to satisfy them. The true object of negotiation is to satisfy the underlying interests of both sides. As professional mediator John Heister explains, when you focus on interests, all of the disputants get on the same side of the table and say, "We have a problem to solve. Based on our common interests, we need to find a solution that meets the needs of each of the stakeholders."[48]

Here is how the strategy works: Your manager asks you to submit a proposal for increasing sales volume. You see it as an important opportunity to link up with another distributor. When you submit your ideas, you learn that management wants to venture further into ecommerce, not to expand the dealer network. Instead of insisting on linking with another dealer, be flexible. Ask to be included in the decision making for additional involvement in ecommerce. You will increase your sales volume (your true interest), and you may enjoy such secondary benefits as having helped the company develop a stronger ecommerce presence.

Be Sensitive to International Differences in Negotiating Style   A challenge facing the multicultural leader is how to negotiate successfully with people from other cultures. Frank L. Acuff notes that Americans often have a no-nonsense approach to negotiation. A key attitude underlying the U.S. approach to negotiation is "Tell it like it is."

A problem with this type of frankness and seeming impatience is that people from other cultures may interpret such remarks as rudeness. The adverse interpretation, in turn, may lead to a failed negotiation. Acuff gives a case example: "It is unlikely in Mexico or Japan that the other side is going to answer 'yes' or 'no' to any question. You will have to discern answers to questions through the context of what is being said rather than from the more obvious direct cues that U.S. negotiators use."[49]

By sizing up what constitutes an effective negotiating style, the negotiator stands a reasonable chance of achieving a collaborative solution. Other cross-cultural differences in negotiation style include these tendencies: Japanese avoid direct confrontation and prefer an exchange of information. Russians crave combat; Koreans are team players; Nigerians prefer the spoken word and Indians the written one.[50] (We caution again, that cultural stereotypes are true much of the time, but not all of the time.)

When negotiating, it is important to recognize that you might want to make another deal, another day, with the same party. As a result, you want to conduct yourself in a dignified way and not attempt to maximize gain for yourself and minimize gain for the other side.

Negotiating and bargaining, as with any other leadership and management skill, require conceptual knowledge and practice. Leadership Skill-Building Exercise 12-3 gives you an opportunity to practice collaboration, the most integrative form of negotiating and bargaining, as well as conflict resolution. Practice in finding options for mutual gains is helpful for the leader because negotiating is a high-impact part of his or her job.

LEADERSHIP SKILL-BUILDING EXERCISE 12-3

Win–Win Bargaining

The class is organized into groups of six, with each group being divided into two negotiating teams of three each. The members of the negotiating teams would like to find a win–win (collaborative) solution to the issue separating the two sides. The team members are free to invent their own pressing issue, or they can choose one of the following:

- Management wants to control costs by not giving cost-of-living adjustments in the upcoming year. The employee group believes that a cost-of-living adjustment is absolutely necessary for its welfare.
- The marketing team claims it could sell 350,000 units of a decorative smart phone case if it could be produced at $10 per unit. The manufacturing group says it would not be feasible to get the manufacturing cost below $15 per unit.

- Taco Bell would like to build in a new location that is adjacent to a historic district in one of the oldest cities in North America. The members of the town planning board would like the tax revenue and jobs that the Taco Bell store would bring, but they do not want a Taco Bell restaurant (or store) adjacent to the historic district.

After the teams have arrived at their solutions through high-level negotiating techniques, the creative solutions can be shared with teammates.

SUMMARY

Open communication between company leaders and employees helps an organization overcome problems and attain success. Effective communication skills contribute to inspirational leadership. Nonverbal skills are also important for leadership effectiveness.

A major feature of communication by leaders is to rely on networks of contacts both in-person and electronically. Without being connected to other people it would be almost impossible for leaders to carry out their various roles. Developing networks of live interpersonal contacts remain an essential method for a leader building relationships, motivating others, and attaining collaboration. Leadership networks include the peer, operational, personal, and strategic.

An important use of the social media is for the leader to build and maintain a professional network. The productive leader is more likely to focus on contacts of relevance or density rather than superficial contacts. The strength-of-ties perspective explains the difference between strong and weak ties. The relationships among the different actors in a network can be broadly classified into two major types: strong versus weak ties and direct versus indirect ties.

Inspirational and powerful communication helps leaders carry out their roles. Suggestions for inspirational and powerful speaking and writing include the following: (1) be credible; (2) gear your message to your listener; (3) sell group members on the benefits of your suggestions; (4) use heavy-impact and emotion-provoking words; (5) use anecdotes to communicate meaning; (6) back up conclusions with data; (7) minimize language errors, junk words, and vocalized pauses; (8) use business jargon in appropriate doses, and (9) write crisp, clear memos, letters, and reports, including a front-loaded message.

Using a power-oriented linguistic style is another way to communicate with inspiration and power. The style includes a variety of techniques, such as downplaying uncertainty, emphasizing direct rather than indirect talks, and choosing an effective communication frame. Leaders can also improve their communication skills by following the six principles of persuasion: liking, reciprocity, social proof, consistency, authority, and scarcity.

Skill can also be developed in using nonverbal communication that connotes power, being in control, forcefulness, and self-confidence. Among the suggestions for nonverbal communication are to stand erect; speak at a moderate pace with a loud, clear tone; and smile frequently in a relaxed manner. A person's external image also plays an important part in communicating messages to others.

Videoconferencing, including telepresence, places heavy demands on nonverbal communication. Videoconferences represent a powerful tool for far-flung managers to make a name for themselves at corporate headquarters. The camera magnifies small nonverbal communication errors, such as scratching your head.

Listening is a fundamental management and leadership skill. Two impediments for the leaders who want to listen well are (1) leaders are already overloaded, and (2) people can listen to more words per minute than others can speak. Leaders have to be careful about listening selectively. A robust communication channel for the leader/manager is to engage in face-to-face communication with direct reports by making the rounds. Such rounds are effective for dealing with morale problems.

Overcoming communication barriers created by dealing with people from different cultures is another leadership and management challenge. Guidelines for overcoming cross-cultural barriers include the following: (1) be sensitive to the existence of cross-cultural communication barriers; (2) challenge your cultural assumptions; (3) show respect for all workers; (4) use straightforward language, and speak slowly and clearly; (5) look for signs of misunderstanding when your language is not the listener's native language; (6) when appropriate, speak in the language of the people from another culture; (7) observe cross-cultural differences in etiquette; (8) do not be diverted by style, accent, grammar, or personal appearance; (9) avoid racial or ethnic identification except when it is essential to communication; (10) be sensitive to differences in nonverbal communication; and (11) be attentive to individual differences in appearance.

Leaders and managers spend considerable time managing conflict, including conflict with outsiders. Resolving conflict facilitates collaboration. Five major styles of conflict management are as follows: competitive, accommodative, sharing, collaborative (win–win), and avoidant. Each style is based on a combination of satisfying one's own concerns (assertiveness) and satisfying the concerns of others (cooperativeness). The collaborative style of conflict management includes agreeing with the criticizer and apologizing. When resolving conflict, people typically combine several of the five resolution styles to accomplish their purpose, such as dominating and accommodating. Which modes of conflict handling to use depends upon a number of variables such as the importance of the issue and the relative power between the parties.

A high-level managerial skill is to help two or more group members resolve conflict between or among them. The most useful approach is to get the parties in conflict to engage in confrontation and problem solving.

Conflicts can be considered situations calling for negotiating and bargaining. Specific negotiating techniques include the following: (1) listen first to investigate what the other side wants; (2) begin with a plausible demand or offer; (3) focus on interests, not positions; and (4) be sensitive to international differences in negotiating style.

KEY TERMS

linguistic style

making the rounds

win–win approach to conflict resolution

✔ GUIDELINES FOR ACTION AND SKILL DEVELOPMENT

A subtle part of being an effective communicator is to avoid language that discourages another person from expressing his or her opinion, or worse, shuts the person up. At times you may feel like putting the lid on a subordinate. However, in the long run silencing your team will backfire because you will lose valuable input. Here are three examples of statements leaders and managers frequently use that clamp down on communication: "I already know that," "Why would you want to change that? It's not broken," and, "Well, it's my decision and I say no."[51]

Another technique for curtailing communication is to react to a comment with a blank stare and no comment of your own. Such behavior implies that you either don't care or are denying the reality of what the person is saying.

Discussion Questions and Activities

1. Now that you have studied this chapter, what are you going to do differently to improve your communication effectiveness as a leader?
2. Find an example of a powerful written or spoken message by a leader. Bring the information back to class to share with others.
3. What do you see as a potential downside to using a power-oriented linguistic style?

4. Why is persuasion considered to be one of the leader's essential tools?
5. Given that people really do defer to experts, how might the leader establish his or her expertise?
6. What should a leader worry about overcoming cross-cultural communication barriers? After all, isn't the leader in power?
7. Some managers avoid developing personal friendships with any direct reports because they do not want to be at a disadvantage in resolving conflict or negotiating with a subordinate. Does this idea seem reasonable to you?
8. Suppose a manager believes that by adding three more staff members, his or her business unit could double in productivity, however there is currently a hiring freeze in the organization. Which negotiating techniques might the manager best use with company executives to receive an exemption from the hiring freeze?
9. What concrete steps can a leader take to demonstrate that he or she respects a group member from another culture?
10. Assume that during a meeting, a middle manager is told by a subordinate that he or she is not fit for the position and should resign. What approach do you recommend that the leader take to resolve this conflict?

LEADERSHIP CASE PROBLEM A

Margot, the Cross-Cultural Communicator

Margot is the sales development manager of an online retailer that specializes in the sale of upscale clothing for men and women, at drastically low prices. Most of the clothing sold stems from reselling of inventory from high-end retailers that have gone out of business, are bankrupt, or liquidating merchandise for other reasons such as needing cash desperately.

Based in Los Angeles, the online store has an office and a distribution warehouse. Yet some sales are shipped directly from the distressed retailers who receive a small payment for making the shipments.

Margot was raised in Mexico. She speaks both English and Spanish fluently, which facilitates her working well in Los Angeles. However, Margot considers herself to be multicultural beyond working well with Americans, Latinos, and Mexican-Americans. "Give me anybody, whatever ethnicity and race, and I'll warm up to that person," she says. Not all the staff members at the company are so convinced about the effectiveness of Margot's multicultural skills.

Derek, the company website designer, who is African-American, said this about Margot: "I love the lady, but sometimes I think she patronizes me. She starts almost all our conversations asking me something about professional basketball. Oh, yes, I know that the vast majority of NBA players are black, but so are almost all the doctors, scientists, and lawyers in Africa. To please Margot, I make a few general comments about basketball so the conversation can proceed."

Lucie, an order-fulfillment specialist, is a Latina raised in Costa Rica. She said that she appreciates Margot's working hard to establish rapport with her, but that she gets tired of Margot so frequently asking her questions about Costa Rican cooking and holidays. "Okay, I was raised in Costa Rica. That doesn't mean that I think about my home country every day. I am here living and working in L.A."

Basil, a purchasing specialist, is the only senior working at the company. He has forty years of experience in merchandising women's clothing. "To me, Margot is like a niece, but I don't think she gets it about dealing with a senior. Margot keeps talking to me about my health, retirement planning, and how I like working with younger people in an online business. I just don't like talking about senior concerns."

Questions

1. What suggestions can you make to Margot about overcoming cross-cultural communication barriers?
2. What might be the factor or factors contributing to any errors Margot might be making in terms of cross-cultural communication?
3. To what extent do you think the three staff members mentioned above are being too harsh in judging Margot's attempts at establishing rapport?

ASSOCIATED ROLE PLAY

One person plays the role of Margot who will be having brief face-to-face interactions today with Derek, Lucie, and Basil. She will be taking her usual approach to establishing rapport with her staff members. Three other students will play the roles of Derek, Lucie, and Basil. All three would prefer that Margot not focus so much on the cultural identity mentioned above. (Most people have more than one cultural identity, such as being Latino as well as a member of Generation Y.) Observers will be alert to how well the cross-cultural interactions go.

LEADERSHIP CASE PROBLEM B

West Coast Wellness on the Go

Heather Wyoming was feeling great because she believed that today would be a turning point. As the director of marketing for West Coast Wellness, she was to meet with the executive committee, which included her boss, the CEO. Heather's purpose was to get approval to hire three new sales and marketing representatives. The meeting to discuss her plans took place at 8:30 A.M. A partial transcript of the meeting follows:

Heather: Thanks so much for meeting with me this morning. In appreciation, you can see that we have snacks that will make you well. All the pastries, doughnuts, and bagels are made without trans-fats. And all the juices served are freshly squeezed.

I am glad to see that you are looking well, because today we are celebrating wellness. West Coast Wellness is on the go. We have signed up six new companies and three HMOs in the last few months to use our services. We have also broken the ground by offering individual memberships.

I need your approval to hire three new sales and marketing representatives so we can keep the momentum rolling on our expansion.

CEO: How much will these new hires *cost* West Coast?

Heather: No cost at all. We will be investing about $30,000 per year for each rep. They will be working on mostly commission. I estimate that each successful rep will bring in a net of about $200,000 in revenue. So there is really no *cost* involved.

Exec Committee Member 1: Yet, Heather, we cannot overlook the fact that you want to bring three new employees on board, a situation that creates an immediate financial liability for West Coast Wellness.

Heather: I understand your point of view. If the reps produce nothing, we lose a lot of money. However, by hiring the right reps we will turn this potential liability into a great asset. I understand the need for prudent financial management, but I think I am asking you to take a prudent risk.

Exec Committee Member 2: The regional economy has cooled down considerably, and there are many layoffs. Heather, what makes you so optimistic that we can expand the market for wellness services?

Heather: I share your concern about the economy. However, keeping employees well is a fabulous investment. We can demonstrate to potential clients that helping employees stay well increases productivity. When employees lose fewer days to absenteeism and less time to tardiness, they are more productive. Another great selling point we have is that when employers use our services, their medical insurance premiums typically go down.

Exec Committee Member 3: Heather, we all share your enthusiasm for wellness—otherwise, we wouldn't be members of the executive committee. But I am a little concerned that the market for our services is saturating. Hiring three more reps might be too optimistic.

Heather: You make a great point, yet awareness of wellness is on the rise. Companies are even giving workers financial rewards to get in shape. Obesity is being attacked on all fronts, and smokers are treated like criminals. Wellness is on the move, and we can get a bigger share of the market.

CEO: Heather, I am proposing to you and the committee that you begin by hiring one new sales and marketing rep. If that person proves to be a good investment, we will authorize you to hire another rep.

Heather: I can buy that logic. Just give me a chance to prove how much I can expand our market. I just want to get started on the path to success. One rep it is for now.

Questions

1. How successful has Heather been at negotiating her demands?
2. Did Heather leave anything on the table?
3. What leadership characteristics has Heather displayed?

ASSOCIATED ROLE PLAY

One person plays the role of Heather, who is committed to hiring three sales representatives for her wellness program. She intends to negotiate fiercely for what she believes is a good investment.

Three other students play the roles of the executive committee members. Observers will comment on the effectiveness of the negotiation.

LEADERSHIP SKILL-BUILDING **EXERCISE 12-4**

My Leadership Portfolio

For this chapter's entry into your leadership portfolio, think through how you have dealt with your opportunities to communicate as a leader in your experiences. Did you have an opportunity to attempt to persuade an individual or group? Did you have an opportunity to be supportive toward another person? Did you have an opportunity to make a presentation on the job or in class? During these communication opportunities, how well did you come across as a leader? Did you impress anybody with persuasive skill or warmth? Carlos, an assistant restaurant manager, made this entry in his portfolio:

> I help manage an upscale restaurant. The wait staff has to be on top of its game when in the dining room. Without superior service, nobody is going to pay our prices, even if the food and wine are good. Late one afternoon, Rick dragged in, looking in no shape to give good service to our guests. He looked worried and distracted. Instead of telling Rick to go home, I took him aside in the office. I asked him to give me a full explanation of whatever problem he was facing. We both sat down, and I poured Rick a cup of coffee. After a minute or so, Rick opened up to tell me about how he rammed the back of his car into a two-foot-high guardrail in a parking lot. His fiberglass bumper split, and he figures it will cost him $650 to replace it. I listened to his whole story without being judgmental. I said I would check with the manager to see if we could give him extra hours this month to earn more money to apply toward his repair. Rick said, "Thanks for listening," and he left our one-on-one session feeling better and looking well enough to face the guests.
>
> I give myself a gold star for having been a supportive leader. Ha! Ha!

 LEADERSHIP SKILL-BUILDING **EXERCISE 12-5**

Evaluating the Communication Skills of an Organizational Leader

So much has been said about the importance of good communication skills for an effective leader. Your assignment is to observe a specific organizational leader of your choice, such as a business executive. Methods of observing an organizational leader include (a) an interview of an executive on a television news channel, (b) finding a brief executive presentation on YouTube or Hulu, and (c) attending a function in which an executive is either giving a talk or interacting with visitors. In preparing your evaluation look for such factors as persuasiveness, adequate grammar and sentence structure, and ability to establish rapport with the receiver of the message.

A side aspect of this assignment is to observe the executive's communication skills with the intent of picking up an idea or two to improve your own communication effectiveness.

▶❚❚ **LEADERSHIP** VIDEO **CASE** DISCUSSION **QUESTIONS**

To view the videos for this activity, you'll need access to the CourseMate that is available for this text. To get access, visit www.CengageBrain.com.

After watching "Metropolitan Bakery," answer the following questions.

1. Do you believe the expectations at Metropolitan Bakery communicated clearly? Explain.

2. What is a linguistic style? How might James Barrett and Wendy Smith Born, co-owners of Metropolitan Bakery, use a linguistic style that gives them power and authority?

3. Define making the rounds. How does Wendy Smith Born use this technique as a leadership skill?

4. James Barrett describes a time in which he worked at learning from European Apprenticeship Program trained chefs. He also talks about what it was like working with U.S. chefs. Describe the differences between the two. According to the text, what are some cultural mistakes to avoid with European cultures?

NOTES

1. Story created based on facts and observations found in the following sources: Susanne Craig, "E*Trade Fills Its CEO Post," *The Wall Street Journal*, March 23, 2010, p. C3; "Steven Freiberg, CEO of E*Trade; Colin Goddard, Former CEO of OSI Pharmaceuticals, Appointed to Hofstra Board," *PressZoom* (http://presszoom.com), January 16, 2001; Amit Chowdhry, "Former Citigroup Exec Steven Freiberg Becomes CEO of E*Trade," *Pulse2* (http://Pulse2.com), March 22, 2010, pp. 1–10.
2. John Hamm, "The Five Messages Leaders Must Manage," *Harvard Business Review*, May 2006, p. 116.
3. Bruce Hoppe and Claire Reinelt, "Social Network Analysis and the Evaluation of Leadership Networks," *Leadership Quarterly*, August 2010, p. 600.
4. Quoted in Ben Worthen, "Battle Stations," December 8, 2008, p. R9.
5. Hoppe and Reinelt, "Social Network Analysis," p. 601.
6. Herminia Ibarra and Mark Hunter, "How Leaders Create and Use Networks," *Harvard Business Review*, January 2007, pp. 40–47.
7. Mark Granovetter, "The Strength of Weak Ties: A Network Theory Revisited," *Sociological Theory*, Volume 1, 1983, pp. 201–233.
8. Quoted in Jim Aley and Brian Bremmer (editors), "Trouble at the Virtual Water Cooler," *Bloomberg Businessweek*, May 2–May 8, 2011, 31.
9. Research reported in Kyle Stock, "For Lying CEOs, 'Team,' Not 'I.'" *The Wall Street Journal*, August 12, 2010, p. C3.
10. Stephen P. Robbins and Phillip L. Hunsaker, *Training in Interpersonal Skills: Tips for Managing People at Work* (Upper Saddle River, N.J.: Prentice Hall, 1996), p. 115. (These findings are still valid today.)
11. Cited in Benice Atufunwa, "The Art of Effective Communication," *Black Enterprise*, November 2009, p. 47.
12. Frank Luntz, "Words That Pack Power," *Business Week*, November 3, 2008, p. 106.
13. Stephen Denning, "Stories in the Workplace," *HR Magazine*, September 2008, pp. 129–132.
14. William Strunk Jr., E. B. White, and Maira Kalman, *The Elements of Style*, 6th ed. (Boston: Allyn and Bacon, 2007).
15. James R. Hagerty, "Dad. What Do You Do at Work? I'm a Leader in Active Safety," *The Wall Street Journal*, November 26, 2010, p. A1.
16. Sherry Sweetham, "How to Organize Your Thoughts for Better Communication," *Personnel*, March 1986, p. 39.
17. Cited in Laura Raines, "Sharpen Your Communication Skills to Stand Out in World of Work," www.ajc.com, March 29, 2011, p. 3.
18. Deborah Tannen, "The Power of Talk: Who Gets Heard and Why?" *Harvard Business Review*, September–October 1995, pp. 138–148.
19. Tannen, "The Power of Talk," pp. 138–148; "How You Speak Shows Where You Rank," *Fortune*, February 2, 1998, p. 156; "Speak Like You Mean Business," *Working Smart* (www.nibm.net), March 2004; "Weed Out Wimpy Words: Speak Up Without Backpedaling, Qualifying," *Working SMART*, March 2000, p. 2.
20. Robert B. Cialdini, "Harnessing the Science of Persuasion," *Harvard Business Review*, October 2001, pp. 72–79.
21. Ibid., p. 79.
22. Several of the suggestions here are from *Body Language for Business Success* (New York: National Institute for Business Management, 1989), pp. 2–29; "Attention All Monotonous Speakers," *Working SMART*, March 1998, p. 1.
23. Drake Bennett, "I'll Have My Robots Talk to Your Robots," *Bloomberg Business Week*, pp. 52–61.
24. Cited in Joann S. Lublin, "Some Dos and Don'ts to Help You Hone Videoconference Skills," *The Wall Street Journal*, February 7, 2006, p. B1.

25. Ibid.

26. Richard M. Harris, *The Listening Leader: Powerful New Strategies for Becoming an Influential Communicator* (Westport, Conn.: Praeger, 2006).

27. Erika H. James, "Selective Hearing Can Lead to a Blind Eye," *The Darden Perspective in First Person*, published in *The Wall Street Journal*, December 4, 2007, p. A16.

28. Linda Dulye, "Get Out of Your Office," *HR Magazine*, July 2006, pp. 99–100; "'Making Rounds' Like a Physician," *Manager's Edge*, February 2006, p. 8.

29. Joyce M. Rosenberg, "Talking with Your Workers Lifts Morale," The Associated Press, October 12, 2009.

30. Trudy Milburn, "Bridging Cultural Gaps," *Management Review*, January 1997, pp. 26–29.

31. Gunnar Beeth, "Multicultural Managers Wanted," *Management Review*, May 1997, p. 17.

32. "When English Is Not Their Native Tongue," *Manager's Edge*, April 2003, p. 5.

33. Kathryn Kranhold, "Lost in Translation," *The Wall Street Journal*, May 18, 2004, p. B1.

34. "Cross-Cultural Communication: An Essential Dimension of Effective Education," *Northwest Regional Educational Library: CNORSE* (www. nwrel.org/cnorse).

35. Siri Carpenter, "Why Do'They All Look Alike'?" *Monitor on Psychology*, December 2000, p. 44.

36. Chris Penttila, "Turf Wars," *Entrepreneur*, March 2007, p. 90.

37. Jeff Weiss and Jonathan Hughes, "Want Collaboration? Accept—and Actively Manage—Conflict," *Harvard Business Review*, March 2005, pp. 92–101.

38. April Castro, "Amazon Closing TX Center Amid Dispute," Associated Press, February 10, 2011.

39. Kenneth Thomas, "Conflict and Conflict Management," in Marvin D. Dunnette, ed., *Handbook of Industrial and Organizational Psychology* (Chicago: Rand McNally, 1976), pp. 900–922.

40. Barbara Kellerman, "When Should a Leader Apologize and When Not?" *Harvard Business Review*, April 2006, pp. 72–81.

41. Elizabeth A. Mannix, Leigh L. Thompson, and Max H. Bazerman, "Negotiation in Small Groups," *Journal of Applied Psychology*, June 1989, pp. 508–517.

42. Patrick S. Nugent, "Managing Conflict: Third-Party Interventions for Managers," *Academy of Management Executive*, February 2002, p. 152.

43. "Questions for Michael Watkins," *Workforce*, December 11, 2006, p. 11.

44. Jeff Weiss, Aram Donigian, and Jonathan Hughes, "Extreme Negotiations," *Harvard Business Review*, November 2010, pp. 68–69.

45. Cited in Brenda Goodman, "The Art of Negotiation," *Psychology Today*, January/February 2007, p. 65.

46. Deepak Malhotra and Max H. Bazerman, "Investigative Negotiation," *Harvard Business Review*, September 2007, pp. 72–78.

47. Cited in Tori DeAngelis, "Achieving Win–Win," *Psychology Today*, November 2008, p. 64.

48. John Heister, "Collaborate to Solve Societal Ills," Rochester, New York, *Democrat and Chronicle*, May 14, 2004, p. 18A.

49. Frank Acuff, *The World-Class Negotiator: An Indispensable Guide for Anyone Doing Business with Those from a Foreign Culture* (New York: AMACOM, 1992).

50. Wendi L. Adair, Tetsushi Okumura, and Jeanne M. Brett, "Negotiation Behavior When Cultures Collide: The United States and Japan," *Journal of Applied Psychology*, June 2001, pp. 371–385.

51. "Avoid Language That Shuts People Up," *Executive Leadership*, January 2008, p. 8.

The **Creative** and **Innovative Aspects** of **Leaders**

LEARNING OBJECTIVES

After studying this chapter and doing the exercises, you should be able to

- Identify the steps in the creative process.
- Identify characteristics of creative problem solvers.
- Be prepared to overcome traditional thinking in order to become more creative.
- Describe both organizational and individual approaches to enhance creative problem solving.

- Explain how the leader and the organization can establish a climate that fosters creativity.
- Identify several leadership practices that contribute to organizational innovation.

CHAPTER OUTLINE

Marissa Mayer is both a leader of highly creative people and a highly creative person herself. Born in 1975, she was for many years the vice president of Search Products and User Experience at Google Inc. Her latest role at the company is vice president of consumer products. Mayer's major responsibility is to run the company's geographic and local services initiatives. These services deal with delivering information and advertising to consumers, based on their geographic location at the moment. Mayer has been personally involved in every product and service Google has offered.

After earning a master's degree in computer science from Stanford University in 1999, Mayer signed on with the fledgling search firm Google. She became the company's twentieth employee and first female engineer. Mayer is a self-described geek, but she is also strongly interested in fashion and runs every day to help stay in top physical condition.

Mayer has many opinions about creativity and innovation stemming from her exceptional business successes. She emphasizes that ideas can come from anywhere, and then you need to build a prototype. You also have to figure out how you are going to capture the imagination and attention of the users and really meet their needs. Every product must walk out the door the way you want it. Feedback on what you offer people is critical for refining your product.

Mayer also believes that to enhance innovation you should share your ideas and projects on the intranet. To keep innovation moving along you need to favor intelligence over experience when hiring. She also believes that creativity adores restraints. "Give people a vision, rules about how to get there, and deadlines. Or give them leather straps and a ball gag."[1]

The perspectives on innovation and the leadership of innovation from one of Google's heaviest hitters fit closely some of the themes in this chapter. Leaders of creativity and innovation are creative themselves, and they make a special effort to engage in leadership and management practices that foster creativity and innovation.

By thinking creatively, a person can form a new enterprise or enlarge an existing one that can keep many people engaged in productive activity. However, the creative idea has to be executed properly for innovation to take place. Although the terms *creativity* and *innovation* are often used interchangeably, **innovation** refers to the creation of new ideas and their *implementation* or *commercialization*. A major focus of innovation is taking organizations built for efficiency and rewiring them for creativity and growth.[2] Creativity is also regarded as essential for an entrepreneurship that launches new businesses and that sustains successful companies after they have attained global scale.[3]

Long-time leadership authority Warren Bennis regards creativity as an essential characteristic of leaders.[4] The role of a creative leader is to bring into existence ideas and things that did not exist previously or that existed in a different form. Leaders are not bound by current solutions to problems. Instead, they create images of other possibilities. Leaders often move a firm into an additional business or start a new department that offers another service.

This chapter emphasizes the development of creativity in the leader. It also explains the nature of creativity and creative people and examines the leader's role in establishing an atmosphere that helps group members become more creative, along with leadership practices conducive to innovation.

STEPS IN THE CREATIVE PROCESS

An important part of becoming more creative involves understanding the stages involved in **creativity**, which is generally defined as the production of novel and useful ideas. A still well-accepted model of creativity developed almost ninety years ago can be applied to organizations. This model divides creative thinking into five stages,[5] as shown in Figure 13-1. Step 1 is *opportunity or problem recognition:* a person discovers that a new opportunity exists or a problem needs to be resolved. One day in 1994, a financial analyst named Jeff Bezos was seated at his desk at the New York hedge fund, D. E. Shaw, when he noticed an astonishing statistic: The number of Internet users was growing by 2,300 percent per year. Bezos thought that there must be some good way to commercialize this development. Bezos was concerned that he or his company had not yet capitalized on the revolutionary development called the Internet. He detected an opportunity for some kind of business, but he did yet know which one.[6]

Step 2 is *immersion.* The individual concentrates on the problem and becomes immersed in it. He or she will recall and collect information that seems relevant, dreaming up alternatives without refining or evaluating them. Bezos grabbed every fact he could about mail order businesses and thought about which ones could be conducted more efficiently over the Internet than by the traditional means, such as phoning in or writing for orders.

Step 3 is *incubation.* The person keeps the assembled information in mind for a while. He or she does not appear to be working on the problem actively, but the subconscious mind is still engaged. While the information is simmering, it is being arranged into meaningful new patterns. Bezos kept thinking about using the Internet for a mail order business while performing his regular work.

Step 4 is *insight.* The problem-conquering solution flashes into the person's mind at an unexpected time, such as on the verge of sleep, during a shower, or

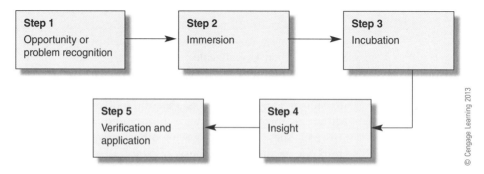

FIGURE 13-1 Steps in the Creative Process.

Creative problem solvers often go through these steps below the level of conscious awareness. Yet being aware of these steps (such as immersing yourself in knowledge) when faced with a challenging problem will often increase the probability of finding a creative solution.

while running. Insight is also called the *Aha! experience:* all of a sudden, something clicks. At some point it clicked in Bezos's mind that books were the commodity for which no comprehensive mail order catalog existed because a catalogue of this nature would be much too large to mail profitably. A catalogue of this type would be ideally suited to the Internet because a vast database could be shared with an almost unlimited number of users. The aha! experience usually arrives after hours of thought and study, as indicated by Step 2, immersion.

Step 5 is *verification and application.* The individual sets out to prove that the creative solution has merit. Verification procedures include gathering supporting evidence, using logical persuasion, and experimenting with new ideas. Application requires tenacity because most novel ideas are first rejected as being impractical. The day after his insight experience, Bezos flew to Los Angeles to the American Booksellers' Convention to learn all he could about the book business. One key fact he found was that the major book wholesalers had already assembled electronic lists of their inventory. Bezos reasoned that the potential new venture only needed one Internet location where the book-buying public could search through the stock and place orders directly.

Because his employer wasn't interested in jumping into the Internet bookselling business, Bezos decided to go into business for himself, founding Amazon.com. He and his wife then drove to Seattle, Washington, to set up the new business, drawing up the business plan as they rolled down the highway in a 1988 Chevy Blazer.

Bezos' opportunity-spotting has evolved into a major business corporation that now sells all kinds of merchandises in addition to books and music, as well as information technology services such as cloud computing. Today, Amazon.com is the largest online retailer in the United States. The end product of Bezos' creative thinking was a business possibility rather than an invention. Nevertheless, businesspeople typically follow the same five steps of creative thought as do inventors. Even though creativity usually follows the same steps, it is not a mechanical process that can be turned on and off. Much of creativity is intricately woven into a person's intellect and personality.

CHARACTERISTICS OF CREATIVE LEADERS

Creative leaders, like creative workers of all types, are different in many ways from their less creative counterparts. They are devoted to their fields and enjoy intellectual stimulation, and they challenge the status quo, which leads them to seek improvements. Larry Page, the cofounder and CEO of Google Inc., has a reputation for challenging the status quo despite the success of the company. Recently he expressed an interest in pushing Google into renewable energy and robotic cars.[7] Above all, creative people are mentally flexible and can see past the traditional ways of looking at problems.

As described next, the specific characteristics of creative people, including creative leaders, can be grouped into four areas: knowledge, cognitive abilities, personality, and passion for the task and the experience of flow.[8] These

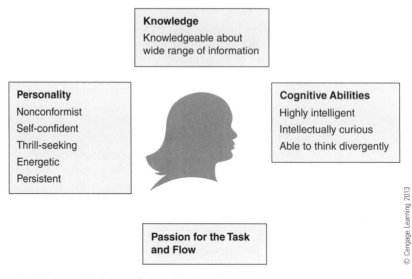

Knowledge
Knowledgeable about
wide range of information

Personality
Nonconformist
Self-confident
Thrill-seeking
Energetic
Persistent

Cognitive Abilities
Highly intelligent
Intellectually curious
Able to think divergently

Passion for the Task and Flow

© Cengage Learning 2013

FIGURE 13-2 Characteristics of Creative Leaders.

Having the right characteristics improves the chances of a person being a creative problem solver and a creative leader.

characteristics are highlighted in Figure 13-2. In addition, we present a formula about human behavior that helps explain how these characteristics lead to creative output. Before studying this information, compare your thinking to that of a creative person by doing Leadership Self-Assessment Quiz 13-1.

Knowledge

Creative problem solving requires a broad background of information, including facts and observations. Knowledge provides the building blocks for generating and combining ideas. Most creative leaders are knowledgeable, and their knowledge contributes to their charisma. A well-known case in point is Steven P. Jobs, the former chief executive of Apple Inc. He contributes design and marketing decisions to most of Apple's key products, and he played a major role in the development of the popular iPhone and iPad. A contributor to Jobs's creativity is his in-depth technical knowledge of computer hardware and software. Jobs said at the peak of his career something to the effect that creativity is the result of having enough dots to connect. (The dots are bits of knowledge.)

An example of connecting dots is the cross-breeding of the iPod Nano with a Nike running shoe. A chip inserted into the shoe turns the shoe into a step counter that is wirelessly connected to a receiver in the iPod Nano. The iPod then displays such information as the number of miles run and calories burned.

LEADERSHIP SELF-ASSESSMENT QUIZ 13-1

The Creative Personality Test

Instructions: Describe each of the following statements as "mostly true" or "mostly false."

	MOSTLY TRUE	MOSTLY FALSE
1. It is generally a waste of time to read magazine articles, Internet articles, and books outside my immediate field of interest.	☐	☐
2. I frequently have the urge to suggest ways of improving products and services I use.	☐	☐
3. Reading fiction and visiting art museums are time wasters.	☐	☐
4. I am a person of very strong convictions. What is right is right; what is wrong is wrong.	☐	☐
5. I enjoy it when my boss hands me vague instructions.	☐	☐
6. Making order out of chaos is actually fun.	☐	☐
7. Only under extraordinary circumstances would I deviate from my To Do list (or other ways in which I plan my day).	☐	☐
8. I often use search engines other than Google just to explore something different.	☐	☐
9. Rules and regulations should not be taken too seriously. Most rules can be broken under unusual circumstances.	☐	☐
10. Playing with a new idea is fun even if it does not benefit me in the end.	☐	☐
11. Some of my best ideas have come from building on the ideas of others.	☐	☐
12. In writing, I try to avoid the use of unusual words and word combinations.	☐	☐
13. I frequently jot down improvements in the job I would like to make in the future.	☐	☐
14. I prefer to stay with technology devices I know well rather than frequently updating my equipment or software.	☐	☐
15. I prefer writing personal notes or poems to loved ones rather than relying on greeting cards.	☐	☐
16. At one time or another in my life I have enjoyed doing puzzles.	☐	☐
17. If your thinking is clear, you will find the one best solution to a problem.	☐	☐
18. It is best to interact with coworkers who think much like you.	☐	☐
19. I would readily accept an assignment to a new product development committee.	☐	☐
20. Tight controls over people and money are necessary to run a successful organization.	☐	☐

QUIZ 13-1 (continued)

Scoring and Interpretation: Give yourself a score of 1 for each answer that matches the answer key:

1. Mostly false	**8.** Mostly true	**15.** Mostly true
2. Mostly true	**9.** Mostly true	**16.** Mostly true
3. Mostly false	**10.** Mostly true	**17.** Mostly false
4. Mostly false	**11.** Mostly true	**18.** Mostly false
5. Mostly true	**12.** Mostly false	**19.** Mostly true
6. Mostly true	**13.** Mostly true	**20.** Mostly false
7. Mostly false	**14.** Mostly false	

Total score: ⎯⎯⎯⎯⎯

Extremely high or low scores are the most meaningful. A score of 15 or more suggests that your personality and attitudes are similar to those of creative people, including creative leaders. A score of 8 or less suggests that you are more of an intellectual conformist at present. Do not be discouraged. Most people can develop in the direction of becoming more creative.

How does your score compare to your self-evaluation of your creativity? We suggest you also obtain feedback on your creativity from somebody familiar with your thinking and your work.

Cognitive Abilities

Intellectual abilities comprise such abilities as general intelligence and abstract reasoning. Creative problem solvers, particularly in business, are often bright but are not at the absolute top end of the brilliance scale. A subtle exception here is that when the creativity centers on highly technical matters, the creative business person is often brilliant. Two examples presented so far in this chapter are Marissa Mayer and Jeff Bezos. Sanjay Jha, presented later, is also brilliant.

Even if extraordinarily high intelligence is not required to be creative, creative people are facile at generating creative solutions to problems in a short period of time. Creative people also maintain a youthful curiosity throughout their lives, and the curiosity is not centered just on their own field of expertise. Instead, their range of interests encompasses many areas of knowledge, and they are enthusiastic about puzzling problems. These mental workouts help sharpen a person's intelligence.

Creative people show an identifiable intellectual style: being able to think divergently. They are able to expand the number of alternatives to a problem, thus moving away from a single solution. Yet the creative thinker also knows when it is time to narrow the number of useful solutions. For example, the divergent thinker might think of twenty-seven ways to reduce costs, but at some point he or she will have to move toward choosing the best of several cost-cutting approaches.

In recent years several business firms have included design school graduates in their product development teams because designers tend to think flexibly. The idea is to search for new options that do not already exist. An example is that Intel works with design students to work on new products for aging baby boomers' future homes.[9]

As in the Amazon.com example, a hallmark of a creative businessperson's intellect is to spot opportunities that others might overlook. Many a creative developer has seen the opportunities in abandoned factories and converted them into loft apartments and offices for small businesses that wanted to operate in an aesthetic environment.

A key issue in relation to the cognitive styles of creative business leaders is whether they should be left-brain dominant (logical and analytical), or right-brain dominant (creative and intuitive). The answer is, "Both." Daniel Pink, a writer who synthesizes psychological research, explains that in the past the most important abilities in any kind of white-collar profession were characteristic of the left hemisphere of the brain. These abilities are the logical, linear, sequential, analytical, and spreadsheet type. Although still necessary, they are no longer sufficient. In the present economy, the abilities that matter the most are artistry, empathy, inventiveness, and big-picture thinking.[10]

Personality

Personality factors or the noncognitive aspects of an individual heavily influence creative problem solving. Creative people tend to have a positive self-image without being blindly self-confident. But because they are reasonably self-confident, they are able to cope with criticism of their ideas, and they can tolerate the isolation necessary for developing ideas. Part of the self-confidence of a creative worker focuses on the belief that he or she can solve problems creatively. Talking to others is a good way to get ideas, yet at some point the creative problem solver has to work alone and concentrate.

Creative people are frequently nonconformists and do not need strong approval from the group. Nonconformity can also mean being a maverick. Richard E. Cheverton observes: "The maverick is really the person who is the focus of creativity in a company, but a lot of people perceive them as jerks because they like to stir the pot. But these are just people driven to accomplish things anonymously. They just want to get things done, and they do not care about office politics or organizational charts. They like to spread the credit around."[11] A maverick personality who is not granted the freedom to develop new ideas is likely to join another firm or start a business.

Closely related to being nonconformists and mavericks, creative workers prefer to search for alternatives than worry about attaining consensus. Josh Linkner, the founder and chairman of ePrize LLC, an interactive promotions company, said that groupthink (striving for consensus at any cost) discourages innovation.[12]

Many creative problem solvers are thrill seekers and risk takers who find that developing imaginative solutions to problems is a source of thrills. Larry

Page, a big risk taker himself, has said that the biggest payoffs at Google have stemmed from risky ideas and investments.[13] Creative people are also persistent, which is especially important for the verification and application stage of creative thinking. Selling a creative idea to the right people requires considerable follow-up. Finally, creative people enjoy dealing with ambiguity and chaos. Less creative people become quickly frustrated when task descriptions are unclear and disorder exists.

Passion for the Task and the Experience of Flow

A dominant characteristic of creative people that is closely related to personality is a passion for the work. More than twenty years of research in industry conducted by Teresa M. Amabile and her associates led to the *intrinsic motivation principle of creativity:* People will be at their creative best when they feel motivated primarily by the interest, satisfaction, and challenge of the work itself—and not by external pressures.[14]

Passion for the task and high intrinsic motivation contribute in turn to a total absorption in the work and intense concentration, or the **experience of flow**. It is an experience so engrossing and enjoyable that the task becomes worth doing for its own sake regardless of the external consequences.[15] Perhaps you have had this experience when completely absorbed in a hobby or some analytical work, or when you were at your best in a sport or dance. (Flow also means *being in the zone*.) The highly creative leader, such as a business owner developing a plan for worldwide distribution of a product, will often achieve the experience of flow.

One of the problems with attempting to be creative under high-pressure conditions is that the pressure may interfere with the intense concentration required for high creativity. Based on her analysis of nearly 12,000 journal entries of workers engaged in creative tasks, Amabile discovered that time pressures may block people from deeply engaging with the problem. People can be creative when they are under heavy time pressures, but only when they can focus on the work.[16]

To fully understand the contribution of personal characteristics to creativity, we note the basic formula of human behavior: $B = f(P \times E)$ (behavior is a function of a person interacting with the environment). In this context, certain personal characteristics may facilitate a leader's being creative, but the right environment is necessary to trigger creative behavior. As will be described later, the right environment includes the leader encouraging creative thinking.

OVERCOMING TRADITIONAL THINKING AS A CREATIVITY STRATEGY

A unifying theme runs through all forms of creativity training and suggestions for creativity improvement: Creative problem solving requires an ability to overcome traditional thinking. The concept of *traditional thinking* is relative, but it generally refers to a standard and frequent way of finding a solution to a problem. A traditional solution to a problem is thus a modal or most frequent solution. For example, traditional thinking suggests that to increase revenue, a retail store should conduct a sale. Creative thinking would point toward other solutions. As an example, a retail store might increase sales by shipping goods for a small fee, or providing for online shopping (of the store's products) in the store.

The creative person looks at problems in a new light and transcends conventional thinking about them. A historically significant example is Henry Ford, who was known for his creative problem-solving ability. A meatpacking executive invited Ford to visit his Chicago plant and observe how employees processed beef. The automotive executive noticed that at one end of the plant whole carcasses of steers were placed on a giant conveyor belt. As the meat traveled through the plant, workers carved it into various cuts until the carcass was consumed. A flash of whimsical insight hit Ford: What if the process were reversed, and all the pieces would become a whole steer again? Ford asked himself, "Why can't an automobile be built that way?" He took his creative idea back to the Ford Motor Company in Detroit and constructed the world's first manufacturing assembly line.[17]

The central task in becoming creative is to break down rigid thinking that blocks new ideas. At the same time, the problem solver must unlearn the conventional approach. Henry Ford unlearned the custom approach to building autos so he could use an assembly line. (In the current era, people who have unlearned the assembly-line approach and switched to customization are considered to be creative!)

Overcoming traditional thinking is so important to creative thinking that the process has been characterized in several different ways. The most familiar is that *a creative person thinks outside the box*. A box, in this sense, is a category that confines and restricts thinking. Because you are confined to a box, you do not see opportunities outside the box. For example, if an insurance executive thinks that health insurance is only for humans, he or she might miss out on the growing market for domestic animal health insurance. Inside the accompanying box insert, you will find several business examples of thinking outside the box.

A caution about thinking outside the box: Workers still need some constraints as to how far outside the box they are permitted to think. You will recall that in the chapter opener, Marissa Mayer stated that creativity adores constraints. Similarly, creativity writer Shawn Coyne contends that when people are told to think outside the box with no constraints they quickly become overwhelmed by the unlimited scope of the task. Effective project leaders establish parameters and prepare their teams for idea generation by pointing them in a specific direction. Coyne also explains that the best ideas come from "thinking inside a very carefully designed box that's not too big or too small."[18] An example might be telling team members that they need to find ways of saving the company energy costs but that no suggestions will be used that are too expensive or result in widespread employee complaints.

Modern Business Examples of Thinking Outside the Box

- Conventional wisdom says that you do not permit competitors to sell products and services in your own store or on your own website. Amazon.com, however, has had a program in place for years that enables the consumer to shop at other online stores through its own website. Amazon.com collects a small commission, and customer experience has been improved, thereby increasing sales at Amazon.
- Conventional wisdom says that sidewalks have to be made out of cement or concrete, and that when tree roots damage the sidewalks, the trees have to go. Lindsay Smith noted that twenty-six trees in her neighborhood in Gardena, California, were being cut down because their roots were damaging the sidewalk. With guidance from U.S. Rubber Recycling, she founded Rubbersidewalks, a company that has installed footpaths made of recycled tires in sixty cities in the United States and Canada. Each square piece can be removed for repairs, thereby saving the destruction of trees. Also, rubber is more compatible with tree roots than is concrete.
- Conventional wisdom said that to rent videos or DVDs you had to visit a physical video or DVD store. Netflix shot out of seemingly nowhere to create a new segment in the movie rental business with a simple business model that allows consumers to rent popular DVDs online and have the movies arrive quickly in the mail, all for a monthly fee. (Now the DVDs can be accessed digitally, as well, and streamed onto the computer monitor or a TV receiver.) Netflix's success spawned competitors, but Netflix still controls a substantial market share.
- Conventional wisdom says that there is not much a pharmacy can do about customers who neglect to refill their prescription, thereby often suffering health consequences, as well as the pharmacy

forgoing revenue. Leadership at CVS/Caremark thought that a proactive approach was needed. A system has been installed to deal with the problem. If a patient on a pharmacy benefit management program has stopped taking his or her drugs, a CVS pharmacist may telephone to remind the patient to order refills. The program is also thought to be a creative way of reducing the number of patients who become so ill that they require hospitalization.

- Conventional wisdom says that banks cannot make home loans to devout Muslims because, according to the Koran (Islam's sacred book), Muslims are forbidden to pay or receive interest. As a consequence, a potential segment of the market was shut out from receiving home mortgages. The University Bank of Ann Arbor, Michigan, developed a unique interest-free program designed for people whose religious beliefs forbid paying interest. The bank developed a mortgage alternative loan transaction (MALT) program that replaces a traditional home loan with a redeemable lease. The bank holds the home in trust, and the customer makes monthly payments to that trust. Each rent payment includes a set amount of savings that builds equity in the property. After the savings account equals the home's original price, the customer owns the home free and clear.

Source: Heather Green, "How Amazon Aims to Keep You Clicking." *BusinessWeek*, March 2, 2009, pp. 034–040; Stacy Perman, "Concrete Decision," *BusinessWeek SmallBiz*, February/March 2007, p. 034; Christopher Stern, "Netflix Braces for Amazon: DVD Rental Company Cuts Fees to Compete," *Washington Post*, October 16, 2004, p. 1E; Matthew Boyle, "CVS: Dispensing Drugs—and Health Reform," *BusinessWeek*, February 23, 2009, pp. 42–43; Karen Dybis, "Banks Offer No-Interest Options for Muslims," *Detroit News*, December 21, 2004 (detnews.com).

ORGANIZATIONAL METHODS TO ENHANCE CREATIVITY

To enhance creative problem solving, most organizations regularly engage in brainstorming. We focus here on new developments in brainstorming and other creativity-enhancing methods. Programs of this nature are applied to actual problems, while at the same time they provide an opportunity to improve creative thinking.

The leader has a dual role in implementing creative problem-solving techniques: He or she facilitates group interaction and also provides a fair share of creative output. The four creativity-enhancing, problem-solving techniques described here are (1) systematically collecting fresh ideas; (2) brainstorming; (3) using the pet-peeve technique; and (4) equipping a kitchen for the mind. A notable point about creativity-enhancing methods is that no one method is likely to be consistently better than any other method. The underlying mechanism is that each creativity-enhancing method helps bring new ideas to the surface. Danny Strickland, an innovation consultant and former chief innovator at Coca-Cola, points out that all of these creativity tools have one simple thing at the heart. "They try to bring in new information that will help change your perspective. If you change the way you think about something, then suddenly new ideas come to mind."[19]

Systematically Collecting Fresh Ideas

Creativity is often referred to as a numbers game, because the more ideas you try, the greater the probability of finding one that works. A notable way of collecting fresh ideas is for employees to furnish them to a company database so that when somebody needs a fresh idea it can be accessed through a company search engine. Posting ideas on an intranet is similar to the database.

A straightforward approach to collecting ideas is for company leadership to engage more of its own staff in the search for innovation. A representative example is Reckitt Benckiser PLC, a British maker of household-cleaning and personal-hygiene products. The company has alerted many of its staff members in purchasing, marketing, and customer relations to be on the lookout for relevant, new market trends. A small in-house team attempts to authenticate reported trends and build on them. The team reports its findings to senior managers who decide which products are worth pursuing. A company spokeswoman said that 40 percent of revenue in a recent year resulted from innovations launched in the three previous years.[20]

To facilitate having fresh ideas, the leader or manager can establish idea quotas, such as by asking staff members to bring one new idea to each meeting. Although the vast majority of these ideas may not lead to innovation, a few good ones will emerge. One reason idea quotas work is that they are a goal. Another is that an environmental need (in this case, the idea quota) is an excellent creativity stimulant.

Brainstorming

The best-known method for creativity improvement is brainstorming, which you have probably already done. Although brainstorming is often condemned as being superficial, it remains a key idea-generation method for even the most advanced technology companies. A notable example is the firm Intellectual Ventures, whose primary mission is to develop inventions, cofounded by Nathan P. Myhrvold, the former chief technology officer at Microsoft.

Myhrvold assembles groups of doctors, engineers, and scientists known for their brilliance, along with in-house inventors and lawyers, for day-long brainstorming sessions. The Intellectual Ventures staff takes ideas from the brainstorming sessions and turns them into patents. Inventors get a share of any eventual royalties.[21]

The Intellectual Ventures application of brainstorming emphasizes the observation that goals are an essential part of the process. The Ventures team focuses on the goal of attaining ideas worthy of a patent. According to the theorizing of Robert C. Litchfield, the various rules of brainstorming can be regarded as goals, including (a) generate quantity, (b) avoid criticism, (c) combine and improve on previous ideas, and (d) encourage free-wheeling.[22]

As a refresher, do Leadership Skill-Building Exercise 13-1. Because the vast majority of employers use brainstorming, it is helpful to have some advanced knowledge of the topic other than that it is simply shouting out ideas.

A key aspect of brainstorming is that all ideas can be steppingstones and triggers for new and more useful ideas. Any idea might lead to other associations and connections. Thus, during the idea-generating part of brainstorming, potential solutions are not criticized or evaluated in any way, so that spontaneity is encouraged.

The derivation of the name "Bing" for the Microsoft search engine illustrates how brainstorming remains important for creativity in business. Interbrand, the firm that was awarded a contract for developing a list of names, assigned

LEADERSHIP SKILL-BUILDING EXERCISE 13-1

Choose an Effective Domain Name

Organize into groups to play *Choose an Effective Domain Name*. Your task is to develop original domain names for several products or services. An effective domain name is typically one that is easy to remember and will capture potential customers in an uncomplicated Web search. One reason this exercise is difficult is that "cybersquatters" grab unclaimed names they think business owners might want, and then sell these names later. For example, a cybersquatter (or domain name exploiter) might develop or buy the domain name www.catfood.com, hoping that an online retailer of cat food will want this name in the future. The owner of catfood.com would charge a company like PetSmart every time a surfer looking to purchase cat food over the Internet entered www.catfood.com and was then linked to PetSmart.

After your team has brainstormed a few possible domain names, search the Internet to see if your domain name is already in use. Simply enter "www" plus the name you have chosen into your browser. Or visit the site of a company like DomainCollection.com. After you have developed your list of domain names not already in use, the team leader will present your findings to the rest of the class.

- Tattoo and body-piercing studios
- Replacement parts for antique or classic autos
- A chain of reading and math learning centers for children
- Alzheimer's disease treatment centers
- Personal loans for people with poor (subprime) credit ratings
- Recycled steel for manufacturers

eight staff members to brainstorm names focused on such themes as "speed" and "relevance." Over a six-week period 2,000 choices were generated. After reducing words that were difficult to type, profane, or being used by another company, about 55 words were submitted to Microsoft. The second two runner ups were Kumo and Hook, and Bing was the ultimate winner.[23] Could Microsoft have saved loads of time and money by having assigned this task to a group of students to do in an hour?

Another variation of brainstorming is to encourage *extreme thinking*. Participants are asked to contribute ideas that would probably work but are so outrageous they could get the group fired. Later, the group figures out a way to narrow the potential solutions.[24] Here are two examples of extreme thinking during brainstorming about product development:

- At Hewlett-Packard, a group suggests that the company exit the desktop computer business because PCs are on the decline and profit margins are shrinking.
- At IBM, somebody suggests that the company capitalize on its great brand name by moving into consumer products such as smart phones, alarm clocks, and pencil sharpeners.

Brainstorming, much like other creative problem-solving techniques, works best in an organizational culture that fosters innovation. It is an integral part of the famous design firm IDEO, Inc., whose employees believe passionately in innovation. As a result, they are able to argue about alternative solutions to problems yet still unite to produce an effective design.[25]

Using the Pet-Peeve Technique

An important part of leadership is for organizational units to find ways to continuously improve their service to external and internal customers. The **pet-peeve technique** is a method of brainstorming in which a group identifies all the possible complaints others might have about the group's organizational unit.[26] Through brainstorming, group members develop a list of complaints from any people who interact with their group. Sources of complaints include inside customers, outside customers, competitors, and suppliers. Although the pet-peeve technique is not well known, it is potentially valuable.

Group members can prepare for the meeting by soliciting feedback on themselves from the various target groups. In keeping with the informal, breezy style of the pet-peeve group, feedback should be gathered informally. Rather than approach target groups with a survey, members might tell others about the upcoming pet-peeve session and then ask in person or electronically, "What complaints can you contribute?"

During the no-holds-barred brainstorming session, group members throw in some imaginary and some humorous complaints. Humorous complaints are especially important, for humor requires creative thinking. After all complaints have been aired, the group can process the information during a later session, when they can draw up action plans to remedy the most serious problems.

A pet-peeve session in the human resources department of a manufacturer of small electronic appliances generated many complaints, including the following:

"A lot of people wonder what we are doing. They think we just fill out forms and create work for ourselves."
"Some line managers think our job is to find good reasons why they shouldn't hire their best job candidates."
"Job candidates from the outside think our job is to shred résumés. They think we throw away or delete 90 percent of the résumés that arrive at the company."

As a result of these penetrating, albeit exaggerated, self-criticisms, the human resources department developed an effective action plan. The department leader arranged brief meetings with units throughout the organization to discuss the department's role and to answer questions.

The pet-peeve technique is potentially valuable for a leader because it can help the group improve its work processes. Because it has a good-spirited touch, it is not likely to be perceived as threatening. Leadership Skill-Building Exercise 13-2 presents an opportunity to practice the pet-peeve technique.

Equipping a Kitchen for the Mind

According to Mike Vance, every business needs a **kitchen for the mind**, a space designed to nurture creativity. The supplies can be ordinary items such as a chalkboard, flip charts, a coffeepot, a refrigerator, a pencil sharpener, and a personal computer with graphics software. Creativity rooms are also sometimes supplied with children's toys, such as dart guns, Frisbees, Nerf balls, and stuffed animals. The purpose of the toys is to help people loosen up intellectually and emotionally, thus stimulating creative thinking.

More important than the equipment within the kitchen for the mind is the existence of a communal meeting place where people can get together to think creatively. Vance contends that even when people's resources are limited, they can still use their ingenuity to produce creative ideas.[27]

A specific example of a kitchen for the mind is the Innovation Kitchen at Nike, a think tank for designers where athletic ambition, art, and mad science

---

LEADERSHIP SKILL-BUILDING EXERCISE 13-2

The Pet-Peeve Technique

Review the description of the pet-peeve technique given in the text. Break into groups of about five contributors each. Each group assumes the role of an organizational unit. (Pick one that is familiar to the group, either through direct contact or through second-hand knowledge. For example, you might assume the role of the auditing group of an accounting firm, the financial aid office at your school, or the service department of an automobile dealer.) Generate a number of real and imagined criticisms of your group. Take the two most serious criticisms and develop an action plan to move your group to a higher plane.

are blended together into ideas that have made Nike the major player in sport shoes and apparel. The Kitchen has been described as a free-range creative play pen, with every type of tool, material, machine, toy, instrument, software, game, and inspirational image is available on the spot. Nike Free, the training shoe that imitates the benefits of running barefoot, was hatched in the Kitchen.[28]

The Morality of Enhancing Creativity

Methods that help generate creative ideas, as well as the leadership and managerial actions to enhance creativity described at various places in this chapter, have ethical and moral consequences. Creativity writer Gerald Sindell emphasizes the need for creative thinkers to place their work within a moral context. He notes that creative work and output never exist in a vacuum. In contrast, every idea and product has potential harmful consequences in minor and major ways.[29]

A relevant example is the smart phone that enables millions of people to communicate readily for business and personal purposes. Yet, the unintended dysfunctional consequences have been enormous. Driving under the influence of smart phones, including texting, is almost as dangerous as driving under the influence of alcohol. Also, productivity suffers enormously as workers become distracted by the ready availability of their smart phone for non-work purposes. Also, some scientists are concerned that excessive use of smart phones can create brain cancer. Hundreds of other products and services also have ethical implications. For example, brilliantly developed financial products, such as derivatives, have also created harm for many consumers.

Sindell recommends that creative workers should imagine all the possible misuses of an innovative product or service, and then take steps to limit the damage from the misuses.[30] Warning labels and informative advertising are at least a step in the right direction.

SELF-HELP TECHNIQUES TO ENHANCE CREATIVE PROBLEM SOLVING

Leaders and others who want to solve problems more creatively can find hundreds of methods at their disposal, all of them aiming to increase mental flexibility. Six strategies and specific techniques for enhancing creative problem solving are presented next and are outlined in Table 13-1. These strategies and techniques support and supplement the organizational programs described previously. An underlying contribution of these techniques is that they facilitate flexible thinking, or viewing the world with open and curious eyes.[31] With such a mental stance, almost anything can spark a new idea. As a warehouse manager you might observe young people rollerblading in the park. With a creative attitude, you might conclude that your logistic specialists would be more efficient if they used Rollerblades rather than walked.

TABLE 13-1 Self-Help Techniques for Creativity Improvement

1. Practicing creativity-enhancing activities
2. Staying alert to opportunities
3. Maintaining an enthusiastic attitude, including being happy
4. Maintaining and using a systematic place for recording your ideas
5. Playing the roles of explorer, artist, judge, and lawyer
6. Engaging in appropriate physical exercise

© Cengage Learning 2013

Practicing Creativity-Enhancing Activities

An established way to sharpen creative thinking is to regularly engage in activities that encourage flexible thinking. If you enjoy photography, put yourself on assignment to take a photograph illustrating a theme. You might, for example, take photographs illustrating the proper use of your company's product. Puzzles of all types are useful in stretching your imagination; many creative people regularly do crossword puzzles. Another mind stretcher is to force yourself to write jokes around a given theme. Can you create a joke about the creativity of a leader?

Learning a second language, including sign language, can facilitate creativity because you are forced to shift mental sets. For example, your second language may require you to remember the gender of every noun and to match the spelling of each adjective to the gender and number (singular versus plural) of the noun.

Leadership Skill-Building Exercise 13-3 gives you an opportunity to practice creative thinking. Doing exercises of this nature enhances creative problem solving.

LEADERSHIP SKILL-BUILDING EXERCISE 13-3

The Multiple Uses Technique

A standard technique for developing creativity is to find multiple uses for ordinary objects. In other words, the person doing the exercise is requested to go beyond conventional thinking in visualizing potential uses for a standard object. The point of the exercise is to develop skill in thinking flexibly. A basic example is that a soup bowl might also be used as a flower pot or paper weight. Working alone or using group brainstorming, identify about six potential uses for the following objects:

1. A paperclip*
2. A brick**
3. A shopping cart

4. An e-mail address
5. A worn out or obsolete cell phone
6. A five-pound reference book

It will be instructive to share solutions with other classmates; for one thing, it helps to determine if your alternative use was not mentioned, or rarely mentioned, by others. Infrequent mention suggests a higher degree of imagination, although not necessarily practicality.

*Finding multiple uses for a paperclip might have been the first creativity development exercise in history.
**Finding multiple uses for a brick might have been the second (or tied for first) creativity development exercise in history.

Staying Alert to Opportunities

A characteristic of creative leaders is that they can spot opportunities that other people overlook. Opportunity seeking is associated with entrepreneurial leadership because the entrepreneur might build an organization around an unmet consumer need. The idea behind the international chain of Starbucks coffee shops began when Howard Schultz, the director of a four-store retail operation called Starbucks Coffee, Tea, and Spice, was attending a housewares convention in Milan, Italy. Schultz noticed the coffee-bar phenomenon. Milan alone had 1,500 of them, all serving trendy beverages such as espresso. Believing that coffee bars would also prosper in the United States, Schultz convinced Starbucks to open one. Schultz left the company to form his own small chain of coffee bars, and then he bought out Starbucks's two founding partners and merged Starbucks with his firm.[32] (What unmet consumer need did Schultz identify?)

Maintaining an Enthusiastic Attitude, Including Being Happy

The managerial leader faces a major hurdle in becoming a creative problem solver. He or she must resolve the conflict between being judicial and being imaginative. In many work situations, being judicial (or judgmental) is necessary. Situations calling for judicial thinking include reviewing proposed expenditures and inspecting products for quality or safety defects. Being judicial is much like a self-imposed restraint on creativity.

Imaginative thinking is involved when searching for creative alternatives. Alex F. Osburn, a former advertising executive and the originator of brainstorming, notes how judgment and imagination are often in conflict:

> The fact that moods won't mix largely explains why the judicial and the creative tend to clash. The right mood for judicial thinking is largely negative. "What's wrong with this? ... No, this won't work." Such reflexes are right and proper when trying to judge.

In contrast, our creative thinking calls for a positive attitude. We have to be hopeful. We need enthusiasm. We have to encourage ourselves to the point of self-confidence. We have to beware of perfectionism lest it be abortive.[33] The action step is therefore to project oneself into a positive frame of mind when attempting to be creative. The same principle applies when attempting to be creative about a judicial task. For instance, a leader might be faced with the task of looking for creative ways to cut costs. The manager would then have to think positively about thinking negatively!

Closely related to enthusiasm as a contributor to creativity is that being in a good mood facilitates creativity. The finding comes from an analysis of diaries or journals. The journal entries showed that people are happiest when they come up with a creative idea. However, they are more likely to have a breakthrough idea if they were happy the day before. One day's happiness is often a predictor of the next day's creative idea.[34]

Maintaining and Using a Systematic Place for Recording Your Ideas

It is difficult to capitalize on creative ideas unless you keep a careful record of them. A creative idea trusted to memory may be forgotten in the press of everyday business. An important suggestion kept on your daily planner may become obscured. Creative ideas can lead to breakthroughs for your group and your career, so they deserve the dignity of a separate notebook, or computer file, or any other storage device that works for you. Recording tools include notebooks or journals, smart phones, index cards, audio recorders, voice mail and e-mail messages sent to you, flip charts, pocket-size notepads, and an idea file/database such as a storage box for index cards.[35] A cautious or forgetful person is advised to keep two copies of the ideas: one at home and one in the office.

Playing the Roles of Explorer, Artist, Judge, and Lawyer

Another creativity-improvement method incorporates many of the preceding methods. Say you want to enhance your creativity on the job. This method calls for you to adopt four roles in your thinking.[36] First, be an *explorer*. Speak to people in different fields and get ideas that can bring about innovations for your group. For example, if you manage a telecommunications group, speak to salespeople and manufacturing specialists.

Second, be an artist by stretching your imagination. Strive to spend about three percent of your day asking what-if questions. For example, the leader of a telecommunications group might ask, "What if some new research suggests that the extensive use of telecommunications devices is associated with high rates of cancer?" Also remember to challenge the commonly perceived rules in your field. A computer services manager, for example, asked why customers really needed printed user manuals. The questioning led to a new company practice that is now standard: placing instruction manuals online.

Third, know when to be a *judge*. After developing some imaginative ideas, at some point you have to evaluate them. Do not be so critical that you discourage your own imaginative thinking. Be critical enough, however, so that you do not try to implement weak ideas. A managing partner in an established law firm formulated a plan for opening two storefront branches that would offer legal services to the public at low prices. The branches would advertise on radio, on television, online, and in newspapers. After thinking through her plan for several weeks, however, she dropped the idea. She decided that the storefront branches would most likely divert clients away from the parent firm, rather than create a new market.

Fourth, achieve results with your creative thinking by playing the role of lawyer. Negotiate and find ways to implement your ideas within your field or place of work. The explorer, artist, and judge stages of creative thought might take only a short time to develop a creative idea. Yet you may spend months or even years getting your breakthrough idea implemented. For example, many tax-preparation firms now loan clients instant refunds in the amount of their anticipated tax refunds. It took a manager in a large tax-preparation firm a long time to convince top management of the merits of the idea.

Engaging in Appropriate Physical Exercise

A well-accepted method of stimulating creativity is to engage in physical exercise. Stephen Ramocki, a marketing professor at Rhode Island College, found that a single aerobic workout is sufficient to trigger the brains of students into high gear—and that the benefit lasted for a minimum of two hours. Gary Kasparov, the chess champion, is a gym fanatic and has an extraordinary intellect. He has credited his physical fitness with boosting his skill in chess.

The fact that creative insights often arise during physical exercise fits the steps on the creative process referred to as immersion and incubation. Another explanation of why exercise facilitates creativity is that exercising pumps more blood and oxygen into the brain. Exercise also enhances activity in the frontal lobe, the region of the brain involved in abstract reasoning and attention.[37] The fact that physical exercise can boost creative thinking should not be interpreted in isolation. Without other factors going for a leader, such as a storehouse of knowledge and passion for the task, physical exercise will not lead to creative breakthroughs.

ESTABLISHING A CLIMATE AND CULTURE FOR CREATIVE THINKING

Leaders need to develop creative ideas of their own to improve productivity and satisfaction. Establishing a climate, or culture, conducive to creative problem solving is another requirement of effective leadership. The point is that top management purposely sets about to take steps to make the organization more innovative. The surge in innovation at Procter & Gamble a few years ago was facilitated by the appointment of a chief innovation officer, a five-fold increase in the number of design managers, and the establishment of an *innovation gym*, a place to train managers in thinking about product design.[38]

A foundation step in fostering organizational creativity is to establish a vision and mission that includes creativity, such as that of DuPont: "Our vision is to be the world's most dynamic science company, creating sustainable solutions essential to a better, safer and healthier life for people everywhere." Vision statements and mission statements set the pace, but they must be supported by the right climate, or organizational culture, and extensive use of the techniques described throughout this chapter.

Information about establishing a climate for creativity can be divided into (1) leadership and managerial practices for enhancing creativity and (2) methods for managing creative workers. To become sensitized to this vast amount of information, do Leadership Diagnostic Activity 13-1. The instrument gives you an opportunity to ponder many of the management and leadership practices that encourage or discourage creative problem solving.

LEADERSHIP DIAGNOSTIC ACTIVITY 13-1

Assessing the Climate for Creativity and Innovation

Instructions: Respond "mostly yes" or "mostly no" as to how well each of the following characteristics fits an organization familiar to you. If you are currently not familiar with an outside organization, respond to these statements in regard to your school.

		MOSTLY YES	MOSTLY NO
1.	Management wants workers to be creative.	☐	☐
2.	People who contribute new and useful ideas often receive financial rewards.	☐	☐
3.	Creative thinking is mostly the responsibility of people in creative jobs such as research and development, and marketing.	☐	☐
4.	Workers are encouraged to spend part of their time coming up with new ideas for products or services.	☐	☐
5.	Creative types rarely get promoted.	☐	☐
6.	The company invests considerable resources in innovation.	☐	☐
7.	Few of our leaders appear to be innovative thinkers.	☐	☐
8.	Innovative thinkers are publicly recognized in our organization.	☐	☐
9.	People are often poked fun at for suggesting a unique idea.	☐	☐
10.	Constructive change is welcome in this organization.	☐	☐

Scoring and Interpretation: The score in the direction of a climate for creativity and innovation is "mostly yes" for statements 1, 2, 4, 6, 8, and 10, and "mostly no" for statements 3, 5, 7, and 9. A score of 7 or higher suggests a climate well suited for creativity and innovation. A score of 4 to 6 is about average, and 3 or below suggests a climate that inhibits creativity and innovation.

Leadership Practices for Enhancing Creativity

Nine leadership and managerial practices are particularly helpful in fostering creative thinking, as revealed by the work of many researchers and observers.[39] The organizational methods already described for enhancing creativity might also be interpreted as leadership practices.

1. *Hire creative people from the outside and identify creative people from within.* The most robust leadership and management practice for enhancing creativity is to hire people with the aptitude for, or track record in, being creative. Creativity training is helpful, yet starting with creative people enhances the potential of training. Part of the same argument is that hiring innovative people helps foster an innovative environment. Arthur D. Levinson, chairman and chief executive of Genentech, the heralded biotechnology firm, says, "If you want an innovative environment, hire innovative people, listen to them tell you want they want, and do it."[40]

FIGURE 13-3 Five Business Organizations Judged to Be Highly Innovative

COMPANY	JUSTIFICATION FOR BEING PERCEIVED AS INNOVATIVE
Apple Inc.	Apple has consistently invented products that have created enormous demand for consumer-oriented digital technology, including the iPad which has been the pacesetter for tablet computers. Business leaders throughout the world admire the creativity of Apple as led by Steve Jobs, and Apple products are now frequently used in the workplace. The legal staff at Apple continually fights off imitators of the company's innovations.
Twitter	Twitter has had explosive growth, and is often regarded as having redefined communication. Although scattered with nonsensical and often dishonest postings, this social networking site is also a vital component of business communication.
LG Electronics	To help launch its penetration into the consumer electronics market, LG management hired top talent from multinational leaders such as IBM and Procter & Gamble.
Trader Joe's	Beloved by its customers, this grocery chain jumped past Whole Foods to become the favorite specialty grocer in the United States. Part of the innovation is in the selection of products that are both low priced and have a gourmet appeal.
Hyundai Motors	Formerly known as a South Korean manufacturer of low-price automobiles, Hyundai is a fierce competitor with a reputation for high quality and excellent styling at a moderate price.

Source: Based partially on information in Michael Arndt and Bruce Einhorn, "The 50 Most Innovative Companies" *Bloomberg Business Week*, April 25, 2010, 38–39; Fast Company Staff, "The World's Most Innovative Companies," *Fast Company*, March 2011, 66–82.

2. *Intellectual challenge.* Matching people with the right assignments enhances creativity because it supports expertise and intrinsic motivation. The amount of stretch is consistent with goal theory; too little challenge leads to boredom, but too much challenge leads to feelings of being overwhelmed and loss of control. The leader or manager must understand his or her group members well to offer them the right amount of challenge. Moderate time pressures can sometimes bring about the right amount of challenge.

3. *Empowerment including freedom to choose the method.* Research with information technology workers in the People's Republic of China supported the idea that an empowering style of leadership facilitates worker creativity. Specifically, when workers are empowered they are more likely to work through the steps for creative problem solving. Part of the creativity was attributed to empowered workers having a sense of self-determination which sparked their creative thinking.[41]

Workers also tend to be more creative when they are granted the freedom to choose which method is best for attaining a work goal (as described in our study of empowerment in Chapter 11). Stable goals are important because it is difficult to work creatively toward a moving target.

4. *Ample supply of the right resources.* Time and money are the most important resources for enhancing creativity. Deciding how much time and money to give to a team or project is a tough judgment call that can either support or stifle creativity. Under some circumstances, setting a time deadline will trigger creative thinking because it represents a favorable challenge. An example would be hurrying to be first to market with a new product. False deadlines or impossibly tight ones can create distrust and burnout. To be creative, groups also need to be adequately funded.

An example of providing the right resources is an eBay process labeled the Garden, which enables engineers to get real customer feedback on innovations. Using the Garden, the engineers observed how customers react to the opportunity to make a choice between an auction and a fixed-price sale. Refinements were then made in giving customers an opportunity to make the choice.[42]

5. *Effective design of work groups.* Work groups are the most likely to be creative when they are mutually supportive and when they have a diversity of backgrounds and perspectives. Blends of gender, race, and ethnicity are recognized today as contributing to creative thought, similar to cross-functional teams with their mix of perspectives from different disciplines. The various points of view often combine to achieve creative solutions to problems. Homogeneous teams argue less, but they are often less creative. Putting together a team with the right chemistry—just the right level of diversity and supportiveness— requires experience and intuition on the leader's part.

A leadership and management practice related to work group design is encouraging face-to-face contact to facilitate innovative thinking. It is more difficult for geographically dispersed workers to think creatively. According to Eric Schmidt, a Google executive, the best programming team is two people programming together. The second-best programming team is everybody fitted into one room. All other variants work less well for innovation.[43]

6. *Supervisory encouragement and linking innovation to performance.* The most influential step a leader can take to bring about creative problem solving is to develop a permissive atmosphere that encourages people to think freely. Praising creative work is important because, for most people to sustain their passion, they must feel that their work matters to the organization. Creative ideas should be evaluated quickly rather than put through a painfully slow review process.

In addition to encouraging innovation, supervisory leaders should promote the idea that innovative thinking improves job performance. A study conducted with 238 pairs of workers and supervisors in four U.S. companies in several different industries supported the importance of employee expectations. When employees believed that innovative thinking would lead to better job performance, they were more likely to solve problems creatively. The supervisor could help in the process by explaining how innovation improves job performance.[44]

7. *Organizational support.* The entire organization as well as the immediate manager should support creative effort if creativity is to be enhanced on a large scale. The company-wide reward system should support creativity, including recognition and financial incentives. Organizational leaders should encourage information sharing and collaboration, which lead to the development of the expertise so necessary for creativity and to more opportunities for intrinsic motivation. Executives who combat excessive politics can help creative people focus on work instead of fighting political battles. In a highly political environment, a worker would be hesitant to suggest a creative idea that was a political blunder, such as replacing a product particularly liked by the CEO.

8. *Have favorable exchanges with creative workers.* Another insight into encouraging a creative climate is for leaders to have favorable exchanges with group members, as defined by LMX theory (see Chapter 6). A study with 191 research and development specialists found a positive relationship between LMX ratings and creativity of workers as measured by supervisory ratings.[45] When group members have positive relationships with their manager, they may have a more relaxed mental attitude that allows the imagination to flow. A useful strategy for enhancing creativity throughout the organization is to emphasize the importance of working with a sense of heightened awareness, of being alert to new possibilities.

9. *Give financial rewards for innovation.* Creativity is self-rewarding to some extent because it is so exciting. Nevertheless, financial rewards for contributions to innovation help sustain a climate of innovation. Jeffrey Wadsworth is the chief executive of the Battelle Memorial Institute, a think tank of 23,000 employees specializing in inventions for profit. He points out that financial rewards for creativity are widespread in industry and universities. "If you publish a patent you get $1,000, or you get $1 in a frame. Or you get a piece of the action moving forward."[46] Another factor is that financial rewards have spurred useful inventions for hundreds of years. A recent example is that, in 2010, three teams shared the Progressive Insurance Automotive award for the first production-ready automotive that can achieve a fuel efficiency of 100 miles per gallon or its energy equivalent.[47]

Methods of Managing Creative Workers

Closely related to establishing organizational conditions favoring creativity is choosing effective methods for managing creative workers. The suggestions that follow supplement effective leadership and management practices in general.[48]

1. *Give creative people tools and resources that allow their work to stand out.* Creative workers have a high degree of self-motivation and therefore want to achieve high-quality output. To achieve such high quality, they usually need adequate resources, such as state-of-the-art equipment and an ample travel budget for such purposes as conducting research.

2. *Give creative people flexibility and a minimum amount of structure.* Many creative workers regard heavy structure as the death knell of creativity. *Structure* for these workers means rules and regulations, many layers of approval, strict dress codes, fixed office hours, rigid assignments, and fill-in-the-blank Web forms or paperwork. (Typically, the leader/manager will have to achieve a workable compromise in this area that stays within the framework of organizational policy. Regular office hours, for example, are a must for team assignments. Also, creative people may need help with meeting deadlines because many creative people do not manage time well.)

Although structure should be minimized, some constraints will foster creativity, such as the leader presenting demands about the cost of the product or service and the deadline for the innovation. Marissa Mayer of Google offers this example: When the company develops a new toolbar, it must work for all users, and it must download fast, even over a modem. Toolbar developers are required to work within these constraints, and the constraints have been found to speed development. Time constraints have also proved useful because failures can be discovered quickly and abandoned quickly.[49]

3. *Give gentle feedback when turning down an idea.* Creative employees are emotionally involved with their work. As a result, they are likely to interpret criticism as a personal attack on their self-worth. (Students often feel the same way about their term papers and projects.)

4. *Employ creative people to manage and evaluate creative workers.* Managers of creative workers should have some creative ability of their own so that they can understand creativity and be credible as leaders. Understanding the creative process is important for evaluating the creative contribution of others. What constitutes creative output is somewhat subjective, but the output can be tied to objective criteria. At Hallmark Cards, Inc., for example, creativity is measured by such factors as how well the creative work sold and how well it performed in a consumer preference test. In general, a manager's intuition about the potential contribution of a creative idea or product still weighs heavily in the evaluation.

The accompanying Leader in Action describes a technology leader who is highly creative, and also aware of the importance of building a creative and innovative organization.

ADDITIONAL LEADERSHIP PRACTICES THAT ENHANCE INNOVATION

Creativity in organizations leads to innovations in products, services, and processes (such as a billing system or safety improvement). All leadership and management practices that enhance creative problem solving therefore also enhance innovation. Here we describe eight additional leadership initiatives that enhance innovation.

1. *Emphasize transformational leadership if possible.* A macro-perspective on a leader's role in fostering innovation is to exercise transformational leadership. As described in Chapter 4, the transformational leader creates an environment of change and growth. Based on case histories, management professors Adegoke Oke, Natasha Munshi, and Fred O. Walumbwa concluded that

LEADER IN ACTION

Sanjay Jha Emphasizes a Culture of Creativity and Innovation at Motorola Mobility

Motorola Inc. recruited Sanjay Jha in 2008 to revitalize the company's Mobile Devices division. His successes led to the spinoff of the division into a new entity called Motorola Mobility, with Jha being appointed as the chairman and chief executive officer a few years later. Before joining Motorola, Jha was the chief operating officer in charge of research and development at Qualcomm, a wireless chip maker. While at the company, he had developed the reputation of the rare engineer with a talent in marketing and a concern for profitability. The Motorola board thought that Jha's qualification could help pull the mobile division out of its long tailspin in terms of market share and financial losses.

Born in India, Jha holds a Ph.D. in electronic and electrical engineering from the University of Strathclyde in Scotland, and a bachelor's degree in engineering from the University of Liverpool in England.

Jha's major technology strategy for increasing the market share of Motorola hand-held devices was to build smart phones based on the Google Android operating system, including the Droid, and the Droid X. Jha says that his key management technique for turning around the division was to require a detailed analysis of each project. Jha adores PowerPoint presentations but studies them carefully before the meeting in which they are used.

To help develop a culture of innovation, Jha guided efforts to help connect the output of engineers to the demands of the market, and give the relevant problems to tackle. When Jha arrived at Motorola, he analyzed that Motorola was not making phones that consumers were willing to purchase. The company was still trying to feed on the enormous successes of the Razr, which had lost its luster in the marketplace.

Jha revamped the organization structure to facilitate innovation. Motorola had been using a hierarchical system in which one executive was in charge of each product or line of business, with engineering and marketing teams of its own. The motto was that when

big mistakes were made, there would be "one throat to choke." Jha shifted the organization structure to a design more typical of technology companies, with centralized groups for major functions, such as engineering marketing, and product management. A council was also created to facilitate groups working out their differences. Jha believed that the mutual accountability reflected in the new organization structure would create the urgency needed for innovation.

To help stimulate innovative thinking, Jha requires every discussion at a meeting to begin with recommendations. Sometimes the PowerPoint presentation is skipped if the recommendation is accepted immediately. Based on his engineering knowledge and talents, Jha carries a caliper in his pocket so he can measure the width of any device because little details like this influence the sales appeal of a hand-held device.

Motorola Mobility will most likely continue to face strong completion, but many company insiders think that Jha can move the company forward. A financial executive at the company said, "Sanjay's passion resonates. You now hear people say, 'I think we've turned a corner.'" The division was sold to Google in 2011 but with no change in Jha's position.

QUESTIONS

1. What does Jha do that contributes to a creative organizational culture?
2. How credible does Jha appear to be as a leader who can enhance creativity and innovation?

Source: Story created from facts and observations in the following sources: "Executive Team: Sanjay Jha," *Media Center* (http://mediacenter.motorola.com), January 2011, 1; Saul Hansell, "How Sanjay Jha Overhauled Motorola's Culture," *The New York Times* (http://bits.blogs.nytimes.com), October 29, 2009, 1–3; Jessi Hempel, "Motorola Gets in the Game," *Fortune*, October 12, 2009, 82–84; Roger Cheng, "Droid Sales Drive Motorola," *The Wall Street Journal*, July 30, 2010, B1; Rolfe Winkler, "Moto Must Weigh Greater Scale," *The Wall Street Journal*, April 8, 2011, C8.

transformational leaders are particularly well suited to jump start the innovation process.[50] This is probably because the transformational leader is good at providing intellectual stimulation. (Jha at Motorola is a good example.)

2. *Continually pursue innovation.* A major characteristic of the Most Admired Companies, as compiled by the Hay Group consultancy for *Fortune*, is constant innovation. Translated into practice, this means that company leaders stay alert to innovative possibilities. Innovation is important because a new technology can make an industry obsolete or place it in grave danger. What will happen to petroleum refineries when (and if) the fuel cell takes hold?

3. *Take risks and encourage risk taking.* "No risk, no reward" is a rule of life that applies equally well to the leadership of innovation. Even in a slow-growth economy, companies cannot win big in the marketplace by doing things just a teeny bit better than the competition. It is necessary to gamble intelligently, shrewdly, and selectively, even during a period of insecurity and instability.[51] Because most new ideas fail, part of taking risks is being willing to go down blind alleys.

4. *Emphasize collaboration among employees.* Most innovations stem from networks, that is, groups of people working in concert. The workers needed for the innovation are often dispersed throughout the organization. Choosing the right leader for a project can be the key to collaboration. The workers chosen to develop new ideas are often top performers in individual areas. However, they may be lacking the connections within the company that are vital for accomplishing the innovation task. For instance, an outstanding engineer might be selected to lead a major project. But a lower-ranking engineer who has worked in more divisions of the company might be a wiser choice because he or she could tap broader knowledge and connections inside the company.

A consumer products company intentionally placed workers together on a project who had developed friendships during a business conference. One result was customized packaging and designs for candy that commanded much higher prices than the company's traditional offerings.[52]

Leaders in multiunit organizations are at an advantage for innovation because workers from the various units can share ideas that would be useful for many different products. For example, if one unit of a medical company developed a patch for delivering medicine to the body, other units might be able to profit from the same technology. The topic of encouraging idea sharing will be reintroduced in Chapter 14.

A more direct way of attaining collaboration is to organize workers into teams for purposes of innovation. Wadsworth from Battelle notes that most of the successful innovations he has seen have come from remarkably complex teams. People from different disciplines, such as accountants, lawyers, and customer service representatives must work together smoothly for innovation to surface.[53]

5. *Avoid innovation for its own sake.* Leaders also have to exercise good judgment: Innovation just for the sake of innovation is not always valuable. Many gadgets are scientific marvels, yet they have limited market appeal. An example is the robot lawnmower, which arouses the curiosity of many people but does not appeal much to consumers. Most companies have loads of interesting ideas floating to the surface, but very few will even translate into a profitable product or service. A survey of 1,090 executives in 63 countries indicated that only 48 percent were satisfied with their return on investments from innovation.[54]

6. *Use loose-tight leadership.* *Looseness* refers to granting space for new ideas and exploration, whereas a tight approach means finally making a choice among the alternatives. Innovation is also enhanced when workers throughout the organization are able to pursue absurd ideas without penalty for being wrong or for having wasted some resources. An axiom of creativity is that many ideas typically have to be tried before a commercially successful one emerges.

7. *Integrate development and production.* Innovation may suffer when the people who develop ideas do not work closely with the people responsible for their production or manufacture. For many years, Japanese companies had moved manufacturing to low-cost countries to save money. Leadership at Canon, Inc., however, has found that the key to creating new products quickly is for the production team to physically work close to the product developers. The result is more input and communication. Although the cost of the product, such as an advanced digital camera, may be higher, its high quality leads to higher consumer demand.[55]

8. *Recognize the hidden opportunities when products and ideas flop.* Many product innovations had their origins in flops and failures because somebody was perceptive enough to recognize the new possibilities that emerged from the setback. Success emerged from the ashes of the products that appeared to be drastic mistakes. Two famous examples follow:

- In 1983, Apple produced Lisa, the first commercial personal computer featuring a graphical user interface (GUI). Lisa sold poorly because it was sluggish and high priced. However, the GUI of Lisa helped to inspire Apple's user-friendly product line including the iMac, the iPod, the iPhone, and the iPad.
- In 1962, McDonald's tested the Hula Burger, a cheese-topped grilled pineapple on a bun for Chicago residents who chose not to eat meat on Friday (a traditional practice for many Christians). Consumers shunned the Hula Burger, and the company learned that meatless didn't have to mean wacky. The next year, a franchise owner developed a tastier alternative for meatless Fridays—the Filet-O-Fish, which became a McDonald's classic.

Not all product failures lead to profitable innovations. In instances of total failure, the leader might have to study what went wrong and encourage the product developers involved to do better in the future.[56]

SUMMARY

A creative idea becomes an innovation when it is implemented or commercialized. Creativity is an essential characteristic of leaders. A creative leader brings forth ideas or things that did not exist previously or that existed in a different form. The creative process has been divided into five steps: opportunity or problem recognition; immersion (the individual becomes immersed in the idea); incubation (the idea simmers); insight (a solution surfaces); and verification and application (the person supports and implements the idea).

Distinguishing characteristics of creative people fall into five areas: knowledge, cognitive abilities, personality, passion for the task, and the experience of flow. Creative people possess extensive knowledge, good intellectual skills, intellectual curiosity, and a wide range of interests. Personality attributes of creative people include a positive self-image, tolerance for isolation, nonconformity, and the ability to tolerate ambiguity and chaos. Passion for the work and flow are related to intense intrinsic motivation. Creative people also enjoy interacting with others. The right personal characteristics must interact with the right environment to produce creative problem solving.

A major strategy for becoming creative is to overcome traditional thinking, or a traditional mental set. Also, it is necessary to break down rigid thinking that blocks new ideas. Yet workers still need some constraints in terms of creative solutions to problems.

Creative thinking can be enhanced by systematically collecting fresh ideas and brainstorming. Goals are an important part of brainstorming. A variation of brainstorming is extreme thinking. A spin off of brainstorming is the pet-peeve technique, in which a group thinks of all the possible complaints others might have about their unit. Some organizations also equip a kitchen for the mind, or a space designed for creativity.

The generation of creative ideas has moral implications. Every idea and product has potential harmful consequences in minor and major ways.

Self-help techniques to enhance creative problem solving include (1) practicing creativity-enhancing exercises, (2) staying alert to opportunities, (3) maintaining enthusiasm and being happy, (4) maintaining and using a systematic place for recording ideas, (5) playing the roles of explorer, artist, judge, and lawyer, and (6) engaging in appropriate physical exercise.

Establishing a climate conducive to creative problem solving is another requirement of effective leadership. A foundation step is to establish a vision statement and mission that include creativity. Specifically, leaders should (1) hire creative people from the outside and identify creative people from within, (2) provide intellectual challenge, (3) empower workers and allow them freedom to choose their own method, (4) supply the right resources, (5) design work groups effectively, (6) have supervisors encourage creative workers, (7) give organizational support for creativity and explain how innovation improves performance, (8) have favorable exchanges with creative workers, and give financial rewards for innovation.

Special attention should be paid to managing creative workers. One should provide excellent tools and resources, give creative people flexibility, turn down ideas gently, and employ creative people to manage and evaluate creative workers.

Eight additional leadership initiatives that enhance innovation are the following: emphasize transformational leadership; continually pursue innovation; take risks and encourage risk taking; emphasize collaboration; avoid innovation for its own sake; use loose-tight leadership; integrate development and production; and recognize hidden opportunities in flops.

KEY TERMS

innovation	**experience of flow**	**kitchen for the mind**
creativity	**pet-peeve technique**	

✔ GUIDELINES FOR ACTION AND SKILL DEVELOPMENT

Although creativity is important for leaders, recent research suggests that being perceived as highly creative has a downside. Creative people are sometimes perceived as quirky, and such a perception can block a person's attempt to climb the leadership and management ladder. In studies conducted with business groups in India, and then repeated with U.S. college students, individuals who expressed more creative ideas were viewed as having less—not more—leadership talent.[57]

The way to get around this potential negative perception is for the imaginative person who wants to climb the leadership ladder, to frequently remind others in a subtle way that he or she is business-oriented. If you are the creative person aspiring to climb the ladder, casually mention such concepts as the return on investment of your ideas, and how your idea might contribute to the bottom line.

Tom Freston has had a long career as a creative leader and manager of creative people. He is now a principal in Firefly3 LLC, a consulting and investment company. Among his previous positions has been the chief executive of the part of Viacom that is home to cable networks such as MTV and VH-I, as well as movie studio Paramount Pictures. Freston offers five tips for managing a creative organization that reinforce several ideas already presented in this chapter.[58]

1. Put great creative people at the top.
2. Ensure that ideas flow from the bottom up with a minimum of hierarchy.
3. Maniacally know your audience.
4. Hire passionate, diverse people.
5. Have a lot of fun.

Discussion Questions and Activities

1. Give an example of creativity in business that does *not* relate to the development or marketing of a product or service.
2. If people are supposed to be the most creative during their early childhood, why not hire an eight-year-old as a product planner for a major consumer company?
3. Is it important for leaders to be creative and innovative? Or, should they simply hire creative and innovative direct reports?
4. In many companies, managerial and professional workers are expected to wear formal business attire to work (such as suits and high heels). What effect do you think this dress code has on creativity?
5. In what way does your current program of study contribute to your ability to solve problems creatively?
6. The opinion has often been expressed that too much emphasis on teamwork inhibits creativity. What do you think of this argument?
7. Why do many people believe that if you emphasize being efficient, such as using the quality-improvement process Six Sigma, creativity and innovation are likely to suffer?
8. Several people have written that Twitter is one of the most creative developments in the history of business and the world in general. What is your opinion about Twitter as a powerfully creative development?
9. What do you think the next great creative breakthrough in business will be that will rival e-commerce and mobile phones in importance? (Loads of product planners and business leaders are waiting for your answer.)
10. Speak to the most creative person you know in any field, and find out if he or she uses any specific creativity-enhancing technique. Be prepared to bring your findings back to class.

LEADERSHIP CASE PROBLEM A

The Rapid Cash Store Needs Ideas

Sam is the CEO of The Rapid Cash Store, a chain of 20 stores whose primary business is to provide payday loans and cash checks for people who typically do not have a bank account. A payday loan is essentially a loan against an upcoming paycheck, such as a person borrowing $100 to be repaid when he or she receives a paycheck within ten days. The paycheck has been signed over to Rapid Cash, and a company representative gives the check to the lender minus the fee charged by Rapid Cash. The checks cashed are often payroll checks for workers whose checks are not directly deposited because they do not have bank accounts.

A criticism of The Rapid Cash Store, as well as other payday lenders, is that their interest rate on loans, if projected on an annual basis, would be about 350 percent. Sam says, "This is an irrelevant criticism. Almost no customer takes out a loan for a year. We provide a useful service at a reasonable fee for people who are strapped for cash. Why look at the annual rate? If you rent a hotel room for one night, it might cost $150. Does anybody complain that the hotel is charging $54,750 per year for the room?"

Despite Sam's defense of his company's practices, as well as those of his industry, he is worried that the mounting criticism of his company might result in lost revenue.

Among the criticisms of The Rapid Cash Store is that it exploits the poor. Furthermore, many large discount retailers are getting in to the business of payday loans and check cashing. For example, the MoneyCenters at Walmart stores cash checks for customers at fees much lower than those charged by payday lenders.

Sam is so worried about the forces against his business that he decides to work on the problem with his top-management team. Sam said that he has been casually talking about the problem with his team, but he hasn't really put the problem on his agenda. Sam sends his team an e-mail about the necessity of finding new sources of revenue for the firm, and he alerts them to a meeting to work on the problem.

At the meeting, Sam says to the group, "The Rapid Cash Store is in trouble. Our revenues only declined 15 percent last year, but the handwriting is on the wall. The criticism of our business model is getting more vocal, with even local politicians turning against us. The big box stores are breathing down our neck.

"I want you as the executive team to come up with a way of finding new sources of revenue for the Rapid Cash."

"No disrespect," said Kim, the director of marketing. "But you are our leader. You are supposed to provide the breakthrough idea that will create a solid future for Rapid Cash. We've often talked about broadening our services, but we usually hit the same brick wall. The most notable idea was the one about installing tattoo parlors in our stores because so many of our customers wear tattoos.

"I think the best idea we had was the one about selling lottery tickets in all the stores. But I think we ran into some potential legal problems."

Sam then said, "I don't disagree that as CEO maybe I should have the next great idea for The Rapid Cash Store. But I don't right now, so that's why I'm asking you for your creative suggestions."

Greg, the CFO, said, "I think that we need to ask an even deeper question than where we can find new sources of revenue. We need to ask where to look and whom to ask about new lines of business."

Questions

1. To what extent do you think it is Sam's individual responsibility to furnish creative ideas for generating new business for The Rapid Cash Store?
2. In response to Greg's comment, where should the management team look for creative ideas for enlarging the revenue of The Rapid Cash Store?
3. From the standpoint of ethics, do you think The Rapid Cash Store should stay in business? Explain your reasoning.

ASSOCIATED ROLE PLAY

One student plays the role of Sam, who, during his meeting with the executive team, presses them to suggest at least one useful idea for expanding The Rapid Cash Store's top line (revenue) by either selling more of existing services or creating a new service. Several other students play the roles of members of the executive team. They enjoy this opportunity of participative decision making as well as the chance to engage in creative thinking. Yet, they also believe that it is Sam's role to exercise strong leadership by pointing The Rapid Cash Store in the right direction. Observers will look to see if this problem-solving session is likely to result in any innovations for The Rapid Cash Store.

LEADERSHIP CASE PROBLEM B

The Food Company New-Product Development Group

Manchester Foods is a large food manufacturer and processor consisting of twenty-one divisions. Many of these divisions are smaller companies purchased in recent years. The executive office, headed by Gerry Ambrose, recently decided to establish a centralized new product development group whose responsibility it would be to develop new food products. Ambrose explained to the group:

"The time has arrived for Manchester to copy what a few successful major food companies are already doing. Effective September 1 of this year, we are establishing our own centralized new-product development group. Following the model of many high-tech companies, the unit will be located offsite. The executive office has chosen Maria Sanchez for this key assignment. Maria was a successful entrepreneur who created Tornado Tacos. Starting in her mother's kitchen, she built a national distribution for her product in three years. We bought Tornado Tacos for its growth and profitability. More importantly, we bought the talent of Maria.

"Tornado Tacos will be headed by Andres Morales while Maria is on indefinite assignment as the manager of the new-product development group. Maria will begin with six imaginative staff members. She and her group can have as much budget as they need as long as it looks like they are on the path to developing successful products."

At this point in Gerry's presentation, Garth Laidlaw, division head of Tiger Pet Foods, waves his hand. "We need clarification, Gerry. You mention that the new group will be funded as long as it looks like it is about to develop successful products. Developing a successful new product is a risky business. About 90 percent of new-product ideas never make it to marketplace. And about half of the 10 percent that do arrive on the market fail within one year."

"I'm aware of these dismal statistics," said Gerry. "But without a push on new product development, Manchester Foods is doomed to stagnation and mediocrity. Let's move forward toward a successful new-product development group. And let us all wish Maria the best of luck."

Three months after the new group was established, Maria received a visit from Gerry who said, "Maria, I get the impression that there is a lot of activity going on here, but it does not seem to be focused activity. Could you give me an update?"

"Gerry, it's premature to expect results. We have been set off company premises so we can proceed at our own pace. This is not a crash program. Don't forget, I had been working in the food business for three years before I thought of the idea for Tornado Tacos."

"It's true that we are not expecting immediate results from the new product group, but you are pretty well funded. Could you please give me a hint about any new product idea you have developed so far?"

Maria answered, "Actually, we are excited about one new idea. It's a form of instant fish called Sudden Seafood. The busy and health-conscious professional will love it. You add boiling water to pulverized seafood, and you get a mashed-potato like substance that is actually tasty seafood. We would certainly be the first on the market."

"Revolting," responded Gerry. "I would definitely turn thumbs down on Manchester investing money to market instant fish. Maybe you should interest our Tiger Pet Foods division in that idea. It could be used when travelling with cats."

Three months later, Gerry revisited Maria at the new-product development site. He said, "I'm just doing an informal check again. What new product idea is your group toying with these days?"

"I think that we have a real winner on the drawing board," said Maria. "The world is sick of wimpy soft drinks that have no real flavor, no gusto, and no boost to the psyche. We have been experimenting with a raspberry-flavored soft drink that has four times the caffeine and three times the sugar of anything on the market, even the energy drinks. Its tentative name is Razzle Razzberry. It's destined to be a winner."

"Hold on Maria. You're running counter culture. Except for energy drinks, the world is moving away from heavy soft drinks toward noncarbonated beverages. You're suggesting a beverage that is practically a narcotic. It sounds like the new-product group might be getting carried away."

"Gerry, it's too bad that you don't like this promising idea. Maybe I could meet with you and the other members of the executive office to discuss the mission of the new-product development group. I don't feel that things are going right."

"It sounds to me like you're getting a little touchy," said Gerry.

Questions

1. What is your opinion of Gerry's approach to evaluating the output of the new-product development group?
2. Do you think that Maria is getting too sensitive to criticism?
3. How do constraints on creativity enter into this case?
4. What is your hunch about the potential success of Sudden Seafood and Razzle Razzberry?

ASSOCIATED ROLE PLAY

One student plays the role of Gerry Ambrose, who is becoming impatient to see results from the new product development group. He believes that the company should start seeing results from the time and money being invested in the new-product development group. As a result, he is visiting Maria at her office. Another person plays the role of Maria Sanchez, who wants to make an important contribution to the company, but believes that creativity should not be rushed. Observers will look to see if the meeting between Gerry and Maria leads to a constructive resolution of their differences of opinion.

 ## LEADERSHIP SKILL-BUILDING EXERCISE 13-4

My Leadership Portfolio

You guessed it: For this chapter's entry into your leadership portfolio, record any creative or innovative idea you have had lately in relation to organizational activity, including school. After recording the idea, ask yourself what prompted you to develop it. If you have not contributed a creative idea recently, your assignment is to develop a creative idea within the next ten days. If possible, make plans to implement the idea; otherwise, it will not lead to innovation. Here is an example of a creative community initiative taken by Alexis, a marketing major:

In my neighborhood, there is a ten-story high-rise building. Practically all of the tenants are senior citizens who live on limited pensions. Some of the folks in the building are in their eighties or even their nineties. The building is old and not particularly warm, especially for people with poor blood circulation. I've often heard friends and family members say that we should do something to help the seniors in the high rise, but nobody seems to go beyond expressing a little sympathy.

Then I got a brainstorm. I thought, "Why not organize a 'Socks for Seniors' program?" My friends and I would buy dozens of pairs of socks that usually sell for about $3.00 a pair from deep discounters like Dollar General. We could raise some of the money by returning bottles and cans with deposits.

A few friends of mine made a bunch of telephone calls, and we raised $175 in no time for our project. Then, one cold night, we visited the high rise, rang a few doorbells, and told the residents what we were up to. We were allowed in to start distributing the socks. The smiles and words of appreciation we received were enormous. My idea is so good, I plan to do it every year. My friends are with me, and we think that if we post this idea on a website, it might spread around the country.

LEADERSHIP SKILL-BUILDING EXERCISE 13-5

The Multimedia Presentation

Here is an opportunity to be creative about the topic of business creativity. Work individually or in groups to develop a multimedia presentation about the importance of creativity in business. By *multimedia*, we refer to using more than one media to develop your presentation. For example, you might make a presentation using bulleted lists, narratives, still photos, video clips, and Internet links. It might also be possible to upload your presentation to a social networking site. The presentation might also include music, art, poetry, or quotations from literary figures. Spoken words might also be considered a medium for delivering your message. If the multimedia presentations are limited to about five minutes, class time might allow for several students, or student groups, to present.

LEADERSHIP VIDEO CASE DISCUSSION QUESTIONS

To view the videos for this activity, you'll need access to the CourseMate that is available for this text. To get access, visit www.CengageBrain.com.

After watching "Scholfield Honda," answer the following questions.

1. How are Scholfield Honda and Honda as a whole using innovation to create growth?
2. List the five steps of the creative process and briefly describe how Lee Lindquist, alternative fuels manager, may have used each step in creating the idea for Scholfield Honda to sell the Civic DX.
3. What is the extreme thinking method, and how might Roger Scholfield and other Honda owners and managers use it to enhance creativity?
4. Do you think that it is important for Roger Scholfield to be creative and innovative? Or should he just hire creative and innovative employees? Explain.

NOTES

1. Story created from facts and observations found in the following sources: Jessica Guynn, "How I Made It: Marissa Mayer, Google's Champion of Innovation and Design," *Los Angeles Times* (www.latimes.com), 1–3; E. B. Boyd, "Google's Marissa Mayer to Take Over Geo and Local Services," *Fact Company.com*, October 12, 2010, 1–2; "Google VP Marissa Mayer's 'Nine Notions of Innovation'," *DaxDesai.com* (www.daxdesai. com), September 30, 2006, 1; Marissa Mayer: V.P. of Search Product and User Experience, Google," *Design Thought Leader*, April 30, 2009,

1; Ujala Shegal, "Marissa Mayer," www. businessinsider.com, October 26, 2010, p. 1.

2. Jena McGregor, "The World's Most Innovative Companies," *Businessweek*, April 24, 2006, p. 64.

3. Teresa M. Amabile and Mukti Khaire, "Creativity and the Role of the Leader," *Harvard Business Review*, October 2008, p. 101.

4. Warren Bennis, "The Challenges of Leadership in the Modern World," *American Psychologist*, January 2007, p. 2.

5. Graham Wallas, *The Art of Thought* (New York: Harcourt Brace, 1926).

6. Josh Quittner, "How Jeff Bezos Rules the Retail Space," *Fortune*, May 5, 2008, pp. 126–132; "Jeff Bezos: Founder and CEO, Amazon.com," *Academy of Achievement* www.achievement. org), August 9, 2010, pp. 1–4.

7. Michael Liedtke, "Google Founder Hopes to Prove He's Ready to Be CEO," Associated Press, April 1, 2011.

8. Teresa M. Amabile, "How to Kill Creativity," *Harvard Business Review*, September–October 1998, pp. 78–79; Darrell K. Rigby, Kara Gruver, and James Allen, "Innovation in Turbulent Times," *Harvard Business Review*, June 2009, pp. 79–86.

9. "The Talent Hunt: Desperate to Innovate, Companies Are Turning to Design Schools for Nimble, Creative Thinkers," *Businessweek*, October 9, 2006, p. 72.

10. Cited in "The Pink Prescription: Facing Tomorrow's Challenges Calls for Right-brain Thinking," *Knowledge@Wharton* (http:// knowledege.wharton.upenn.edu) June 10, 2009.

11. Cited in Anita Bruzzi, "Seek Out Creative Free Spirit," Gannett News Service, October 31, 2000. See also William C. Taylor and Polly LaBarre, *Mavericks at Work: Why the Most Original Minds in Business Win* (New York: William Morrow, 2006).

12. Tim Devaney, "ePrize Exec Says Creativity Key to Detroit's Future," *The Detroit News* (www. detnews.com), February 18, 2011, p. 1.

13. Cited in "Larry Page on How to Change the World," *Fortune*, May 12, 2008, p. 84.

14. Amabile, "How to Kill Creativity," p. 79.

15. Mihaly Csikszentmihalyi, "If We Are So Rich, Why Aren't We Happy?" *American Psychologist*, October 1999, p. 824.

16. Cited in Bill Breen, "The Six Myths of Creativity," *Fast Company*, December 2004, pp. 77–78.

17. "Putting Creativity into Action," *Success Workshop*, supplement to *The Pryor Report*, April 1996, p. 1.

18. Cited in Dawn Klingensmith, "Give Your Team Direction," CTW Features, March 8, 2011. Based on information in Shawn Coyne, *Brainsteering: A Better Approach to Breakthrough Ideas* (New York: HarperCollins, 2011).

19. Quoted in Duane D. Stanford, "Coke's Chief Innovator Brings Together Consumer Need and Business Fit," *The Atlanta Journal-Constitution* (ajc.com), November 11, 2007.

20. John Bessant, Kathrin Moslein, and Bettina von Stamm, "In Search of Innovation," *The Wall Street Journal*, June 22, 2009, p. R4.

21. Michael Orey, "Inside Nathan Myhrvold's Mysterious New Idea Machine," *BusinessWeek*, July 3, 2006, pp. 54, 57.

22. Robert C. Litchfield, "Brainstorming Reconsidered: A Goal-Based View," *Academy of Management Review*, July 2008, pp. 649–668.

23. Burt Helm, "The Dubbing of 'Bing'," *Business Week*, June 15, 2009, p. 23.

24. "Hold a Creativity Session," *Manager's Edge* May 2006, p. 6.

25. Michael Schrage, "Playing around with Brainstorming," *Harvard Business Review*, March 2001, pp. 149–154; "Stock a Room to Improve Brainstorming," *Business Management Daily* (www.businessmanagement daily.com), March 18, 2011, p. 1.

26. Anne Sagen, "Creativity Tools: Versatile Problem Solvers That Can Double as Fun and Games," *Supervisory Management*, October 1991, pp. 1–2.

27. Cited in Robert McGarvey, "Turn it On: Creativity Is Crucial to Your Business' Success," *Entrepreneur*, 1996, p. 156.

28. Ellen McGirt, "Artist. Athlete. CEO." *Fast Company*, September 2010, p. 68.

29. Gerald Sindell, *The Genius Machine: The 11 Steps That Turn Raw Material into Brilliance* (Novato, Calif.: New World Library, 2009).

30. Sindell, *The Genius Machine*, p. 40.

31. Juanita Weaver, "The Mental Picture: Bringing Your Definition of Creativity into Focus," *Entrepreneur*, February 2003, p. 69.

32. Scott S. Smith, "Grounds for Success," *Entrepreneur*, May 1998, p. 120.

33. Alex F. Osburn, quoted in "Breakthrough Ideas," *Success*, October 1990, p. 38.

34. Breen, "The Six Myths of Creativity," p. 78.

35. Chuck Frey, "Ten Power Tools for Recording Your Best Ideas," *Innovation Tools* (www.innovationtools.com), December 10, 2003.

36. "Be a Creative Problem Solver," *Executive Strategies*, June 6, 1989, pp. 1–2.

37. Richard A. Lovett, "Jog Your Brain: Looking for a Creative Spark? Hop to the Gym," *Psychology Today*, May/June 2006, p. 55.

38. Tim Brown, "Change by Design," *Businessweek*, October 5, 2009, p. 54.

39. Amabile and Khaire, "Creativity and the Role of the Leader," pp. 100–109; "How to Kill Creativity," pp. 80–81; Teresa M. Amabile, Constance N. Hadley, and Steven J. Kramer, "Creativity Under the Gun," *Harvard Business Review*, August 2002, pp. 52–61; Giles Hirst, Daan van Kippenberg, and Jing Zhou, "A Cross-Level Perspective on Employee Creativity: Goal Orientation, Team Learning Behavior, and Individual Creativity," *Academy of Management Journal*, April 2009, pp. 280–293.

40. Quoted in Jena McGregor, "25 Most Innovative Companies," *BusinessWeek*, May 14, 2007, p. 52.

41. Xiaomeng Zhang and Kathryn M. Bartol, "Linking Empowering Leadership and Employee Creativity: The Influence of Psychological Empowerment, Intrinsic Motivation, and Creative Process Engagement," *Academy of Management Journal*, February 2010, pp. 107–128.

42. Interview with EBay CEO John Donahoe, "How eBay Developed a Culture of Experimentation," *Harvard Business Review*, March 2011, p. 95.

43. "How Google Fuels Its Idea Factory," *Business Week*, May 19, 2008, p. 58.

44. Feron Yuan and Richard W. Woodman, "Innovative Behavior in the Workplace: The Role of Performance and Image Outcome Expectations." *Academy of Management Journal*, April 2010, pp. 323–342.

45. Pamela Tierney, Steven M. Farmer, and George B. Graen, "An Examination of Leadership and Employee Creativity: The Relevance of Traits and Relationships," *Personnel Psychology*, Autumn 1999, pp. 591–620.

46. Quoted in "The Profit Motive," *The Wall Street Journal*, September 27, 2010, p. R11.

47. Eric S. Hintz, "Creative Financing," *The Wall Street Journal*, September 27, 2010, p. R8.

48. Shari Caudron, "Strategies for Managing Creative Workers," *Personnel Journal*, December 1994, pp. 104–113; Chris Pentila, "An Art in Itself," *Entrepreneur*, December 2003, pp. 96–97.

49. Marissa Ann Mayer, "Creativity Loves Constraints," *Businessweek*, February 13, 2006, p. 102.

50. Adegoke Oke, Natasha Munshi, and Fred O. Walumbwa, "The Influence of Leadership Process on Innovational Processes and Activities," *Organizational Dynamics*, January-March 2009, pp. 64–72.

51. Keith H. Hammonds, "No Risk, No Reward," *Fast Company*, April 2002, pp. 81–93.

52. Rob Cross, Andrew Hargadon, Salvatore Parise, and Robert J. Thomas, "Together We Innovate," *The Wall Street Journal*, September 15-16, 2007, p. R6.

53. "The Profit Motive," p. R11.

54. Survey cited in Richard Evans, "A Cost–Benefit View of Innovation," *Los Angeles Times* (www.latimes.com), March 4, 2007.

55. Sebastian Moffett, "Separation Anxiety," *The Wall Street Journal*, September 27, 2004, p. R11.

56. Jena McGregor, "How Failure Breeds Success," *Businessweek*, July 10, 2006, pp. 42–45.

57. Jennifer Mueller, Jack A. Goncalo, and Dishan Kiamdar, "Recognizing Creative Leadership: Can Creative Idea Expression Negatively Relate to Perceptions of Leadership Potential?" *Journal of Experimental Social Psychology*, March 2011, pp. 494–498; "A Bias against 'Quirky'? Why Creative People Can Lose Out on Leadership Positions," *Knowledge@Wharton* (http://knowledge.wharton.edu), February 16, 2011, pp. 1–3.

58. Matthew Karnitschnig, "Mr. MTV Moves Up," *The Wall Street Journal*, January 9, 2006, B1.

Thinking Strategically and Managing Knowledge

14

LEARNING OBJECTIVES

After studying this chapter and doing the exercises, you should be able to

- Describe the nature of strategic leadership.
- Explain how to use the SWOT model to assist in strategic planning.
- Identify a number of current business strategies.
- Describe how leaders contribute to the management of knowledge and the learning organization.

CHAPTER OUTLINE

Ursula Burns became Chairman and CEO of Xerox Corporation in 2009, starting as a summer intern in 1980. Raised in the low-income Lower East Side section of New York City, Burns received a bachelor's of science degree in mechanical engineering from the Polytechnic Institute of New York University in 1980. Later she earned a master's degree in the same field from Columbia University. Early in her career, Burns focused on highly technical problem solving, and she later gradually worked her way into solving managerial and strategic problems.

After completing her internship, Burns was invited to accept assignments in product development and planning. After being a member of and leading a variety of business teams between 1992 and 2000, Burns was promoted to senior vice president for corporate strategic services. Her broad experience in product development, marketing, and global research elevated her status and reputation. Burns was appointed president of Xerox in 2007. When Burns became CEO and chair, she received world-wide publicity as the first African American woman to lead a major business corporation.

The chair and CEO of American Express, Kenneth L. Chenault, who knows Burns well because she serves on his board, praises her leadership skills: "Ursula knows where she wants to lead and she articulates it exceptionally well. That's one of the things that make her an inspirational leader."

Burns spearheaded the Xerox shift toward earning more of its revenue from services rather than relying so heavily on the income from copying machines, printers, and related equipment. Xerox was on the offensive to advance its strategy for the digital age. In 2010, Xerox repositioned itself further into services with the acquisition of Affiliated Computer Services, Inc., a business process outsourcing firm. (For example, ACS processes medical insurance claims.) Burns said that Xerox saw a great company in ACS. It was diversified but lacked having a strong brand. It also needed technology and automation to improve its efficiency, as well as a global reach. "And we have all three."

To Burns, the nature of Xerox's business is that the company enables its customers to concentrate on their true business while Xerox takes care of their document-intensive processes behind the scenes. Xerox chooses the right technology to get the job done, and performs it on a global scale.[1]

The story about CEO and chair Ursula Burns illustrates how leaders must continually think through the very nature of their business and the direction in which the firm is headed. A key leadership role is to form a **strategy**, an integrated, overall concept of how the firm will achieve its objectives.[2] In this chapter, we approach strategic leadership by emphasizing the leader's role rather than presenting extensive information about business strategy. First, we examine the nature of strategic leadership and describe a frequently used tool for development strategy, SWOT analysis. We then examine the strategies that leaders most frequently use to bring about success. Following that is a description of a leader's contribution to an important thrust in strategy, knowledge management, and developing a learning organization.

THE NATURE OF STRATEGIC LEADERSHIP

Strategic leadership deals with the major purposes of an organization or an organizational unit, and therefore has a different focus than leadership in general: Strategic leadership emphasizes balancing the short-term and long-term needs of the organization to ensure the enduring success of the organization.

Leaders engage in strategic leadership when they act, think, and influence in ways that promote the competitive advantage of their organization.[3] For our purposes, **strategic leadership** is the process of providing the direction and inspiration necessary to create or sustain an organization. Netflix founder Reed Hastings provided strategic leadership because he developed a concept for an organization, developed the organization, and inspired large numbers of people to help him achieve his purpose. Furthermore, developing a major presence on the Internet was an example of direction setting by Hastings.

Strategic leadership is a complex of personal characteristics, thinking patterns, and effective management, all centering on the ability to think strategically. Do Leadership Self-Assessment Quiz 14-1 to explore your orientation toward thinking strategically. Our approach to understanding the nature of strategic leadership will be to describe certain associated characteristics, behaviors, and practices, as outlined in Figure 14-1. The information about transformational leadership presented in Chapter 4 is also relevant here.

High-Level Cognitive Activity of the Leader

Thinking strategically requires high-level cognitive skills, such as the ability to think conceptually, absorb and make sense of multiple trends, and condense all of this information into a straightforward plan of action. The ability to process information and understand its consequences for the organization in its interaction with the environment is often referred to as *systems thinking*. Systemic thinking means that the person thinks in terms of a system, and the process gets quite complex.[4] For instance, part of systemic thinking would be

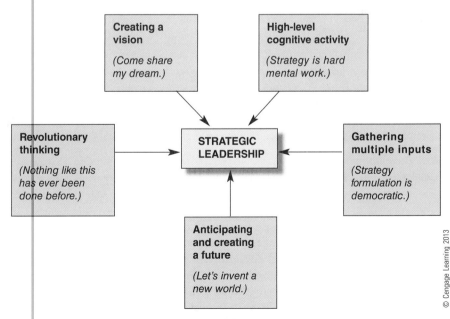

FIGURE 14-1 Components of Strategic Leadership.

© Cengage Learning 2013

LEADERSHIP SELF-ASSESSMENT QUIZ 14-1

Are You a Strategic Thinker?

Instructions: Indicate your strength of agreement with each of the following statements: SD = strongly disagree, D = disagree, N = neutral, A = agree, SA = strongly agree.

	SD	D	N	A	SA
1. Every action I take on my job should add value for our customers, our clients, or the public.	1	2	3	4	5
2. Let top management ponder the future; I have my own job to get done.	5	4	3	2	1
3. Strategic thinking is fluff. Somebody down the organization has to get the job done.	5	4	3	2	1
4. A company cannot become great without an exciting vision.	1	2	3	4	5
5. What I do on the job each day can affect the performance of the company many years into the future.	1	2	3	4	5
6. It is rather pointless to develop skills or acquire knowledge that cannot help you on the job within the next month.	5	4	3	2	1
7. Strategic planning should be carried out in a separate department rather than involve people throughout the organization.	5	4	3	2	1
8. It makes good sense for top management to frequently ask itself the question, "What business are we really in?"	1	2	3	4	5
9. If a company does an outstanding job of satisfying its customers, there is little need to worry about changing its mix of goods or services.	5	4	3	2	1
10. Organizational visions remind me of pipe dreams and hallucinations.	5	4	3	2	1
11. I like the idea of an organization sending a group of managers and professionals to an off-site strategic planning session every couple of years or so.	1	2	3	4	5
12. Strategy formulation is a bureaucratic exercise that usually gets the organization nowhere.	5	4	3	2	1

Scoring and Interpretation: Find your total score by summing the point values for each question. A score of 52 to 60 suggests that you already think strategically, which should help you provide strategic leadership to others. Scores of 30 to 51 suggest a somewhat neutral, detached attitude toward thinking strategically. Scores of 12 to 29 suggest thinking that emphasizes the here and now and the short term. People scoring in this category are not yet ready to provide strategic leadership to group members.

Skill Development: Reflecting on your ability to think strategically is useful because leaders at all levels are expected to see the big picture and point people in a useful direction.

to investigate how parts of a system react and interact to each other and external factors. Suppose a company leader decides to reduce expenditures for research and development. He or she should analyze how the cutback will affect marketing and sales in the next several years.

Long-term thinking is a key part of strategy. A CEO might work with a twenty-five-year perspective regardless of whether he or she would be with the same firm in twenty-five years.

Emphasizing the cognitive activity of the leader helps emphasize that the leader plays a major role in strategy formulation. The leader must think through what makes the organization distinct, and define its purpose. Creativity and insight are required to achieve these profound conclusions. Most great companies start with great purposes formulated by the founder. A sterling example is IKEA's intent to offer customers "a wide range of well-designed, functional home furnishing products at prices so low that as many people as possible can afford them."[5] Typically the purpose comes from intuition rather than extensive analysis. Mintzberg believes that synthesizing information and thinking ahead is more important than strategic planning in developing useful business strategy.[6]

As one moves up the hierarchy, more problem-solving ability and imagination are required to handle the task environment effectively. To engage in strategic management and leadership, a person must have conceptual prowess. An organization will be successful when the cognitive abilities of its leaders are a good fit with the nature of the work. This is one of many reasons that tests of problem-solving ability correlate positively with success in managerial work.[7]

Creative problem solving is also important because the strategic leader has to develop alternative courses of action for shaping the organization. Furthermore, asking what-if questions requires imagination. For example, at Ford Motor Co., Alan Mullaly asked, "What if we sold off our luxury brands, terminated the Mercury line, and concentrated on Ford—would we be a stronger company?" (He was right.)

Gathering Multiple Inputs to Formulate Strategy

Many strategic leaders arrive at their ideas for the organization's future by consulting with a wide range of interested parties, in a process similar to conducting research to create a vision. Jeff Bezos explains that even though he developed the original concept for Amazon.com, many others now contribute to the strategic direction of the company. Amazon has a group called the S Team (S meaning senior) that keeps current on what the company is working on and digs into strategy issues. The team meets for about four hours every Tuesday, along with a twice-a-year two-day meeting to explore new directions for Amazon. As a result of this type of collective strategy formulation, the company continues to use new business models such as letting competitors offer their wares on the Amazon website, as well as more recently providing cloud computer services.[8]

Gathering multiple inputs has the added benefit of building morale. Whirlpool Corporation earns the support of line workers by placing volunteers on strategic teams with midlevel managers and senior executives. The production workers contribute to decisions that affect Whirlpool facilities in the United States. They travel to other countries with executives to new manufacturing facilities to help top management gain a better perspective on production and workforce issues.[9] As a result, Whirlpool leadership can make crisper strategic decisions about production and work force issues.

Anticipating and Creating a Future

A major component of leadership is direction setting, which involves anticipating and sometimes creating a future for the enterprise or organizational unit. To set a direction is also to tell the organization what it should be doing. To set a productive direction for the future, the leader must accurately forecast or anticipate that future. Insight into tomorrow can take many forms, such as a leader's making accurate forecasts about consumer preferences, customer demands, and the skill mix needed to operate tomorrow's organization. A truly visionary leader anticipates a future that many people do not think will come to pass. A classic example is that in the early days of xerography, market research indicated that most people polled saw no need for a product to replace carbon paper.

Creating the future is a more forceful approach than anticipating the future. The leader, assisted by widespread participation of team members, creates conditions that do not already exist. He or she must ask questions about the shape of the industry in five to ten years and decide how to ensure that the industry evolves in a way that is highly advantageous to the company. Furthermore, the leader must recognize the skills and capabilities that must be acquired now if the company is to occupy the industry high ground in the future.

Creating the future has been conceptualized as reinventing an industry. Entrepreneurial leaders frequently engage in such activity. A classic example is in order: C. K. Prahalad explains that the shoe industry is a good illustration of reinvention. Nike and Reebok have fundamentally reinvented their industry and consequently are fast-growing businesses in a mature industry. One factor is that they have changed the price-performance relationship in the industry. Both companies have introduced high technology, new materials, large-scale advertising, and global brands. None of these factors was so pronounced previously in the shoe industry.[10] A more modern example of creating the future was the development of the iPad by the late Steve Jobs and his product designers at Apple Inc. Hand-held computers had existed before, but nothing of the nature of the iPad. Industrial applications of the device spread rapidly including using them to display products as well as the owner's manual for the Kia automobiles and S.U.V.s.

So how much time should an executive leader invest in plotting the future? Jack Welch, the General Electric CEO emeritus, recommends that leaders should devote from 20 percent to 30 percent of their time plotting the future.[11] Faced with so many urgent operational problems, few business leaders could probably spend that much time on the future. About 5 percent of work time invested in plotting the future might seem more realistic.

Revolutionary and Contrarian Thinking

Using even stronger terms than *reinventing an industry*, Gary Hamel characterizes strategy as being revolutionary. According to Hamel, corporations are reaching the limits of incrementalism. Incremental improvements include squeezing costs, introducing a new product a few weeks earlier, enhancing quality a notch, and capturing another point of market share. These continual improvements enhance an organization's efficiency and are therefore vital to a firm's success, but they are not strategic breakthroughs or radical innovations.[12]

Although incrementalism may not classify as true strategy, incremental changes can move an organization forward in a major way. A few years ago, Domino's Pizza, Inc., was at a crossroads. Flat sales led management to closing 108 U.S. stores, and the company faced a perception that its pizza tasted like cardboard. Domino leadership took a risk and changed its 49-year-old pizza recipe to feature a garlic-seasoned crust with a top layer of mozzarella and provolone cheeses fused together by a sauce flavored with red pepper. Online marketing was enhanced, and the company rebranded itself by publicly admitting that its former pizza was not so tasty. The incremental changes resulted in about an 11 percent increase in sales and a regaining of market share.[13]

To be an industry leader, a company's leaders must think in revolutionary terms. Revolutionary companies such as Amazon.com and Netflix create the rules for others to follow. According to Hamel, any strategy that does not seriously challenge the status quo is not actually a strategy. What passes for strategy in most companies is often sterile and unimaginative.

Strategy expert Michael Porter agrees with the revolutionary aspect of business strategy by insisting that a key component of strategy is deliberately choosing to be different.[14] Being different sometimes refers to having an expansive and elegant concept of the future of a business.

A variation of choosing to be different is to engage in contrarian thinking, in which the leader rejects conventional wisdom, much like the investor who trolls for hidden value in out-of-favor stocks. Jim Lanzone is the former CEO of Ask.com. Lanzone rejects the wisdom that success involves striving to be an industry leader. "You can be the fourth-ranked search engine, like we are, and still be doing very, very well," says Lanzone. He says his guiding principle (or strategy) was to stay focused on improving search results rather than on distractions such as e-mail or blog services.[15]

Creating a Vision

We have already mentioned visions in this book, including the description in Chapter 4 of the vision component of charismatic leadership. Here we examine the concept of vision in more depth, because visions are an integral part of strategic leadership. One of the most important challenges of high-level leadership is to create a shared vision that will motivate organizational members to perform well.[16] Whether the effort takes place is also a function of the leader's behavior and personality. Otherwise a carefully crafted vision written anonymously and emitted by e-mail would be a strong motivator.

The final vision statement is relatively short. James R. Lucas, a specialist in vision formulation, writes that a carefully considered and articulated vision helps us know who we are and who we are not. The vision also points to what we do successfully and what we do not, which activities we should take on and which we should avoid.[17] An example of a short vision statement that appears to be motivational is the statement Marc Benioff, the founder of

Salesfor.com: "In ten years I want us to be the largest and most important enterprise cloud computing company."[18] (A few more specifics about developing a vision statement are presented in the Guidelines for Action and Skill Development section of this chapter.)

Articulating a clear vision helped get several great companies off the ground when the company founders were seeking funding from venture capitalists. When Sergey Brin and Larry Page were planning to launch a company, they had no business experience and no track record, yet they had a powerful one-line vision. They told investors at Sequoia Capital, "We deliver the world's information in one click." The investors liked the vision statement, and invested in the company called Google.[19] The Google statement might be classified as dealing with a *mission* because it relates to the present, not the future. However, even the smartest minds in business often use *mission* and *vision* interchangeably.

In companies that believe strongly in visions and strategic goals, all activities throughout the company are supposed to support the vision and goals. For example, at Salesforce.com, company leadership expects workers at all levels to make suggestions for enhancing cloud computing service to other companies.

Most high-level leaders think strategically, and the accompanying Leader in Action insert describes a leader who is well known for his strategic thinking.

LEADER IN ACTION

Famous J. P. Morgan Banker Jamie Dimon Thinks Big

James (Jamie) Dimon is chair and chief executive of J. P. Morgan Chase & Co., the biggest bank in the United States. For example, it is the biggest credit-card issuer in the country, and it is also number one in auto loans. Dimon insists that no financial institution is too big to fail, not even J. P. Morgan Chase.

One of Dimon's most dramatic accomplishments was to cooperate with the U.S. government in agreeing to purchase Bears Stearns Company in 2008 when the latter was close to collapse. The government was concerned that if Bears Stearns declared bankruptcy, negative ripple effects would be felt throughout the industry. J. P. Morgan Chase similarly rescued Washington Mutual.

Dimon is credited with having had the wisdom and long-range point of view to prevent his bankers from succumbing to the extreme greed that made many bankers rich but destroyed their firms and reduced the net worth of so many investors. Among Dimon's

initiatives was to make sure his bank had enough capital on hand to survive an emergency. He also avoided risky loans such as adjustable rate mortgages (ARMs), and invested lightly in packages of mortgage securities known as collateralized debt obligations (C.D.O.'s)

Dimon favors the strategy of a large bank providing for one-stop shopping. He argues that consumers who want credit cards also need home mortgages, and small business that needs loans may also want the services of an investment banker. According to Dimon, "Economies of scale are a good thing. If we didn't have them, we'd still be living in tents and eating buffalo."

At Dimon's admission, J. P. Morgan Chase did make some errors, but he saw enough trouble brewing to avoid the catastrophes of investment banks such as Lehman Brothers. J. P. Morgan Chase encountered some losses in credit cards and home mortgages. Dimon is in favor of some bank regulations but not others. Among the practices Dimon favors for regulatory reform are the mortgage business, better control over investments called derivatives, and fees for overdrafts on checking accounts. However, he is opposed to creating "a weed of bureaucracy that could wind around our ankles and necks," thereby interfering with the entrepreneurial spirit. Dimon is particularly opposed to the Consumer Financial Protection Agency, which would allow states to introduce stricter regulations. To help prevent what he considers to be over-regulation, Dimon visits Washington, D.C., to meet with members of both parties to plead his case.

In defending interest-rate increase on credit cards, Dimon argues that all businesses are selective about what merits a charge. For example, restaurants give you the table cloth and silverware for free but charge a lot for the food. Credit-card companies provide the service of convenience for free, but must then charge interest to pay their expenses, which include absorbing the loss on people who do not pay back their loans.

QUESTIONS

1. Identify several examples of strategic thinking displayed by James Dimon.
2. In what way might Dimon acting as a lobbyist be part of strategic thinking?

Source: Story created from facts and observations found in the following sources: Charles Ferguson, "Jamie Dimon: The Survivor Shapes the Debate," *Time*, May 2, 2011, p. 124; Roger Lowsenstein, "Jamie Dimon: America's Least-Hated Banker," *The New York Times* (www.nytimes.com), December 1, 2010, pp. 1–15; Anita Raghavan, "Master Banker, Master Schmoozer," *Forbes*, November 30, 2009, pp. 90–98; Shawn Tully, "Jamie Dimon's SWAT Team," *Fortune*, September 13, 2008, pp. 64–78; Robin Sidel, "In a Crisis, It's Dimon Once Again," *The Wall Street Journal*, March 17, 2008, pp. C1, C2.

Leadership Effectiveness and Strategy Implementation

Carefully crafting a strategy and vision is not sufficient for its effectiveness. The strategy and vision must also be implemented or executed by the leader/manager. Part of being an effective leader is to implement a strategic initiative. A basic example is that Domino's managers throughout the organization successfully implemented the strategic initiative of upgrading pizza quality.

A study in a medical setting demonstrated that when leaders across the organization were perceived to be effective, it was more likely that strategic change would take place. In this study, strategic change was defined as the change over a two-year period in overall patient satisfaction with access and service. The strategic change was to compete not on cost of medical care, but on quality and service. When the large health care organization attempted to provide low-cost service, it tended to be perceived as too bureaucratic and impersonal. The participants in the study were 280 physicians in 8 specialty departments working in 6 medical centers for a total of 40 departments. Approximately 50,000 patient survey evaluations were used to measure satisfaction.

The physician rated their leaders on six items reflecting strategic leadership. Leaders at three levels were rated: CEOs, medical center leadership, and department leadership. Measures of strategic leadership included in the items were assessments of the degree to which the leader articulated a strategy, created a vision, provided measurable objectives, rewarded progress in the change effort, dealt with resistance, and motivated medical staff to change. To repeat, when leaders at the three levels were rated positively, ratings of strategic change were more likely to be positive.[20]

CONDUCTING A SWOT ANALYSIS

Strategic planning helps a manager lead strategically. **Strategic planning** encompasses those activities that lead to the statement of goals and objectives and the choice of strategy. Quite often, a firm arrives at its strategy after completing strategic planning. In practice, many executive leaders choose a strategy prior to strategic planning. As mentioned earlier, at times intuition and judgment is more important than planning in the creation of a strategy. Once the firm has the strategy, such as forming strategic alliances, a plan is developed to implement it.

Quite often, strategic planning takes the form of a **SWOT analysis**, a method of considering internal strengths and weaknesses as well as external opportunities and threats in a particular situation. A SWOT analysis represents an effort to examine the interaction between the particular characteristics of your organization or organizational unit and the external environment, or marketplace, in which you compete.[21] The framework, or technique, is useful in identifying a niche the company has not already exploited. The components of a basic version of SWOT are described next.

Internal Strengths

The emphasis in this step is assessing factors within the organization that will have a positive impact on implementing the plan. (In some versions of SWOT analysis, an analysis of the external environment is included in this step.) What are the good points about a particular alternative? What are your advantages? What do you do well? Use your own judgment and intuition, and also ask knowledgeable people. As a business owner, you may have a favorable geographic location that makes you more accessible to customers than your competitor is. Another strength is that you may have invested in state-of-the art equipment that became available only recently.

A successful example of capitalizing on internal strengths took place when Hewlett-Packard Corp. regained the lead over Dell Inc. in PC sales. Within weeks after arriving at HP to run the company's PC business, Todd Bradley concluded that HP was fighting Dell on the wrong battlefield. HP was mobilizing its resources to compete with Dell where Dell was strong, in direct sales via the Internet and phone. Instead, Bradley decided that HP should capitalize on its strength—retail stores where Dell had no presence at the time. Bradley worked on better distribution of the PCs, along with building better relations with retailers. (An effective leader never neglects relations.) As a result of capitalizing on the retail strengths, HP reclaimed its number one position in the sale of personal computers.[22]

Internal Weaknesses

Here the strategy developer takes a candid look at factors within the firm that could have a negative impact on the proposed plan. Consider the risks of pursuing a particular course of action, such as subcontracting work to a low-wage country (outsourcing). What could be improved? What is done badly? What should be avoided? Examine weaknesses from internal and external perspectives. Do outsiders perceive weaknesses that you do not see? (You may have to ask several outsiders to help you identify these weaknesses.) Are there products, services, or work processes your competitors perform better than you do? You are advised to be realistic now and face any unpleasant truths as soon as possible. Again, use your judgment, and ask knowledgeable people. As a manager or business owner, you may have problems managing your inventory, or you may have employees who are not up to the task of implementing a new plan or venture.

External Opportunities

The purpose of this step is to assess socioeconomic, political, environmental, and demographic factors among others to estimate what benefits they may bring to the organization. Think of the opportunities that await you if you choose a promising strategic alternative, such as creating a culturally diverse customer base. Use your imagination, and visualize the possibilities. Look for interesting trends. Useful opportunities can derive from such events as the following:

- Changes in technology and markets on both a broad and narrow scale
- Changes in government policy related to your field
- Changes in social patterns, population profiles, lifestyles, and so forth.

External Threats

The purpose of this step is to assess what possible negative impact socio-economic, political, environmental, and demographic factors may have on the organization. There is a downside to every alternative, so think ahead, and do contingency planning. Ask people who may have tried in the past what you are attempting now. Answer questions such as:

- What obstacles do you face?
- What is your competition doing?
- Are the required specifications for your job, products, or services changing?
- Is changing technology changing your ability to compete successfully?

Despite a careful analysis of threats, do not be dissuaded by the naysayers, heel draggers, and pessimists. To quote Nike, "Just do it."

Carrying out a SWOT analysis is often illuminating in terms of both pointing out what needs to be done and putting problems into perspective. Although much more complex schemes have been developed for strategic planning, they all include some analysis of strengths, weaknesses, and opportunities. Leadership Skill-Building Exercise 14-1 gives you an opportunity to conduct a SWOT analysis.

LEADERSHIP SKILL-BUILDING **EXERCISE 14-1**

Conducting a SWOT Analysis

In small groups, develop a scenario for a SWOT analysis, such as the group starting a chain of panini restaurants, pet-care service centers, or recycling centers for electronic devices. Because you will probably have mostly hypothetical data to work with, you will have to rely heavily on your imagination. Group leaders might share the results of the SWOT analysis with the rest of the class. Conducting a SWOT analysis reinforces the skill of thinking strategically about a course of action. A key challenge in preparing this hypothetical SWOT analysis is to make a distinction between internal and external forces.

A SAMPLING OF BUSINESS STRATEGIES FORMULATED BY LEADERS

We have been focusing on the process by which leaders and managers make strategic decisions. Also of interest to leaders and potential leaders is the content of such decisions. Business strategies are often classified according to their focus of impact: corporate level, business level, or functional level. Corporate-level strategy asks, "What business are we in?" Business-level strategy asks, "How do we compete?" And functional-level strategy asks, "How do we support the business-level strategy?" Some of the business strategies listed next might cut across more than one of these three levels. The first three of these strategies are the generic strategies espoused by Michael Porter.[23]

1. *Differentiation.* A differentiation strategy seeks to offer a product or service that the customer perceives as being different from available alternatives. The organization may use advertising, distinctive features, exceptional service, or new technology to gain this perception of uniqueness. What differentiates one of your favorite products? A challenge with the differentiation strategy is that if the product or service is successful, competitors move in quickly. Groupon, the popular website specializing in local shopping deals by placing consumers into groups, was an immediate sensation. The business model required no special technology, and soon other websites were in competition, including one backed by Amazon.com.[24] Facebook has also developed a service for groups of consumers to obtain deals.

2. *Cost leadership.* A basic strategy is to produce a product or service at a low cost in order to lower the selling price and gain market share. Aldi, a chain of deep-discount food stores, is the eighth largest retailer in the world. The company capitalizes on the bargain hunter who accepts private labels, limited choices, and paying 25 cents to use a grocery cart. The choice of fewer brands helps cut costs. Aldi does not accept credit cards or checks and encourages customers to bring their own bags. An investor in urban grocery stores said, "Now it's private label that is attractive, that has nutritious labels on it, and that are part of the corporate strategy."[25] A variety of general merchandise stores, such as Dollar General and Family Dollar, implement the cost leadership strategy.

3. *Focus or niche.* In a focus strategy, the organization concentrates on a specific regional market or buyer group. To gain market share, the company will use either a differentiation or a cost leadership approach in a targeted market. The focus strategy is a natural, common-sense approach to business because it is difficult to serve every customer well. A focus strategy is about the same thing as finding a *niche*, or your place in the market. Almost every successful business venture was found by locating a niche, including Enterprise Auto, which began its road to prominence by supplying rental autos to people whose vehicles were under repair at a body shop. An example of successful, well-planned focus marketing strategies is as follows:

- Instead of competing directly with eBay, several smaller online auctions stick to a narrow, successful niche, giving them an identity that facilitates sales. An example is StubHub, Inc., which competes with eBay as a middleman for ticket sales to sporting events, concerts, and other spectator activities.[26]

4. *High quality.* A basic business strategy is to offer goods or services of higher quality than the competition does. Leaders continue to emphasize quality, even if there is less explicit emphasis today on formal quality programs than in the past. Important exceptions are the Six Sigma programs that emphasize statistical approaches to attaining quality. Leaders at GE and 3M, for example, emphasize Six Sigma. One reason that quality is classified as a strategy is that it contributes to competitive advantage in cost and differentiation. Because many customers now expect high quality, a quality strategy must be supplemented with other points of differentiation, such as supplying customized features and services that customers desire. How about Tiffany & Co. or the Swiss Army knife for a quality strategy?

Drifting away from a strategy of high quality can damage an organization's reputation and sales. A few years back, Toyota Motor Corp. had to recall millions of automobiles and trucks because of a variety of electronic and mechanical problems. President Akio Toyoda blamed some of the problems on excessive focus on growth. He said that the rapid expansion had "attracted much praise from outside the company and some people just got too big-headed and focused too excessively on profit."[27] The implication was that Toyota's strategy of high quality was diminished.

5. *Imitation.* If you cannot be imaginative, why not imitate the best? Manufacturers of popular digital devices such as digital cameras and smart phones use an imitation strategy. The company waits for the right time to introduce a lower-priced competitor. Benchmarking is a form of learning by watching. One company emulates the best practices of another company, usually without outright stealing the product or service ideas of another company. The automotive industry is rampant with one company imitating another. Next time you are in a busy parking lot or driving on the highway, see how many hoods and auto grilles you can find that resemble a Mercedes.

6. *Strategic alliances.* A modern business strategy is to form alliances, or share resources, with other companies to exploit a market opportunity. A strategic alliance is also known as a *virtual corporation*. Strategic alliances have become more common as leaders in the high-tech industry attempts to capitalize on the strengths of other companies. A few years ago, Microsoft and Facebook formed a strategic alliance in which Microsoft became the exclusive third-party advertising platform partner for Facebook, and Microsoft invested in Facebook. A Microsoft executive said, "Making this investment and expanding the partnership will position Microsoft and Facebook to better take advantage of advertising opportunities around the world."[28]

Strategic alliances sometimes take the form of marketing partnerships in which the two parties benefit considerably when the products or services go well together—hence, the strategic alliance between Papa John's pizza restaurants and Six Flags theme parks. The partnership requires that only Papa John's pizza be sold on Six Flags properties. This helps Six Flags make contact with consumers at approximately 1,100 Papa John's restaurants located within a 100-mile radius of a Six Flags theme park.[29]

7. *Growth through acquisition*. A standard strategy for growth is for one company to purchase others. Growth in size is important, but companies may also purchase other companies to acquire a new technology or complete a product line. Buying a new technology is often less expensive than investing huge sums in R&D that might not yield a marketable product. Cisco Systems, Inc., achieved much of its growth by purchasing smaller companies, and much of General Electric's growth over the years can be attributed to acquiring other companies.[30]

Another form of growth by acquisition is for a company to attain all of its growth by reviving old brands that have a good reputation but have been undernourished. The Jarden Corporation has 20,000 employees through ownership of such niche brands as Coleman (outdoor products), Bicycle (playing cards), and Crock-Pot (cooking).[31]

8. *High speed and first-mover strategy*. High-speed managers focus on speed in all of their business activities, including product development, sales response, and customer service. Believing that time is money, they choose time as a competitive resource. It is important to get products to market quickly because the competition might get there first or might deliver a product or service more rapidly. Getting to market first is also referred to as the first-mover strategy. Starbucks was the first national chain of coffee bars. The many storefronts served as marketing devices to acquire more customers.

Moving in after a product or service in already successful will sometimes best the first-mover strategy. A classic example is that Visicalc, the first desktop computer spreadsheet program, lost ground as Lotus took over the field with its 1-2-3. Soon, Microsoft's Excel dominated the field.

9. *Product and global diversification*. A natural business strategy is to offer a variety of products and services and to sell across borders to enhance market opportunities. Coca-Cola Co. exemplifies a company that thrives on both global and product diversification. Coke now generates 75 percent of its revenue and operating profit from countries outside the United States. Despite the company's reputation for relying too heavily on Coke, it has acquired many smaller brands of beverages in recent years, including the purchase of the organic beverage company Honest Tea of Bethesda in 2011. A key point of the acquisition is that Honest Tea is a growth company, and many consumers have made a move toward health and wellness in their beverage consumption.[32]

Sometimes a company with a strong reputation for delivering one product or service will branch out to capitalize on the allure of its brand. Victorinox Swiss Army Brands Inc., the manufacturer of the famous Swiss Army Knife, has experienced reasonable success selling watches, luggage, clothing, and fragrances carrying its brand.[33]

Global diversification is such a widely accepted strategy that the burden of proof would be on a business leader who shunned globalization.

10. *Sticking to core competencies.* Many firms of all sizes believe they will prosper if they confine their efforts to the activities they perform best—their core competencies. Corporate strategist Jim Collins calls this the *Hedgehog concept:* becoming very good at one thing in a world of companies that spread themselves into many areas where they lack depth.[34] Many firms that expanded through diversification later trimmed back operations to activities on which they had built their reputation. A representative example is aluminum giant Alcoa, which exited the plastic-wrap and some automotive businesses to re-specialize in aluminum mining and production. Part of the reason given was that Alcoa could compete better if it eliminated the distraction of plastic wraps.[35]

A return to core competency is sometimes done because straying from the company's mission and strategy backfired. William Simon, the head of the U.S. division of Wal-Mart, noted that part of his strategy included returning to the "Every Day Low Prices" theme that the company popularized. The company had veered away from offering low prices consistently and instead discounted some items while raising prices on others. Simon modified the strategy to win back some of the core customers—households earning between $30,000 and $70,000 annually—that Wal-Mart had been losing to dollar stores.[36]

11. *Brand leadership.* As obvious as it may appear, succeeding through developing the reputation of a brand name can be considered a business strategy. The opposite strategy is to build components for others, build products that others market under their names, or be a commodity, such as cinder blocks. Jeffrey Bezos of Amazon has implemented a relentless brand leadership strategy to the point that his company has become almost synonymous with online retailing. The ultimate goal of the brand leadership strategy is to make Amazon the best-known destination for purchasing anything that might be for sale on the Internet.

According to research company Interbrand, the world's ten leading brands in order of brand strength are (1) Coca-Cola, (2) IBM, (3) Microsoft, (4) Google, (5) GE, (6) McDonald's (7) Intel, (8) Nokia (9) Disney, and (10) Hewlett-Packard.[37] By building the reputation of their brands, senior management (assisted by countless thousands of workers) has helped these companies succeed financially.

12. *Focus on environmental sustainability.* Yet another strategy is for company leadership to focus on being green, that is, engaging in many activities that help sustain the external environment. Among the myriad activities fitting the green strategy would be using solar panels and wind turbines for as much energy as possible, using recycled paper, and encouraging employees to car pool. (Many of these green initiatives were presented in Chapter 5.)

A specific example of the green strategy was formulated by Chief Executive Office Peter Löscher of the German conglomerate Siemens. Shortly after becoming CEO he focused on green business to assure the company's future. Löscher increased the proportion of Siemens that sells sustainability-focused customers products such as light bulbs, high-speed trains, and factory control systems. Siemens also generates considerable revenue from the sale of wind power, solar energy, and energy-conserving electricity grids. About one-quarter of Siemens employee are classified as *green-collar workers* because they produce or market resource-efficient products.[38] Note that the green strategy of Siemens focuses on customers rather than the company itself.

13. *Competitive advantage through hiring talented people.* A powerful strategy for gaining competitive advantage is to build the organization with talented, well-motivated people at every level. The most urgent need in building great companies is to find and keep great people. Microsoft and Amazon.com, along with elite business consulting firms, are examples of firms that explicitly use the hiring-talented-people strategy. Talented people may need some leadership direction, but they will think of new products and services and develop effective work processes.

All of these impressive strategies have limited impact unless they are implemented properly, meaning that effective management must support strategic leadership. To repeat, visions must be followed up with execution. Based on case research in many companies, Michael Beer and Russell A. Eisenstat found that strategies are sometimes not implemented correctly because top management is not aware of problems that threaten the business.

In many organizations, it is difficult for leadership to hear the unfiltered truth from managers down below. Beer and Eisenstat developed a method whereby a task force of the most effective managers collects data about strategic and organizational problems. Task force members present their findings to senior managers in the format of an honest conversation. As a result of these discussions, senior managers can make the right moves to adjust strategy.[39] For example, the task force might discover that the true reason a strategy is not working well is that the top management team is not granting enough decision-making authority to the business units. If the business unit leaders were empowered more fully, they could perform better.

KNOWLEDGE MANAGEMENT AND THE LEARNING ORGANIZATION

Another thrust of leaders is to help their organizations better adapt to the environment by assisting workers and the organization to become better learners. To accomplish this, the leader manages knowledge and cultivates a learning organization. **Knowledge management (KM)** is a concerted effort to improve how knowledge is created, delivered, and applied.[40] When knowledge is managed effectively, information is shared as needed, whether it be printed, stored electronically, or rests in the brains of workers. Managing knowledge helps create a **learning organization**—one that is skilled at creating, acquiring, and transferring knowledge and at modifying behavior to reflect new knowledge and insights.[41]

Knowledge Management

Knowledge management (KM) deals with a cultural focus on knowledge sharing. Managing knowledge is an important leadership role because so few organizations make systematic use of the collective wisdom of employees. Loads of information is often collected in databases, such as on the intranet, but little systematic use is made of the information. Here we look at the general format of KM programs.

Knowledge management has three components, as revealed by the research and observations of Thomas H. Davenport, Laurence Prusak, and Bruce Strong.[42] *Knowledge creation* is used to spur innovation. Programs for creating knowledge solicit ideas, insights, and innovations from many sources, including rank and file workers, customers, and business partners, instead of relying exclusively on the research and development staff. For example, more than 40 percent of Procter & Gamble products have a component from external sources that is up from 10 percent six years ago.

Knowledge dissemination through information technology is the most frequent activity within knowledge management. Methods of sharing knowledge include company intranets, web portals, and databases. Information is consolidated in one place so that it is more accessible to potential users. An example is to make an intranet a one-stop information shop designed to support critical jobs and work processes. For example, Intel places on one website all of the information workers need to make a capital purchase. *Knowledge application* is the process of getting workers better at what they do. Many organizations have discovered that the most effective way of encouraging workers to apply knowledge is through basic practices such as mentoring, on-the-job training, and workshops.

General Format of KM Programs   Knowledge management systems sometimes take the form of a computer-based system for collecting and organizing potentially useful information. Yet many effective systems rely on person-to-person exchange of information. For example, many companies in the field of communication technology, including Google, place white boards on the premises so technology workers can easily exchange ideas face-to-face.

We have emphasized how important it is for leaders to use anecdotes to communicate meaning. Narratives also play a major role in knowledge sharing, as Thomas Davenport illustrates in this anecdote (developed before the days when the company in question had achieved such negative publicity):

> As part of its knowledge management initiative, British Petroleum rolled out some videoconferencing technology for rapidly sharing ideas. Soon after, one of their gas drills broke down in the North Slope of Alaska. BP's leading expert in gas turbines

was working in the North Sea; it would have taken him twenty hours to fly to Alaska. Instead of putting him on a plane, BP patched him into the North Slope via video-conferencing, and he worked with on-site technicians to pinpoint the problem and get the drill back on-stream. They finished the job in just thirty minutes. That story quickly circulated throughout BP. In time, it found its way into other organizations. Because it gave real-world evidence of a dramatic improvement, the story became part of knowledge-sharing lore.[43] [Note that the human touch was helpful in selling a technology-based method of knowledge sharing.]

An advance in knowledge management is to deliver information just in time, or at the point at which it is most needed. For example, Partners HealthCare System, Inc., embeds knowledge into the technology that physicians use so that retrieving the knowledge is no longer a separate activity. When a staff physician orders medicine or a lab test, the order-entry system automatically checks his or her decision against a huge clinical database as well as the patient's own medical record. Just-in-time delivery of knowledge is also useful in business. Customer service representatives at Hewlett-Packard and Dell work with computer systems that give them immediate access to information to help them respond to customer problems.[44] In this way, the representative does not have to have reams of information in his or her head.

Whatever advanced technology is used to implement knowledge management, it works best in an organizational culture that values knowledge and encourages its dissemination. A study conducted in 121 new-product development teams and 41 subsidiaries of a high-technology company quantified another factor that influences knowledge sharing. Professional workers are less likely to hoard knowledge when there is less competition across the organizational units.[45]

The organizational subculture shapes our assumptions about what constitutes knowledge, and which knowledge is worth managing.[46] Professional workers in the finance division of Gap, Inc., might think that watching MTV on company time or surfing the Internet is a waste of company time. In the merchandising division, however, watching MTV and Internet surfing might be perceived as a valuable way of understanding clothing trends.

Think through your attitudes toward sharing knowledge by taking Leadership Self-Assessment Quiz 14-2. Then, to round out your understanding of knowledge management, do Leadership Skill-Building Exercise 14-2.

The Learning Organization

A learning organization can be viewed as a group of people working together to enhance their capacities to create the results they value.[47] Organizational leadership, however, must usually take the initiative to create the conditions whereby such enhancement of capacities, or learning, takes place. Toward this end, several firms have created a position labeled chief knowledge officer (CKO), or its equivalent. The major justification for creating such a position is that in many companies, human skills, intuition, and wisdom are replacing capital as the most precious resource. Chief knowledge officers seek to disperse those assets throughout the firm and convert them into innovations. They are

LEADERSHIP SELF-ASSESSMENT QUIZ 14-2

My Attitudes toward Sharing Knowledge

Instructions: Indicate how much you agree with the following statements: disagree strongly (DS); disagree (D); neutral (N); agree (A); and agree strongly (AS).

	DS	D	N	A	AS
1. I have often helped other students with their homework.	1	2	3	4	5
2. In brainstorming sessions, I usually hold back from giving my best ideas because I do not want them stolen.	5	4	3	2	1
3. I enjoy helping another person with a work or school problem.	1	2	3	4	5
4. I would be willing to submit some of my best ideas to a company database, such as an intranet.	1	2	3	4	5
5. I am concerned about submitting my most creative ideas on a term paper because these ideas could be stolen.	5	4	3	2	1
6. I enjoy working as part of a team and sharing ideas.	5	4	3	2	1
7. I get a little suspicious when a coworker or fellow student attempts to pick my brain.	1	2	3	4	5
8. It upsets me if I do not receive full credit for my ideas.	5	4	3	2	1
9. If I had a great idea for a screenplay or novel, I would not tell anyone about it before I was finished with the idea.	5	4	3	2	1
10. I have often let other people know about a good method I developed to improve work efficiency.	1	2	3	4	5
				Total score: _____	

Scoring and Interpretation: Tally your score by adding the numbers you circled or checked.

- **40 or higher:** You are generous with respect to knowledge sharing and would probably fit well in an organization that practices knowledge management.

- **20–39:** You have average attitudes toward sharing knowledge, with a mixture of enthusiasm and skepticism about knowledge sharing.

- **1–19:** You are quite cautious and guarded about sharing ideas. Unless you become more willing to share your ideas, you would not fit well in an organization that emphasized knowledge management.

Note: *You are authorized to share this quiz with as many people as you would like.*

in charge of systematically collecting information and connecting people with others who might have valuable information.

Here we look at a variety of leadership practices and attitudes that facilitate organizational learning.

Transformational versus Transactional Leadership and Organizational Learning Recent research in a large European financial services firm has brought into sharper focus the leader's role in organizational learning. One major finding was that transformational leadership behaviors contribute significantly

LEADERSHIP SKILL-BUILDING EXERCISE 14-2

The Knowledge-Sharing Investigation Teams

A challenge with the idea of knowledge sharing is to know what knowledge should be shared among company members. The class is organized into knowledge-sharing investigation teams. Members of each team contact two people working in a support, technical, sales, professional, or managerial position in a profit or nonprofit organization. Ask the contact persons what knowledge would be valuable to share in their place of work. Communicate using the easiest method, whether it be a phone call, a text message, or a tweet.

Discuss your findings in a group, and perhaps add opinions of your own as to what knowledge would be worthwhile sharing in an organization. Arrive at a conclusion about five specific types of knowledge within an organization worth sharing. Share your findings with members of the other groups in the class.

to encouraging workers to pursue exploratory innovation. An *exploratory innovation* deals with finding new products, services, processes, or technology. An example would be a bank finding an entirely new service to offer to the public, such as a relocation service for geographically transferred employees. Another major finding was that transactional leadership behaviors facilitate improving and extending existing knowledge and are associated with *exploitative innovation*.[48] Exploitation relates to learning ways to make incremental improvements in existing products, services, or processes. An example would be a bank developing a line of credit specifically geared toward the one-person enterprise. The example cited of improving the tastiness of Domino's pizza is another example of exploitative innovation.

Leadership Initiatives for Enhancing the Learning Organization A wide variety of leadership initiatives can create and enhance a learning organization. Understanding them will help you grasp the concept of what a leader might do to enhance organizational learning.[49]

A major building block of a learning organization is a *supportive learning environment*. Several factors comprise a supportive learning environment. Employees should not fear being belittled or marginalized when they disagree with their manager or coworkers or ask naïve questions. Instead, they should feel comfortable about expressing disagreement or puzzlement. Differences in opposing views should be both accepted and appreciated. Supportive learning also includes being open to new ideas and having the time to think and reflect. In many organizations, a person seen looking out the window would be assumed to be daydreaming rather than thinking about work-related problems.

A second building block of a learning organization is *concrete learning processes and practices*. One example would be for a company to hold debriefing sessions discussing what went right or wrong with a recent program of placing product advertisements as temporary tattoos on the foreheads of paid participants.

A third building block is *leadership that reinforces learning*. For example, when leaders actively question and listen to employees, dialogue and debate as well as learning are encouraged. Most of the behaviors in the rest of this section would fit the building block of leadership that reinforces learning.

A top-level leader should *create a strategic intent to learn*. Organizational learning then becomes a vehicle for gaining competitive advantage. *Creating a shared vision* enhances learning as organization members develop a common purpose and commitment to having the organization keep learning. If workers at all levels believe that the company is headed toward greatness, they will be motivated to learn to help deliver greatness.

In a learning organization, *employees are empowered to make decisions and seek continuous improvement*. The idea is to develop a community of learning in which every worker believes that he or she can contribute to a smarter, more effective organization.

Systems thinking is almost synonymous with organizational learning. The leader helps organization members regard the organization as a system in which everybody's work affects the activities of everybody else. Systems thinking also means keeping the big picture foremost in everybody's mind and being keenly aware of the external environment. In addition to the big picture of systems thinking, the leader must encourage the little picture of *personal mastery of the job*. As team members gain personal mastery of their jobs, they contribute to *team learning*, an essential part of a learning organization. Team learning centers on collective problem solving in which members freely share information and opinions to facilitate problem solving.

Action learning, or learning while working on real problems, is a fundamental part of a learning organization. Participants in action learning are asked to work in teams to attack a significant organizational problem, such as decreasing the cycle time on a project. In the process of resolving an actual work problem, the participants acquire and use new skills, tools, or concepts. As the project progresses, new skills are applied while working with the problem. For example, if the team learned how to eliminate duplication of effort in one aspect of the work process, it would look to eliminate duplication at other points in the cycle.

Learning from failure contributes immensely to a learning organization. A company that diversified into an area unsuccessfully might analyze why it failed, and then not repeat the same mistake. *Encouraging continuous experimentation* is another important practice for crafting a learning strategy. The leader encourages workers to learn from competitors, customers, suppliers, and other units within the organization.

For organizational learning to proceed smoothly, workers throughout the organization must have the *political skills to make connections with and influence others*. For example, if a production technician discovers an effective method of reducing water consumption, he or she must have the skill to sell an influential person on the merits of this idea.

A final perspective on creating the learning organization is that the leader must encourage organizational members to think creatively—to imagine possibilities that do not already exist. Research synthesized by Yukl suggests that a comprehensive way for leaders to enhance organizational learning is to "Develop, implement, and support programs and systems that will encourage and reward the discovery of new knowledge and its diffusion and application in the organization."[50] Instead of merely adapting to the environment, the organization engages in the type of breakthrough thinking described in our previous discussions of creativity and strategic leadership.

SUMMARY

Strategic leadership deals with the major purposes of an organization or organizational unit and provides the direction and inspiration necessary to create, provide direction to, or sustain an organization. Strategic leadership has five important components: (1) the high-level cognitive activity by the leader, (2) gathering multiple inputs to formulate strategy, (3) anticipating and creating a future, (4) revolutionary and contrarian thinking, and (5) creating a vision.

Creating a vision is an integral part of strategic leadership. The final vision statement is relatively short. After formulating a vision, the leader should be involved in its communication and implementation. A carefully considered and articulated vision helps us know who we are and who we are not. The vision also points to what we do successfully and what we do not, which activities we should take on and which to avoid. In companies that believe in visions and strategic goals, all activities throughout the company are supposed to support the vision and goals.

Carefully crafting a strategy and vision is not sufficient for effectiveness. The strategy and vision must also be implemented or executed by the leader/manager. A study in a large healthcare organization demonstrated that when leaders at all levels were perceived to be effective, it was more likely that strategic change would take place.

Strategic planning quite often takes the form of a SWOT analysis, taking into account internal strengths and weaknesses and external opportunities and threats in a given situation. A SWOT analysis examines the interaction between the organization and the environment.

Strategic leaders use many different types of business strategies, including the following: (1) differentiation, (2) cost leadership, (3) focus or niche, (4) high quality, (5) imitation, (6) strategic alliances, (7) growth through acquisition, (8) high speed and first-mover strategy, (9) product and global diversification, (10) sticking to core competencies, (11) brand leadership, (12) focus on environmental sustainability, and (13) competitive advantage through hiring talented people.

Another strategic thrust of leaders is to help their organizations adapt to the environment by assisting workers and the organization to become better learners. To accomplish this feat, the leader manages knowledge and cultivates a learning organization. Knowledge management focuses on the systematic sharing of information, including being able to deliver information just in time. Knowledge management consists of knowledge creation, dissemination, and application.

The leader has many roles in a learning organization. Transformational leaders tend toward encouraging exploratory innovation, whereas transactional leaders tend toward encouraging exploitative (increments in what already exists) innovation.

Major leadership initiatives for creating a learning organization include creating a strategic intent to learn, creating a shared vision, and empowering employees to make decisions and seek continuous improvements. Also important is encouraging systems thinking, encouraging personal mastery of the job, and team learning. Action learning, or learning while working on real problems, learning from failures, and encouraging continuous experimentation are also part of the learning organization. Workers must have the political skills to make connections and influence others. Encouraging creative thinking is also part of the learning organization.

KEY TERMS

strategy	strategic planning	Knowledge management (KM)
strategic leadership	SWOT analysis	learning organization

✔ GUIDELINES FOR ACTION AND SKILL DEVELOPMENT

To make sure that all workers understand the company's vision of where it wants to go, the vision statement should have certain key characteristics:[51]

1. **Brief.** The statement should be short enough so employees can recall it with ease. It has been suggested that a vision should fit on an adult-size T-shirt.
2. **Verifiable.** A verifiable vision is one that ten people could agree that an organization has achieved.
3. **Focused.** Vision statements often contain too many ideas. It is better to focus on a major goal such as the vision of Ford Motor Company: "Employee involvement is our way of life." (Notice that this vision is about human resource management, not about a product or brand.)
4. **Understandable.** A major purpose of the vision statement is that employees will know where the organization wants to go and how to help it get there. Being understandable is therefore a key quality of the vision statement. Terms such as *world class* and *leading edge* might be subject to wide interpretation. The following component of the H&R Block vision statement would be understandable by most company employees: "Quality products, excellent service, reasonable fees."
5. **Inspirational.** To inspire, a vision statement should make employees feel good about working for the organization and should focus them on measurable business goals.

Organizations cannot rely on CKOs alone to manage knowledge. The entire knowledge process must be embedded in the position of line manager.[52]

Discussion Questions and Activities

1. Why is creative thinking required to develop a strategy for an organization? Why couldn't a leader simply use a search engine to find a good strategy?
2. How might a business strategy deal with a topic other than products or services?
3. In what way can a business strategy motivate and inspire employees?
4. How could you adapt a business strategy to guide you in your own career as a leader?
5. Many top-level managers say that they want lower-ranking managers to think strategically. How can a middle manager or a first-level manager think strategically?
6. Why might finding a niche for the organization be the most important activity of a strategic leader?
7. Working alone or with several team members, provide a recent example of revolutionary thinking by a company.
8. During the Great Recssion, many consumers who had previously shopped at traditional supermarkets shifted to doing basic shopping at dollar stores and discount department stores. Furthermore, some of these shoppers remained loyal to the low-priced stores after the recession. What are the strategy lessons here?
9. In what way might doing a good job of knowledge management give a company a competitive advantage?
10. Why do you think it has been so difficult for researchers to prove that knowledge management pays dividends to an organization?

LEADERSHIP CASE PROBLEM A

Mike Duke of Wal-Mart Digs Into the Business

Wal-Mart Stores, Inc., (or *Walmart*) is regarded as the world's biggest business enterprise, with about $425 billion in annual sales, and 8,500 stores worldwide. More than 200 million customers and members are served each week in 15 countries. President and CEO Mike Duke is the number one leader of this giant enterprise, and only the fourth such executive in the company's history—not including founder Sam Walton. Before becoming CEO in 2009, Duke had been the highly successful chairman of the company's international division.

Among Duke's job experiences prior to the international assignment were logistics work early in his career, and the director of U.S. sales. Lee Scott, the previous Wal-Mart CEO said Duke is a better manager than he is: "I think it's his ability to deal with data, his ability to set a schedule and follow that schedule, and to get all of the things done that he needs to get done. Mike is disciplined ..." PepsiCo CEO Indra Nooyi describes Duke as a person "who's very unassuming, a very, very global thinker, and a very worldly person."

Duke's concerns as chief executive include merchandising and store displays. Shortly after becoming CEO, he studied the effects of a company program called Project Impact that freshened up stores, giving them a cleaner, less cluttered look. Customers liked the new look, but because less merchandise was stocked, sales suffered. Duke jumped in to increase the number of product offerings to the days before project impact. When Duke visits stores he makes observations such as whether bananas are priced competitively and enough underwear is on the shelves. (Underwear is one of Wal-Mart's best-selling items.)

During 2010–2011, Wal-Mart was coping with seven consecutive quarters of sales declines in stores. Duke expressed concern that partly attributable to increases in gas and food prices, many Wal-Mart customers were running out of money before the end of the month. A large proportion of Wal-Mart customers live paycheck to paycheck, so they shop in bulk at the beginning of the month and decrease purchases when their funds diminish. Because of rising good prices, Duke said that Wal-Mart was charging more for some fresh groceries and reducing prices on many non-food items such as electronics.

Duke embraces the Wal-Mart mission statement, "Saving people money so they can live better." He believes that technology will continue to have a major impact on shopping because prices are more transparent through such means as social media. Duke said to his managers, "And what kind of retailer wins in a time of price transparency? You got it, the price leader. We need to really churn the productivity loop and deliver on our Every Day Low Price business model everywhere. We will win on price leadership, and we will win big."

To enable customers to save and have a better life, Duke announced at a shareholder meeting that four strategies are necessary for building the Next Generation Wal-Mart:

1. Become a truly global company.
2. Understand the business challenges that retailers will face and solve them.
3. Play an even bigger leadership role on social issues that matter to our customers.
4. Keep our culture strong everywhere.

Questions

1. Which business strategy does Wal-Mart obviously emphasize?
2. To what extent do the strategies Duke lists really constitute business *strategy*?
3. To what extent should the president and CEO of the world's largest company be concerned about merchandising details such as whether enough underwear is on the shelf?
4. What strategic suggestions might you have to help Wal-Mart overcome declining sales should that problem arise again?

Source: Original case created from facts and observations found in the following sources: Brian O'Keefe, "Meet the CEO of the Biggest Company on Earth," *Fortune*, September 27, 2010, pp. 80–94; "Walmart CEO Mike Duke Outlines Strategies for Building the 'Next Generation Walmart'," *Walmart Corporate*, June 4, 2010, pp. 1–2; Parija Kavlianz, "Wal-Mart: Our Shoppers are 'Running out of Money'," *CNNMoney.com* (http://money.cnn.com), April 28, 2011, pp. 1–2; Miguel Bustillo, "New Chief at Wal-Mart Looks Abroad for Growth," *The Wall Street Journal*, February 2, 2009, pp. B1, B6; Anne D'Innocenzio, "Mike Duke, Wal-Mart CEO," *Huffpost Business* (www.huffingtonpost.com), November 21, 2008, pp. 1–2.

ASSOCIATED ROLE PLAY

The Wal-Mart Strategy Team

Organize into teams of about six students because Mike Duke has selected you to come up with a strategy for Wal-Mart to supplement existing strategy. Duke tells you via e-mail, "Be as courageous as you want in giving me a strategy suggestion. We are the world's biggest company, but it doesn't mean that we are perfect, or that we cannot be toppled by a competitor. Be bold. Think big. I'm a Georgia Tech grad, so I know a good idea when I see one." You have about thirty minutes to arrive at a new strategy for Wal-Mart. An alternative is to spend some supplementary time outside of class working on the problem. Brainstorm by e-mail or social media if you would like.

LEADERSHIP CASE PROBLEM B

"Superintendent Briggs Is Busy Creating Visions Today"

Mary Briggs is the superintendent of schools of a city school district comprised of more than 60 schools, including pre-kindergarten, elementary, middle, and high schools. The school district has approximately 50,000 students enrolled at any one time. Many of the students are doing well, but the school district is also beset with many problems. Fewer than 50 percent of the students graduate from high school, and only about 10 percent of the high school graduates are considered ready for college or employment.

The local press, many parent groups, and the office of the mayor voice frequent complaints about the low performance of the city schools. Some people blame the teachers and the school principals for the problems. Others blame the parents and the neighborhood influences for the problems. Still others blame the problems of the school district on Superintendent Briggs, who, as the leader, should be able to fix most of the problems facing the district, they believe.

A member of the school board recently asked Mary Briggs what she perceived to be the most important part of her job. Briggs replied, "I do visions. As a leader my job is to help create a better future for the schools, our students, and our teachers. I see a great future for our schools in which most of our students develop the skills and intellect to prepare them for the modern world. Many of our students will become leaders in our society, no matter what field they enter."

The school board member replied, "Thanks, Dr. Briggs, but I thought you might be working on problems like there not being enough money in the food program for our poorest students."

During the workday, school principals and vice principals often send Briggs e-mails asking her advice for dealing with an immediate problem, such as a student physically assaulting a teacher or another student in the classroom. Usually it takes about twenty-four hours to receive a response.

As an alternative to sending Briggs an e-mail about an important operational problem, some principals or vice principals will attempt to get through to her on the telephone. Usually, the calls go to voice mail. On occasion, the call does get through to Briggs' administrative assistant. A response from the assistant that has come to irritate many of the principals and vice principals, is "Sorry, Superintendent Briggs is busy creating visions today. So she cannot talk with you unless this problem is a total emergency." As a result, the phrase "Superintendent Briggs is busy creating visions today" has become a punch line for many jokes among principals, vice-principals, and teachers.

1. As a strategic leader, what error might Mary Briggs be making?
2. To what extent should a school superintendent be spending more time on strategy than operational problems?
3. What advice might you offer Briggs to enhance her leadership image in her school district?

ASSOCIATED ROLE PLAY

The Union Leader Meets with the Visionary Superintendent

One student plays the role of the head of the teacher's union in the school district just described. The union leader believes firmly that Mary Briggs is not devoting enough time to working on operational problems, such as dealing with teacher complaints about classroom assaults. The union leader has arranged a face-to-face meeting with Briggs. Another student plays the role of Briggs who will probably defend her role as a visionary for the school system who cannot spend too much time on mundane, operational problems.

LEADERSHIP SKILL-BUILDING EXERCISE 14-3

My Leadership Portfolio

A major part of being a strategic leader is to think strategically. Entrapped by the necessities of the small tasks facing us daily, it is easy to "think little" instead of "think big" as required to be a strategic thinker. A "little thinker" might attend a leadership seminar and spend five minutes demanding a $5.00 rebate because he or she was served ill-prepared food at lunch. A "big thinker" might reflect on the same poorly prepared meal as a lesson in the importance of employees' taking care of small details to ensure customer satisfaction. For this installment in your leadership portfolio, enter into your journal how you capitalized—or did not capitalize—on the opportunity to think strategically during the last week, or so. An example follows:

My friend and I visited a large shopping mall on Saturday morning. We noticed a large number of vehicles, both autos and small trucks, circling around within a block of the mall entrance. The drivers were obviously looking for a parking spot close enough so they could avoid walking the block, or so, necessary if they parked farther from the entrance.

My friend is a fitness nut, so he said the parking space chasers could do themselves a favor by parking a long distance from the mall entrance. In this way they could get a little physical exercise. A strategic flash went through my mind. If I, or perhaps the First Lady, could launch a national campaign for parking a distance away from mall entrances, we could make some headway on two of the major problems facing our society. First, physical inactivity is becoming almost as big a killer as smoking. Second, think of all the gas people are wasting. On a national scale, think of all the gas we would save if people would stop circling around looking for spaces. Besides, those little extra blocks of gas consumption add up. My strategic brainstorm could lead to more fitness and less energy consumption in our country.

LEADERSHIP SKILL-BUILDING **EXERCISE 14-4**

Developing a Business Strategy for an Appliance Repair Chain

Imagine that you and a few classmates are the management team of a business that is almost dead—a chain of household appliance repair stores. Over the years, your business has been declining steadily. A major contributing factor is that most people just replace rather than repair appliances such as television sets, DVD players, irons, heaters, hair dryers, and electric razors.

Today you are holding a business strategy session focused on the survival of your business. Be as bold as possible in your thinking, but keep in mind that your probably do not have much cash on hand and that your borrowing power is limited. Within thirty minutes, see if you can construct at least a tentative path for the survival of your appliance-repair business.

▶❚❚ **LEADERSHIP** VIDEO **CASE** DISCUSSION **QUESTIONS**

To view the videos for this activity, you'll need access to the CourseMate that is available for this text. To get access, visit www.CengageBrain.com.

After watching "Evogear," answer the following questions.

1. What is strategic leadership? How does the founder of Evo, Bryce Phillips, provide strategic leadership?

2. Is Evo a learning organization? Explain why or why not.

3. What are the four components of a SWOT analysis? Briefly conduct a SWOT analysis for Evo.

4. List the three generic business strategies promoted by Michael Porter. Which of these three strategies does Evo use most? Explain.

NOTES

1. Story created from facts and observations found in the following sources: Dana Mattioli, "Xerox Touts Its Business-Services Side," *The Wall Street Journal*, September 2, 2010; Geoff Colvin, "Ursula Burns: Less than a Year into the Job, the Xerox CEO is Already Transforming the Company," *Fortune*, May 3, 2010, pp. 96–102; Jerome Nathaniel, "Chairman and CEO of Xerox to Speak at Commencement," *www.campustimes.org*, April 7, 2011, pp. 1–4; Sonia Alleyne, "Most Powerful Women in Business," *Black Enterprise*, February 2010, pp. 88–89.

2. Donald C. Hambrick and James W. Fredrickson, "Are You Sure You Have a Strategy?" *Academy of Management Executive*, November 2001, p. 48.

3. Richard L. Hughes and Katherine C. Beatty, *Becoming a Strategic Leader: Your Role in Your Organization's Enduring Success* (San Francisco: Jossey-Bass, 2005).

4. J. Brian Atwater, Vijay R. Kannan, and Alan A. Stephens, "Cultivating Systemic Thinking in the Next Generation of Business Leaders," *Academy of Management Learning & Education*, March 2008, p. 13.

5. Cynthia Montgomery, "Putting Leadership Back in Strategy," *Harvard Business Review*, January 2008, pp. 54–80.

6. Henry Mintzberg, *Managing* (San Francisco: Berrett-Koehler, 2009), p. 162.

7. Bruce J. Avolio and David A. Waldman, "An Examination of Age and Cognitive Test Performance Across Job Complexity and Occupational Types," *Journal of Applied Psychology*, February 1990, pp. 43–50.

8. Julia Kirby and Thomas A. Stewart, interview with Jeff Bezos, "The Institutional Yes," *Harvard Business Review*, October 2007, p. 76; "Amazon.com Apologizes for Multi-Day Cloud Computing Outage," *Los Angeles Times* (www.latimes.com), April 29, 2011, p. 1.

9. Samuel Greengard, "Leveraging a Low-Wage Workforce," *Workforce Online*, February, 2004.

10. Strategy Session with C. K. Prahalad, *Management Review*, April 1995, pp. 50–51.

11. Cited in "Jack Welch on Doing and on Dreaming," *Executive Leadership*, September 2009, p. 1.

12. Gary Hamel, "Revolution vs. Evolution: You Need Both," *Harvard Business Review*, May 2001, p. 150.

13. Jaclyn Trop, "Domino's Delivers on Its Turnaround Plan," *The Detroit News* (www.detnews.com), December 4, 2010, pp. 1–3.

14. Keith H. Hammonds, "Michael Porter's Big Ideas," *Fast Company*, March 2001, p. 153.

15. Susanna Hamner and Tom McNichol, "Ripping Up the Rules of Management," *Business 2.0*, May 2007, p. 63.

16. Adam Bryant, *The Corner Office* (New York: Times Books), 2011.

17. James R. Lucas, "Anatomy of a Vision Statement," *Management Review*, February 1998, p. 26.

18. Quoted in Victoria Barret, "The Web's Big Upstart," *Forbes*, December 6, 2010, p. 74.

19. Carmine Gallo, "Be a Visionary Leader," *The Ladders.com Executive Coach* (TheLadders.com), January 23, 2008.

20. Charles A. O'Reilly, David F. Caldwell, Jenifer A. Chatman, Margaret Lapiz, and William Self, "How Leadership Matters: The Effect of Leaders' Alignment on Strategy Implementation," *Leadership Quarterly*, February 2010, pp. 104–113.

21. Several ideas for this version of SWOT are from "SWOT Analysis," *Business Owner's Tool Kit*, November 8, 1999 (www.toolkit.cch.com/text/p02_4341.asp); "Performing a SWOT Analysis," in *Business: The Ultimate Resources* (Cambridge, Mass.: Perseus Publishing, 2002), pp. 226–227.

22. Christopher Lawton, "How H-P Reclaimed Its PC Lead over Dell: Shifting Battlefield to Stores Was Key; Help from Vera Wang," *The Wall Street Journal*, June 4, 2007.

23. Michael Porter, *Competitive Strategy* (New York: The Free Press, 1980), pp. 36–46.

24. Brad Stone and Douglas MacMillan, "Groupon's $6 Billion Snub," *Bloomberg Business Week*, December 13-December 19, 2010, p. 7.

25. Stephanie Clifford, "Where Wal-Mart Failed, Aldi Succeeds," *The New York Times* (www.nytimes.com), March 20, 2011, pp. 1–4.

26. Nick Wingfield, "Taking on eBay," *The Wall Street Journal*, September 15, 2004, p. R10.

27. Norihiko Shirouzu, "Toyoda Rues Excessive Profit Focus," *The Wall Street Journal*, March 2, 2010, p. B3.

28. "Facebook and Microsoft Expand Strategic Alliance," *Microsoft News Center* (www.microsoft.com), October 7, 2007, p. 1.

29. Melanie Haiken, "Innovative Partnering: Papa John's and Six Flags," *Time* (*Business 2.0* insert), December 11, 2006, p. 2.

30. Rolfe Winkler, "Cisco Grapples With Shock to System," *The Wall Street Journal*, July 13, 2011, C16.

31. www.jordan.com; Telis Demos, "The New King of Name Brands," *Fortune*, July 7, 2008, pp. 86–90.

32. Danielle Douglas, "Coca-Cola May Be Preparing to Acquire Honest Tea," *Capital Business* (www.washingtonpost.com), February 7, 2011, pp. 1–2

33. Joe Mandak, "Zippo's Burning Ambition Lies in Retail Expansion," Associated Press, March 23, 2011.

34. George Anders, "Homespun Strategist," *The Wall Street Journal*, January 6, 2004, p. B1.

35. Robert Guy Matthews, "Why Firms Are Returning to Their Roots," *The Wall Street Journal*, October 22, 2007, p. A2.

36. Miguel Bustillo, "With Sales Flabby, Wal-Mart Turns to Its Core," *The Wall Street Journal*, March 21, 2011, p. B1.

37. "Best Global Brands 2010," *Interbrand* (www.interbrand.com), © 2011.

38. "How Siemens Got Its *Geist* Back," *Bloomberg Business Week*, January 31 – February 6, 2011, pp. 18–20.

39. Michael Beer and Russell A. Eisenstat, "How to Have an Honest Conversation about Your Business Strategy," *Harvard Business Review*, February 2004, pp. 82–89.

40. Thomas H. Davenport, Laurence Prusak, and Bruce Strong, "Putting Ideas to Work: Knowledge

Management Can Make a Difference, but It Needs to Be More Pragmatic," *The Wall Street Journal*, March 10, 2008, p. R11.

41. David A. Garvin, "Building a Learning Organization," *Harvard Business Review*, July–August 1993, p. 80.

42. Davenport, Prusak, and Strong, "Putting Ideas to Work," p. R11.

43. Bill Breen, "Hidden Asset," *Fast Company*, March 2004, p. 95.

44. Thomas H. Davenport and John Glaser, "Just-in-Time Delivery Comes to Knowledge Management," *Harvard Business Review*, July 2002, pp. 107–111.

45. Morten T. Hansen, Marie Louise Mors, and Bjorn Lovas, "Knowledge Sharing in Organizations: Multiple Networks, Multiple Phases," *Academy of Management Journal*, October 2005, p. 790.

46. David W. De Long and Liam Fahey, "Diagnosing Cultural Barriers to Knowledge Management," *Academy of Management Executive*, November 2000, pp. 115–117.

47. Robert M. Fulmer and J. Bernard Keys, "A Conversation with Peter Senge: New Developments in Organizational Learning," *Organizational Dynamics*, Autumn 1998, p. 35.

48. Justin J. P. Jansen, Dusya Vera, and Mary Crossan, "Strategic Leadership for Exploration and Exploitation: The Moderating Role of Environmental Dynamism," *Leadership Quarterly*, February 2009, pp. 5–18.

49. The three building blocks are from David A. Garvin, Amy C. Edmondson, and Francesca Gino, "Is Yours a Learning Organization?" *Harvard Business Review*, March 2008, pp. 110–114. The rest of the list is from the following sources: Robert M. Fulmer and Philip Gibbs, "The Second Generation Learning Organizations: New Tools for Sustainable Competitive Advantage," *Organizational Dynamics*, Autumn 1998, pp. 7–20; Peter M. Senge, *The Fifth Discipline* (New York: Doubleday, 1990); Thomas P. Lawrence, Michael M. Mauws, Bruno Dyck, and Robert F. Kleysen, "The Politics of Organizational Learning: Integrating Power into the 4I Framework," *Academy of Management Review*, January 2005, pp. 180–191; Joe Raelin, "Does Action Learning Promote Collaborative Leadership?" *Academy of Management Learning & Education*, June 2006, pp. 152–168.

50. Gary Yuyl, "Leading Organizational Learning: Reflections on Theory and Research," *Leadership Quarterly*, February 2009, p. 50.

51. "Making Vision Statements 'Visionary,'" *Manager's Edge*, December 1998, p. 1.

52. Neil Gross, "Mining a Company's Mother Lode of Talent," *Business week*, August 28, 2000, p. 137.

The **Development** of **Leaders** and **Succession Planning**

LEARNING OBJECTIVES

After studying this chapter and doing the exercises, you should be able to

- Explain how leaders develop through self-awareness and self-discipline.

- Explain how leaders develop through education, experience, and mentoring.

- Summarize the nature of leadership development programs.

- Describe the nature of leadership succession.

CHAPTER OUTLINE

Many people have heard about those brave and highly skilled men and women who are members of the New York Fire Department. They fight fires in buildings and subways, and they rescue people trapped in vehicular accidents. Now a select number of these firefighters are helping develop corporate leaders.

The FDNY Firefighter for a Day Team Challenge was developed to share the New York City Fire Department's team building and leadership practices with members of corporations. The setting for the training is the FDNY training academy. Participants are exposed to state-of-the-art training simulators to strengthen teamwork and leadership skills.

The key component of the challenge is that corporations compete in teams of four people where they receive hands-on training designed to improve team building, leadership, communication, and problem-solving skills. A major goal of the program is to help leaders become more skilled at dealing with a crisis.

On a given day of training, to enhance their leadership skills, managers from about two dozen different companies joined with some of their employees to simulate being firefighters on a given afternoon. Teams of four wear firefighter gear, including gas masks. Supervised by New York City firefighters, the four-person teams go through emergency drills, particularly rushing into burning buildings and rescuing passengers from simulated subway accidents.

Leadership skills are needed, as the four-person teams quickly make assignments within the group to deal with a building fire or a subway accident. The program coordinators from the FDNY recommend that each team have one senior official and several nonmanagerial employees.

Scott Parel, of the major law firm Weil, Gotshal, Manges, offered this comment about the firefighter training: "A truly incredible and unique experience. You will leave with valuable team building and leadership skills and a new sense of pride and respect for the FDNY."

Malinda Robey reacted to her experience in these words: "The FDNY Firefighter for a Day Team Challenge is a once in a lifetime, must-do experience! I now have a newfound respect for New York's bravest, the FDNY."[1]

The leadership development program (yet another type of offsite training) just described illustrates the importance companies place on developing the leadership ability of managers and other personnel. The previous chapters in this book have included information and activities designed to develop leaders and enhance their effectiveness. This chapter describes how self-development can enhance leadership effectiveness, as well as the processes organizations use to develop current and future leaders. Such activities and processes are typically referred to as leadership development, or management development. One reason that leadership development is important is because unless top-level management assigns high priority to leadership development and succession planning, the company will experience a steady attrition in talent. As a result, it will be difficult for the company to cope with an upheaval such as acquiring a company with a different operating style and organizational culture.[2]

Having a separate chapter about leadership development is based on the belief expressed in Chapter 1 that leaders are both born and made. Leadership talent can therefore be developed. As Sharon Daloz Parks observes, leadership is not exclusively about having the right traits but also involves behaviors. And these behaviors can be taught because they can be translated into doable tasks, such as learning to coach.[3] We add that traits can also be developed to some degree, as described in this chapter.

In addition to describing various approaches to leadership development, this chapter also describes leadership succession. Leadership succession is included here because an important part of leadership development is being groomed for promotion. The text concludes with a glimpse of the challenges newly appointed leaders face.

DEVELOPMENT THROUGH SELF-AWARENESS AND SELF-DISCIPLINE

Leadership development is often perceived in terms of education and training, job experience, and coaching. Nevertheless, self-help also contributes heavily to developing leadership capabilities. Self-help takes many forms, including working on one's own to improve communication skills, to develop charisma, and to model the behavior of effective leaders. Two major components of leadership self-development are self-awareness and self-discipline.

Leadership Development Through Self-Awareness

An important mechanism underlying self-development is **self-awareness**, insightfully processing feedback about oneself to improve one's effectiveness. Business ethicist Joseph L. Badaracco Jr. points out that leaders should learn more about themselves if they want to succeed. An example is that if you want to lead other people, you first need to reflect on how well you can manage yourself.[4]

According to two specialists in leadership assessment, many big mistakes in careers and organizations result from gaps in self-awareness.[5] For example, a managerial leader might observe that three key group members left her group over a six-month time span. The leader might defensively dismiss this fact with an analysis such as, "I guess we just don't pay well enough to keep good people." Her first analysis might be correct. With a self-awareness orientation, however, the leader would dig deeper for the reasons behind the turnover. She might ask herself, "Is there something in my leadership approach that creates turnover problems?" She might ask for exit-interview data to sharpen her perceptions about her leadership approach.

Chris Argyris has coined the terms *single-loop learning* and *double-loop learning* to differentiate between levels of self-awareness.[6] **Single-loop learning** occurs when learners seek minimum feedback that might substantially confront their basic ideas or actions. As in the example of the high-turnover leader, single-loop learners engage in defensive thinking and tend not to act on the clues they receive. Argyris offers the example of a thermostat that automatically turns on the heat whenever the room temperature drops below 68 degrees Fahrenheit (20 degrees Celsius).

Double-loop learning is an in-depth type of learning that occurs when people use feedback to confront the validity of the goal or the values implicit in the situation. The leader mentioned earlier was engaged in double-loop learning when she questioned the efficacy of her leadership approach. To achieve

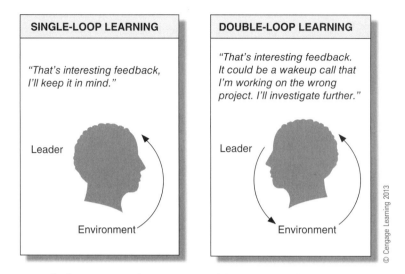

FIGURE 15-1 Single-Loop Learning Versus Double-Loop Learning.

double-loop learning, one must minimize defensive thinking. Many people are blind to their areas of incompetence, and do not know their vision is blocked. Figure 15-1 illustrates the difference between single-loop and double-loop learning.

An important contribution of double-loop learning is that it enables the leader to learn and profit from setbacks. Interpreting the reason that a setback occurred may help the leader to do better the next time. Faced with a group in crisis, a leader might establish a vision of better days ahead for group members. The leader observes that the vision leads to no observable changes in performance and behavior. Perhaps the group was not ready for a vision. In a comparable situation in the future, the leader might hold back on formulating a vision until the group is headed out of the crisis.

A fruitful area of self-awareness is for leaders to recognize their standing on two key dimensions of leadership: forceful versus enabling leadership, and strategy versus operational. Bob Kaplan explains that the leader should not go overboard on each dimension, such as being too forceful or too enabling (empowering). A leader should also not spend so much time strategizing that operations become neglected, or so much time focusing on operations that strategy is neglected. The process of self-awareness on these two dimensions is much like volume control—raise or lower the volume to get the best result. Figure 15-2 outlines this area of self-awareness in terms of the extremes, or being lopsided. Leaders can take the Leadership Versatility Index®, which enables them to find their standing on the two dimensions of leadership. The ideal point is to be just right in forcefulness versus enabling, and strategic versus operational. Feedback from others helps a leader become self-aware of his or her standing on these two dimensions.[7]

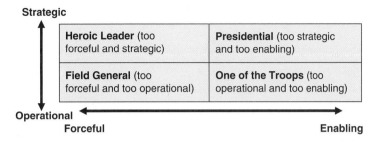

FIGURE 15-2 Four Kinds of Lopsided Leaders.

Source: Based on concepts from Bob Kaplan with Rob Kaiser, *The Versatile Leader: Make the Most of Your Strengths—Without Overdoing It* (San Francisco: Pfeiffer, 2006).

Leadership Development Through Self-Discipline

As with other types of personal development, leadership development requires considerable self-discipline. In the present context, **self-discipline** is mobilizing one's effort and energy to stay focused on attaining an important goal. Self-discipline is required for most forms of leadership development. Assume, for example, that a leader is convinced that active listening is an important leadership behavior. The leader reads about active listening and also attends a workshop on the subject. After the reading and workshop are completed, the leader will need to concentrate diligently in order to remember to listen actively. Self-discipline is particularly necessary because the pressures of everyday activities often divert a person's attention from personal development.

Self-discipline plays an important role in the continuous monitoring of one's behavior to ensure that needed self-development occurs. After one identifies a developmental need, it is necessary to periodically review whether one is making the necessary improvements. Assume that a person recognizes the developmental need to become a more colorful communicator as a way of enhancing charisma. The person would need self-discipline to make the conscious effort to communicate more colorfully when placed in an appropriate situation. Leadership Self-Assessment Quiz 15-1 contains an interpersonal skills checklist that will help you identify your own developmental needs related to interpersonal relationships.

A specific example of a leader addressing a developmental need is advertising account manager Samantha Reeb-Wilson who recognized that honing her negotiation skills might accelerate her career. She said, "In my role, we try to figure out the best way to solve a client's business problems, and that requires laying out an argument and defending it." As a result, she signed up for a seminar on persuasive argument at a women's leadership program at her alma mater, Barnard College.[8]

A key part of making self-awareness and self-discipline vehicles for personal development is to have a healthy belief in personal growth. According to psychology professor Carol Dweck, some people have a healthy belief in growth, whereby they assume that they will develop their talents during their

LEADERSHIP SELF-ASSESSMENT **QUIZ 15-1**

The Interpersonal Skills Checklist

Instructions: Following are a number of specific aspects of behavior that suggest that a person needs to improve his or her interpersonal skills related to leadership and influence. Check each statement that is generally true for you. You can add to the reliability of this exercise by asking one or two other people who know you well to rate you. Then compare your self-analysis with their analysis of you.

DEVELOPMENTAL NEEDS AND AREAS FOR IMPROVEMENT

1. I am too shy and reserved. ☐
2. I bully and intimidate others frequently. ☐
3. I tell others what they want to hear rather than emphasizing the truth. ☐
4. I have trouble expressing my feelings. ☐
5. I make negative comments about group members too readily. ☐
6. Very few people pay attention to the ideas I contribute during a meeting. ☐
7. My personality is not colorful enough. ☐
8. People find me boring. ☐
9. I pay too little attention to the meaning behind what team members and coworkers are saying. ☐
10. It is very difficult for me to criticize others. ☐
11. I am too serious most of the time. ☐
12. I avoid controversy in dealing with others. ☐
13. I do not get my point across well. ☐
14. It is difficult for me to make small talk with others. ☐
15. I boast too much about my accomplishments. ☐
16. I strive too much for individual recognition instead of looking to credit the team. ☐
17. Self-confidence is my weak point. ☐
18. My spoken messages are too bland. ☐
19. My written messages are too bland. ☐
20. I relate poorly to people from cultures different from my own. ☐
21. I read people poorly. ☐
22. I display a lot of nervous mannerisms when I am working in a group. ☐
23. I do a poor job of making a presentation in front of others. ☐
24. I multitask, such as receiving a phone call, while talking to another person face-to-face. ☐
25. _____ ☐

(Fill in your own statement.)

Now that you (and perhaps one or two others) have identified specific behaviors that may require change, draw up an action plan. Describe briefly a plan of attack for bringing about the change you hope to achieve for each statement that is checked. Ideas might come from personal development books or from leadership development and human relations workshops. After formulating an action plan, you will need self-discipline for its successful implementation. For example, if you checked, "People find me boring," you might want to expand your fund of knowledge by extensive reading and by talking to dynamic people. You will then need the self-discipline to continue your quest for ideas and to incorporate some of these ideas into your conversation.

Another approach to this exercise is for each student to choose one developmental need, combined with an action plan, that he or she is willing to share with others. Next, students present their developmental need and action plan to the rest of the class. After all students have presented, a class discussion is held about whatever observations and generalizations students have reached.

personal and work lives. In contrast, others possess a fixed mindset, whereby they believe that talents are innate and will carry them to the top without the need for modification.[9]

DEVELOPMENT THROUGH EDUCATION, EXPERIENCE, AND MENTORING

Much of leadership development takes place through means other than self-awareness and self-discipline or leadership development programs. Leadership is such a comprehensive process that almost any life activity can help people prepare for a leadership role. Three important life and work experiences that contribute to leadership development are education, experience as a leader, and mentoring. In the next several pages, we look at the link between each of these three factors and leadership.

Education

Education generally refers to acquiring knowledge without concern about its immediate application. If a potential leader studies mathematics, the logical reasoning acquired might someday help him or her solve a complex problem facing the organization. As a result, the leader's stature is enhanced. Reading biographies and autobiographies about successful people is a good source of ideas about leadership. Formal education is positively correlated with achieving managerial and leadership positions. Furthermore, there is a positive relationship between the amount of formal education and the level of leadership position attained.

The correlation between education and leadership status, however, may not reflect causation. Many people get the opportunity to hold a business leadership position *only if* they have achieved a specified level of education. A more important issue than the statistical association between leadership and formal education is *how* education contributes to leadership effectiveness.

Most high-level leaders are intelligent, well-informed people who gather knowledge throughout their career. The knowledge that accrues from formal education and self-study provides them with information for innovative problem solving. Being intellectually alert also helps them exert influence through logical persuasion.

Experience

On-the-job experience is an obvious contributor to leadership effectiveness. Without experience, knowledge cannot readily be converted into skills. For example, you will need experience to put into practice the appropriate influence tactics you studied in Chapter 10. Leadership experience also helps build skills and insights that a person may not have formally studied. Many company leadership development programs focus on giving participants varied experiences, such as Yum Brands requiring that executive leaders obtain experience managing a store.

Challenging Experiences The best experiences for leadership development are those that realistically challenge the manager, including dealing with stressful problems. Creating an environment for development requires that an organization first rid itself of the belief in survival of the fittest. The goal of leadership development is to provide meaningful development opportunities, not to push managers to the point where they are most likely to fail.[10] An example of a stretch experience for many managers is being placed in charge of an organizational unit with low productivity and morale. The manager would need to apply many leadership skills to improve the situation.

Today, well-regarded business executive James Smisek is the CEO of the world's largest airline carrier, United/Continental. He developed his airline leadership skills the hard way as part of the team that rescued Continental from near death in the mid-1990s—an extremely challenging experience. The turnaround has become a classic case study.[11]

Failure is a special type of challenging experience that contributes enormously to reaching one's leadership potential. One reason is that people who have never failed have avoided taking big risks. Richard Branson, the flamboyant chair of Virgin Atlantic Airways Limited, claims that "the best developer of a leader is failure." An effective way of capitalizing on failure is to reflect on what you might do differently in the future. Ask yourself questions such as "What would have to change inside me to enable me to do things differently?"[12] For example, perhaps the project failed because you did not provide enough guidance to the group and did not communicate a sense of urgency. In the future, you might lead with more control and assertion. Table 15-1 lists a number of powerful learning experiences for developing leadership and managerial skills.

An important part of capitalizing on challenging experiences is for the leader or manager to be given leeway in choosing how to resolve the problem. A team

TABLE 15-1 Powerful Learning Experiences for Developing Leadership Skills

Research with managers has revealed fifteen types of powerful learning experiences that contribute to one's development as a leader and manager.

1. *Unfamiliar responsibilities*. Responsibilities are new, quite different, or much broader than previous ones. As a result, the situation requires skills and abilities beyond a person's current competencies.

2. *Proving yourself*. There is pressure to show others that one can get the job done.

3. *Developing new directions*. The leader is responsible for starting something new, implementing a reorganization, or responding to rapid changes in the business environment.

4. *Inherited problems*. The manager must fix problems created by a former manager or is handed the responsibility for problem employees.

5. *Downsizing decisions*. The manager must make decisions about shutting down operations or reducing staff.

6. *Dealing with problem employees*. The group members lack adequate experience, are incompetent, or are resistant.

7. *Facing high stakes*. The manager is faced with tight deadlines, pressure from senior management, high visibility, and responsibility for success and failure.

8. *Managing business complexity*. The job is large in scope, and the manager is responsible for multiple functions, groups, products, customers, or markets.

9. *Role overload*. The size of the job requires a large investment of time and energy. An example is that suddenly you deal with a customer request far beyond the capacity of the company to handle.

10. *Handling external pressure*. The manager is forced to deal with external factors that affect the business, such as negotiating with unions or government agencies or coping with serious community problems.

11. *Having to exert influence without authority*. To accomplish the job, it is necessary to influence peers, higher management, external parties, or other key people over whom one has no formal control.

12. *Adverse business conditions*. The business unit faces a drop in revenues or a drastic budget cut. For example, it becomes necessary to raise funds from investors and you have to be humble and almost beg for money.

13. *Lack of top management support*. Senior management is reluctant to provide direction, support, or resources for the manager's major work activities or for a new project.

14. *Lack of personal support*. The manager is excluded from key networks and receives little encouragement from others about the work activities.

15. *Difficult boss*. A personality clash with the boss is evident, or he or she is incompetent.

Source: Adapted from C. McCauley, M. Ruderman, P. Ohlott, and J. Morrow, "Assessing the Developmental Components of Managerial Jobs," *Journal of Applied Psychology* 79, 4 (1994), pp. 544–560. Copyright © 1994 by the American Psychological Association. Adapted with permission. Point 1 is also derived from Gretchen M. Spreitzer, "Leadership Development Lessons from Positive Organizational Studies," *Organizational Dynamics*, Issue No. 4, 2006, p. 307. Points 7 and 12 are also derived from "Moments of Truth: Global Executives Talk about the Challenges That Shaped Them as Leaders," *Harvard Business Review*, January 2007, pp. 16, 17.

leader, for example, might be told, "Increase productivity by 10 percent and, at the same time, decrease costs by 10 percent." The team leader would have the developmental opportunity of finding a solution to this challenge.

Extremely challenging experiences are sometimes referred to as **crucibles**— critical events and experiences that more often reflect failure than grand success. The crucible demands that leaders step up and do something they have never done before, such as rescuing a failing business or rebuilding after a hurricane has struck a key business location.[13]

Sources of Experience   The two major developmental factors in any work situation are work associates and the task itself.[14] Work associates can help a person develop in myriad ways. An immediate superior can be a positive or negative model of effective leadership. You might observe how your boss skillfully confronts a cost overrun problem during a staff meeting. You observe carefully and plan to use a similar technique when it becomes necessary for you to confront a problem with a group. In contrast, assume that your boss's confrontational approach backfires and the group becomes defensive and recalcitrant. You have learned how not to confront. Members of upper management, peers, and reporting staff can also help a worker profit from experience. For example, by trial and error, the worker might learn which type of praise is best for influencing others.

Work-related tasks can also contribute to leadership development because part of a leader's role is to be an effective and innovative problem solver. The tasks that do most to foster development are those that are more complex and ambiguous than a person has faced previously. Starting a new activity for a firm, such as establishing a dealer network, exemplifies a developmental experience.

An extreme approach to developing leadership skills is to be assigned responsibility for an area in which you lack the appropriate skills or knowledge of the business. An example would be appointing an operations manager as the director of marketing. According to Matt Paese of Development Dimensions International, leadership ability is the most effective way of succeeding in areas where you lack technical expertise. Among the specific leadership skills would be consulting with people who have the necessary expertise and exuding self-confidence, yet not being arrogant.[15]

Broad Experience   Many aspects of leadership are situational. A sound approach to improving leadership effectiveness is therefore to gain managerial experience in different settings. An aspirant to executive leadership is well advised to gain management experience in at least two different organizational functions, such as marketing and operations.

A widespread practice is to assign managers to cross-functional teams to give them experience in working with other disciplines. The more urgent the purpose of the team, the more likely meaningful leadership development will take place. Achieving broad experience fits well with the current emphasis on growth through learning new skills rather than a preoccupation with vertical mobility. For example, more professionals today than in the past are willing to take a lateral move instead of a promotion if there is an opportunity to acquire new skills. For example, the manager of market research might be content to become a sales manager (a position at about the same level) in order to enhance his or her skill portfolio.

A particularly effective type of broad experience early in a career is to perform technical work in one's specialty, and combine it with front-line supervision. A representative example is Justin Welke, a 26-year-old who began as an operations training at a Nestlé factory:

> At a factory in Illinois, Welke quickly implemented a handful of cost-cutting initiatives related to his packaging degree from Michigan State University. At the same time, he supervised a team of twenty production workers. Welke's performance was recognized, and he was given a new assignment in a Utah plant where he then managed forty-four hourly workers, some older than his parents. Welke said, "Wow, I have a chance to get front-line leadership experience. That's something I couldn't get in a corporate role."[16]

As implied by double-loop learning, experience is the most beneficial when the person extracts value from what is happening. A new term for an attribute of people who show good potential for leadership positions because they profit from experience is *catalytic learning capability*. People with this capability have the capacity to scan for new ideas, the intellectual skills to absorb them, and the practical intelligence to translate that new learning into production action for customers and organizations.[17] For example, Justin Welke, the packing specialist and supervisor, noticed that some pallets were not being used to capacity. He decided to restack cases to make room for ten more on a pallet, saving the company an estimated $60,000 per year.

The leadership portfolio that you have been maintaining will help you capitalize on experience as a source of leadership development.

Mentoring

Another experience-based way to develop leadership capability is to be coached by an experienced, knowledgeable leader. Quite often this person is a **mentor**, a more experienced person who develops a protégé's abilities through tutoring, coaching, guidance, and emotional support. Mentoring others is an important leadership responsibility. In some companies, such as Safeway, every manager from the CEO on down is supposed to be an active mentor.[18] The mentor, a trusted counselor and guide, is typically a person's manager. However, a mentor can also be a staff professional or coworker. An emotional tie exists between the person mentored and the mentor. To personalize the subject of mentoring, test your attitudes toward the process by taking Leadership Self-Assessment Quiz 15-2.

Informal versus Formal Mentoring   Mentoring is traditionally thought of as an informal relationship based on compatibility or spark between two personalities. In reality, employers often formally assign a mentor to a new employee to help him or her adjust well to the organization and to succeed. Belle Rose Ragins and John L. Cotton conducted a study comparing the effectiveness of informal versus formal mentoring programs for men and women.[19] Three occupations were studied: engineering (male dominated); social work (female dominated); and journalism (gender integrated). Formal mentoring programs were used in all three of these occupations.

LEADERSHIP SELF-ASSESSMENT QUIZ 15-2

My Attitudes Toward Mentoring

Instructions: Answer "Generally Agree" or "Generally Disagree" to the following ten statements.

	GENERALLY AGREE	GENERALLY DISAGREE
1. Many times in life I have taught useful skills to younger family members or friends.	☐	☐
2. Few people would be successful if somebody else had not given them a helping hand.	☐	☐
3. I would enjoy (or have enjoyed) being a Big Brother or Big Sister.	☐	☐
4. Experienced workers should be willing to show the ropes to less experienced workers.	☐	☐
5. I would like to be considered a good role model for others in my field.	☐	☐
6. I have very little concern that if I shared my knowledge with a less experienced person, he or she would replace me.	☐	☐
7. At least one of my teachers has been an inspirational force in my life.	☐	☐
8. I am willing to drop what I am doing to help somebody else with a work or study problem.	☐	☐
9. I am willing to share my ideas with others, even if I do not receive any credit.	☐	☐
10. Helping others contributes toward becoming immortal.	☐	☐

Scoring and Interpretation: This quiz does not have a precise scoring key. However the more of the statements that you agree with, the more likely you have the proper mental set to be a mentor.

Source: Andrew J. DuBrin, *Coaching and Mentoring Skills,* First Edition, © 2005, p. 161. Adapted with permission of Pearson Education, Inc., Upper Saddle River, N.J.

Protégés with informal mentors received greater benefits than protégés with formal mentors. Informal mentors were also perceived as more effective. The protégés with informal mentors reported that their mentors provided more career development and psychological and social support than protégés with formal mentors. Protégés with informal mentors also reported higher incomes. A possible explanation for these findings is that people who are able to attract their own mentor are more career-driven and have the type of interpersonal skills that help one earn a higher income.

Another approach to mentoring is **shadowing**, or directly observing the work activities of the mentor by following the person around for a stated period of time, such as one day per month. The protégé might be invited to strategy meetings, visits with key customers, discussions with union leaders, and the like. The protégé makes observations about how the mentor handles situations, and a debriefing session might be held to discuss how and why certain tactics were used.

Online, or virtual, mentoring is popular because sending e-mail messages and social media posts helps overcome barriers created by geography, limited time, and voice mail. The protégé might pose a career or work question to the mentor and receive a helpful reply that day. A major advantage of online mentoring is that it offers a wide pool of possible mentors and better matches between the mentor and the person mentored. Going online, you might be working in Chicago, yet have a good fit with a manager in San Francisco or London.

One innovation in online mentoring are websites that link mentors and mentored employees via profiling software, modeled after dating websites. Another innovation is virtual mentoring that makes face-to-face contact rare. With one system, an employee searching for a mentor logs onto an intranet and enters up to three career interests or skills he or she wants to develop. "Literally, in a matter of seconds you get a list of possible mentors throughout the company all over the world," says Kevin D. Gazzara, program manager of "Leading Through People" at Intel.[20]

Despite the efficiency advantage of online mentoring, some face-to-face contact with a mentor is recommended to help keep the relationship vibrant. Can you imagine somebody recommending you for promotion after having communicated with you exclusively by e-mail and a website?

Effective Mentoring Behaviors   Because many mentors are leaders, effective mentors are likely to engage in many of the behaviors of effective leaders described throughout this book. Interviews with professionals in service firms, such as consultancies and accounting firms, suggest that the following behaviors in particular are characteristic of a good mentor:

- Highly credible, and whose integrity shows through whether the message delivered is positive or negative
- If necessary, will tell you things you do not want to hear, but listens to you
- Interacts with you in a way that makes you want to improve your effectiveness
- Makes you feel secure enough to be willing to take risks
- Helps boost your self-confidence enough to put aside your inner doubts and fears
- Encourages you to set stretch goals for yourself
- Presents opportunities and points to challenges you might not have seen on your own[21]

The behaviors just listed are examples of contributions by a mentor that can assist the protégé develop as a leader.

Impact on Leadership   Mentors enhance the career of protégés in many ways, such as by recommending them for promotion and helping them establish valuable contacts. High-level leaders sometimes use mentors as a way of obtaining useful feedback. Coaching can be a component of mentoring. Mentors demonstrating a high level of involvement tend to coach apprentices on how they handle certain leadership assignments. The mentor is usually not physically present when the protégé is practicing leadership. Alternatively, the protégé recaps a leadership situation and asks for a critique. Wendy Lopez, the operations manager for a payroll services firm, recounts a mentoring session with her boss about a leadership incident:

> I explained to Max [her mentor and the vice president of administration] that I had some trouble motivating my supervisors to pitch in with weekend work. We had received a surge of new clients because many firms had decided to downsize their own payroll departments. Our group was having trouble adjusting to the new workload. Instead of operations running smoothly, things were a little spastic. Although I tried to explain the importance of getting out the work, the supervisors were still dragging their heels a little.
>
> Max reviewed the incident with me. He told me that I might have helped the supervisors take a broader view of what this new business meant to the firm. Max felt I did not communicate clearly enough how the future of our firm was at stake. He also suggested that I should have been more specific about how pitching in during an emergency would benefit the supervisors financially.
>
> With Max's coaching behind me, I did a much better job of enlisting cooperation the next time an emergency surfaced.

Another way in which mentors further the development of potential leaders is to help them understand the political aspects of the organization. Many career professionals search for ways to navigate the tough and competitive terrain of the world of business, and such navigation is difficult without being mentored.[22]

A challenge in having a strong mentor is to at some point graduate from mentorship. Your mentor may have given you credibility and connections for a long time, but at some point you have to emerge from the shelter of that shadow in order to be perceived as a leader with your own strengths. Detaching yourself from a strong mentor is often facilitated by a few accomplishments of your own, outside your mentor's jurisdiction.[23]

The Importance of Having More than One Mentor   Case histories collected by Dawn E. Chandler and Lillian Eby emphasize the importance of having a backup mentor. The problem is that mentoring relationships are often fragile, and problems can occur. One potential problem is that the mentor might perceive the protégé to be a rival and therefore attempt to damage the latter's career through such means as badmouthing. A more common problem is that the mentor may wind up neglecting the protégé because the former becomes preoccupied with his or her own job responsibilities. Having more than one mentor at a time helps alleviate both problems.[24]

LEADERSHIP DEVELOPMENT PROGRAMS

A time-honored strategy for developing prospective, new, and practicing leaders is to enroll them in leadership development programs. Many management development programs are also aimed at leadership development. The difference, however, is that management development programs offer courses that cover hundreds of topics within the functions of planning, organizing, controlling, and leading. About 20 percent of all money spent on employee training and

TABLE 15-2 A Sampling of Leadership Development Programs Offered by Universities and Training and Development Firms

The Executive Program (four-week program for senior executives involved in the strategic management of their firms)

The Exceptional Leader: Action Steps for Leadership Formation

Reinventing Your Business Strategy

Business Ethics for the Professional Manager

The Disney Approach to Leadership Excellence

Leading Change and Innovation

Transforming Your Leadership Strategy

Building Better Work Relationships

Implementing Successful Organizational Change

Managing People for Maximum Performance

Portfolio Management

Developing Exemplary Leaders: Key Practices for Achieving Results

The Voice of Leadership: How Leaders Inspire, Influence, and Achieve Results

The People Side of Great Business

Capitalizing on Social Media for Marketing and Internal Communications

Developing and Managing a Successful Technology and Product Strategy

Note: Organizations offering such seminars and courses are the Wharton School of the University of Pennsylvania, the University of Michigan Business School, the University of Chicago Graduate School of Business, the Cornell University School of Industrial and Labor Relations, the Massachusetts Institute of Technology, MIT Sloan School of Management, the Center for Creative Leadership, the Center for Management Research, the American Management Association, Dale Carnegie Training, the World Business Forum, Stanford Executive Briefings and DVD Programs. and the Disney Institute.

development is invested in leadership training and development. Table 15-2 lists a sample of leadership development programs.

Leadership development has become a heavy priority for many major business and government organizations. A case in point is the opinion of Eric Wiseman, the CEO of VF Corp, which carries such brands as Wrangler, Lee, and Nautica. In formulating his plans for growth, he said, "I need a strong financial lever, and that's never been more important than it is now. I need brands that are winning against the competition. And I need talent. Money and brands don't do me any good if I don't have the talent."[25]

An analysis conducted by *Fortune* concluded that no matter what business a company is in, the real business is building leaders. Without a cadre of effective current and future leaders, a company would lose its competitive edge. Part of the reason is that leaders are either responsible for providing innovative ideas or for creating the conditions that foster innovation (refer back to Chapter 13). One of the forces compelling companies to develop leaders is the world economy's shift from dependency on financial capital toward human capital. The general picture of developing leaders is to make such development part of the culture, including mentoring and offering constructive feedback on performance.[26] The more specific picture of leadership development is presented next.

Developing and training leaders is far more complex than merely sending aspiring leaders to a one-week seminar. The leadership development program has to be appropriately sponsored, carefully designed, and professionally executed.

Types of Leadership Development Programs

In practice, the various programs for developing leaders often overlap. For ease of comprehension, we divide these programs into seven categories: feedback-intensive programs, those based on skills, conceptual knowledge and awareness, personal growth, socialization, action learning, and coaching and psychotherapy.

Feedback-Intensive Programs   As implied at many places in this text, an important vehicle for developing as a leader is to obtain feedback on various aspects of your behavior. **A feedback-intensive development program** helps leaders develop by seeing more clearly their patterns of behaviors, the reasons for such behaviors, and the impact of these behaviors and attitudes on their effectiveness. Such a program also helps leaders or potential leaders find more constructive ways of achieving their goals.

An instructive point about feedback-intensive programs, as well as practically all forms of leadership development, is that the person being developed needs to follow up. If you learn that you tend to shut people off with an angry smirk on your face, unless you practice removing that smirk, you have not gained much from the feedback. In the words of leadership coach Marshall Goldsmith, "If you go to a class and don't do any follow-up, it's a complete waste of time."[27]

Skill-Based Programs   Skill training in leadership development involves acquiring abilities and techniques that can be converted into action. Acquiring knowledge precedes acquiring skills, but in skill-based training the emphasis is on learning how to apply knowledge. A typical example would be for a manager to develop coaching skills so he or she can be a more effective face-to-face leader. Skills training, in short, involves a considerable element of how to.

Five different methods are often used in skill-based leadership training: lecture, case study, role play, behavioral role modeling, and simulations. Since the first three methods are quite familiar, only the last two are described here. *Behavioral role modeling* is an extension of role playing and is based on social learning theory. You first observe a model of appropriate behavior, and then you role-play the behavior and gather feedback. A person might observe a video of a trainer giving positive reinforcement, then role-play giving positive reinforcement. Finally, the classroom trainer and the other participants would offer feedback on performance.

Simulations give participants the opportunity to work on a problem that simulates a real organization. In a typical simulation, participants receive a hard copy or computerized packet of information about a fictitious company. The participants are given details such as the organization chart, the company's financial status, descriptions of the various departments, and key problems facing the organization and/or organizational units. Participants then play the roles of company leaders and devise solutions to the problems. During the debriefing, participants receive feedback on the content of their solutions to problems and the methods they used. The group might be told, for example, "Your decision to form a strategic alliance was pretty good, but I would have liked to have seen more group decision making."

A pioneering approach to simulations for leadership development is the use of multiple online role-playing fantasy games such as *Star Wars Galaxies*. One component of *Galaxies* is to make useful products and then market the products on game planets. Players advance by keeping the supply chain filled and satisfying customer demands. The players who lead teams in these online fantasies hone their business leadership skills. According to the developers of this type of simulation, the computer game helps develop the leadership skills of speed, risk taking, and the acceptance of leadership roles as being temporary.[28] Participants who have previously acquired gaming skills are fascinated by this approach to leadership development.

Conceptual Knowledge and Awareness Programs A standard university approach to leadership development is to equip people with a conceptual understanding of leadership. The concepts are typically supplemented by experiential activities such as role playing and cases. Conceptual knowledge is very important because it alerts the leader to information that will make a difference in leadership. For example, if a person studies how a leader brings about transformations, he or she can put these ideas into practice. The World Business Forum is a leadership development program for well-established managers that offers considerable conceptual knowledge. The presenters are well-known executives, business professors, and authors. For example, Howard Schultz of Starbuck's makes a presentation called "Managing Vision and Culture: The Makings of a Global Brand." Table 15-2 presents examples of the types of conceptual knowledge contained in leadership development programs.

One of the reasons for the continuing acceptance of university-based conceptual knowledge programs for leadership development is that these programs often address topics of immediate concern to business. For example, when the world was facing a financial crisis in 2008, several management development programs brought in economists who had first-hand knowledge of financial crises.

Personal Growth Programs Leadership development programs that focus on personal growth assume that leaders are deeply in touch with their personal dreams and talents and that they will act to fulfill them. Therefore, if people can get in touch with their inner desires and fulfill them, they will become leaders. A tacit assumption in personal-growth training programs is that leadership is almost a calling. The executive leadership development program at PepsiCo, Inc., focuses on personal growth and business topics such as corporate strategy, ethics, and bringing about change and innovation. Jim Loehr, the psychologist heading the program, challenges the participants to reflect about their lives and identify something they want to change that will give them more energy and improved motivational skills.[29]

Socialization Programs From the company standpoint, an essential type of leadership development program emphasizes becoming socialized—becoming acclimated to the company and accepting its vision and values. Senior executives make presentations in these programs because they serve as role models who thoroughly understand the vision and values participants are expected to perpetuate.[30] Many of the other types of programs presented so far also include a segment on socialization, particularly in the kickoff session. Quite frequently the chief executive makes a presentation of the company's vision and values.

The Walt Disney World Resort exemplifies a company that emphasizes leaders, as well as other workers, understanding the organizational culture in order to function well. Lee Cockerell, the former executive vice president at Disney, said this about his efforts at employee development: "I thought of myself a chief environmentalist—keeping the culture alive during tough times. The number one factor of any business is good customer service. And the quality of leadership directly translates to better [profit] margins."[31]

Action Learning Programs A directly practical approach to leadership development is for leaders and potential leaders to work together in groups to solve organizational problems outside their usual sphere of influence. You will recall that action learning is part of the learning organization, as described in Chapter 14. Much of the development relates to problem solving and creativity, yet collaborating with a new set of people from your firm can also enhance interpersonal skills.

Action learning is also referred to as experiential learning, and a key proponent is Boeing. The company has been strongly interested in employee wellness for a long time. A few years ago, as part of an action learning project, a group was assigned the task of studying ways to make Boeing facilities tobacco free.[32] As part of the action learning members have ample opportunity to develop team leadership skills.

A variation on action learning for leadership development is to assign managers to socially responsible projects that are not part of company operations. Natural Cosmeticos of Brazil sends managers to work full time organization and building nongovernmental organizations, such as hospitals, clinics, and community centers. The responsibility helps develop leadership skills as well as a first-hand view of the importance of social responsibility.[33]

Action learning often carries with it an element of consciousness raising because the leaders might develop a first-hand awareness of the challenges facing another group. An example of this type of activity took place at Ford Motor Company. Functional and unit business heads talked with board members, managers, and staff members at Homes for Black Children, an adoption agency in inner city Detroit, Michigan. The Ford leaders shared life stories, day-to-day challenges, and goals with their nonprofit counterparts.[34] When the

Ford executives helped the agency leaders deal with some of the problems facing Homes for Black Children, action learning took place.

Coaching and Psychotherapy   Executive coaching as described in Chapter 7 is clearly a form of leadership development because the managers coached receive advice and encouragement in relation to their leadership skills. A coach, for example, might advise a leader that giving more recognition for good performance would make him a more dynamic leader.

Another highly personal way of enhancing leadership effectiveness is to undergo treatment for emotional problems that could be blocking leadership effectiveness. For example, a leader who has difficulty giving recognition might not improve in response to coaching. The person might have underlying problems of being so hostile toward people that he or she really does not want to boost their morale. Psychotherapy might help, but positive changes are not always forthcoming. Psychiatrist Kerry Sulkowicz notes that change does not always take place quickly. However, executives are accustomed to getting quick results, which can make them highly motivated patients.[35] In general, leaders who score low on the personality dimension of emotional stability might become more effective in their interpersonal relationships with the benefit of psychotherapy. Some of the bizarre behavior exhibited by executives, such as swearing at and belittling subordinates, sexually harassing subordinates, and arbitrarily firing workers, are symptoms of psychological problems.

Although online learning supplements leadership development, face-to-face interaction with other leaders and course presenters will most likely remain popular. Leadership development programs for C-level executives are unlikely to be conducted online because executives believe that face-to-face contact with professors and other executives is an important part of the learning process.

Many companies evaluate their leadership development programs to see if they are cost effective. In a large company, for example, a comparison would be made of the ratings from superiors and subordinates for those leaders who participated in the program versus those who did not. Another method of evaluating the outcome of a leadership development program would be to compare the financial results of participants versus nonparticipants.

The accompanying Leader in Action insert illustrates the importance that a CEO of a professional services firm places on leadership development.

LEADERSHIP SUCCESSION

In a well-managed organization, replacements for executives who quit, retire, or are dismissed are chosen through **leadership succession**, an orderly process of identifying and grooming people to replace managers. Succession planning is vital to the long-term health of an organization, and therefore an important responsibility of senior leadership. Instead of engaging in a flurry of activity after a key person leaves the organization, the planning is done in an orderly way over time. Succession planning is linked to leadership development

LEADER IN ACTION

Deloitte CEO Barry Salzberg Focuses on Leadership Development

Barry Salzberg has spent his entire thirty-four-year career in one place, climbing the corporate ladder at Deloitte LLP. From his first unsupportive manager at the New York–based professional services firm to the mentors who helped pull him up through the ranks, Salzberg learned to lead and be led. He became the CEO of Deloitte in the United States in 2007, and four years later the global chief executive officer of Deloitte Touche Tohmatsu Limited.

His message for the next generation of leaders is that the old leadership hierarchy no longer works. "Gone is the day of the old command-and-control environment, the climb-the-ladder model, in which the employee kept quiet and didn't say too much beyond what was asked and tasked," Salzberg told his audience at a Wharton Leadership Lecture. "Gone, too, is the densely layered organizational hierarchy and dinosaur-like structures that are too slow and lumbering for today's environment."

Instead, Salzberg said, today's leadership needs to be flat and transparent. And to thrive in an ever-changing world, companies must actively commit to cultivating younger leaders throughout the organization, encouraging older leaders to pass on what they know. "No longer is leadership about a few exceptional leaders at the top of the organization. Rather, the future is about exceptional teams and the leaders within those teams who can out-maneuver, out-manage, and out-innovate their competition."

Leaders today must also be transparent, said Salzberg. "In today's social media environment, it's fascinating to see how in ten seconds what you say is spread throughout the organization. There are few hiding places."

As Salzberg grew and matured in the organization, he took on many leadership roles and became a partner in 1985. "Then, as now, you need an advocate to make partner. You need a mentor," he pointed out. "While mentoring was naturally part of the process, it was not a hard-and-fast requirement. Rather, it was something you did if you kind of felt like it. It was optional, and nobody really monitored it. As I look back on it, the old model left too much to chance as far as developing leaders."

Salzberg's new approach to developing leadership is a stand-alone, bricks-and-mortar university where Deloitte professionals can go to teach and learn—a $300 million initiative. The 100-plus acre campus in Westlake, Texas, is dedicated to the idea that leaders must learn from other leaders. "Call it 'apprenticeship' if you will. It's an age-old model for turning the young into the talented, experienced professionals and leaders."

The university gives Deloitte professionals a chance to share their experience and wisdom with the next generation. "The best leaders are generous with their experience, time, and understanding that leadership is a life-long journey that is best made with trusted companions. If you have become a leader, the likelihood is that someone mentored you. Someone helped you. Someone championed your career."

QUESTIONS

1. Which style of leadership described at any place in this text does Salzberg appear to be advocating?
2. What advice about developing yourself as a leader might you take away from Salzberg's comments?
3. What is your opinion of the probable return on investment from a professional services spending $300 million on constructing a leadership university?

Source: Excerpted and adapted slightly from "Deloitte CEO Barry Salzberg on Leadership as 'the Norm, Not the Exception'," *Knowledge @Wharton* (http://knowledge.wharton.upenn.edu), May 11, 2011, pp. 1–3.

in two important ways. First, being groomed as a successor is part of leadership development. Second, the process of choosing and fostering a successor is part of a manager's own development.

A concern about succession planning is that it is often done poorly, which results in leaders who are a poor fit for their responsibilities. Ram Charan reports that two out of five CEOs fail in their first eighteen months. The failure results from a variety of factors, such as making poor decisions about new products, demoralizing the organization, or engaging in highly unethical practices. One of the most important approaches to successful succession planning is to develop enough strong leaders within the company.[36]

Our approach to understanding the leadership aspects of succession focuses on five topics: (1) how the board chooses a new chief officer; (2) succession planning at GE and P&G; (3) the emotional aspects of leadership succession; (4) developing a pool of successors; and (5) growing inside-out leaders. Understanding these factors should lead to more success in new appointments to leadership positions.

How the Board Chooses a Successor

A major responsibility of the board of directors is to select a successor to the chief executive, typically a CEO. The general approach is to follow standard principles of human resource selection, such as thoroughly screening candidates, including speaking to several people who have worked with the individual. Conducting a background investigation to uncover any possible scandalous or illegal behavior is also important. When the successor is an outsider, boards consistently use executive search firms (also known as *headhunters*) to locate one or several candidates. Even when the board has an outside candidate in mind, a search firm might be hired to act as an intermediary.

George D. Kennedy, a person with experience on many boards, provides a few specifics of a representative approach to selecting an internal candidate for the top executive position. First, the information from a development program for successors must be carefully reviewed, including documentation of performance. Second, the board should have direct and regular contact with all of the promising candidates. Some of the contact should be formal; for example, the candidate should make regular presentations at board meetings. Informal connections are also important. Board members should invest the time to develop a feel for the personal chemistry of the candidates through such means as casual conversations over dinner and lunch.[37] (Because some of the decision making about succession is based on subjective judgments, it is imperative for CEO candidates to be skilled at organizational politics and influence tactics.)

Succession Planning at General Electric and Procter & Gamble

General Electric is often noted for its progressive and thorough management techniques. Its system for identifying and developing talent is considered exemplary. Leadership development is so important to the company that CEO Jeffrey Immelt reportedly invests 30 percent of his time to the process. GE-trained executives are in high demand at other business firms.

Much of this activity is linked closely to succession planning. Board members are closely involved in an ongoing evaluation of the company's 130 highest-ranking managers. Twice a year, directors scrutinize about 15 of these people. The information they use comes from lengthy interviews with the managers, their managers, former associates, and group members. Directors investigate the managers' strengths and weaknesses, make suggestions for leadership development, and discuss future assignments. While Jack Welch was CEO at GE, he emphasized ruthless honesty in evaluating the performance of managers and the businesses they represented. Should the day arrive when a manager must be chosen to replace a higher-level manager, the board will be prepared to make an independent decision rather than have to give automatic approval to an insider's recommendations.[38]

Key advantages of the GE system for identifying successors are that it is based on multiple opinions and that it tracks longitudinal performance. Yet the system may still be replete with political biases. The board members, for example, are not exempt from giving high ratings to the people they like the best or to people who have personal characteristics similar to theirs.

Another famous company, Procter & Gamble, has a rigorously developed succession program. Labeled Build from Within, it tracks the performance of every manager in great detail, making sure that he or she is ready for promotion. Each of the top fifty leadership positions has three replacement candidates in line. Most replacements are from within, helping reduce the 50 percent fail rate often attributed to promoting outsiders into key positions. A key part of developing successors is to give high-potential managers broad experience, such as being the assistant manager for Cascade detergent, then taking on assignments in Canada and Asia.[39]

The Emotional Aspects of Leadership Succession

Leadership succession should not be regarded as a detached, objective management process. Even financially independent executives are likely to experience an emotional loss when they are replaced; they might yearn for the power and position they once possessed. Leadership succession in family-owned firms is a highly emotional process for many reasons. Family members may fight over who is best qualified to take the helm, or the owner and founder may not feel that any family member is qualified. An intensely emotional situation exists when the owner would like a family member to succeed him or her, yet no family member is willing. The business may therefore have to be sold or simply abandoned; in any case, its identity will be lost.

The emotional aspects of leadership succession are also evident when a business founder is replaced by another leader, whether or not the enterprise is a family business. After the sale of his or her company, the business founder often stays on in some capacity, perhaps as a consultant or chair. Watching the new owner manage the business can be uncomfortable for the founder. The issue transcends concerns about delegation. Entrepreneurial leaders typically are emotionally involved in the firms they have founded and find it difficult to look on while somebody else operates the firm.

Emotional reactions to leadership succession also take place at the work-group level, as described in a theory recently developed by Gary A. Ballinger and F. David Schoorman. For example, when a departing leader is well liked by the group or team, it will be more difficult for the new leader to exert his or her authority or to be accepted. Another problem is that when the previous leader was well liked, turnover in the group will be higher and productivity might be lower. Yet, on the positive side, if the previous leader was disliked, turnover might be lower and productivity might be higher.[40]

Developing a Pool of Successors

Developing a pool of successors goes beyond succession planning, which usually involves identifying one or two candidates for a specific job. The steps involved in developing a pool of successors (or succession management) follow:[41]

- Evaluate the extent of an organization's pending leadership shortage.
- Identify needed executive competencies based on the firm's future business needs, values, and strategies.
- Identify high-potential individuals for possible inclusion in the pool, and assess these individuals to identify strengths and developmental needs to determine who will stay in the high-potential pool.
- Establish an individually tailored developmental program for each high-potential candidate that includes leadership development programs, job rotation, special assignments, and mentoring. Rising stars should be given the opportunity to change responsibilities every three to five years.
- Select and place people into senior jobs based on their performance, experience, and potential. While in these positions, the leaders should have access to board members including making presentations. The managers develop a sense of what matters to directors, and directors get to see firsthand the talent in the pipeline.
- Continuously monitor the program and give it top management support.

Developing a pool of candidates, therefore, combines evaluating potential with giving high-potential individuals the right type of developmental experiences. To the extent that these procedures are implemented, a leadership shortage in a given firm is less likely to take place.

To help preserve a strong pool of candidates for future assignments, financial services giant Aetna focuses on mentoring young managers with high potential. A specific program is that eight high-level Aetna managers, including chief executive Ronald Williams, meet one-on-one with eight target candidates for an hour each month for a year. To qualify, the protégés must have at least a decade of experience at the company and have received high perfor-mance evaluations.[42]

Growing Inside-Outside Leaders

A continuing debate related to succession planning is whether a company should promote an insider or an outsider, to a top position. Research and analysis suggest that promoting insiders with an outside perspective may be the best solution. Joseph Bower found in his analysis of 1,800 successions that companies performed substantially better when they appointed insiders to CEO. Other researchers have reached similar conclusions. Promotion from within also offers the advantage of more hope to insiders because they believe they have more opportunity for advancement within their own company.

Company insiders promoted to a top position know the company, its culture, and its people but often do not see clearly the need for radical change. Also, their many political ties may inhibit them from making some necessary person-nel shifts. Outsiders may recognize the need for a new approach but may be limited because they do not understand the company culture or the industry. Bower recommends that companies nurture *insider-outsiders*—internal candi-dates who have developed an outside perspective.

Insider-outsiders are frequently those who have considerable experience away from the company mainstream (and away from headquarters), and experience in taking on challenging opportunities. Before being selected as CEO of Procter & Gamble, A. G. Lafley, for instance, worked for years build-ing the Chinese cosmetics division of the company rather than P&G's core business.[43]

A recent study indicated that board members who are appointed as CEO outperformed other types of candidates because they represent a strong blend of insider and outsider. Board members have more company knowledge than a pure outsider. Yet at the same time they don't have the constraints of a pure insider with respect to making politically unpopular decisions or bring about painful changes. For example, it is often difficult for an insider to lay off a well-liked but under-performing executive. James McNerney at Boeing is an example of a board member who took over as CEO, and then performed quite well as the new company leader. (The former CEO resigned following a sex scandal.)[44]

CHALLENGES OF BEING A NEW LEADER

People participate in leadership development programs for two broad purposes: (1) preparing to become a leader for the first time, or (2) enhancing their leadership skills for a current position or advancement into more lead-ership responsibility. Everything that has been written in this book and discussed in your leadership course fits these two broad purposes. Another way of preparing for becoming a leader for the first time is to think through some of the inevitable challenges in the role. The information about the rewards and frustrations of occupying a leadership role in Chapter 1 points to the challenges of occupying a formal leadership position for the first time. In addition, consider these five additional challenges for the first time leader:

1. *Uncertainty about how much time to spend leading versus doing individual tasks.* From the first-level supervisor of entry-level workers to the chairperson of the board, leaders spend some time as individual contributors, including preparing budgets, thinking of ideas for new products, and making financial deals. As a new leader, you have to work with your manager and perhaps your direct reports to find the right balance between doing and leading.

2. *Overcoming the resentment of the people in the group who wanted your leadership position.* If you are selected from among the group to be the new leader, you will have to deal with the resentment and envy of several direct reports who wanted your position. It can be helpful to deal openly with the issue with such statements as, "I know that other people would be equally qualified to be the leader of the group. Yet management has chosen me for this position, at least for now. I respect your expertise, and I need your contribution. I also want your respect for me in my job as the chosen leader."

3. *Building relationships and fostering teamwork quickly enough.* As a new leader, a high priority is to build constructive relationships with subordinates as quickly as possible, using many of the techniques described in Chapter 6. Several direct reports who were your former coworkers may attempt to manipulate you and take advantage of prior friendships to receive special treatment. It is essential to build a professional, merit-based team climate as soon as possible. In the words of career coach Aya Fubara Eneli: "Friendships work best between equals. If you were already friends with some of the staff, expect those relationships to change. It's difficult to be a friend while giving orders and judging performance."[45]

4. *Having realistic expectations about how much you can accomplish right away.* The role of a leader/manager is not like that of a house painter—you typically do not see sparkling results right away. Patience is necessary. Many organizational leaders as well as elected officials proclaim, "Everything will be different from day one." Leadership involves building relationships, so the process will take time.

5. *Overcoming the need to be liked by everybody.* The most admired leaders at every level are rarely liked by everybody. By the nature of their roles, leaders make decisions that not everybody agrees with. The changes you bring about may hurt the feelings of some people and jeopardize their positions. Your role is to establish and implement goals that will result in the greatest good.

Leadership Skill-Building Exercise 15-1 may give you a few good insights into the type of leader you are becoming and how well you fit the role of a new or experienced leader.

LEADERSHIP SKILL-BUILDING EXERCISE 15-1

Building for the Future

Our close-to-final skill-building exercise, the use of a feedback circle, encompasses many aspects of leadership covered in this and the previous fourteen chapters. Ten members of the class arrange their chairs in a circle. One person is selected as the feedback target, and the other nine people take turns giving him or her supportive feedback. Assume it is Linda's turn. Each person in the circle gives Linda two pieces of feedback: (a) her best leadership attribute, and (b) how she needs to develop for the future. The feedback should take about thirty seconds per feedback

giver. After receiving input from all of the circle members, Linda is free to comment. It is then the next person's turn to be the feedback target.

Class members who are not in the circle observe the dynamics of what is happening and report their observations after the circle finishes. With diligence, the whole process will take about ninety minutes. If time permits, a new feedback circle can form. Alternatively, the class can break into several circles that operate simultaneously, or run just one circle with ten volunteers.

SUMMARY

Leadership and management development are widely practiced in a variety of organizations and take many forms, including self-development. Self-awareness involves the insightful processing of feedback about oneself to improve personal effectiveness. Single-loop learning occurs when learners seek minimum feedback that may substantially confront their basic ideas or actions. Double-loop learning occurs when people use feedback to confront the validity of the goal or values implicit in the situation; it enables the leader to learn and profit from failure. A promising area of self-awareness is for leaders to recognize their standing on two key dimensions of leadership: forceful versus enabling, and strategy versus operational.

Leadership development requires considerable self-discipline. For example, self-discipline is needed to monitor one's behavior to ensure that the necessary self-development takes place.

Education, leadership experience, and mentoring are all major contributors to leadership development. Most high-level leaders are intelligent, well-informed people who gather knowledge throughout their career. The best experiences for leadership development are those that realistically challenge

the manager. An important part of capitalizing on challenging experiences is for the leader/manager to be given leeway in how to resolve the problem. Two important aspects of leadership experience are work associates and the task itself (such as a complex and ambiguous assignment). An extreme approach to developing leadership skills is to be assigned responsibility for an area in which you lack the appropriate skills or knowledge of the business.

Broad experience is important for leadership development, as suggested by membership on a cross-functional team. An effective type of broad experience early in a career is to perform technical work in one's specialty, combined with front-line supervision. People with catalytic learning capability have good potential for leadership because they profit from experience.

Another experience-based way to develop leadership capability is to receive mentoring. Although usually an informal relationship, mentoring can also be assigned. A study showed that informal mentors typically were more helpful to a person's career than formal mentors, and informal mentoring is also associated with higher income.

The human resource department often coordinates a formal mentoring program. Shadowing is a form of mentoring. Mentors enhance the career of protégés in many ways, such as by recommending them for promotion and helping them establish valuable contacts. Also, the mentor can serve as a model for effective (or ineffective) leadership. Having more than one mentor is helpful because a mentoring relationship can fail.

Feedback-intensive development programs help leaders develop by seeing more clearly their patterns of behavior, the reasons for such behaviors, and the impact of these behaviors and attitudes on their effectiveness. Skill training in leadership development involves acquiring abilities and techniques that can be converted into action. Such training involves a considerable element of *how to*. Five methods of skill-based training are lecture, case study, role play, behavior role modeling, and simulations. During simulations, participants play the role of company leaders and devise solutions to problems. Feedback on performance is provided.

A standard university approach to leadership development is to equip people with a conceptual understanding of leadership. The concepts can be applied to leadership situations. Personal growth experiences for leadership development assume that leaders are deeply in touch with their personal dreams and talents and will act to fulfill them. Another emphasis in these programs is learning who you need to be. From the company standpoint, an essential type of leadership development is becoming socialized in the company vision and values. Action learning is a directly practical approach to leadership development and may be directed at areas outside the participant's expertise.

Coaching and psychotherapy are two highly personal ways of developing as a leader. Psychotherapy is called for when the leader has emotional problems that lower his or her effectiveness.

Leadership succession is linked to leadership development because being groomed as a successor is part of a leader's development. Boards of directors use standard selection methods in choosing a CEO. In addition, they look for both formal and informal contact with insiders. When recruiting an outsider, organizations often employ executive search firms. General Electric and Procter & Gamble are examples of companies that use rigorous succession planning. Leadership succession is highly emotional for the leader who is being replaced, especially when a founder sells a business. The succession problem in a family business often leads to conflict among family members. Large family-run businesses are more likely to identify leadership successors. One way to cope with potential shortages of leaders is to identify a pool of high-potential individuals and provide them with developmental experiences. Research and analysis suggest that promoting company insiders with an outside perspective may be the best solution to succession through an internal versus an external candidate.

One way of preparing for becoming a first-time leader is to think through some of the inevitable challenges in the role, including the following: uncertainty about how much time for leading versus doing individual tasks; overcoming resentment of people who wanted your job; quickly building relationships and fostering teamwork; having realistic expectations about quick accomplishments; and overcoming the need to be liked by everybody.

KEY TERMS

self-awareness	crucibles	feedback-intensive development program
single-loop learning	mentor	leadership succession
double-loop learning	shadowing	
self-discipline		

✔ GUIDELINES FOR ACTION AND SKILL DEVELOPMENT

A major determinant of whether a person will develop as a leader later in life is the *motivation to lead*. Typically this motivation develops early in life.

The motivation is manifested in such activities as volunteering for leadership roles, as well as taking the initiative to lead in sport, club, or neighborhood activities.[46] It is therefore important to assume leadership roles in both work and personal life as early in your career as possible.

An important method for enhancing both the acceptance and the effectiveness of leadership development is needs analysis, the diagnosis of the needs for development. A needs analysis is based on the idea that there are individual differences among leaders and future leaders. For example, Jasmine might have excellent conceptual knowledge about leadership but limited team experience. She might be a good candidate for outdoor training. Jordan might be an excellent team leader with limited conceptual knowledge. He might be a good candidate for a leadership development program concentrating on formal knowledge about leadership. Sources of data for assessing leadership developmental needs include the following:

1. Self-perceptions of developmental needs, including the results of many of the diagnostic instruments presented in this text
2. Perceptions by superiors, subordinates, and peers of the person's developmental needs, including 360-degree survey results
3. Psychological evaluation of developmental needs
4. A statement of organizational needs for development, such as the importance of leaders who can deal effectively with diversity (within the company, with customers, and globally)

Multiple sources of data are useful because of possible errors in perception, biases, and favoritism.

Discussion Questions and Activities

1. Assuming that you have the physical capabilities, would you be willing to participate in the FDNY Firefighter for a Day Team Challenge as part of your leadership and teamwork skills development? Explain your logic.
2. Many business executives believe that playing team sports helps a person develop as a leader. Based on your knowledge of leadership development, where do you stand on this issue?
3. Where can a person get some honest feedback about his or her leadership ability?
4. Suppose you aspired to become a senior manager in a large company. How would working as an office supervisor, production supervisor, or manager in a quick-service restaurant help you achieve your goal?
5. Why is being a member of a cross-functional team considered to be helpful experience for a future leader?
6. A recent leadership development activity is to train accounting managers in humor to help them relate better to both subordinates and clients. How reasonable does this specific approach to leadership development seem to you?
7. Identify at least one developmental need with respect to leadership skills for the current president of the United States. Point to any specific behavior of the president that indicates the need for the particular development you specify. (Attempt to be objective rather than political in your answer.)
8. What can you as a parent, future parent, or close relative do to help a child under ten years old become a leader later in life?
9. Ask an experienced leader what he or she thinks is the most effective method of developing leadership skills. Bring your findings back to class.
10. Now that you have completed a course in leadership, what do you think of this ancient adage: "Leadership shouldn't be a popularity contest."

LEADERSHIP CASE PROBLEM A

Malcolm Eyes the Executive Suite

Malcolm Gupta comes from a family whose members include many successful business executives, including his parents. Since he was a teenager, Malcolm has been fascinated with the prospects of becoming a corporate executive. In addition to more typical teenage interests, Malcolm would frequently read the business section of his local newspaper, *The Wall Street Journal* and *Forbes*. He also enthusiastically read biographies of business executives including Warren Buffet, Donald Trump, and Martha Stewart.

Malcolm studied industrial engineering as an undergraduate, thinking that such a program would give him a solid base for understanding the operations of a business. He followed up his undergraduate degree with an MBA, with an emphasis on leadership and organizational behavior. Malcolm said to himself, his family, and friends repeatedly, "I know I have what it takes to get to the corner office."

With first-rate interpersonal skills to match his solid education, Malcolm was well received by an on-campus recruiter for a major player in the high-tech field, a manufacturer of computer equipment and services. He was chosen to a management training program in which he would be given approximately one-year assignments in several business functions. His initial assignment was as a member of a team whose purpose was to help reduce the manufacturing costs of desktop computers.

Six weeks after being assigned to the team, Malcolm informed his team leader that he was developing his skills in Mandarin Chinese, a language he had studied in college. As Malcolm explained to his team leader, "Chinese is going to help me because so much of our manufacturing is outsourced to China. And besides, a second language can only be an asset for a future executive leader."

After about fifteen months on the team, Malcolm was appointed as the supervisor of an order-fulfillment group within a distribution center of the company within the same manufacturing complex.

Upon accepting the distribution-center assignment, Malcolm told his new manager, "I will do my best to be an outstanding performer here. But I am wondering if spending time in a distribution center will really enhance my credentials for becoming an executive in this company."

Upon completing his eighteen-month supervisory assignment, Malcolm's performance was evaluated. His boss noted that his performance was slightly above average but that he seemed a little too focused on his career ambitions and not focused enough on the good of the company. Malcolm's next assignment was as a team leader of a logistics group that kept track of the flow of equipment that manufactured overseas. Given that about 80 percent of the company's manufacturing was globally outsourced, logistics was highly valued at the company.

A few weeks after Malcolm began his new assignment, he met with his company assigned mentor, Jessica Magnum, a manufacturing executive. Asked how his work was going at the company, Malcolm replied: "Maybe you can help me. I'm enjoying my work, but I think that my career is inching along, when I should be making big strides. I would like to be assigned to a strategy team, or maybe a new product development team. In this way I would get the experience and the visibility I need to move more quickly into the corner office."

Jessica responded, "Malcolm, I think highly of you, but your idea of career progress is old fashioned. You need to focus more on performance than promotion."

Questions

1. In what way is this case about leadership development?
2. What would you recommend that Malcolm do to facilitate his path to an executive position?
3. To what extent do you think Jessica's comment is justified?

ASSOCIATED ROLE PLAY

Malcolm's Big Aspirations

One person plays the role of Malcolm who has arranged to have a brief meeting with Peter, the director of management and organization development at the company. Malcolm wants to plead his case that he has the potential to be an executive in the company. He wants to make sure that he is not overlooked by the company. Peter listens but wants to avoid making any commitments to Malcolm. At the same time, Peter thinks that perhaps Malcolm is expecting too much too soon from the company. Observers might want to look for signs of leadership potential Malcolm displays during his interview.

LEADERSHIP CASE PROBLEM B

No-Holds-Barred Feedback in Aspen

Ten managers representing ten different organizations gathered at a resort in Aspen, Colorado, during late summer. The purpose was a three-day leadership development seminar, with Virginia Abrazzo as the seminar leader. For two-and-one-half days, the group engaged in a variety of activities, including lectures about strategic leadership, problem-solving groups, and scavenger hunting. The group also dined together and went on nature hikes in the mountains.

As the group gathered for its final leadership-development session, Abrazzo instructed the group, "Here we are for the grand finale. All of you have been working together, and most likely observing each other, since you arrived here two-and-one-half days ago. You are now going to experience something that could change your life, as well as make you a better leader.

"Every manager in this room is going to receive candid feedback from the nine other managers who have worked with you at our leadership development seminar. We begin by placing one of you in the center of a circle, or the hot seat. Each of the other nine participants, one by one, will look you in the eye and give you feedback about you, as a person and as a leader. After you have received your feedback from the nine other participants, you will be given a few minutes to respond."

Loads of nervous laughter arose from the group. One of the participants, Gary, said, "What's going on here? How is this ridiculous exercise going to help me get a better return on investment for our stockholders?"

Virginia replied, "Gary, you are being too defensive. Let's give this a try. You'll see the value later."

Next, Virginia smiled and said, "Who would like to go first?" Stan, an operations head from an office-building construction company, said, "I feel suicidal today, so I'll go first." Stan's feedback proceeded as follows:

Marilyn: Stan, I think you are a nice guy. I would like to have a beer with you. But I think you try too hard to be liked. Ease up a bit on your likeableness.

Bud: Stan, I don't think you are as nice as you appear on the surface. It's a little bit of a façade. When you get serious, you are a determined tiger. I think the combo makes you a really effective leader.

Derek: Hey, Stan, I noticed that you look a little nervous when you are under pressure. Like right now. If you could control your nervous tics, you would be a better leader. Look, you are scratching your face right now.

Sara: Stan, I think you really have it as a leader. I notice that you can talk financials with the best of us. Yet at the same time you are likeable and approachable. I'm going to give you a gold star and a hug.

Gerry: You didn't make much of an impression on me, either good or bad, Stan. And that could be a problem. A leader should stand out. You need to have a stronger presence.

Bill: Stan, I notice that you are hesitant to criticize, even when you know the other person is wrong. Remember the other day when Marilyn had the wackiest idea about downsizing I ever heard? I could tell from your face that you disagreed with her strongly, yet you just smiled.

Lori: Don't let all this negativity get you down, Stan. You are a straight shooter with lots of potential. I think you just need to tweak your being firm with people a little. You could be just a little more assertive.

Hugh: You look pretty good to me as a leader. But can't you change your hairdo? The way you style your hair makes you look like Donald Trump. Are you imitating The Donald because you are in the building development business? [Burst of laughter from the group.]

Nancy: I find it interesting that another man would be so concerned about your hairstyle, Stan. I think you have loads of leadership qualities. Yet, I think you need to improve a little on how comfortably you feel working with woman as equals. I noticed a little sexist behavior, like pulling out the chair for me when I entered the conference room.

Stan: Thanks for all the feedback. Maybe I felt suicidal for a good reason. But seriously, I have learned a lot that will help me. I recognize that I also have a lot to work on to develop further as a leader.

Stan left the hot seat with a smile. Attention then shifted to giving feedback to the other nine participants.

Questions

1. What value, if any, do you see in this type of feedback for purposes of leadership development?
2. What specific suggestions for development do you think Stan should take away from this feedback session?
3. If you were Virginia, the seminar leader, would you have reacted to Hugh's feedback about Stan's hairstyle? Why or why not?

ASSOCIATED ROLE PLAY

Recovering from Negative Feedback

One person plays the role of a participant in the Aspen feedback experience who has received negative feedback from all nine members of the group. The participant feels crushed and overwhelmed (as will happen in some of these feedback groups). A question arises as to whether this person has been emotionally damaged by the feedback experience. Another person plays the role of Virginia, who signals to the group member to step outside on the porch so the two can discuss the feedback. Virginia wants to repair the damage, yet she still believes that the participant has received some useful feedback for his or her development.

Observers will look to see how badly the participant has been damaged, and how effective Virginia is in helping that person.

LEADERSHIP SKILL-BUILDING EXERCISE 15-2

My Leadership Portfolio

The final entry for your leadership portfolio deals more with the future than the present. As you build your leadership career in either a formal or informal leadership position, update your journal from time to time, perhaps once a quarter. Review what experiences you have had that contribute to your development as a leader. Entries might take forms such as the following:

- In January, my company sent me to a seminar about dealing with difficult people. I came away with a few good insights about helping to turn around a difficult person, such as explaining how his or her behavior was hurting productivity and morale. I also learned that many difficult people are crying out for attention, so I will try to pay more attention to a difficult person should I encounter one.

• We had a major flood in the area last week, and our office became inundated. We had to do

something quick before we were damaged so badly that we could not serve our customers. Our supervisor was out of town. I called her on her cell phone and asked for her authorization to be in charge of organizing our salvage operation. I spearheaded an effort that helped salvage a lot of equipment and computer records. I think I really polished my crisis management skills.

LEADERSHIP SKILL-BUILDING EXERCISE 15-3

Analyzing a Local Leader

As an individual or group project, identify a leader in your community who you would like to analyze from the standpoints of strengths, weaknesses, and needs for development. Among the possibilities of a leader to analyze would be a prominent business person, the president of your learning institution, or an athletic coach. Use information from any-where in the text, plus your own thoughts, to

identify both the positive and negative personal characteristics, along with the developmental needs of this particular leader.

If this is a group project, look to see if there is any consistency across groups with respect to the traits, behaviors, and developmental needs of the leader chosen. If you think the analysis is constructive, you might send a copy to the leader in question.

LEADERSHIP VIDEO CASE DISCUSSION QUESTIONS

To view the videos for this activity, you'll need access to the CourseMate that is available for this text. To get access, visit www.CengageBrain.com.

After watching "Flight 001," answer the following questions.

1. What is a mentor? How might Brad John and John Sencion, co-founders of Flight 001, use mentoring to aide Emily Griffin in her development

as a leader? Would it be more beneficial for Griffin to receive formal or informal mentoring? Explain.

2. Describe the importance of on-the-job experience in the development of a leader. How has Emily Griffin, manager of crew development, used experience to grow?

3. Explain how Emily Griffin contributes to the development of leaders.

NOTES

1. Story created from facts and observations presented in the following sources: "FDNY Firefighter for a Day Team Challenge," *New York City Fire Department* (www.nyc.gov/html/events), 2001; "FDNY Firefighter for a Day Team Challenge," *FDNY Foundation* (www.fdnyfoundation.org), 2011; Garry Kranz, "Special Report: Leadership Development, from Fire Drills to Funny

Skills," *Workforce Management*, May 2011, pp. 28–29.
2. Jeffrey M. Cohn, Rakesh Khurana, and Laura Reeves, "Growing Talent as If Your Business Depended on It," *Harvard Business Review*, October 2005, p. 64.
3. Sharon Daloz Parks, *Leadership Can Be Taught: A Bold Approach for a Complex World* (Boston: Harvard Business School Press, 2005).

4. "Leadership in Literature: A Conversation with Business Ethicist Joseph L. Badaracco Jr." *Harvard Business Review*, March 2006, p. 55.

5. Robert Hogan and Rodney Warrenfeltz, "Educating the Modern Manager," *Academy of Management Learning and Education*, March 2003, p. 74.

6. Chris Argyris, "Teaching Smart People How to Learn," *Harvard Business Review*, May–June 1991, pp. 99–109; Argyris, "Double-Loop Learning, Teaching, and Research," *Academy of Management Learning and Education*, December 2002, p. 206.

7. Bob Kaplan with Rob Kaiser, *The Versatile Leader: Make the Most of Your Strengths—Without Overdoing It* (San Francisco: Pfeiffer, 2006).

8. Rita Pyrillis, "Programs Help Women Take the Lead," *Workforce Management*, January 2011, p. 3.

9. Cited in Jared Sandberg, "Cubicle Culture: Why Learn and Grow on the Job? It's Easier to Feign Infallibility," *The Wall Street Journal*, January 22, 2008, p. B1.

10. Morgan W. McCall, "Leadership Development Through Experience," *Academy of Management Executive*, August 2004, pp. 127–130; Jean Martin and Conrad Schmidt, "How to Keep Your Top Talent," *Harvard Business Review*, May 2010, p. 58.

11. Geoff Colvin, "Airline King," *Fortune*, May 2, 2011, p. 50.

12. "How Great Leaders Benefit from Failure," *Manager's Edge*, November 2004, p. 3.

13. Robert J. Thomas, "Life's Hard Lessons," *HR Magazine*, June 2008, p. 143.

14. Richard L. Hughes, Robert C. Ginnett, and Gordon J. Curphy, *Leadership: Enhancing the Lessons of Experience* (New York: McGraw-Hill/Irwin, 2006), pp. 58–61.

15. Joann S. Lublin, "Leadership Skills Ease Stressful Promotion to Uncharted Area," *The Wall Street Journal*, July 3, 2007, p. A7.

16. Lindsey Gerdes, "The Best Places to Launch a Career," *Business Week*, September 14, 2009, p. 36.

17. Douglas A. Ready, Jay A. Conger, and Linda A. Hill, "Are You a High Potential?" *Harvard Business Review*, June 2010, p. 82.

18. Ann Pomeroy, "Cultivating Female Leaders," *HR Magazine*, February 2007, p. 48.

19. Belle Rose Ragins and John L. Cotton, "Mentor Functions and Outcomes: A Comparison of Men and Women in Formal and Informal Mentoring Relationships," *Journal of Applied Psychology*, August 1999, pp. 529–550. Similar observations are reported by Kathy Kram in Jared Sandberg, "With Bad Mentors, It's Better to Break Up Than to Make Up," *The Wall Street Journal*, March 18, 2008, p. B1.

20. Donna M. Owens, "Virtual Mentoring," *HR Magazine*, March 2006, p. 106.

21. Thomas J. DeLong, John J. Gabarro, and Robert J. Lees, "Why Mentoring Matters in a Hypercompetitive World," *Harvard Business Review*, January 2008, p. 117.

22. Wendy Harris, "Making the Connection: Mentors, Sponsors, and a Network You Can Count On," *Black Enterprise*, February 2007, p. 114.

23. Lublin, "Protégé Finds Mentor Gave Her a Big Boost, but Shadow Lingers," *The Wall Street Journal*, September 7, 2004, p. B1.

24. Dawn E. Chandler and Lillian Eby, "When Mentoring Goes Bad," *The Wall Street Journal*, May 24, 2010, p. R3.

25. Quoted in Fay Hansen, "What the CEO Wants," *Workforce Management*, July 20, 2009, p. 18.

26. Geoff Colvin, "Leader Machines," *Fortune*, October 1, 2007, pp. 98, 101–102.

27. Jared Sandberg, "The Sensitive Me," *The Wall Street Journal*, April 11, 2006, p. B1.

28. Byron Reeves, Thomas W. Malone, and Tony O'Driscoll, "Leadership Online Labs," *Harvard Business Review*, May 2008, pp. 58–66.

29. Carol Hymowitz, "PepsiCo Chief Executive Asks Future Leaders to Train Like Athletes," *The Wall Street Journal*, September 9, 2003, p. B1.

30. Jay A. Conger and Beth Benjamin, *Building Leaders: How Successful Companies Develop the Next Generation* (San Francisco: Jossey-Bass, 1999), p. 79; Conger, "Can We Really Train Leadership?" www.strategy+leadership.com, 2006.

31. Quoted in Emily Shearing, "Speaker Brings Disney Magic to Leadership Talk," *Democrat and Chronicle*, Rochester, New York, May 26, 2010, p. 5B.

32. Nancy M. Davis, "Leading by Example: How the HR Chief Overseas the Drive to Train Leaders at Boeing Co.," *HR Magazine*, December 2008, p. 44.

33. "How Four Top Companies Mold Leaders," *Executive Leadership*, June 2010, p. 1.

34. Philip Mirvis, "Executive Development Through Consciousness-Raising Experiences," *Academy of Management Learning & Education*, June 2008, pp. 173–188.

35. Cited in Carol Hymowitz, "More CEOs Seek Psychotherapy," *The Wall Street Journal*, June 22, 2004, pp. B1, B3.

36. Ram Charan, "Ending the Succession Crisis," *Harvard Business Review*, February 2005, pp. 72–81; Charan, *Leaders at All Levels* (San Francisco: Jossey-Bass, 2008).

37. Jay W. Lorsch and Rakesh Khurana, "Changing Leaders: The Board's Role in CEO Succession," *Harvard Business Review*, May–June 1999, p. 100.

38. Linda Grant, "GE: The Envelope, Please," *Fortune*, June 26, 1995, pp. 89–90; George Anders, "When Filling Top Jobs Inside Makes Sense—And When It Doesn't," *The Wall Street Journal*, January 16, 2006, p. B1; Bill Conaty and Ram Charon, *The Talent Masters: Why Smart Leaders Put People Before Numbers* (New York: Crown Business, 2010); Fay Hansen, "Training the Top at GE," *Workforce Management*, June 9, 2008, p. 26.

39. Mina Kimes, "P&G's Leadership Machine," *Fortune*, April 13, 2009, p. 22.

40. Gary A. Ballinger and F. David Schoorman, "Individual Reactions to Leadership Succession in Workgroups," *Academy of Management Review*, January 2007, pp. 118–136.

41. William C. Byham, "Grooming Next-Millennium Leaders," *HR Magazine*, February 1999, pp. 46–50; Joseph Weber, "The Accidental CEO," *BusinessWeek*, April 23, 2007, p. 68.

42. Victoria Barret, "Talent Search," *Forbes*, March 1, 2010, p. 26.

43. Joseph L. Bower, "Solve the Succession Problem by Growing Inside-Outside Leaders," *Harvard Business Review*, November 2007, pp. 90–96.

44. James M. Citrin and Dayton Ogden, "Succeeding at Succession," *Harvard Business Review*, November 2010, pp. 29–31.

45. Quoted in Sonja D. Brown, "Congratulations, You're a Manager, Now What?" *Black Enterprise*, April 2006, p. 104.

46. Ronald E. Riggio and Michael D. Mumford, "Introduction to the Special Issue: Longitudinal Studies of Leadership Development," *The Leadership Quarterly*, June 2011, p. 454.

GLOSSARY

NOTE: The number in brackets following each term refers to the chapter in which the term first appears.

Achievement motivation Finding joy in accomplishment for its own sake. [3]

Assertiveness Forthrightness in expressing demands, opinions, feelings, and attitudes. [3] As a cultural value, the degree to which individuals are (and should be) assertive, confrontational, and aggressive in their relationships with one another. [2]

Apprising Influence tactic in which influence agent explains how carrying out a request or supporting a proposal will benefit the target personally, including advancing the target's career. [10]

Authenticity Being genuine and honest about your personality, values, and beliefs, as well as having integrity. [3]

Autocratic leader A person in charge who retains most of the authority for himself or herself. [8]

Bandwagon technique A manipulative approach in which one does something simply because others are doing likewise. [10]

Centrality The extent to which a unit's activities are linked into the system of organized activities. [11]

Charisma A special quality of leaders whose purposes, powers, and extraordinary determination differentiate them from others. [4]

Coalition A specific arrangement of parties working together to combine their power. [10]

Coercive power The power to punish for noncompliance; power based on fear. [11]

Commitment The most successful outcome of a leader's influence tactic: The person makes a full effort. [10]

Compliance Partial success of an influence attempt by a leader: The person makes a modest effort. [10]

Co-opt To win over opponents by making them part of your team or giving them a stake in the system. [10]

Consensus leader The person in charge who encourages group discussion about an issue and then makes a decision that reflects general agreement and that group members will support. [8]

Consideration The degree to which the leader creates an environment of emotional support, warmth, friendliness, and trust. [8]

Consultative leader A person in charge who confers with group members before making a decision. [8]

Contingency approach to leadership The contention that leaders are most effective when they make their behavior contingent upon situational forces, including group member characteristics. [9]

Cooperation theory A belief in cooperation and collaboration rather than competitiveness as a strategy for building teamwork. [6]

Core self-evaluations A broad personality trait that captures bottom-line self-assessment, composed of self-esteem, locus of control, generalized self-efficacy, and emotional stability. [3]

Corporate social responsibility The idea that organizations have an obligation to groups in society other than owners or stockholders and beyond that prescribed by law or union contract. [5]

Creative self-efficacy An employee's belief that he or she can be creative in a work role. [13]

Creativity The production of novel and useful ideas. [13]

Crisis leadership The process of leading group members through a sudden and largely unanticipated, intensely negative, and emotionally draining circumstance. [9]

Cross-cultural training A set of learning experiences designed to help employees understand the customs, traditions, and beliefs of another culture. [2]

Cultural intelligence (CQ) An outsider's ability to interpret someone's unfamiliar and ambiguous gestures the way that person's compatriots would. [2]

Cultural sensitivity An awareness of and a willingness to investigate the reasons why people of another culture act as they do. [2]

Debasement The act of demeaning or insulting oneself to control the behavior of another person. [10]

Delegation The assignment of formal authority and responsibility for accomplishing a specific task to another person. [11]

Democratic leader A person in charge who confers final authority on the group. [8]

Dependence perspective The point of view that a person accrues power by other being dependent on him or her for things they value. [11]

Diversity training A learning experience designed to bring about work-place harmony by teaching people how to get along better with diverse work associates. [2]

Double-loop learning An in-depth style of learning that occurs when people use feedback to confront the validity of the goal or the values implicit in the situation. [15]

Drive A propensity to put forth high energy into achieving goals and persistence in applying that energy. [3]

Effective leader One who helps group members attain productivity, including good quality and customer satisfaction, as well as job satisfaction. [8]

E-leadership A form of leadership practiced in a context where work is mediated by information technology. [6]

Emotional intelligence The ability to do such things as understand one's feelings, have empathy for others, and regulate one's emotions to enhance one's quality of life. [3]

Employee network (or affinity) group A group of employees throughout the company who affiliate on the basis of a group characteristic such as race, ethnicity, sex, sexual orientation, or physical ability status. [2]

Empowerment Passing decision-making authority and responsibility from managers to group members. [11]

Engagement The current buzzword for the commitment that workers make to their employers. [7]

Entitlement In relation to unethical behavior by executives, the idea that some CEOs lose their sense of reality and feel entitled to whatever they can get away with or steal. [5]

Equity theory An explanation of motivation contending that employee satisfaction and motivation depend on how fairly the employees believe they are treated in comparison to peers. [7]

Ethical mind A point of view that helps the individual aspire to good work that matters to their colleagues, companies, and society in general. [5]

Ethics The study of moral obligations, or separating right from wrong. [5]

Evidence-based leadership or management The approach whereby managers translate principles based on best evidence into organizational practices. [9]

Executive coaching A one-on-one development process formally contracted between a coach and a management-level client to help achieve goals related to professional development and/or business performance. [7]

Expectancy An individual's assessment of the probability that effort will lead to correct performance of the task. [7]

Expectancy theory A theory of motivation based on the premise that the amount of effort people expend depends on how much reward they can expect in return. [7]

Experience of flow An experience so engrossing and enjoyable that the task becomes worth doing for its own sake, regardless of the external consequences. [13]

Expert power The ability to influence others because of one's specialized knowledge, skills, or abilities. [4]

Farsightedness The ability to understand the long-range implications of actions and policies. [3]

Feedback-intensive development program A learning experience that helps leaders develop by seeing more clearly their patterns of behaviors, the reasons for such behaviors, and the impact of these behaviors and attitudes on their effectiveness. [15]

Flexibility The ability to adjust to different situations. [3]

Future orientation As a cultural value, the extent to which individuals engage (and should engage) in future-oriented behaviors such as delaying gratification, planning, and making investments for the future. [2]

Gender egalitarianism As a cultural value, the degree to which a culture minimizes, and should minimize, gender inequality. [2]

Global leadership skills The ability to exercise effective leadership in a variety of countries. [2]

Goal What a person is trying to accomplish. [7]

Hands-on leader A leader who gets directly involved in the details and process of operations. [10]

Humane orientation As a cultural value, the degree to which a society encourages and rewards, and should encourage and reward, individuals for being fair, altruistic, and caring others. [2]

Implicit leadership theories Personal assumptions about the traits and abilities that characterize an ideal organizational leader. [10]

Influence The ability to affect the behavior of others in a particular direction. [10]

Information power Power stemming from formal control over the information people need to do their work. [11]

In-group collectivism As a cultural value, the degree to which individuals express, and should express, pride, loyalty, and cohesiveness in their organizations and families. [2]

Initiating structure Organizing and defining relationships in the group by activities such as assigning specific tasks, specifying procedures to be followed, scheduling work, and clarifying expectations of team members. [8]

Innovation The process of creating new ideas and their implementation. [13]

Insight A depth of understanding that requires considerable intuition and common sense. [3]

Instrumentality An individual's assessment of the probability that performance will lead to certain outcomes. [7]

Integrity Loyalty to rational principles, thereby practicing what one preaches, regardless of emotional or social pressure. [5]

Internal locus of control The belief that one is the prime mover behind events. [3]

Kitchen for the mind A space designed to nurture creativity. [13]

Knowledge management (KM) A concerted effort to improve how knowledge is created, delivered, and applied. [14]

Leader–member exchange model (LMX) An explanation of leadership proposing that leaders develop unique working relationships with group members. [6]

Leadership The ability to inspire confidence and support among the people who are needed to achieve organizational goals. [1]

Leadership diversity The presence of a culturally heterogeneous group of leaders. [2]

Leadership effectiveness Attaining desirable outcomes such as productivity, quality, and satisfaction in a given situation. [1]

Leadership Grid® A framework for specifying the extent of a leader's concern for the production and people. [8]

Leadership polarity The disparity in views of leaders: they are revered or vastly unpopular, but people rarely feel neutral about them. [4]

Leadership style The relatively consistent pattern of behavior that characterizes a leader. [8]

Leadership succession An orderly process of identifying and grooming people to replace executives. [15]

Leading by example Influencing others by acting as a positive role model. [10]

Learning organization An organization that is skilled at creating, acquiring, and transferring knowledge and at modifying behavior to reflect new knowledge and insights. [14]

Legitimate power The lawful right to make a decision and expect compliance. [11]

Linguistic style A person's characteristic speaking pattern. [12]

Machiavellians People in the work-place who ruthlessly manipulate others. [10]

Management openness A set of leadership behaviors particularly relevant to subordinates' motivation to voice their opinion. [8]

Management by storytelling The technique of inspiring and instructing group members by telling fascinating stories. [4]

Making the rounds The leader casually dropping by constituents to listen to their accomplishments, concern, and problems and to share information. [12]

Mentor A more experienced person who develops a protégé's abilities through tutoring, coaching, guidance, and emotional support. [15]

Micromanagement The close monitoring of most aspects of group member activities by the manager or leader. [6]

Morals An individual's determination of what is right or wrong influenced by his or her values. [5]

Multicultural leader A leader with the skills and attitudes to relate effectively to and motivate people across race, gender, age, social attitudes, and lifestyles. [2]

Multicultural worker A worker who is convinced that all cultures are equally good and enjoys learning about other cultures. [2]

Normative decision model A view of leadership as a decision-making process in which the leader examines certain factors within the situation to determine which decision-making style will be the most effective. [9]

Open-book management An approach to management in which every employee is trained, empowered, and motivated to understand and pursue the company's business goals. [6]

Organizational politics Informal approaches to gaining power through means other than merit or luck. [11]

Outcome Anything that might stem from performance, such as a reward. [7]

Participative leader A person in charge who shares decision making with group members. [8]

Partnership A relationship between leaders and group members in which power is approximately balanced. [1]

Path-goal theory An explanation of leadership effectiveness that specifies what the leader must do to achieve high productivity and morale in a given situation. [9]

Performance orientation As a cultural value, the degree to which a society encourages (or should encourage) and rewards group member for performance improvement and excellence. [2]

Personal brand Also, the *brand called you*, or your basket of strengths that makes you unique. [4]

Personal magnetism A captivating, inspiring personality with charm and charismatic-like qualities. [10]

Personal power Power derived from the person rather than from the organization. [11]

Personalized charismatic A charismatic leader who exercises few restraints on the use of power in order to best serve his or her own interests. [4]

Pet-peeve technique A method of brainstorming in which a group identifies all the possible complaints others might have about the group's organizational unit. [13]

Positive psychological capital An individual's positive psychological state of development, characterized by four psychological resources: self-efficacy, hope, optimism, and resilience. [11]

Power The potential or ability to influence decisions and control resources. [11]

Power distance As a cultural value, the degree to which members of a society expect, and should expect, power to be distributed unequally. [2]

Practical intelligence The ability to solve everyday problems by using experience-based knowledge to adapt to and shape the environment. [3]

Prestige power The power stemming from one's status and reputation. [11]

Pygmalion effect The situation that occurs when a managerial leader believes that a group member will succeed, and communicates this belief without realizing it. [8]

Referent power The leader's ability to influence others through his or her desirable traits and characteristics. [4]

Resistance The state that occurs when an influence attempt by a leader is unsuccessful: The target is opposed to carrying out the request and finds ways to either not comply or do a poor job. [10]

Resource dependence perspective The view that an organization requires a continuing flow of human resources, money, customers and clients, technological inputs, and materials to continue to function. [11]

Reward power The authority to give employees rewards for compliance. [11]

Self-awareness Insightfully processing feedback about oneself to improve personal effectiveness. [15]

Self-discipline The ability to mobilize one's efforts to stay focused on attaining an important goal. [15]

Self-efficacy The confidence in one's ability to carry out a specific task. [7]

Self-leadership The idea that all organizational members are capable of leading themselves, at least to some extent. [11]

Servant leader One who serves constituents by working on their behalf to help them achieve their goals, not the leader's own goals. [8]

Shadowing An approach to mentoring in which the trainee follows the mentor around for a stated period of time. [15]

Single-loop learning A situation in which learners seek minimum feedback that might substantially confront their basic ideas or actions. [15]

Situational Leadership II (SLII) A model of leadership that explains how to match the leadership style to capabilities of group members on a given task. [9]

Socialized charismatic A charismatic leader who restrains the use of power in order to benefit others. [4]

Strategic contingency theory An explanation of sources of power suggesting that units best able to cope with the firm's critical problems and uncertainties acquire relatively large amounts of power. [11]

Strategic leadership The process of creating or sustaining an organization by providing the right direction and inspiration. [14]

Strategic planning Those activities that lead to the statement of goals and objectives and the choice of strategy. [14]

Strategy An integrated, overall concept of how the firm will achieve its objectives. [14]

Substitutes for leadership Factors in the work environment that provide guidance and incentives to perform, making the leader's role almost superfluous. [1]

SWOT analysis A method of considering internal strengths, weaknesses, and external opportunities and threats in a given situation. [14]

Team A work group that must rely on collaboration if each member is to experience the optimum success and achievement. [6]

Teamwork Work done with an understanding and commitment to group goals on the part of all team members. [6]

Territorial games Also referred to as turf wars, political tactics that involve protecting and hoarding resources that give one power, such as information, relationships, and decision-making authority. [11]

360-degree feedback A formal evaluation of superiors based on input from people who work for and with them, sometimes including customers and suppliers. [8]

Time orientation As a cultural value, the importance nations and individuals attach to time. [2]

Tough question One that makes a person or group stop and think about why they are doing or not doing something. [8]

Transformational leader A leader who brings about positive, major changes in an organization. [4]

Trust A person's confidence in another individual's intentions and motives and in the sincerity of that individual's word. [3]

Uncertainty avoidance As a cultural value, the extent to which members of a society rely (and should rely) on social norms, rules, and procedures to lessen the unpredictability of future events. [2]

Upward appeal A means of influence in which the leader enlists a person with more formal authority to do the influencing. [10]

Valence The worth or attractiveness of an outcome. [7]

Virtuous cycle The idea that corporate social performance and corporate financial performance feed and reinforce each other. [5]

Vision The ability to imagine different and better conditions and ways to achieve them. [4]

Whistleblower An employee who discloses organizational wrongdoing to parties who can take action. [5]

Win–win approach to conflict resolution The belief that after conflict has been resolved, both sides should gain something of value. [12]

Work orientation As a cultural value, the number of hours per week and weeks per year people expect to invest in work versus leisure, or other non-work activities. [2]

NAME INDEX

ORGANIZATION INDEX

SUBJECT INDEX